The
LASERDISC
FILM GUIDE

The LASERDISC FILM GUIDE

Complete Ratings for
the Best and Worst
Movies Available on Disc

1993–1994 Edition

Jeff Rovin

ST. MARTIN'S PRESS—NEW YORK

Acknowledgments

Thanks to Bob Stephens, laserdisc columnist for the *San Francisco Examiner*, who contributed a number of reviews; to Vincent DiFate, who contributed expertise; to Mike Betker at Image Entertainment, who contributed laserdiscs; to Jamie Ludowitz and David Wallace, who contributed information; and to Gordon Van Gelder at St. Martin's Press, who contributed editorial know-how.

THE LASERDISC FILM GUIDE. Copyright © 1993 by Jeff Rovin. All rights reserved. Printed in the United States of America. No part of this book may be used or reproduced in any manner whatsoever without written permission except in the case of brief quotations embodied in critical articles or reviews. For information, address St. Martin's Press, 175 Fifth Avenue, New York, N.Y. 10010.

Design by Judy Christensen

Library of Congress Cataloging-in-Publication Data

Rovin, Jeff.
    The laserdisc film guide : complete ratings for the best and worst movies available on disc / Jeff Rovin.
       p. cm.
    ISBN 0-312-08703-9 (pbk.)
    1. Videodiscs—Catalogs. 2. Motion pictures—Catalogs.
3. Videodiscs—Evaluation. I. Title. II. Title: Laser disc film guide. III. Title: Laserdisc film guide.
PN1992.95.R68 1993
016.79143'75—dc20   92-33340
                                                    CIP

First edition: February 1993

10 9 8 7 6 5 4 3 2 1

Attention: Schools and Businesses
St. Martin's Press books are available at quantity discounts with bulk purchase for educational, business, or sales promotional use. For information, please contact:
Special Sales Department, St. Martin's Press
175 Fifth Avenue, New York, N.Y. 10010

Contents

Introduction	ix
Japanese Laserdiscs	xiii
Abbott and Costello Meet Frankenstein	1
The Adventures of Don Juan	2
The Adventures of Milo and Otis	3
After Hours	3
Akira Kurosawa's Dreams	4
The Alamo	5
Alexander Nevsky	6
Aliens	7
Anastasia	8
Annie Hall	10
Apocalypse Now	11
Arachnophobia	13
The Assassination of Trotsky	14
Avalon	15
Babette's Feast	15
Backdraft	16
The Band Wagon	17
Barry Lyndon	18
Batman	19
Battle of the Bulge	20
The Bear	21
Beauty and the Beast	22
Becket	23
Bedazzled	25
Being There	25
Ben-Hur	27
Betsy's Wedding	29
The Bible . . . In the Beginning	30
Bird on a Wire	30
Black Rain	31
Blazing Saddles	32
Blue Velvet	33
Born on the Fourth of July	34
Brainstorm	35
Broken Lance	36
The Brood	37
The Buddy Holly Story	37
Bye Bye Birdie	38
Caligula	39
The Cardinal	40
Carnival of Souls	41
Casablanca	42
The Chase	43
Chinatown	44
Chinese Roulette	46
Christmas in Connecticut	46
Cinema Paradiso	47
Citizen Kane	48
Cleopatra	49
A Clockwork Orange	50
Close Encounters of the Third Kind	52
The Cocoanuts	53
Conan the Barbarian	54
The Court Jester	56
Crazy People	57
The Creature from the Black Lagoon	58
Curse of the Demon	58
Dances with Wolves	60
Dangerous Liaisons	60
Darkman	62
The Day the Earth Stood Still	63
Deliverance	64
Dial M for Murder	65
Dick Tracy	66
Die Hard	67
The Dirty Dozen	68
Dirty Harry	69
Dr. Cyclops	70
Dr. Jekyll and Mr. Hyde	71
Dr. Strangelove or: How I Learned to Stop Worrying and Love the Bomb	72
Doctor Zhivago	73
Dollman	75
The Doors	75
Double Indemnity	76
Dracula	77
Earthquake	78
The Eddy Duchin Story	80
Edward Scissorhands	81
Elmer Gantry	82
Empire of the Sun	83
Enemies, A Love Story	84

Title	Page
Ernest Goes to Jail	85
The Errand Boy	85
E.T. The Extra-Terrestrial	87
Excalibur	88
The Exorcist	89
The Exorcist III	90
Fame	91
Fantasia	92
Far from the Madding Crowd	94
Fiddler on the Roof	95
Field of Dreams	96
Fiend Without a Face	97
First Men in the Moon	98
A Fish Called Wanda	99
Five Easy Pieces	100
The Flame and the Arrow	101
Flatliners	102
Forbidden Planet	102
Frankenstein	104
From Here to Eternity	105
Full Metal Jacket	106
Gandhi	107
Ghost	108
Glory	109
The Godfather	110
Going Places	111
The Golden Voyage of Sinbad	112
Goldfinger	114
Gone With the Wind	116
Gonza the Spearman	118
Goodbye, Mr. Chips	119
Goodfellas	120
Grand Prix	120
Graveyard Shift	121
The Great Escape	122
The Great Race	124
The Grifters	124
The Guardian	125
Gunga Din	126
Hairspray	127
The Hallelujah Trail	127
Hamlet	129
Hardware	130
The Hard Way	131
Harlem Nights	132
Harper	133
Havana	133
Head	134
Henry & June	135
Henry: Portrait of a Serial Killer	136
Henry V	137
Hercules	138
The Hindenburg	139
Home Alone	140
Horror of Dracula	141
How the West Was Won	142
The Hunger	143
The Hunt for Red October	144
Ice Station Zebra	145
I Love You to Death	146
Impromptu	147
Invasion of the Body Snatchers	148
It's a Mad Mad Mad Mad World	149
It's a Wonderful Life	151
Jacob's Ladder	152
Jason and the Argonauts	153
Jesus Christ Superstar	154
The Jolson Story	155
Journey to the Center of the Earth	156
Khartoum	157
King Kong	159
King of Kings	162
A Kiss Before Dying	163
The Krays	164
Kronos	165
Kwaidan	166
Lady Jane	167
Last Tango in Paris	168
The Last Temptation of Christ	169
Lawrence of Arabia	170
The Leopard Man	171
Licence to Kill	172
Lionheart	173
Little Big Man	174
The Little Mermaid	175
Lolita	176
The Longest Day	177
Love Among the Ruins	178
The Magnificent Seven	179
The Manchurian Candidate	180
Manhattan	181
Maniac Cop 2	182
March of the Wooden Soldiers	182
The Marrying Man	184
Meet Me in St. Louis	184
Memphis Belle	186
Metropolis	186
Mr. and Mrs. Bridge	187
Monty Python's Life of Brian	188
Monty Python's The Meaning of Life	189
Mountains of the Moon	190
The Music Man	191
Mutiny on the Bounty	192
The Naked Jungle	194
Near Dark	194
Nicholas and Alexandra	195

None but the Brave	196	The Silence of the Lambs	251
North by Northwest	197	Singin' in the Rain	252
The Nutty Professor	198	Sleeping with the Enemy	253
Ocean's Eleven	199	Some Like It Hot	254
On Dangerous Ground	200	Son of Dracula	254
On Her Majesty's Secret Service	201	Sorcerer	256
On the Town	202	The Sound of Music	257
Our Man Flint	203	The Spy Who Loved Me	258
Pacific Heights	204	Stagecoach	259
Patton	205	Star Trek—The Motion Picture	261
Penn & Teller Get Killed	206	Star Wars	263
The Perfect Weapon	207	Stone Cold	264
Peter Pan	207	A Streetcar Named Desire	265
Phantom of the Opera	208	Sunset Boulevard	266
The Philadelphia Story	210	Superman	267
The Pink Panther	211	Tales from the Darkside: The Movie	268
The Pirates of Penzance	212		
Planet of the Apes	213	The Tall Guy	269
Plan 9 from Outer Space	215	10	270
The Poseidon Adventure	216	The Ten Commandments	271
Predator	217	The Terminator	272
Predator 2	218	Terminator 2: Judgment Day	273
Pretty Woman	219	That's Entertainment!	275
The Princess Bride	220	Them!	276
The Producers	221	This Is Spinal Tap	277
The Professionals	221	The Three Caballeros	278
Psycho	222	Thunderbolt and Lightfoot	279
PT 109	223	To Have and Have Not	280
The Punisher	225	Top Gun	281
Quigley Down Under	226	Touch of Evil	282
The Raiders of the Lost Ark	227	The Toxic Avenger	283
The Rainmaker	228	Toy Soldiers	284
Re-Animator	228	Tremors	285
Rear Window	229	Truth or Dare	286
Red River	230	Twenty Million Miles to Earth	286
Return of the Dragon	231	2001: A Space Odyssey	287
Reversal of Fortune	232	Ulzana's Raid	290
Ride the High Country	233	Uncle Buck	290
Robin and Marian	234	The Untouchables	291
Robin Hood: Prince of Thieves	235	Victor/Victoria	292
Romancing the Stone	237	Viva Las Vegas	293
The Rookie	238	The War of the Roses	294
Rosemary's Baby	238	War of the Worlds	295
The Ruling Class	239	Weekend at Bernie's	296
The Russia House	240	West Side Story	297
The Sea Hawk	241	When Dinosaurs Ruled the Earth	298
Sea of Love	242	White Palace	300
The Searchers	243	Who Framed Roger Rabbit	300
Seven Brides for Seven Brothers	244	Wild at Heart	302
The Seven Samurai	245	The Wild Bunch	302
The Seventh Seal	246	Wings of Desire	304
She-Devil	247	The Wizard of Oz	305
The Shining	248	Wolfen	306
A Shot in the Dark	250	Women in Love	307

Women on the Verge of a Nervous Breakdown	308	Yankee Doodle Dandy	311
		Young Man with a Horn	312
The Wonderful World of the Brothers Grimm	308	Zombies on Broadway	313
		Zorba the Greek	313
The Yakuza	310	Zulu	314

Introduction

If you're reading this, you probably own a laserdisc player already and don't need to be told about all the machine's wonderful abilities—but just in case you still haven't taken the plunge, here are some of the advantages a laserdisc player offers:

- The picture is 60 percent sharper than that of videotape.
- The music is of the same quality as that of compact discs, and it allows you to experience movies in digital Surround Sound if you've got four or five speakers.
- The films on laserdisc regularly boast special features unavailable anywhere else, such as trailers, cut scenes, interviews, etc. (You'll find more detailed information on these extras in the entries for each film.)
- Laserdisc players are compatible with the new televisions currently in production, and plans to integrate laserdisc technology with personal computer technology are moving ahead.

Laserdisc players were introduced in 1978 and might have caught on much earlier if they hadn't made their debut at roughly the same time as videocassette recorders. Even though only a few prerecorded cassettes were available in the late 1970s, videotapes offered one feature that laserdiscs do not as yet: the ability to tape movies and programs from the TV. (Record-once discs will be on the market soon.)

Consumers who *did* prefer laserdiscs to videocassettes faced another problem: They couldn't tell which format was going to click. The laserdisc we know and love today was marketed by Magnavox as MagnaVision, with software provided by MCA's DiscoVision; at the same time, RCA's SelectaVision videodisc—which played discs by using a diamond-tipped needle, much like a record player—was being promoted. Early laserdisc players and discs had a high defect rate, and consequently MCA folded its software tent by 1982, with SelectaVision following two years later.

Only Pioneer had faith in the format. The electronics giant built a state-of-the-art processing plant in Japan, took over MCA's plant in Carson, California, and almost single-handedly kept the laserdisc format from disappearing—though its success in Japan must also be acknowledged (see page xiii).

The industry gained a stronger foothold in the market with the introduction of compact discs in 1983. Digital laser technology caught on first with classical-music buffs and soon spread to the wide world of popular music as consumers became aware of the superiority of CD sound over LPs or tape sound. In 1984, Pioneer introduced the first "combiplayer," a machine that spun both CDs and laserdiscs. It was expensive ($1,200), but the idea was excellent.

Another important event in 1984 was the Voyager Company's entry into the field. Their Criterion Collection of discs was dedicated to releasing the best possible versions of classic films, with extensive supplementary material and a CAV format to enhance the viewing experience: Their first two releases were *Citizen Kane* and *King Kong*. MCA jumped back into the laserdisc game a year later, releasing Encore Edition laserdiscs of their classics *The Bride of Frankenstein*, *Animal Crackers*, and *Scarface*. Paramount introduced digital audio sound in their laserdiscs in 1984. In 1985, MGM/UA issued *Manhattan* in the letterboxed format, and Criterion followed suit in 1986 with the first of its many letterboxed movies, thus encouraging many movie buffs to make the switch to laserdiscs and bring wide-screen films into their own homes. Laserdiscs had finally found their niche.

In 1988, Image Entertainment struck licensing deals with a number of major studios to distribute products, and MCA Universal released *E.T.*, which sold an unprecedented 63,000-plus copies. Laserdiscs had begun to become a force in the marketplace. Pioneer offered a low-priced ($600) combiplayer in 1989, and sales took off.

By 1991, *most* software companies (that is, those who produced the laserdisc films, as opposed to the hardware companies who made the actual laserdisc machines) were offering laserdisc versions of films on the same day as the videotape versions became available. No one's surprised, anymore, when popular titles routinely sell more than 100,000 laserdisc copies. *Fantasia* has sold nearly twice that number to date.

Laserdiscs are no longer just for collectors. Consumers have become savvy not just to the better picture but to the extraordinary sound capabilities of laserdiscs—Surround Sound, digital sound-field processing, and more (see Glossary, page 316).

Then there's letterboxing, the laserdisc's unique tribute to film as an art form. Through this process, films are transferred to laserdisc with the original aspect ratio of the film intact; that is, the entire wide-screen theater image is recreated on your monitor (with black bands called "mattes" masking the unused portions of the screen above and below the image). All the characters, action, and sets appear—nothing has to be lopped off the sides in order to fit the action on a TV monitor.

There may not be a touchier subject among collectors than letterboxing. Those who want to see a movie exactly as the director intended, without artificial cuts or distracting pans, are delighted by this technique. Nothing is lost to television—but the price to pay is in the height of the image. Letterboxing sacrifices height for width, and there are plenty of viewers who like to have their TV screens filled from top to bottom.

Obviously, the letterboxed *Ben-Hur* is going to look like a pencil on a nineteen-inch screen. Just as obviously, however, losing half of the 2.66:1 image is going to hurt the film on *any* monitor. But seeing all of the Mona Lisa is better than just seeing her eyes. Reading all of *Moby-Dick* is better than reading the Classics Illustrated edition. And seeing all of *The Magnificent Seven* is better than seeing "The Magnificent Three" or "Four." If a director feels that he or she can become involved in the process and make a creative transfer without letterboxing—as William Friedkin did with *Sorcerer*—that's fine. Otherwise, accepting the fact that *any* theatrical film is going to be compromised on the TV screen, the director's vision should be recreated as faithfully as possible. Only letterboxing permits that.

If letterboxing is a controversial topic among laserphiles, one thing is not: the issue of sound, image, and quality. A laserdisc player should indulge one's fondness for films that look beautiful and sound great.

Unfortunately, just because a movie is on laserdisc, that doesn't mean it's very good. There are sloppy, hurried transfers; crummy pressings; scratched or faded source materials; and, of course, just plain lousy films. So, before you spend anywhere from $25 to $125 on a laserdisc, you should know exactly what you're getting.

This book is a guide to the complete package, using a "no stars" to ★★★★★ rating system to grade the video and audio quality, as well as the quality of the movie itself. It tells you what's good and bad about the transfer, whether it's CLV or CAV, whether there are chapters—scenes numbered for easy access—who manufactured it, what kind of supplementary material is offered, and also summarizes the plot, provides some history of the film, and points out a few filmmaking blunders, as well—visible microphones, shadows of spectators or cameras, continuity mistakes, and so on—telling you exactly where to find them on the disc.

There are nearly seven thousand domestic laserdiscs available today, and the number of titles grows by a dozen or two each month. Nearly half of these discs are feature films. In this volume—the first of a proposed series—three hundred of these are covered: great films that may or may not have been given great transfers (such as *Citizen Kane* and *Fantasia*), popular films that may or may not look good on laserdisc (*The Sound of Music* and *Top Gun*), films that look and sound dazzling on laserdisc but may have little else to offer (from *Crazy People* to *Toy Soldiers*), and so on.

We've also tried to provide a sampling from every genre, the best work of the most honored or prolific directors, and even some "just plain fun" titles such as *The Nutty Professor, Plan 9 from Outer Space,* and *The Toxic Avenger.*

As you buy discs or read through this book, you'll notice that certain manufacturers can almost always be counted on to release quality discs—though Criterion stands out. While some of its catalogue is covered in this book, the rule of thumb is this: If Criterion releases it, you'll be getting what is *likely* to be the best source material and best transfer available. There are exceptions: Years after Criterion's releases of *King Kong, 2001: A Space Odyssey,* and *Singin' in the Rain,* other companies found better source material or were able to make better transfers. Upgrades are always going to be a part of laserdisc collecting, but, *for the most part,* Criterion discs can't be beat.

For the present, laserdisc collectors must contend with one problem: acquiring new discs. If you live in Manhattan or Los Angeles, there are plenty of dealers who stock a bounty of new and old titles. But if you live in a small town, you can't just drive down to the local mom-and-pop video store.

Fortunately, you can get new releases pretty quickly via mail order. From personal experience, I recommend Laser Island in Brooklyn, NY (718–743–2425), which deals in domestic and imported discs, gets ample supplies of new titles, and gets discs to you promptly.

Barr Digital (800–274–7002) is excellent with domestic titles, if you can wait a week or so to have them in your hot little hands; you may want to, since they give a 12.5 percent discount on all titles *or* coupons that can be redeemed for free discs. Their inventory of old discs isn't extensive, however, and you may have to wait three or four weeks for a back-ordered title. However, they are *very* cheerful there in Redmond, Washington.

Other collectors have had happy dealings with Starship Industries (703–430–8692), Laser World (800–343–9211), Ken Crane's (800–624–3078; in California, 800–626–1768), Tewksbury Audio & Video (908–832–9064), and Dave's Video (800–736–1659). The latter has a very deep inventory of old titles.

Columbia House Laserdisc Club has a membership plan that works like any book or CD club: Buy three discs for a low price and agree to buy two more over the next year at list price. Each purchase after you fulfill your commitment earns you bonus dollars that can save you a bundle on future purchases. It's worth joining if you buy a lot of discs, but call first to make sure they have what they're advertising (you may jump, as many did, at the letterboxed *The King and I,* only to find they didn't get it for months), and be certain that you're not buying a disc that has since been remastered: As of this writing, the company is still offering the original, inferior versions of *Manhattan, Apocalpyse Now, How the West Was Won,* and others that have subsequently been given better transfers. It's better to stick with recent titles from these folks.

There are two excellent laserdisc periodicals: Scott Hughes's *LaserScene Monthly* (37 Dorland Street, San Francisco, CA 94110) and Douglas Pratt's *Laser Disc Newsletter* (PO Box 420, East Rockaway, NY 11518–0420), both of which are published monthly and are available by subscription.

A few words about running times. They've been listed as they appear on the discs, which usually includes the supplementary material. (Criterion discs tend to list just the film running time, since much of their supplementary material is designed to be stepped through at the viewer's pace.) Running times may also be affected by time compression or by added scenes and, thus, may not always jibe with what's listed in film books such as *Leonard Maltin's TV Movies and Video Guide* (an annual reference book which is the best such guide on the market).

And now, pleasant viewing!

Japanese Laserdiscs
—Mel Neuhaus, Laser Island

"They've got *Von Ryan's Express!*" a friend of mine shouted with joy over the phone.

It was sometime in 1984, and what he'd said seemed rather odd, since no such entry had appeared in any of the software reports I'd seen. The answer came when I went to the then-slim racks of laserdiscs at Tower and saw for myself: It was a Japanese import. And there were others.

The obvious questions immediately began whirlpooling through my head. What language are they in? What else is available? What is the quality?

Helter-skelter rummaging through racks there and elsewhere revealed other American titles that weren't available on domestic labels, films such as *Taps, Cruising, Bus Stop, Foreign Correspondent, Letter from an Unknown Woman, Make Mine Music, Melody Time, The Undefeated,* and many others.

I remember ripping the (far more sensible) heavy-duty, loose-fitting shrink wrap off *Von Ryan's Express* and watching, in horror, as Frank Sinatra, Trevor Howard, Edward Mulhare, and the rest of the cast spoke English while Japanese subtitles appeared in the lower part of the frame. I tried to eliminate the white titles by pressing every button on the remote, but to no avail. Only later did I discover that just some titles, such as *The Seven Year Itch* and *Song of the South* had bilingual tracks (though the latter used subtitles for the song lyrics). Within five minutes, though, I was oblivious to the subtitles, and for the next ninety-five minutes (or however long it took Von Ryan nearly to reach his destination) I was hooked. The idea that there was an entirely different library of films out there, many with superior audio and video, added to my delight.

When I started Laser Island a few years later, much had occurred. First, the dollar/yen situation had gotten out of control, so that titles that had been only five dollars or so more than domestic discs were now double the price. Second, fed up with the red tape involved in bringing over these films, Tower had given up on the import market. Third, the Japanese were manufacturing laserdiscs like mad.

Part of this mania was fueled by the enormous success of *karaoke* in Japan. The sing-along phenomenon flashes song lyrics on the screen, allowing consumers (or patrons at a *karaoke* bar) to sing while watching vocal-less vignettes or narratives on the screen. At present, there are more than 13,000 *karaoke* titles available and their sales account for 40 percent of the laserdisc business in Japan. (Concerts/music videos comprise 30 percent; foreign films—mostly American—account for 23 percent more; and how-to, sports, etc., make up the rest.)

At Laser Island, I sell nearly twice as many Japanese discs as I do domestic laserdiscs. To understand fully why a laserphile would pay twice as much for an import with Japanese subtitles, it's important to understand the phrase *collector conscious*. Until recently, laserdiscs were almost exclusively a collector's medium, and the Japanese tuned into this with a vengeance. Back in the Stone Age (for laserdiscs, that was the early 1980s), while U.S. manufacturers were releasing laserdiscs such as *Say Yes, Hardbodies, The Yum-Yum Girls,* and bad transfers of *Blazing Saddles, Deliverance,* and other movies, the Japanese were pressing major action and fantasy films (still the two most popular genres here and abroad) in superdeluxe letterboxed editions and, occasionally, in CAV. Furthermore, many of them were encoded with the then-new technology of digital sound. No one in the United States was doing that sort of thing (Criterion had yet to make its debut).

The initial selections I was able to offer were a movie fan's dream come true: *Forbidden Planet, 2001: A Space Odyssey, Where Eagles Dare, El Cid* (which is still not available domestically), *Kelly's Heroes*, and others. Hammer horror fans were treated to uncut 35mm transfers of *The Vampire Lovers, Frankenstein and the Monster from Hell*, and others. Then there were the Ray Harryhausen classics such as *Valley of Gwangi, The Three Worlds of Gulliver*, a digital/CAV *Clash of the Titans*, and a CAV documentary about this master special-effects man's career. Equally important was the availability of the classy Italian shockers from Dario Argento, Mario Bava, Lucio Fulci, and Michel Soavi.

The appearance of these films in gorgeous, uncut transfers caused many American film buffs to go out and purchase their first players. The delight of collectors was indescribable as they discovered that many of these films were letterboxed, and some ran almost forty minutes longer than American theatrical or videotape versions. The Japanese version of *The Fall of the Roman Empire*—a much underrated film—finally tells us what happened to Anthony Quayle's character, who in all of the American versions simply disappears! The Tom Cruise film *Legend* contained the lovely Jerry Goldsmith score, and not the Tangerine Dream music that appears on the domestic release. The disc of *55 Days at Peking* includes Andy Williams singing "So Little Time," which was hitherto available only on the album of the sound track.

But there was more: At least twenty-five Toho monster classics, long in demand by collectors, were now available in (where applicable) full Tohoscope wide-screen editions. These gems from the 1950s and 1960s included the original *Godzilla, Rodan, Mothra, King Kong vs. Godzilla*—Japanese cuts often running a good twenty minutes longer than the American versions, without added, made-in-America scenes (*Godzilla*, without Raymond Burr, is a more satisfying film). Not to be outdone, Daei soon debuted their Gamera series, starring the giant, jet-propelled monster turtle.

Martial-arts students were able to study their favorite practitioners in dozens of bloody, thrill-packed adventures (one in 3-D, glasses included), while more sober fans of Asian films could collect wide-screen versions of *Ran* or *Fires on the Plain*.

In the late 1980s, when domestic manufacturers were still giving us notoriously bad panned-and-scanned laserdiscs, the Japanese were giving us superior wide-screen versions of films such as Schwarzenegger's *Raw Deal* (known as *Gorilla*) and *The Mission*. It didn't take long for American home-video companies to catch on: Soon, MGM/UA, MCA Universal, Criterion, and Image Entertainment began to copy the ambitious release schedules of the Japanese. Not to be outdone, the Japanese retaliated by digging into the more obscure, highly collectible works of important American and European filmmakers, past and present. Soon, imports of Fritz Lang's super-rare *Hangmen Also Die*, Bill Forsyth's quirky *Housekeeping*, Buñuel's *Belle de Jour*, Chabrol's *Leda* and *Les Biches*, Welles's *F for Fake* and *The Trial*, Fellini's *Amarcord* and *The Clowns*, and many others began arriving on these shores. When the Americans picked up on that trend, the Japanese started issuing the likes of *Stephen King's It* miniseries and the feature-length pilot of *The Flash* TV series, demonstrating yet another direction in which imports are headed.

Do Japanese citizens collect American-pressed discs? Yes they do, and avidly. Collectors from Tokyo regularly ask us to supply them with anything that's gotten a superior transfer or is not available in their own catalog—such as the letterboxed editions of *The Great Race* or *King of Kings* and obscure releases such as *The Long, Long Trailer* and *Yours, Mine and Ours*—both featuring Lucille Ball, a big Japanese favorite.

What's next? At the moment, the Japanese still excel at animation, pop, rock, and jazz, categories in which they collectively produce between thirty and fifty times the American output. And they're working hard on finding ways to pack sixty minutes of material on each side of a five-inch laserdisc (in contrast to the present twelve-inch ones).

Whatever happens, one thing is certain: The two laserdisc "superpowers" are going to keep each other on their toes. Quality and diversity will be the key to success, and laserdisc fans are going to be the beneficiaries.

Abbott and Costello Meet Frankenstein (1948) ★★★★
Director: Charles Barton
Running Time: 83 minutes

What a fine, fine movie this is, a grade-A production that succeeds as horror and comedy. It works because the horror is played straight by some of the best actors ever to work in the genre, and the comedy is vintage Abbott and Costello.

When a pair of crates arrives from Europe, Florida shipping clerks Chick Young (Bud Abbott) and Wilbur Grey (Lou Costello) deliver them to McDougal's House of Horrors. However, the contents—the real Count Dracula (Bela Lugosi) and Frankenstein's Monster (Glenn Strange)—up and leave, for which McDougal (Frank Ferguson) blames our heroes. Dracula heads to a castle in the bayou and links up with scientist Sandra Mornay (Lenore Aubert) in an effort to give the Monster a subservient brain—that of unsuspecting Wilbur. Meanwhile, insurance investigator Joan Raymond (Jane Randolph) is staying close to Wilbur to try and find McDougal's exhibits, while good-hearted Lawrence Talbot (Lon Chaney, Jr.), aka the Wolf Man and an old enemy of the Count's, comes to America and links up with Wilbur and Chick in an effort to destroy Dracula.

Eventually, Wilbur is spirited away to the castle, Talbot and Chick rescue him, Dracula and the Wolf Man die after a vicious battle, the Frankenstein Monster is burned to death, and our heroes have a run-in with the Invisible Man (Vincent Price).

This was Abbott and Costello's twenty-second film, and one Costello hadn't even wanted to make; he felt the script wasn't particularly funny, and producer Robert Arthur had to talk him into doing it. (Arthur reported that Costello and Abbott both kept up their spirits during the making of the film by throwing cream pies at crew members, often going through a dozen a day.)

The film was the team's first big hit in four years and revitalized their careers, though it also brought about a string of increasingly worse "meets the monsters" movies: *Abbott and Costello Meet the Killer, Boris Karloff* (1949); *Abbott and Costello Meet the Invisible Man* (1951); *Abbott and Costello Meet Dr. Jekyll and Mr. Hyde* (1953), and the absolute worst of them all, *Abbott and Costello Meet the Mummy* (1955). (None of these is available on laserdisc, though *Abbott and Costello Meet the Invisible Man* is quite good and *should* be.)

The movie also gave Lugosi, Chaney, and Strange one last night in the moonlight as the monsters that made them famous. All made the most of it, turning in fine and energetic performances. (Watch the scene in which the Monster tosses Aubert out the window: When Strange hurt his ankle, Chaney donned the Frankenstein makeup and did the scene for him.)

The camera angles are inventive, the makeup by Bud Westmore (not their creator, Jack Pierce) is as impressive as ever, and, best of all, we're treated to some great transformation scenes—Talbot into the Wolf Man and Dracula into a bat (and vice versa). The sets are also terrific, especially Dracula's lab and the castle cellar.

Look for the wire holding up the bat at frame 24.00 on side one; and is that the entire wall shaking or just the reflection of the lamp at 28531 on side two?

The Disc
Video: ★★★½
Audio: ★★★ (monaural)
Chapters: Just one (for the trailer)
Format: CLV (side one), CAV (side two)
Source: MCA Home Video

The print used for the film is in very good shape. Despite some grainy patches, there are nice gray tones and deep blacks, and a fairly sharp focus. Lines and scratches are minimal.

The CAV side contains some of the film's best special effects, and you'll enjoy frame-by-framing your way through them.

The audio has a bit of background

noise and is a bit hissy and raw, though not as bad as you'd expect from a movie this age.

MCA Home Video has been releasing other vintage Abbott and Costello films on laserdisc: highly recommended are very good transfers of *In the Navy* and *Keep 'Em Flying* (both 1941).

Not recommended is their newly released *The Naughty Nineties* (1945), one of the duo's worst films, little more than a series of their old sketches, including a truncated "Who's on First."

The Adventures of Don Juan (1948) ★★★★½
Director: Vincent Sherman
Running Time: 111 minutes

Errol Flynn was a great action star whose reputation was built on a dozen movies, made between the mid-1930s and the early 1940s. Because of drinking, chain-smoking, carousing, drug use, and illness, Flynn's best years were well behind him when he made this film. Though he was only thirty-nine, he looked much older.

Yet, *The Adventures of Don Juan* is arguably his finest movie. He was still relatively trim and could wear period costumes like no one before or since; he was still graceful and could handle a sword (though future movie Tarzan Jock Mahoney did the more difficult stunts, including the climactic jump down the staircase); he still oozed charm; and he had a terrific supporting cast, magnificent sets, and a powerful Max Steiner score behind him. And he had one thing more: a world-weariness that gave his Juan a depth none of his other swashbuckling roles possessed. What could have been more *right* for Flynn than to play a man whose sexual prowess precedes and haunts him, allowing him neither peace nor a chance to nurture real love?

Returning to Spain after spending time in England, Juan is appointed instructor at the fencing academy in the court of the weak-willed King Philip III (Romney Brent) and his beautiful, wise wife, Queen Margaret (Viveca Lindfors). There, Juan fends off more passes from women than thrusts from his pupils. Genuinely devoted to the queen—and in love with her—Juan and his sidekick, Leporello (Alan Hale), learn of a plot hatched by the evil Duke de Lorca (Robert Douglas) to seize power for himself. With the help of his fencing students, Juan thwarts Lorca's men (who include Captain Alvarez, played by a youthful Raymond Burr), after which he leaves the palace so that his love for the queen will remain chaste.

The Adventures of Don Juan was only a modest commercial success: Despite the use of stock footage from both *The Adventures of Robin Hood* (1938; the escape from Nottingham Castle) and *The Private Lives of Elizabeth and Essex* (1939; Essex's return from Cadiz) to help keep the budget down, the film cost nearly $3 million—a whopping sum that it didn't recover. It was the last big-budget picture in which Flynn would appear; his later action films, such as *Adventures of Captain Fabian* (1951) and *Against All Flags* (1952), are chintzy, rather pathetic affairs. *The Adventures of Don Juan* is a thrilling, fitting, and touching epitaph for the legendary star.

The actress in the carriage at the end of the film is Nora Eddington, Flynn's second wife.

The John Barrymore *Don Juan* (1926) is also available on laserdisc. Although not a talkie, it was the first film to feature sound effects and music (albeit limited) on a record running along with the film. A year later, this same Vitaphone process was used for *The Jazz Singer*—generally regarded as the first talkie, although the dialogue was limited to a handful of Al Jolson songs and the rest was silence.

The scenario is considerably different from that in the Flynn film: In Italy, Juan falls in love with a young woman who is also being wooed by a member of the powerful Borgia family. Naturally, Juan wins the girl and carries her off to Spain. The movie doesn't have the sweep of other silent epics, but it's got Barrymore, who gives an entrancing performance.

The Disc

Video: ★★★★★
Audio: ★★★★ (monaural)
Chapters: No
Format: CLV
Source: MGM/UA Home Video

It can be argued that this is the most spectacular domestic Technicolor disc on the market today. The picture is so clear and the colors so real that the film almost looks 3-D. You can study the detailed workmanship on the sets and costumes, and even the difference between Errol Flynn's haircut and that of his stunt double is obvious on the disc.

While you'll yearn for a *bit* more body in the Steiner score—which is so evocative of the genre that it was reused in *Zorro, The Gay Blade* (1981)—the dialogue and sounds couldn't be better.

The 1926 film is in surprisingly good shape. The print has its share of scratches but nothing catastrophic, and the ambitious audio provides a great deal of texture despite being predictably tinny.

The Adventures of Milo and Otis (1989) ★★★½

Director: Masanori Hata
Running Time: 76 minutes

Milo is an irrepressible kitten; Otis a practical pug-nosed puppy. The two animals are friends; and when Milo's curiosity gets him swept down a river, Otis dutifully sets out after him. The two become separated, and the film follows their respective adventures in the woods, along the shore, and in the snow; fighting carnivorous foes and finding unlikely allies; their romances with the cat Joyce and pug-nosed Sandra; and their eventual reunion.

The Japanese filmmaker spent four years filming his animals (look-alike Milos and Otises were used to keep the characters from aging *too* much), and—along with his twenty trainers—did as little prodding as possible to get them to do what they were supposed to. When the animals came up with interesting "bits" on their own, Hata changed the story to incorporate them.

The events in this film seem somewhat more artificial than those in *The Bear* (see page 21), the animals doing many things they simply wouldn't do in real life (like playing hide-and-seek). But the results are entertaining for adults as well as for children, and the animal actors are adorable. Besides, whenever the action does sputter or something implausible occurs, there's Dudley Moore as the narrator, pulling us along with the whimsical and inventive voices he created for the characters.

The film was originally released in Japan in 1986 as *Koneko Monogatari* and ran fourteen minutes longer.

The Disc

Video: ★★★★½
Audio: ★★★ (Surround)
Chapters: Yes
Format: CLV
Source: RCA Columbia Pictures Home Video

The Adventures of Milo and Otis is simply beautiful to look at. The colors are lifelike, the image is sharp, and there's barely any grain, even in the night scenes. The film isn't letterboxed, but that's fine: The close-ups of the animals seem that much larger. The scenery looks fine, even with the edges missing.

The digital audio is in Surround, but you won't experience it as fully as they did in Japan because of Moore's narration. It's necessary, of course, but the sounds of nature have been turned way down to accommodate him. It's *very* disappointing that a separate track wasn't provided for Moore. Isn't that what laserdisc technology is all about?

After Hours (1985) ★★★★½

Director: Martin Scorsese
Running Time: 97 minutes

The movie's just over an hour and a half, but you'll feel as though you've spent an eternity stuck in downtown New York.

Paul Hackett (Griffin Dunne) is a young executive who meets Marcy Franklin (Rosanna Arquette) at a diner. Though it's nearly midnight, he goes down to the SoHo loft she shares with sculptress Kiki (Linda Fiorentino). En route, his money flies out the open cab window—an omen of things to come. It turns out that Marcy's a deeply troubled young woman, but things get worse when Paul storms out on her. Each new scene brings a fresh crisis or eccentric character as Paul tries to get back home; standouts among the crackpots he meets are waitress Julie (Teri Garr), who's still living in the 1960s; Mister Softee driver and vigilante Gail (Catherine O'Hara); and bartender Tom (John Heard), who turns out to have something unfortunate in common with Paul—namely, a suddenly dead girlfriend named Marcy Franklin.

Scorsese imparts virtually every sound (ticking clocks, whispers, ringing phones) and every inanimate object with menace; his camera darts, glides, and floats as though it's wired directly to Paul's overwrought nervous system. Except for a rather abrupt, strangely unsatisfying resolution, the movie is a perfect nightmare, a real-life *Invasion of the Body Snatchers* in which only Paul knows what's real but can't get anyone to believe him.

Griffin Dunne is the perfect Everyman, and he gives a performance reminiscent of vintage Gene Wilder; they even sound alike at times. All the other players are perfect, too.

Look for future TV star Bronson Pinchot as Paul's coworker in the film's opening minutes and comedians Cheech and Chong as a pair of crooks.

The Disc
Video: ★★★★½
Audio: ★★★★★ (monaural)
Chapters: Yes
Format: CLV
Source: Warner Home Video

Scorsese's film has been given a first-class remastering, with magnificent color, a sharp, perfect picture, and slight letterboxing. Though the old disc was opened up rather than panned-and-scanned, the matte emphasizes the director's superlative horizontal composition.

The digital sound is gloriously clear. The audio is so well done, in fact, that if you pipe it through rear speakers, you'll swear it's Surround Sound.

Akira Kurosawa's Dreams (1990) ★
Director: Akira Kurosawa
Running Time: 120 minutes

Akira Kurosawa is one of the world's great filmmakers and with the exception of Kubrick, he has made more classic films than any living director, from *Rashomon* (1951) to *Ran* (1985). *Akira Kurosawa's Dreams*, though heartfelt and brilliantly made, is *way* short of being one of them.

The film consists of eight blackout-style tales of varying length and tone. The most successful are "Crows," in which a museumgoer is drawn into a Van Gogh painting, walks through several of the artist's works, and meets the crusty painter himself (stiffly played by director Martin Scorsese), and "Village of the Watermills," a sweet, sensitive ecological tract in which a Japanese Yuppie compares notes with a centenarian in a bucolic village.

The rest of the tales are either self-indulgent, heavy-handed, preachy, or just plain naïve; key offenders are "Mount Fuji in Red," with its nuclear power plant meltdown, and "The Weeping Demon," an anti–atom bomb lament. Yes, some of the images are incredibly beautiful. Yes, many of the special effects created by George Lucas's Industrial Light and Magic shop are stunning. But no matter how attractive the package, handwringing is still handwringing, and you expect more from this director.

One dream, planned by Kurosawa but never filmed, featured a man soaring across land and space with an angel. The conceptual paintings executed by Kurosawa look beautiful, and it's a shame he opted not to include this segment.

The Disc
Video: ★★★★★
Audio: ★★★★★ (Surround)
Chapters: Yes, including subchapters for each tale
Format: CLV (sides one and three), CAV (side two)
Source: Warner Home Video

As seriously flawed as the movie is, you won't find a more impressive disc on the market. The letterboxed image is awash with hypnotic colors, from the subtle blues in "The Blizzard" (if you can stay awake to enjoy them) to the bloodred waters in "The Weeping Demon" to the vibrant primary colors of "Crows."

The sound is even better. You won't hear a lot from your rear speakers, but when you do—you'll feel as in "The Blizzard" and "Mount Fuji in Red"—you'll feel as though you've been drawn into the heart of a maelstrom. The sensory delights are *constant* and are reason enough to own the disc.

The Alamo (1960) ★★★½
Director: John Wayne
Running Time: 172 minutes

John Wayne hadn't intended to star as Davy Crockett in his "dream film," much of the $12 million budget for which came from Wayne's own pocket. He wanted to direct the movie and play a small part as Sam Houston. However, the distributor felt that his name was needed to ensure box-office success, and he reluctantly donned the coonskin cap. (The double duty cost him thirty pounds and drove his cigarette habit up to five packs a day though he assumed a dual function again in 1968 for his hawkish *The Green Berets*.)

Despite the personal cost, *The Alamo* is a film of which Wayne was justifiably proud, an epic fictionalized account of how and why Crockett, Jim Bowie (Richard Widmark), and their men came to the mission to join the command of gentleman soldier Col. William Barret Travis (Laurence Harvey, who starts out with a pretty good southern accent, then reverts to his native British).

If the movie isn't much of a history lesson, it's grand entertainment, and the final siege is an eye-filling spectacle awash with explosions, stirring charges, and nearly as many extras as fought in the original battle. A recreation of the Alamo was constructed in Brackettville, Texas, where it remains a popular tourist attraction.

Contrary to popular belief, the film made a lot of money, though Wayne didn't see a penny: Debts forced him to sell his shares for a quick financial infusion.

The Disc
Video: ★★★★½
Audio: ★★★★★ (Surround)
Chapters: Yes
Format: CLV
Source: MGM/UA Home Video

This disc looks and sounds so good that, except for a few scenes that are a *touch* faded, you'd never guess the picture was over thirty years old. Letterboxed, with digital sound, it wraps you in the action—and, unfortunately, in some of John Wayne's hokiest speeches (his "Republic" discourse would be painful if he wasn't so *sincere*). What's most amazing about the video are the details the disc finds, particularly as the Mexicans take up their positions outside the fort: Every color, epaulet, and button is as vivid as can be. The overture, intermission music, and exit music are included.

MGM had previously offered this disc at 172 minutes, which is still a terrific set. However, they've recently released the original director's cut, which includes thirty minutes of material that had been snipped shortly after the film's release and was believed lost. Most of the scenes go far in bringing the characters to life, and are very welcome additions. For the most part, the material—from a 70mm print found in Toronto—intercuts perfectly with the older footage.

The boxed set also features a terrific "making of" featurette, which offers interviews with filmmakers, footage of the building of the reconstructed Alamo, and other gems.

The Green Berets is also available in a first-rate letterboxed laserdisc from Warner Home Video. That movie, unfortunately, remains intact. The battle scenes are terribly impressive, though.

Alexander Nevsky (1938) ★★★★★
Director: Sergei Eisenstein
Running Time: 107 minutes

In March of 1938, Hitler annexed Austria and it became clear to Soviet leaders that one day they'd have to defend themselves against the Reich. Communist party heads turned to Eisenstein—who had directed *Potemkin* (1925) and other patriotic films—to make a heart-swelling pro-Soviet epic that would fire the public and strengthen its resolve. The result was a film version of the historic thirteenth-century struggle between the Russian people and the merciless Teutonic knights.

Though living the quiet life of a fisherman, Novgorod's Prince Alexander Nevsky (Nikolai Cherkassov, a member of the Supreme Soviet) is aware of the menace on Russia's western border. Learning that the city of Pskov has fallen, he accedes to the peoples' plea to raise an army and lead it against the invaders; at his side are the bold Vassily Bouslay (Nikolai Okhlopkov) and Gavrilo Olexitch (Alexander Abrikossov), both of whom are vying for the hand of Olga (Vera Ivacheva), who has agreed to wed whoever proves to be the bravest.

On April 5, 1262, after several skirmishes, the force of crudely armed Russian peasants meets the armored, mounted, well-armed Teutonic army on the frozen Lake Tchoudsk. The battle is fierce, but the Russians gain the upper hand; victory is assured when the ice cracks and the invaders' heavy armor drags them down. As for Olga, though she chooses Gavrilo, Vassily is more than happy to wed Vassilissa (Anna Danilova), a warrior woman he met on the battlefield.

To modern eyes, some aspects of *Alexander Nevsky* will seem crude. Bits of action in the battle scenes were sped up, no one bleeds when they're stabbed or axed, the ice obviously isn't ice, the romance is hokey, and the sound is tinny due to the primitive recording techniques that existed in the Soviet Union at the time. (Eisenstein hadn't even made a "speaking" film until the unfinished *Bezhin Meadow*, 1935 to 1937.)

The movie still possesses awesome emotional power, however, particularly in light of the real-life carnage that was to follow. From the burning of the babies in Pskov to the victory celebration in Novgorod, Eisenstein created images that spoke both to the moment and to all time. Visually, the work remains a landmark film: For sheer impact and originality, Eisenstein's screen compositions, ingenious cutting, costuming (especially the helmets), barren landscapes, and use of black, white, and gray tones have rarely been matched. His grotesque helmets alone have inspired countless filmmakers, most notably John Boorman in *Excalibur* (see page 88).

Cherkassov, the Charlton Heston of Russia (he also played Ivan the Terrible; see below), is the embodiment of honor, courage, humanity, and resolve; if the real-life Alexander wasn't like Cherkassov, he should have been. All the supporting players are also perfectly cast, especially Vladimir Erchov as the icy Grand Master of the Teutons, Sergei Blinnikov as the Russian traitor Tverdila, and Naoum Rogojin as the ratlike black monk.

Eisenstein commissioned Sergei Prokofiev to write the score, and the director was so impressed with the finished product that he recut portions of the climactic battle to fit the music rather than have the composer alter the music. The suite created from the score remains a recording and concert staple.

Eisenstein's epics *Ivan the Terrible, Part One* and *Ivan the Terrible, Part Two*, 1942 to 1946, are also available on laserdisc. They have the scope and technical brilliance of *Alexander Nevsky* and tell a fascinating tale, though they lack the soul of Eisenstein's earlier work. The director died before he could film part three.

The Disc
Video: ★★½
Audio: ★★
Chapters: Yes
Format: CLV
Source: Corinth Video/Image
    Entertainment

The print used by Corinth has its strengths and weaknesses. The strengths are strong blacks, whites, and gray tones, the weaknesses being a snowstorm of negative dirt in spots (such as the beginning of side two), severe scratches in others, and occasional image warping. In fairness to Corinth, it should be pointed out that even the best prints of *Alexander Nevsky* have many of these problems.

The sound is more disappointing. As mentioned previously, the quality was never very good, and Prokofiev had to record his score quickly, with a bare-bones orchestra. But there's still a good deal of hiss in the digital audio, which prevents the viewer from turning up the volume to compensate.

The dialogue is in Russian, obviously, but the manner in which it's delivered is important: The voices are acceptably clear on the disc.

Aliens (1986) ★★★★
Director: James Cameron
Running Time: 154 minutes

Back in the mid-1970s, Dan O'Bannon wrote a screenplay called *They Bite*, about extraterrestrials terrorizing a spaceship. The idea wasn't particularly novel: author A. E. van Vogt had used it in his 1939 story "Black Destroyer," and so had the 1958 film *It! The Terror from Beyond Space*, among others. But it was still a viable subject, and writer Ron Shusett worked with O'Bannon on a second draft called *Star Beast*, which had just one alien killing people in order to reproduce.

After hitting box-office gold with *Star Wars*, Twentieth Century–Fox was on the prowl for another science fiction project with sequel potential: They bought the script, British director Ridley Scott was brought aboard (he had previously directed the stylish *The Duellists* in 1977), and *Alien* was under way. Scott—who conceived of the film as a cross between *The Texas Chainsaw Massacre* and *Star Wars*—hired artist Hans Rudi Giger to design a creature and spaceships that had his unique "biomechanics" look.

The 1979 film was a huge hit, recounting the tale of the space trawler *Nostromo*, which answers a distress call from a nearby world. One of the crewmen is attacked by a crablike "face-hugger" that plants an egg in his body. When the newborn is sufficiently grown, it explodes from the crewman, matures quickly, and attempts to impregnate or kill the other crew members. Only Ellen Ripley (Sigourney Weaver) survives, managing to open an air lock and suck the alien into space, then climbing into hypersleep for a well-deserved rest—a long one.

In the sequel, Ripley is found after drifting for fifty-seven years. She learns that a colony has been established on planet LV-426, where the alien was found—and, coincidentally, communication with the 157 colonists has suddenly gone dead. Reluctantly, she agrees to join a U.S. colonial marine rescue mission. Unknown to her, mission leader Carter Burke (Paul Reiser) has been charged with sneaking an alien back for bioweapons research by allowing it to impregnate one or more members of the mission. But Burke turns out to be just one of the team's problems. The colony has been overrun by the eight-foot-tall aliens, and everyone is dead except for a nine-year-old girl, Rebecca "Newt" Jorden (Carrie Henn). Ripley takes the girl under her wing, loses her when they try to flee, and has to face a huge, powerful queen alien in order to get her back.

Like Cameron's previous film, *The Terminator* (see page 272), the action in *Aliens* is breakneck and intense. The suspense is heightened by the design of the colony—multileveled but claustrophobic, full of places for evil aliens to hide.

Weaver is astounding. Ripley's strength comes from a mixture of anger, love, and fear, colors that make her utterly believable (unlike, for example, Linda Hamilton's comic book–deep heroine in Cameron's *Terminator 2: Judgment Day*). Michael Biehn is terrific as Corporal Hicks, and Lance Henriksen is great (as usual) as the android Bishop.

The film is flawed by two problems, one minor and one major. The minor problem: Burke gets off too easily. The supplemental material explains what was planned for him, and that would have been much more satisfying.

The major problem is the film's many anachronisms. This is the future. They've got videophones; spaceships; suspended animation; androids. Marines will *not* be talking like surfers or using expressions that are already starting to creak. Even if United Airlines is still around, marines won't have *Fly the friendly skies* written on their helmets. (Would marines today have Civil War–era slogans on their armor?) The barrage of 1980s lingo is distracting and wrongheaded and makes it very difficult for us to believe in the characters.

There's also a nagging question, though Cameron probably had an explanation in some draft of the script: Newt looks the same age when the first alien hits the colony as she does when the marine ship *Sulaco* arrives, and one of the impregnated colonists is still alive when Ripley finds her. This means that only a few days *tops* have passed between losing contact with the colony and the ship's arrival. How come the space soldiers had to go into hypersleep?

Thanks to the skill of Cameron and his stars, the film manages to ride over these failings and is a crackerjack entertainment that (surprised no one says it in the film) ain't over till it's over.

By the way, that's a yogurt and milk mixture Bishop has for blood.

The Disc

Video: ★★★
Audio: ★★★★½ (Surround)
Chapters: Yes
Format: CAV
Source: Fox Video

If you're a science fiction or action fan, you've got to have this disc. When *Aliens* was released, Cameron had to cut it so it wouldn't run over a certain length. Many important scenes were dropped, and these have been restored. Not only do they add enormously to the excitement, they make Ripley a much fuller character (for example, she had a daughter, and the girl's fate explains why Ripley is so passionately protective of Newt). A sequence on colonial LV-426 is also an eye-opener. Notes included with the boxed set explain in detail which scenes have been added or changed.

In addition to being restored, the film has been letterboxed, which makes it superior to the previously released CBS/Fox Home Video pan-and-scan edition. Unfortunately, that version did not suffer from the grain that plagues this one. Cameron supervised the transfer, so it's shocking that some scenes are sharp, crystal-clear, while others are a bit fuzzy, with grain that's all over them like a face-hugger. Portions of the film are also very dark, though at least video noise isn't a problem. The colors are generally solid and accurate.

The audio is splendid: extremely clear, with wonderful use of stereo and rear channels. If you've got subwoofers, watch out for falling plaster. The gross, slurping audio effects also sound terrific.

Anastasia (1956) ★★

Director: Anatole Litvak
Running Time: 105 minutes

Anna Anderson died without ever proving that she was Grand Duchess Anastasia, daughter of the last Russian Czar, Nicholas II. The reason was simple: She wasn't. On July 16, 1918, Nicholas, his wife, Alexandra, their five children, and four aides were shot to death in the cellar of a house in remote Ekaterinberg. According to all accounts, Anastasia fainted at the onset of the attack; waking and screaming, she was bayoneted and clubbed to death by members of the execution party. Afterward, all of the bodies were trucked to a mine where they were hacked to pieces, doused with gasoline, and burned in a bonfire. Remaining body parts were destroyed with sulfuric acid, including Anastasia's.

Surviving relatives of the Czar pronounced Anna Anderson's claim to be false. However, that didn't stop people from wondering—or Marcelle Maurette from writing a play that Twentieth Century–Fox turned into a movie.

It's ten years after the murder and, in Paris, the opportunistic General Bounine (Yul Brynner) and two colleagues have been raising money to search for Anastasia, promising investors a share of the £10 million being held by the Bank of England for the Grand Duchess, should she ever be found. When the con men have to produce an Anastasia or go to jail for fraud, Bounine enlists an amnesiac young refugee from an insane asylum (Ingrid Bergman) to pretend to be Anastasia. He schools her in courtly manners and she comes to believe that she is, in fact, the Russian Grand Duchess. Bounine presents her to relatives and former members of the court, but their endorsements are not unanimous. He gains an audience with Anastasia's grandmother, the Dowager Empress (Helen Hayes). In time, the "unmeltable icicle" of a woman is convinced; but before Anastasia can be betrothed to her childhood sweetheart, Prince Paul, she and Bounine realize they've fallen in love, and they run off together.

It's arguable which generated more public interest: Anna Anderson's quest or the saga (briefly explained in the gatefold jacket) of how, in 1949, star Bergman abandoned her husband, Dr. Petter Lindstrom, and daughter Pia to live with Italian director Roberto Rossellini. Condemnation of the actress was widespread, and she was still persona non grata when director Litvak insisted on casting her as Anastasia. Studio head Darryl F. Zanuck reluctantly agreed. And though her husband threatened to kill himself if Ingrid left him in Paris while the movie was shot in England, she went anyway. (She said she had three reasons for going: The marriage was crumbling, they needed the money, and it was simply too good a part to turn down.)

The story *is* a fascinating one, but the movie is a disappointment. The actors are all very good (though, at forty-one, Bergman looked a bit old to be playing the twenty-seven-year-old), but *Anastasia* is top-heavy with exposition and soap opera, and there are only a few truly memorable scenes: the early confrontation between Anastasia and her late father's chamberlain, who is both skeptical of and rude to the woman; Bounine's first meeting with the Dowager Empress at the theater, where her disdain for him is absolute; and the Empress's surprise visit to the hotel room to meet this woman she's *convinced* is a false Anastasia.

Interesting when viewed as a companion piece to *Nicholas and Alexandra* (see page 195) but not worth it on its own.

The Disc

Video: ★★★½
Audio: ★★★★½ (Surround)
Chapters: Yes
Format: CLV
Source: CBS Fox Video

This is a beautiful movie, and the disc does a very good job of capturing that beauty. Though the Deluxe process has given a slight brownish cast to the colors, it isn't as bad as one might expect from that wretched company. The image is generally very sharp and grain is kept to a satisfactory minimum.

This CinemaScope film has been given a wide letterbox, which is good: Since so much of the movie is talk, you want to see who's being spoken to.

The sound is grand, full-bodied and resonant, with an exceptional sense of depth (a striking impression of distance is created by the train that goes by regularly outside Bounine's window). You'll feel like you're in the concert hall during the performance of *Sleeping Beauty*. The Surround Sound aspects are limited primarily to Alfred Newman's score.

The extras consist of Movietone footage of the film's New York and Hollywood premieres—nice but skimpy. Fox missed a great opportunity to include newsreel footage and photographs of Nicholas II and his family.

Annie Hall (1977) ★★★★★
Director: Woody Allen
Running Time: 94 minutes

Watching director/actor Allen's progression toward *Annie Hall* is a dizzying experience. In his films *Take the Money and Run* (1969), *Bananas* (1971), *Everything You Always Wanted to Know About Sex (But Were Afraid to Ask)* (1972), *Sleeper* (1973), and *Love and Death* (1975), Allen continually grew in style and ambition without abandoning his lovable, helpless, neurotic persona.

As polished and insightful as *Sleeper* and *Love and Death* are, no one quite expected the brilliance of *Annie Hall*, the story of the superficially confident, successful, and idealistic New York comic Alvy Singer (Allen) and his relationship with a mercurial, transplanted Midwesterner, aspiring singer Annie Hall (Diane Keaton, whose real surname is Hall—Keaton was her mother's maiden name—and whose friends call her Annie). What makes *Annie Hall* unique in the Allen filmography is that the old "make 'em laugh" Allen and the serious Allen are in perfect harmony.

Allen shot nearly 50 percent more material than he ended up using, and much of the movie's final structure came about in the editing room. The picture was originally a stream-of-consciousness film called *Anhedonia*—the inability to enjoy life—which, according to cowriter Marshall Brickman, was about Alvy "examining his life [which] consisted of several strands. One was a relationship with a young woman, another was concern with the banality of the life that we all live, and a third was an obsession with proving himself . . . to find out what kind of character he had." Allen says, "The thing was supposed to take place in my mind [but] none of that worked." He cut the film down until it was just the story of himself and Annie, losing many scenes that he and Brickman both loved (for example, a scene straight from *Invasion of the Body Snatchers* in which Rob tries to substitute a pod double for our hero; a sequence set in Eden; a visit to hell; Alvy interpreting a dream for Annie's mother [Colleen Dewhurst]; and more).

Although the final film was more focused, Allen still eschewed chronology and embraced whatever technique best suited the point he was trying to make: subtitles to reveal what the characters are really thinking, animation, silent movie–style slapstick, split screen, talking to the viewer, the surreal (Annie stepping out of her body to comment on what's happening), and so on.

The film also benefits from impeccable casting. In addition to Allen stock player Tony Roberts, who is perfect as the shallow, trendy Rob, Paul Simon is ideal as Annie's airy, superficial mentor, Tony Lacey; Christopher Walken is frighteningly convincing as her troubled brother, Duane; Colleen Dewhurst has a short but effective role as her mother; and both Carol Kane and Shelley Duvall are memorable as Alvy's lovers. And one mustn't forget the movie's highlight, the guest appearance by Marshall McLuhan.

Look for model/actress Shelley Hack as the "empty" pedestrian Allen talks to at the end of chapter fifteen, Sigourney Weaver as Allen's date at the end of the film, and Jeff Goldblum as a partygoer at Lacey's home.

Apart from his next comedy, *Manhattan* (see page 181), Allen has had trouble coming close to the artistic and commercial high-water mark of *Annie Hall*. With the exception of *Hannah and Her Sisters* (1986), *Radio Days* (1987), and *Crimes and Misdemeanors* (1989), his comedies and near-comedies *Stardust Memories* (1980), *A Midsummer Night's Sex Comedy* (1982), *Zelig* (1983), and *Broadway Danny Rose* (1984) have been amusing but generally slight affairs, while his dramas—*Interiors* (1978), *September* (1987), *Another Woman* (1988), and *Alice* (1990)—have been curiously uneven. Or have we just come to expect too much from the man who gave us this masterpiece?

Most Allen's films are available on laserdisc.

The Disc
Video: ★★★
Audio: ★★½ (monaural)
Chapters: Yes
Format: CLV
Source: Criterion and MGM/UA Home Video

Allen's film is one of subdued lighting and monochrome, and that presents some problems for both versions of the film. It's less noticeable on the Criterion disc, though both are equally dark in a number of places (the Adlai Stevenson rally, Keaton's nightclub debut, and more).

The discs are mildly letterboxed, which is essential to the film. Allen has many important wide-screen scenes—for example, "Touch my heart with your foot" and dinner at the Halls's—which look ridiculous cropped (which MGM/UA's original release was).

The audio is clean and clear on both discs.

**Apocalypse Now
(1979) ★★★★½**
Director: Francis Coppola
Running Time: 155 minutes

In 1939, Orson Welles was set to make his first film, an adaptation of Joseph Conrad's 1902 novel, *Heart of Darkness*. The "heart of darkness" of the novel refers not just to the jungle—through which a steamer captain goes in search of the mad, megalomaniacal ivory trader Kurtz, who has made himself a king—but also the feral human heart. After preproduction work was completed, the film was deemed too expensive and was abandoned. Welles made *Citizen Kane* instead.

In 1969, Coppola and writer John Milius made plans to go to Vietnam and shoot, in 16mm, a transplanted version of the story. George Lucas was slated to direct. However, Warner Brothers refused to let the filmmakers subject themselves to actual warfare, and every other studio passed on the film. Coppola made *The Godfather* instead.

After shooting *The Godfather, Part II*, Coppola decided to revive his Vietnam film. Lucas was involved with *Star Wars*, so Coppola decided to direct the project himself—though it was no longer possible to shoot in Vietnam. Since the U.S. government didn't want to lend him the hardware he needed, the director made an agreement with Philippine president Ferdinand Marcos to shoot the film there and borrow his air force. With a budget of $13 million and a proposed sixteen-week shooting schedule, Coppola headed for the Philippines in February 1976.

In his version of Conrad's tale—which was based on soldiers' experiences in the war—Capt. Benjamin L. Willard (Martin Sheen) is sent upriver in a patrol boat to find and assassinate Green Beret Col. Walter E. Kurtz (Marlon Brando), who has set up an empire and built a fiercely loyal army just over the border in Cambodia. At first, Willard is reluctant about the mission, never having had to kill an American before. As he journeys through Vietnam, he becomes more reluctant still: Reading through Kurtz's dossier, he comes to admire the bold, independent officer. Ultimately, however, he confronts Kurtz and realizes that whatever the colonel was before, he is completely mad now—and Willard does what he came to do.

Coppola has said he set out to make "the most vulgar, entertaining, exciting, actionful" film he could, because he wanted "people to come see it." What he did not expect, however, were the countless, seemingly insurmountable problems that got in his way from start to finish. After a week of filming, he decided that the actor playing Willard—Harvey Keitel—was not right for the part (this after the part had already been turned down by Robert Redford, Jack Nicholson, Gene

Hackman, Steve McQueen, and actors whom Coppola had made stars: Al Pacino and James Caan). Martin Sheen was hired to replace him, but the director's problems were far from over. He had trouble with Marcos's air force, which was frequently called away to fight rebels, sometimes in the middle of a shot. Each day, different pilots would show up on locations, making the previous day's rehearsals useless.

Shooting dragged on into the summer, when heat and humidity plagued the crew. A typhoon hit, wrecking many of the sets and causing the production to close down for two months; it resumed in July 1976 and slogged on until March of the following year, when Sheen had a heart attack. He was out of commission for six weeks, during which time Coppola did long shots with a double (such as the spear attack on the boat). Then Marlon Brando arrived to contribute his three weeks of shooting. To Coppola's horror, Brando hadn't read *Heart of Darkness*, didn't know his lines, and (no kidding!) didn't really have a handle on the character. He was also ninety pounds heavier than he was supposed to be to play the gaunt Kurtz. Coppola changed his concept of the character and then turned Brando and Sheen loose in improvisations. The actor managed to get some of his lines right, and the director finally had to *stop* shooting the final confrontation—though even when it was done, he wasn't sure it was exactly what he wanted.

After spending $31 million—the overages were personally guaranteed by the director—on a 238-day shoot, Coppola returned to the United States to assemble his film. It was scheduled to open in April 1978, but Coppola continued to juggle, edit, and rethink it. He cut out many of Brando's improvisations and, among other scenes, an extensive ghostlike sequence in which Willard comes upon a fog-enshrouded French plantation whose occupants are living in the past. The film finally premiered in August of 1979 and was an international smash.

Milius had always regarded *Apocalypse Now* as a retelling of the *Odyssey*. Lieutenant Colonel Kilgore (Robert Duvall), the air cavalry officer whose helicopters give Willard and his boat a lift, is the Cyclops who had to be deceived to get results; the Playboy Bunnies who entertain troops at the transportation center are the Sirens; and so on. However, the film plays more like *Alice in Wonderland*, with Mad Hatters, Mock Turtles, and Queens of Hearts galore and sights that become more and more surreal: the giant bullets rimming the Playboy arena, the helicopter in a tree, the tiger in the jungle, the jet in the river. By the time they reach the bridge at the border of Cambodia—brightly lighted, like an amusement park Ferris wheel—*everyone* is mad, from the soldiers fighting there to Willard's boatmates. It's positively nightmarish, with Willard—the assassin—the one sane figure.

From top to bottom, the cast is extraordinary. Sheen plays the Oliver North–like hero just right, and Brando projects a world-weariness that Coppola was able to use to make his submission to death more believable. Dennis Hopper is frighteningly out in space as the nameless photojournalist who lives in the Kurtz compound and worships the colonel, and Robert Duvall's performance as Kilgore is, of course, legendary. Everyone remembers his "I love the smell of napalm in the morning" line, but *everything* about his work is memorable, from his walk—with his shoulders pulled back like a taut bow—to his loving discourses about surfing. Coppola himself appears as the director filming the soldiers at 4/28:29 on side one.

Technically, the film is also a marvel. The two attacks on the patrol boat are terrifying, but there may not be a more incredible sequence than Kilgore's helicopter attack on the beach: This scene will make you wish the film were all CAV so you could freeze each stunning frame. It's one of the film's many ironies that while decrying "the horror, the horror" of war, it gets the red blood flowing with the spectacular, savage assault.

Hearts of Darkness, by the director's wife, Eleanor, is available on laserdisc and should be seen. Never has a filmmaker's highs and lows, torments and exhilarations, been captured with greater insight than in this exciting, inspiring feature-length documentary on the making of *Apocalypse Now*.

The Disc

Video: ★★★★★
Audio: ★★★★★ (Surround)
Chapters: Yes
Format: CLV (sides one, two, three), CAV (side four, consisting solely of the titles)
Source: Paramount Home Video

The disc is as perfect as you could want. There are a couple of *very* minor flaws in the master element, but that's *it*. The colors are striking, the letterbox framing is just right, and the sharpness of the image is unbelievable. There's no video noise, and the only grain you'll find is grain Coppola wanted in the original film.

The audio kills. Normal stereo separation sounds fine, but the Surround Sound —remixed from the six-track master— will wipe you out. If you thought that *Die Hard* was the last word in helicopter assaults, be prepared for a postscript.

Arachnophobia (1990) ★★½
Director: Frank Marshall
Running Time: 110 minutes

Entomologist Dr. James Atherton (Julian Sands) takes photographer Jerry Manley (Mark L. Taylor) and a research party deep into a Venezuelan jungle, where they discover a new breed of spider. Unfortunately, one of the arachnids—whose venom is instantly toxic—bites Manley and he dies; the male spider slips into the photographer's coffin and rides back with him to rustic Canaima, California. There, it exits the coffin, is snatched by a bird, kills the would be predator, and sets up housekeeping in a barn.

The barn is owned by Dr. Ross Jennings (Jeff Daniels), who has just moved from San Francisco with his wife, Molly (Harley Jane Kozak), and their children, Tommy (Garette Patrick Ratliff) and Shelley (Marlene Katz). Ross wants to lead the simple life of a country GP, but his life is anything but quiet as the spider mates with a domestic house spider, breeds lethal soldiers, and sends them out to kill. After several deaths, and the inability of exterminator Delbert McClintock (John Goodman) to contain the creatures, Jennings (who, naturally, has a crippling fear of spiders) sends for Dr. Atherton and the battle is joined.

This was the inaugural film of Disney's Hollywood pictures division and was produced by Steven Spielberg's Amblin Entertainment, with longtime Spielberg producer Marshall making a competent directorial debut. *Arachnophobia* was not the box-office blockbuster the Disney folks had expected, part of which was due to the idiotic marketing campaign, which sold the film as a "thrill-omedy." Hollywood Pictures would have been far more successful if they'd dared viewers to sit through the film. For his part, Marshall dropped the ball in the chills department: His spiders are ominous and photographed with a wonderful eye for drama, but they're never creepy-crawly *gross*. He didn't want to alienate the squeamish but then why bother making a movie about killer spiders?

It was also a terrible idea to throw in a rather unusual home-improvement tool (at 4/43:43 on side one): Once you see it, you know how the movie ends.

The performances are fine, though too many are on the broadly comic side, especially Goodman and Stuart Pankin as the bumbling Sheriff Lloyd Parsons. A special salute goes to the team that worked the very convincing mechanical spider boss.

The Disc

Video: ★★★★
Audio: ★★★½ (Surround)
Chapters: Yes
Format: CLV
Source: Hollywood Pictures Home Video

For the most part, the transfer is beautiful. The image is razor-sharp and the colors are generally solid. There's only the barest hint of grain in a few scenes (such as the predawn opening), and there's no video noise. The movie has been mildly letterboxed.

The audio is pleasing, though Surround effects are surprisingly pedestrian: They pop only during the jungle scenes and during the climactic spider attack on the house.

The Assassination of Trotsky (1972)
Director: Joseph Losey
Running Time: 103 minutes

Richard Burton had had a string of flops when he undertook *The Assassination of Trotsky* and he was hopeful that the film would turn his fortunes around. "For one thing," he said when filming began in Rome, "the lines I have to speak are Trotsky's own. That is a decided advantage." For another, he was working with Losey (*The Boy with Green Hair* [1948], *These Are the Damned* [1962]), a filmmaker of talent and vision. Unfortunately, Losey found it impossible to communicate effectively with the international cast and crew, and the results were a confused, heartbreaking disaster.

The film covers the last four months in the life of the exiled Russian revolutionary Leon Trotsky, who had lost a power struggle with Stalin after the death of Lenin. At the time, he was living in Mexico City behind high protective walls in the Avenida Viena, Coyoacan, tending to his pet rabbits, writing articles, books, and letters, and spending time with his wife and followers. The recreation of his compound is amazingly exact, and the events themselves are all accurate. Even the state of decay of his friend Robert Sheldon Harte's body when it was recovered from a lime pit is precisely the way it looked. But there's no drama because key events are missing (it isn't clear that Trotsky moves after the daring Siqueiros raid), character motivation is never fully explained, and performances are either melodramatic or flat. There's also too much padding: *long* and pointless scenes of a May Day parade, the assassin on a boat, shots of "meaningful" murals, a painfully bloody bullfight (the Trotsky/bull metaphor is *way* overdone), and more.

Burton tries hard, but he's undercut by the confusing editing and his ill-advised decision to skip the Russian accent. Trotsky spoke fluent English, but it *was* accented.

French star Alain Delon plays the Stalin-sent assassin, Ramon Mercader, a.k.a. Frank Jacson. He took the part of the trembling, unlikable killer to prove "I am an actor. I have been fighting for ten years to make people forget that I am just a pretty boy with a beautiful face." Though the murder is also recreated with great accuracy, the face is all you'll be watching, since his scenes play flat. Romy Schneider chews the scenery relentlessly as his lover, Sylvia Ageloff.

For the record, Jacson spent twenty years in jail for the murder. He died in Cuba in 1978.

The Disc
Video: no stars
Audio: ★ (monaural)
Chapters: No
Format: CLV
Source: Republic Pictures Home Video

You think the film is bad? Wait'll you get a load of the miserable presentation. Republic was either desperate for product or else has a complete disdain for the consumer (or both): The picture is absolutely terrible—seriously red or pale, often indecipherable in dark scenes, full of breaks and dust, and with *the ragged bottom of the image* showing constantly. And it's grainy to boot. The titles are letterboxed, showing you just how much of the film is lost to cropping—though letterboxing the whole film wouldn't have helped much.

The dialogue is frequently inaudible or muffled, and there are a number of dropouts. Background hiss and crackles are minimal at the beginning but become a serious problem as the film progresses.

An example of the lack of care that was taken with the package is indicated by the fact that on the jacket the manufacturer gets the date of the film wrong by fifteen years!

Avalon (1990) ★★★½
Director: Barry Levinson
Running Time: 126 minutes

In English legend, Avalon was a place of healing, the vale to which Arthur asked to be taken after being mortally wounded by Mordred. In this film, Avalon is the name of the Baltimore neighborhood in which the Krichinsky family settles—the hoped-for haven that turns out to be as illusory as the one to which Arthur went.

The film begins in 1914, and we follow the Krichinsky brothers as they try to build a life for themselves, their wives, and their children. Of all the brothers, Gabriel (Lou Jacobi) feels the strongest about the importance of family ties, and it's he who complains the most when one brother moves to the suburbs: He may be bettering himself, but he's also breaking up the family. Ironically, it's Gabriel who lays the ax to the root when he arrives late for Thanksgiving dinner and discovers that the turkey has been carved without him. He leaves and is true to his word never to return.

The film expands, then, to tell the tale of second-generation cousins Issy "Kirk" (Kevin Pollak) and Jules "Kaye" (Aidan Quinn) and their families, the wildly successful department store they open—and how they deal with the awful tragedy that ensues.

If you come from a family with a European background, chances are that you've lived at least part of this film. It will be bittersweet, painful, and uplifting for those viewers and enlightening for others. Levinson covers a lot of territory in the autobiographical film, yet it never feels rushed (at times, in fact, it's actually a bit lethargic) and it steeps you so thoroughly in these people and their times that you won't want to leave. It is Levinson's most moving film since *Diner* (1982), which is about the director's youth in Baltimore, and more heartfelt and sincere than his overrated *Rain Man* (1988).

Joan Plowright deserves special mention for her work as Eva Krichinsky: If the film has a Greek chorus, this wise and touching soul is it. The widow of Laurence Olivier, Plowright has given rare but exceptional performances in films such as *Brimstone and Treacle* (1982) and *I Love You to Death* (see page 146). She should get out *much* more often!

The Disc
Video: ★★★★½
Audio: ★★★ (Surround)
Chapters: No
Format: CLV
Source: RCA/Columbia Home Video

The film has been given a mild letterbox and a loving transfer. Despite the many dark or monochromatic scenes, there is a minimal amount of grain—*very* minimal. For the most part, colors are rock-solid and there is no video noise. In almost every shot, the image positively glows.

The audio doesn't have very many grandstanding moments, but the clarity and detail help to project the intimacy of the family gatherings.

Babette's Feast (1987) ★★★★
Director: Gabriel Axel
Running Time: 102 minutes

Paris-born Axel, who divides his time between Denmark and Paris, works primarily in theater and has directed only eight movies since 1959. None of these received much recognition or many commercial engagements in the United States until *Babette's Gastebud—Babette's Feast*. Earlier films, such as *The Red Mantle* (1967), a tale of passion and revenge set in eleventh-century Iceland, and *The Popular Toy* (1968), a comedy about pornography, just didn't have the kind of appeal that finds an international audience.

Babette's Feast is different. Set in 1871 with flashbacks, it stars Brigitte Federspiel and Bodil Kjer as spinster sisters Martina and Philippa, respectively, who live together in a small coastal village in Jutland. The daughters of a deeply devout minister, they carry on his work after he dies, tending to the small group of acolytes he left behind—a mission that, over the decades, has prevented them all from truly living.

Enter Babette Hersant (Stephane Audran), whose husband and son were slain in the civil war that overthrew the French emperor. She is sent to Jutland by a friend, Parisian opera singer Achille Papin (Jean-Philippe Lafont), who once lived in Denmark and gave lessons to (and loved) Philippa. Babette is engaged to work as the sisters' housekeeper in exchange for room and board.

Babette's sole remaining tie with France is playing the lottery, and when she wins a small fortune she prepares a feast for the sisters, their stoic guests, and the visiting General Lorenz Lowenhielm (Jarl Kulle). What the repast reveals about each character is the beautiful heart and soul of the film, one you'll savor—like the guests their meal—for quite some time.

The film is based on a short story by Isak Dinesen, and the performances, especially by Kulle, are exceptional. The general's parting words to Philippa are some of the most heartfelt and poignant you'll ever hear in a film, and the movie gets richer with repeated viewings.

The Disc

Video: ★★★
Audio: ★★★ (stereo)
Chapters: No
Format: CLV
Source: Orion Home Video/CinemaDisc Collection

The image is rather grainy (somewhat more so than in the original film), and the colors are drab, but the picture is acceptably sharp. Only the titles are letterboxed—which isn't really a drawback except during certain shots of the feast, where characters are lost on the sides.

The movie is strong enough to survive these problems, and you'll forget them soon enough not just because the characters are so interesting but because the audio is superb. The quiet clatter of the utensils and dishes make a bigger impact on the characters than the thundering surf and storms that batter Jutland, and the audio treats these gentle sounds with great respect. They bring the feast to life, the perfect use of digital sound to create atmosphere.

Babette's Feast is in Danish and French with yellow subtitles that capture most of the nuance of the language.

Backdraft (1991)★★
Director: Ron Howard
Running Time: 135 minutes

When Ron Howard is on target, he works wonders, making us care about his characters, as in *Splash* (1984), *Cocoon* (1985), and *Parenthood* (1989). When he misses the mark, he misses by a mile, as in *Gung Ho* (1986) and *Willow* (1988). Add *Backdraft* to the latter list. Howard tells the story of brothers Stephen and Brian McCaffrey (Kurt Russell and William Baldwin) of Engine Company 17 in Chicago, the sons of a heroic fireman who died in a blaze. Stephen is the hardened veteran who has been trying to prove himself a worthy bearer of the McCaffrey name; Brian is the Fire Academy rookie who wants to earn the respect of his brother.

This predictable, insipid soap froths against a background of arson as fire inspector Donald Rimgale (Robert De Niro, wasted) seeks to prove that a very knowledgeable arsonist has been setting fires for a very specific reason. He's right, of course, though viewers will be way ahead of him as to who and why. Donald Sutherland has a small but chilling role as jailed arsonist Ronald Bartel, a Hannibal Lecter–like figure who advises the department about the firebug.

Russell and Baldwin are good, and Scott Glenn is typically sturdy as fireman John Adcox. But the script is a rickety framework for the dazzling fire stunts and special effects (the exploding rooftop, among other set pieces, is a miniature seamlessly combined with live actors) and for eerily beautiful shots of crawling, dancing flames. If only there were chapter marks to get through the rest of the drivel.

The Disc
Video: ★★★½
Audio: ★★★½ (Surround)
Chapters: No
Format: CLV (sides one and two), CAV (side three)
Source: MCA/Universal Home Video

With all of the fire scenes, video noise was a hellish problem for MCA, and they've done a good though not perfect job of controlling it. Grain is a minor problem in a few scenes, though otherwise the picture is sharp, glossy, and colorful.

The letterboxing captures the film's spectacular fires perfectly, though a bit of the picture has been dropped on the sides. A pan-and-scan version has been opened up slightly and captures the drama perfectly, though the incredible action scenes are somewhat eviscerated. The CAV side is flawless.

The audio is *so* exciting during the fire scenes, you'll overlook the fact that there isn't much to listen to the rest of the time. The only caveat is that the musical score is laid on *way* too thick both front and rear.

The Band Wagon
(1953) ★★★★
Director: Vincente Minnelli
Running Time: 113 minutes

After the success of *Singin' in the Rain* (see page 249), which was about the making of a movie, producer Arthur Freed filmed *The Band Wagon*, which is about the making of a play. *The Band Wagon* has some of the earlier film's daffiness, but it has bittersweet elements that make it less fun.

Instead of the silent-film era giving way to the coming of sound, *The Band Wagon* is about aging movie star Tony Hunter (Fred Astaire), whose film career has come to an end. To shake the depression and boredom, Hunter agrees to star in a musical written by Lester and Lily Marton (Oscar Levant and Nanette Fabray, playing characters based on the film's screenwriters Betty Comden and Adolph Green). Unfortunately, the man they engage to direct the play is hamola Broadway actor/director/playwright Jeffrey Cordova (Jack Buchanan). The play is about a children's writer who starts penning lurid mysteries, but Cordova views it as a Faust story and stages it accordingly, with fiery reds, a devil, and Dantean spectacle. It bombs in New Haven; if that wasn't depressing enough for Tony, he's in love with his costar, pampered prima ballerina Gabrielle Girard (Cyd Charisse), who's very tight with her jealous choreographer, Paul Byrd (James Mitchell).

Tony isn't one to wallow in depression, however. With the help of his young and enthusiastic costars, and an increasingly sweet Gaby, he reformulates the play and opens on Broadway as the musical Lily and Lester had intended. It's a smash, and both his career and private life take a decided turn for the better.

The two big male musical stars at MGM—Gene Kelly and Fred Astaire—were known for rather different styles of dancing: Kelly for his muscular tap and acrobatics, Astaire for his graceful tap and ballroom style. Nonetheless, there was a rivalry between the two, and in this film Astaire not only does what he did best but also invades Kelly territory with a surreal production number such as the ones Kelly danced and choreographed in *An American in Paris* (see comments in *On the Town*), and *Singin' in the Rain*. The number *Girl Hunt: A Murder Mystery in Jazz* is brilliantly choreographed and danced; Astaire was fifty-three at the time yet moved like a man half his age.

Cyd Charisse, who had a decade of film experience behind her and had danced with Kelly in *Singin' in the Rain*, handles the various dance styles expertly, while pianist Oscar Levant is his typically entertaining or annoying self, depending upon your point of view. (Levant, too, was "borrowed" from *An American in Paris*).

Giving the film added appeal are the songs themselves. "That's Entertainment" has become a standard, but "A Shine on Your Shoes" and "Triplets" are the real showstoppers. In the former, Astaire stops at a penny arcade on Forty-second Street and does a marvelous tap with the shoe-shine man; in the latter, he, Fabray, and Buchanan play babies complaining about one another. The trio do the number dressed as toddlers and, incredibly, dance on their *knees*, to which baby shoes have been attached.

If the somewhat familiar story and characters prevent *The Band Wagon* from being the classic *Singin' in the Rain* has become, it's darn close—and that's not bad.

Watch for Ava Gardner's delightful unbilled cameo in Grand Central Station. (Also look for the shadow of the camera operator on the "Electricity Is Life" attraction in the foreground moments after Astaire has knocked over the cans: 11/24868 CAV.)

The Disc

Video: ★★★★★
Audio: ★★★★ (monaural)
Chapters: Yes
Format: CLV and CAV editions
Source: MGM/UA Home Video

The Band Wagon is one of the three best Technicolor discs presently available (*The Adventures of Don Juan* [see page 2] and—naturally—*Singin' in the Rain* are the others). It looked very good on the original disc, released in 1987, but the remastered edition will startle you with its solid colors and sense of depth—especially the CAV edition. The sharpness of the picture and solidness of the colors are simply unbelievable.

Apart from a few minor blemishes—and they are minor indeed—the print is immaculate as can be. In the CAV edition, freeze-frame 5975 in chapter three: Astaire is hidden behind the newspaper, but if your monitor is large enough, you can actually see him reflected in the window of the train.

The digital audio has the limited dynamic range you'd expect from a film of this era, but that's an observation, not a complaint. The film sounds just fine.

The extras include one of Cyd Charisse's dance numbers that was cut from the film and, on the CAV edition, the original trailer.

Barry Lyndon (1975) ★★★★
Director: Stanley Kubrick
Running Time: 185 minutes

William Makepeace Thackeray's wonderfully satirical *The Luck of Barry Lyndon*, published in 1844 in *Fraser's Magazine* (retitled *The Memoirs of Barry Lyndon Esq., by Himself* when published in book form) is the saga of Irish rogue Redmond Barry, who, after fighting a duel, is forced to flee Ireland. Serving in the Seven Years War as a soldier for the English and then their allies the Prussians, he falls in with the Chevalier de Balibari—who, it turns out, is actually his uncle, Cornelius Barry. The two make their living as gamblers, during which time Barry weds the widowed Countess of Lyndon. He dislikes and abuses her young son, Lord Bullingdon, who runs away from home; however, Barry couldn't be more doting to their own boy, Bryan, who dies tragically. When Bullingdon reaches adulthood, he returns, wounds Barry in a duel, and offers him a pension if he'll leave the country. Barry goes but is left penniless by the death of the Countess. He spends his remaining days in Fleet Prison, tended to by his mother.

Kubrick's film stops short of the death of the Countess but is otherwise generally faithful to the novel. It's a sad, memorable film that draws the viewer into its impeccable recreation of the era. The director, a renowned travel hater, shot the picture entirely in England and created painterly images of unparalleled beauty and authenticity; thanks to new film stocks, even the candlelit scenes were shot using only available lighting.

In fact, the film's major flaw is how much Kubrick was in love with these images, letting far too many of them go on *way* too long. Kubrick the screenwriter knew just what to snip from Thackeray but not from his own film.

Ryan O'Neal took some hits from the critics for his quiet, unassuming portrayal and for an accent that sounds too practiced. While the part could have used some of the impishness of Albert Finney's *Tom Jones* (1963), O'Neal brings convincing affection to his relationship with the Chevalier (Patrick Magee, who is superb) and equally convincing hatred to the relationship with Bullingdon (Leon Vitali, whom you will love to hate). Unfortunately, it's difficult to judge Marisa Berenson's work as the Countess: She doesn't get to say much and, more often than not, is simply posed by Kubrick to complete his photographic paintings. They receive excellent support from Hardy Kruger as Captain Potzdorf and Marie Kean as Mrs. Lyndon, and from members of the Kubrick repertory company: Philip Stone (Graham), Steven Berkoff (Lord Ludd), and Leonard Rossiter (Captain Quin).

The Disc
Video: ★★★★½
Audio: ★★★★ (monaural)
Chapters: Yes
Format: CLV
Source: Warner Home Video

This disc is a *vast* improvement over the earlier cropped version. Except for a few scenes that aren't quite as sharp as they should be, the transfer is nearly perfect. The colors are rich and subtle, there isn't a trace of grain—even in the candlelit scenes—and, despite all the reds and browns, there's no video noise. The letterboxing is quite mild, but all of Kubrick's magnificent compositions are intact.

The audio is a little hollow in spots—a virtue of Kubrick's preference for recording sounds on location rather than dubbing them in later—but the sound effects and music have exceptional range.

The film is presented with its original intermission.

Batman (1989) ★★★½
Director: Tim Burton
Running Time: 126 minutes

When cartoonist Bob Kane created Batman in 1939, he envisioned him as a mysterious, frightening creature of the night. A pair of chintzy movie serials emphasized slam-bang action, and in 1966 the hit TV series took a camp approach, as did the motion picture *Batman* of the same year, which starred the TV cast.

A year after the success of *Superman* in 1978, producers Benjamin Melnicker and Michael Uslan tried to get a Batman movie going: At one point, the project seemed ready to roll with Peter O'Toole as the villainous Joker. However, it languished until director Tim Burton came aboard. Burton, a former Disney animator who had directed the surprise outré hits *Pee-wee's Big Adventure* (1985) and *Beetlejuice* (1988), was deemed the perfect man to helm a Batman true in look and spirit to the original comic-book character.

Boy, did he. The plot—such as it is—tells us why millionaire Bruce Wayne (Michael Keaton) became the hero, why petty crook Jack Napier (Jack Nicholson) became the villain, and lurches forward as the Joker plots to murder everyone in Gotham City and Batman tries to stop him. What the film *really* is about are these two people, both of whom are psychotic, one only less so than the other, and the sparks that happen when they clash. Oddly, though neither Keaton nor Nicholson look like the respectively muscular and lanky comic-book characters, the movie works. You *believe* these two are crazy enough to do what they do for a living. Burton integrates them nicely into his settings, though it should be noted that Sam Hamm's original script contained many wonderful touches that were dropped from the finished film—for instance, Batman explaining that he wears the golden symbol on his chest so that enemies will shoot at it and not at his face (an idea lifted from Frank Miller's 1986 graphic novel *The Dark Knight Returns*).

There are some nice action scenes (and some bad ones, such as the totally unbelievable climax outside the cathedral tower), and long stretches of nothing happening as Vicki Vale (Kim Basinger) looks into Batman's background or chats it up with Wayne's butler Alfred (a wonderful Michael Gough), or when the Joker disfigures works of art, cuts paper dolls, and dances under his Macy's-like balloons—forever, it seems.

The late Anton Furst's stand-out art direction accurately creates the look described in the script, as though hell had broken through the pavement and kept on growing, and Danny Elfman's fresh, driving score is magnificent. Both help the film through its numerous slow stretches.

The Disc
Video: ★★★★★
Audio: ★★★★★ (Surround)
Chapters: Yes
Format: CLV
Source: Warner Home Video

The scene in which Batman crashes through the skylight, then races the Batmobile through the city will *probably* become the scene you use to show the uninitiated the power and range of laserdiscs. From the tinkling of the shattered glass to the roar of the engine, the scene's a dazzler.

But so is the rest of the disc. You'd understand if it wasn't this good: The movie is dark, but the colors and blacks are glossy, the details are incredible, and there's no grain or noise. This is one of the great ones.

The letterboxing is not severe and captures most of the original screen image.

The stereo separations are superb, and the Surround Sound is a *lot* of fun: Shut the main speakers while the family is looking for a cab at the beginning and just soak up all the ambient sounds.

Battle of the Bulge (1965) ★★
Director: Ken Annakin
Running Time: 156 minutes

Begun on December 16, 1944, the Battle of the Bulge—also known as the Battle of the Ardennes—was Hitler's last major counteroffensive of World War II. The plan was to prevent the Allies from reaching Germany by splitting the Americans from the British in Belgium, capturing Antwerp, and blocking Allied supply routes while destroying the isolated armies. Believing Hitler to be beaten, the Allies were taken totally by surprise; fortunately, a combination of stiff Allied resistance and depleted German resources saw the tide turn after December 24, though it wasn't until February 7 that the Allies regained the territory they'd lost.

In the early 1960s, star-driven films about World War II were enjoying great success at the box office. Movies such as *The Guns of Navarone* (1961), *The Longest Day* (see page 177), and *The Great Escape* (see page 122) not only had a domestic audience, they had international appeal, as well. The market for these films continued well into the Vietnam era: Witness the success of *The Dirty Dozen* (see page 68), *Where Eagles Dare* (1969), and *Patton* (see page 205).

The fierce, lengthy Battle of the Bulge was an ideal subject for a big movie of this sort. Unfortunately, while the film has a star-studded cast, exciting battles, and first-class production values, it lacks strong characters and more than a hint of historical accuracy (a disclaimer at the end of the film acknowledges that characters and events were "generalized" and "synthesized"). It was a costly flop.

American reconnaissance officer Lieutenant Colonel Kiley (Henry Fonda) believes that a German offensive is imminent, but he can't convince General Grey (Robert Ryan) or Colonel Pritchard (Dana Andrews) of that. It isn't until the German colonel Hessler (Robert Shaw) makes serious inroads into Allied territory that the commanders agree to take action. Fortunately, Lieutenant Weaver

(James MacArthur) and the obnoxious black marketeer Guffy (Telly Savalas) are on hand to stop Hessler and his panzers by setting their tanks ablaze with oil drums. Elsewhere, macho Sergeant Duquesne (George Montgomery) and scrappy Major Wolenski (Charles Bronson) more or less single-handedly destroy the rest of the German army.

While the history is worthless and the characters (except for Hessler) are two-dimensional, the scenery and battles are awe-inspiring. Made in the "you are there" Cinerama process and shot entirely in Spain (the Sierra de Guadarrama provided real snow, not fake-looking movie snow), the film puts you in diving airplanes, in jeeps on winding roads, on the end of 88mm tank cannons, and slams you into walls. You won't know much about what really happened when it's all over, but you will feel as if you've been through a war. The only flaws in the physical production are the occasional use of obvious miniatures—buildings, tanks, and trains—but these are minor complaints.

The Disc
Video: ★★★★★
Audio: ★★★★★
Chapters: Yes
Format: CLV
Source: Warner Home Video

Shot in Ultra Panavision with seven-channel sound, *Battle of the Bulge* couldn't look or sound better. The picture is so sharp, you can practically count the snowflakes, and there's no loss of detail in night scenes or dark interiors. The print is almost entirely free of grain or defects.

The letterboxing doesn't quite capture the full wide-screen image of the 70mm original, but it comes close enough. The windowboxed titles will show you just how much you're missing.

The audio is stunning. Viewers with Surround Sound will have tank treads rolling right over them, explosions carrying from front to back, and just listen to those musical *pings* on side three, chapter five, when Henry Fonda is flying in a fog. To get clearer sound than that, you'd have to have someone playing a triangle next to your TV. The overture, entr'acte, and exit music are included.

Battle of the Bulge was shortened by nearly ten minutes after its initial road-show engagement; a few slow spots and a rather nasty assassination attempt against Hessler were cut. These scenes have not been restored; reportedly, no one knows where they are, and a major restorative effort is unlikely.

The Bear (1989) ★★★★½
Director: Jean-Jacques Annaud
Running Time: 92 minutes

Annaud's film *Quest for Fire* (1981) was a flawed but amazing accomplishment: a feature-length film about cave people made virtually without dialogue. *The Bear* is even more amazing: It was made with very little dialogue and partly without human stars.

Based on the novel *The Grizzly King* by James Oliver Curwood, and set in British Columbia in 1885, the film follows the adventures of the young bear cub Douce (Youk), who, after losing his mother in a rockslide, befriends an adult Kodiak bear, Kaar (Bart), who's been wounded by a pair of hunters. The two pelt traders—Bill (Jack Wallace) and Tom (Tcheky Karyo)—continue tracking the animals, eventually bringing in dogs and their handler (Andre Lacombe) to assist. The chase continues, Kaar finds love, the bears bond, and we're even allowed a peek at Douce's dreams and a mushroom-induced hallucination—in which frogs, bees, and butterflies take on all kinds of bizarre forms and characteristics—before the final showdown, high in the mountains. The resolution is at once satisfying and moving.

The director spent $24 million and exposed 1 million feet of film (twice that of an "ordinary" feature) to get the trained bears to do exactly what he wanted; in those few cases where he couldn't, "robot" bears built by Jim Henson's Creature Shop were used. They intercut seamlessly with the genuine article. The only reality stretching that should have been avoided was the (apparent) dubbing of a child's voice for that of the bear cub: it's easy enough to identify with Douce without having made him more "human."

Though *The Bear* was an international smash, it flopped in the United States. While children *will* find some segments slow, this is a film the whole family can enjoy, a highbrow variant of *The Adventures of Milo and Otis* (see page 3).

The Disc

Video: ★★★★★
Audio: ★★★★★ (Surround)
Chapters: No
Format: CLV
Source: RCA/Columbia Home Video

Except for a few night scenes that are a shade too dark and a bit of video noise in some of the camp-fire sequences, the transfer is perfect, a real delight. The film was shot in the Canadian northwest and in the Dolomites in northern Italy, and it looks magnificent in this letterboxed presentation. (The incredible scene in which Douce confronts the mountain lion on the riverbank just doesn't work the same panned-and-scanned.)

The colors are true to life, the image is sharp as can be, and for most of the film you'll feel as though you're looking out a window.

The audio is both intimate and epic, and the separation throughout is outstanding. From the hunters' voices to the cracking camp-fire to the river and animal sounds, the stereo and Surround effects are a constant joy.

Beauty and the Beast (1946)
★★★★½
Director: Jean Cocteau
Running Time: 92 minutes

The story "La Belle et la Bête," written by Mme. Marie Leprince de Beaumont, was originally published in *Magasin des Enfans* in 1756—though the story had many precedents. It has also been filmed many times, beginning with a French short subject made in 1899 and then most recently in 1991 as an opulent but sanitized Disney feature. Even *King Kong* (see page 159) owes a debt to the tale. However, Cocteau's elaborate and beautiful film remains the finest screen version; indeed, it's one of the best screen fantasies ever made.

Stopping at an eerie castle in the woods, an elderly (unnamed) merchant (Marcel André) plucks a rose to bring to his daughter, Beauty (Josette Day). A leonine Beast (Jean Marais) appears and tells him that either he must die for taking the rose or his daughter must take his place. The Beast allows the merchant to return home and put his affairs in order; upon learning what transpired, the devoted Beauty races to the Beast's castle to take her father's place. In time, Beauty gets over her initial revulsion and she and the Beast become close friends; he trusts her so much that he permits her to go home and visit her ailing father, pointing out that he'll die of grief if she doesn't return in one week. In an additional show of his trust, he also gives her the key to his treasure pavilion.

Back home, Beauty's greedy lover Avenant (also played by Marais), her brother Ludovic (Michel Auclair), and her greedy sisters Félicite (Mila Parély) and Adelaide (Nane Germon) learn of the treasure and plot to steal it. Avenant and Ludovic head to the castle and get into the pavilion. A statue of Diana inside the pavilion fires an arrow into Avenant; he becomes a Beast and dies; and when Beauty's timely return prevents the Beast from dying, he becomes human again.

Cocteau, a novelist, artist, and poet, had made only one previous film, *The Blood of a Poet* (1930), a very personal, surreal, nonnarrative work that tries to address this question: Whence comes poetry and how and why does the poet suffer? Afterward, he wrote, painted, and indulged in opium until his intimate friend Marais—with whom he had worked on the stage—convinced him to make *Beauty and the Beast*. As Marais had anticipated, the film made him a screen star and rekindled Cocteau's desire to make movies. He wrote and/or directed many movies thereafter, most notably *Orpheus* (1950) and *The Testament of Orpheus* (1959).

Beauty and the Beast has its slower passages—mostly those involving the folks back home—but it's also Cocteau's most accessible work, with a straightforward narrative and alternately dreamlike and nightmarish visuals: Beauty literally gliding along the floor of a castle hallway; the candles that light by themselves; the living arms that support the candelabras; and the faces that are part of the architecture but are also alive. Virtually every scene has shots that are treasures: Watch, for example, even the simple fade at 15476, the three main characters positioned so that they "become" the windows and doors in the next shot.

The sound design is equally masterful, especially the rasping voice of the Beast.

A strikingly handsome actor, Marais is alternately sad, feral, and noble as the Beast, brash and dashing as Avenant. (He's also braver: The "lake" where the Beast goes to drink was really a sewage ditch.) His performance is helped considerably by his makeup, which remains among the most effective and expressive ever created for a fantasy film. Watch how even the ears move when the Beast, with Beauty, hears the buck in the distance.

Day is a sweet Beauty and her pale, blond looks contrast nicely with the dark settings, but there isn't much to the part; the wicked sisters have the meatier roles.

The scenes set in Beauty's home were shot at Rochecorbon, a manor located in the Loire valley. The film took six months to make, as postwar shortages of lighting equipment and film stock, terrible weather, and sickness beset the production. The diary Cocteau kept during the making of the film is full of anguish, but he was able to channel his pain into the film.

It took five hours to apply the Beast's makeup and two to put on the hands, which is why he occasionally wore gloves. Cocteau himself usually applied the makeup.

Despite some inaccuracies, the episode of *Cinematic Eye* included on the disc provides interesting insights into the film.

The Disc
Video: ★★★
Audio: ★★½ (monaural)
Chapters: Yes
Format: CAV
Source: Criterion

This is the second time the film has been put on disc (Embassy Entertainment did so in 1986), and it's only a slight improvement.

The master element is in moderately good shape; some scenes having excellent contrast and a pristine image, others are gray or scratchy. (Some of that is the fault of the different film stocks Cocteau was forced to use and the fact that there never *were* any really terrific prints of the film.) The subtitles are quite clear, though the beauty of Cocteau's language and the subtleties of the French are lost. (For example, the Beast and Beauty address each other with the formal *vous* ("you"), which underscores the distance between them.)

The audio is thin, but, again, it's probably as good as it'll ever get.

The only reasons to upgrade to the more expensive disc are the excellent CAV (no jitters at all) and some nice supplementary material. Though the *Cinematic Eye* show (a South Carolina public-television presentation) has a few terrific clips from other films and from artwork that inspired Cocteau, the lecture itself is film-school pretentious. Conversely, the late film historian Arthur Knight presents an interesting running commentary on the film's audio track.

The disc also includes the complete text of the original 1756 story.

Becket (1964) ★★★★½
Director: Peter Glenville
Running Time: 148 minutes

In 1161, England's King Henry II realized he had to pay less attention to solidifying his holdings on the continent and more to domestic troubles. One of his chief problems was the Church. The clergy was furious with Henry for siphoning off Church monies for his wars, while he resented the fact that ordinary citizens were able to seek justice in ecclesiastical courts rather than in the civil courts of the king. There were tit-for-tat exchanges between the two factions. When Archbishop Theobald died, Henry saw it as a perfect opportunity to bring the Church under his control. On June 3, 1162, he appointed his friend and chancellor Thomas à Becket the new archbishop. Much to Henry's surprise and disappointment, Becket took his new post seriously, looking after the Church and not after Henry. The men fought bitterly until, in 1170, four courtiers who heard Henry rail against the archbishop took it upon themselves to slay him.

The relationship between the two men forms the basis of Jean Anouilh's brilliant and accurate play *Becket*, which had its Broadway debut in 1960, starring Anthony Quinn as the king and Laurence Olivier as Becket. When the play's director was asked to make a film version, producer Hal Wallis wanted him to use bigger box-office names (or, at least, a bona fide English actor for the king). Peter O'Toole had just become a star thanks to *Lawrence of Arabia*, and his manic intensity was exactly right for Henry; Burton was also a box-office draw after *Cleopatra*, and he was cast as the pious Becket.

As it turned out, the actors played off one another brilliantly and struck sparks with the other actors as well, especially John Gielgud as King Louis of France (with whom the beleaguered Becket allies himself), Pamela Brown as Becket's backbiting queen, and Martita Hunt as the embittered queen mother. Given wise, sassy, and insightful dialogue by Edward Anhalt—which follows the play very closely—they make this a stirring and memorable film.

The Lion in Winter (1968), which picks up Henry many years later, was Peter O'Toole's second and equally memorable turn as the king, with Katharine Hepburn as his wife, Eleanor of Aquitaine.

The Disc

Video: ★★½
Audio: ★★★★ (Surround)
Chapters: Yes
Format: CLV
Source: MPI Home Video

If only the disc were as good as the movie! The colors are all right in brightly lighted scenes, but there's a lot of darkness that shouldn't be there. Watch as Henry enters the cathedral at the beginning of the film: Even his bright red cape is lost in darkness. Henry and Becket are practically silhouettes in their important meeting on the beach. There are faint traces of grain and video noise here and there.

At least the film is letterboxed, enabling you to watch all the actors who fill the wide screen: Once you've seen the film, try to imagine, Henry-less, the scene in which his mother and wife chatter on about him while he's perched on the windowsill, far left, or the naming of Becket as chancellor (you'd lose one or the other as Becket kneels).

There's some moiré on the staircases and shimmering in the gold and silver of costumes, tapestries, and the like, but it's all quite tolerable.

The audio is excellent. The Surround doesn't give the rear speakers much (basically, just the music louder than the dialogue), but the stereo and clarity of the sound are delightful.

The film's trailer is the only extra.

The Lion in Winter is available in a surprisingly good transfer—surprising given the fact that technology has improved considerably since the transfer was done in 1986. Though there's some cropping of the nonanamorphic image, the colors are solid, the picture is very sharp, and the monaural sound is beautifully clear. The Embassy Home Entertainment/Pioneer release is a tough one to find, as copies tend to get snapped up quickly.

Bedazzled (1967) ★★★★
Director: Stanley Donen
Running Time: 104 minutes

After graduating from Oxford, Peter Cook and Dudley Moore teamed with fellow alumni Jonathan Miller and Alan Bennett to form the comedy act Beyond the Fringe (nearly a decade before Monty Python), which was a multimedia hit. Later, Moore and Cook went off to form their own act and make movies. Their first film was *The Wrong Box* (1966), costarring Michael Caine and Peter Sellers, a black comedy about family members jockeying for an inheritance. Next up was their co-written *Bedazzled*, which has become a cult classic.

Short-order cook Stanley Moon (Moore) is desperately in love with waitress Margaret (Eleanor Bron) but lacks the courage to ask her for a date. Enter George Spiggot (Cook)—that is, the Devil, who offers Moon seven wishes in exchange for his soul. Moon agrees, but, as he quickly discovers, his wishes must be *very* specific or George will find a way to turn each of them into hell on earth. (For example, Stanley uses one wish to make Margaret fall in love with him. George grants it but also makes her married and unwilling to cheat on her husband.)

Considering the desperate, often frantic quality Moore brings to this role—as he does to his best parts, such as the single-minded lover in *10* (see page 270), the outgoing drunk in *Arthur* (1981), the revolutionary ad executive in *Crazy People* (see page 57)—it's amazing how Cook's underplayed, monotone Prince of Darkness is the scene stealer. Stanley may be hungry for love, but George is director Donen's personification of everything that's wrong with modern society, right down to the magic words he uses: "Julie Andrews!" As such, Cook not only gets the best lines—including endless sexual double entendres—but he's constantly performing hilarious bits of mischief.

Then there's Raquel Welch, who has a small—make that minor—role as Lillian Lust, one of the Seven Deadly Sins. Even if the movie was terrible, she'd be worth the disc's hefty price tag: Watching her serve Stanley breakfast in bed and dance at a party George throws for his Sins, one is reminded just *why* she was the preeminent female sex symbol of the era. (That obviously crossed the mind of Fox Video's art director, as well. There are seven photos from the movie on and in the gatefold jacket: Six are of Welch.)

Fans of *When Dinosaurs Ruled the Earth* (see page 298): look for caveman Tara (Robin Hawdon) as Randolph, the harp teacher.

The Disc
Video: ★★½
Audio: ★★½
Chapters: Yes
Format: CLV
Source: CBS Fox Video

Bedazzled was shot with a dreary color scheme, and the colors have browned even more due to the Deluxe color process. Apart from the reds in George's office, there's very little life to the disc. But the news isn't all bad: The disc boasts a generous letterbox. Moore and Cook *are* the movie, and when they're on opposite sides of the screen—which is often—it's necessary to see them both.

The audio has only one problem: Despite digital encoding, the dialogue is still slightly muffled, a result of the original recording, which wasn't terribly good to begin with. That, compounded by the English accents, will make it necessary to scan backward to pick up a few of Cook's mutterings. And due, apparently, to faulty recording during the billiards scene, Cook and Moore had to redub their lines; their stuttering companion did not, and his dialogue is scratchy and barely comprehensible.

Being There (1979) ★★★★★
Director: Hal Ashby
Running Time: 130 minutes

Peter Sellers spent seven years lobbying studios, producers, and anyone who would listen in order to make a film of Jerzy Kosinski's 1971 novel *Being There*. Sellers even had a director in mind: Hal Ashby, whose dark comedy *Harold and Maude* he'd seen and loved. Ashby couldn't get the film made either, so he and Sellers promised that whoever managed to get it going first would bring the other in.

As it happened, both hit at the same time. Sellers struck box-office gold thanks to *Return of the Pink Panther* (1975) and its sequels, and Ashby batted one out of the park with *Coming Home* (1978). As a result, they were finally able to make their labor of love.

Being There is the story of childlike Chance the gardener (Sellers) who has never seen the outside of his employer's house and knows the world only through TV. Upon his employer's death, Chance is evicted. Wandering about, he's struck by a car belonging to Eve Rand (Shirley MacLaine) and is taken to the Washington, D.C., mansion of her powerful husband, the ailing Benjamin (Melvyn Douglas), an Armand Hammer–type confidant of the President (Jack Warden). The Rands misunderstand their guest and think that "Chauncey Gardiner" is a businessman whose company has failed due to the economic climate. Though Benjamin's private doctor, Robert Allenby (Richard Dysart), suspects that Chauncey is exactly the simple man he appears to be, everyone else in Washington and the media regard him as an economic messiah: By tale's end, he's well on his way to becoming President of the United States. (The end of the movie also offers a shot that upends everything you think you knew about Chance and compels you to sit through the picture again and watch it with a rather different eye, such as checking out the graffiti on the wall after Chance leaves his home at the beginning.)

Being There is a fable about America, a society in which appearance is more important than substance. The title refers to the fact that simply by being there, Chance becomes the clay that others use to express what they believe or need or want to feel.

Shot in part at George Vanderbilt's enormous home in Asheville, North Carolina—Biltmore—*Being There* is as gentle and affecting a movie as you'll ever see. Douglas, MacLaine, Warden, and Dysart are wonderful, Richard Basehart makes a strong impression as the Russian ambassador Vladimir Skrapinov, and David Clennon (Miles of *thirtysomething*) is typically untrustworthy as lawyer Thomas Franklin, who evicts Chance and reenters his life when he becomes famous.

Then there's poor, perpetually underrated Sellers. He made only two more films—including the terrible *The Fiendish Plot of Dr. Fu Manchu* (1980)—before his death from heart failure at the age of fifty-four. He'd always been a tense, excitable man: Tragically, even his beloved *Being There* had exacerbated his condition. Sellers's widow, Lynne Frederick, recalls that just days before filming began, the actor still hadn't "found" the character to his satisfaction. He taped various accents and listened to them. "The FBI, the CIA, and the KGB can't trace his background when they try," she says, so "he couldn't have an accent tied to a particular locality." She says that one would be "too New Yorkerish, another too West Coast, a third too Deep South." After fretting for weeks, the actor finally based the voice on the intonation and speech pattern of comedian Stan Laurel. He rehearsed the walk with equal doggedness, using a video camera to tape it until he got what he wanted. Sellers also wore himself down with little things, such as Ashby's decision to use outtakes from a scene (not in the finished film) in which Sellers continually flubs a line (which is probably *why* it wasn't in the finished film). Upon seeing the outtakes tacked on under the closing titles, Sellers fired a telex to the director that screamed that the clips "do a grave injustice to the picture for the sake of a few cheap laughs. It breaks the spell; *do you understand?*" Sellers's ire was misplaced: The outtakes remind the audience that this "American" is British, and that he worked damn hard on the film.

The Disc
Video: ★★★
Audio: ★★½
Chapters: Yes
Format: CLV
Source: Warner Home Video

Though most of the film is generally sharp, some scenes are on the soft side and there's a lack of detail in most of the dark sequences. A slight graininess pervades the mansion scenes, though that would have been difficult to avoid, given the wood-panel brownness in almost every shot. Despite the preponderance of browns and reds, there's hardly any noise.

The edges of the nonletterboxed image are lost, though all the vital information is here.

The audio has a mild but distressing hiss throughout, especially noticeable because most of the characters in the film are so soft-spoken.

Ben-Hur (1959) ★★★½
Director: William Wyler
Running Time: 211 minutes

MGM was in a bad way financially when they decided to put everything they had into a new film version of Lew Wallace's 1880 novel, *Ben-Hur: A Tale of the Christ*. The previous screen adaptation, made in 1926 for a then-staggering $4 million, starred Ramon Novarro and Francis X. Bushman and was a huge success (and is available on laserdisc).

MGM hoped that lightning would strike twice and budgeted the film at an unprecedented $15 million. But the gamble made sense: Their Roman-era epic *Quo Vadis?* had been a success in 1951, *The Ten Commandments* (1956) had made a bundle for Paramount, and *Ben-Hur* was a well-known property. The story also contained all the elements for cinematic success: love, spectacle, revenge, and the triumph of faith.

The novel itself was inspired by a railway-car debate between Civil War officer Wallace and philosopher Robert Ingersoll about the divinity of Jesus. Researching the life of Christ, Wallace decided to present his own beliefs in the form of a story about Judah Ben-Hur, an aristocratic Jew who is wrongly accused by his ambitious Roman friend Messala of trying to murder the new governor of Judea. Judah is sent to be a galley slave and his mother and sister are imprisoned.

After rowing for the fleet for three years, Judah is granted his freedom when he saves the life of the tribune Quintus Arrius during a battle; returning to Judea, Judah meets the benevolent sheik Ilderim, cripples Messala in a chariot race (kills him in the film), learns that his mother and sister have become lepers, cures them by taking them to see Jesus (in the novel, Jesus heals them before his death, not after), and falls in love with a young woman, Esther, the daughter of the merchant Simonides.

Though the film dropped a number of supporting characters, rearranged events slightly, and (mercifully) eschewed Wallace's tongue-hobbling dialogue ("I give him thanks; and praise him thou, for of his favor I have wherewith to give thee great reward, and I will"), the film is still remarkably faithful to the novel. Wyler worked wonders with the movie, never letting his characters get swallowed up by the spectacle: Jesus giving Judah water in the desert is every bit as memorable as the chariot race. (The production took its toll on producer Sam Zimbalist, though, who collapsed and died during the filming of the epic.)

Despite its huge financial success and haul of Oscars (eleven—still a record), it would be a mistake to call *Ben-Hur* a great film. It's an entertaining, engrossing, and often moving film—but its piety and extraneous subplots overwhelm what the story *really* is about: the relationship between Judah and Messala (Charlton Heston and Stephen Boyd). As Heston has said, "Even while we were shooting it, we came to realize that the story is not really a story of the Christ, no matter what Lew Wallace says, and it's certainly not a story of Ben-Hur and Esther, a totally implausible relationship which has no structural function. It's a love story between Ben-Hur and Messala, and the destruction of that love, its turning to hate and revenge."

The movie is not helped by erratic casting. Stephen Boyd is a stoic but unexciting Messala: The Irish-born actor had limited film experience before being cast and wasn't comfortable with the classic-style dialogue. He also labored painfully behind brown contact lenses throughout the shoot (Wyler didn't want his villain to be blue-eyed). Haya Harareet is simply terrible as Esther, and though her casting was an attempt to give the picture at least one authentic Middle Eastern star, the Israeli stage actress was never at ease in front of a camera or speaking English. Alabama native Cathy O'Donnell, who had been memorable in Wyler's *The Best Years of Our Lives* (1946), was too all-American for the role of Judah's sister, Tirzah. (This was her last film; she died in 1970 at the age of forty-five).

On the plus side, Hugh Griffith steals every scene he's in as the boisterous, horse-loving Ilderim; Jack Hawkins is excellent as Arrius; Frank Thring makes a haughty Pontius Pilate; and Martha Scott is proud and loving as Judah's mother (unnamed in the novel, she's Miriam in the film). This was Scott's second turn as Heston's mother: She also played Moses's mother, Yochabel, in *The Ten Commandments*, and the two would costar again in the popular *Airport 1975* (1974).

As for Charlton Heston's Ben-Hur, it's difficult to imagine anyone else in the role. MGM tried: The part was originally offered to Burt Lancaster, who turned it down because he couldn't swallow the film's religious views. Rock Hudson was approached but had other obligations; Italian actor Cesare Danova was considered, but his accent was too thick and there wasn't time to fix it. Wyler had just worked with Heston (as the villain) in *The Big Country* (1958) and had originally considered him for Messala. With no other Ben-Hurs at his disposal, he went with Heston.

Heston has dignity, strength, and compassion. He's convincing as the loving son and friend, and even more so as the hardened galley slave and charioteer. And unlike Boyd (whose double has brawnier arms), the actor did all his own driving in the race, save for the jump over the wrecked chariots. (And contrary to rumor, no one died during the filming of the race. The only accident occurred when Joe Canutt, doubling for Heston during the jump, was flipped from the chariot. Fortunately, he managed to hold on and pull himself in. The first part of the accident is still in the film, followed by a close-up of Heston climbing back into the chariot.)

After the film's release, there was a very public dispute between Wyler and the Writers Guild over their refusal to allow cowriter Christopher Fry a screen credit, though Heston thanked him when accepting his Best Actor Oscar. Gore Vidal also contributed to the screenplay.

The picture's success saved MGM, though the studio lost a big chunk of those earnings when the remake of *Mutiny on the Bounty* sunk (see page 192).

The Disc

Video: ★★★
Audio: ★★★½ (Surround)
Chapters: No
Format: CLV
Source: MGM/UA Home Video

MGM/UA caught flak from some consumers for the letterboxed edition of the film. *Ben-Hur* was shot in the widest of the wide-screen ratios (2.66:1) and it's presented here in its full, ribbon-long glory. Fans of the film won't mind: They get to see all eight horses on the screen when Heston and Boyd are locked wheel-to-wheel in the chariot race. However, consumers who don't cherish the movie *quite* so much and/or hate letterboxing to begin with won't appreciate the long, narrow image.

Obviously, *any* movie on video is a compromise, but this particular film is still infinitely better in full letterboxing than when panned-and-scanned or even slightly cropped. William Wyler learned a great deal about working in the wide-screen process when he made *The Big Country*, and in *Ben-Hur* he utilized the farthest reaches of the screen not just for spectacle but for people. His nativity, the toast when Ben-Hur and Messala first meet, Judah gazing out at Rome from Arrius's window (a very effective miniature, not a painting): All fill the screen completely. Wyler was not a capricious director; if he put something in the frame, he meant it to be seen. So just move in closer to the TV and enjoy!

Technically, the disc is good but not great. The exteriors are sharp and richly colored. But where the interiors and night scenes are concerned, the image is a *little* soft and the reds are a bit runny.

The digital audio is very clear, and Miklos Rozsa's score is glorious. The stereo separation is good, but Surround is a misnomer: The rear channels give you pretty much what you're getting from the front speakers.

A 1992 remaster is slightly brighter and sharper, though not by so much that owners of the original should bother upgrading.

Fans of Heston epics should *definitely* pick up the Japanese import of *El Cid* (1961), which is frankly a better film but isn't available on a domestic laserdisc. The mildly letterboxed disc boasts superb color and magnificent stereo.

Betsy's Wedding (1990) ★★
Director: Alan Alda
Running Time: 94 minutes

If Alda was trying to be the poor man's Woody Allen, he succeeded. *Betsy's Wedding* is full of Allenisms—Alda talking to the ghost of his father, the clash of ethnic and white-bread cultures—but it's devoid of real intelligence and finesse. There are some fascinating characters here, but the director (who also wrote the screenplay) hasn't given them anything interesting to do.

Builder Eddie Hopper (Alda) is the father of bride-to-be Betsy (Molly Ringwald), whose in-laws-to-be are an old-money contrast to the blue-collar Hoppers. Eddie insists on paying for the wedding and goes to his rich brother, Oscar (Joe Pesci), for a loan. Oscar is heavily involved with the mob; in exchange for the loan, Eddie must hire Stevie Dee (Anthony LaPaglia), the decent, exceedingly formal nephew of crude mob boss Georgie (Burt Young). Stevie gets paid an outrageous amount of money for doing absolutely nothing on the job site—where he falls hopelessly in love with Eddie's other daughter, Connie (Ally Sheedy), a police officer. He woos her relentlessly but with the utmost respect. Meanwhile, Oscar's wife, Gloria (Catherine O'Hara), is secretly out to undermine her husband's real estate deals because he's a philanderer who can be hurt only through his bankbook.

Naturally, all hell breaks loose when these characters get together for Betsy's wedding—beneath a tent as shaky as many of the relationships—during a storm that personifies the tumult in their lives.

Alda is flat in his role, his wife, Lola (Madeline Kahn), is a *really* annoying worrywart, and the mob subplot is just not funny. The sporadic appearances of Joey Bishop as Eddie's father are embarrassingly out of place as Alda reaches for a sentiment that's way beyond his grasp. What keeps the movie from being a total bust are O'Hara's sneaky maneuverings and LaPaglia's utterly enchanting courtship of Sheedy. He gives a touching, inspired performance, one of the most original in years, and he almost makes the disc worth the price. (LaPaglia is also the sole asset of the abominable *One Good Cop* [1991] as Michael Keaton's doomed partner. If Hollywood lets him, this actor's going to do some great work.)

The Disc
Video: ★★★½
Audio: ★★★★ (Surround)
Chapters: Yes
Format: CLV
Source: Touchstone Home Video

The film was shot in muted tones, so the colors are a little on the subdued side. But the image is very sharp and there's hardly any grain or video noise. The film is helped by its full-screen image, which allows you to savor O'Hara and LaPaglia.

The audio is excellent and the film is full of delightful background noises even in the most mundane settings.

The Bible ... In the Beginning (1966) ★
Director: John Huston
Running Time: 172 minutes

This is a reverent film. The Twentieth Century–Fox logo appears without fanfare; even the souvenir book sold during the film's road-show engagement was printed on subdued matte-finish paper instead of the traditional glossy stock.

Too bad it's a terrible movie, as well. Though it clocks in at over two and a half hours, *The Bible ... In the Beginning* feels as if it were the fifteen-hour epic producer Dino de Laurentiis originally planned (with directors such as Welles, Visconti, and Fellini helming different segments). Actually, the film is just the Bible in the *very* beginning, covering less than half of Genesis. It begins with a lengthy travelouguelike Creation, followed by the stories of Adam and Eve (Michael Parks and Ulla Bergryd, both naked and discreetly photographed); Cain slaying Abel (Richard Harris and Franco Nero); Noah (John Huston, laying on the paternal shtick with a trowel); Nimrod (Stephen Boyd) and the Tower of Babel; Abraham, Sarah, and Hagar (George C. Scott, Ava Gardner, and Zoë Sallis); Sodom and Gomorrah and the flight of Lot and his ill-fated wife (Gabriele Ferzetti and Elenora Rossi Drago, with Peter O'Toole as the Three Angels of Doom); and God's testing of Abraham.

Except for the effective slaying of Cain (with the jawbone of an ass, borrowed from DeMille's 1949 *Samson and Delilah*) and the relatively brief Tower of Babel sequence, which has impressive moments of spectacle, the film anesthetizes rather than inspires. The tale of Sodom and Gomorrah in particular dares to be bland and the cities' destruction—by a mushroom cloud superimposed on the desert!—has to be one of the dopiest images ever put on the screen.

This was de Laurentiis's second biblical epic, the first having been the far superior *Barabbas* (1962). The failure of the $18 million epic ended the cycle of biblical films that had begun with DeMille's *Samson and Delilah*, leaving the good book as fodder for an occasional TV miniseries.

The Disc
Video: ★
Audio: ★½
Chapters: Yes
Format: CLV
Source: CBS Fox Video

In 70mm, presented in the wide-screen Dimension-150 process, the movie was at least an imposing experience. The colors were bright and the sound was full of low-register rumblings.

Practically none of this is captured on the disc. Here, the Garden of Eden is so full of grain (the video kind) that the picture is nearly indecipherable in places. And there's a vertical line toward the left of the screen that comes and goes throughout the film: This isn't the kind of print for which you should have to pay big bucks. Daylight scenes are bright enough, but night scenes and all of those set in Sodom and Gomorrah are murky and washed-out. There's also a good deal of noise in the darker colors.

The letterboxing preserves the film's spectacle, especially during the building and populating of the Ark and the numerous desert sequences. Otherwise, it has little dramatic effect.

The digital stereo is merely serviceable. When the audio *should* shine, as during the flood, it fails to deliver the goods.

Bird on a Wire (1990) ★★½
Director: John Badham
Running Time: 110 minutes

Fifteen years ago, drug-running Richard Jarmin (Mel Gibson) was granted immunity in exchange for his testimony against crooked feds. With the help of agent Lou Baird (Jeff Corey), he was placed in the federal witness protection program. Now, one of those crooked agents, Eugene Sorenson (David Carradine), has been released from prison and, with the help of Lou's replacement, corrupt agent Joe Weyburn (Stephen Tobolowsky), he goes gunning for the stoolie. Coincidentally, Jarmin's ex-lover, Marianne Graves (Goldie Hawn), bumps into Jarmin at a Detroit gas station. When Sorenson and his partner, Albert Diggs (Bill Duke), arrive in town, she helps Jarmin escape and they end up on the run, desperately looking for Lou, the only man who can help them.

Action fans, this one's for you. There's a terrific car chase, a motorcycle chase that's almost as good, and a plane versus helicopter battle worthy of the James Bond crew.

Gibson fans, this is a present for you, too. Lots of close-ups of the charming, ponytailed star, and even a few shots of his bare butt. And he's just *so* secure, he even pretends to be an effeminate hairdresser in the film. (Too bad he doesn't get to show any emotion, as when his employer at the gas station dies because of him.)

Hawn fans, you get to see her butt, too.

Feminists, stay away. Icy, high-powered lawyer Hawn makes mincemeat of two men in the film's opening scenes, then spends the rest of the movie shrieking and playing the "Laugh-In" dumb blonde. It's incredible that she went along with this.

Suspense fans, watch *North by Northwest* instead (see page 197). This is one of those movies where billions of bullets are fired and no one is hurt, where bad guy's guns jam at *just* the right moment, where there are more holes in the logic than in the bullet-ridden scenery (how *did* Mel and Goldie pay for the hotel room after she refused to play chambermaid?), and where the climax in a zoo's jungle habitat fails to generate an ounce of suspense since no fall, punch, or wound seems to hurt our heroes.

Badham's *The Hard Way* (see page 131) was a better movie that did much worse at the box office. Goldie's thriller *Deceived* (1991) bombed. Moral: Gibson really *is* worth all that money they pay him.

The Disc
Video: ★★★½
Audio: ★★★½ (Surround)
Chapters: Yes
Format: CLV
Source: MCA/Universal Home Video

The film is available in both letterbox and pan-and-scan versions. Both are identical in terms of quality, though the latter cramps the action scenes and also hurts the drama, such as the buckshot-from-the-behind operation, with Goldie on the left and Mel on the right.

The picture is supersharp, thanks to a 70mm source print, and only a handful of scenes have grain. Video noise is kept to a minimum except for the final sunset, which is awash with it—and can *anyone* read those closing credits?

The audio is excellent, with very good Surround effects. Though the music is pushed a bit too hard from the rear speakers, you'll have to keep the sound turned up or you'll miss the sirens, barking dogs, horses, train, and the very fine effect of the crashing plane, the sound moving slowly into the rear speakers as it plows toward you.

Black Rain (1989) ★★½
Director: Ridley Scott
Running Time: 125 minutes

Scott may well be the unluckiest director in the business. Except for *Legend* (1985), which was stunning to look at but empty as a drum, his films have all been impressive: *The Duellists* (1977), *Alien* (1979), *Blade Runner* (1982), *Someone to Watch Over Me* (1987), *Black Rain*, and *Thelma*

& Louise (1991). Yet only *Alien* and *Black Rain* have been box-office successes. They were also his least original works, *Alien* having been inspired by previous works (see page 7) and *Black Rain* telling a predictable, formulaic story reminiscent of *The Yakuza* (see page 310)—albeit with Scott's characteristic style and drive.

Michael Douglas stars as New York homicide Detective Sergeant Nick Conklin, who, with his partner, Charlie Vincent (Andy Garcia), happens to collar Japanese thug Sato (Yusaku Matsuda) in Manhattan. The duo escorts him to Japan, where they are duped into turning him over to gangsters rather than the police. Against the wishes of the authorities, the Americans stick around and hunt the criminal down, aided by their one friend, Assistant Inspector Masahiro Matsumoto (Ken Takakura, who looks at times amazingly like Jack Webb) and by a transplanted Chicagoan, bar girl Joyce Kingsley (Kate Capshaw, who is terrible).

Black Rain is an easy movie to pick apart. There are plot holes (the good Japanese cops were just standing around at the front of the plane, hands in their pockets, while the baddies helped their boss off the back?), improbable developments (Nick manipulates Masahiro and the police much too easily), and some really unlikely chases (in one, heavy smoker Nick, on foot, keeps pace with Sato's motorcycle!). But Scott's visuals are hypnotic, his pacing frenetic, and he does a good job showing how the two cultures, which lock horns at first, slowly mesh.

Douglas is good as the world-weary, single-minded Nick, and Takakura is excellent as Masahiro, who struggles against his training as a team player to aid the "cowboy" from America. Garcia is less intense than he was in films such as *The Untouchables* (see page 291) but is a congenial enough screen presence; John Spencer (of TV's "L.A. Law") gets short shrift as Oliver, Nick's one-man fan club on the NYPD.

You'll like this one a lot if it's only a rental.

The Disc
Video: ★½
Audio: ★★★★ (Surround)
Chapters: No
Format: CLV
Source: Paramount Home Video

It's disgraceful that an *A* film should be given such a shoddy transfer. It's grainy from start to finish, the colors are drab, the picture is never quite sharp enough, and there's an abundance of red noise.

The film is available in letterboxed and pan-and-scan editions. The latter tells the story just fine, though important reaction shots are lost and the film's location photography is much less impressive.

The audio is quite satisfying, however. The stereo separations are excellent and the rear speakers are always busy with screeching tires, gunshots, traffic, conversation in the bar, and so on. In fact, the rear channels tend to overwhelm the dialogue at times and should be turned well down from maximum levels.

Blazing Saddles (1974) ★★★★
Director: Mel Brooks
Running Time: 90 minutes

Blazing Saddles was Mel Brooks's third film, following *The Producers* (see page 221) and the obscure *The Twelve Chairs* (1970). Though not as technically polished or lavish as his next effort, *Young Frankenstein* (1974), *Blazing Saddles* is the most consistently funny—and tasteless—of Brooks's films.

The film tells about a former laborer, Bart (Cleavon Little), who is appointed sheriff of the redneck town of Rock Ridge. With the help of a drunken gunfighter, the Waco Kid (Gene Wilder), Bart brings law to the West, promotes racial understanding (sort of), and thwarts the plans of megalomaniacal attorney general Hedley Lamarr (a wonderfully unctuous Harvey Korman) to take over the town and clean up when the railroad comes through.

The movie was the brainchild of writer Andrew Bergman, who went to Brooks with his screenplay *Tex-X*, about a black man out west. The two assembled a group of writers—including Richard Pryor—who wrote a brilliant parody of Western clichés and stereotypes. (Pryor was actually Brooks's first choice to star in the film, but studio executives were scared off by the comedian's history of volatility and so nixed him.)

Little is smooth as Bart—but he isn't Pryor. Wilder is surprisingly restrained as the drunken gunslinger, and Madeline Kahn's brief turn as chanteuse Lili Von Shtupp is a hoot.

The Disc
Video: ★★½
Audio: ★★ (monaural)
Chapters: No
Format: CLV
Source: Warner Home Video

The colors are bright on this remastered disc, and the focus is fairly sharp—a contrast to the terrible colors and very soft image of the previous edition. However, there are some very grainy sequences, and the movie still suffers from too much bad panning-and-scanning. Rather than jump-cutting left or right when characters are on opposite sides of the screen, the camera pans quickly—and often. Viewers may suffer whiplash as the telecine operator rushes to catch all the participants in the infamous campfire scene.

The sound isn't as muffled, warped, and just plain awful as in the original release, but it isn't as crisp and zingy as it should be.

Blue Velvet (1986) ★★★★
Director: David Lynch
Running Time: 120 minutes

While walking beside a field, college student Jeffrey Beaumont (Kyle MacLachlan) discovers a severed human ear (the entranceway to the brain and nightmares?) and takes it to Detective Williams (George Dickerson). Williams is reluctant to discuss it, but his daughter, Sandy (Laura Dern), tells Jeffrey she heard her father say something about nightclub singer Dorothy Vallens (Isabella Rossellini) in connection with the ear. Jeffrey goes to Dorothy's apartment when she's out and hides in the closet. When she returns, he eavesdrops as Frank Booth (Dennis Hopper) arrives and makes violent love to her. Learning that Frank has kidnapped Dorothy's husband, Don, and son, Donnie, and has made her his love slave, Jeffrey follows him and is savagely beaten. However, he refuses to abandon the case and eventually learns the secret of the ear—and has a final, deadly confrontation with Frank.

Director Lynch has taken Bobby Vinton's song "Blue Velvet" and changed it from a starry-eyed dating song into a brutal, fatalistic study of good versus evil, showing the savage world that lies under the watered lawns, rose gardens, and the amiable order of small-town Lumberton. He often takes a satiric approach that undercuts the tough and honest sexual content, but the inconsistent tone doesn't destroy the power of the whole.

MacLachlan is a bit too stolid for the part, but Rossellini is painfully open and sensuous, and Hopper pushes freakish evil to the edge (and often over it), cranking himself up with an oxygen mask and laughing at the rest of us from somewhere in the stratosphere. Dean Stockwell is very good as his pale cohort Ben, who at times seems more vegetable than human.

Blue Velvet isn't for everyone, but those wiling to endure its horrors will find it revealing and provocative.

The Disc
Video: ★★★★
Audio: ★★★½ (Surround)
Chapters: Yes
Format: CLV
Source: Warner Home Video

This new letterboxed edition is a welcome replacement for the poor transfers of the old pan-and-scan edition and the dark, inadequately letterboxed Japanese import. The wide-screen framing dramatizes not only the entrances (especially that of Dern) and conversations but also shows us the menacing or perverse activites going on in the periphery. It is absolutely essential to the film.

The source material is in excellent shape, and the transfer is extremely good. The colors are accurate, there's no bleeding, and brightness levels are excellent, even in the darker scenes. The blacks are also very solid, and there's only occasional video noise and grain.

The audio is clear, there's a fair amount of ambient sound for stereo and Surround systems both, and Angelo Badalamenti's lyrical synthesizer score sounds very good.

Born on the Fourth of July (1989) ★★★½
Director: Oliver Stone
Running Time: 145 minutes

After piloting himself to the top of the box-office heap with *Top Gun* (1986), Tom Cruise made *The Color of Money* (1986) and *Cocktail* (1988), both popular successes, then clawed his way to critical respectability with *Rain Man* (1988) and *Born on the Fourth of July* (credibility he very nearly squandered with *Days of Thunder* in 1990).

Born on the Fourth of July was based on the autobiographical work by Ron Kovic—a consultant on the 1978 film *Coming Home*—who went to Vietnam full of the fighting spirit and came home paralyzed from the waist down. The project had been kicking around Hollywood for years, but, thanks to the success of *Platoon* (1986), Stone was able to get it made. He chose Cruise, he said, because "he was the closest to Ron Kovic in spirit. They certainly had the same drive, the same hunger to achieve, to be the best, to prove something." And he had box-office appeal, something the downbeat story needed. (Only Cruise's face, not Kovic's handicap, was pictured in print ads.)

The film briefly covers Kovic's early years, playing war with his friends, dating, and participating in sports and striving to win. Spurred by a "my country right or wrong" philosophy, he enlists in the marines, is maimed during battle, and returns to the United States for rehabilitation. Over the next few years, his experiences in VA hospitals, with anti-war activists, with his former girlfriend Donna (Kyra Sedgwick), and with the parents of a marine he accidentally killed convince him that the war is wrong and turn him into a passionate protester. The movie ends in 1976, when Kovic—a man far removed from the boy who went to war—addresses the Democratic National Convention in New York.

Full of pain, anger, and unsettling images—and, as is normal for Stone, lacking humor of any sort—this is a powerful movie, one that's not easy to watch. It was obviously tough to make, and Cruise deserves accolades for his effort. The truth is, though, the part was beyond him. He's just right as the gung ho, unquestioning kid and, later, is convincing enough as he struggles with his wheelchair and rages at his fate. But for all that, his performance lacks texture. He's unable to express degrees of suffering or hostility with equal ease or understatement; the performance falls far short of what Jon Voight accomplished in *Coming Home*, or what other young actors could have done with the part.

Stone's *Platoon* costars, Willem Dafoe and Tom Berenger, have small roles as another crippled veteran and a marine sergeant recruiter, respectively. The late Abbie Hoffman appears as an activist.

The Disc
Video: ★★
Audio: ★★★★ (Surround)
Chapters: No
Format: CLV
Source: MCA/Universal Home Video

Born on the Fourth of July was shot in a monochromatic color scheme; while the sepia tones are effective dramatically, they create a lot of problems on the disc. Video noise and grain are ever-present, and the sharply focused image can't overcome these distractions.

The film is available in both letterboxed and pan-and-scan editions: The former is preferable not only because of Stone's wide-screen compositions but because it makes the grain slightly less obvious. Only viewers who want Cruise's face looming large will find the pan-and-scan version rewarding.

The audio is extremely clear, and the Surround is used sparingly but to great effect.

Brainstorm (1983) ★★
Director: Douglas Trumbull
Running Time: 107 minutes

This film is important for two reasons. First: It broke the blacklist against actor Cliff Robertson. Executive David Begelman had issued and cashed a ten-thousand-dollar check made out to Robertson, and, when the actor saw the non-income listed on his taxes and blew the whistle, he didn't work for years—until gutsy Trumbull, making this film for Begelman at MGM, asked, "Say ... you wouldn't mind if I used Cliff for the part of Alex Terson, wouldja?"

Second: *Brainstorm* was nearly completed when star Natalie Wood drowned in 1981. With $12 million already invested in the film, the cash-strapped studio decided to try and collect the insurance, saying the picture simply couldn't be finished. But once again, Trumbull stuck it to them. He made one change in the script (actor Joe Dorsey, as Hal Abramson, delivered some exposition originally written for Wood) and told the insurers that no ... he'd have no problem completing the film for another $6 million. That was cheaper than $12 million, so the money was paid and the film was finished.

Unfortunately, the results don't justify Trumbull's heroic efforts. The film is about a brain-wave machine that records thoughts and emotions and allows them to be played back into the mind of the creator or another person. Wood and Christopher Walken play estranged husband and wife research scientists Karen and Michael Brace, Robertson is their boss, and Louise Fletcher is Lillian Reynolds, a delightfully crusty scientist. Karen and Michael are beset by government "we gotta have this" types, by reblossoming love, and by people who insist on abusing the invention.

Worse than all the clichés is how badly the movie bobbles the ball when it enters territory later explored by *Flatliners* (see page 102), as Lillian tapes her death, which Michael plays back and reexperiences. Trumbull's bubbly, angel-filled vision of the afterlife is like a mall at Christmas, and just as vapid. What a crashing disappointment from start to finish!

Trumbull—who masterminded many of the special effects in *2001: A Space Odyssey* and *Close Encounters of the Third Kind* (see pages 287 and 52) and also directed *Silent Running* (1971)—had originally intended to feature the "thought/dream/emotion–visualization" scenes in his Showscan technique, a 70mm process that runs the film through the camera at nearly twice normal speeds, creating a phenomenally clear projected image. That would have given the "trips" more power. But Showscan doesn't work with normal projectors, and the cost of refitting theaters was prohibitive. Thus, he settled for a regular 35mm image during "normal" scenes, jumping to a wide-screen 70mm image for the rest. It was quite effective in theaters but underscores the truism that Hollywood never seems to learn: If you don't come up with a good script, you don't end up with a good movie.

The Disc
Video: ★★★★
Audio: ★★★★½ (Surround)
Chapters: Yes
Format: CLV
Source: MGM/UA Home Video

Sadly, the 35mm/70mm–size jumps are gone here: The entire film is letterboxed the same, from start to finish (though it's an improvement over the previous pan-and-scan edition).

The segments shot in 70mm are *extremely* sharp, though the 35mm imagery is also very good. The colors are solid, and there are relatively few grain or noise-related imperfections.

The audio is very good throughout, but it really packs a punch during the 70mm segments: The original six-track experience of these scenes is superbly recreated, and rear-channel effects are gloriously effective.

The film's trailer is included.

Broken Lance (1954) ★★★½
Director: Edward Dmytryk
Running Time: 98 minutes

Irishman Matthew Devereaux (Spencer Tracy) has come to America and built a cattle empire out west. Now, it's the 1870s and he's in his fifties, but he's still driven. He's hard on his three sons by his first wife—Ben (Richard Widmark), Mike (Hugh O'Brian), and Danny (Earl Holliman)—but generous and gentle with Joe (Robert Wagner), his smart, hardworking son by current wife "Señora" Devereaux (Katy Jurado), a Comanche. When water pollution caused by a copper mine kills some of Matt's cattle, he goes to the foreman and asks that the runoff be diverted. The foreman refuses, and Matt destroys the place; the company sues the rancher, and though Horace (E. G. Marshall), the governor, owes his job to Matt, he doesn't like the fact that his daughter, Barbara (Jean Peters), has been seeing half-breed Joe. Horace refuses to appoint a sympathetic judge and, to spare his father a certain prison sentence, Joe takes the blame for what has happened. He's sent away for three years: Matt dies while his beloved son is in jail, Joe's mother goes back to live with her people, and Joe's half-brothers run the ranch.

When Joe returns, it's the proverbial "good news/bad news" situation. The good news is that Barbara has waited for him. The bad news is that his half-brothers don't want him around and take steps to see that—alive or dead—he relocates.

The film is a solid, engrossing drama—"Bonanza" with substance (the TV show premiered five years later with roughly the same structure and two characters having the same names—coincidence?) or *King Lear* out west. You expect greatness from Tracy, and when you get it you can't help but be in awe of what he does: Whether he's reassuring his wife, dressing down the governor, or being downright antagonistic to the prosecutor in court, he's a marvel. Jurado is wise and warm, Widmark has always been terrific as a heavy, and Wagner brings more heft than usual to his role. Peters—who married Howard Hughes in 1957—is lovely but unimpressive, and Holliman whines no more or less than usual.

The film is also a very personal statement for Dmytryk, who was sentenced to prison in 1947 for having Communist affiliations. After spending six months in jail, the distinguished director went into exile and then in 1951 appeared again before the House Committee on Un-American Activities and turned in other supposed Reds, which got him off the blacklist. The anger and shame he felt are clearly stated in *Broken Lance*, with its self-serving politicians, persecution of the innocent, and corrupt judicial system.

The Disc
Video: ★★
Audio: ★★★ (Surround)
Chapters: Yes
Format: CLV
Source: CBS FOX Video

The film has a moderately sharp picture, with little grain and no video noise. However, the Deluxe colors are reddish and rather faded, which is particularly detrimental to the spectacular scenery (filmed in the Santa Cruz valley in Arizona). There's also a problem with bleeding reds and flesh tones.

The film has been generously letterboxed, including almost the entire original CinemaScope image.

The audio is quite nice, everything as clear as can be. However, the Surround Sound is underwhelming, little more than

The Brood (1979) ★★★
Director: David Cronenberg
Running Time: 92 minutes

Director David Cronenberg broke into the mainstream in 1983 with his moderately entertaining film version of Stephen King's plodding novel *The Dead Zone*. He followed that with *Videodrome* (1983), *The Fly* (1986), *Dead Ringers* (1988), and *Naked Lunch* (1991), works of polish with flashes of extraordinary power.

However, Cronenberg's movies were more compelling when he made them on a comparative shoestring, when he used ideas and mood to compensate for the lack of budget. His first film, *They Came from Within* (1975), was about a parasite that unleashes a victim's sexual desire; he followed that with *Rabid* (1977), starring porn star Marilyn Chambers as a woman who goes in for plastic surgery and comes out a vampire.

However, Cronenberg really hit his stride with *The Brood* (and, in 1981, with *Scanners*, about murderous telepaths). Art Hindle stars as Frank Carveth, whose wife, Nola (Samantha Eggar), was abused as a child and is abusing their own child, five-year-old Candice (Cindy Hinds). Nola is sent for treatment to the Somafree Institute of Psychoplasmics in Toronto, where Dr. Hal Raglan (Oliver Reed) is very secretive about what he's doing for her. Meanwhile, strange, dwarfish creatures kill Nola's mother, Juliana Kelly (Nuala Fitzgerald), her father, Barton (Henry Beckman), and Candy's teacher, Ruth Mayer (Susan Hogan)—creatures that Frank investigates, ties to Somafree, and follows in a surprising nail-biter of a climax.

Art Hindle is an acceptable lead, but let's face it: Very few performers can threaten Oliver Reed and sound convincing. Reed dominates the screen as few actors can, and his presence in this film helps to sell its loopy ideas. Samantha Eggar is a terrific psychopath, a dramatic change from the victim she played in *The Collector* (1965) or the dim-bulb love interest in *Doctor Doolittle* (1967).

Most of the creatures were played by seven-year-old girls from a school in Ontario, though the lead monster is Felix Silla, who was the robot Twiki on the "Buck Rogers" TV series and Cousin Itt of "The Addams Family" TV series.

Interestingly, the name of the school in Cronenberg's film is the Krell school: *Forbidden Planet* (see page 102), with its alien Krel civilization, features a creature conceptually similar to the Brood. The name of Raglan's institute is, of course, a nod to the "delicious" hallucinogen used in Huxley's *Brave New World*.

The Disc
Video: ★★
Audio: ★★ (monaural)
Chapters: Yes
Format: CLV
Source: Nelson Entertainment/Image Entertainment

The film is generally grainy (many of the interiors were shot that way), with a lot of minor scratches; beneath it all, the image is a little soft, though the colors are relatively strong. Though the film isn't letterboxed, cropping is insignificant.

The digital audio gets the job done cleanly and without distortion.

The Buddy Holly Story (1978) ★★★½
Director: Steve Rash
Running Time: 113 minutes

Headstrong, successful, and brilliant, Buddy Holly was the most innovative rock 'n' roller of his day. The Texas-born singer/composer was just beginning to stretch his musical wings when he died in a plane crash in 1959. Popular music would not have been what it is without him (he inspired the Beatles, among others) and it's much, much less than it would have been had he lived.

In 1975, director Jerry Friedman began shooting *Not Fade Away* for Twentieth Century–Fox, a film about Holly (Steve Davies) costarring Bruce Kirby and Gary Busey as his band, the Crickets—Joe B. Mauldin and Jerry Allison, respectively. But the studio wanted a lighthearted period romp like *American Graffiti* (1973) and the director wanted to make a movie about the conflicts among the band members and (fictionalized) enmity with contemporary black groups. One-third of the way through filming, Fox pulled the plug.

Another Holly project got going late in 1977, and someone who had seen the *Not Fade Away* footage suggested the Texas-born Busey for the lead role. The actor/guitarist/singer auditioned and was hired and gave a riveting, career-making performance.

The film follows Holly from his days of writing and recording rock demos in his garage, through his rise to fame and whirlwind romance and marriage to Maria Elena Santiago, to his break with the Crickets and his final tour. Certain events were changed for dramatic resonance (Holly's parents didn't discourage Buddy, as shown in the film; the Crickets did the bulk of their early recording in Clovis, New Mexico, not in New York; Holly had his front teeth broken in Australia, not prior to an "Ed Sullivan Show" gig, etc.), and the names and personalities of the (still-living) Crickets were changed. Don Stroud costars as drummer "Jesse" and Charles Martin Smith plays bassist "Ray Bob," making for two fewer permissions the producers had to obtain.

That said, the movie is incredibly faithful in spirit to the life of Holly. Part-time Cricket Niki Sullivan was particularly impressed with Busey's work: "That was just the way Buddy was," he says. "Busey picked up a lot of Buddy's mannerisms—how, I don't know."

Like only a handful of movies before it, the music wasn't lip-synched. What you hear is what Busey, Stroud, and Smith sang and played as the cameras rolled. The liberties are excusable: This is rousing and affecting entertainment.

The Disc
Video: ★★½
Audio: ★★★ (stereo)
Chapters: No
Format: CLV
Source: Columbia Pictures Home Video

The Buddy Holly Story was shot on a small budget in as many real locations as possible—not for authenticity but to minimize the cost of building sets. Low light in the concert and evening scenes was a real problem; and while the excessive grain isn't the disc's fault, it doesn't make for an eye-pleasing experience. Moreover, a mild letterbox would have been helpful: Shots of the band are a mite snug.

The live music has a raw, vital edge that really comes across on the disc and the stereo separation is excellent. The rest of the audio is—well, all right.

Bye Bye Birdie (1963) ★★★½
Director: George Sidney
Running Time: 112 minutes

When Elvis Presley was drafted early in 1958, lyricist Lee Adams and composer Charles Strouse (who later wrote *Annie* and the infamous *Nick & Nora*) teamed to write a Broadway musical fictionalizing the event. They bought the rights to the novel *Let's Go Steady* by Warren Miller and Raphael Millan, intending to work their drafted rock singer Conrad Birdie (named after singer Conway Twitty) into that. But there wasn't enough pizzazz to the story, or opportunities for music, so they scrapped the novel and decided to create an original story. A number of librettists were interviewed (including Mike Nichols) before they settled on TV sketch writer Michael Stewart. The result was *Bye Bye Birdie*, which opened on Broadway in 1960 and ran for over a year. (An ill-advised sequel, *Bring Back Birdie*, opened and closed quickly in 1981.)

When rock star Conrad Birdie (Jesse Pearson) is drafted, struggling songwriter Albert F. Peterson (Dick Van Dyke, making his film debut) is convinced his career is finished: Conrad was about to record one of his songs and make him rich and famous. Fortunately, Albert's secretary and girlfriend, Rosie DeLeon (Janet Leigh, a knockout with her black hair), doesn't give up so easily. Contacting Ed Sullivan (playing himself), she arranges to have the pre-induction Birdie sing a Peterson song on Sullivan's show, where he'll also plant a farewell kiss on an average teen-age girl.

The girl Rosie selects from the ranks of the Birdie fan club is Kim McAfee (Ann-Margret) and Birdie's arrival in Sweet Apple, Ohio, creates havoc in the town, in the McAfee household, and with Kim's jealous boyfriend, Hugo (Bobby Rydell). Things go from bad to worse when time constraints force the Sullivan people to cut the number, leaving just Conrad and the kiss and forcing Albert to resort to rather unorthodox means to get his song on the air.

The original Broadway cast consisted of former nightclub performer Van Dyke, with Chita Rivera as Rosie (choreographers Gower and Marge Champion had turned the parts down). Dick Gautier was Birdie, Susan Watson was Kim, and Paul Lynde played Kim's father, Harry. Lynde repeated the role in the film, and he's terrific.

For the movie Kim, the producers went with Ann-Margret. Born in Sweden (Ann-Margret Olsson) and discovered by George Burns (who else?) while she was performing in a cabaret, Ann-Margret appeared in *Pocketful of Miracles* (1961) and *State Fair* (1962) before making *Bye Bye Birdie;* her pink pants and cascading red hair are among the picture's greatest assets. Maureen Stapleton is hilarious as Albert's self-made martyr of a mother, Mae, whose coming is always announced by the squeal of her crepe-soled shoes.

In addition to the solid cast, there are timeless songs and some fun choreography—though the dance steps are very much rooted in the early 1960s and will seem more than a little foolish to modern teens. The numerous Khrushchev and Goldwater references also may escape them.

For an *A*-level production, the picture has some surprisingly shoddy special effects. The animation during the "Put on a Happy Face" number looks chintzy and watch when Leigh steps outside her body and her double walks from behind the gazebo. The alignment of the two images is *way* off and she seems to appear from thin air! You can also see the reflection of the kids in the "invisible" Plexiglas ramp used to scoot the tortoise up the stairs.

The Sweet Apple town square was later used in the *Back to the Future* films.

The Disc
Video: ★★★½
Audio: ★★★ (stereo)
Chapters: Yes
Format: CLV
Source: Pioneer Special Edition

The picture quality varies wildly in the film. In some scenes, there's a great deal of video noise—especially in the flesh tones—and the picture is slightly out of focus, while in other shots the colors are glossy and the image is supersharp. Fortunately, there are many more good scenes than bad.

The image is letterboxed on the recently released disc, which renders the pan-and-scan version obsolete: The split screen in "Going Steady" and the choreography in virtually all of the numbers demand the full screen.

The audio is clear and the separation is excellent, though, unfortunately—and inexcusably—the stereo tracks are reversed. (Corrected discs have been promised.)

Kim's surname is misspelled on the jacket, using the spelling from the Broadway Show, not the film.

Caligula (1979) ★
Directors: Tinto Brass (principal photography), Giancarlo Lui and Bob Guccione (additional scenes)
Running Time: 143 minutes

Ever since he was a starving painter/photographer living in Europe, Bob Guccione has wanted to be taken seriously as an artist. Thanks to the success of his *Penthouse* magazine, Guccione was able to shoot for the moon in a $15 million motion picture. Unfortunately, all he proved was that he could create a very expensive *Penthouse* spread.

Caius Caesar Germanicus (called Caligula because of the *caligae*, the small military boots, he wore as a child) ruled Rome from thus A.D. 37 to A.D. 41. The movie, "adapted from an original screenplay by Gore Vidal," actually gets much of the history right. Caligula's predecessor Tiberius was probably smothered; the new emperor was supported against his rival Tiberius Gemellus by the praetorian prefect Macro; Caligula is said to have had an incestuous relationship with his sister, Drusilla; he wed the sexually aggressive Caesonia; and he was carnally adventurous himself. The deaths of Caligula and his family are accurately portrayed.

Alas, there's too much sex for this to be taken seriously as drama and too much talk for it to work as pornography. Moreover, while exposed privates are plentiful in this unrated, unedited version, the sexual escapades are for the most part gauzily soft-core (there *are* a few graphic exceptions) as Guccione strove to put art on the screen.

Malcolm McDowell is much better than many of the scenes demand (sodomizing a man, performing necrophilia, pimping the wives of senators, etc.) and Peter O'Toole has some fun as the mad, disfigured Tiberius. John Gielgud as the cynical Nerva has the good fortune to slit his wrists in the first reel. (All of these distinguished actors signed aboard based on the Vidal script. When Guccione reshaped it, they were obliged to stick around.)

Teresa Ann Savoy is surprisingly endearing as Drusilla, and Helen Mirren—who went on to greater things (starring roles in *Excaliber, 2010*, and many others)—is the best thing about the film, playing the sexy, ambitious Caesonia.

Guccione has wanted to follow up this film with *Catherine the Great*, about the Russian empress who, legend (wrongly) has it, attempted to have intercourse with a horse. One suspects that somehow, someday, he'll get the movie made.

The Disc
Video: ★½
Audio: ★★ (monaural)
Chapters: No
Format: CLV
Source: Penthouse Video/Image Entertainment

The disc is the best it can be, but that's not saying much. The cinematography throughout is dark and murky, with one amateurish zoom after another. As a result, the disc looks grainy and has no detail at all, particularly in the dark scenes. The lack of letterboxing costs a bit of information but mostly during the dramatic sequences: Guccione knew enough to position the bare bottoms center screen.

The digital sound is a little bit better. The dialogue is very clear—too bad so little of it is worth listening to. There are virtually no sound effects (unless you include moaning and a gurgling disemboweling) and the music is inconsequential.

Spring for the wonderful *I, Claudius* instead, available in an excellent boxed set.

The Cardinal (1963) ★★★
Director: Otto Preminger
Running Time: 175 minutes

Otto Preminger was a blunt, gruff man who tended to make heartfelt but clunky films. The Austrian-born filmmaker believed passionately in freedom and human dignity, and his movies, most notably *The Moon Is Blue* (1953), *The Man with the Golden Arm* (1955), and *Anatomy of a Murder* (1959), are remembered more for the daring social ground they tilled than for their artistic merit. *The Cardinal* is no exception. (Even the *making* of his films often stirred controversies. While shooting this one in Austria, Preminger was denied permission to film at the National Library: The minister of education issued a statement that said it wouldn't be good for morale to have the arrival of the Nazis in Austria filmed there. In an equally public statement, Preminger asked the minster why he hadn't issued a similar statement back in 1938.)

Based on Henry Morton Robinson's ponderous bestseller (though Robert Dozier is credited with the screenplay, Preminger said, "Almost all of it was rewritten by Gore Vidal"), *The Cardinal* follows the rise of clergyman Stephen Fermoyle (Tom Tryon) from parish priest to cardinal. The picture is riveting when it deals with Church politics, race relations in the South, and the rise of Nazi Germany; when it lumbers into intermarriage and the temptation of the flesh, it becomes bad soap opera—no, make that *very* bad soap opera.

Tom Tryon is sincere but stiff as the "vain, ambitious Roman puppy" who matures over the course of the film, but Raf Vallone and John Huston are superb as ideological rivals, Cardinal Quarenghi and Cardinal Glennon. Carol Lynley is kittenish as Stephen's sister Mona and later as her own daughter Regina! John Saxon gives a good performance as her Jewish fiancé, Benny Rampell.

The late Tryon (*I Married a Monster from Outer Space*, *The Longest Day*) gave up acting two years later after working with the tyrannical Preminger a second time (*In Harm's Way*) and became a bestselling novelist (e.g., *The Other*).

It's interesting to speculate how his career might have gone differently if his first major film—*Something's Got to Give* (1962)—had not been aborted due to the temperamental behavior of star Marilyn Monroe.

The Disc
Video: ★★★½
Audio: ★★★ (Surround)
Chapters: Yes ... but only for fans of composer Jerome Moross, as they access the overture, intermission, and closing music!
Format: CLV
Source: Hal Roach Studios/Image Entertainment

From the fragile beauty of the opening titles to the brutal, climactic Nazi assault on the Austrian Church, the letterboxed film is rich with memorable images. The Panavision 70 cameras didn't miss a detail of the period sets and costumes, and the disc does them justice. The colors aren't as strong as they were in theaters, but the master element is in remarkably good shape.

The digital sound is clear, though the only real Surround aspect is rear-speaker channeling of Jerome Moross's powerful score.

Carnival of Souls (1962)
★★★★
Director: Herk Harvey
Running Time: 96 minutes

A woman and her companions drive off a bridge and drown—though the woman, Mary Henry (Candace Hilligoss), staggers from the water sometime later, surprised to be alive. Leaving town and taking a job as a church organist, she has frequent, unsettling visions of a pale, deathlike man (Herk Harvey), and now and then she seems to tune out of reality, neither seen nor heard by the people around her. Finally, with the nervous avidity of birds seeking prey, the dead come for Mary en masse, dancing and darting about. Realizing that she died in the crash, she reluctantly joins them in their dance of death at the Saltair pavilion.

Carnival of Souls is an amazing film. It's full of creepy suggestions of mortality and infinity: The swirling vortex of the river, the requiemlike dirges of the organ, and the landscape itself—blank skies, empty horizons, and open roads—seem to make the ordinary world disappear. The film does all it can to help the viewer enter Mary's nightmare, sharing its horrors and unnerving clamminess.

A triumph of low-budget filmmaking, *Carnival of Souls* was shot in Lawrence, Kansas, by industrial filmmaker Harvey. The filmmaker chose local amateur actors for his film and they imbue *Carnival of Souls* with a regional quality that gives it the air of a documentary. A few of the performers stand out, such as Harvey and Frances Feist as Mary's landlady; Sidney Berger is less effective as John Linden, whose interest in Mary is purely sexual: His Method acting falls way short of the Brando-esque levels he seems to *think* he's reaching.

Hilligoss is strong in the lead, giving a natural, understated performance.

Carnival of Souls is correctly regarded as a classic of its kind: It's unique, chilling, and memorable.

The Disc
Video: ★★★½
Audio: ★★
Chapters: Yes
Format: CLV
Source: VidAmerica

This restored edition of *Carnival of Souls* is sixteen minutes longer than most earlier versions shown on television and in the art houses. The print is Harvey's own and it is in pretty good shape; the transfer is excellent for a film of its age. The contrast is good, though the blacks aren't terribly glossy and the whites have a hint of gray to them. Nonetheless, this movie clearly demonstrates the advantage of laserdiscs when it comes to penetrating darkness and revealing detail in dim scenes. A lot of the movie is lost on videotape: For example, it's difficult to distinguish the pavilion from the landscape, to tell what's going on when Mary's car runs off the road at night, and much more. The details are all discernible on the laserdisc.

The sound is good but not great. While the audio has been digitized, the sound actually improves when the analog tracks are used.

The only extra is a short introduction to the film by the director, in which he gives a brief history of its distribution and critical reaction.

Casablanca (1942) ★★★★★
Director: Michael Curtiz
Running Time: 103 minutes

Humphrey Bogart's portrayal of café owner/gambler Rick Blaine in *Casablanca* became the prototype for the cynical yet sentimental romantic hero who was to dominate movies until the arrival of the antihero in films such as *Easy Rider* and *Five Easy Pieces* (see page 100). He's self-protectively disengaged from the pain of the living, and when he says, "I stick my neck out for nobody," the viewer can hardly wait for the inevitable: the arrival of Ilsa Lund (Ingrid Bergman), for whom he *will* stick his neck out. And who could blame him? In an era when directors routinely filled the screen with dramatic close-ups of beautiful actresses, none was more stunning than Ms. Bergman.

Rick operates his café in wartime Casablanca, which is officially administered by France's Vichy government. Because the city is a stopover for people on their way to Lisbon and freedom, this is where the Nazis have their last chance to catch political enemies.

Rick maintains a strict neutrality until his former lover, Ilsa, arrives: Having abandoned him, she is now married to freedom fighter Victor Laszlo (Paul Henreid). Uncharacteristically, Rick had agreed to conceal letters of transit given to him by Resistance worker Ugarte (Peter Lorre), which are the only way that Laszlo and his wife can get out of the city. Meanwhile, Capt. Louis Renault (Claude Rains)—whose cooperation with the Nazis is halfhearted at best—and Maj. Heinrich Strasser (Conrad Veidt) conspire to make sure Laszlo does not leave. A struggle for control of the letters of transit ensues: When Ilsa finally offers herself to Rick in exchange for Laszlo's freedom, he does the "right" thing and helps the two of them escape.

The film's images are memorable, yet even more imposing is the dialogue, some of which has worked its way into our colloquial treasury: Bogart's "Here's looking at you, kid," and the immortal "Play it again, Sam"—a misquotation of what Ilsa actually said ("Play it, Sam. Play 'As Time Goes By.'"). But the lines are so redolent of the film's smoky nightclubs, of its gardenias and gin, that the exact phrasing is almost incidental.

Incredible as it is in retrospect, Bogart

and Bergman were not the filmmaker's only choices for the parts: George Raft, Ronald Reagan, Hedy Lamarr, and Ann Sheridan were also under consideration. Although it's also difficult to believe, the making of the film was a chaotic affair. According to Ms. Bergman, "From the very start Hal Wallis, the producer, was arguing with the writers ... and every lunch time Mike Curtiz argued with Hal Wallis. There had to be all sorts of changes in the script. So every day we were shooting off the cuff: every day they were handing out the dialogue and we were trying to make some sense of it."

She added that originally they were going to shoot two endings: one in which she flew off in the airplane with her husband and one in which she stayed with Bogart. The first ending they shot was the one that ended up in the film, with Bogart and Rains walking off together, Bogart saying the famous "Louis, I think this is the beginning of a beautiful friendship." Ms. Bergman recalled that after filming it, everyone said, "'That's just perfect, a wonderful closing line.' But they hadn't known it was the closing line until they heard it."

The film was inspired by an unproduced play called *Everybody Comes to Rick's*.

The Disc

Video: ★★★★ (Criterion); ★★★½ (MGM/UA)
Audio: ★★★ (monaural)
Chapters: Yes
Format: CLV or CAV
Source: Criterion or MGM/UA Home Video

The CAV and CLV Criterion versions of the film are the best ones available, with a good sharp picture, very good contrast (given the smokiness of the original image), and excellent source material.

The sound is clear and acceptably free of hisses and pops.

The Criterion CAV edition's extras are mouth-watering: a collection of publicity photos, the original trailer, the treatment for a planned sequel, a second analog track Lux Radio broadcast of the story, a sample of the colorized version, and newsreel footage of the city. Both versions offer Ronald Haver's audio commentary.

MGM/UA's CLV edition is less than half the price of the Criterion CAV version. The picture and sound quality are very nearly as good as the more expensive edition and will satisfy anyone who can live without all the extras.

Both the CLV and CAV MGM/UA editions include the documentary, "You Must Remember This," about the making of the film; the CAV edition has two versions of the original trailer as well as a commemorative booklet.

The Chase (1966) ★★½
Director: Arthur Penn
Running Time: 135 minutes

Novelist/playwright/screenwriter Horton Foote is best known for works that evoke small-town American life. His screenplay for *To Kill a Mockingbird* (1962) was widely praised and, much later, he turned out splendid scripts for *Tender Mercies* (1983) and *The Trip to Bountiful* (1985).

Foote also wrote the 1952 novel and play on which *The Chase* is based, drawing on things he saw and experienced while growing up in Wharton, Texas. Lillian Hellman wrote the screenplay, bringing to the tale her own talent for creating psychological conflict. Unfortunately, the union of these two great talents resulted in nothing more than a southern *Peyton Place* with class struggles and racial relations factored into the suds—an interesting failure, but most definitely a failure.

The Chase is set in Tarl County, Texas, where the leisure pursuits during the long, hot summer are enjoying the sexual revolution and getting drunk. Tycoon Val Rogers (E. G. Marshall) calls the shots in the county, though his biggest disappointment is the fact that his son Jake (James Fox) doesn't have a happy marriage—which isn't to say Jake's *entirely* unsatisfied: He's been fooling around with Anna Reeves (Jane Fonda), the wife of convict Bubber Reeves (Robert Redford).

When Bubber breaks out of prison, it has a domino effect on Jake and Anna and on everyone who comes into contact with them—which, in this small town, is everyone. Fear, jealousy, prejudice, and distrust well up and bubble over, and Sheriff Calder (Marlon Brando) not only has to find Bubber, he has to keep the townspeople from destroying him and one another. The film ends powerfully and unsettlingly, with madness reminiscent of *The Day of the Locust* and—reflecting the violent mood of America at the time—with two deaths that can be regarded as a psychodramatic reenactment of the John Kennedy/Lee Harvey Oswald killings.

The Chase is a frustrating film. The story and cast are good, the white-collar/old-money relationships are well drawn—and, at one point, it was probably a very good film. But producer Sam Spiegel did what he'd done to David Lean's *Lawrence of Arabia* (see page 170): He cut it down. In the case of *The Chase*, though, he didn't just pare, he reedited and dropped scenes. What remains is worth seeing, but it's not what it might have been.

Brando dominates the film, but there are memorable performances from Robert Duvall as Val Rogers's timid vice president, Edwin Stewart, Henry Hull as the aloof "observer" Mr. Briggs, and Bruce Cabot as bartender Sol. Redford and Fonda are too neat and articulate for their parts as white trash (Redford had originally been slated to play Brando's role but asked for the change) and Marshall and Fox overplay and underplay, respectively. John Barry's excellent, brooding score was commissioned by Spiegel.

The Disc
Video: ★★★
Audio: ★★★ (monaural)
Chapters: Yes
Format: CLV
Source: Pioneer Special Editions

The print used for this new, letterboxed edition is nearly as frustrating as the film. It starts out with rich, saturated colors that, at the first reel change (side one, 6/20:50), go pale and stay that way for the bulk of the reel. The next reel change (at 8/40:07) restores the solid colors, but they get washed out again at the next change, and so on.

The image is generally very sharp, and the print itself is in very good condition. There's slight grain in many of the night scenes but very little video noise (even when, by some accident, the reds *do* manage to show some life!).

The audio is free of background noises but loses some of the fullness of the bass in Barry's score, and more than a couple of Brando's mumblings will require a quick backward scan. Other than that, the film sounds fine.

Chinatown (1974) ★★★★★
Director: Roman Polanski
Running Time: 131 minutes

In Los Angeles of 1937, while working on what he *thinks* is just another case of spying on a philandering spouse, private eye Jake Gittes (Jack Nicholson) is inadvertently involved in the murder of his subject, an honest water commissioner named Hollis Mulwray (Darrell Zwerling). Fascinated by the commissioner's widow, Evelyn (Faye Dunaway), Gittes investigates the murder—even after a (nameless) hood (director Polanski) cuts open his nose and tells him to back off. His search leads him into a realm of power and corruption as he learns that Evelyn's father, multimillionaire Noah Cross (John Huston), and his partners have been working to divert water in an effort to maximize the value of a vast amount of land they've purchased.

The swindle isn't the only shock awaiting Gittes, however. He learns the true nature of Evelyn's relationship with her father and is unable to prevent the tragic, if inevitable, conclusion.

The film was inspired by the Owne River valley scandal of 1908 and the characterizations are pure Raymond Chandler. But Polanski—whose wife, Sharon Tate, was brutally murdered in Los Angeles in 1969—brings his own dark vision to the story, stripping the characters of hope and barely allowing his protagonists to cling to their dignity.

Nicholson mixes humor and honor in what may well be his most memorable performance. His Gittes is skeptical, proud, and clever—*too* clever, as it turns out, because what he forces Evelyn to reveal changes him forever, and not for the better. Dunaway's Evelyn is untrustworthy, defensive, and bitter, a perfect contrast to Gittes—and to the lascivious, cruel, and corrupt Noah. Never has the expression "Lord, oh Lord," been uttered as hypocritcally as when he feigns horror over the climactic murder.

Chinatown—whose title is a bleak metaphor, a place where events large and small are simply written off—is a stunning, heartbreaking masterpiece.

The sequel, *The Two Jakes* (1990), is heartbreaking for other reasons.

"I said I'd play Gittes again only if we could come up with a unique script about the same character at some other point in his life," Nicholson has said. "Like what Shakespeare did, writing two separate plays about Mark Antony at specific junctures."

Screenwriter Robert Towne had originally planned the Gittes saga as a trilogy, examining the decline of Southern California value and culture. *The Two Jakes* aspired to a more pessimistic, world-weary tone than the cynical original and first went before the cameras in 1987. However, it was aborted due to squabbles between Towne—who was directing—and producer and former actor Bob Evans, who had been cast as Berman. Towne didn't feel Evans was up to it, Evans refused to leave, and the picture was shut down after $3.5 million had been spent.

Two years later, Nicholson—still keen to reprise his role as Gittes—tried to get the project going again with Bernardo Bertolucci, John Huston, or Mike Nichols directing. They turned him down, so he decided to direct it himself and to do rewrites on his own when Towne decided to stay away from the project. Why not? It wasn't *his* $19 million at risk.

The story is a good one: In postwar L.A., developer Jake Berman (Harvey Keitel) thinks his wife, Kitty (Meg Tilly), is having an affair with his partner. Gittes helps Jake track them to a motel in order to catch them in the act. But a gun goes off, the partner is killed, and his wife, Lily Bodine (Madeleine Stowe), thinks that Berman and his wife were behind the whole thing so they could collect her husband's share of the business.

Unfortunately, Nicholson didn't pull it off. His picture is poorly paced (though three minutes shorter than *Chinatown*, it plods) and it's confusing, something he recognized himself when he added his character's voice-over narration. The film was so muddled, in fact, that its original release date was pushed back nine months so that Nicholson could make *some* sense of the thing. At ★½, this one's a rental at best.

The Disc

Video: ★★★★½
Audio: ★★★½ (monaural)
Chapters: No
Format: CLV (sides one and two), CAV (side three)
Source: Paramount Home Video

The first version of *Chinatown* was panned-and-scanned and crapped up. It lost a *lot* of the image and was terribly grainy.

The recent wide-screen edition gives the film the respect it deserves, with saturated colors (and some attendant video noise), a minimum of grain, and a sharp picture. Considering the size of the picture area, the amount of details in the darker scenes is amazing.

Depending upon your monitor, this wide-screen edition (and also *The Two Jakes*) will either be letterboxed or windowboxed. Paramount went to the very edge of the film image to get *everything* onto the screen.

The audio is solid and clear, and Jerry Goldsmith's suave, tense, nostalgic score has been isolated on a separate analog track.

The Two Jakes is also available on a laserdisc, letterboxed or not, and Paramount Home Video has done a very good job with a very difficult film. While the transfer will *seem* inferior, especially on the nonwide-screen edition—dark in spots, pale in others, the focus soft here and there—that's exactly how the film looked on the screen.

The nonletterboxed edition was opened slightly into the safety area. The CAV capacity on side three is perfect.

The audio quality is excellent, with some fine Surround effects.

Chinese Roulette (1976)★
Director: Rainer Werner Fassbinder
Running Time: 82 minutes

A film buff who wrote for and acted in politically radical plays as part of his Anti-Theater troupe, Fassbinder segued into feature films when he was twenty-four and directed more than forty movies between 1969 and his death in 1982. His spare-looking films dwell, often fanatically, on social or political issues, carried along by dialogue rather than by dramatics or stylish cinematography. *The Marriage of Maria Braun* (1978) was his international breakthrough, the tale of a soldier's wife who builds a postwar industrial empire; it's the director's best film. His mammoth fifteen-hour-plus *Berlin Alexanderplatz* (1980), set in Germany in the 1920s, is also a magnificent film; neither is available on laserdisc.

The earlier *Chinese Roulette* is available, though it's a plodding film filled with people who are either aloof (which they mistake for sophistication) or who hate. Angela (Andrea Schober) is a crippled young girl whose soul is considerably more twisted than her legs. Because each of her parents began having a supposedly secret affair when she fell ill and blame her for their unhappiness, Angela arranges a cruel payback: She fixes things so that her mother, father, and their lovers show up at the family country estate, Traunitz Castle, at the same time. The adults try to be oh so civilized about the turn of events, but everything comes apart when Angela organizes a game of Chinese roulette that consists of questions such as "If you were a car, what kind would you be?" This degenerates into anger and then to gunplay, though death is a breath of fresh air after all the lofty "saint-mother-whore" observations.

There's some clever staging as Fassbinder shows rather than explains how the characters feel toward one another and how those feelings shift as the awkward holiday progresses. But that's not enough to sustain interest in the characters or the film.

The Disc
Video: ★½
Audio: ★★ (monaural)
Chapters: Yes
Format: CLV (side one), CAV (side two)
Source: CinemaDisc Collection/Image Entertainment

The mildly letterboxed film is only marginally better than videotape: The image is fuzzy, the colors are drab, and there's very fine grain throughout.

The audio is mostly talk and is rather hollow-sounding. The subtitles are easy to read.

The CAV side is uneven, with some sections steady and others jittering for three or four frames in a row.

Christmas in Connecticut (1945) ★★★
Director: Peter Godfrey
Running Time: 102 minutes

If *Double Indemnity* (see page 76) gives us a Barbara Stanwyck to fear, this movie gives us one to love all over again—and reminds us just what a fine and versatile actress she was.

Smart Housekeeping columnist Elizabeth Lane (Stanwyck) writes about the recipes she cooks for her husband and child on their beautiful farm in Connecticut—even though she lives alone in a small New York apartment and can't cook even an egg. She gets all of her recipes from her good friend Felix Bassenak (S. Z. Sakall), a restaurateur. Meanwhile, after his ship is torpedoed, sailor Jefferson Jones (Dennis Morgan) ends up in a naval hospital and nurse Mary Lee (Joyce Compton) falls in love with him—though not vice versa. Mary Lee feels that Jones would be more receptive to marriage if he was to experience home and hearth firsthand, and she writes to *Smart Housekeeping* publisher Alexander Yardley (Sydney Greenstreet), suggesting that hero Jones spend Christmas with the Lane household. Yardley thinks the idea is terrific and orders Lane to be Jones's Christmas host at her farm—and invites himself along, as well. It's up to the panic-stricken writer and her even more panicked editor, Dudley Beecham (Robert Shayne), to come up with a husband, a farm, and a baby.

This is a dated film, one in which publishing companies were run by czars instead of by corporations and a woman's worth was defined by mink coats and men. But it's also a smart, clever, funny film with a wonderful cast and nice screwball touches.

With a huge, roaring fireplace, a big trimmed tree, perfectly frosted windowpanes, and sleigh rides through rolling fields of snow, it evokes Christmas as only a movie can—made entirely in a Hollywood soundstage!

The Disc
Video: ★★½
Audio: ★★★ (monaural)
Chapters: Yes
Format: CLV
Source: MGM/UA Home Video

The disc was transferred from a master element that is flawed by a few scratches here and there. Too bad that's not the only problem! While the focus is generally sharp, the picture alternates between clarity and grain for no apparent reason. Some scenes also have a slightly gray cast, though contrast on the whole is very good.

Despite some tinny patches, the audio is clear and has nice resonance in the middle range.

The disc has one terrific extra: The program opens with the hilarious 1946 Bugs Bunny cartoon *Acrobatty Bunny*. The color is rich and the sound very good.

Cinema Paradiso (1989)
★★★½
Director: Giuseppe Tornatore
Running Time: 123 minutes

Alfredo (Philippe Noiret) is an aging projectionist in a small town in southern Italy after the World War II. He befriends fatherless Salvatore (played, as he ages, by Salvatore Cascio, Mario Leonardi, and Jacques Perrin). Salvatore adores the movies, and the projectionist and the theater become his surrogate father and mother, his sanctuary and schoolroom. The only dark cloud in both their lives is the local priest, Father Adelfio (Leopoldo Trieste), who prescreens each of the films and forces Alfredo to remove the kisses. However, Adelfio can't stop the teenaged Salvatore from pursuing real-life kisses outside the theater, and the film moves deftly between its rite-of-passage story line and its glorious love letter to the magic of the movies.

Told in flashbacks—the adult Salvatore is a successful filmmaker based in Rome—*Cinema Paradiso* was shot in Tornatore's hometown outside of Palermo and was only the director's second film (after *The Professor* in 1986). The performances are naturalistic and touching. While there are slow spots, just let the last scene wash over you: You'll forget them all and experience nothing but joy (shared with Salvatore) about life and the art form the film celebrates.

The Disc
Video: ★
Audio: ★★★ (monaural)
Chapters: Yes
Format: CLV (sides one and two), CAV (side three)
Source: CinemaDisc Collection/Image Entertainment

Despite its merits, the film is tough to watch because of consistent fuzziness and excessive video noise. The colors are acceptable but no better and there is occasional grain. Given the popularity of the film, the unexceptional quality of the transfer is both surprising and disappointing.

The CAV side—with the "kiss" footage—is jitter-free.

The film is subtitled, but the second audio channel has rather cleverly been used for the dubbed sound track. For once, viewers *can* have a foreign film both ways! (And the dubbed version doesn't hurt the film much: Frenchman Noiret is dubbed in the Italian version, anyway.)

The audio in both versions is fine, though the mesmerizing Ennio Morricone score is a bit clearer in the subtitled version.

Citizen Kane (1941) ★★★★★
Director: Orson Welles
Running Time: 119 minutes

As a child, Orson Welles excelled at everything: painting, writing, acting, magic tricks, piano playing—the works. At the age of six, he was already staging productions of Shakespeare's plays in his living room. Skipping college and traveling around the world, Welles returned to the United States, worked on Broadway, and, with John Houseman, formed the Mercury Theatre in 1937. The company moved to radio the following year; among their productions was the famous "War of the Worlds" broadcast, which convinced thousands of listeners that Grovers Mills, New Jersey, was under attack by martians.

The financially strapped RKO Studios lured the twenty-four-year-old wunderkind to Hollywood in 1939 with the promise of giving him complete artistic freedom in exchange for a movie that (they hoped) would pay off at the box office. Welles set about writing a screen adaptation of Joseph Conrad's *Heart of Darkness* (see *Apocalypse Now*) and planning a film of the novel, but he abandoned that; he also worked on projects called *The Smiler with the Knife* and *Mexican Melodrama*. Then he met screenwriter and former newspaperman Herman Mankiewicz, who wanted to make a movie about newspaper mogul William Randolph Hearst—or someone like him. Welles loved the idea not just for its dramatic potential but because it appealed to his "bad boy" nature to be able to tweak the nose of a giant. Mankiewicz wrote the screenplay, Welles added to it, and *Citizen Kane*—originally called *American* by Mankiewicz and then *John Citizen, U.S.A.* by Welles—went into production.

The film covers the years 1870 to 1940, jumping back and forth in the life of newspaper czar Charles Foster Kane (Welles). On his deathbed, Kane utters the word *Rosebud* and expires. In an effort to discover who or what *Rosebud* is, reporter Thompson (William Alland) interviews people who knew Kane when he was a young newspaper publisher, devoted husband to Emily Norton Kane (Ruth Warrick), and an aspiring politician destroyed (prophetically) by his love for singer Susan Alexander (Dorothy Comingore), his inability to make her a major star, and his increasing bitterness and reclusiveness. Among the people Thompson visits are Kane's old friends and coworkers Jedediah Leland (Joseph Cotten), Mr. Bernstein (Everett Sloane), and Susan. Thompson learns a lot about Kane but never what *Rosebud* means; that discovery is left for the audience alone and, though dismissed by some as pop psychology and armchair Freud, it succeeds in bringing us closer to Kane than any of the characters in the film ever got.

After it was completed, *Citizen Kane* was very nearly killed by people fearful of Hearst's power. Through influential Hollywood friends, Hearst tried to buy the film from RKO and have it destroyed. His newspapers sabotaged it and other RKO films with bad publicity or the cold shoulder. Despite the kind of publicity a studio would kill for, RKO had trouble getting the film to the public because theater chains refused to show the picture. It played here and there, it vanished, and it resurfaced over the years in art houses—usually bad 16mm prints, which, however awful they were, could not dim its genius. As the controversy faded and the film was (finally) allowed to stand on its own merits, people began to appreciate its timeless characterizations and immense visual power. When film schools began to sprout like weeds in the mid-1960s, the movie became a staple of curricula; books were written about it; and by the end of the decade it was widely regarded as the greatest American film—perhaps the greatest film—ever made.

In summarizing one of the greatest and most tragic characters in cinema, Welles said that Kane's "greatest error"—the fatal flaw in his character—"was that of the American plutocrats of those years, who believed that money automatically conferred a certain stature to a man." He stated, "Kane arrives at having a certain class but never greatness." (Welles added that even "if he had been poor, Kane would not have been a great man but one thing is sure and that is that he would have been a successful man.")

Citizen Kane cost $686,000 to make—not *wildly* expensive but enough to hurt RKO—and its failure doomed Welles to a life of struggle in Hollywood and Europe. Never again would he be given the freedom he enjoyed on his first film; in spite of that, he managed to make magnificent, original films such as *The Magnificent Ambersons* (1942), *The Lady from Shanghai* (1948), *Macbeth* (1948), and *Touch of Evil* (see page 282). Still, any film buff's got to ache at the thought of what Welles *might* have been able to achieve if Hearst and his bullies hadn't sunk his masterpiece.

Future superstar Alan Ladd appears briefly as the pipe-smoking reporter.

The new Criterion disc was transfered a frame at a time, each shot nursed to its best possible condition, and the results are stunning. The black and white film has never looked better (just as Criterion claims), with detail and nuance that will surprise and delight you.

The sound is limited somewhat by the recording technology of the time, but, despite some faint hissing and a few minor, extraneous noises, you'll be amazed at the clarity and range of the audio. Bernard Herrmann's driving, ominous score is especially well served by the presentation.

Extras on the CAV edition include interviews with film professionals about *Citizen Kane*, as well as production art, storyboards, the original trailer, photographs, and scenes cut from the script.

The only problem with the set is the packaging: Instead of boxing it, Criterion has put the three discs in a gatefold jacket. Close it up for too long and the discs will *warp*.

The Turner print of the film isn't *quite* as strong in the dark scenes, where some details are lost and the gray tones aren't as rich. The print is in good shape, though, and the focus is very sharp throughout.

Turner's audio is a little rinky-dink in the upper ranges, though it's quite satisfactory otherwise.

Criterion also has done a superlative job with *The Magnificent Ambersons*, a CAV presentation containing the storyboards, shooting script, audio-track commentary, and more. Criterion also has a CLV edition of Welles's overrated *Confidential Report* (1955), aka *Mr. Arkadin*, a return to *Citizen Kane* territory and the life of a rotten millionaire.

The Disc

Video: ★★★★★ (Criterion); ★★★½ (Image)
Audio: ★★★★½ (Criterion); ★★★½ (Image)—both monaural
Chapters: Yes
Format: CLV or CAV (Criterion); CLV (Image)
Source: Criterion or Turner Entertainment/Image Entertainment

Cleopatra (1963) ★★★½

Director: Joseph Mankiewicz
Running Time: 246 minutes

It's difficult to say which caused more of a stir: the events covered in the film—the arrival of Julius Caesar in Egypt (48 B.C.) his love for Queen Cleopatra, his assassination, the subsequent power struggle between Mark Antony and Octavian, and the deaths of lovers Antony and Cleopatra (66 B.C.)—or the press generated by lovebirds Elizabeth Taylor and Richard Burton when they made the movie.

The press coverage started early on, when Taylor signed for a then-unprecedented $1 million to play the Queen of the Nile, then suffered a near-fatal bout with staphylococcal pneumonia after shooting began in England. Her illness caused a lengthy production delay, forcing stars Stephen Boyd (Mark Antony) and Peter Finch (Julius Caesar) to withdraw due to prior commitments. They were replaced by Burton, fresh from playing King Arthur in Broadway's *Camelot*, and Rex Harrison, who was hired after Trevor Howard turned the producers down.

To preserve Ms. Taylor's health, the $5 million sets that had been built in damp England were abandoned and plans were made to shoot the film in Hollywood. However, various TV series as well as George Stevens's *The Greatest Story Ever Told* (ultimately postponed) were due to occupy fully the Fox lot, so the new sets were constructed in sunny Rome. This helped to propel the budget to a still-impressive $37 million—along with smaller things, such as Liz agreeing to go to Italy only if her personal physician came along for a fee of $25,000 plus expenses. There was talk of replacing the demanding actress with Fox starlet Joan Collins—but with so much money riding on the production, and no other box-office name in the film, Liz stayed.

Was all the fuss and expense worth it? Sure—if you weren't a Twentieth Century–Fox stockholder. The studio ultimately had to sell off most of their back lot (which is now Century City) to pay for the film. Elizabeth Taylor was never more beautiful, and, though her alternately shrill and stilted delivery remains an aesthetic sinkhole, she's bolstered by a literate script and superb performances by Harrison, Burton, and Roddy McDowall (Octavian). And the sets are *truly* epic: You'll go back to the film repeatedly just to gawk.

The Disc
Video: ★★★★
Audio: ★★★★ (Surround)
Chapters: Yes
Format: CLV
Source: CBS Fox Video

The spectacle of *Cleopatra* has been captured in all its glory by this letterboxed presentation, made even more appealing by lush colors and a generally sharp, grain-free picture.

The digital sound is crisp and powerful, with good stereo separation and effective use of the rear channels during the battles and crowd scenes. The overture, entr'acte, and exit music are included.

The five-sided boxed set restores footage snipped from the original film by Darryl F. Zanuck, the response of the fractious studio head to complaints from critics that the movie was too long. The set also offers a twenty-minute featurette, "Cleopatra's Fourth Star," an interesting behind-the-scenes look at the making of the sets, along with star-studded footage of the film's opening in New York, Los Angeles, and Washington, D.C.

A Clockwork Orange (1971)
★★★★★
Director: Stanley Kubrick
Running Time: 137 minutes

After making *2001: A Space Odyssey* (see page 287)—which ended with a shot of the messianic Star Child—Stanley Kubrick went back to the future, opening *A Clockwork Orange* with a shot of the murderous Alex DeLarge (Malcolm McDowell), setting the tone for a far less hopeful film. Now, it's no longer apes but, rather, teenagers that gather around a fallen foe, beating him with sticks. At roughly the same time that the spaceships of *2001: A Space Odyssey* are doing their weightless ballet, Alex and his friends are engaged in a ballet of flying bodies as they fight Billyboy and *his* thugs.

Based on Anthony Burgess's 1962 novel—whose title refers to "the attempt to impose upon man ... laws and conditions appropriate to a mechanical creation"—the movie opens as young Alex and gang members Dim (Warren Clarke), Georgie (James Marcus), and Pete (Michael Tarn) go about their nightly "ultraviolence"—brawling, running cars off the road, and, tonight, stopping at the home of Mr. and Mrs. Alexander (Patrick Magee and Adrienne Corri), where they beat and cripple Mr. Alexander and rape his wife, who dies soon thereafter.

The following night, resentful of Alex's dictatorial leadership and also for setting his criminal sights too low, his fellow ruffians turn on him. He subdues them with a violent outburst; later, during a robbery, Dim hits him with a milk bottle, temporarily blinding him. (Spiked milk got him up for the crime; getting spiked with milk brings him down.) The police apprehend him.

After spending time in prison, Alex volunteers for the experimental Ludovico technique: While under the influence of drugs, he's forced to watch violent films, the combination causing him to become physically ill at the thought of violence. Sent out into the world, Alex is unable to defend himself when he's beaten up by Dim and George, who are now police officers. Ironically, he falls in with subversives, led by Mr. Alexander (who doesn't recognize him at first), who are working to overthrow the government. Alex becomes a pawn of both factions and a cause célèbre; in the end, not only does the government operate on him to reverse the effects of the "cruel" Ludovico treatment, it rewards the hoodlum with a position of importance.

Burgess wrote the novel based on his own experiences during World War II, when a trio of GIs beat and raped his wife, who later died. Rock star Mick Jagger had wanted to play Alex in an aborted film version in 1964, but it remained for Kubrick, with his clout, to put the controversial story before the cameras. His generally faithful adaptation (which includes some of the novel's Nadsat slang, the Russian/English hybrid spoken by the teenagers) is one of the great ones, interweaving sociology, politics, ethics, and theology to create an unflinching, brutal, and poetic work. People who saw *A Clockwork Orange* in the theaters never forgot it; over twenty years later, the film retains its awesome power.

Malcolm McDowell is so good that despite the other fine work he's done—especially *Time After Time* (1979), in which he plays author H. G. Wells—he has never escaped the shadow of Alex. Afterward, Kubrick's muse also must have been pretty well wasted: His three subsequent films, *Barry Lyndon*, *The Shining*, and *Full Metal Jacket*, have been of variable quality.

One question, though: Why, in such a technically perfect film, did Kubrick choose to insert a quick, cheesy earthquake shot from *One Million Years B.C.* (1966) in Alex's first reverie. The visual is fake, grainy, and jarringly inappropriate. Compare this to the pains Kubrick took to get the point-of-view shot when Alex leaps out the window in a suicide attempt: He had the camera encased in polystyrene and threw it out the window six times to get the footage he wanted.

A Kubrick film wouldn't be complete without subtleties and *A Clockwork Orange* has those, from the visual symbolism of trying to fit a square peg in a round hole (the sky and the circle in the prison courtyard, side two, 3/18.55) to the Experimental Serum 114 given to Alex at the Ludovico center. It was the destruction of a CRM 114 unit on board the B-52 in *Dr. Strangelove* (see page 72) that made the recall of the plane impossible and World War III inevitable. Obviously, the director feels programmed behavior is as terrible as nuclear holocaust.

On a less weighty note, the actor who plays Mr. Alexander's companion Julian is Dave Prowse, who wore the Darth Vader costume in *Star Wars* and its sequels. And check out the continuity flub with the clipboard on side two, 4/20:48, and the reference to Alex as Alex Burgess in the newspapers—even though he clearly states that his surname is DeLarge.

The Disc

Video: ★★★★
Audio: ★★★½ (monaural)
Chapters: Yes
Format: CLV
Source: Warner Home Video

There's reason to rejoice that a letterboxed edition has replaced the old cropped version and the transfer—personally supervised by the director—is very good. There *are* flaws; for example, there's a red gash, dead center, that appears at 8/29:26 on side one and stays there for quite some time, and greater care could have been taken with some of the trickier shots, such as the backlighted bedroom meeting between Alex and his postcorrective adviser, P. R. Deltoid (Aubrey Morris), in which Deltoid's head looks as fuzzy as a cotton ball. However, except for the solid orange and blue title cards, which bleed all over the screen, the reds and browns are excellently handled. The other colors are equally solid.

The letterboxing allows you to enjoy the director's powerful compositions, not to mention allowing all four "droogs" to appear on screen at the same time.

The audio is very good. The opening strains of the title music—adapted from Henry Purcell's "Music for the Funeral of Queen Mary"—are so strong that they make you ready and willing to forgive the disc its flaws—which include a slightly sibilant sound track, the result of the digital processing.

This version of the film is the original X-rated edition; the subsequent R-rated release clipped a few shots from the *William Tell* Overture sex sequence (which, incidentally, took twenty-eight minutes of "real" time to shoot).

Close Encounters of the Third Kind (1977) ★★★★½

Director: Steven Spielberg
Running Time: 137 Minutes

Despite its disregard for the laws of physics and pacing, *Close Encounters of the Third Kind* is a great film; it is, in addition, a great *American* film, with its emphasis on the pioneering, exploratory spirit, its celebration of technology, and its childlike energy.

Roy Neary (Richard Dreyfuss), an Indiana utility worker, is an Everyman who has a close encounter with an alien spacecraft one night. He receives a subconscious impression from the extraterrestrials, a vague *shape* that he seeks to identify with increasing obsessiveness, costing him his wife, Ronnie (Teri Garr), and family and very nearly his sanity.

At the same time, other people have received the same "signal": Nearly as preoccupied as Neary are single mother Jillian Guiler (Melinda Dillon), especially after the E.T.s kidnap her four-year-old son, Barry (Cary Guffey). Meanwhile, UFO specialist Claude Lacombe (French director François Truffaut) has secretly arranged a landing site for the aliens at Devil's Tower in Wyoming. In time, Roy, Jillian, and others realize that the columnar rock formation was the image implanted in their minds, and they desperately make their way to the historic first meeting between humans and spindly beings from another world. Not everyone who keeps the rendezvous gets to go away with the aliens—but even those who remain behind are changed in mind and spirit (though how they'll function again in the mundane real world is a mystery).

Fresh from the success of *Jaws* (1975), Spielberg decided to make a film about UFOs—long a favorite topic of his—and began working on a script he called *Watch the Skies*, a title inspired by the last line of the 1951 science fiction classic *The Thing from Another World*. When he'd roughed the script out, the director turned it over to Paul Schrader to finish. The author of such bleak, gritty films as *The Yakuza* (see page 310) and *Taxi Driver* (1976), Schrader took a less optimistic view of the encounter, so Spielberg rewrote it (with the uncredited help of John Milius—see *Conan the Barbarian*—and Jerry Belson, and input from UFO expert J. Allen Hynek).

Filmed on actual locations and in a pair of abandoned dirigible hangars outside of

Mobile, Alabama (to accommodate the large sets and keep the story and visuals a secret), the picture underwent tinkering, sometimes radical, as it progressed. Spielberg was constantly changing the design of the aliens. Jim Henson worked on Muppet-like creatures that failed to satisfy the director, while a giant transluscent marionette looked silly. At one point, he had costumed children on roller skates so they'd seem to float; mostly, though, they just fell over. Finally, Carlo Rambaldi—who had made the unwieldly, life-size mechanical King Kong for the classic film's miserable 1976 remake—came up with a cable-operated alien that Spielberg liked. That and nonskating costumed children were used to portray the aliens.

A preview audience reacted negatively to Jiminy Cricket singing "When You Wish Upon a Star," and that, too, was excised from the film's climax.

The biggest change of all, however, came nearly two years after the film's release. Hurt by criticism that the middle section dragged (when Neary builds a huge sculpture of Devil's Tower in his living room), Spielberg cut the section and tightened the film in other spots, added new scenes, and included a million-dollar peek inside the alien spacecraft at the end. *Close Encounters—The Special Edition* was the result.

The $20 million film is magnificent and awe-inspiring in either version (or both together; see *The Disc*) and, unlike other science fiction films made in the seventies, the special effects by Douglas Trumbull (of *2001: A Space Odyssey* fame) are as fresh and impressive as the day the film opened. Though the music suffers from John Williams' tendency to overinflate every measure with bombast, his five-note melody is haunting and instantly evokes the film and its theme of hope and magic.

Difficult to believe that this movie is from the same director who gave us the soppy *E.T.* (see page 87) and the miserable, misguided, no-sense-of-wonder *Hook.*

The Disc

Video: ★★★★★ (Criterion); ★★ (RCA/Columbia
Audio: ★★★★★ (Surround) (Criterion); ★½ (RCA/Columbia)
Chapters: Yes (Criterion)
Format: CAV or CLV (Criterion); CLV (RCA/Columbia)
Source: Criterion or RCA/Columnbia Home Video

RCA/Columbia's panned-and-scanned version of *The Special Edition* will satisfy those who want to fill their screens with a big picture. But the colors are slightly off, the image is way too grainy in spots, and the Devil's Tower sequence is stripped of its awesome scope. The sound throughout is slightly distorted and unpleasant.

The Criterion discs are stupendous. Not only are they properly letterboxed but the colors are stunning. Just *look* at that red soil on the hill near Devil's Tower.

The audio is perfect, with heavenly trebles and devilish basses.

The CAV edition not only offers a wealth of supplementary material—storyboards, UFO sketches, deleted sections of script, and so on—it allows the viewer to see the original film and/or program in the *Special Edition* footage, as well. It is, in short, a complete version of the film. The CLV edition offers no supplementary material and only the original 1977 edition.

The Cocoanuts (1929) ★★★½

Directors: Joseph Stanley and Robert Florey
Running Time: 93 minutes

Prodded by their mother, Minna, Leonard, Adolph, Julius, Herbert, and Milton Schoenberg went into vaudeville as a musical team, but it wasn't until they turned to comedy that they began to make a name for themselves, literally as well as figuratively. By the time they reached Broadway in 1924, in the musical comedy

I'll Say She Is, they were Chico, Harpo, Groucho, Zeppo, and Gummo Marx.

Their second show was the hit *The Cocoanuts* (1925), in which their personal comedic styles were set: cigar-smoking, ad-libbing Groucho, with his fake mustache and eyebrows and crouched walk; harp-playing, horn-honking pantomimist Harpo; malapropian Chico; and romantic straight man Zeppo. (Gummo left early in the team's career.) The show ran for three years, and their unique, hilarious combination of words and visuals was deemed perfect for sound films. In 1929, *The Cocoanuts*—with musical numbers by Irving Berlin—was made into a movie, shot in the Astoria Studios just outside of New York (so the brothers could commute and continue to appear nightly in their show *Animal Crackers*).

The Cocoanuts is still very much a stage play, although the brothers toned down the manic performances somewhat. Groucho stars as Mr. Hammer, owner of the Hotel de Cocoanut on Cocoanut Beach in Florida. Zeppo is his long-suffering employee Jamison, while Chico and Harpo (that's what they're called) are pickpockets who come for what they hope will be a profitable visit. Meanwhile, the wealthy Mrs. Potter (Margaret Dumont) and her daughter, Polly (Mary Eaton), are also guests; Polly is in love with young Bob Adams (Oscar Shaw), though her mother disapproves of the poor fellow. Mrs. Potter prefers the Continental Harvey Yates (Cyril Ring)—who, unknown to her, is plotting with his lover, Penelope (Kay Francis), to steal Mrs. Potter's $100,000 diamond necklace. Naturally, Bob is accused of the crime—and, just as naturally, the Marx Brothers help prove his innocence.

The romantic fluff is dated, but the comedy and Irving Berlin tunes are timeless. Among the classic Marx bits in this film are the "viaduct" dialogue between Groucho and Chico, the "door routine" with intricate comings and goings between two hotel rooms, and the property auction where Groucho has informed Chico how to "bid up" the lots—and, predictably, Chico screws up.

Most of the Marx Brothers films are available on laserdisc, and many are better than this one. But *The Cocoanuts* is a wonderful testament to their developing talent and to a film industry still in transition between silents and sound. As such, it is an important film ... and, of course, wildly funny to boot.

MCA is to be congratulated for leaving the film's original Paramount logo intact.

The Disc

Video: ★★★
Audio: ★★★ (monaural)
Chapters: Yes
Format: CLV
Source: MCA/Universal Home Video

There probably isn't a millimeter of the film that isn't scratched *somehow*, but, considering its age, *The Cocoanuts* is in very good shape. Most of the print is very sharp, with good contrast beneath the scratches and mild grain. The only serious breach occurs at the reel change at 8/5:22; both the picture and sound go fuzzy until the next change, at 10/16:36.

The sound, too, is better than you'd expect. Careful digital processing has resulted in no hiss whatsoever; the pops and crackles that are present are faint and found on the source material. Except for that one reel change, most of the dialogue is surprisingly crisp.

Conan the Barbarian (1982)
★★★
Director: John Milius
Running Time: 129 minutes

The Conan stories of Robert E. Howard weren't much as literature, but they were unmatched for their muscular violence, odd and eerie characters, and exotic locales in the mythical Hyborian Age. Prolific pulp writer Howard penned twenty-six Conan stories in all, most of which were published between 1932 and 1936.

John Milius's most effective movies manifest that same kind of aggressive power, such as *The Wind and the Lion* (1975) and *Farewell to the King* (1989). But, like Howard, his fascination with thews and/or hardware often causes him to lose sight of story and characterization, which hurt *Red Dawn* (1984), *Flight of the Intruder* (1990)—and *Conan the Barbarian*.

When his village is attacked and his parents slain by the leader of a cannibalistic snake cult, Thulsa Doom (James Earl Jones), young Conan is sold into slavery. Growing to manhood, Conan (Arnold Schwarzenegger) becomes a gladiatorial Pit Fighter who is eventually freed by his owner. With the thief Valeria (Sandahl Bergman) and the Mongol Subotai (Gerry Lopez), Conan accepts a commission from King Osric (Max von Sydow) to rescue his daughter from Doom. Together, the trio invades his stronghold, the Mountain of Power. As they escape with the princess, Valeria is slain and Conan plots vengeance: After luring Doom's forces into one bloody trap after another, the hero faces his old nemesis and lops off his head.

The movie is high on action and atmosphere, but the dialogue is spare and what's there is a mix of the insipid and mystical mumbo jumbo. That's a shame, because the casting couldn't have been more on the money. Schwarzenegger is perfect as the feral and cynical Conan, while Bergman—who did the memorable topless dance in Bob Fosse's *All That Jazz* (1979)—is a smart, lithe heroine. With some sharp, revealing exchanges between the two, and less shallow posturing from Doom, this could have been a movie with real substance, sort of a *Seventh Seal* with muscles and viscera. (It was cowritten by Milius and Oliver Stone—who has gone on to better things.)

In a sequel, *Conan the Destroyer* (1984), directed by fantasy-film veteran Richard Fleischer (*20,000 Leagues Under the Sea* [1954] and *Fantastic Voyage* [1966]) a somewhat tamed (PG instead of R-rated) barbarian is hired to escort a princess on a dangerous mission. He's accompanied by the feisty Zula (Grace Jones) and the grim Bombaata (Wilt Chamberlain), who provide some sparks in this action-packed but unatmospheric film. In Fleischer's *Red Sonja* (1985), Schwarzenegger played the Conan-like Kalidor, with Brigitte Nielsen as Robert E. Howard's sword-swinging barbarian heroine.

Both films are available on laser, in panned-and-scanned versions only.

The Disc

Video: ★★★
Audio: ★★½ (monaural)
Chapters: Yes
Format: CLV (sides one and two), CAV (side three)
Source: MCA/Universal Home Video

This is a satisfying remaster, despite the fact that—for some unfathomable reason—there are a number of grainy daylight scenes compared to relatively clear nighttime ones. Watch the daytime preparations for battle on side three and Doom's evening rally later on: The difference in clarity is striking. The grain wasn't present in the original film. Video noise is a minor problem in a few spots.

Those distractions aside, the disc has generally strong colors and is perfectly letterboxed, capturing all of the original screen image. While this doesn't affect the characters, who tend to cluster together, it lets you enjoy the elaborate sets and rough-hewn Spanish countryside. (The sequel was filmed in Mexico, on the transformed sets from *Dune*).

The digital sound is clear but frustrating. It's curious that Milius chose to make the film monaurally, particularly after *Star Wars* and *Raiders of the Lost Ark* proved the appeal of Dolby stereo. Two of the movie's greatest assets are its drumming, Prokofiev-like score by Basil Poledouris (a Milius schoolmate) and bludgeoning sound effects. On the disc, these have a flatness you simply don't expect from a fantasy film of this era.

The film's trailer is included.

A panned-and-scanned version of the film is available, but it doesn't do justice to the film's epic look. Moreover, while there's less grain, the colors are somewhat paler overall and the image is softer than in the remastered edition. These same criticisms apply to the sequel and to *Red Sonja*.

The Court Jester (1956)
★★★★½
Directors: Norman Panama and Melvin Frank
Running Time: 101 minutes

Catskills comic and nightclub entertainer Danny Kaye made his Broadway debut in 1939 in *The Straw Hat Revue*. Two years later, he became the talk of the town by singing "Tchaikovsky" in *Lady in the Dark*, batting out fifty-four Russian names in just over a half minute. He made his movie debut in 1944 and his grace, charm, wit, and vocal abilities—singing and mimicry—helped make successes of *The Secret Life of Walter Mitty* (1947), *The Inspector General* (1949), *Hans Christian Andersen* (1952), *White Christmas* (1954), *The Five Pennies* (1959), and, of course, *The Court Jester*. He died in 1987 at the age of seventy-four.

The Court Jester is a perfect showcase for Kaye's talents, but it's also an endlessly clever film with more twists than a bag of Twizzlers. The ambitious Roderick (Cecil Parker) has slaughtered the royal family and named himself king of England. However, one survivor—a babe, with the telltale purple pimpernel birthmark on its backside—has fallen into the hands of the Robin Hood–like Black Fox (Edward Ashley), who is determined to place the infant on the throne. Among the Fox's soldiers are Hubert Hawkins (Kaye) and Captain Jean (Glynis Johns). To help achieve their goal, Hawkins and Jean waylay Giacomo (John Carradine), who's on his way to the castle to become the new jester. Hawkins takes his place, not knowing that Giacomo is also an assassin and that the evil Sir Ravenhurst (Basil Rathbone) has engaged him to kill the king's other advisers: With them out of the way, Ravenhurst will be able to control Roderick completely. Meanwhile, the witch Griselda (Mildred Natwick) enchants Giacomo so that he falls in love with the king's daughter, Princess Gwendolyn (Angela Lansbury), who returns his love and refuses to marry the powerful Sir Griswold (Robert Middleton), who demands to meet Giacomo in a joust.

The movie gets even more complicated, and the way these and other plot threads interweave will put a smile on your face and keep it there. One classic bit follows another, from the numerous exchanges of "Get it? Got it! Good," to the hurried knighting of Hawkins so he can joust Griswold, to the witch's attempt to poison Griswold before the fight by placing poison in the vessel with the pestle (not to be confused—as Hawkins does—with the chalice from the palace or the flagon with the dragon). The joust itself is a comic masterpiece as lightning magnetizes Hawkins's armor. There's even a Sir Locksley in the film, for Robin Hood fans.

Johns has never been more catlike-sexy, Lansbury is blissfully love-struck and comically out of touch with reality, and Rathbone—at sixty-four—has lost none of the sneering evil he'd displayed as Errol Flynn's foil, Sir Guy, in *The Adventures of Robin Hood* (1938).

It's Kaye's show, however, and he steals it without trying. He's particularly amazing during the duel with Rathbone: Flynn and Douglas Fairbanks, Sr., were considered swashbucklers nonpareil, but Kaye was their equal. Rathbone, a seasoned swordsman, said he "had never fenced before but after a couple of weeks of instruction Danny could completely outfight me. His reflexes were incredibly fast and nothing had to be shown or explained to him a second time. His mind worked like a camera." (Because of his age, Rathbone had to be doubled in several shots of the duel by Ralph Faulkner.)

Except for one or two slow spots (the song sung to the babe and Kaye's belabored old-man disguise), this is a perfect film.

The Disc
Video: ★
Audio: ★½ (monaural)
Chapters: Yes
Format: CLV
Source: Paramount Home Video

The Court Jester is on the top of the needs-to-be-remastered list. The picture is faded throughout and discolored in a few spots (the image goes red when Hawkins is hiding behind the curtains in the Princess's chambers); not one scene has the beauty laserphiles have come to expect from Technicolor transfers. There are also numerous scratches in the source material, some of which drag on for several minutes. The VistaVision image is also trimmed a little on all four sides. This doesn't hurt the film or any of Kaye's scenes dramatically, though characters do get sliced off (for example, Rathbone, during the climactic duel, at 3/43:04 on side two).

The sound has many distracting crackles and pops throughout, though there's no hiss.

Crazy People (1990) ★½
Director: Tony Bill
Running Time: 91 minutes

This movie's like a day in Disneyland: lots of waiting around for a few moments of fun. What *should* have been a biting black comedy about advertising ends up being a rosebush with a couple of thorns.

Dudley Moore continues his seemingly irreversible slide into box-office oblivion as advertising executive Emory Leeson, who suddenly decides to create ads that tell the truth. Shocked, his coworker Stephen Bachman (Paul Reiser) and meanie of a boss Charles F. Drucker (J. T. Walsh) have him committed to the Bennington Sanitarium in the country (actually, Virginia). When Emory's ads accidentally get printed and become a smashing success, he agrees to go back to work for Drucker but only if he can operate out of the asylum with the other inmates as his assistants. Drucker agrees, and Emory forms a special bond with Kathy Burgess (Daryl Hannah), a love-starved claustrophobic/agoraphobic.

After a variety of personal and professional crises, which include a showdown with Drucker and the greedy asylum boss, Dr. Horace Koch (Ben Hammer), Emory and his colleagues become the toast of Madison Avenue.

The film's highlights are the ads themselves, which are crude but hilarious, as is a presentation before Sony executives in which the inmates, temporarily deprived of Emory's help, fail to make any sense whatsoever. The rest of the movie, particularly the soppy relationship between Emory and Kathy, is flat. The major problem is the fact that, except when he loses his mind, Moore never gets to cut loose: *He's* the stabilizing force at Bennington, which deprives the film of a valuable and necessary source for manic humor. Among the inmates, David Paymer (the subway spirit from *Ghost*) is very good as George Cartelli, whose vocabulary consists entirely of the word *hello*. However, most of the other inmates have disorders that aren't funny and/or whose humor quickly wears thin.

The Disc
Video: ★★★★½
Audio: ★★★★ (Surround)
Chapters: No
Format: CLV
Source: Paramount Home Video

Crazy People is a terrific-looking and -sounding disc. The picture is nearly perfect: Except for just a *sprinkling* of grain here and there, the image is bright, sharp, and so clear that it looks three-dimensional at times. The film was shot TV-safe, and practically nothing is lost to cropping.

The audio is superclear, and the Surround capacity gives the film a lot of depth, with phones, birds, voices, and other sounds floating from behind. The first scene in the agency will cause you to pause the film to see whether *your* phone is ringing.

Like the film, the disc was a flop—so

chances are you'll find chains offering it at a good price (Tower has it for under fifteen dollars). For the money, or as a rental, it's a worthwhile audiovisual experience.

The Creature from the Black Lagoon (1954) ★★½
Director: Jack Arnold
Running Time: 79 minutes

When a strange Devonian fossil hand is found in Brazil, Dr. Carl Maia (Antonio Moreno) takes it to his old student David Reed (Richard Carlson). Reed convinces the PR–hungry Dr. Mark Williams (Richard Denning) to have his California aquarium underwrite an expedition to find the rest of the skeleton. Williams agrees, and they're joined on the boat *Rita* by scientist Kay Lawrence (Julie Adams), Dr. Edwin Thompson (Whit Bissell), and Captain Lucas (Nestor Paiva) and his helpers. Upon reaching the Black Lagoon—untouched and unchanged for some 150 million years—the group finds the living fish man itself, who not only takes unkindly to the intruders but lusts after the beautiful Ms. Lawrence. This leads to some violent encounters (surprisingly so, for the time) and the shooting of the Creature, who sinks, inert, to the bottom of the Lagoon—until the sequels, that is.

Shot entirely on the back lot at Universal Pictures, the film is sunny and rather leisurely and generates only sporadic moments of suspense. But the acting and conflict are better than average, and the Creature is one of the greatest monsters ever made for a movie: sleek, humanoid in shape and behavior, but still alien and unsettling, and even sexy, in its own lanky, scaly, big-shouldered way. The creature suit was made of sponge rubber and was worn by swimmer Ricou Browning, who was fed air through a hose between takes. Browning was selected because of his unique style of swimming, which he describes as "similar to the top-water freestyle stroke." He adds that wearing the suit "was very much like swimming with your overcoat on."

Pay close attention to the scene when the creature swims below Ms. Adams for the first time: Not only is it cinematic poetry (as poetic as something like this can be, anyway) but you'll see where *Jaws* (1975) came from—music and all.

The film was followed by a pair of sequels: *Revenge of the Creature* (1955), in which the monster is captured and brought to an aquarium, and *The Creature Walks Among Us* (1956), in which the Gillman is surgically altered to be more human. Neither is available on laserdisc.

The Disc
Video: ★★★
Audio: ★★★ (monaural)
Chapters: No
Format: CLV (side one), CAV (side two)
Source: MCA/Universal Home Video

While it's good to see the venerable monster classic available in MCA's Encore Edition series, it's too bad the studio didn't make a 3-D transfer (as they did with the videotape version in 1980). The picture plays fine "flat," but in 3-D—despite some blurry effects here and there—it's a killer.

The transfer is very good, though not as spectacular as other Encore Editions. The above-water scenes are clear and sharp, but the underwater and night scenes tend to be on the murky side—dimmer than in pristine prints of the film. Flaws in the master element are very minimal.

The sound is faintly hissy, on a par with many other films this old, but pops and crackles are rare.

The CAV is rock-steady.

Curse of the Demon (1957) ★★★½
Director: Jacques Tourneur
Running Time: 95 minutes

Even after his colleague Professor Henry Harrington (Maurice Denham) dies while investigating an English devil cult, psychologist John Holden (Dana Andrews) refuses to believe in the supernatural. Picking up the investigation where the professor left off, Andrews—aided by Harrington's niece Joanna (Peggy Cummins)—looks into the affairs of cult leader Julian Karswell (Niall MacGinnis). During his first meeting with Karswell, Holden is secretly passed a slip of paper inscribed with runic symbols: Soon thereafter, the psychologist is informed that he will be destroyed by a demon unless he can return the paper to Karswell without the cultist's knowledge. Holden is dubious at first—but, after several brushes with the supernatural, becomes a believer and manages to give the paper back to Karswell ... moments before the huge demon arrives, picks up the satanist, and pounds the life out of him.

As in his earlier films (see *The Leopard Man*), Tourneur very much wanted to be inconclusive about the existence of the supernatural: Each death attributed to the demon, every occult event, *could* have been caused by something else going on at the time. (Karswell is running along a train track, a train approaching, when the demon snatches him up.) But the film's producer, aware of the box-office appeal of a garish monster, insisted that Tourneur show the demon. He does so at the beginning and end of the film—quite effectively as it turns out—but Tourneur was never happy with the notion of the monster or its actual execution in the film.

The disc features the complete English print of the movie (though it doesn't sport the British title, *Night of the Demon*), containing twelve minutes of footage not seen in the American release. The footage clears up some narrative lapses: For example, a visit with Mrs. Hobart (Janet Barrow) reveals how Holden was able to get permission to hypnotize her son—former cult member Rand Hobart (Brian Wilde)—to ask about the demon. And Holden's trip to Stonehenge to check the runes on the monument against those on his paper gives credence to his otherwise-abrupt transformation from nonbeliever to believer.

If the film has a serious flaw, it's Andrews's Holden, who's just *too* arrogant for us to care whether he's ripped to pieces or not. And the big cat that attacks him in Karswell's estate, Lufford Hall—well, Andrews just doesn't tussle with fake animals with the panache of Johnny Weissmuller or Steve Reeves.

On the other hand, there's a wonderfully chilling performance by MacGinnis (best known as Zeus in *Jason and the Argonauts*; see page 153), and the supporting players are all very good. Production designer Ken Adam, who does some eerie work here, went on to design the James Bond films.

The movie was based on the M. R. James story "Casting the Runes," published in 1911. In it, Karswell is hounded by Edward Dunning, and events occur more or less as they do in the film. The demon never makes an appearance in the story: Karswell dies after Dunning passes him the runic writing and a stone falls off a church, killing him.

The Disc
Video: ★★★
Audio: ★★★½ (monaural)
Chapters: No (despite what it says on the jacket)
Format: CLV
Source: Columbia Pictures Video

This is a frustrating disc. It ranges from beautifully crisp to annoyingly hazy, often from one shot to the next. Part of this is due to Tourneur's lighting: For example, Holden's nighttime approach to Lufford Hall and his subsequent flight through the woods are starkly lighted and they look great. Yet the scene inside the house is dim and grainy. The entire movie is like that, though—bliss!—most of the supernatural scenes look first-rate. The film was shot flat, so the lack of letterboxing doesn't hurt.

The audio crackles a bit now and then, but not so much that it's a bother. Despite a bit of tinniness, the sound is clear enough so that the accents are never a problem. Highlights are the windstorm and lightning, which are booming and powerful, and the sounds of the demon's arrival have "chalk on a black board" clarity.

Dances with Wolves (1990)
★★★
Director: Kevin Costner
Running Time: 181 minutes

Union Lt. John Dunbar (Kevin Costner) has had it with war and warmongers and with a civilization that isn't terribly civilized. Requesting a transfer to the frontier so he can "see it before it's gone," he's sent to a remote outpost in the Dakotas. There, he encounters the Sioux—men of varied temperaments such as Kicking Bird (Graham Greene) and Wind in His Hair (Rodney A. Grant). White man and Indians get to know one another slowly and warily until, finally, Dunbar is accepted as one of the tribe. The Indians call him Dances with Wolves after he's seen doing just that, and they allow him to take the white woman Stands with a Fist (Mary McDonnell) as his wife and fight alongside them against their enemies—who include Indians and cavalry alike. In the end, as more soldiers arrive in the Great Plains, the Indians and Dunbar are forced to move on, into the winter of their civilization.

The film was adapted by Michael Blake from his own novel, and no one can fault Costner for his earnestness and intent, or for his courage. He stood up to the producers when they wanted to cut his budget and slice his movie down to something a little shorter (though he did cut nearly an hour's worth of footage). He also bore up admirably under the rigors of a physically difficult film, including a nasty spill during the buffalo hunt. He gives a sensitive performance and, as a debut director, elicits proud and powerful performances from others. There's a lot of good in this film.

It's unfortunate, however, that Costner used his film to compensate for the portrayal of Indians in Hollywood Westerns: He diminished the credibility and integrity of his message by stereotyping the soldiers in a way that's historically inaccurate and very difficult to swallow. Nearly every white man in the film is a redneck who shoots wolves and horses and people for recreation. The Civil War was madness, as Costner suggests—but wasn't abolition as important a cause as the rights of Indians? Genocide (not just against the Plains Indians but against all native North and South Americans) demands to be remembered and memorialized, but not with a convert's lopsided view that undermines the effectiveness of the presentation. In films such as *Cheyenne Autumn* (1964), classier filmmakers such as John Ford took the Indian "side" with a better, more balanced presentation. See also the phenomenal *Little Big Man*.

The Disc
Video: ★★★★
Audio: ★★★★ (Surround)
Chapters: Yes
Format: CLV
Source: Orion Home Video/Image Entertainment

The film is available in both panned-and-scanned and letterboxed editions. Even though the latter doesn't include all of the original image, it obviously does a much better job of capturing the awe-inspiring vistas and the buffalo hunt than the cropped version. Since Costner tends to bunch his characters together, the drama isn't affected by the unmatted version—though the characters *are* cramped at times. The subtitles in the letterboxed edition appear largely below the picture.

The film suffers from a bit of grain here and there (more so in the letterboxed edition), though the colors are bright and sharp in both.

The audio is full and clear and the stereo separations are extremely good, though, apart from the buffalo hunt, the Surround aspect is disappointing. The gatefold jacket contains interesting observations about the film.

Dangerous Liaisons (1988)
★★★★½
Director: Stephen Frears
Running Time: 120 minutes

Pierre-Ambroise-François Choderlos de Laclos (1741–1803) was a French artillery officer, a leader in the French Revolution, and the author of the novel *Les Liaisons Dangereuses* (1782), a work that lacks even a hint of humor: The characters are mean and unsentimental, and its reputation as literature is a distant second to its reputation as erotica. It was banned in many places, despite the fact that the author clearly disapproved of the wicked and ribald activities of the corrupt hero and heroine.

Two centuries later, Christopher Hampton turned the novel into a successful stage play, giving antagonists the Marquise de Merteuil and the Vicomte de Valmont a wicked sense of humor and the play a sense of fun. Alan Rickman did a wonderful job as Valmont onstage.

For the film version, Hampton and director Frears (*My Beautiful Launderette* [1985] *Sammy and Rosie Get Laid* [1987] and, later, *The Grifters* [1990]) relied on a quartet of magnificent actors to give the film an even greater sense of puckishness—and tragedy.

In pre-Revolutionary France, former lovers the Marquise (Glenn Close) and the Vicomte (John Malkovich) woo and destroy others foolish enough to fall in love with them; they keep score and, later, compare notes. When Merteuil's young lover, the Chevalier Danceny (Keanu Reeves), leaves her for virginal Cecile (Uma Thurman), the Marquise challenges Valmont to seduce the girl before her wedding day. He accepts, while also working to despoil the seemingly incorruptible Madame de Tourvel (Michelle Pfeiffer). He succeeds on both accounts, but his surprising remorse about de Tourvel leads him to reevaluate his life and, ultimately, to surrender it.

The great strength of the film is the fact that no matter how nasty the leads become, no matter what deception or spite they work, the viewer likes them and doesn't want to see them fail. Valmont in particular is like a great athlete playing for a team you hate: You feel a little dirty rooting for him, but the moves he makes, the words he utters, the glances he gives, are all so perfectly calculated that you can't resist him. And the Marquise, beneath her icy exterior, is so vulnerable, you can (and will) hurt for her when she is ostracized by the society that's so important to her.

Close is superb; she is, by any reckoning, the greatest American actress working today. Malkovich is more prissy than the knife-sharp Alan Rickman was on the Broadway stage, but he's superb. Pfeiffer is good, but, except for the fact that she's playing against type, she isn't in a class with the others. Sly and sexy Thurman makes the most of her brief screen time, though Reeves is woefully out of place in a period piece.

Another film version, *Valmont*, directed by Milos Forman, was released in 1989. Played by a younger cast—Annette Bening, Colin Firth, Meg Tilly, Henry Thomas (of *E.T.*), and Fairuza Balk (Dorothy in *Return to Oz*)—the film has spunk and a very good script, but it lacks the bitterness, bitchiness, and textured performances of the Frears film.

The Disc

Video: ★★½
Audio: ★★★ (Surround)
Chapters: Yes
Format: CLV
Source: Warner Home Video

The movie's colors were muted and grainy in the theaters but not *this* muted and grainy. The picture isn't *quite* as sharp as it should be, though details in the sets and costumes come through well enough.

The mild letterbox captures most of the original imagery. The sound track is full of appealing directional effects and ambient audio that brings the time and place very much to life. Unfortunately, a hiss pervades much of the film and will force you to keep the volume turned lower than you might like. The dialogue is acceptably clear.

Valmont is available on laserdisc in a panned-and-scanned version, which hurts the drama and the film's look; the picture is on the soft side, with some very grainy passages. The audio is very good.

Darkman (1990) ★★
Director: Sam Raimi
Running Time: 96 minutes

It wouldn't be accurate to describe *Darkman* as a *Batman* clone: It borrows more from *Phantom of the Opera* (see page 208). Unfortunately, it didn't borrow enough: For a movie that draws from the superhero and horror genres, *Darkman* is surprisingly dull.

Dr. Peyton Westlake (Liam Neeson) is on the verge of perfecting synthetic skin when his world falls apart—literally. Mobster Robert G. Durant (Larry Drake) and his thugs go to the lab looking for papers that were left there by the scientist's girlfriend, lawyer Julie Hastings (Frances McDormand). The papers document illegal payments that would destroy the empire of Durant's boss, construction magnate Louis Strack, Jr. (Colin Friels). The criminals blow up the lab. Westlake, his face disfigured and his mind warped in the blast, sets up a new lab in a condemned warehouse. Swathed in bandages and garbed in a black coat and slouch hat, he becomes Darkman, committed to bringing down Durant and Strack with the help of his synthetic skin—which, though unstable, briefly allows him to impersonate other people.

The plot is a very skeletal framework on which to hangs the heart of the movie: Darkman's enemies trying to stop him as he violently and sadistically exterminates them. Director Raimi showed a real gusto for the grotesque in his *The Evil Dead* (1980) and *The Evil Dead 2* (1988), and there are some predictably sadistic but cute touches here, such as Durant's collection of severed fingers. There are also clever and ambitious moments—for example, showing Darkman's torment by having the camera go into one eye, roll around inside his disordered brain, and emerge from the other eye.

There aren't enough of these, however, to do more than generate an occasional "Wow!" The rest of the film is undermined by budgetary constraints and the fact that Raimi seemed unable to decide whether he wanted to make a gothic action film or a Three Stooges comedy. The changes in tone are *that* pronounced, most noticeably in the action centerpiece of the film, Darkman hanging on to a cable suspended from Durant's helicopter, being swung around buildings and over freeway traffic. Raimi has his hero dash across the top of a truck, his legs churning like the Roadrunner, excuse himself when he's smashed through an office window, and perform other shtick. What works in a Marvel Comic plays like broad, dumb comedy on the big screen. Subpar special effects also hurt the scene. The climax, with Darkman, Strack, Durant, and Hastings on top of an unfinished skyscraper, also suffers from cheesy special effects: Look for the wires supporting McDormand, surprisingly visible at 34.04.

Neeson's performance is out of control, while McDormand seems bored. She probably was, given the flatness of the role. The movie is really propped up by Drake (*L.A. Law*'s Benny Stulwicz), who has the suave meanness of a prime James Bond villain.

Danny Elfman's score is evocative, though portions seem to have been lifted from *Alexander Nevsky* (see page 6).

The Disc
Video: ★★★★½
Audio: ★★★★½ (Surround)
Chapters: No
Format: CLV
Source: MCA/Universal

You want vivid close-ups of Darkman's charred face, of Durant's finger collection, of the fake composites? This disc gives them to you with loving clarity. Whether the scene is dark, light, or smoky, the picture is nearly perfect, marred only by rare spots of video noise and grain.

Darkman is not letterboxed but loses nothing in the transition.

You won't have any complaints about the wonderfully clear Surround Sound either, with ambient audio that's as interesting as the bombastic helicopters, explosions, and traffic.

The Day the Earth Stood Still (1951) ★★★★★
Director: Robert Wise
Running Time: 92 minutes

Robert Wise has attributed the longevity of his film to two factors: "It has a strong moral thrust, and we will always be fascinated by the belief in the existence of life in other parts of our universe—especially life that is wiser than we are."

That's true now, but in the 1950s the film had one thing more going for it: As far as science fiction films were concerned, it was an era of discovery with no established, successful formulas to follow. As a result, *The Day the Earth Stood Still* was able to invent a lot of them.

The film begins in space, and after the camera floats through Earth's atmosphere and sails above an ocean, we realize we're experiencing a point-of-view shot, an alien ship descending from turbulent space into the soft, reflective light of our world. Yet, it is in *our* world where chaos lies. The federation represented by the alien Klaatu (Michael Rennie) knows this, and he has a plan to prevent us from spreading our violence to other worlds.

Klaatu is gunned down when he emerges from his ship and, after a short stay in the hospital, lives among us for a time as Mr. Carpenter (Christ references, anyone?), befriending Helen Benson (Patricia Neal) and her son, Bobby (Billy Gray), as well as the Einstein-like scientist Dr. Barnhardt (Sam Jaffe). Klaatu asks for a meeting of the world leaders and doesn't get it; since the seven-foot-tall robot Gort (Lock Martin), mutely guarding his flying saucer, isn't evidence enough of his power, Klaatu temporarily shuts down all of Earth's electrical impulses. The authorities respond by shooting Klaatu again, this time killing him, and it's up to Helen to get to Gort and utter the immortal words "Klaatu barada nikto" before the robot reduces our world to a burned-out cinder.

Gort fetches Klaatu's body and brings him back to life (another Christ reference), and the alien delivers a message to Dr. Barnhardt and a group of scientists: He's leaving Gort behind to enforce pacifism. If we continue in our violent ways, the robot will destroy our world. (The movie ignores the moral complexity such tyrrany would cause, subscribing to the dubious proposition that the end justifies the means. It also ignores the question of an apocalyptic accident a malfunctioning Gort might cause.) With that, the prince of peace leaves . . . wiser but not much better.

The Day the Earth Stood Still was based on Harry Bates's 1940 short story "Farewell to the Master," from which only the alien, the robot, and the mission were retained. The filmmakers abandoned Bates's twist, that the robot (called Gnut) turns out to be the master, and Klaatu the servant. But what they brought to the property was a look and sound that is still striking. A few highlights: Watch when Klaatu abruptly appears in the TV room of a boardinghouse and fear sweeps those gathered in this normally secure place as they glance toward the alien's intrusive silhouette. Or the wonderfully creepy scene in which Helen and Klaatu are trapped in an elevator when the alien shuts down Earth's power. Or the breathtaking first view of the spaceship's interior, as Klaatu goes along a circular walkway that leads to the ship's instruments. The scene is lighted from below and we see beautiful dark, triangular patterns, radiant lines, and curvilinear distortion in areas of light. And, of course, there's the frightening scene when Gort's ominous shadow crosses a corrugated wall as he approaches Helen, who's so terrified that she can barely utter the phrase that will save her—and the planet.

As important as the look of the film is Bernard Herrmann's alternately ominous and ethereal score. Herrmann was a rude, arrogant man and a pain in the neck to work with, but he wrote brilliant movie music, whether it was for science fiction, thrillers (*Psycho*), drama (*Citizen Kane*), or fantasy (*Journey to the Center of the Earth*).

The casting is also just right. Michael Rennie was the third choice to play Klaatu; Spencer Tracy and Claude Rains had been approached but had turned the part down. Seen today, it's difficult to imagine anyone but the ascetic, imperious, occasionally smug Rennie in the part. After acting in films for fifteen years, this was his big break: Unfortunately, it also typecast him. Though he was the apostle Peter in *The Robe* (1953) and starred in Disney's popular *Third Man on the Mountain* (1959), he also ended up playing a *lot* of aliens and superbeings, especially toward the end of his career. He died in 1971.

Patricia Neal is as fine a performer as one could reasonably expect to find in a science fiction film, and she went on to distinguish herself in films such as *Hud* (1963). Lock Martin had been a movie-theater doorman and was hired simply because he was over seven feet tall.

Look for actor Ben Gazarra as a soldier riding in a jeep near the end of the film.

The Disc
Video: ★★★
Audio: ★★
Chapters: No
Format: CLV
Source: CBS/Fox Home Video

Considering the film's age, the image is pretty sharp. There are no major flaws, other than the usual wear and tear you'll find on a movie this old. The image darkens briefly but distressingly at 12:20 on side one and loses considerable detail for over a minute at 12:50 on side two.

The audio is good, but it is impoved somewhat by switching to the analog tracks: The music is fuller and richer, with additional details in the strings (it sounds as though some of the high notes were clipped off by the digitization).

Deliverance (1972) ★★★★½
Director: John Boorman
Running Time: 109 minutes

James Dickey's best-selling 1970 novel is a chilling tale of four suburbanites who go deep into the "red-neck South" for a canoe ride from Oree to Aintry in north Georgia, through land that will be submerged when a new dam is finished. En route, Ed Gentry and Bobby Trippe are assaulted by two backwoodsmen; one sodomizes Bobby and the other is about to have his way with Ed when Lewis Medlock and Drew Ballinger return to the camp. Lewis, an expert field archer, kills one man, the other flees, and the men decide to bury their victim rather than go to the highway patrol and stand trial before a jury of the man's family members. But the four suburbanites still have to finish the journey down the Cahulawassee, and the nightmare is far from over.

The novel is narrated by Ed—the most grounded man of the bunch—and the film is also told more or less from his point of view. The events and dialogue follow Dickey's more or less exactly, including the famous "Dueling Banjos" sequence (though the terrifying "squeal like a pig" exchange was invented for the film). Most of the cuts come at the expense of Ed's home life.

Deliverance is a gripping film, slow to build and then relentless in its horror, right down to Ed's final, nightmarish vision. Jon Voight is perfect as Ed; Ned Beatty made a memorable screen debut as Bobby; Ronny Cox's role as Drew was also his movie debut; and Burt Reynolds leapt to the ranks of movie superstars with his magnetic performance as Lewis, the man Dickey describes as willing to go to "any means ... to hold on to his body and mind and improve them, to rise above time."

Author Dickey appears as Sheriff Bullard; Ed O'Neill plays a highway patrolman.

The Disc
Video: no stars
Audio: ★★½ (monaural)
Chapters: No
Format: CLV
Source: Warner Home Video

This may be the most pitiful-looking laserdisc on the market. Several minutes of action are annoyingly squeezed under the titles, and the rest of the film is panned with sudden jerks. Or should that read *by* jerks? The picture is fuzzy, reddish, and incredibly dark: Voight's trip up the cliff consists of shot after shot of near-solid black. The videotapes look better than this.

Apart from intermittent crackles on the sound track, the audio is fairly clear.

A remastered letter box edition is being readied for release by Warner Home Video.

Dial M for Murder (1954)
★★★½
Director: Alfred Hitchcock
Running Time: 105 minutes

Hitchcock was having a difficult time with an original script he was working on when he decided to dump it and film Frederick Knott's play *Dial M for Murder*. Paring the talky melodrama down to its bare bones, he created a riveting (if *still*-talky) film.

American crime novelist Mark Halliday (Robert Cummings) is having an affair with Margot Mary Wendice (Grace Kelly), the wife of former tennis champion, now sporting goods salesman, Tony Wendice (Ray Milland). Learning of her infidelity, Wendice makes plans to blackmail an old crony, Swan Lesgate (Anthony Dawson), into murdering her. When things don't go as planned, Wendice *still* thinks he has a way to fix his philandering wife—though to say more would be to spoil the film's many ingenious twists and turns. As with most Hitchcock films, there are *many* of these, along with one big surprise: the fact that we're actually rooting for that heel Wendice!

If the film has any flaws (apart from some awful process photography that places the Hollywood-based players in London), it's the *vast* amount of exposition that Wendice delivers during his meeting with Swan (close attention must be paid), as well as the casting of Cummings: It's difficult to imagine Grace Kelly dumping Milland for the boyish, geeky American. Cummings is woefully outclassed by Milland: Watch, for example, what Milland is able to suggest just by his posture, shot from behind, while Cumming's character discusses the notion of the perfect crime.

This was Grace Kelly's first film for Hitchcock; she followed it with *Rear Window* (1954) and *To Catch a Thief* (1955). It was while the latter film was being shot on the French Riviera that she met her future husband, Prince Rainier III, and they married a year later.

Hitchcock was fascinated by movie technology, and he shot *Dial M for Murder* in 3-D. However, the fad was on its way out before the film was released, and there were only a few 3-D engagements. Still, the film was designed in such a way that it still suggests amazing depth. The director didn't thrust objects at viewers as most filmmakers did; he was more subtle. During Wendice's first meeting with Swan, for example, notice how Hitchcock placed the lamp in many of the shots—close to the camera, creating a sense of space even without 3-D. And, of course, there's the famous shot of Kelly's outstretched arm, pictured on the jacket, which is still very effective "flat."

Note, incidentally, how the colors on the wall behind Kelly change during the trial sequence to match the color of the dresses she's wearing. And check out the continuity blunder (rare for the meticulous Hitchcock) with the cane at 14.56 in chapter four.

The Disc
Video: ★★
Audio: ★★★ (monaural)
Chapters: Yes
Format: CLV
Source: Warner Home Video

The print used for the transfer is in very good shape, though the colors are not as bright as they should be. Typical of this is the red on Milland's face as he's standing over the fireplace, which lacks the hellish glow it should have. For the most part, the fleshtones are flat and at times have that "colorized" look; many of the dark scenes are *too* dark. The Warner Color process is to blame: It's virtually the same as Eastman Color, which results in a softening of the image over time.

The sound gets a little raw during the middle of chapter eleven on many discs, but is otherwise solid enough and hiss-free.

The intermission card is included at the end of side one; there are no other extras.

If you're not familiar with the story, don't read the chapter stops on the back of the jacket: They give the thing away!

Dick Tracy (1990) ★½
Director: Warren Beatty
Running Time: 105 minutes

In 1931, cartoonist Chester Gould created the comic strip "Plainclothes Tracy," about a square-jawed Chicago detective. He sold it to the Chicago Tribune–New York News Syndicate, which retitled the strip "Dick Tracy." Over the years, it became renowned for its grotesque villains, violence, and fanciful gadgets, such as the famous two-way wrist radio, closed-circuit TV, and iodine blowguns. This was perfect stuff for the movies. In fact, several movies were made from the strip in the 1940s, the best of which starred Ralph Byrd as Tracy.

Add to this great mix the man who directed the superlative *Reds* (1981), top-of-the-line actors and/or stars, a budget of $35 million, and what have you got? Impossible as it is to believe, an incredibly *boring* movie.

In a nutshell, Big Boy Caprice (Al Pacino) is trying to eliminate rival mobsters, take over their rackets, and effectively run the city. He and his chief henchman, Flattop (William Forsythe), are also trying to get rid of Tracy (Warren Beatty), who is hunting them. And Tracy isn't the only one hunting the crooks: The mysterious villain known as No Face is also after Caprice and control of the city. While Tracy deals with these bad pennies, he's also got to look after an orphan named the Kid (Charlie Korsmo), work up the courage to propose to his longtime girlfriend, Tess Trueheart (Glenne Headly), and avoid the advances of Caprice's moll, singer Breathless Mahoney (Madonna).

The brightly colored sets and costumes, Danny Elfman's Gershwinesque score, the makeup and casting—all are candy for the eyes and ears. There's nothing wrong with the look or sound of the film. It's the script and lethargic pacing that do it in. As a character, Tracy is boring beyond belief, a problem compounded by the fact that Beatty is too old for the part and doesn't even *look* like Gould's drawings. His relationship with Tess is two-dimensional; Caprice rants and kills without ever being truly menacing; and the action is flat. The fight in the Kid's shed is sped up and comically exaggerated—and could Tracy's escape from the building ledge have been staged any slower or shot from more boring angles? Even the climactic shoot-out and ensuing fight at the bridge are a lot of sound and fury with no sense of danger.

If only Beatty had understood or even read the comic strip, there *was* a story to be told! In Gould's first episodes, Tracy (who is not a cop) and Tess announce their engagement to her parents. As they do, crooks break into the Trueheart home and murder her father, Emil, knock Tracy out when he attacks them, and kidnap Tess. When the numb Tracy wakes, he joins the force to exact vengeance, then weeps as he visits Tess's traumatized mother in the hospital.

Pacino is entertaining as he chews up the scenery and spits it in the faces of the other actors; Dustin Hoffman has fun with the crooked Mumbles; Paul Sorvino is properly disgusting as Lips Manlis; and James Caan is oily as the corrupt Spaldoni. Madonna isn't bad at all and looks swell (she's a ringer for the evil Maria from *Metropolis* in her first close-up). Mandy Patinkin, Charles Durning, Kathy Bates, Estelle Parsons, Michael J. Pollard, Henry Silva, Catherine O'Hara, and Dick Van Dyke are enjoyable in small roles. In this film, all you *get* are small pleasures.

The Disc
Video: ★★★★½
Audio: ★★★★★ (Surround)
Chapters: Yes
Format: CAV and CLV editions
Source: Touchstone Home Video

There seems to be a rule in the industry: The worse a movie is, the better the transfer. The job done by Touchstone Home Video is a killer. But before we get to that—

The jacket says, "*Dick Tracy* is presented in the aspect ratio in which the movie was originally filmed." This is not true. The movie isn't letterboxed; and while the image has been opened up and includes *most* of the original screen image, it's not all here. You'll notice slight panning-and-scanning at times, such as when Big Boy hangs up the phone and moves toward Flattop (side four, chapter two). But Beatty's compositions are fairly tight, and everything of importance is on the screen.

The colors and resolution are phenomenal. There's a lot of body to the tones, nothing is lost in the film's many shadows, and there is no grain to speak of. Considering all the primary colors in the film, the dearth of video noise is astonishing.

Likewise, the audio is so spectacular, it's worth sitting through the movie just to listen to it. Whether it's a car barreling through a wall, Pacino grumbling under his breath, dogs barking, Madonna singing, or Elfman's score swelling around us, it's all a treat.

The CAV version is recommended, not because it's any better but because you'll want to freeze-frame the incredible matte-painted skylines, some of the makeup, and the Kid ducking in front of the (miniature) train. (Unfortunately, you may experience some jitter on every other frame of side one.)

Rollercoaster Rabbit, the Roger Rabbit cartoon that played with the film in theaters, has not been included. Presumably, the Touchstone (Disney) folks plan to make a separate collection of these.

Die Hard (1988) ★★★★★
Director: John McTiernan
Running Time: 127 minutes

By helping Arnold Schwarzenegger score his biggest success up until that time—*Predator* (1987)—former TV-commercial director McTiernan proved that he was one of the best of the new crop of action directors. His next film, *Die Hard*, catapulted him to the top of the heap. It also made a box-office star of Bruce Willis, though he has managed to become a white dwarf in subsequent films.

John McClane (Willis) is a New York cop who visits his estranged wife, Holly Gennaro McClane (Bonnie Bedelia) at her office in Los Angeles. While he's there, the building is taken over and sealed off by Hans Gruber (Alan Rickman) and his terrorists, who plan to steal $640 million in negotiable bearer bonds from the safe of the Nakatomi Corporation. While the police and the authorities fumble about, and Nakatomi personnel are murdered, McClane works to stop the terrorists single-handedly—and steer clear of the FBI, who believe him to be one of them.

Die Hard is such a powerful, damn-the-torpedoes action film that the few lapses in logic (such as how the hero is able to *stand* after all the punishment he takes) are gladly overlooked. The action scenes are classics—the edge-of-your-seat cat-and-mouse chases through the building, the elevator-shaft explosion, and the helicopter attack on the skyscraper whose roof is rigged to explode, with McClane and Nakatomi employees on top. Just how *good* a job McTiernan does with the action is clear when you look at director Renny Harlin's *Die Hard 2* (1990), in which McClane stumbles into a terrorist plot at Washington, D.C.'s Dulles Airport while waiting for Holly's plane. Though it has some good lines ("Just the fax, ma'am") and a few impressive action sequences, the film hasn't got the relentless momentum or sheer dazzling style of *Die Hard*.

What makes *Die Hard* even more appealing are the people that the spectacular events surround. Except for William Atherton as Thornburg, who is an insulting caricature as a pushy, immoral reporter, the characterizations are perfect—especially Willis as the Everyman hero, Rickman as the scrupulously polite monster, and Reginald Veljohnson as Sgt. Al Powell of the LAPD, the only one who believes that McClane is on their side.

McTiernan went on to score another hit with *The Hunt for Red October* (see page 144), while Willis imploded with *Hudson Hawk* and *The Last Boy Scout* (both 1991).

The Disc
Video: ★★★★★
Audio: ★★★★★ (Surround)
Chapters: Yes
Format: CLV
Source: CBS Fox Video

Both *Die Hard* films are excellent laserdisc titles, with only the slightest grain and video noise in some scenes working against them. They're sharp as can be, and both discs are letterboxed to a point just shy of the original aspect ratios.

The audio of the first film is explosive, with the chopper attack a favorite demonstration sequence for laserphiles who want to show off the medium to the uninitiated. However, it isn't *all* bombast: Watch how effective the "quiet" explosion is atop the tower in the long shot.

Die Hard 2 features a CAV side three and a trailer for the original film. The audio is comparatively tame, though there are still a couple of terrific Surround effects.

The much-panned *Hudson Hawk* is available panned-and-scanned; the film isn't as bad as you've heard, but the disc is mediocre, with washed-out colors and sharp but unspectacular sound (surprising, given all the action).

The Last Boy Scout is letterboxed, with stronger colors, excellent Surround, and a plot as improbable as they come. Still, Willis and costar Damon Wayans are fun to watch, and there are some neat stunts.

The Dirty Dozen (1967)
★★★★
Director: Robert Aldrich
Running Time: 150 minutes

Possibly the best of the manly, superhero war movies, *The Dirty Dozen* plays as well today as when it was released. Yes, there's sexism. Yes, it's as improbable as any war movie you'll ever see. And yes, these are cold-blooded murderers and rapists we're rooting for. But it's so much fun, and the final forty-five minutes are so tense, that you'll forgive it its flaws.

Less than two months before D-day, tough, independent Maj. John Reisman (Lee Marvin) is given an impossible mission: to disorient the Nazis on the eve of the invasion by attacking a château in France used as a retreat by German officers. His unit will consist of twelve criminals, several of them condemned men, and he has six weeks to train them for the mission. The inmates include Joseph Wladislaw (Charles Bronson), Robert Jefferson (Jim Brown), former mobster Victor Franko (John Cassavetes), the misogynistic (to put it mildly) religious fanatic Archer Maggott (Telly Savalas), the slow-witted Vernon Pinkley (Donald Sutherland), and the powerful Samson Posey (Clint Walker).

Unfortunately, not all of the enemies are German: Reisman's rival, Col. Everett Dasher Breed (Robert Ryan), would love for the group to fail, and it takes a daring move by the dozen during war games to set him straight. The cons's ingenuity also convinces the dubious General Worden (Ernest Borgnine) that the men are ready for their dangerous mission.

Alas, when they reach the château, their luck runs out. Though the attack itself is carefully planned, one of the men cracks in the early stages, causing exciting, spectacular, and deadly improvisation—deadly for both sides.

The movie packs in a lot of narrative and is necessarily superficial (more so than the E. M. Nathanson novel on which it is based), but it has flashes of wit and humor, memorable characterizations, and bristling action. All of the performers are good, though Cassavetes and Sutherland are standouts.

The hit film belatedly spawned three made-for-TV movies—*The Dirty Dozen: The Next Mission* (1985), starring Marvin and Borgnine; *The Dirty Dozen: The Deadly Mission* (1987), starring Savalas and Borgnine; and *The Dirty Dozen: The Fatal Mission* (1988), starring Savalas and Borgnine—and a short-lived TV series. None is available on laserdisc.

The Disc
Video: ★★★½
Audio: ★★★★ (stereo)
Chapters: No
Format: CLV
Source: MGM/UA Home Video

The Metrocolor has gone slightly red and faded in spots, and there are more scratches and marks on the print than you might expect. For the most part, however, the image is perfectly sharp.

The letterboxed film is in every way superior to the panned-and-scanned effort released in 1984, though the widescreen presentation doesn't affect the drama as much as the spectacular assault.

The digital stereo has just a few directional effects, and there are occasional dropouts (at least two of Bronson's lines are lost, and it isn't just because he's mumbling). But the audio is generally sharp and showcases the bombastic explosions and brassy score perfectly.

The lengthy trailer gives us interviews with the stars about their characters, but there's more puffery here than insight.

Dirty Harry (1971) ★★★★
Director: Don Siegel
Running Time: 102 minutes

After years of toiling in minor roles in films such as *Francis in the Navy* and *Tarantula* (both 1955), Clint Eastwood went to Spain, where he made a series of "spaghetti Westerns" directed by Sergio Leone. These films—*A Fistful of Dollars* (1964), *For a Few Dollars More* (1965), and *The Good, the Bad, and the Ugly* (1966)—featured Eastwood as the silent, violent "Man with No Name," and made him an international star. He returned to Hollywood a conquering hero and made films such as *Hang 'Em High* (1968), *Where Eagles Dare* (1969), *Paint Your Wagon* (1969)—*singing*, for God's sake, with Lee Marvin—and *Kelly's Heroes* (1970). But it was *Dirty Harry* that gave him his first good contemporary role, and thereafter some of his best movies would be set in modern day, such as *Play Misty for Me* (1971), which he also directed, *Every Which Way but Loose* (1978), and *Tightrope* (1984).

Silent, magnum-toting San Francisco police inspector Harry Callahan (Eastwood) is on the trail of Scorpio (Andy Robinson), a vicious killer who demands $200,000 or he'll kill his hostage. The mayor (John Vernon) wants to pay; Harry wants to find and shoot the killer. Eventually, Harry captures Scorpio. But because he entered the man's residence without a warrant, illegally seized evidence, and tortured the suspect (shooting him, then stepping on the wound to find out where the abducted girl is hidden), the confessed killer goes free—and kidnaps a busload of school children. Fortunately, Harry intercepts Scorpio and makes sure he won't go free again.

Despite an inconsistent visual style that ranges from gritty, evening news–like (the would-be suicide) to slick, Indiana Jonesish (the final bus ride), *Dirty Harry* has a consistent philosophical point of view: The law is a ass. The movie takes an especially dim view of the then-recent *Miranda* rule (*Miranda* v. *Arizona*, 1966), in which the rights of the accused must be upheld to the letter. According to the film, the only valid law is that of Harry, who cares nothing about rights, only about right.

Social commentary aside, the movie is tense, breathlessly edited, and well acted, with excellent use of the San Francisco locations (particularly some dizzying shots from the tops of buildings). No one plays a determined, confident, smart-mouthed hero like Eastwood does and he's a powerful presence even to the small screen. He plays well off Reni Santoni as his partner, the college-educated Chico, whom he comes to admire after a rocky start.

Look for the name of Eastwood's son Kyle spray painted on the subway wall (chapter eight, 51.10).

The film spawned four sequels: *Magnum Force* (1973), *The Enforcer* (1976), *Sudden Impact* (1983), and *The Dead Pool* (1988). *Sudden Impact* (source of the famous "Make my day" line) is the best of these, featuring some nice chemistry between Eastwood and costar Sondra Locke, and recreating some of the shadowy tension of the original film. All of these films are available on domestic laserdiscs.

The Disc
Video: ★
Audio: ★★★½ (stereo)
Chapters: Yes
Format: CLV
Source: Warner Home Video

Warner must feel that two of its most successful films don't *need* good laser transfers. How else can one explain the sorry state of this film and *The Exorcist* (see page 90)? *Dirty Harry* has some intentionally gritty shots, such as the scene when Harry rides the cherry picker to the rooftop, but this transfer is too often opaque: The scene in chapter five where Harry drags the trash can over to the apartment window to look inside is a solid mass of black: no highlights, no details—nothing. Even many of the daylight scenes have grain (chapter six, 33.36, for example).

As a glance at the action under the squeezed titles will tell you, the movie needs a letterbox. If there's a scene with three or more people in it, you can be sure you're going to lose one or two of them. When Chico's standing to the right of the map in a strategy session, you don't even realize he's in the room until he speaks! The transfer almost always keeps Eastwood on the screen, thought.

The audio, reprocessed for stereo, has excellent separation, and the sound effects are clear and powerful. The dialogue is on the quiet side, a situation exacerbated by Eastwood's whispered delivery. It's a bad idea to turn up the volume, though, because some kind of blast is always lurking around the corner.

A new, letterbox edition has been announced, and *has* to be an improvement.

Dr. Cyclops (1940) ★★
Director: Ernest B. Schoedsack
Running Time: 106 minutes

The career of director Schoedsack is a lot like this movie: a few big things completely overshadowing the many little things he created. Schoedsack gave us epic, engrossing movies such as *The Most Dangerous Game* (1932), *King Kong* (see page 159), and *The Last Days of Pompeii* (1935), yet lost his way with uninspired potboilers such as *Blind Adventure* (1933), *Long Lost Father* (1934), and *Trouble in Morocco* (1937).

Dr. Cyclops is something of a hybrid, featuring the best and worst of the director, incredible spectacle undermined by very thin melodrama.

Albert Dekker stars as Dr. Alexander Thorkel (that's Thor-KEL), a biologist who has been studying ways of reshaping organic molecules by using radiation. After two years at his laboratory in a remote Amazon jungle, his eyes are failing him (hence the film's title) and he sends for three colleagues: Dr. Rupert Bulfinch (Charles Halton), Dr. Mary Robinson (Janice Logan), and Bill Stockton (Thomas Coley). The trio helps Thorkel at a crucial point in his research, after which he thanks them and tells them to go home. The indignant scientists refuse—so he uses radioactivity to shrink them to doll-size, along with their surly guide, Steve Baker (Victor Kilian), and his own servant, Pedro (Frank Yaconelli). When Thorkel slays Bulfinch, the others manage to escape, survive the predatory animals (which had been cleverly introduced in the background during the "normal-sized" scenes), destroy Thorkel, and return to their original size.

Considering the cinematic potential inherent in the subject, the special effects are a letdown. The photographic processes used to combine Thorkel and the animals with the shrunken people (primarily rear-screen projection and split screen) are very convincing but made interaction impossible. The only real interplay occurs when a giant human hand constructed for the film grabs Bulfinch, but the prop is unwieldy and fails to generate much excitement. The oversized sets are truly magnificent, however, and are responsible for much of the film's appeal.

Why didn't Schoedsack hire Willis O'Brien, who had worked wonders for him on *King Kong*? For one thing, the cost of the many impressive, outsized sets built for *Dr. Cyclops* precluded the added expense of O'Brien's costly stop-motion models. For another, color film stock was not yet versatile enough to accommodate O'Brien's technique without excessive grain. Even in 1949, when Schoedsack and O'Brien teamed for *Mighty Joe Young*, they shot it in black and white.

Dramatically, the film is also a bust, alternately lethargic and hurried, and Dekker is disappointingly tepid as a mad scientist. A Lionel Atwill or Peter Lorre in the role would have livened things up considerably. The little people are even less interesting. With the exception of the feisty Halton, who dies much too early, the shrunken folk are either dull or just plain crabby.

Frank Reicher, who played the skipper in *King Kong*, appears briefly as Professor Kendall.

The Disc

Video: ★★★★★
Audio: ★★★½ (monaural)
Chapters: Yes
Format: CLV (side one), CAV (side two)
Source: MCA/Universal Home Video

Poor as the movie is, the disc is well worth owning. It's the only horror/science fiction film from this era that was shot in color (why didn't they give us a Technicolor *Son of Frankenstein* instead?), and the radiation greens and electric blue/whites are dazzling to behold. They just didn't *put* colors like those in *Gone With the Wind*! The prologue alone, done in glowing greens with a hint of purple, is worth the price of the disc. (It's also a delightfully nasty scene, filmed as an afterthought when the producers realized what a dull movie they'd concocted. Unfortunately, there wasn't time or money to fix anything else.)

The vivid colors give the sets a remarkable sense of depth, and you'll spend a lot of time freeze-framing the images on side two. Video noise and grain are practically nonexistent. The print is nearly pristine.

The audio is quite clear; and while nothing very exciting ever happens, that isn't the fault of the disc. Background noise is *very* low.

Dr. Jekyll and Mr. Hyde (1932)
★★★★½
Director: Rouben Mamoulian
Running Time: 98 minutes

Working as a banker in 1920, Frederic March ended up in the hospital after an attack of appendicitis. Lying there, taking stock of his life, the twenty-three year-old decided that what he really wanted to do was act. Within months, his natural talent and youthful good looks won him a part on the stage, and he was making silent films within weeks after that.

Though March made many great films, including *The Best Years of Our Lives* (1946) and *Inherit the Wind* (1960), it is for this version of the 1886 Robert Louis Stevenson novel (*The Strange Case of Dr. Jekyll and Mr. Hyde*) that he is perhaps best remembered. Certainly it demonstrates the actor's remarkable range. Trying to find a way to subvert the animal nature of humankind, Dr. Henry Jekyll inadvertently releases his own feral side as Mr. Hyde. At first, the bestial creature emerges only when Jekyll drinks his potion; later, though, Hyde appears at will—more monstrous in manner and appearance each time. Jekyll's activities manage to hurt both the woman who loves him,

Muriel Carew (Rose Hobart), and the tart enslaved by Hyde, Ivy Parson (Miriam Hopkins). His efforts ultimately bring tragedy and death to himself and to Ivy.

March is brilliant as the quiet, driven Jekyll and wonderfully theatrical as the murderous, apelike Hyde. The makeup is extremely effective—March seems genuinely liberated by it—and the transformations are quite good. In several scenes, infrared light was used to create the changes without a cut, bringing out lines and shadows applied before the cameras rolled but unseen in a visible light.

Ms. Hopkins is sad and memorable as the sensual, terrified Ivy.

This was only director Mamoulian's third film, but he had mastered the camera and did some remarkable things with it: The opening scenes are told entirely from Jekyll's point of view (the mirror shot is amazing), and some of the cutting is as fresh today as it was in 1932.

March tied with Wallace Beery (in *The Champ*) for the Best Actor Oscar before the award became uselessly politicized (think how Alfred Lunt must've felt: He was the only other nominee, for *The Guardsman*). Also available on disc are the 1941 Spencer Tracy version—which emphasizes (poorly) the psychological rather than the physical transformation of Hyde—and the unintentionally campy 1970 Kirk Douglas *musical.*

The Disc

Video: ★★★
Audio: ★★½ (monaural)
Chapters: Yes
Format: CLV
Source: MGM/UA Home Video

When MGM remade the film with Tracy, the studio bought the March version from Paramount and buried it so there would be no competition for the new film. Mamoulian's film remained unseen for just over a quarter of a century, until a print was located for a Mamoulian tribute. Now, not only is the best Hyde of them all back but there are over sixteen minutes worth of film that had been snipped during its late-1930s reissue. (It isn't clear whether this was done by censors after the establishment of the puritanical Production Code or by the studio to enable theaters to squeeze in an extra showing each day. The latter seems likely, because what was cut were neither the most frightening nor the most suggestive parts of the film). The version presented on this disc hasn't been seen since the original run of the film.

Not surprisingly, there are splices, scratches, and other imperfections in the source material, but the contrast is generally very good and the disc itself is the best that can be expected.

The digital sound is a understandably tinny (sound films were only half-a-decade old), but it's hardly enough to detract from the film.

Dr. Strangelove or: How I Learned to Stop Worrying and Love the Bomb (1964)
★★★★½
Director: Stanley Kubrick
Running Time: 94 minutes

Peter George's novel *Red Alert* (1960; published in England two years earlier as *Two Hours to Doom*) and Eugene Burdick and Harvey Wheeler's *Fail Safe* (1962) are the preeminent novels about accidental nuclear war. The latter was effectively filmed in 1964 by Sidney Lumet; through a fine film, the straightforward, depressing drama was a box-office disappointment, obviously not what a button-wary world wanted. Kubrick, on the other hand, turned George's novel into a black comedy—though that was not the director's original intention.

"As I kept trying to imagine the way in which things would really happen," Kubrick has said, "ideas kept coming to me which I would discard because they were so ludicrous." It occurred to him, then, that "the only way to tell the story was as a black comedy ... where the things you laugh at most are really the heart of the paradoxical postures that make a nuclear war possible."

Instead of George's tale in which the

President tries to help the Soviets shoot down the renegade planes and, after a rouge gets through, is faced with the prospect of destroying Atlantic City to satisfy the enemy, Kubrick tells the tale of mad Gen. Jack D. Ripper (Sterling Hayden), who, convinced that Communists are polluting his "precious bodily fluids," orders SAC to attack the Soviet Union. While Group Capt. Lionel Mandrake (Peter Sellers) tries to convince Ripper to issue the recall code, the only marginally less insane Gen. Buck Turgidson (George C. Scott) attempts to convince President Merkin Muffley (also Sellers) to launch an all-out attack on the Communists. Meanwhile, the crew in the cockpit of the Russia-bound B-52 *Leper Colony* has its own problems as Maj. T. J. Kong (Slim Pickens), Bombardier Lothar Zogg (James Earl Jones), and their crew mates dutifully prepare for the attack—despite jammed bomb-bay doors. Ultimately, the plane gets through and triggers a Soviet Doomsday machine that destroys the world. (Kubrick shot but cut a climactic pie fight that breaks out in the U.S. war room.)

The performances are uniformly brilliant, with the late Sellers—a sorely misused genius in too many films—shining as Mandrake, Muffley, and presidential adviser Dr. Strangelove. (He was originally slated to play Kong as well, but a broken ankle made it impossible for him to crawl around the cockpit set.)

Sadly, author George ended his life with a gun in 1966; he was forty-one.

The Disc

Video: ★★★½ (Columbia)★★★★★ (Criterion)
Audio: no stars (Columbia); ★★★★★ (Criterion) (both monaural)
Chapters: No (Columbia); yes (Criterion)
Format: CLV (Columbia); CAV (Criterion)
Source: Columbia Pictures Home Video or Criterion

There may not be a classic film in worse shape on laserdisc than Columbia's presentation of the movie. There are numerous scratches and splices, and the black and white film lacks contrast.

The sound is shockingly bad. Many of Mandrake's and Turgidson's lines are spoken quickly and are indecipherable. You'll have to turn the bass down and treble up to catch a lot of it.

Though expensive, Criterion's two-disc version is worth the additional cost. Except for a few nicks and scratches on the source material, the print is in excellent shape. The image is supersharp, and every tone from black to white is perfectly rendered. The audio is clear as can be, and the freeze-frames are perfect. Note how as Slim Pickens goes through the survival kit, his voice says "Vegas" though his lips clearly mouth "Dallas." The change was made shortly before the film's release due to the assassination of President Kennedy.

Columbia's disc isn't letterboxed, and Criterion's is—sort of. Kubrick shot some of the film using a 1.33:1 ratio, and some of it 1.66:1. A section of the disc's extensive supplementary material explains why. Chances are, though, you'll be so riveted by the film you'll hardly notice the occasional shifts in the shape of the image.

Doctor Zhivago (1965) ★★★★
Director: David Lean
Running Time: 200 minutes

Boris Pasternak got himself into trouble with his 1957 novel *Doctor Zhivago:* Although the Communist party had no quarrel with his account of the imminent Russian Revolution and its aftermath, they felt that Zhivago's conversations with his Uncle Kolya, among others, contained overt anti-Marxism, and that the novel itself was tainted by its sympathetic view of religion. When the novel was published abroad, Pasternak won the Nobel Prize—and bravely stood up to the torrent of official criticism and censure in the Soviet Union. He died three years after finishing the novel.

Director David Lean (*Bridge on the River Kwai, Lawrence of Arabia*) was drawn to the material because of its sweep and intimacy, and he approached Peter O'Toole to star. O'Toole turned him down, which smarted; Lean had made him a star. He went, next, to O'Toole's *Lawrence of Arabia* costar Omar Sharif, who agreed to play the young doctor/poet Yuri Andreievich Zhivago.

Upon the death of his mother, young Yuri (Sharif's son Tarek) goes to live with Alexander and Anna Gromeko (Ralph Richardson and Siobhan McKenna). Becoming a general practitioner in Moscow, he has several chance meetings with Larisa "Lara" Feodorovna Guishar (Julie Christie), who is betrothed to revolutionary Pavel "Pasha" Pavlovich Antipov (Tom Courtenay). Yuri marries the Gromekos's daughter, Antonia "Tonya" Alexandrovna (Geraldine Chaplin), and serves on the Ukrainian front during World War I, where he falls in love with Lara, who went to work as a nurse when her husband enlisted (he became the powerful revolutionary known as Strelnikov and abandoned her). Yuri and Lara are separated upon his return to Moscow; the turmoil of the Revolution forces the doctor to move his family to their country estate in Varykino. There, he meets Lara again and has an affair that ends when he's waylaid by Red partisans and forced to serve as their medic. Eventually, he defects, makes his way back to Lara, and learns that his family has fled Varykino. Unfortunately, Strelnikov has been defeated and Lara is wanted by the authorities. Yuri convinces her to leave under the protection of the powerful lawyer Victor Komarovsky (Rod Steiger)—a former lover of Lara's mother who once raped the girl. Yuri fares poorly without her, and is eventually found and rescued by his influential half brother Yevgraf (Alec Guinness). About to embark on a new career in a hospital, Yuri spots Lara in a streetcar and dies of a heart attack chasing after her.

Shot in Spain and Finland, the $11 million film sticks closely to the novel, save for necessary cuts and an inspired framing story in which Yevgraf interviews a girl (Rita Tushingham) who may or may not be the daughter of Yuri and Lara (scenes derived from the epilogue of the novel). More so than in previous films, Lean gets carried away with clunky symbolism (for example, when Yuri and Lara first brush at 20:05 on side one, he cuts to a sparking wire) and lays on slabs of exposition to explain the political scene (Strelnikov interviewing Zhivago, or Klaus Kinski as the soldier Kostoyed railing about injustice on the train to Varykino). But you forgive the missteps because everything around them is so good: the romance, the grandeur of the images, and the scope and importance of the events.

The cast is uniformly superb, particularly the unsung Steiger.

Interestingly, all of the ice outside and inside the Varykino estate is fake, and that magnificent Moscow street on which the protesters are massacred was built in forced perspective, the buildings constructed increasingly smaller so that they *appear* to be receding far into the distance.

The Disc

Video: ★★★½
Audio: ★★★★ (Surround)
Chapters: No
Format: CLV
Source: MGM/UA Home Video

Doctor Zhivago is a film that has always demanded a wide-screen presentation, and MGM/UA Home Video is to be commended for having made it one of the first in their Deluxe Letterbox Edition series.

Though it clips just a bit off the sides, the letterboxing retains most of Lean's grand, linear images, such as the train crossing the stark white landscape, the carriage arriving at Varykino, and the battles. The pan-and-scan version of the film has a clear picture, but it's like watching the film in a snow globe.

On the whole, the new transfer is good: The picture is very bright and clear, with no loss of detail and hardly any grain. Unfortunately, the focus is slightly soft and the colors are a little weak, particularly in scenes with muted color schemes. There are no subtleties in the snow, though that's a virtue of the shrunken size of the image and not the transfer.

The crisp audio offers excellent stereo separation and, though the effects are limited, good Surround Sound (trains, gunfire, etc.). The classic score—delicate one moment, swelling the next—sounds great: You'll be reaching for your hanky from the first strains of the balalaika!

The overture and entr'acte are included.

Dollman (1991)
Director: Albert Pyun
Running Time: 83 minutes

There's nothing wrong with low-budget films—or exploitation films. Done well, they can be a lot of fun. But done badly, they're enough to make you want to turn in your player.

Dollman was done badly—*very* badly. Tim Thomerson stars as Brick Bardo, a crime-fighter on Arturos, a planet ten thousand light-years from earth. When the evil floating head, Sprug (Frank Collision), flees into space, Bardo gives chase. They end up on earth, where the Arturosians are one-sixth the size of humans. Sprug falls in with South Bronx drug lord Braxton Red (Jackie Earle Haley), while Bardo allies himself with single mother and antidrug activist Debi Alejandro (Kamala Lopez). Before the fireworks are through, Sprug is killed by Red, Red is blown away by Bardo and his protoblaster, and we're left to wonder why the people on Arturos speak English—colloquial English at that.

Director Pyun made a promising start in films with the underappreciated action film *The Sword and the Sorcerer* (1982), starring Lee Horsley. After that, he seemed to lose it: Lately, his career has been marked by such stinkers as the straight to video *Captain America* (1989), the amateurish *Kickboxer 2* (1991)—and *Dollman*.

About half the film is padding: shots of the streets, of gunplay that goes on and on, of banal dialogue. The rest is Thomerson doing a bad Clint Eastwood impression, Lopez lecturing people in the neighborhood or fighting off attackers, and Collision or Haley barking out threats. What few special effects there are are unexciting and/or uncovering: Most of the time, to save money, Pyun simply shows things from Bardo's point of view.

What the film *really* is is dull, man.

The Disc
Video: ★★★½
Audio: ★★★½ (Surround)
Chapters: No
Format: CLV
Source: Full Moon Entertainment

Despite the budgetary constraints, Pyun has made a decent-looking film. The colors are fairly punchy, and grain is minimal. The biggest problem is plentiful video noise in the reds.

The film is not hurt at all by cropping.

The sound is crisp and full, with good separation and some excellent (albeit limited) Surround effects.

At the end of the disc is Full Moon's Video Zone, which includes a "pat yourself on the back" making-of featurette, and a generous look at clips from the company's other films (such as the cult hit *Trancers*).

The Doors (1991) ★★½
Director: Oliver Stone
Running Time: 140 minutes

Very few rock 'n' roll fans are ambivalent about the Doors. Many found lead singer Jim Morrison's lyrics and style profoundly poetic; others regarded them (and him) as shallow and pretentious, his suffering-artist persona as carefully sculpted as his Alexander the Great locks. But whatever one thinks of the Doors, there is no confusing their sound, style, or dark lyrics for those of any other band. Morrison once said, "I am interested in anything about revolt, disorder, chaos," and the band's songs certainly reflect that bent. They also reflect Morrison's belief that drink and drugs released the bohemian artist in him, enabled him to "reach the mental through the physical." Substance abuse lead to his death in 1971, at the age of twenty-seven.

Oliver Stone's film goes through the motions of searching for the real Morrison (Val Kilmer). It looks at his failed college career, at the genesis of the Doors, and at the group's rise to fame—all in quick, powerful, but disconnected scenes. Before long, they're famous and Morrison is hobnobbing with the likes of Andy Warhol (Crispin Glover), marrying a witch, hanging out from windows, having sex with every woman that smiles at him, letting his fellow band members down, and drinking or drugging himself into one stupor after another.

The film is a study in Morrison's excesses, weaknesses, and mysticism—but, strangely, his art is absent. The poet isn't here, only the clown and the jerk. What Stone *has* accomplished is to make a time machine of incredible audiovisual power, recreating the era and its sensibilities as completely as he did in *Platoon* (1986) and *Born on the Fourth of July* (see page 34). He's also captured the look and sound of the Doors: Anyone familiar with concert or documentary footage will find it faithfully recreated. And the three surviving band members agree that Kilmer's performance is eerily exact, from the singer's dervishlike dancing to the poses he struck in his photo sessions with Gloria Stavers (Mimi Rogers). The singing is also remarkably right, a mixture of both Morrison and the actor.

(Two liberties that were taken with the facts are worth nothing: There was no "Light My Fire" TV commercial. Morrison didn't *snarl* the verboten word *higher* at Ed Sullivan's cameras; he simply sang the song as normal.)

The rest of the casting is perfect: Kyle MacLachlan as keyboardist Manzarek, the pompous musical genius; Kevin Dillon as drummer John Densmore, who is perpetually disgusted by Morrison's antics; and Frank Whaley as bemused, timid guitarist Robby Krieger. Unfortunately, Stone—who never did much with women in his films before—does nothing with them here. Meg Ryan looks exactly like Morrison's long-suffering lover, Pamela Courson, but Stone presents her as a ditz (she wasn't), while Kathleen Quinlan as Morrison's witch-wife, Patricia Kennealy, is little more than a scheming vamp (she wasn't, and she has become a respected fantasy writer.)

Stone himself appears as the college film professor; singer Billy Idol—still hobbling after a motorcycle accident—makes a brief appearance at the bar; Densmore is the technician recording Morrison's *An American Prayer;* and Patricia Kennealy herself is the head witch at the marriage ceremony.

Manzarek didn't like the film, claiming that it missed Morrison's sensitive, intellectual side; he replied to it by making the documentary *The Soft Parade*. Available on laserdisc, it's an ideal companion piece.

The Disc

Video: ★★★★½
Audio: ★★★★★ (Surround)
Chapters: Yes
Format: CLV
Source: Live Home Video/Image Entertainment

With garish colors, many of them pulsing, psychedelic-bright, the film could have been a laser disaster. But the transfer is beautiful, with a sharp image (even the stars are bright pinpoints) and only occasional noise in the reds and browns. The letterboxing is crucial; and while the mammoth concert scenes lose *some* of their impact on the small screen, you can turn up the volume to compensate.

The sound is full and engulfing, but the quieter passages—such as the hotel-room interview—are also exquisite.

Double Indemnity (1944)
★★★★
Director: Billy Wilder
Running Time: 107 minutes

For the most part, the novels of author James M. Cain are about ambitious, rotten people doing ruthless things to get what they want, be it a lover or wealth or both. That's true of *The Postman Always Rings Twice* and *Mildred Pierce*, both of which were made into successful motion pictures, and it's also true of *Double Indemnity*, which was published in 1943.

Insurance salesman Walter Neff (Fred MacMurray) and Phyllis Dietrichson (Barbara Stanwyck) plot to do away with the unhappy woman's insensitive oil-executive husband on a train, thus allowing them to collect on a $100,000 double-indemnity insurance policy. Things go as planned—or do they? Back at Pacific All Risk Insurance, Neff's superior, Barton Keyes (Edward G. Robinson), smells a six-foot-tall rat and continues to nose around even after the police have finished their investigation, declaring the man's death an accident. Neff eventually learns that Phyllis has been using him for her own reasons, and they get what they deserve—from each other.

The funny, intricate screenplay was co-written by Wilder and Raymond Chandler, the master hard-boiled novelist to whom Cain has often been compared. The dialogue is pure Chandler; and if you're not a fan of his clever, metaphoric style, you may find it a bit *too* snappy. The script was originally turned down by MacMurray, who loved the part but feared that fans accustomed to seeing him in light comedies would hate him as a sleaze. Wilder talked him into taking it, and he's wonderful as the lust-filled, fast-talking Neff. Platinum blond Stanwyck is every inch his equal, an icy lady who's as quick to thaw as she is to freeze again. However, *both* stars are overshadowed by Robinson, whose gruff but compassionate claims manager has the best and funniest lines—and is the only admirable character in the film.

Double Indemnity was remade for TV in 1973 with Richard Crenna and Samantha Eggar, and it also inspired the 1981 film *Body Heat*.

The Disc
Video: ★★★½
Audio: ★★★
Chapters: Yes (just for the trailer)
Format: CLV
Source: MCA/Universal Home Video

Considering how badly so many half-century-old black and white films look, *Double Indemnity* is a surprise. The print is generally clean, with good contrast. The image ranges from sharp and moderately glossy to *very* sharp and glossy.

The audio is a bit thin in the upper ranges, but the sound is clear and very satisfying for a film this old.

The trailer is typical melodrama from the era.

Dracula (1979) ★★½
Director: John Badham
Running Time: 109 minutes

On paper, it was so *right*. Fresh from his previous year's run as Broadway's sensual Count Dracula, Frank Langella would star as the vampire. Laurence Olivier would play vampire hunter Van Helsing. John Badham, stylish director of *Saturday Night Fever* (1977), would helm the project, and John Williams (*Star Wars*) would write the score. How could the screen version of *Dracula* miss?

Well, it didn't—not entirely. But it isn't the classic it should have been.

Based on the 1927 Hamilton Dean/John L. Baldsterston play—which is a tight adaptation of the then-thirty year-old Bram Stoker novel—the film brings Dracula directly to England (as opposed to both the novel and the 1931 Bela Lugosi film, which spends time in Transylvania). In England, Dracula dines on his neighbor Mina Van Helsing (Jan Francis) while deciding that her friend Lucy Seward (Kate Nelligan) should be his immortal bride. Though Mina dies and is reborn as a vampire, the Count fails to claim Lucy for eternity thanks to Mina's grieving father (Olivier) and Lucy's stolid fiancé, solicitor Jonathan Harker (Trevor Eve).

What's good about the film are Langella, who gives a surprisingly restrained performance (surprising, considering his flamboyant stage interpretation), Kate Nelligan as his strong-willed foil, and Donald Pleasence as Dr. Seward, the somewhat loony head of the local insane asylum. Williams's sweeping score is appropriately melodramatic, and the sets are very impressive. As for the rest . . .

Olivier was ill during the making of the film and he looks tired. Getting through the film with a consistent Eastern European accent monopolized his once-prodigious energies, and the one-time master of nuance hams relentlessly. Yet, bad Olivier is better than the painfully nondescript Harker, who, even at the prospect of losing his fiancé to an immortal monster, is unable to shuck his Victorian stolidness. Worst of all, however, is the film's climax. Dracula has skewered Van Helsing in the hold of a ship and, with his dying breath, the fearless vampire killer weakly flings a hook at Dracula, which somehow manages to impale him and hoist him up the ship's mast, where he's cooked by the sun. When the Count is finished disintegrating, his cape flutters off like a hang glider, comic book–style shorthand to let us know *he may not be dead*!

A runner-up for worst scene of the film is the laser-drenched seduction of Lucy, which is anachronistic and distracting. It's surprising Badham didn't cast Travolta as Dracula.

Despite the film's polish and lavish production values, Bela Lugosi's *Dracula*, Christopher Lee's *Horror of Dracula* (see page 141), and Francis Coppola's *Bram Stoker's Dracula* (1992) remain the definitive screen interpretations of the Count to date.

The Disc

Video: ★★★½
Audio: ★★★½ (Surround)
Chapters: Yes
Format: CLV
Source: MCA/Universal Home Video

Dracula caused a furor among laserphiles because director Badham opted to make changes in the film before its letterboxed laser release. He tinkered with some of the music (for example, changing the recording playing on the phonograph at Dr. Seward's dinner for Dracula) and, more significantly, muted the colors of the film considerably. This is especially apparent during scenes set at Carfax Abbey, Dracula's home. Badham had always wanted to make his *Dracula* more like a black and white film with splashes of color (read: red); now he's done it. Viewers who enjoyed the rich tones of the original should stick with the much richer panned-and-scanned laserdisc release. Others will find this rendition generally satisfying and appropriate to the subject.

Color aside, this version is still atmospheric, every stone and cobweb crisply rendered in the transfer. There is very little grain or video noise, and the generous letterbox puts the entire original image up there on the screen.

The audio is exquisite. Langella has an incomparable voice, and it sounds terrific. Though the Surround effects are limited mostly to the music and the screaming of inmates at Dr. Seward's asylum, the storm is powerful.

The original theatrical trailer is included.

The Lugosi *Dracula* is also available on disc in a restored edition. The film is generally clear and sharp, though the sound is hollow and raspy (talkies were still young). Yet without music, and with only minimal sound effects and camera movement, this early *Dracula* is still much creepier. Moreover, the film is faithful to the way the play was performed with Lugosi, hinting at the power he must have had on stage.

Earthquake (1974) ★½
Director: Mark Robson
Running Time: 123 minutes

Architectural engineer Stuart Graff (Charlton Heston) is married to Remy (Ava Gardner), the bitchy daughter of his boss, Sam Royce (Lorne Greene, who was seven years old when Ava was born). The marriage is on the rocks, so Graff seeks solace in the arms of widow Denise Mitchell (Geneviève Bujold), whose husband died on a job to which Graff had assigned him (King David metaphors, anyone?). Miles Quade (Richard Roundtree) is a motorcycle stunt driver trying to make it big. Jody (Marjoe Gortner) is a grocery-store worker and army reservist who lusts after beautiful young Rosa (Victoria Principal). Lew Slade (George Kennedy, the best actor in the film) is a tough, headstrong cop who gets into trouble for wrecking Zsa Zsa Gabor's hedge during a chase. Lloyd Nolan is the compassionate Dr. Vance.

Cowriter Mario Puzo's original script was much grittier than the finished film, in which the soapsuds are lathered on thick and with less interesting results than in other films of this genre, such as *The Poseidon Adventure* (see page 216). Heston—who had script approval—fought hard to have his character die in the film: He felt it was implausible for Graff to have his "mean wife killed and neat girlfriend left alive while he rebuilds Los Angeles." It was a nice sentiment, but did it really matter in this picture?

The much vaunted Earthquake effects are extremely erratic. Some, such as the collapse of the highway and the Capitol Records Building, are dazzling; others, such as the optical *warping* of a building at 6:34 on side two (it doesn't collapse; it just bends), are embarrassingly bad. And watch for the goof at 12:32 on side two: You can see the shards of glass planted in the woman's face *before* she's hit by the falling window. Roughly half the effects were created using miniature models, many of which were built on special shakers so they'd look as if they were being rattled apart rather than pulled down. (The term *miniature* is somewhat misleading, though: The model of the Hollywood Dam was fifty-six feet wide.) Matte paintings were used to show the city in ruins—fire and smoke were superimposed over the art—while close-ups of people dodging debris were executed by having cranes rain debris on stunt actors on Universal's back lot. The scene in which Miles outraces the water from the broken dam was actually shot on the studio tour's flood attraction—and looks about as convincing. (Note the scene in which Miles first demonstrates his motorcycle track. The stuntman's fall from the top of the loop was unplanned and was incorporated into the film. He never *did* make a complete circuit, which is why it's accomplished in the film through editing.)

The film's continuity is also very sloppy: Watch, for instance, as Heston clearly stops in the doorway on side one, 4:52; when the angle changes at 4:53, he's still walking through the door. There are countless editing gaffes like that throughout the film.

Scenes of actress Debralee Scott in a 707 trying to land in L.A. during the quake were cut before the film's release, along with a lot of footage of Jody protecting Rosa postquake. Mercifully, these have not been restored for laserdisc. Walter Matuschanskayasky is, of course, Walter Matthau, who did the cameo in the film for his friend Robson.

Earthquake was the first film to use the short-lived gimmick Sensurround, which used low frequencies in the audible and subaudible range, fed through special speakers, to "shake" the theater in tandem with the onscreen earthquake. The process was subsequently used for *Midway* (1976), *Rollercoaster* (1977), and the theatrical release of the pilot for TV's *Battlestar Galactica* (1979).

The Disc
Video: ★
Audio: ★★★½ (stereo)
Chapters: Yes (for trailer only)
Format: CLV (sides one and two), CAV (side three)
Source: MCA Home Video

Bad as the film is, it's weakened considerably by the presentation. Most damaging is the panning-and-scanning, which loses over one-third of the image at any given time. When Dr. Vance says, "This used to be a helluva town, Officer," there's no officer on the screen, as Kennedy is cropped off to the right. To see how badly the film is hurt, watch the theatrical trailer at the end, which *is* letterboxed:

The nifty shot of the Volkswagen literally flying off the highway at 35333 is missing from the film itself.

In fact, the clarity of the trailer is infinitely better than that of the film. There, the colors and sharpness are perfect; in the film, the colors are solid, but the image throughout is slightly grainy and fuzzy.

The audio is generally quite clear and the earthquake sounds have a lot of body, though subwoofers are required actually to bring the Sensurround experience home.

The Eddy Duchin Story (1956)
★★★
Director: George Sidney
Running Time: 123 minutes

Hollywood has always pounced on trends, and when *The Glenn Miller Story* (1954) and *The Benny Goodman Story* (1955) made money, Columbia figured that the combination of late, great pianist Eddy Duchin, memorable music, and star Tyrone Power couldn't miss.

They were right.

Born in Cambridge, Massachusetts, in 1910, Duchin studied to be a phramacist. At the age of nineteen, he decided to pursue a career in piano—and that's where we meet him in the film, a bushy-tailed hopeful arriving in New York. He meets socialite Marjorie Oelrichs (Kim Novak), who helps him get a job with bandleader Leo Reisman (Larry Keating); by 1930, Duchin has married Marjorie and founded his own band. But Marjorie dies after giving birth to a son, Peter, and Eddy blames the boy for her death.

While serving as a naval officer in the Pacific during World War II, Duchin encounters a young native boy (Warren Hsieh) whose loneliness underscores what Peter must be feeling at home. Eddy goes back and, with the help of his manager, Lou Sherwood (James Whitmore), and Peter's nanny, Chiquita (Victoria Shaw), he gets to know his son (Rex Thompson). Eddy and Chiquita fall in love and marry, though their time together is brief, because Eddy becomes terminally ill with leukemia. (He died in 1951, which is suggested in the film by having him literally disappear from the keyboard.)

Director Sidney wasn't known for maudlin movies—that is, *Anchors Away* (1945) and *Scaramouche* (1952)—but he served up the melodrama here as if he were a stockholder in Kleenex. Subtle it isn't, though it must be said that Power's "Chopsticks" duet with young Hsieh is a scene of such power and eloquence that it elevates the entire movie.

Power does extremely well with this part, which was one of his last. He'd always been a charismatic leading man but had recently spent a lot of time on the stage, honing his talents as an actor. It showed. As for Novak, she doesn't so much act as pose (a recurring problem with her). Fortunately, she dies before it becomes tiresome.

Famed pianist Carmen Cavallaro played the Duchin songs on the sound tack, which were very adeptly fingered by Power, who was coached on Duchin's style by pianist Nat Brandwynne. Power is especially impressive in the "Dizzy Fingers" number that opens chapter five, side one. (While you're on that side, go to the end of chapter four, when Eddy and Marjorie go strolling in Central Park in the 1930s. The Empire State Building is sporting the two-hundred-foot-tall antenna that had not yet been erected.)

Duchin himself appeared in the films *Mr. Broadway* (1932), *Coronado* (1935), and *1937 Hit Parade*, a facet of his career not touched on in the movie.

The Disc
Video: ★★½
Audio: ★★★½ (Surround)
Chapters: Yes
Format: CLV (sides one and two), CAV (side three)
Source: Columbia Pictures Home Video/ Pioneer Special Edition

Despite having been shot in Technicolor, *The Eddy Duchin Story* doesn't have the punchy colors one associates with the process. The hues are frequently pale and wishy-washy, though the picture itself is strong and sharp.

The CinemaScope film has been generously letterboxed, allowing us to see—among other things—all eighty-eight keys when Power plays.

The digital audio is clear and excellent. Cavallaro's playing sounds fresh and resonant, despite the age of the film, and the Surround effects work.

Viewers who like this sort of film will also enjoy *Sincerely Yours* (1955), with Liberace as an aspiring concert pianist who loses his hearing. The movie is pure corn, terribly acted, but with some wonderful musical interludes. Unfortunately, though the image is generally sharp, the colors are washed out and/or dead wrong in spots (orange skin tones, for example). The print is also unacceptably ragged in many places, and the audio is somewhat tinny.

Edward Scissorhands (1990)
★★★½
Director: Tim Burton
Running Time: 105 minutes

As he proved in *Pee-wee's Big Adventure* (1985), *Beetlejuice* (1988), and *Batman* (see page 19), former Disney animator Burton has a fresh, original imagination, and) knows how to tell a story using visuals. Conversely, he doesn't really know, yet, how to get the most out of his actors, and wouldn't know a good script if one fell through a skylight and hit him on the head. That *Edward Scissorhands* works is a tribute to his visual genius and wonderfully skewed view of the world.

Holed up in a dark, old castle high on a hill above pastel-hued suburbia, a nameless inventor (Vincent Price) decides to build himself a companion, a robotic little boy. Unfortunately, he dies before the lad (Johnny Depp) is quite finished: He still possesses pasty flesh, a moplike hairdo, and scissors for hands. Enter Peg (Dianne Wiest), an Avon lady who comes calling at the castle, finds the orphaned Edward Scissorhands, and takes him home with her.

At first, Edward is all the rage—trimming hedges, clipping dogs, fixing salads, and giving haircuts. But when Peg's daughter Kim (Winona Ryder) becomes *too* friendly with the teen, her boorish boyfriend Jim (Anthony Michael Hall) tricks the naïve boy into robbing a house. The community turns on Edward, who, like the Frankenstein Monster pursued by angry villagers, returns to his dreary retreat. There, the movie takes some surprising turns that fill the screen with horror and wonder, the heart with joy, and the eyes with tears.

Edward Scissorhands is a magical fable with the sensibilities of *Peter Pan* and *Beauty and the Beast* (see pages 207 and 22). It's sentimental but not mawkishly so; the many observations about society and its values may not be particularly fresh, but they're generally on target. And like a modern-day Chaplin, right down to his black and white appearance, Depp is a touching, splendid Edward.

If only the rest of the characters weren't so broad or thin (Alan Arkin is wasted as Peg's husband, Bill) and the dialogue so banal, this would have been one for the time capsule.

The Disc
Video: ★★★★
Audio: ★★★★★ (Surround)
Chapters: Yes
Format: CLV
Source: Fox Video

The movie is bathed in soft shades, all of which are gorgeously captured on the disc. The image is sharp as a scissor and is almost completely free of noise. Why only four stars, then? Because the movie needed a mild letterbox at least and doesn't have it. Characters fall off the sides and, with a director as visual as Burton, *any* loss of picture is detrimental. Shame on Fox for not offering the film both ways.

The audio is excellent and, while there are no ear-popping effects, the Surround Sounds are like delicious little h'ors d'oeuvres served here and there throughout the film. Conversely, Danny Elfman's score is a full-blown meal, washing over and around you with a mesmeric impact that rivals the film's visuals.

Elmer Gantry (1960) ★★★★
Director: Richard Brooks
Running Time: 147 minutes

Author Sinclair Lewis created an unprecedented stir with the publication of his novel *Main Street* (1920), which exposed the destructive provincialism of small-town America. He gave business people a black eye in *Babbitt* (1922), assaulted the scientific community in *Arrowsmith* (1925)—which won him a Pulitzer Prize—and took on evangelists in *Elmer Gantry* (1927).

In the novel, Gantry is an ex-football player who becomes an ordained minister and, through a blend of stolen sermons, good looks, and a knack for self-promotion, becomes the head of a powerful midwestern church. Director Richard Brooks had been wanting to film the book for over a decade, but studios felt it was dangerous to attack religion—even the charlatan kind practiced by the hero of Lewis's novel. Finally, Brooks bought the rights and wrote a screenplay. Burt Lancaster committed to star in the project before a production deal was even in place; his popularity guaranteed that someone would put up the money for the film, and he felt it should be made. He also wasn't stupid: It was a hell of a part.

With Lancaster's (sometimes-unwelcome) input, Brooks rewrote the script and changed the story and the character of Gantry considerably, making him not just a con man but a man who was searching for something. In the film, set during Prohibtion, Gantry (Lancaster) becomes a salesman after getting thrown out of a theological seminary for seducing the deacon's daughter, Lulu Bains (Shirley Jones), in the church. Lacking self-respect and unable to make ends meet, he happens upon a revival meeting held by the angelic Sister Sharon Falconer (Jean Simmons). He finagles an audience with her and she allows him to address her congregation. Feeding on the crowd, he delivers a hell-raising sermon and, against the advice of her cautious aide, William Morgan (Dean Jagger), Sharon allows Gantry to join the organization.

Gantry helps promote Sister Falconer into the big time. But there are pitfalls: Reporter Jim Lefferts (Arthur Kennedy), who is covering Falconer for the *Zenith Times-Dispatch*, files an unfavorable story that threatens to derail them; and Lulu, now a prostitute, resurfaces and blackmails Gantry and the church. Gantry and Falconer survive it all, though there is no avoiding the act of God (an angry God?) that ultimately destroys the ministry.

Although the film is dated (Gantry's excesses seem mild compared to contemporary evangelists) and the film's many moral questions are dealt with in a fairly didactic manner, *Elmer Gantry* is still a powerful motion picture thanks to sharp dialogue and a great cast. Lancaster bats this one out of the park; as he has said, "Some parts you fall into like an old glove. Elmer really wasn't acting. It was me." However, his Bible-beating performance doesn't overshadow the quiet dignity of Simmons, the deep bitterness of Jones (you'll never see Shirley Partridge in *quite* the same light), and the articulate cynicism of the splendid Kennedy (who would play a virtually identical role in *Lawrence of Arabia* two years later; see page 170).

Note the clever salute to author Lewis in the film, and watch for an amazing gaffe: At chapter five, 11:49, a contemporary car drives right through the picture, behind Gantry.

The Disc
Video: ★★★
Audio: ★★★ (monaural)
Chapters: Yes
Format: CLV
Source: MGM/UA Home Video

Eastman Color film stock is far from reliable, and the colors in this remastered edition look somewhat worn—not *awful* but not vibrant, either. The film is also hurt by a slight softness to the image, some color noise in the reds and flesh tones, and a bit of grain. There are also a few scratches in the master element.

The sound is good and free of extraneous noises, although there are a couple of dropouts.

Empire of the Sun (1987) ★★
Director: Steven Spielberg
Running Time: 203 minutes

British writer James Graham Ballard was born in Shanghai in 1930, imprisoned in a civilian POW camp by the Japanese when they occupied eastern China at the beginning of World War II, and never saw England until 1946. His experiences in crowded Shanghai and in the camp inspired him to write a different kind of science fiction than most of his peers: He didn't bother with aliens and time machines but concentrated instead on tales of apocalypse and urban disaster. After reading his autobiographical tale and seeing the movie Spielberg made from it, you'll understand why. (It will also come as no surprise that, as soon as he was old enough, airplane buff Ballard joined the RAF.)

Jim Graham (Christian Bale) is a precocious lad who loves airplanes, enjoys a life of luxury, and takes it all for granted until the Japanese arrive and he and his parents try to flee Shanghai. Jim is separated from them and, half-starved, falls in with merchant seaman and crook Basie (John Malkovich). In exchange for food, Jim agrees to show Basie around the rich houses outside the city. Unfortunately, they're captured by the Japanese and incarcerated in a camp beside Japan's Soochow air base.

The two spend the next four years there, Jim befriending Dr. Rawlins (Nigel Havers) and also learning to steal from and soft-soap the Japanese. And he watches the planes, even saluting the enemy pilots who fly them. When Allied planes attack the base, Jim plays dead, the fleeing Japanese leave him, and the boy embarks on a long and difficult trek back to civilization and his parents.

No doubt about it, as he proved in his Indiana Jones movies, Spielberg can mount a big film with stunning action sequences. Unfortunately, he hasn't the foggiest idea what to do with people. Like the planes and props and landscape, they further his tale without revealing who they are or what makes them tick—other than in the most simplistic terms. Once in a while, Spielberg hits the elusive emotional notes he's striving for, as when James risks himself to save the doctor from a beating. The rest of the time, he resorts to childish and/or insincere manipulation, as when the three Japanese fliers salute James.

The actors are all good, especially newcomer Bale, who convincingly grows from obnoxious to indomitable. It's a shame that he and the others had nothing interesting to say.

The Disc
Video: ★★★★
Audio: ★★★★ (Surround)
Chapters: Yes
Format: CAV or CLV
Source: Warner Home Video

The most disappointing aspect of this disc is that the letterboxing is so mild. The film's spectacle is its principal asset, and a wider image—truer to the original film—would have made it more enjoyable.

Despite wisps of video noise here and there, the film boasts an excellent image, with a sharp picture and rich colors. Spielberg uses a lot of primaries and they are extremely vibrant.

Though John Williams's cascading and celestial score tends to overwhelm the dialogue in far too many scenes, the audio is flawless otherwise. The stereo separations are very good, especially when planes zip from side to side. However, considering the size of the film and the number of airplane and crowd scenes, it's surprising how restrained the Surround Sound is. It's used to emphasize, not bludgeon: For example, as the camera pans to reveal more and more slave laborers on side two, 2/15:25, the sound also begins to build, slowly filling the rear channels. It's an expert use of the medium.

Side four contains an interesting "making of" featurette. Considering all the work and good intentions that went into the film, you'll feel awful that it didn't turn out better.

Enemies, A Love Story (1989)
★★★★½
Director: Paul Mazursky
Running Time: 120 minutes

During World War II, gentile Polish girl Yadwiga (Margaret Sophie Stein) hid her former Jewish employer, Herman Broder (Ron Silver), in a hayloft to save him from the Nazis. After the war, Herman is told that his wife, Tamara, is dead; indebted to Yadwiga, he brings her to New York and marries her in a civil ceremony. His erstwhile maid is a loving but simple woman; for excitement, he sees young, passionate Masha (Lena Olin), a concentration camp survivor estranged from her husband, Leon (Paul Mazursky).

Herman has his hands full juggling his livelihood—he earns a modest living writing for Rabbi Lembeck (Alan King, who should have done less shtick and more acting)—and two women ... which is when Tamara (Anjelica Huston) comes back into his life. Having survived two bullet wounds, spent time in Russia, and finally made her way to the United States, Tamara resumes her bickering with Herman just about where they had left off years before. As if things weren't complicated enough, both Masha and Yadwiga get pregnant; Herman marries the former in a Jewish ceremony and now has three wives.

Enemies, a Love Story is quite faithful to the 1972 novel by the late Yiddish author Isaac Bashevis Singer, who based his work on the experiences of Holocaust survivors. It's a stunningly photographed film, a time machine that brilliantly evokes the year—1949—the places—from Coney Island to the Bronx to the Catskills—and, of course, the people. As Singer himself sums up his work, the characters are not just victims of the Nazis, they are "victims of their own personalities and fates."

The characters in the film are studies in contrasts: Herman is an intellectual who is ruled by his sexual appetite; Masha is an intellectual who uses her body to get what she wants; Yadwiga is a woman of limited intellect who is desperately trying to improve her mind and ignores her body; and Tamara is a woman whose body and mind have been battered by the Nazis, yet she is the wisest and strongest of them all.

This is an alternately funny and deeply depressing film, one that isn't about the most likable folks in the world, but they're people you won't soon forget. The acting couldn't be better, and Huston proves the difference between acting with an accent and passing off an accent and mannerisms as acting (i.e., Meryl Streep in just about any role).

The only other film based on Singer's works was Barbara Streisand's 1983 film *Yentl*.

The Disc
Video: ★★
Audio: ★★★½ (Surround)
Chapters: Yes
Format: CLV
Source: Media Image Entertainment

The laserdisc is something of a disappointment. The original film has flat, monochromatic color schemes, but within those boundaries the colors are fairly distinct. Here, though the picture is sharp enough, the hues are run-together muddy. There's also a great deal of grain that wasn't present in the theaters, and the nonletterboxed image not only seems to put the characters in a vise, it damages some of the film's stunning visuals of the crowded city, desolate wintery streets, and the Coney Island boardwalk.

The audio is much better, for the most part clear and clean. The Surround effects are minimal, but when they happen—for example, the rumbling of the el or the howling of the wind—they draw you right into the film.

The biggest problem with this disc is that copies may skip a few frames at a time (the action looks jerky for a second), especially on the second side. It *looks* time-compressed but isn't—just a crummy manufacturing job.

Yentl is available in a very satisfying laserdisc with a sharp picture and good Surround Sound.

Ernest Goes to Jail (1990)
★★★
Director: John Cherry
Running Time: 81 minutes

The accident-prone, dull-witted Ernest P. Worrell (Jim Varney) burst upon the American consciousness in TV commercials, then graduated to feature films in *Ernest Goes to Camp* (1987). That surprise hit was followed by *Ernest Saves Christmas* (1988), *Ernest Goes to Jail*, and *Ernest Scared Stupid* (1991).

Ernest Goes to Jail is the best of the lot, an appealing blend of dump slapstick and character-driven humor. Working as a janitor in a Howard County bank, Ernest dreams of becoming a bank clerk and is encouraged by young, loving bank employee Charlotte Sparrow (Barbara Bush . . . no, not *that* Barbara Bush). Summoned for jury duty, Ernest happens to be a dead ringer for death-row crime czar Felix Nash. When Ernest's jury visits the Dracup Maximum Security Prison, Nash arranges a switcheroo, leaving him free to work at the bank and plot its robbery while also wooing Charlotte. Meanwhile, the hapless Ernest is slated for execution. Miraculously surviving among the toughs at Dracup, Ernest fries but doesn't die: His visit to the chair turns him into Electroman, packed with superhuman powers and determined to save the bank and Charlotte from Nash.

Varney will either delight or annoy you as Ernest, but he's really a surprise as

Nash—cruel, rough, and completely believable. However, Gailard Sartain and Bill Byrge are the unbilled highlights of the film, turning in excellent comic performances as a pair of hapless bank guards, the gung ho Chuck and over-the-hill Bobby.

If you don't turn the film on expecting the Marx Brothers or Monty Python, and you can round up a couple of kids to watch with you, you'll have a lot of fun: I *dare* you not to laugh when the bank chair stalks the magnetized Ernest or Chuck and Bobby try out their invisible wall to protect the bank.

The Disc
Video: ★★★½
Audio: ★★★★½ (Surround)
Chapters: Yes
Format: CLV
Source: Touchstone Home Video

Ernest Goes to Jail may very well have the gaudiest color scheme of any film in cinema history, dominated by shocking purples, pinks, reds, blues, and oranges. There's video noise here and there but, considering the potential problem areas, the transfer is surprisingly stable. Grain is also a problem at times, but otherwise the picture is clean and sharp. The film isn't letterboxed but was shot TV-safe and translates just fine.

The audio has the kick of a big-budget action movie, with Surround Sound you just don't get in any other film, such as a runaway floor polisher, an attack by filing cabinets, and Worrell's postexecution electric discharges.

The Errand Boy (1961) ★★½
Director: Jerry Lewis
Running Time: 93 minutes

Like Woody Allen, Jerry Lewis *might* have become a very good director in time. Don't laugh: He showed flashes of comic brilliances in many of his movies, especially this one. *The Nutty Professor* (see page 198) is not only a good Jerry Lewis movie, it's a good movie *period*.

Lewis and his nightclub partner Dean Martin made seventeen films for other directors from 1949 to 1956, after which Lewis not only starred in an amazing thirty-two solo features, but directed many of them, as well. If they have a common failing, it's the fact that Lewis relies extensively on pratfalls and goofy faces. He never developed his verbal wit, and his attempts at bathos were almost always maudlin.

Nowhere are his strengths and faults better exemplified than in *The Errand Boy*. Lewis stars as Morty Tashman, a klutz hired to work as a studio messenger in order to spy on employees and help curtail financial waste. Morty stumbles from one disaster to another, the pivotal one being when he opens a huge bottle of champagne at a party and showers the studio chief and one of his top actresses. The accident is captured on film, the studio realizes it has a comedic genius on its hands, and Morty becomes a star. (Yes... *Pee-wee's Big Adventure* [1985] owes a big debt to this film.)

Many of the gags work, and one is a classic: Morty, sitting in the studio head's chair, faces an empty boardroom and silently mouths the instruments on the sound track, delivering a musical "speech." The miming is inventive and the scene is a riot. Morty's mispronunciation of complicated names is amusing, his efforts to eat lunch on the lot while action scenes erupt around him are hilarious (four surprise guest stars appear at the end of the scene), and the aforementioned champagne shower is a hoot. Morty's accidental redubbing of a movie (which isn't caught until a sneak preview, of course) is also very funny.

Other gags fall flat, go on too long, or are predictable, such as the convertible in the car wash, Morty being mistaken for a dummy, and Morty crashing a musical number, and the serious stuff is embarrassingly bad: Two "sweet" scenes with puppets that come to life and talk about life, love, and friendship will have you reaching for the scan button, while a director giving a *long* lecture to studio executives about art and craft will send you looking for a brick.

Still, this was only the second film Lewis directed (*The Bellboy*, the year before, was his first) and he can be forgiven his trespasses... this time. Unfortunately, in subsequent films, he ended up recycling shtick and blackout-style gags until the style was passe. His fans stayed with him until the late sixties; though he's made films occasionally, his last starring vehicle, *Cracking Up* (1983), was never even released.

The Disc

Video: ★★★★
Audio: ★★★ (monoaural)
Chapters: Yes
Format: CLV
Source: International Video
    Entertainment/Image Entertainment.

This mildly letterboxed disc is a Lewisophile's dream, a perfect print of the black and white film, with a generally sharp image, a very satisfactory range of gray tones, and very little grain.

The digital audio is a little thin in a few spots, but this is basically a silent film to begin with, so that's not a problem. There is no background noise.

The extras consist of lobby cards, posters, behind-the-scene photographs, and the trailer. The latter features takes not used in the champagne sequence—long shots in which the guy holding the bottle clearly is *not* Jerry Lewis.

Other Lewis films recently released on laserdisc are his first solo effort, *The Delicate Delinquent* (1957), in which he becomes a police officer (the picture is not letterboxed, and the source material is in so-so shape); *The Bellboy* (1960), which is *truly* a silent film for Lewis, who doesn't speak until the end (the letterboxed presentation is in very good shape); and *The Ladies' Man* (1961), a gorgeous Technicolor film in which Lewis plays a handyman in a girl's school.

E.T. The Extra-Terrestrial (1982) ★★

Director: Steven Spielberg
Running Time: 115 minutes

Fans of a movie *loathe* being hit with complaints about plot holes. If you like a movie, you overlook the lapses. If you don't, you use it to support your case. Well, there's a black hole in *E.T.* so powerful that it sucks the rest of the movie right in.

Early in the film, a cuddly little alien is left behind when its ship takes off. The creature stands there, helpless, watching as it leaves. Later, the E.T. and a gaggle of kids are being chased by bad guys. To escape, the E.T. levitates itself, the kids, and their bicycles. Question: Why didn't the extraterrestrial fly after the ship at the beginning? Yes, of course—because then (as John Ford said of *Stagecoach*; see page 259) there'd be no movie. In this case, that wouldn't have been such a bad thing.

Three million light-years from home, the stranded E.T. wanders into a suburban backyard, where young Elliott (Henry Thomas) befriends it and forms a mental bond with the creature. (Later, Elliott gets drunk when the creature does, yet neither of them uses the mind link after that, when it could have helped the alien stay out of trouble.) Elliott hides the alien in his home, sharing the secret with his younger sister, Gertie (Drew Barrymore), and older brother, Michael (Robert McNaughton), but keeping it from their divorced mom, Mary (Dee Wallace).

Building a satellite dish, the creature phones home for a ship to come and get it—but before the spacecraft arrives, mean authorities led by Keys (Peter Coyote) find E.T. Acting quickly, Elliott and his friends steal the truck carrying E.T., load the alien onto a two-wheeler, and form a bicycle motorcade to hurry the creature to the rendezvous site. The ship arrives, E.T. waddles aboard after a tearful farewell, and the vessel paints a rainbow in the sky as the ship darts away.

The rainbow is an inspired touch. So's a Halloween night out, with E.T. spotting a kid dressed like Yoda from *The Empire Strikes Back* (see *Star Wars*) and recognizing the fellow alien. And after all the contrived sentiment, there's the *genuinely* moving moment when the dog tries to leave with the departing E.T. The rest is just a space-Lassie film, with the same trite conventions done bigger and with more pretention. Americans took it to their bosom and made it the most successful film of all time ... but we're not to blame. Spielberg was smart enough to push all the right family-film buttons in his usual slick way. (When he tried again with the contemptible, condescending, and even more obvious *Hook* [1991], audiences stayed home.)

For most of the film, E.T. was actually one of two performers in a costume, two-foot-seven-inch Tamara de Treaux or two-foot-ten-inch Pat Bilson, with mechanical elements and robotic limbs created by Carlo Rambaldi (who constructed the lead alien in *Close Encounters of the Third Kind* [see page 52]). Legless teenager Matthew de Merritt got inside the costume and walked on his hands during the inebriation scene.

Incidentally, that's *This Island Earth* (1955) E.T. is watching after the Tom and Jerry cartoon. Now *that's* a science fiction film!

The Disc

Video: ★★
Audio: ★★★½ (Surround)
Chapters: No
Format: CLV or CAV
Source: MCA Home Video

Surprisingly, the disc is nothing to phone home about—considering what a stickler Spielberg is for the "artistic integrity" of his films on home video. Though the colors are moderately strong and the image is fairly sharp, there are varying levels of grain or mud or video noise in practically *every* shot, and some scenes are extremely dark.

The CAV edition is slightly punchier than the CLV version but not enough to justify the extra cost.

The letterboxed image captures all of the director's carefully planned widescreen designs.

The audio is crisp, with good stereo separation, though ambient sounds are minimal: Only John Williams's majestic score truly benefits from the rear channels.

Excalibur (1981) ★★★★½
Director: John Boorman
Running Time: 141 minutes

Morte d'Arthur by fifteenth-century author Sir Thomas Malory has become the definitive work on the legend of King Arthur. Written while the politically active Malory was in prison, it incorporated elements that had not been a consistent part of Arthurian tradition—such as the quest for the Holy Grail—and made them so. Though not reliable as history some eight hundred years after the fact, it is brilliant mythmaking.

The story of King Arthur has been told many times in motion pictures. Its most dreadful incarnation is *Knights of the Round Table* (1953), starring the woefully miscast Robert Taylor and Ava Gardner as Lancelot and Guinevere, with Mel Ferrer earnest as Arthur. It was the basis for Disney's *The Sword in the Stone* (1963), which recounts how Arthur learned about life by living it as a succession of different animals (!), and of course there's the musical *Camelot* (1967), starring Richard Harris as Arthur, Vanessa Redgrave as Guinevere, and Franco Nero as Lancelot, and *Monty Python and the Holy Grail* (1975), which is another herd of coconuts altogether.

John Boorman's *Excalibur* towers above them all, an alternately glittering and dark epic of human passions that covers English history from the rise and fall of Uther Pendragon (Gabriel Byrne) through the birth, rule, and death of his son, King Arthur (Nigel Terry). Along the way, it tells of Arthur's relationship with his wife, Guenevere (Cherie Lunghi), her infidelity with his bravest knight, Lancelot (Nicholas Clay), the plans of Arthur's wicked half sister Morgana (Helen Mirren) to usurp the throne for their son, Mordred (Robert Addie), the quest of Sir Perceval (Paul Geoffrey) for the Holy Grail, and the king's friendship with the quixotic wizard Merlin (Nicol Williamson).

That's an ambitious lot of story to tell, but Boorman pulls it off without seeming to cram it all in, and he works in several powerful themes to boot: the age of wizards giving way to the age of men, the king as the personification of the land and its people, and the search for the Grail as a spiritual quest. One of his few missteps is having the characters stop to *explain* these things: We got it, John.

A masterful visual stylist—Boorman also directed *Deliverance* (see page 64), *The Emerald Forest* (1985), and *Hope and Glory* (1987), as well as the turkeys *Zardoz* (1974) and *Exorcist II: The Heretic* (1977) —the director outdoes himself here. Shot in Ireland, the film alternates between moody medieval sets and landscapes and celestial images of gleaming armor, fiery skies, and a golden Camelot. Many of the images will take your breath away.

The cast is also perfect, and it's difficult to believe that Terry, the noble Arthur, is the same actor who played the sniveling Prince John in *The Lion in Winter* (1968). Williamson stirred some critical controversy with his glib, youthful Merlin, but it's a delightful, original interpretation that gives the film some pizzicato among all the otherwise-ominous bowings. Look for Liam Neeson (*Darkman*) and Patrick Stewart (*Star Trek: The Next Generation*) as Gawain and Leondegrance, respectively.

The Disc
Video: ★★
Audio: ★★★★ (monoaural)
Chapters: Yes
Format: CLV
Source: Warner Home Video

The orginal transfer didn't get the special handling it required, and was worth ★★. Far too many of the scenes were grainy, and details were lost in the shadows. The panning-and-scanning was well-done: you still lost portions of the picture—such as Perceval being scrolled off the left side of the screen when Arthur kills Mordred, but at least you got to see him standing there before the picture inches over to the combatants.

The newer, letterboxed transfer—to which the ratings above apply—is splendid. The picture is sharp, the colors are strong, and though grain is still a problem, it's a flaw inherent in the original print (i.e., the flung sword spinning toward the lake at the end).

The use of music by Wagner and Orff was inspired, and even viewers familiar with their works will find that *Excalibur* quickly makes them its own. The sound is terrific, and the rest of the audio is also powerful and clear. The original transfer is monaural, though it's extremely crisp.

The discs offer the original R-rated version, not the eviscerated PG cut, which loses, among other things, details of Arthur's conception.

Knights of the Round Table is available in a newly remastered letterboxed edition, which doesn't even have vivid color to recommend it. *Camelot* has also been remastered, wide-screen and looking (and sounding) very lovely indeed!

The Exorcist (1973) ★★★★
Director: William Friedkin
Running Time: 122 minutes

Actress Chris MacNeil (Ellen Burstyn) is shooting a movie at the Georgetown University campus when her twelve-year-old daughter, Regan (Linda Blair), becomes distant, then (apparently) mentally ill. Medicine and psychiatry are helpless to prevent Regan's physical and psychological deterioration, so her desperate mother contacts psychiatric counselor Father Damien Karras (Jason Miller). After interviewing the girl, Karras has good news and bad news for Chris: The good news is that she may be possessed by the devil. Karras recommends an exorcism and the church assigns veteran Father Merrin (Max von Sydow), with Karras assisting.

The men work long and hard over Regan (her raspy demon voice provided by actress Mercedes McCambridge): Merrin dies during the ordeal, and Karras finishes the job by taking the demon within himself and then committing suicide. (Or so it seems: See *The Exorcist II*.)

The Exorcist arrived on the heels of William Peter Blatty's huge best-seller (which was inspired by a real-life exorcism on a young boy in 1949). While patrons were busy fainting and even vomiting in theaters and moviemakers were grinding out cheap imitations such as *Abby* and *Beyond the Door*, psychologists were either deriding the film's graphic horror or explaining why it was cathartic for us.

Seen today, however, *The Exorcist* seems a lot tamer than it did before Freddy Krueger and Jason Voorhees began carving people up on Elm Street and at Crystal Lake. And some of the special effects—innovative then—are crude by contemporary standards. The movie still has that magnificent slow build, the many effective "boos," and its powerful exorcism. It also has a very moving performance by Miller and a deft, funny one by Lee J. Cobb as Lieutenant Kinderman, who's investigating a murder that may have been committed by Regan. Burstyn is also good, but her bitchy, prima-donna character is tough to like: Father Merrin should have tossed some holy water her way while he was busy exorcising demons.

Robbed of its ability to shock, and removed from the controversy and mass hysteria that possessed theatergoers, *The Exorcist* isn't nearly the ultimate horror show its reputation makes it out to be, however. (That honor still belongs to Robert Wise's brilliant 1963 film *The Haunting*, which is long overdue for a letterboxed laserdisc release.)

The Disc
Video: ★★
Audio: ★★ (Surround)
Chapters: Yes
Format: CLV (sides one and two), CAV (side three)
Source: Warner Home Video

See the photograph on the front of the jacket? That's approximately the quality of the color you'll find on this remastered disc. The film has gone brownish, and details are lost in shadows or washed out in daylight scenes (watch Karras's face go white, and not from fear, during his first meeting with Chris). Throughout, there are also slight but annoying color shifts from shot to shot—as when Kinderman and Karras first meet—and grain is a problem in numerous scenes.

The movie hasn't been letterboxed, which is a mistake. The sandstorm in Iraq just about fits on the screen, and there are times (as during that first Karras/Chris meeting) when the fronts of both faces barely get onto the screen. At least this remastered disc hasn't been time-compressed, as the original one was.

But if you think the picture's bad, try *listening* to what the characters are saying. To understand more than half of what Karras and his friend Father Dyer (Reverend William O'Malley) talk about in Karras's apartment, you'd better have the script in your lap. You'll have to crank up the treble to pick up the muffled dialogue.

The fine Surround effects are the only really strong aspect of the audio and they make some scenes even more effective than they were in theaters.

The Exorcist III (1990) ★★½
Director: William Peter Blatty
Running Time: 111 minutes

After the success of *The Exorcist*—both novel and movie—author Blatty resisted writing a sequel because he couldn't think of a way "the story might continue credibly." He had nothing to do with *Exorcist II: The Heretic* (1977), a visually stunning but dopey tale in which Father Lamont (Richard Burton) learns that young Regan MacNeil (Linda Blair) hasn't been entirely exorcised, so he undertakes to finish the job. (The movie is available as a Japanese import.)

Based on Blatty's 1983 novel *Legion*, *The Exorcist III* ignores the second film and picks up with Father Damien Karras (Jason Miller). It seems he didn't die after falling down the stairs, despite severe brain damage. And as punishment for his role in the exorcism, the devil allowed him to be possessed by the spirit of the newly executed Gemini Killer (Brad Dourif). Feigning amnesia, Karras was taken to a psychiatric ward, where the killer's spirit has spent fifteen years regenerating Karras's damaged brain cells. Now that that's done, the spirit goes out to murder just as Gemini did in the old days. And all the trapped spirit of Father Karras can do is sit and watch the horror.

George C. Scott gives one of his best performances in years as Gemini's old foe Lieutenant Kinderman (continuing the role Lee J. Cobb played in the first film). Ed Flanders is affecting and funny as his friend Father Dyer (another holdover from the original, Karras's clergyman friend played by Reverend William O'Malley in the original), and Brad Dourif shines—despite huge slabs of expository dialogue—as the killer. Miller doesn't have much to do except look pained, and both Nicol Williamson and Viveca Lindfors are wasted in small parts as the exorcist Father Morning and a possessed nurse. The late Colleen Dewhurst (the former Mrs. Scott) provides the voice of the disembodied spirit.

Blatty had previously directed *The Ninth Configuration* (1980), based on his novel *Twinkle, Twinkle, Killer Kane*—a seriocomic tale of a psychiatrist who is more troubled than his patients. His second film is ambitious, very well made, and frequently chilling. Bloodshed and shock effects are kept to a minimum until the climax, and there are many effective "boos." Unfortunately, the narrative is often confusing and the final showdown is a major letdown, coming on suddenly and ending quickly. You'll find yourself thinking back to the long, agonizing exorcism in the first film and wondering why Blatty decided to rush and skimp here, of all places.

The Disc
Video: ★★★★
Audio: ★★★★★ (Surround)
Chapters: Yes
Format: CLV
Source: CBS Fox Video

Since so much of this movie is anticipation of something happening, you'll be watching the screen closely, enjoying the crisp, relatively grain-free transfer and strong, stark colors. Though the movie is not letterboxed, nothing is missing (in the Cell 11 sequence, for example, both characters are still visible on opposite ends of the screen).

The digital audio is mesmerizing. The stereo is impressive, but the Surround is *truly* spectacular. It's fun but unobtrusive one moment—the bustle of the hospital or the circling of a helicopter, for example—then opens wide to swallow you whole whenever something demonic is in the offing.

The Ninth Configuration is available on laser, a very good transfer with fine digital sound.

Fame (1980) ★★½
Director: Alan Parker
Running Time: 134 minutes

Fame is one of those movies you'll like and admire, though you'll wish you could've *enjoyed* it more.

The movie doesn't so much have a plot as a direction, covering the lives of a group of students at New York City's High School for the Performing Arts, from audition to graduation. The students include ebullient, vulnerable Coco (Irene Cara), sensitive Montgomery (Paul McCrane), brash but secretly insecure Ralph (Barry Miller), cocky ace dancer Leroy (Gene Anthony Ray), high-tech innovator Bruno (Lee Curreri), and sheltered Doris (Maureen Teefy). Among the teachers are the thorny Shorofsky (Albert Hague) and the strong-willed Mrs. Sherwood (Anne Meara).

English director Parker came to movies via TV commercials and had previously made the all-kids gangster musical *Bugsy Malone* (1976) and the brutal *Midnight Express* (1978). *Fame* has the energy and charm of the first and the intensity of the second, but it's just too episodic to satisfy. Though the episodes are entertaining while they're happening—especially the cafeteria jam and the dancing-in-the-streets "Fame" number—and each of the kids has some powerful moments, there are so many characters that we don't always see how and why they grow—just that they have. Coco falling for a porn photographer's scam and Ralph's disastrous stand-up gig are the notable exceptions.

The film was the basis for the TV series, which aired from 1982 to 1987.

The Disc
Video: ★★★
Audio: ★★★★★ (Surround)
Chapters: Yes
Format: CLV
Source: MGM/UA Home Video

The movie looks like an overcast day in Manhattan, dark and monochromatic—which is as it should be. It's the kids who are colorful. Unfortunately, part of the look is intentional and part of it is grain, which even this recently remastered edition can't fix.

Minor letterboxing would have helped relieve the claustrophobia in some of the dance and classroom scenes, but the cropping isn't a serious drawback.

The audio, however, is exceptional. Everything from the subtlest sounds to the busiest orchestrations are wonderfully clear, and there are some startling directional and Surround effects.

The theatrical trailer is included.

Fantasia (1940) ★★★½

Directors: Samuel Armstrong (Bach's Toccata and Fugue in D Minor and the *Nutcracker* Suite); James Algar (*The Sorcerer's Apprentice*); Bill Roberts and Paul Satterfield (*The Rite of Spring*); Hamilton Luske, Jim Handley, and Ford Beebe (the *Pastoral* Symphony); T. Hee and Norman Ferguson (*Dance of the Hours*); Wilfred Jackson (*A Night on Bald Mountain* and "Ave Maria")
Running Time: 162 minutes

Fantasia came about due to a chance encounter between Walt Disney and conductor Leopold Stokowski in 1937. The famed conductor was dining alone at a restaurant when Disney invited him to his table to discuss a short subject he was planning featuring Mickey Mouse as the hero of composer Paul Dukas's *The Sorcerer's Apprentice*. Disney had been making musical cartoons for nearly a decade, since his adaption of Saint-Saëns's *Danse Macabre* as a "Silly Symphony" short, *The Skeleton Dance* in 1929. This one was planned to recapture Mickey's lost impishness and restore him to his former glory, his popularity having been overshadowed by the precocious Donald Duck.

Stokowski agreed to edit and conduct the score for *The Sorcerer's Apprentice*, and he also suggested several other classical pieces that would make excellent short subjects. Disney was receptive to the idea and, as the cost of the opulent *The Sorcerer's Apprentice* mounted, he decided to make several other shorts and string them together as a feature, which was the only way he'd ever make back what he was spending.

Disney never did anything half heartedly, however, and as soon as he was committed to the feature—which ended up costing a staggering $2.28 million—he began thinking of ways to make it a cinematic experience. There had been experiments in wide-screen processes—screens were still roughly square back then—and Disney explored using one of these. Unfortunately, while it was technically feasible, the cost of shooting the picture that way, not to mention replacing existing screens in movie theaters, made it impractical. However, his accountants could *not* talk him out of using a stereo process that his technicians came up with. Called Fantasound, it required the installation of a thirty-thousand dollar system in each theater showing the film. Only one dozen units were completed before the government—preparing for war—made it impossible to get components for the remaining sixty-four units he'd planned to construct. Ultimately, the pressure to recoup his investment without spending more money forced Disney to release the film using a normal sound track for all but a few key engagements.

While it was in production, *Fantasia* was known simply as *The Concert Feature;* it was given its release title by default when no one could think of a better one. And how did it fare? Disastrously. Because foreign markets were cut off by the onset of war, and because *Fantasia* was regarded as a highbrow entertainment, it did not make money during its initial release or even in subsequent reissues. It went through the roof only when acid-trippers and potheads of the late 1960s discovered its "psychedelic" pleasures. Disney (who died in 1966) did not live to see this happen. He summed up his feelings about the film in 1961, when it was still in the red: "We made it and I don't regret it. But if we had it to do all over again, I don't think we'd do it."

Summarizing the segments is pointless, though there are some facts worth mentioning.

- Johann Sebastian Bach's Toccata and Fugue was written for organ, and was transcribed for orchestra by Stokowski. This was a sentimental favorite for the conductor, who had began his career as a church organist.
- Tchaikovsky considered his *Nutcracker* ballet and the suite he created from it to be among his weaker works.
- *The Sorcerer's Apprentice* is

based on a tale first told by the Greek writer Lucian some two thousand years ago.
- *The Rite of Spring*—the only piece in the film by a then-living composer—did not please Igor Stravinsky. Stokowski had shortened and reorchestrated all of the film's selections. Upon hearing it, Stravinsky complained, "The horns play their glissandi an octave higher in the 'Danse de la Terre.' The order of the pieces had been shuffled, too, and the most difficult of them eliminated—though this did not save the musical performance, which was execrable." He categorized the animation as "unresisting imbecility." Nonetheless, he'd accepted Disney's payment of five thousand dollars and had no legal recourse against the studio.
- Beethoven wrote his *Pastoral* Symphony as a response to composer Justin Knecht's composition "A Musical Portrait of Nature," a popular piece that he loathed.
- In the *Pastoral* Symphony, look for the penciled guidelines in the sky in the first shot of the rainbow, indicating where the arc was to be laid down. (Cleaning the negative for its fiftieth anniversary reissue *did* have its drawbacks!)
- Though unnamed in the film, the solo ballerina who introduces *Dance of the Hours* is Mlle. Upanova; the prima ballerina is named Hyacinth Hippo; and her suitor is Ben Ali Gator.
- The version of *Night on Bald Mountain* used in the film is *nothing* like the Mussorgsky original, which was written for the ballet *Mlada*. Rather, it's based on Rimsky-Korsakov's orchestral tone poem, which used just a few passages from the original work. Stokowski cut it further, adding scratchy violins where they certainly do *not* belong.
- The actual Bald Mountain is located near Kiev; the demon in the film is named Tchernobog. Actor Bela Lugosi did some modeling for the animators working on the devil, though his poses weren't what they wanted and only a few hand gestures found their way into the film.
- The lyrics sung in the "Ave Maria" segment are not those of composer Schubert but were written for the film by novelist Rachel Field.
- Because of the film's high cost, one segment, featuring Debussy's *Claire de Lune*, was dropped, though it was finished and used as the *Blue Bayou* segment of *Make Mine Music* in 1946.
- The sections featuring the musicians and narrator Deems Taylor were the first live-action sequences ever shot for a Disney film. (Live-action footage had been shot to guide animators in previous films, but that footage was never incorporated into the finished product.) Ironically, the orchestra seen in these segments is not the one that performs in the film. These are Hollywood musicians; the score was recorded in Philadelphia by Stokowski's Philadelphia Orchestra.

All of which brings us to the question, How good *is* the film? It's been called a classic, the greatest animated film ever made, but those judgments are colored by the film's noble intentions and innovation. Stokowski very definitely defiled much of the music with his arrangements, and it can be argued that the images in many of the pieces do the same, most notably the ersatz geology lesson accompanying *The Rite of Spring*—which, in parts, moves as slowly as the evolving life-forms—and the dated Ivy League male centaurs and girl-next-door female centaurs in heat in the *Pastoral* Symphony. The "Ave Maria" segment is lovely to look at, but so's a Christmas card.

Having said that, there are many memorable segments as well, with *A Night on Bald Mountain* topping the list—chaos and evil never having been portrayed as effectively as they are here. The dinosaur segment of *The Rite of Spring* is also memorable, as is the storm sequence from the *Pastoral* Symphony. Despite a too-cutesy Mickey Mouse, *The Sorcerer's Apprentice* has its moments, and the "Chinese Dance," "Russian Dance," and "Waltz of the Flowers" make up for the rest of the boring *Nutcracker* Suite episode. These are moments that transcend both the desecration of the music and the very basic question of whether a classics-illustrated version of the music was needed at all.

In the souvenir program for the film's premiere, it said, "Note: From time to time the order and selection of compositions on this program may be changed." It was Disney's intent to constantly reshape the film, adding and deleting segments. That didn't happen during his lifetime, but it's going to happen now: *Fantasia Continued* will be released in 1996, with several new segments replacing old ones. The studio hopes that, at long last, this process will be ongoing.

The Disc
Video: ★★★★
Audio: ★★★★ (Surround)
Chapters: Yes
Format: CAV or CLV
Source: Walt Disney Home Video

The source for the transfer was a print struck from the film's original nitrate negative, which was cleaned and restored frame by frame for the film's fiftieth anniversary reissue. The print itself was made using a fine-grain film emulsion not available in 1941, making this, in many ways, the best version of *Fantasia* ever. For the transfer to disc, further color restoration was accomplished using Quantel's Harry Paint Box system. You can't fault the effort, even if the results aren't perfect.

The lines in the picture are generally supersharp—*The Sorcerer's Apprentice* is astounding—the colors are bright, and the original 1.33:1 aspect ratio has been retained. The only drawback is that many scenes are darker on disc than they were in the theaters, especially the "Arab Dance" sequence of the *Nutcracker* Suite and several shots in *A Night on Bald Mountain*. This will frustrate fans who were hoping for the ultimate *Fantasia*. The problem is the result of a tradeoff: In trying to keep the reds "down" and noise-free, portions of the picture came out dark.

Daylight scenes are generally vibrant, however; and given all the solid reds, blues, and so on, it's remarkable that there *isn't* any noise.

The original Fantasound stereo process was a Surround system in itself, recorded with thirty-three microphones. For the disc, a Dolby Surround duplicate of the original Fantasound separations was created using Stokowski's original guide sheets. The separation and Surround effects on the home version are very good. The sound *is* a bit raw in spots—for example, during the opening measures of the *Pastoral* Symphony—and the tracks have degenerated in a few places, with a noticeable loss of volume. But considering its age, the sound will still impress you.

The CAV set includes a lavishly illustrated commemorative program, a commemorative lithograph from *The Sorcerer's Apprentice* (could've lived without this kind of pointless bonus), a lengthy and informative CLV "making of" feature, and the original (CLV) theatrical trailer. *Missing* from the disc is the intermission, which occurred after *The Rite of Spring* only during the film's original release.

Although *Fantasia* is no longer officially available, many stores bought a large inventory of the title, as did some mail-order houses.

Far from the Madding Crowd (1967) ★★★
Director: John Schlesigner
Running Time: 169 minutes

Author Thomas Hardy was fascinated—preoccupied, in fact—with the contrasts of love, especially quiet devotion versus unbridled passion. Nowhere in his works is that theme better expressed than in his 1874 novel, *Far from the Madding Crowd*, which takes its title from poet Thomas Gray's "Elegy Written in a Country Churchyard" (1751).

The film follows the novel closely, the saga of young Bathsheba Everdene (Julie Christie), who inherits a farm in 1865. She spurns the advances of devoted, dependable shepherd Gabriel Oak (Alan Bates) and doting, wealthy neighbor Boldwood (Peter Finch) and marries dashing, impetuous soldier Francis Troy (Terence Stamp), who had abandoned his true love, Fanny Robin (Prunella Ransome), when she inadvertently showed up at the wrong church and left him standing at the altar. Months later, when Robin dies in childbirth, Troy is consumed with guilt; faking his own drowning, he leaves to join a circus. Boldwood resumes his wooing of Bathsheba, Gabriel continues to love her in silence—and, of course, Troy ultimately returns. One of her lovers dies, one ends up in prison for killing him, and she goes off with the survivor.

The film is *way* too long, largely because the director allows too many scenes to go on and on (Troy demonstrating his prowess with a sword, Gabriel curing the sheep, a cockfight, etc.). But the performances are all first-rate and the Dorset countryside is breathtaking. If it isn't *Doctor Zhivago*—which it was clearly trying to emulate, down to the casting of Christie—it is an historical soap opera with class.

The Disc
Video: ★★
Audio: ★★½ (Surround)
Chapters: No
Format: CLV
Source: MGM/UA Home Video

Undoubtedly, MGM/UA used the best print they could find, but while the source material is relatively free of dirt and scratches, the colors are badly faded. Only the reds have any zing, and they're fairly noisy. There's a fair amount of grain in many scenes, though the transfer is somewhat redeemed by a sharp picture and a generous letterbox.

The audio has a slight background hiss but is otherwise free of defects. The dialogue bleeds considerably into the rear speakers, making the Surround Sound more or less a duplication of what's up front.

A note to the makers of discs: Try not to choose photos—such as the one on the back of this jacket—that show one of the main characters' graves!

Fiddler on the Roof (1971)
★★★★
Director: Norman Jewison
Running Time: 180 minutes

There was an uproar in theater circles when it was announced that Israeli actor Chaim Topol would be starring as Tevye the milkman in the film adaptation of the Broadway hit *Fiddler on the Roof*. Zero Mostel had created the part in 1964, and he was certainly well known to moviegoers, thanks to starring roles in *A Funny Thing Happened on the Way to the Forum* (1966) and *The Producers* (see page 221). But the filmmakers felt that it would help overseas box office to have the star of the London stage version in the film, so the thirty-six-year-old Topol was cast, aged to look like the much older Tevye, a milkman in the Eastern European village of Anatevka.

Tevye lives at home with his wife, Golde (Norma Crane) and five daughters, the three eldest of whom are Tzeitel (Rosalind Harris), Hodel (Michele Marsh), and Chava (Neva Small). When the matchmaker Yente (Molly Picon) pairs Tzeitel with wealthy butcher Lazar Wolf (Paul Mann), the girl rebels, declaring to her shocked father that she would prefer to wed the poor tailor Motel (Leonard Frey). Reluctantly, Tevye bends tradition and allows his daughter to choose her husband. He bends it again when Hodel decides to marry anticzarist revolutionary Perchik (Michael—later Paul Michael—Glaser). However, when Chava falls in love with non-Jewish Fyedka (Raymond Lovelock), Tevye disowns her.

Shadowing and finally dominating these domestic matters is an increasingly virulent anti-Semitism, which ultimately destroys the village and scatters its inhabitants.

Tevye is the Jewish people personified, wrestling with problems of assimilation and diaspora, and Topol gives an alternately strong and compassionate performance, dominating the film with his vigor and that powerful voice. Though Mostel's overburdened but optimistic Tevye was closer in spirit to the character in the original stories by Yiddish author Sholem Aleichem, there is no denying the effectiveness of Topol's portrayal.

The rest of the cast is very good, and songs such as "Tradition," "If I Were a Rich Man," "Miracle of Miracles," "Sunrise, Sunset," and others retain their ability to stir despite too many years as Muzak fare.

The Disc

Video: ★★
Audio: ★★½ (Surround)
Chapters: Yes
Format: CLV
Source: MGM/UA Home Video

The film, which was shot on location in Lakenik, Yugoslavia, has a subdued color scheme that, on the big screen, was evocative of the hard life in Anatevka. In this letterboxed edition, the colors are drabber still, there's far too much grain, and the dark scenes are extremely muddy (for instance, the engagement scene at the tavern). The whites tend to bleed, especially on side four where there's a lot of snow and white skies.

The wide-screen presentation does, however, capture the beauty of the choreography, particularly during the "L'Chaim" and bottle dance numbers.

The jacket says Surround Sound, but you're basically getting the same rear-speaker stereo as you are in the front. The separation is very good, the music full-bodied and the voices and sound effects clear, but don't expect Fruma-Sarah's banshee wails to go washing over you as she swoops by.

The entr'acte and original theatrical trailer are included.

Field of Dreams (1989) ★★★½
Director: Phil Alden Robinson
Running Time: 106 minutes

Field of Dreams was inspired by author W. P. Kinsella's sentimental 1982 book *Shoeless Joe*, in which a voice like "that of a ballpark announcer" tells Iowa farmer Ray Kinsella, "If you build it, he will come"—"it" being a baseball diamond and "he" being "Shoeless" Joe Jackson, the Chicago White Sox left fielder dishonored for his part in allegedly throwing the 1919 World Series.

In the film as in the novel, Kinsella (Kevin Costner) plows under his cornfield to do as the voice asks. Though his wife, Annie (Amy Madigan), and the community think Kinsella's nuts, Jackson (Ray Liotta) does indeed show up—along with other members of the team. Unfortunately, Kinsella has no crops and no money, but, when foreclosure looms, the voice tells Ray, "Ease the pain," and he ends up in Boston, where he meets once-radical author Terence Mann (James Earl Jones; it was J. D. Salinger in the book). Together, the two get a third message, "Go the distance," and make their way to Minnesota, where they meet aged Archibald "Moonlight" Graham (Burt Lancaster), who had given up baseball to become a doctor. Driving back to Iowa, Ray and Terence meet Graham as a young man (Frank Whaley) and give him a lift.

Back in Iowa, Graham gets to fulfill his dream of playing against the pros, the jaded Terence has his faith restored, people with imagination see the baseball players play (everyone else sees nothing), the farm is saved, and Ray is reconciled with his father, John (Dwier Brown), who is also dead but shows up to play ball with his son.

Kinsella's book is terrific, full of wide-eyed wonder and glorious insights. The movie strives to equal it, but it is hamstrung by fits of mush and Kinsella's frenetic drive to solve the mystery of the ghostly messages. That it ultimately overcomes these pitfalls is due to the actors: Jones, who moves from grandiose self-importance to easy humor as the film progresses; Lancaster, who is modest, reflective, and very touching; Liotta, who captures Jackson's disciplined athleticism and offers a rhapsodic monologue about his beloved sport; and, of course, Costner.

Costner's got no range, but the effectiveness of the entire film hinges on the final line ("Dad . . . wanna have a catch?"). That Costner musters just enough emotion to sell it justifies the use of this bland performer.

Director John Sayles's excellent drama *Eight Men Out* (1988), about the scandal itself, is not available on either a domestic or imported laserdisc.

The Disc
Video: ★★★★
Audio: ★★½ (stereo)
Chapters: No
Format: CLV
Source: MCA Home Video

MCA has done a terrific job with the transfer. The colors are accurate and generally strong and the picture is sharp. Grain and noise are rarely a problem. The film was not a wide-screen film and nothing important is lost by the unobtrusive panning-and-scanning.

The sound is also very good, with James Horner's swelling Coplandesque score never overpowering the actors, and abundant richness in ambient detail. There is one problem, though: The stereo tracks are reversed, which is distracting enough that you'll want to switch some jacks before watching.

Fiend Without a Face (1958)
★★½
Director: Arthur Crabtree
Running Time: 75 minutes

At U.S. Air Force Interceptor Command Experimental Station #6 (there's a mouthful), located in Winthrop, Manitoba, Canada, the United States is experimenting with a new form of atom-powered radar intended for use in spying on Soviet missile launches. Meanwhile, people in the small town begin to die, their brains and spinal cords sucked from their bodies through two holes in the backs of their necks—which, rather improbably, the locals blame on the atomic reactor. Investigating the deaths, Maj. Jeff Cummings (Marshall Thompson) visits Barbara Griselle (Kim Parker), whose brother was the first victim. He also meets her employer, Professor R. E. Walgate (Kynaston Reeves), who's conducting research in telepathy. It turns out that while he was trying to stimulate his brain in order to give his thoughts physical form, Walgate diverted power from the reactor whenever it was in use. This power created beings able to exist independent of his brain, feeding on nuclear energy and also needing to drain human intellect in order to survive and reproduce.

While Walgate is busy confessing, the creatures attack his home. The size and shape of human brains, they use antennae to see and move, and they leap about by curling their spinal-cord attachments and pushing off. As townspeople and soldiers blast the fields, Cummings reaches the reactor, blows it up, and kills the monsters. (There's no mention of whether the town was obliterated by the radiation shower.)

Based on Amelia Reynolds Long's short story "The Thought Monsters" (published in 1930) and with more than a few ideas and visuals borrowed from *Forbidden Planet* (see page 102)—such as the reactor gauges lighting up as the creatures become more powerful—the movie is a mixed bag. There are some good ideas, but the script is uninspired. For instance, the filmmakers put their hero in a graveyard—what better place for a "boo" or two?—and then have none of the creatures show up. And there are some *really* silly parts, as when an officer offers Cummings a cigarette even though he's already smoking one. The acting's also nothing to write home about—Barbara was devoted to her brother, yet she sure seems chipper after his horrifying death—the sets look like cardboard, and there's too much padding—stock footage of jets zipping around and radars turning.

Fortunately, what one buys the disc to see—the monsters—doesn't disappoint. The creatures are primarily stop-motion models, animated by K. L. Ruppel in Germany (Ruppel apparently has no other science fiction film credits). Though the animation is crude, the creatures are eerie and effective: The slurping sounds they make when they move, the bloody messes they become when shot, and the lumpy pools they become at the end make them without a doubt *the* most wonderfully disgusting monsters of the era. And there may not be a more bizarre scene in movie history than when one of the mouthless creatures vainly tries to blow out the fuse on the dynamite being used to destroy the reactor.

Thompson, the only "name" actor in the film, had a successful career playing juvenile roles in the 1940s and early 1950s; he also appeared in the science fiction film *It! The Terror from Beyond Space* (1958; not available on laserdisc), which was the inspiration for *Alien* (1979), and he was Dr. Marsh Tracy on the TV series "Daktari."

The Disc
Video: ★★
Audio: ★½
Chapters: No
Format: CLV
Source: Republic Pictures Home Video

Though you can't expect *Fiend Without a Face* to look like *Citizen Kane*, this is still a disappointing disc. The first few minutes look awful, full of negative dirt and scratches; when that clears up, you're left with a print that's moderately soft, without rich blacks or clean whites. The forest sequence that ends side one is *way* too dark, though the climactic attack is in good shape. Indeed, it was foolish of Republic not to do the second side in CAV.

Though the dialogue and slurpy sounds are all very clear, there's a hiss on the sound track and an inherent tinniness that are worse than they should be. A fair amount of the dialogue sounds hollow and muffled, due to not terribly sophisticated recording during the making of the film.

First Men in the Moon (1964)
★★★
Director: Nathan Juran
Running Time: 104 minutes

Special effects artist Ray Harryhausen — *Twenty Million Miles to Earth* (see page 286); *Jason and the Argonauts* (see page 153) and *The Golden Voyage of Sinbad* (see page 112)—had long wanted to film H. G. Wells's 1901 novel *First Men in the Moon*. However, according to Harryhausen, his producer, Charles H. Schneer, felt that "Inasmuch as people were planning to go to the moon in a very short space of time, it would no longer be as shocking a thing as it was in the Victorian period." The duo began preparing Wells's 1901 novel *Food of the Gods* for the screen instead, when scriptwriter Nigel Kneale came up with a framing story for the moon tale that would prevent it from becoming outdated when men actually did land on the moon.

In the present day, a United Nations lander sets down on the moon. As the international crew explores the lunar surface, they find artifacts from the year 1899 (rotted . . . on the airless moon?) and trace their owner, Arnold Bedford (Edward Judd), to a nursing home in England. He tells the investigators how, in 1899, the scientist Joseph Cavor (Lionel Jeffries) invented an antigravity paint that took the two of them and Bedford's fiancée, Kate Callender (Martha Hyer), to the moon. The trio encountered a race of antlike beings known as Selenites, ruled by the wise and all-powerful Grand Lunar. Horrified by the human capacity for violence, the Selenites didn't want the terrestrials to leave, lest others follow and bring warfare to the moon. Ultimately, Bedford and

Callender managed to escape, though Cavor remained behind.

After Bedford recounts his tale, TV cameras with the UN crew capture their discovery of crumbling ruins, all that's left of the Selenite civilization, which was destroyed by the cold germs Cavor had brought with him from earth.

The film takes a few liberties with the original story: For example, Wells didn't include a woman in the journey, and the Selenites kill Cavor in the novel so the secret of Cavorite will die with him. But otherwise, it's quite faithful and, except for its scientific naïveté—sound in space, a muddy lunar surface (the water is *where?*), decay on the moon, normal gravity in the spaceships that land there, and so on—the movie is a charmer.

The performances are perfect—especially that of Jeffries—the sets are magnificent, and Harryhausen's special effects generally work. The spaceflight scenes aren't as convincing as they seemed in 1964, and the children wearing Selenite costumes are only moderately successful, but the Grand Lunar is as eerie an alien as you'll ever encounter, the giant insectlike "moon cows" are impressive, and the actors are expertly composited with the miniature sets. The score by Laurie Johnson is one of the unheralded masterpieces of the genre.

Peter Finch not only has a cameo, he has his own chapter stop!

The Disc
Video: ★★★★
Audio: ★★★★ (monaural)
Chapters: Yes
Format: CLV (side one), CAV (sides two and three)
Source: Pioneer Special Edition

You couldn't ask for a more colorful transfer. Although the image isn't always razor-edged, that's due more to the techniques used to create the special effects than to the condition of the print (which happens to be very good). The fairy-tale colors on the moon—with its giant crystals, bubbling liquids, and multihued creatures—are captured to perfection. The letterboxing is essential: This was Harryhausen's first wide-screen film, and he put interesting objects and life-forms in every corner of the screen.

Sound is important to the atmosphere of the film, from the thudding landing of Cavor's ship to the whispering voice of the Grand Lunar, and the digital audio does it justice. The dynamic range isn't as wide as the brassier sections of the score demand, but that's a relatively minor drawback. There is no background noise.

Unfortunately, the jacket art commissioned for the disc is amateurish—simply terrible. Why don't these people wise up and go to competent paperback artists who *know* the genre, be it science fiction, western, or war?

A Fish Called Wanda (1988)
★★★★★
Director: Charles Crichton
Running Time: 108 minutes

George Thomason (Tom Georgeson—no kidding!) is the leader of a gang that commits a successful jewel heist. Two of the gang members—Wanda Gershwitz (Jamie Lee Curtis) and her lover, Otto (Kevin Kline), turn him in so they can keep the take for themselves, after which Wanda intends to steal Otto's share. Only Ken (Michael Palin) remains loyal to George.

Unfortunately, before he was arrested, George rehid the gems, and Wanda tries to find out where by cozying up to George's barrister, Archie Leach (John Cleese, adopting Cary Grant's real name). Locked in a stale marriage, Archie is receptive to her advances, drawing Otto's insane jealousy. As for Ken, he's got his hands full trying to kill elderly Eileen Coady (Patricia Hayes), the only witness to George's involvement in the crime. And that's just the first *third* of the film! It gets more complicated still.

With former Monty Pythonites Cleese (who wrote the screenplay) and Palin on board, bad taste is to be expected and the film does not disappoint. Ken is the brunt of countless cruel barbs because of his stuttering; dogs and fish are slaughtered (including the fish of the title, who plays a key role in the plot); coitus interruptus is the order of the day; Otto is invigorated by the smell of his own armpits; and the language is particularly colorful.

Don't be put off, though: The movie is a riot from start to finish, with original and quirky characters, brilliantly witty dialogue, nifty plot twists, and perfect performances; Kline gives one of the most manically comic performances *ever*, and you'll go back to the disc over and over just to savor his unbridled madness. (And in case you were wondering, the spelling of his CIA alias is Manfredjinsinjen.)

A Fish Called Wanda is reminiscent of the sharp, snappy comedies produced at the English Ealing Studios between 1938 and 1959. These included many of director Crichton's films, most significantly *The Lavender Hill Mob* (1951), starring Alec Guinness as Holland, a quiet bank clerk, who enlists a souvenir manufacturer and a pair of crooks to help him steal bullion and smuggle it in the form of small, tacky souvenir Eiffel Towers. As with George's gang, nothing goes right. The film is not available on laserdisc.

The Disc
Video: ★★★½
Audio: ★★★½ (monaural)
Chapters: Yes
Format: CLV
Source: CBS Fox Video

The image is not quite as sharp as it should be, and there's a bit of video noise in the reds and browns, but the colors are strong and there's not a great deal of grain. Though the film isn't letterboxed, the action is centered and nothing is lost.

The sound is very clear, and you won't have a problem with the British accents.

Five Easy Pieces (1970) ★★★★
Director: Bob Rafelson
Running Time: 98 minutes

Jack Nicholson got the role of drunken lawyer George Hanson in *Easy Rider* (1969) after Rip Torn dropped out. The film ended Nicholson's long tenure in grade-Z movies that began with *The Cry Baby Killer* (1958) and included *The Little Shop of Horrors* (1960), *The Terror* (1963), and *Hell's Angels on Wheels* (1967). After *Easy Rider*, he did *On a Clear Day You Can See Forever* for the money, then teamed with friend Rafelson—with whom he cowrote *Head* (see page 134)—to make *Five Easy Pieces*.

Nicholson stars as Los Angeles oil-rig worker Bobby Eroica Dupea, who lives with waitress Rayette Dipesto (Karen Black) and has nothing to look forward to but bowling with coworker Elton (Billy "Green" Bush) and going to motels with nymphs like Betty (Sally Ann Struthers). When Elton is arrested for having jumped bail, Dupea decides to drive to Seattle to visit his father, who has recently suffered a stroke. Once there, he cavorts with his brother's fiancée, Catherine Van Ost (Susan Anspach), but he isn't any happier in his family's upper-class world than he was with his own blue-collar life. Ultimately, he chucks it all—including Rayette—and hitches a ride to Alaska.

The film was written by Adrien Joyce (aka Carol Eastman), a friend of Nicholson's who wrote the role specifically for the actor, basing the famous diner scene (in which Bobby tries, in vain, to order a side of wheat toast) on a confrontation Nicholson had had with a waitress in Pupi's on Sunset Strip. Nicholson—who improvised Bobby's remarkable speech to his paralyzed father—says that the part was autobiographical in many ways and that "in playing the character, I drew on all the impulses and thoughts I had during those years when I was having no real acceptance."

Five Easy Pieces isn't a perfect film. As a product of the sixties, it's self-consciously meaningful (Betty's dimple story tries to explain too much in a contrived little fable) and it drags (Bobby doesn't want the kind of home life Elton has, a point that is made and remade). But it's full of real insights as well, conveyed by remarkable performances. Nicholson's work is subtle, affecting, and tragic, a reminder of how good he was before films such as *The Shining* (see page 248), *The Witches of Eastwick* (1987), and *Batman* (see page 19) turned him into a raving self-parody. Black is also excellent, as is Helene Kallianiotes as Palm Apodoca, the militant lesbian hitchhiker Bobby picks up on the way to Puget Sound.

The heading of chapter twenty on the jacket should clarify the title for those who don't get it.

The Disc
Video: ★★★
Audio: ★★★ (monaural)
Chapters: Yes
Format: CLV
Source: Criterion Collection

There's mild grain throughout the film, and the image is on the soft and slightly reddish side. But keeping in mind that this was a low-budget film made at a time when color stock was cheap and impermanent, it looks better than it has a right to.

The letterboxing is mild, and flaws in the source material are very minimal.

The audio is somewhat rough and hollow, due to the film's low production values. But everything is audible and the sound fits the look of the film.

The Flame and the Arrow (1950) ★★★½
Director: Jacques Tourneur
Running Time: 88 minutes

Burt Lancaster is one of the rare movie stars who has done everything—action, drama, comedy—and, more importantly, has done it all well.

Fine as he was in films such as *From Here to Eternity* and *Elmer Gantry* (see pages 105 and 82), fans cherish his two swashbucklers above all. In *The Flame and the Arrow* and *The Crimson Pirate* (1952), the former circus acrobat did all of his own stunts and flashed more teeth than any actor in history. Even Errol Flynn wasn't as flamboyant as Lancaster, whose style here is more reminiscent of Douglas Fairbanks, Sr. (a childhood hero of Lancaster's).

The Flame and the Arrow is the better of the two films, a *Robin Hood*-like epic set in medieval Lombardy about the efforts of mountain man Dardo the Arrow (Lancaster) to reclaim his son, Rudi (Gordon Gebert), who's been kidnapped by the evil Hessian invader Ulrich (Frank Allenby). The first-rate cast also features Robert Douglas as the traitorous Alessandro (see *The Adventures of Don Juan*), a ravishing Virginia Mayo as Dardo's love interest, Anne (Ulrich's niece), and Lancaster's old circus crony Nick Cravat as Piccolo. The dazzling stunts by these two cry out for repeated viewings.

To prove to the press and moviegoers that he'd actually *done* his own stunts, movie newcomer and coproducer Lancaster toured with the film, recreating many of the feats. As he quipped at the time, "I've got a couple thousand bucks in that picture. What's a neck?"

The Crimson Pirate features similar stunt work, Lancaster playing Captain Vallo, leader of a pirate band that helps lead a revolt against Spanish tyranny in the Caribbean. Lancaster and Cravat are as good as in the earlier film, though the story and action drift farther into parody than *The Flame and the Arrow*. (There is, however, the scene-stealing performance by Torin Thatcher as a sarcastic pirate.)

The Disc
Video: ★½
Audio: ★★★ (monaural)
Chapters: No
Format: CLV
Source: Warner Home Video

Damn shame that this is not a better disc! The colors are reddish and the picture dark, spoiling many of the gorgeous night scenes, particularly those set in Dardo's forest camp. It's still well worth owning, but you'll wish Warner had treated this treasure with greater respect.

The audio is much better, with only faint background noise. Unlike *The Crimson Pirate*, the musical score in *The Flame and the Arrow* is nothing to write home about.

The picture on *The Crimson Pirate* is considerably brighter, though night scenes and interiors are still darker than they should be.

Flatliners (1990) ★★½
Director: Joel Schumacher
Running Time: 111 minutes

Nelson (Kiefer Sutherland) is a medical student who, like the guy staring up at Clint Eastwood's gun in *Dirty Harry*, just *gots* to know what death is all about. He figures he can find out by dying for a minute or two and having another student revive him before he *stays* dead. Nelson convinces fellow students Rachel (Julia Roberts), Labraccio (Kevin Bacon), Joe (William Baldwin), and Steckle (Oliver Platt) to go along with his scheme. But things get out of hand. Like contestants in a Bizarro-world game of "Name That Tune," each student wants to stay dead *longer* than the one before, making it tougher to bring them back.

Great premise, but what do these precocious kids find on the other end of the River Styx? Nothing more profound than unpleasant events from their past, things that traumatized them and made them feel guilty. The participants in these events come back with them into their real lives, and the students must find ways to atone before the demons beat them silly or make them crazy: Rachel finds her suicidal father; Labraccio, a black girl she used to tease; Nelson, a kid he accidentally killed; and Joe, the girls he has secretly videotaped during sex.

There are quantum physicists who believe that time is a stream flowing in both directions, that our lives are loops and that we drop back into some earlier part when we die—either a good part (heaven) or a bad part (hell). That's an intriguing premise, but the director does nothing with it. All he's done is make a gothic and atmospheric horror film (shot mostly at the University of Chicago) with an existential twist.

Flatliners is kept moving by uniformly strong performances, with Bacon a standout. (It's also the film where Sutherland and Roberts met, spawning a horror story of a *different* sort.)

Director Schumacher also made the superior vampire film, *The Lost Boys* (1987). See also *Jacob's Ladder*, which covers some of the same ground far more effectively.

The Disc
Video: ★
Audio: ★★★★½ (Surround)
Chapters: No
Format: CLV
Source: RCA/Columbia Pictures Home Video

With its saturated colors, especially blues, this film was clearly a technician's nightmare. Unfortunately, RCA/Columbia hasn't risen to the challenge. There's color noise all over the place, limiting image sharpness to the few scenes in which colors don't bleed all over (there's more noise on side one than two, but just barely).

The film is letterboxed, though it cheats somewhat to lessen the matte: The edges of the pictures are missing. Though no information is lost, it costs the characters a little breathing space.

The audio is far more satisfying, with eerie effects and booming Surround. Schumacher would've made a great radio director.

Forbidden Planet (1956) ★★★★
Director: Fred McLeod Wilcox
Running Time: 99 minutes

There would not have been a "Star Trek" if there hadn't been *Forbidden Planet*.

Not only did *Forbidden Planet* prove that a planet's surface could be created convincingly on a soundstage, it took a workaday approach to technology, transplanted the naval hierarchy to space, placed the stargoing humans under the aegic of a peaceful "federation," and presented an antagonist that's far afield from the typical bug-eyed outer space monsters of films that had preceded it. The monster in *Forbidden Planet* is a monster of the mind, and its trigger—megalomania and suppressed (?) incest—paved the way for the semi-adult science fiction of "Star Trek" a decade later. Not-so-coincidentally, *Forbidden Planet* is set in the twenty-third century of the original series "Star Trek."

United Planets Cruiser C-57-D arrives at the planet Altair-4 to find out what has happened to the research ship *Bellerophon*, which was sent there twenty years earlier. The C-57-D crew—led by Comdr. John J. Adams (Leslie Nielsen) and Lt. C. X. "Doc" Ostrow (Warren Stevens)—finds only two people on the planet: Dr. Edward Morbius (Walter Pidgeon) and his daughter, Altaira "Alta" (Anne Francis). The two live in extreme comfort, assisted by their powerful robot, Robby (voice by Marvin Miller). Morbius explains that the rest of the *Bellerophon* crew was slaughtered by a planetary force when they tried to leave: Only he and his wife, since deceased, were spared.

When Adams refuses to leave the planet and, further, romances pretty, naïve Alta, the planetary force returns: a huge lionlike creature that repeatedly attacks C-57-D. Adams and Doc visit Morbius, looking for answers, and are taken on a tour of the incredible machinery built by a civilization known as the Krel, which perished in a single night twenty centuries before. In time, Adams discovers why: The Krel had constructed a machine that creates matter by mere thought and, unwittingly, they used it to project subconscious hatred all across the planet. "Monsters from the Id" slew the Krel. Now, thanks to the machine, Morbius is sending out his own Id Monster to destroy the people who threaten his empire (as his fellow settlers had) ... and his daughter. Morbius confronts the monster and is destroyed by it.

Forbidden Planet is loosely based on Shakespeare's *The Tempest*, with Morbius/Prospero, Alta/Miranda, Robby/Ariel, and the Id Monster/Caliban. At the time when the idea was presented to MGM, science fiction films tended to be sensational, low-budget affairs. However, the studio liked the concept for what was then known as *Fatal Planet*, and budgeted it at just under $1 million—four times higher than most films of this type. By the time it was finished, the film cost $1.9 million, a big chunk of which was eaten up by the special effects. These included cartoon animation of the Id Monster created by Walt Disney animators, headed by Joshua Meador. (Disney loved science fiction films and was happy to rent out his artists.)

Surprisingly few aspects of the film are dated, and some are remarkably prophetic, such as the filament-thin camera. The performances are relaxed and realistic, the electronic score is evocative, and the sets and special effects are still wondrous. The tour of the underground Krel complex looks cartoony, but it very definitely creates an impression of size, and the Id Monster's final attack on the ship, with the invisible creature outlined in the beams of the electric fence, is mesmerizing. That the film lost the special effects Oscar to *The Ten Commandments* was due to the Cecil B. DeMille publicity juggernaut and not to lact of merit.

The Disc

Video: ★★★★★ (Criterion); ★★½ (MGM/UA)
Audio: ★★★★★ (stereo; Criterion); ★★ (stereo, MGM/UA)
Chapters: Yes (Criterion)
Format: CAV (Criterion); CLV (MGM/UA)
Source: Criterion or MGM/UA Home Video

First, forget about the old pan-and-scan release. The movie is hash in that format. One of the two letterboxed releases, the MGM/UA edition offers the advantage of being one-third the price. The *disadvan-*

tage is that to lessen the letterbox, the company has lopped off the extreme sides of the image and opened up the safety area, exposing a large number of splice marks in the early stages. If you just want to see the film, that's the one to buy. But if you're a fan, or if you really want to appreciate *Forbidden Planet*, the Criterion version is a must.

The picture on the Criterion version is considerably more solid and three-dimensional than its counterpart, though the colors of both versions are as full and beautiful as the usually weak Eastman Color will allow: At times, you'll feel as though you can walk right into the picture. The images on the two releases are extremely sharp, though the MGM/UA edition has a fair amount of video noise. Criterion's edition has insignificant levels of noise and grain.

The stereo sound on the Criterion version is also much fuller and completely free of extraneous noise. If you've never heard the film in stereo, the power of the separations will startle you. Perfect CAV frames on the Criterion edition will allow you to study the monster, the Krel artifacts, the other special effects, and—perhaps most disappointingly—Anne Francis's bodysuit when she's supposedly skinny-dipping.

However, the most important plus on the Criterion disc are the extras. There are cut scenes, different versions of scenes in the film, voice tests for the robot and Id Monster, a look at footage *before* the special effects had been added, the original screen treatment, and much, much more. For a fan, these alone justify the high price tag.

Contrary to what the jacket says, the correct spelling is Krel.

Frankenstein (1931) ★★★★
Director: James Whale
Running Time: 71 minutes

The advent of high-tech filmmaking has upped the levels of shock gore considerably, and contemporary fans tend to dismiss pre-1970s thrillers as creaky and ineffective. (See *Phantom of the Opera*.) *Frankenstein* is a powerful exception, and those who have seen it do not speak condescendingly of it.

In 1818, Mary Wollstonecraft Shelley published her novel *Frankenstein, or the Modern Prometheus*, about a Swiss scientist, Victor Frankenstein, who uses corpses to create an artificial eight-foot-tall creature whose "yellow skin scarcely covered the work of muscles and arteries beneath." After roaming, misunderstood, on the fringes of society, the disconsolate creature strands himself on an Arctic ice floe.

In the 1931 film, Dr. Henry Frankenstein (Colin Clive) cobbles his creature together from the bodies of the dead, accidentally provides him with a *disfunctio cerebri*, which his inept aide, Fritz (Dwight Frye), had stolen in lieu of a normal brain, and brings him to life with lightning. Fleeing, the Monster accidentally drowns a little girl, Maria (Marilyn Harris), when he innocently tosses her in a lake to watch her float like a flower. He is pursued by angry villagers and eventually cornered in a windmill, which is burned to the ground. (The monster, however, doesn't die: he returns in *The Bride of Frankenstein*, 1935.)

Bela Lugosi, who had made a powerful impression as the stage and screen Dracula, was originally slated to play the Monster. However, he back out when he discovered that, unlike the novel, the part had no dialogue. Enter the forty-four-year-old Karloff, a former truck driver and bit player whose career was made by the success of the film. Karloff did more fine work in the horror field than any other actor; he was able to elicit audience understanding and sympathy even in the most villainous of roles, and no amount of makeup—whether as the Frankenstein Monster, the Mummy, the Ghoul, or in any other parts—could conceal those expressive eyes and hands.

Colin Clive's lunatic enthusiasm also contributes a great deal to the effectiveness of *Frankenstein*. He mined the Gothic vein further in *The Bride of Frankenstein* and *Jane Eyre* (1934); he died in 1937 at the age of thirty-nine. Mae Clarke, who plays Henry's fiancée, Elizabeth, had little to do in this film; she made a much greater impact the same year getting a grapefruit in the face from James Cagney in *The Public Enemy*.

And, of course, there's Jack Pierce's classic makeup. Pierce was one of the true geniuses of the genre; though he died a forgotten man, his work in the Universal horror films will never be forgotten. His Monster, Wolf Man, and Mummy are the definitive versions of these creatures.

After *The Bride of Frankenstein*—a brilliant work, in which Henry (Clive) and his insane ally Dr. Septimus Pretorious (Ernest Thesiger) create a female companion (Elsa Lanchester) for the Monster (Karloff)—Universal gave us *Son of Frankenstein* (1939)—with Karloff's last portrayal of the monster, Basil Rathbone as Wolf von Frankenstein, and Bela Lugosi's immortal work as Ygor—*The Ghost of Frankenstein* (1942), *Frankenstein Meets the Wolf Man* (1943), *House of Frankenstein* (1944), *House of Dracula* (1945), and *Abbott and Costello Meet Frankenstein* (see page 1). Only the first three films and the last are available on laserdisc.

The Disc

Video: ★★½
Audio: ★
Chapters: Yes
Format: CLV (side one), CAV (side two)
Source: MCA/Universal Home Video

Although there are some splices, skipped frames, and bits of negative dirt, it's unlikely—and sad—that there probably will never be a better version of this film. The contrast is okay—no more. However, the quality of the movie itself, and the famous restoration (a 16mm insertion in the 35mm print) of the monster's playful drowning of little Maria, makes this a must-have title.

The audio track is even worse than the picture, with extensive clicks and pops, some warbling, and an overall thinness (a result of the early sound recording).

The supplemental material is fairly good, though, and includes a trailer and seventy-seven stills. There are repeats of seven major sections of the movie on the jitter-free CAV side, for closer examination.

From Here to Eternity (1953)
★★★★
Director: Fred Zinnemann
Running Time: 118 minutes

Author James Jones drew upon his own war experiences to write his first novel, *From Here to Eternity* (1951), a once-controversial work of power, sexuality, and frank language. (The title was taken from the phrase in Kipling's poem "Gentlemen Rankers," "damned from here to eternity.") Though director Zinnemann (*High Noon* [1952]) brought the burning passions of the best-seller down to a steamy smoulder, they were still pretty hot for the time. While tame by today's standards, the film remains a fascinating character study.

After being replaced as first bugler by a friend of the topkick, Pvt. Robert E. Lee Prewitt (Montgomery Clift) transfers from the bugle corps to the rifle outfit of Capt. Dana Holmes (Philip Ober). Unfortunately, Holmes expects Prewitt to box for him; when he refuses, the captain leans on him. This earns Prewitt the sympathy of Lorene (Donna Reed), a "bad girl" who works at a local soldiers' club, and spunky Angelo Maggio (Frank Sinatra), who has his *own* problems with the sadistic Sgt. "Fatso" Judson (Ernest Borgnine). Sgt. Milton Warden (Burt Lancaster) also feels badly for Prewitt, though he's more interested in wooing Holmes's wife, the beautiful but distant Karen (Deborah Kerr).

Despite the loss of some minor players and detail (the novel is over eight hundred pages long), the characters are fully sketched and their stories skillfully interwoven.

Clift is sturdy but limited by the unflappable righteousness of his character, and he's dominated by his costars. Lancaster has a quiet disdain for officers in general and Holmes in particular, but he serves with respect and propriety. Thus, when he lets himself go—whether making love to Kerr on the beach, standing up to Fatso, or fighting the Japanese—his sense of liberation is palpable. (Incidentally, Lancaster was once asked whether the sand caused any problems during the legendary beach scene. He replied, "Well, there was sand on Deborah's lips, but I'll tell you—it tasted like sugar to me.")

Donna Reed, a farm-raised beauty who had played wholesome young ladies since 1941, is the most convincing prostitute with a heart of gold you'll ever see. She alternates between bitterness, drive, and compassion with an intensity that will surprise those who know her only as one of TV's most famous moms.

From Here to Eternity was a comeback vehicle for Frank Sinatra, who had suffered a hemorrhage of the vocal cords in 1952. He pursued the part of Maggio vigorously, winning it over Eli Wallach—whom the director preferred—by agreeing to take a "slap in the face" fee of eight thousand dollars; Sinatra even abandoned his wife, Ava Gardner, on location in Africa to submit to a humiliating screen test. (This is the role that inspired the famous "horse head in the bed" sequence in *The Godfather*.)

Lancaster and Kerr also won their roles after others had abandoned them. Robert Mitchum couldn't come to terms with Columbia and bowed out; Joan Crawford was slated to play Karen but argued with the studio over her costumes.

One actor did not fare so well: Look for TV's Man of Steel George Reeves in a small part. The actor's role was originally larger, but preview audiences muttered, "There's Superman," and most of his scenes were deleted.

The film was remade as a limp TV movie in 1979, which became a short-lived TV series.

The Disc
Video: ★★
Audio: ★★ (monaural)
Chapters: No
Format: CLV
Source: Columbia Pictures Home Video

This a film seriously in need of remastering. The contrast in the black and white source material is okay, but it's not nearly as vivid as it should be. The night scenes—never terribly strong in the movie, many of them having been filmed "day for night" using filters—are especially gray. The transfer is moderately sharp, and the print is largely unblemished.

The nondigital sound isn't awful, but it's no better than on the videotape version: On disc, those ocean waves should sound like thunder and the attack on Pearl Harbor should reverberate. All of the dialogue is clear, despite a low, pervasive hiss and general tinniness.

Full Metal Jacket (1987) ★★★
Director: Stanley Kubrick
Running Time: 117 minutes

Though *Full Metal Jacket* is set in Vietnam, it illuminates that conflict far less than other films on the subject, such as the underrated *Go Tell the Spartans* (1978) or the wildly overrated *Platoon* (1986). Instead, Kubrick use the subject of Vietnam to wrestle, yet again, with the themes of war and dehumanization (see *Dr. Strangelove* and *A Clockwork Orange*).

Based on Gustav Hasford's novel *The Short Timers*, the film is divided into two sections, following Private "Joker" (Matthew Modine) through basic training on Parris Island, then through his stint as a *Stars and Stripes* reporter in Vietnam, where he's present for the Tet Offensive and a long, agonizing shootout in Hue City. Basic training is by far the strongest section, due to the performances of real-life drill sergeant Lee Ermey as Sergeant Hartman, and Vincent D'Onofrio as Private "Gomer Pyle," a slow-witted recruit whose beating at the hands of his fellow soldiers and final confrontation with Hartman are scenes you won't soon forget.

Things slow down in Vietnam until the last third of the movie, when a sniper holds Joker's platoon at bay. The horror and intensity of the scene is underscored by Kubrick's unmatched ability to move a camera, making the viewer very much a part of the action. But the film ends without resolving or even illuminating the fascinating duality of Joker (i.e., of us all): He's a man of peace who has just fought like hell, and he's going out to fight some more.

In addition to being unfinished and unfocused, the script is full of unresolved themes (the gun/manhood relationship, carefully developed in the first half, is dropped completely in the second) and is frustratingly episodic, with scenes fading out rather than ending. Unlike Kubrick's masterful *Paths of Glory* (1957), in which World War I is the background for a story about treachery and scapegoating, *Full Metal Jacket* serves up the director's observations without the glue of a strong narrative.

A notorious nontraveler, Kubrick had palm trees brought to England and shot the "location" scenes on the outskirts of London. Hue City looks more like Stalingrad with fronds, alas.

The Disc
Video: ★★½
Audio: ★★★ (monaural)
Chapters: No
Format: CLV
Source: Warner Home Video

The picture is generally bright and sharp, but the vivid colors are too often compromised by a light coat of grain. And the grain is inconsistent: Some nighttime scenes are window-clear, while many daylight scenes are not. There's also an abundance of video noise, from the sunset in basic training to the fires in Hue City. Some scenes even suffer from *flesh-tone* noise.

Though the film isn't severely hurt by the lack of a matte—Kubrick hasn't shot anything *really* wide-screen since *2001: A Space Odyssey*—the dehumanization stressed by long corridors or tight enclosures or blasted battlefields is somewhat undermined by cropping.

The audio is clear and full-bodied, solid if unspectacular in the upper and lower ranges.

Gandhi (1982) ★★★★
Director: Richard Attenborough
Running Time: 187 minutes

For twenty years, former actor Attenborough (*The Great Escape*) had been trying to put the life of Gandhi on the screen. Alec Guinness had always been attached to the project, but by the time Attenborough was finally able to put it together—raising $20 million from independent investors and another $7 million from the Indian government—Guiness was too old. The director turned to stage actor Ben Kingsley, whose only previous film had been the disastrous 1972 adaptation of Alistair MacLean's *Fear Is the Key*.

What a choice. Like Peter O'Toole as T. E. Lawrence or F. Murray Abraham as Salieri, it's one of those rare and exciting unions of the actor and the part he was born to play. Half-Indian and born Krishna Banji, Kingsley brought dignity, vulnerability, and humor to the part, which he prepared for each day by learning his lines and then meditating in his hotel room, surrounded by pictures of Gandhi.

Mohandas Karamchand Gandhi—called Mahatma ("great-souled")—was a lawyer trained in England, and the film begins with his arrival in South Africa in 1893, where he helped win political rights for Indian settlers. It was there that Gandhi first advocated the use of nonviolent resistance, and to great effect. Though he supported the British during World War I, he turned on them thereafter, forming the Satyagraha movement, which employed a policy of passive resistance intended to paralyze the nation and force the British out. The film touches the major points of his crusade and ends with his assassination in 1948.

The film unfolds at a slow, careful pace—but after two decades of trying, one could hardly blame Attenborough for wanting to leave nothing out. And though the precise nature of some of the political entanglements is confusing, the literate, sensitive script never fails to communicate the essence of what's going on.

In addition to Kingsley's uncanny performance, the film features Candice Bergen as famed photographer Margaret Bourke-White, Martin Sheen as the American journalist Walker, and a supporting cast of superb British actors—Trevor Howard, John Mills, John Gielgud, Ian Charleson (*Chariots of Fire*), and Edward Fox—among them. Daniel Day-Lewis appears briefly as one of three kids who confront Gandhi.

Surprisingly—in light of *Gandhi*'s success—*Nine Hours to Rama* (1963) is not available on laserdisc. Filmed in India and starring Horst Buchholz and Jose Ferrer, this little-seen film about the events leading up to the assassination would make a nice Pioneer Special Edition wide-screen companion to Attenborough's film.

The Disc
Video: ★★★½
Audio: ★★★★ (Surround)
Chapters: Yes
Format: CLV
Source: Pioneer Special Editions

This new, letterboxed remastering is a considerable improvement over the old RCA/Columbia Pictures Home Video edition—which should tell you how bad *that* one was. Mild grain is present throughout much of the film, though the colors are generally true to life and there is almost no video noise.

The letterbox is a *bit* of a disappointment. While it faithfully recreates the film's look *in general*, it still lops a bit off the sides to lessen the matte. Given the fact that a pan-and-scan version already exists, cheating on the letterbox like this is silly and inexplicable.

The audio is fine. Though the Surround Sound doesn't have many opportunities to bowl the viewer over, the stereo separation and ambient audio are excellent.

Ghost (1990) ★★★½
Director: Jerry Zucker
Running Time: 127 minutes

Investment counselor Sam Wheat (Patrick Swayze) is murdered, and his ghost sticks around to look after his girlfriend, Molly Jensen (Demi Moore), who's in danger from the same man that had Sam bumped off—his corrupt coworker, Carl Bruner (Tony Goldwyn). However, Sam can only communicate with Molly through fruity psychic Oda Mae Brown (Whoopi Goldberg), who Sam also coerces into stealing $4 million in drug money that Carl had been laundering. That causes Carl to become desperate; and when he goes after Molly, Sam—who has since mastered the ability of interacting with objects in the physical world—is waiting. In the end, Carl dies and goes to hell, while Sam finally heads for heaven, where he promises to wait for Molly.

The crime plot is very secondary to the love story, which is the film's raison d'être and made it a box-office smash. So *what* if Sam and Molly get all full of clay in one scene and are whistle-clean the next. So what if the dead Sam has to learn from another ghost how to pick up material objects and yet has no trouble standing on floors or climbing stairs. While it would have been nice if there had been some internal consistency, the movie doesn't exist for that. It exists to define undying love, which it does in the most wonderfully calculated, tear-jerking way imaginable.

Swayze and Moore are sexy and sweet as the lovers, but the film is owned by Goldberg and her inspired, eccentric performance. Ironically, Goldberg—whose career was ice-cold at the time—wasn't the producers' first choice for the part:

She says, "I had to wait (six months) for them to decide they had seen everybody possible."

The Disc
Video: ★★★★½
Audio: ★★★★ (Surround)
Chapters: No
Format: CLV (sides one and three), CAV (side two)
Source: Paramount Home Video

Ghost is available in both letterbox and nonwide-screen editions. The latter isn't pan-and-scan but is opened up into the safety area; a *bit* of picture is lost on the edges, but more imagery—albeit, not what the director intended us to see—is visible on the top and bottom. The dramatic compositions are occasionally ruined, but at least the bulk of the picture is there.

The quality of the image in both versions is superb. The colors are vivid and accurate, the picture is sharp and bright—even in the dark, details are shiny—and there are only isolated pockets of video noise and grain, as well as stray bits of dirt on the master. (This is a recent film, Paramount: Was this the *cleanest* print you could find?)

The audio is sharp, with many appealing directional effects and all kinds of ambient sounds for the rear channels. However, big, booming Surround effects are minimal, occuring during the subway scenes and at the climax.

Fans of this film, and of romantic films with a bit more substance (you'll pardon the pun) should have a look at director Anthony Minghella's *Truly, Madly, Deeply* from Touchstone Home Video. Juliet Stevenson stars as Nina, whose boyfriend Jamie (Alan Rickman) dies, returns as a ghost, brings ghostly friends to her flat (to watch videos), and interferes with her new romance with George (Bill Paterson). The acting and dialogue are first-rate, and the stereo transfer is solid. The nonletterboxed film plays fine.

Glory (1989) ★★★★½
Director: Edward Zwick
Running Time: 122 minutes

Zwick, one of the cocreators of television's "thirtysomething," atones for that series with this exceptional film.

After being shaken and wounded in the bloody battle of Antietam, young Robert Gould Shaw (Matthew Broderick) is sent home to Massachusetts to recuperate. While there, he—the Harvard educated son of abolitionist parents—is asked to lead a newly created black regiment; he accepts, despite his own concerns about the reliability of blacks as soldiers.

With second-in-command Cabot Forbes (Cary Elwes), Shaw turns the men of the Fifty-fourth into a crack outfit, anchored by the bitter, powerful Trip (Denzel Washington) and Sgt. John Rawlins (Morgan Freeman). Shaw changes, too, from a young man who was disoriented in combat to a leader of men who is first into battle—not only against the Confederates but against prejudice among Union soldiers and officers. The final cement—the event that unites the black soldiers and white commanders for all eternity—is the futile attack against the Confederates' well-fortified Fort Wagner on Morris Island, South Carolina, on July 18, 1863. The battle began at sundown and lasted just under three hours; of the 624 men of the Fifty-fourth, 281 were either killed or wounded, including the twenty-five-year-old Colonel Shaw. The fort wasn't taken.

(Not shown in the movie is how the Confederates were infuriated by having to fight black troops, which strengthened their resistance, and how they displayed their contempt for Shaw by burying him in a mass grave with his black soldiers.)

Glory implies that the Fifty-fourth alone tried to take Fort Wagner: In truth, they were one of several regiments, which included the Sixth Connecticut, Third New Hampshire, Forthy-eighth New York, and many others—all white. That aside, the film is quite accurate, an alternately uplifting and wrenching account. The only weak link is Broderick, who, apart from never quite nailing down the accent, turns in a generally flat performance.

But he's surrounded by uniformly strong actors—Washington, Freeman, and Elwes are superb—a rich script, fine production values, and three harrowing battle scenes, all of which will help to explain the Civil War and the men who fought in it better than any textbook could.

The Disc
Video: ★★★★★
Audio: ★★★★★ (Surround)
Chapters: No
Format: CLV
Source: RCA/Columbia Home Video

Mildly letterboxed (the film was not a wide-screen effort, so the scant matte does the job), the film boasts a super-sharp picture with glorious colors that shine through even morning mists, the fog of battle, and the dark of night. There's no grain or noise of which to speak.

The sound is perfect, with spectacular Surround effects: They're not constant, but they're awesomely thrilling when they're used. You won't find very many audio/video passages on any disc that are more involving than the opening salvos of the evening portion of the final attack.

The Godfather (1972)
★★★★★
Director: Francis Ford Coppola
Running Time: 176 minutes

The Godfather was viewed as a risky project for films. Paramount bought the rights to the Mario Puzo story back in 1966, before the book was written; in the interim, their mob film *The Brotherhood* (1968) bombed and the studio wasn't sure there was a market for Puzo's tale. When the book became a huge best-seller, they changed their mind.

Even so, to help keep the budget down, the studio engaged Coppola to direct instead of some big, expensive name. Coppola's films had all flopped—most recently, *Finian's Rainbow* (1968) and *The Rain People* (1969, with James Caan)—but he'd cowritten *Patton* (see page 205) and was regarded as a filmmaker of some potential. Coppola collaborated with Puzo on a script that combined what Paramount wanted (violent action) with what they wanted (the inner workings of the mob family), after which Coppola and producer Albert S. Ruddy turned to the matter of casting.

Don Vito Corleone was the key role, of course. George C. Scott was considered and dismissed (too temperamental); Burt Lancaster and Ernest Borgnine campaigned hard for the part; and Laurence Olivier was actually offered it (he declined due to poor health). Meanwhile, Coppola and Ruddy both stumped for Brando, but Paramount said his string of flops had made him box-office poison—and, besides, he was forty-seven and Corleone was in his sixties and aged from there.

Brando wanted the part and, for the first time in his career, agreed to a screen test; Coppola took a video camera to the actor's house and, after applying his own makeup (including toilet paper to fill out his cheeks), Brando did a silent scene with a cup of coffee and a cigar. The screen test won Paramount over, and with the help of makeup master Dick Smith (who created the makeup in *The Exorcist*) Brando became Corleone. Also cast were Coppola's friend James Caan, New York stage actor Al Pacino—who had made only two films prior to this and who was offered the part after Jack Nicholson turned it down—and the director's sister Talia Shire.

The film begins in 1945 with the marriage of Corleone's daughter, Connie (Shire), to bookmaker Carlo Rizzi (Gianni Russo). Corleone's youngest son, Michael

(Pacino), has just returned from the war and has brought girlfriend Kay (Diane Keaton). Michael doesn't want to join the family "business," but after his father is gunned down he's forced to change his mind, shooting rival gang leader Virgil Zollozzo (Al Lettieri) and crooked police captain McClusky (Sterling Hayden). Michael goes to Sicily to wait for things to cool down, during which time the rival families fight for control of the New York underworld. After the murder of his brother Sonny (Caan), Michael becomes the new Godfather, consolidating his power in one of the most extraordinary sequences in all of filmdom, the crosscutting between Michael at a baptism and the bloody slaughter of his rivals.

Because of the success of the novel, Coppola and Ruddy were able to convince Paramount to boost the original budget from $2 million to $6 million; it was money well spent, as *The Godfather* surpassed *The Sound of Music* (see page 257) to become the most successful film in history.

Though Coppola said the only sequel he'd ever consider was *Abbott and Costello Meet the Godfather*, he continued the saga with *The Godfather, Part II* (1974), which was based on early and later portions of the book they'd been forced to cut, jumping between Michael's career as the Don and the early days of Vito Corleone (Robert De Niro) as a young immigrant. It, too, was a success, and for years Paramount wanted a third film. There was even talk about Sylvester Stallone continuing the saga. Perhaps frightened by those prospects—and by a series of failures that had left his own prospects dim—Coppola finally consented to make *The Godfather, Part III* (1990), which covers Michael's twilight years and the rise of his aggressive nephew Vincent Mancini (Andy Garcia). A less violent tale centered around the "murder" of Pope John Paul I and the Vatican banking scandal—and with the infamously bad performance of the director's daughter, Sofia, as Michael's daughter, Mary—the third film had flashes of the old *Godfather* power, but it did disappointing business.

The Disc
Video: ★★½
Audio: ★★★ (monaural)
Chapters: No
Format: CLV
Source: Paramount Home Video

The first two *Godfather* films were recently remastered and are only marginally better than the original transfers. Granted, the films are tough ones to get right, with extremes of dark and light and troublesome color schemes (a lot of dark brown rooms). Still, they deserve better than this. Many scenes are muddy, and others look pale. And, frankly, to have remastered the films without letterboxing them was just plain dumb. Few filmmakers compose shots as skillfully as Coppola, and those images lose their balance and impact.

The digital audio is good but no better. Background noise is very minimal, but the upper ranges don't have the clarity they should.

The Godfather, Part III is in much better shape, with a sharp, attractive picture, bold colors—resulting in a bit of video noise—and excellent audio with effective stereo separation.

The three films, plus a fascinating documentary, are available as a boxed set, though the discs are the same ones used for the individual releases.

Going Places (1974) ★★★½
Director: Bertrand Blier
Running Time: 118 minutes

Twenty-five-year-old Jean-Claude (Gerard Depardieu) and his twenty-three-year-old pal Pierrot (Patrick Dewaere) are rude, misogynistic petty thieves who roam around France molesting women and stealing cars. One of their victims, shampoo girl Marie-Ange (Miou-Miou), is a "cold fish" whom the young studs are unable to excite. On a train, a young mother leaves them to be with her nerd of a husband. At a bowling alley, two other girls have the temerity to dump them. Fearing that they're losing their appeal, the lads dress handsomely, wait outside a prison, and follow the first woman who's released, Jeanne Pirolle (Jeanne Moreau), who's been in jail for ten years. They woo her, treat her to new clothes and a meal, and before long she seduces them.

However, Jeanne's got serious psychological problems, as well as a loony son who makes them accomplices to a murder. Marie-Ange comes back into their lives just in time to join the boys as they flee the law.

Going Places is a very funny film with some touching moments. Its attitude toward women is repugnant—even by the standards of French cinema—and you'll find yourself resisting and resenting it. But two things turn it around: Jeanne's revealing monologue at the restaurant and her ultimate fate, and the fact that it's a virgin who unlocks Marie-Ange's passion after the brutes have failed. The movie doesn't let these two off the hook for what they've done, and its humor comes at their expense, inspired by their ineptness as thieves and lovers.

Depardieu and Dewaere are a terrific team. Depardieu continued to create off-center contemporary characters until his international breakthrough *The Return of Martin Guerre* (1982), about a sixteenth-century peasant who returns to his family after seven years and may, in fact, be an imposter; more recently, he has starred in *Cyrano de Bergerac* and *Green Card* (both 1990). Young Dewaere committed suicide in 1982.

The Disc
Video: ★½
Audio: ★★★ (monaural)
Chapters: Yes
Format: CLV
Source: CinemaDisc Collection/Image Entertainment

Given the poor-quality color stock being used in the seventies, especially in Europe, it's surprising this film doesn't look worse. The colors are generally drab, there's very mild grain throughout, and you won't find many details in the dark. But the picture is fairly sharp and the master element is in very good shape. It's not unwatchable.

The film is very mildly letterboxed, accurately recreating the original 1.43:1 screen image. The subtitles are white, which creates problems when the two stars are dressed in white.

The audio is clear, with virtually no background noise.

The Golden Voyage of Sinbad (1973) ★★½
Director: Gordon Hessler
Running Time: 106 minutes

After a disappointing series of box-office failures—*Jason and the Argonauts*, *First Men in the Moon* (see pages 153 and 98), and *Valley of Gwangi* (1969)—producer Charles H. Schneer and special effects master Ray Harryhausen returned to the scene of their biggest hit, *The 7th Voyage of Sinbad* (1958), to tell further adventures of the Arabian knight.

This time, Sinbad (John Phillip Law) lands in the kingdom of Marabia, whose benevolent Grand Vizier (Douglas Wilmer) has been horribly disfigured in a fire caused by the evil Koura (Tom Baker). The sorcerer covets the throne for himself, but the only way either man can hold power is by obtaining three pieces of an amulet and depositing them in the Fountain of Destiny in the land of Lemuria, which lies beyond the Sea of Mists. Sinbad agrees to take the Grand Vizier there—with Koura in hot pursuit and using all kinds of dark magic against the heroes. In a nice surprise, Koura manages to reach the Fountain of Destiny first and wins the prize of invisibility. Unfortunately, he's so giddy with delight that he carelessly steps into the fountain, his outline becomes visible, and Sinbad runs him through.

Law makes a terrific Sinbad, and Wilmer is wonderful as the Grand Vizier. Baker (see *Nicholas and Alexandra*) is way over the top, but that's what movie wizards are supposed to be. Caroline Munro is stunning as Sinbad's love interest, the servant girl Margiana, and John Garfield, Jr. (son of the actor) is good as Koura's aide Achmed.

However, the real reason to see the film, as always, is Harryhausen's special effects work. Two scenes in the film are among the finest he's ever done: Powered from afar by Koura, the vacant-eyed figurehead of Sinbad's lateen rigger comes to life and battles the sailors; and a statute of the six-armed goddess Kali does an incredible exotic dance and then attacks Sinbad with a half-dozen flashing swords. The animation, composite photography, and choreography of these scenes are dazzling.

There are also some disappointing sequences. The Cave of the Oracle is a bore, as are the green-skinned natives on Lemuria. The climactic fight between Koura's cyclopean centaur and Sinbad's golden gryphon is also a letdown: Not only is the fight tame but the gryphon comes from nowhere. (Budgetary restrictions forced Harryhausen to eliminate a scripted scene in which the creature was initially seen as a stone guardian near the fountain.)

There were also problems with film stock, so that the colors in the special-effects scenes don't always match the prefilmed live-action footage, such as the (miniature) floor segment under Kali on side two at 8/29054. And watch for the gaffe on the ship deck when the Homunculus drops the amulet: Sinbad picks it up, then picks it up again.

The film's no classic, but the highlights will bring you back to the disc every now and then.

The Disc
Video: ★★½
Audio: ★★★ (monaural)
Chapters: Yes
Format: CLV (side one), CAV (sides two and three)
Source: Pioneer Special Edition

Once again, a disc has been remastered for the collector's market without being letterboxed. Granted, it's not a *big* deal with this 1.66:1 film, but there *are* times when a mild matte would have made the film more enjoyable. The centaur's-eye view of Sinbad is off-center at 6/23229 on side two, while Sinbad is entirely missing from the right side of the screen while battling Kali on side two at 10/36665.

That aside, the transfer is good, though far from perfect. Grain was a problem with the original film, due to the superimposition processes employed by Harryhausen, but it's a bit worse here. Scratches and dirt also show up in various spots throughout the film, while reds and blues are a bit noisy in places, especially in the Cave of the Oracle.

The CAV frames are all perfectly steady and will be used quite a bit by Harryhausen fans who want to try to pick apart his effects. (Hint: The spear on side three, 6/24187, is *entirely* miniature. The actor isn't holding a thing.)

The audio has some oomph and Miklos Rozsa's score sounds fine. The only problems are in the upper-register sounds —swords, shrieks, violins—which are rather shrill.

As part of its Special Edition series, Pioneer has recently released remastered, CAV editions of *The 7th Voyage of Sinbad* (1958), *The 3 Worlds of Gulliver* (1959), and *Mysterious Island* (1961). The transfers are excellent, with perfect freeze-frames and clear digital sound. Apart from the Harryhausen effects and Bernard Herrmann score, there's little to recommend these films—though fans will find those reasons enough! (Note: The yellowish look to some of the special effects scenes in *The 3 Worlds of Gulliver* and *Mysterious Island* is a virtue of the sodium-vapor process used to create some of the composite images in those films. It's *not* the fault of the transfer.)

Valley of Gwangi—about a valley inhabited by dinosaurs in turn-of-the-century Mexico—is available in a newly mastered laserdisc from Warner Home Video. Great dinosaur effects; the rest is sheer tedium.

Goldfinger (1964) ★★★★
Director: Guy Hamilton
Running Time: 111 minutes

Goldfinger, written in 1959, is one of the most entertaining of Ian Fleming's James Bond novels (it was the seventh). It recounts the ambitious plot of Auric Goldfinger to poison the water supply of the town surrounding Fort Knox, blow open the vault, and steal one thousand tons of gold, carting the booty away on a Russian freighter. The plan is foiled by agent Bond, who, though captured by Goldfinger, is able to alert authorities of the plot by taping a note under an airplane toilet seat. His plan thwarted, the villain and his bodyguard, Oddjob, try to escape on a private jet, with Bond still their captive. Agent 007 manages to break a window, and Oddjob is sucked out, enabling Bond to strangle Goldfinger.

The tone of the novel varies from the glib to the grotesque (Goldfinger always kills by shooting victims through the right eye). Conversely, the $2.5 million film version rarely strays from the glib, even when a man's body is crushed, along with his car, in a scrap yard. The third Bond film, *Goldfinger* was the first runaway hit of the series, becoming the second-most-popular film of the year (right behind *Mary Poppins*) and establishing both the cocky tone and futuristic look for the Bond films that followed.

Some changes were made in the plot. Goldfinger (Gert Frobe) has been smuggling gold out of Britain, and the Bank of England is concerned about the detrimental effect on the economy. Bond (Sean Connery) is asked to find out how Goldfinger's doing it and stop him. Following Goldfinger to the Continent, he tracks him to a factory, where he watches as the criminal's car is dismantled and its solid gold parts, forged in England, are melted down. Unfortunately, Bond is captured and taken to the United States, where Goldfinger holds him hostage as he undertakes Operation Grand Slam: Using airplanes commanded by Pussy Galore (Honor Blackman), he plans to release poison gas around Fort Knox, enter, and detonate a nuclear device. By irradiating the American gold supply, he will not only destroy the nation's economy but the value of his own gold will increase considerably.

However, Bond's sexual prowess turns the lesbian Pussy into an ally; after alerting the authorities, she sprays the troops with a harmless gas. Once Goldfinger and his men are inside, the troops spring to life and attack. Bond electrocutes Oddjob (Harold Sakata) and, during the subsequent fight on the plane, it's Goldfinger who gets sucked out the window.

For many fans, *Goldfinger* is one of the top three of the sixteen "official" Bond films produced by Cubby Broccoli—*On Her Majesty's Secret Service* and *The Spy Who Loved Me* (see pages 201 and 258) being the other two. (The non-Broccoli *Casino Royale* [1967] and *Never Say Never Again* [1983] are not considered to be part of the canon, even though the latter stars Sean Connery.) Based on the longest book of the series, *Goldfinger* also happens to be the shortest and tightest Bond film.

After the fantasy of *Dr. No* (1962) and the harder-edged realism of *From Russia with Love* (1963), *Goldfinger* moved the series comfortably to the middle, from which it rarely strayed. It deftly blends sex, gadgetry, and action before those elements became formularized. It gives us our memorable first look at the Secret Service's technological Q Branch and Bond's gadget-laden Aston Martin. (The "spy"-tech elements were such a hit that in the next opus, *Thunderball* [1965], the producers tried to one-up *Goldfinger* by opening with an improbable jet-pack escape from an enemy's estate and a rather absurd water-jet for the car. Things got even more out of hand with the fifth film, *You Only Live Twice* [1967] which, among other ill-advised bits, has a helicopter lowering a giant magnet, plucking a carload of evildoers off the road, and dumping it into the ocean.)

Connery was at his most assured, interesting, *and* interested in *Goldfinger*. His cool confidence, wit, broad knowledge, and catlike grace are in perfect harmony and made it impossible for anyone else ever to own the part, though others have done a fine job playing Bond. (Connery hadn't even been the producers' first choice for Bond: Before making *Dr. No*, they'd considered Cary Grant, David Niven, Richard Burton, and even Jimmy Stewart! But budgetary constraints forced them to seek new talent, and after interviewing dozens of potential Bonds they reduced the selection to two actors. Connery got the nod; the runner-up was future Bond Roger Moore.)

The movie also provided the hero with his most savvy foil: an equally wisecracking villain. "You expect me to talk?" Bond snaps as he lies spread-eagle on a table, a laser beam approaching his crotch. "No, Mr. Bond," Goldfinger says gloatingly. "I expect you to *die!*" Though Frobe's voice was dubbed (the actor's accent was too heavy), he certainly looks like the "thick... out of proportion" figure described by Fleming. And though he acts as in control as Bond, you can see the anger and ambition always bubbling beneath the surface. Sakata was perfect as Oddjob, the powerful bodyguard who flings his metal-brimmed hat like a deadly Frisbee. He was every bit as popular as Bond with kids who saw the film when it was released!

Honor Blackman—the pre–Diana Rigg star of the TV series "The Avengers"—is perfect as Galore, although the character's lesbianism was toned down considerably from the novel. She and Ursula Andress (from *Dr. No*) remain the most memorable of the "Bond girls." Shirley Bassey's rendition of the title song gave the series the first of its many pop-chart hits.

Though some of the stunts aren't up to the standards of later films, they're impressive enough, as is the Fort Knox set. Designer Ken Adam freely admits that he has no idea what the place really looks like—but if it doesn't resemble the set, it *should*.

The Disc

Video: ★★★★½
Audio: ★★★★½
Chapters: Yes
Format: CAV or CLV
Source: Criterion

Except for a few flaws and very slight color washout in the pretitle section of the film, this is a nearly perfect disc. The print is gloriously colorful and sharp, without grain or other marks.

The letterbox frames the film just right, enabling you to enjoy the action and sets as they were meant to be seen.

The digital audio is also excellent and, if you wish, you can tune out the dialogue and listen to the music and sound effects, which are top-notch. There's also audio commentary from Hamilton, Adam, editor Peter Hunt, and writer Richard Maibaum (on the CAV edition only).

In addition to the audio extras, the package includes the trailer, a well-stuffed photo file, and ads for various Bond-related products.

There's also a pan-and-scan CLV edition available from MGM/UA. Apart from losing some of the image area, the source material isn't as good and the wonderful extras are missing.

All of the Broccoli Bond films are available on laserdisc, the first three in both letterbox (Criterion) and panned-and-scanned editions. The remainder of the films are letterboxed from MGM/UA except for *The Man with the Golden Gun*.

Dr. No and *From Russia with Love* are brilliant in their Criterion editions, much less so in the panned-and-scanned versions from MGM/UA and even worse in the previous CBS/Fox incarnations. The remaining Connery films—*Thunderball, You Only Live Twice,* and *Diamonds Are Forever* (1971)—letterboxed from MGM/UA are of good to very good quality.

Never Say Never Again and *Casino Royale* are available panned-and-scanned; the Japanese edition of *Never Say Never Again* is letterboxed.

Gone With the Wind (1939)
★★★★★
Director: Victor Fleming
Running Time: 232 minutes

Gone With the Wind transcends its actual merits. It's terrific and epic entertainment, but a *lot* of films are terrific and entertaining. What makes *Gone With the Wind* so important to us—to our culture and to our hearts—is not just what it is but also what it stands for.

Margaret Mitchell began writing *Gone With the Wind* in 1926. For nearly a decade, she'd write on slips of paper and stuff them in envelopes; when she finally sent the nearly completed manuscript to a publisher, it was crammed into a suitcase. Published in 1936, the novel became a huge best-seller, evoking the old South through characters so vivid, they appealed to people the world over.

The story is a grand one: Raised on the plantation Tara in northern Georgia, headstrong Scarlett O'Hara is distraught when she learns that aristocratic Ashley Wilkes is to marry his cousin, Melanie Hamilton. She marries Charles Hamilton out of sheer petulance, but he dies in the war and Scarlett falls in love with dashing blockade-runner Capt. Rhett Butler. Despite their mutual attraction—and Rhett's daring rescue of Scarlett and Melanie during Sherman's march on Atlanta—the two spark off one another. When the Civil War ends and Rhett refuses to lend Scarlett the money to pay the taxes on Tara, Scarlett weds Frank Kennedy, who will. A member of the Ku Klux Klan, Kennedy dies in a raid—and this time, Scarlett weds Rhett. But their life together is filled with friction and, after a miscarriage and the death of their daughter, Rhett suffers Scarlett's disdain and seeming indifference. He leaves for good even as, for the first time in their relationship, a frightened Scarlett begs him to stay.

Producer David O. Selznick bought the rights to the book upon its publication. When it became a best-seller, he realized that everyone had their own idea who should play Scarlett and Rhett. A survey showed that nearly half the readers of the book wanted Bette Davis to play Scarlett; the distant runner-up was Katharine Hepburn. Problem was, Selznick and Davis didn't click, he didn't want Hepburn, and so he screen-tested sixty other actresses. Finally, he narrowed the choice down to three: Jean Arthur, Joan Bennett, and Paulette Goddard (whose tests *were* excellent). He still hadn't reached a decision when it came time to film the burning of Atlanta (actually old sets, including the huge native gate from *King Kong* [1933], which had to be razed to make way for the *Gone With the Wind* sets). During the fire, he was introduced to onlooker Vivien Leigh by his brother, Myron, who said, "I want you to meet Scarlett O'Hara." Selznick screen-tested and hired the little-known British actress for a meager fifteen thousand dollars. (Southerners were pleased—better to have an English woman as Scarlett than a Yankee like Davis.)

Casting Rhett presented a different kind of problem. The public was unanimous in wanting Clark Gable for the part, but Gable himself was reluctant to do it. "I cannot say that I did not want to play Rhett," he said later. "I did. But he was too popular. Miss Mitchell had etched him into the minds of millions, each of whom knew exactly how Rhett would look and act. It would be impossible to satisfy them all, or even a majority." He added, "I didn't want the part for money, marbles or chalk." (He himself thought that Ronald Colman should have played the part.) However, Gable was under contract to MGM and had no say in what parts he could or couldn't accept. When Selznick set up a coproducing arrangement with the studio for the film, Gable was part of the deal.

The public loved Leigh and Gable in the roles, and favorable reaction was also unanimous toward Leslie Howard as Ashley, Olivia de Havilland as Melanie, and Thomas Mitchell as Scarlett's father, Gerald. TV's Superman, George Reeves, plays one of Scarlett's beaux, Stuart Tarleton, and Butterfly McQueen is perfect as the young, panic-prone slave Prissy. Rand

Brooks and Carroll Nye were Charles Hamilton and Frank Kennedy.

At a cost of $3 million, *Gone With the Wind* was the most expensive—and longest—film made up until that time. It also became the most successful film in history and would hold the crown until *The Sound of Music* knocked it down to number two in 1965.

There were many reasons for its success. On the one hand, it's a very satisfying condensation of the novel. (Though Sidney Howard received full credit for the screenplay, contributions were made by F. Scott Fitzgerald, Ben Hecht, and John Van Druten, among others.) All of the major characters were included, though whittled down considerably, and much of the dialogue was retained, albeit with some interesting changes—most notably Rhett's snide "Cheer up, maybe you'll have a miscarriage," becoming "Maybe you'll have an accident" to satisfy the infamous movie censorship board known as the Hays Office. However, Selznick steadfastly refused to change Rhett's parting line, "My dear, I don't give a damn" (though the word *Frankly* was added up front). After much haggling, the censors agreed to let him have his *damn*, but Selznick was fined five thousand dollars.

The film is also a stunning visualization of the novel, with unparalleled art direction by William Cameron Menzies, lush Technicolor opulent sets, the spectacular burning of Atlanta and the unforgettable shot of Scarlett among the sea of wounded soldiers.

And the casting was just *right*. The surveys notwithstanding, Selznick followed his instincts and they turned out to be just what the public wanted. Not until *The Godfather* (see page 110) would a filmmaker's vision and audience expectations be so perfectly in synch.

Yet, memorable as the film is, what is perhaps most significant about *Gone With the Wind* today is that it's the shining achievement of lost Hollywood: the lavish studio sets and costumes, the lush Max Steiner score, the romantic close-ups and lighting and staging. Never before or since did it come together like this. And, of course, the film is a paean to the studio system that made it possible: the moguls who wielded absolute power (but, unlike the powerful Hollywood businesspeople of today, *loved* to make movies), and the stars who were discovered by them and had parts manufactured for them. *Gone With the Wind* was the triumph of this system, the ultimate Hollywood movie—in every way, a piece of Americana whose likes we'll never see again.

The Disc

Video: ★★★½
Audio: ★★★½ (monaural)
Chapters: Yes
Format: CAV or CLV
Source: MGM/UA Home Video

It's ironic that the CLV sleeve of this quintessential American film is boldly stamped in back "Made in Japan."

The CLV and CAV fiftieth-anniversary editions are of equal quality and are better in every way than the previous MGM/UA Home Video release. However, as satisfying as the new versions are overall (thanks to an extremely sharp image, both struck from the same master), both have some problems.

Scattered throughout its length, roughly half the film is in perfect Technicolor, with accurate flesh tones and saturated colors that really sing. The film's painterly look and awesome silhouettes come through exquisitely. Other sections, however, are very slightly reddish, and there are isolated areas of grain and some very mild video noise. Negative dirt, scratches, and stains that come and go on individual frames are also a problem.

The audio—which includes the music for the overture, intermission, and entr'acte—was transferred from a newly discovered nitrate optical track. The dialogue is fine, but the upper and lower registers of the sound track are on the tinny side. The music is especially vulnerable—though, having said that, nothing can stop those powerful opening strains from weaving their spell.

Though the CAV edition has a few interesting extras, fans of the film should get the CLV version and also pick up *The Making of a Legend: Gone With the Wind*, a superb feature-length documentary about the making of the film. Released by MGM/UA Home Video, it contains rare behind-the-scenes footage, interviews, screen tests, film of the premier, and a complete history of the film.

Gonza the Spearman (1986)
★★½
Director: Masahiro Shinoda
Running Time: 126 minutes

The Japanese playwright Monzaemon Chikamatsu (1653–1724) wrote both Kabuki dramas and puppet plays known as *joruri*. The most popular of these were his historical dramas (*jidaimono*) and his domestic plays (*sewamono*). *Yari No Gonza Kasane, Spearman Gonza's Illicit Love* combines elements of both and has always been one of his most popular works.

This faithful film adaptation is a complex tale of love, lust, and honor. In the early 1700s, the provincial lord Ichinoshin (Takashi Tsumura) is called to Edo for a year. While he's away, the samurai Bannojo (Shohei Hino) makes it clear to the lord's wife, Osai (Shima Iwashita), that he's interested in her. However, she is repulsed by him and has her eye on Gonza (Hiromi Go). Gonza is betrothed to Bannojo's sister Oyuki (Misako Tanake), even though Bannojo doesn't like the spearman.

Meanwhile, in Edo, Ichinoshin fathers an heir. To celebrate back home, the family schedules a tea ceremony: Whoever officiates over the ceremony will bring honor and certainly a promotion on himself. Bannojo and Gonza vie for the honor, Gonza rashly visiting Osai to cut a deal, agreeing to marry her young daughter in exchange for the inside track on the ceremony. The two are seen together by Bannojo, and he accuses them of adultery. Trapped, the two run off and are pursued by a justifiably upset Ichinoshin and various family members.

The movie is slow—*very* slow. Shinoda dwells at length on the tea ceremonies, the fixing of hair, a card game, and conversations that underscore points of honor over and over. The pace isn't helped by the director's straightforward style, which is more like a filmed stage play than cinema. But it's also erotic and the characters are extremely well developed; you get to know the people behind the strict code of ethics. Viewers who stick with the movie will be rewarded with a fascinating look at a hero torn between love and ambition and a woman who has prestige but yearns for love.

The Disc
Video: ★
Audio: ★★★ (monaural)
Chapters: Yes
Format: CLV (sides one and two), CAV (side three)
Source: Kino on Video/Image Entertainment

Alas, the picture on the screen looks nothing like the sharp, colorful photos on the back. For the most part, the letterboxed picture is grainy and soft, with colors that are dark and muddy. If you're expecting the beauty of *Kwaidan* (see page 166), you'll be disappointed. The print is also dirty and scratched in spots: For most of chapter six, a vertical green line dances along the right side of the image.

Though most of the still frames on the CAV side jitter, you'll be able to single-frame through the climax and watch as Gonza's blood shoots from under his clothing, not from his wound, and study how Osai's blood is matted in, spraying up without ever coming down again.

Gonza the Spearman is also hurt by the worst subtitles ever put on a film: Almost every word breaks up—some are unreadable—and letters often bleed off the screen to the right.

The sound is solid, though most American viewers won't be listening to the dialogue, and sound effects are relatively sparse. The sound track does have a nice resonant bass, though.

Goodbye, Mr. Chips (1969) ★★
Director: Herbert Ross
Running Time: 156 minutes

In 1933, author James Hilton (*Lost Horizon*) was having trouble coming up with a story for *British Weekly*. The deadline was fast approaching and he needed the money; after a sleepless night and a long bicycle ride the next morning, he came home and began writing *Goodbye, Mr. Chips*. Four days later, the charming novelette was finished. Hilton later said that the story was "written more quickly, more easily, and with fewer subsequent alterations than anything I had ever written before, or have ever written since."

The story was filmed in 1939 with Robert Donat and Greer Garson; Donat's performance is the highlight of the handsome but creaky film. Ever on the lookout for new projects, producer Arthur P. Jacobs—despite the disastrous failure of his costly musical *Doctor Doolittle* (1967)—thought that a musical version of the Hilton tale was a good idea. He was wrong; the changes he made made it even more wrong.

In the original story, schoolmaster Mr. Chipping of the Brookfield School meets out-of-work governess Katherine Bridges while bicycling. The liberated woman teaches Chips to open up; love is followed by marriage is followed by the death of Katherine and child during childbirth. Thereafter, Chips struggles through a bitter conflict with the egotistical headmaster Ralston and difficulties during World War I.

In the Jacobs version—which begins in 1924 instead of the turn of the century—Katherine (Petula Clark) is an actress whom Arthur Chipping (Peter O'Toole) meets after being dragged to a performance of *Flossie from Fullom*. The two seem to have nothing in common until they meet again while touring Greece (an excuse for the cast and crew to go there). They marry and Katherine not only shakes up Chips but turns the staid old school on its ear. After her death during the Blitz, Chips tearfully retires.

Written by playwright Terence Rattigan (*Separate Tables*), the film jettisoned the charm (never mind the narrative) of Hilton's original, but it has its moments thanks to a sensitive performance by O'Toole and then-wife Sian Phillips as Katherine's eccentric friend, Ursula Mossbank. Clark is okay as the soubrette, though the character is never asked to do more than act outrageous or look gooey-eyed at Chips. (Lynn Redgrave would've been better, but the producers opted, instead, for a charted pop singer. The film bombed, anyway.) Michael Redgrave makes for a sympathetic headmaster.

Leslie Bricusse has done some great scores—for *Doctor Doolittle*, *Scrooge* (1970), and *Willy Wonka and the Chocolate Factory* (1971), among others—but this isn't one of them. There isn't a memorable, hummable song among them and, worse, they slow the film down and spoil what would otherwise have been some effective moments.

Ross made his directorial debut on the film (doing far too much zooming in and out) but went on to better things, such as *Play It Again Sam* (1972) and *The Turning Point* (1977).

The Disc
Video: ★½
Audio: ★★★★ (stereo)
Chapters: Yes
Format: CLV
Source: MGM/UA Home Video

Considering that the film was shot using the impermanent Metrocolor process, the colors aren't bad—somewhat faded, occasionally muddy, but not as awful as some. Unfortunately, the transfer is fuzzy, particularly during the Pompeii sequences. Given that the film was shot in 70mm, the quality of the picture is a crashing disappointment.

At least the letterbox allows all the characters to appear onscreen, which helps the drama somewhat.

When taken in tandem with the picture, the exceptionally clear audio sounds as if it belongs with another film. Though stereo separations are minimal, the depth of the sound is excellent.

The film's overture, entr'acte, and exit music are included, as is the original trailer, which makes the movie look much better than it is.

Speaking of awful musicals, Pioneer has released *Lost Horizon* (1973) as part of its Special Edition series. The Burt Bacharach and Hal David songs are catchy, but they feel shoe-horned into the script, and both Sally Kellerman and Liv Ullmann are obviously embarrassed to be singing them. Peter Finch, John Gielgud, and Michael York fare somewhat better. Excellent, colorful transfer, except for wear-and-tear on scenes salvaged from the archives for this presentation.

Goodfellas (1990) ★★★★
Director: Martin Scorsese
Running Time: 146 minutes

Based on journalist Nicholas Pileggi's best-seller, *Wiseguy*—the reminiscences of real life gangster Henry Hill (who is presently living under the government's witness protection program)—*Goodfellas* is the story of how Hill (Ray Liotta), raised in an Italian section of Brooklyn, joins, serves, and then betrays the mob. Leisurely but fascinating, the early part of the movie emphasizes what it is about the mob that appeals to Hill, and follows the comaraderie that grows between the eager-to-please boy and seasoned mobsters James Conway (Robert De Niro), Paul Cicero (Paul Sorvino, who has never been better), and Tommy DeVito (Joe Pesci)—especially after the kid is arrested for the first time and the guys congratulate him for "losing his cherry."

After Hill woos and weds Karen Hill (Lorraine Bracco), his life goes into decline, and the film chronicles his move into cocaine peddling, his own addiction, and the tragic betrayal of his friends.

The film is the flip side of *The Godfather* (see page 110), a view of a crime family from the bottom up rather than from the top down. It's not about the criminals' attempts to become legitimate businesspeople but, rather, about a Jabez Stone who makes a deal with the devil and then has to pay—very nearly losing his soul in the process.

Goodfellas belongs to Liotta, who played Shoeless Joe Jackson in *Field of Dreams* (see page 96), and he is mesmerizing. He receives excellent support from Lorraine Bracco (who has managed to stink up her career with *Radio Flyers* and *Medicine Man*), from Sorvino and De Niro (both of whom spend too much time in the background), and from Pesci as the explosive, doomed Tommy.

Director Scorsese's mother, Catherine, appears as Mrs. DeVito.

The Disc
Video: ★★★★½
Audio: ★★★★★ (Surround)
Chapters: Yes
Format: CLV
Source: Warner Home Video

This generously letterboxed transfer does a great job with a difficult film. What grain there is was present in the original image, and the only problem is in the reds, which are often way too noisy. (However, if the picture had been toned down to keep them quiet, it would have been *way* too dark.) Otherwise, the colors are perfect, the image is very sharp, and the picture is wonderfully clear, even in the dark scenes.

The audio is magnificent. Stereo separation is dazzling, and the rear speakers skillfully draw the viewer into Scorsese's world. Just *try* not to jump when there are gunshots.

Grand Prix (1966) ★½
Director: John Frankenheimer
Running Time: 175 minutes

Here's how *this* stinker came about: Unable to get tickets to see Laurence Olivier on the London stage as Othello, director Frankenheimer decided to go to Le Mans and watch the race. It occurred to him, then, that a race like this would be the perfect subject for an $8 million Cinerama ("Puts *you* in the picture!") presentation.

In theory, yes. In practice, however, the director of magnificent films such as *The Manchurian Candidate* (see page 180), *Seven Days in May* (1964), and *The Train* (1965) failed to pull it off. He went to the starting gate with a line up of stereotypes: Pete Aron (James Garner), the reckless, cynical loner who lives for racing and winning; his archenemy, Scott Stoddard (Brian Bedford), whose career and marriage are clouded by the death of his racing brother; Pat (Jessica Walter), Scott's bored wife and Pete's mistress; Louise Frederickson (Eva Marie Saint), a "what are they trying to prove by racing?" fashion-magazine editor (that certainly qualified *her* as an expert on the sport); aging champion Jean-Pierre Sarti (Yves Montand); his wife, Monique Delvaux (Genevieve Page), who runs a huge French car company; and single-minded Japanese industrialist Izo Yamura (Toshiro Mifune, making an embarrassingly stilted English-language film debut as a character modeled after car czar Soichiro Honda). He teams with Pete so that his cars will make a mark on Grand Prix racing. (The Japanese had modest goals for their automobiles back then.) There's also a crazy Sicilian racer, Nino Barlini (Antonio Sabato), racing groupie Lisa (a lovely Françoise Hardy), and magnate Agostino Manetta (Adolfo Celi), who was modeled after Enzo Ferrari.

Though the characters are clichéd and badly sketched, the racing scenes come close to salvaging the film. Frankenheimer's use of wide-angle lenses and innovative cinematography during the racing scenes is dazzling; these scenes looked great on the giant Cinerama screen, and they're still heart-in-the-throat thrilling on this disc. If only there were a *story*!

Perhaps things would have been different if Frankenheimer had had more time to cut the two hundred miles of film he shot. Location photography proved to be a logistical nightmare, and he wrapped in mid-October, which left him six weeks to have the film ready for its long-planned Christmas release. Even experienced filmmakers make bad calls under that kind of pressure. But knowing one reason *why* the movie turned out so badly doesn't make it any more endurable.

It took nearly a quarter of a century for a worse racing film to come along—*Days of Thunder* (1990)—which has even shallower characters and less exciting racing footage.

The Disc

Video: ★★★½
Audio: ★★★½ (Surround)
Chapters: No
Format: CLV
Source: MGM/UA Home Video

Though the film doesn't look as fresh as other Cinerama films from the era—such as *The Hallelujah Trail* and *Battle of the Bulge* (see pages 127 and 20)—it doesn't look as badly as it might have. The Metrocolor is somewhat red and/or pale in many places, and there's a good deal of grain in the nighttime scenes. For the most part, however, the letterboxed image is clearly focused and the racing scenes will throw you back in your seat.

The audio is also satisfying, despite its flaws. Though there's weakness in the high and low frequencies (you won't be able to crank this up without decay and distortion), the middle-range sounds are very acceptable, and there are some excellent directional effects.

Maurice Jarre's infectious, souped-up theme sounds great, and the overture is included.

Graveyard Shift (1990)

Director: Ralph S. Singleton
Running Time: 89 minutes

Drop the *f* and you've said it all. There isn't a redeeming aspect of this film, based on the Stephen King short story about a drifter, John Hall (David Andrews), who goes to work at Maine's Bachman Mills (get it, King fans?), where people have been disappearing from the rat-infested cellar. Not even the shell-shocked Vietnam vet exterminator (Brad Dourif) can get to the bottom of things.

To find out what's been offing the workers, Hall, his newfound girlfriend, Jane Wisconsky (Kelly Wolf), foreman Warwick (Stephen Macht), and three other workers decide to go downstairs and clean the place up. What they discover is a labyrinthine subbasement inhabited by a giant bat, which proceeds to pick off the cleanup crew one by one.

The film's only inspired moment? A shot of a character reading *Ben* in the diner. Character motivation? Forget it. Warwick is mean-spirited and Hall remote for reasons that are *never* revealed; everyone else is just plain stupid. The monster's got the only motivation, though how it got there is also never explained. Personality? Sucking cigarette smoke up the nose passes for characterization in this film. Not even the big bloodsucker scores: As giant, meat-eating Muppets go, this one's seriously fake. The matte paintings of the monster's subterranean lair, supervised by master Albert Whitlock (see *The Hindenburg* and *Earthquake*) are distressingly bad, and the vocal effects contributed by Hanna-Barbera veteran Frank Welker fall way short of chilling.

An hour and a half will never, ever seem so long.

The Disc

Video: ★★★
Audio: ★★ (Surround)
Chapters: No
Format: CLV
Source: Paramount Home Video

Mildly cropped, there's only that much less of this movie to hate. The colors are very solid and the picture extremely clear in the daylight scenes, somewhat grainy in many of the darker scenes. Video noise is kept to a satisfying minimum.

Technically, the sound is very good, but the Surround is abused. The constant (unexplained) background "thunder"—spooky at first—quickly becomes annoying. When you go through the mill at the opening of the film, you figure you're going to be in for a real audio treat: There's clacking and shuffling everywhere. Unfortunately, use of the rear speakers is dunning and loud, and you'll tire of it quickly.

The Great Escape (1963)
★★★★
Director: John Sturges
Running Time: 173 minutes

After *The Magnificent Seven* (see page 179), Steve McQueen made *The Honeymoon Machine* (1961), *Hell is for Heroes* (1962), and *The War Lover* (1962)—the latter two well below his potential.

McQueen had wanted to shoot a new version of *Beauty and the Beast*, but those plans fell through; he didn't want for work, however, as Carl Foreman offered him a role in the war film *The Victors* and John Sturges asked him to go to Germany with him to make *The Great Escape*. McQueen had worked with Sturges before and accepted *The Great Escape* with the provision that a riproaring motorcycle chase be added for the star. Though there wasn't one in the original escape *or* the script, Sturges agreed. (*The Victors*, with George Peppard, was a major bomb.)

Based on the book by Paul Brickhill, *The Great Escape* was written by James Clavell and W. R. Burnett and recounts—with some accuracy—an escape that occurred in 1944 (not 1942, as in the film) from Stalag Luft III. The daring breakout is organized by Roger Bartlett (Richard Attenborough, based on real-life organizer Roger Bushnell), who plans to take 250 men through three separate tunnels. The film covers the planning, digging, escape, and aftermath, focusing on the activities of "Scrounger" Bob Hendley (James Garner; a fictitious part), "Tunnel King" Danny Velinski (Charles Bronson), "Forger" Colin Blythe (Donald Pleasence), Australian "Manufacturer" Louie Sedgwick (James Coburn, with an unconvincing accent), "Disposal" Eric Ashley-Pitt (David McCallum), "Surveyor" Cavendish (Nigel Stock), "Intelligence" MacDonald (Gordon Jackson), and "Cooler King" Virgil Hilts (McQueen, inspired by George Harsh, who, in real life, failed to get out of the camp).

Only seventy-nine men are able to escape and, as in real life, only three make it to freedom: Fifty men are executed outright and twenty-six are scattered throughout other POW camps.

Of the escapees, McQueen gives the Germans the roughest time, stealing a motorcycle and leading them on a dandy race through the countryside. McQueen did all his own riding except the heart-stopping jump over the barricade, which was executed by his lookalike friend Bud Ekins. McQueen wasn't happy about the substitution (the insurance company made the call), nor was he pleased with his character's seeming ambivalence about being sent to the cooler (solitary confinement) over and over: He felt Hilts should've kicked and screamed all the way and, like Ives (Angus Lennie), his neighbor in the cooler, shown *some* signs of stress once there.

McQueen's "cool" plays perfectly, however, a contrast to the glib Garner and Coburn, intense Bronson, and dead-serious British cast. Some critics have complained that the film never gets into the minds of the men and, with the exception of Bartlett, that's true. However, Sturges's decision to emphasize the clever preparations for the escape, its claustrophobic execution, and its suspenseful aftermath is also legitimate; both *The Elusive Corporal* (1962) and *The Password is Courage* (1963) are more tightly focused, introspective accounts of POWs, and who even *remembers* those films today?

An unbearably dull two-part TV movie sequel, *The Great Escape II: The Untold Story* (1988) stars Christopher Reeve as an ex-POW who, after the war, leads his fellow inmates on a mission of vengeance. Donald Pleasence costars as an SS officer. The film is not available on laserdisc.

The Disc

Video: ★★★½ (MGM/UA); ★★★★ (Criterion)
Audio: ★★★½ (monaural) (both versions)
Chapters: No (MGM/UA); Yes (Criterion)
Format: CLV (side four of the Criterion version is CAV—though before you rush out and buy it, be aware that the motorcycle jump is on side three)
Source: MGM/UA Home Video or Criterion

Time to replace that old CBS/Fox Home Video pan-and-scan edition: The newer letterboxed presentations are the only way to see this film.

The prints used for both versions are in excellent condition, and the transfers are generally quite sharp. Mildly grainy shots are scattered throughout, though the colors are very solid (except for the flesh tones in the MGM/UA version, which are so bright, the characters look sunburned at times; check out Garner at the airfield). That the colors are as vivid as they are is quite an accomplishment considering the earth and gunmetal colors that dominate the film and the fact that wretched Deluxe was the color of choice.

The Criterion edition has a slightly milder letterbox.

Apart from some minor dropouts on side two of the MGM/UA version, the digital audio on both is very clear: Fans of the score will be particularly pleased with the solidity of the music.

The MGM/UA disc is less than half the price of Criterion's package, but Criterion version gives you knockout extras: military photos of the camp and prisoners, over 250 production stills, script excerpts, and interviews with Sturges, Bernstein, and Eakins.

MGM/UA has included the action-packed trailer, giving away the film's best action scenes (as does the disc's selection of photos for the gatefold jacket).

The Great Race (1965) ★★
Director: Blake Edwards
Running Time: 160 minutes

It's the early days of this century, and the Great Leslie (Tony Curtis) and Professor Fate (Jack Lemmon) are rivals on the daredevil circuit. More than once, the snarling, mustachioed, black-garbed Fate has tried to kill his dressed-in-white, gleaming-teeth colleague, but every effort to sabotage Leslie's stunts backfires. Finally, Fate sees a way to destroy his foe. When Leslie organizes a New York–Paris automobile race (yes, automobile race—heading west, across the Bering Sea), Fate and his numbskull aide, Max (Peter Falk), enter a souped-up, heavily artilleried vehicle, determined to kill Leslie en route. Also partaking in the race is suffragette Maggie Dubois (Natalie Wood), who's covering the event for the press. Once they set off, it's one fight, pratfall, crash, and disaster after another, which leave the two men neck and neck as they head for the finish line.

Blake Edwards set out to make the greatest slapstick comedy in history, but not only was he working in the shadow of *It's a Mad Mad Mad Mad World* (see page 149), he didn't have the cast of comics to pull it off. Lemmon is great, the oiliest screen villain since Henry Kleinbach in *March of the Wooden Soldiers* (see page 182). But Curtis is stiff and unfunny, and Natalie Wood is *grossly* unamusing, with a fake smile and feminism that rings totally false. (She once said she liked making the film but hated the results, determining—rightly—that slapstick was not for her). Keenan Wynn is sturdy as Leslie's aide, Hezekiah, and George Macready and Larry Storch have their moments as General Kuhster and the rootin' tootin' Texas Jack, respectively.

The variable acting wouldn't have mattered so much if the gags were funny. They're not. The race starts out with the amusing destruction of the cars of the other entrants, after which its downhill. There's a long, unfunny brawl that wrecks the Silver Palace Saloon out west, clunky high jinks with a polar bear in Alaska, and a highly contrived pie fight in Pottsdorf. The only highlights in the entire second half are a terrific swordfight, played straight, between Leslie and the wicked Rolfe Von Stuppe (Ross Martin), and the last shot in the film, which involves the Eiffel Tower and is the film's best gag.

The Disc
Video: ★★★★
Audio: ★★★★ (Surround)
Chapters: Yes
Format: CLV
Source: Warner Home Video

The transfer on this letterboxed edition is extremely bright and detailed, so at least you'll have something to look at when there's nothing worth watching. The picture is relatively free of video noise, and there's no grain of which to speak. A generous letterbox gives Edwards's gags the elbowroom they need.

The audio really sings, and the stereo effects are of epic dimensions, from explosive backfiring motors to a storm in the Arctic. The Surround aspect is limited to music and spillover from the front speakers.

Henry Mancini's lively overture, entr'acte, and exit music are included.

The Grifters (1990) ★★★
Director: Stephen Frears
Running Time: 119 minutes

Frears doesn't make happy movies. Having worked as an assistant to Lindsay Anderson (*If . . .* , 1968) and other "angry young men" of the sixties, he began directing small films in 1971 before clicking in the mainstream with *My Beautiful Launderette* (1985). He followed it with films such as *Prick Up Your Ears* (1987), *Sammy and Rosie Get Laid* (1987), and *Dangerous Liaisons* (see page 60).

The Grifters is his darkest film. Based on the novel by Jim Thompson—a pulp writer whose work was also the basis for Sam Peckinpah's *The Getaway* (1972)—

it's about a trio of con artists: Lily Dillon (Anjelica Huston), who travels from racetrack to racetrack making large bets to change the odds in favor of her criminal employers; her son, Roy (John Cusack), a shortchange artist; and his girlfriend, Myra Langry (Annette Bening). After Roy is badly beaten up by a bartender who catches him in a scam, the women come together to care for him. Roy's well-being becomes secondary to the multifaceted rivalry between the women; in his pathetic world, even love turns out to be a con, a fact that leads to the film's unexpected and horrifying conclusion.

Cusack describes the film as "psychologically violent" and "really disturbing," and spending two hours with these people in their seedy world is *not* a pleasant experience. It's also not as illuminating as you might expect. Lily had Roy when she was young and wasn't there for him in a motherly way, so her motivation now is a complex mix of guilt, Oedipal love, and jealousy; she's fascinating, and Huston's performance is incredible. The other two leads are vaguely drawn, despite the best efforts of Bening and Cusack.

This is a good film, though it hasn't got the kind of depth or style that'll bring you back for subsequent looks.

The Disc
Video: ★
Audio: ★★★ (stereo)
Chapters:
Format: CLV
Source: HBO Video

The Grifters is a grainy, monochromatic film, and the transfer has only made matters worse. The colors have a runny, "colorized" look in spots, and there's grain aplenty. The image is not terribly sharp; the titles are letterboxed, which gives you an idea of what you're missing due to the mild cropping.

The audio is perfectly clear, with some very nice separation effects in the dialogue. Still, the sound doesn't make the film *that* much better: Catch it on HBO.

The Guardian (1990) ★
Director: William Friedkin
Running Time: 92 minutes

Ah, how hopes were high for Friedkin's return to the genre, the fine director's first horror film since *The Exorcist* (see page 89). The idea for the film *sounded* pretty fruity—a young woman sacrifices kids to a sacred tree—but Friedkin would pull it off, right?

'Fraid not. The movie is just as idiotic as it sounds. Los Angeles advertising executive Phil (Dwier Brown) and his wife, Kate (Carey Lowell), hire nanny Camilla (Jenny Seagrove) to look after their infant. (Shouldn't that Le Fanu-ish name have been a tipoff that something wasn't quite right about the lady?) Unknown to them, Camilla is actually a druid devoted to sustaining an ancient tree, sustaining it with the lives of babes. In return, the tree protects Camilla, slaughtering—among others —some bikers who menace Camilla.

Though this embarrassing travesty has more holes than an old sock, the biggest is this: After having killed a number of people, the tree doesn't lift a twig to stop Phil from chain-sawing it to death. Even Friedkin's occasionally eerie touches can't rescue the movie from that plot hole or from the hyperactive performances.

As human-killing-foliage films go— from the vintage *Woman Eater* (1959) to *The Little Shop of Horrors* (1960 and 1986) to *Poltergeist* (1982)—this one is the worst ... all bark and no bite.

The Disc
Video: ★★★★½
Audio: ★★★★★ (Surround)
Chapters:
Format: CLV
Source: MCA/Universal Home Video

Too bad such a stunning transfer was wasted on a loser like this. The colors are robust, the image is supersharp, and there's detail even in the many dark and night scenes. The transfer is marred only by a hint of grain. The film is not letterboxed, but Friedkin framed his shots with TV in mind, so nothing is lost.

The audio is as detailed and rich as can be, and the Surround Sound will make you feel as if the tree and its victims are in the room with you.

Gunga Din (1939) ★★★½
Director: George Stevens
Running Time: 117 minutes

Rudyard Kipling's *Barrack-Room Ballads* (1892) is a volume of poems honoring the British soldier, and "Gunga Din" is the most famous of these. It celebrates a Hindu water carrier who served with a British regiment in India, and concludes with the famous passage, "You're a better man than I am, Gunga Din."

Aware of the big box-office grosses of movies about British imperialism—films such as *The Lives of a Bengal Lancer* (1935) and *The Charge of the Light Brigade* (1936)—producer Edward Small bought the rights to "Gunga Din" and hired William Faulkner to write a screenplay that Howard Hawks was to direct. Feeling that Faulkner's script lacked pizzazz, Hawks engaged Ben Hecht and Charles MacArthur to make revisions. They scrapped most of Faulkner's work and came up with a *Gunga Din* that was less Kipling and more Alexandre Dumas—the Three Musketeers in India.

When the telegraph from the village of Tantrapor is cut, soldiers from the British army post at Muri are sent north to find out what happened. Headed by the rollicking Sergeants Cutter (Cary Grant), MacChesney (Victor McLaglen), and Ballantine (Douglas Fairbanks, Jr.), the soldiers learn that the Thuggee murder cult has been revived to serve the goddess Kali. Following the brave water carrier Gunga Din (Sam Jaffe) to a distant temple of gold, Cutter learns that's where Thuggee guru (Eduardo Ciannelli) holds court. Din leaves to get word to the others, and Cutter is taken prisoner. MacChesney and Ballantine are also captured and survive by holding the guru prisoner. However, they are helpless to warn their onrushing men that they're headed into an ambush. Fortunately, Din is able to make it to the top of the temple with a bugle and alerts the soldiers before being killed. Arriving at the camp, correspondent Rudyard Kipling (Reginald Sheffield) writes his poem in time for it to be read at Din's funeral.

Those who encounter *Gunga Din* today, for the first time, can't understand what all the fuss was about. The battle scenes are unrealistic (punches rarely seem to connect, and the cameras were undercranked to speed up the action), it has a condescending view of the Indians, and the characters subscribe to the insane notion that killing is fun. But to hold it accountable for the prevailing attitudes of the time just wouldn't be cricket. *Gunga Din* remains the favorite film of many men who saw it when young, and no wonder: Its heroes are smart-mouthed bad boys who do what they want and get away with it.

The film also has terrific performances, not just by the three principals but by Jaffe and the spidery Ciannelli—plus all the spectacle $1.9 million could buy at the time, which was considerable.

The film was shot outside Lone Pine, California, in the Alabama Range, where the producers constructed the army post, Tantrapor, and the temple. The final battle was shot with nine hundred extras crawling all over Mt. Whitney.

The Disc
Video: ★★
Audio: ★★ (monaural)
Chapters: Yes
Format: CLV
Source: Turner Home Entertainment/ Image Entertainment

If you are a fan, keep your fingers crossed that one day someone will find a better print of the film from which to make a transfer. The disc features restored footage, which is nice (the Kipling scenes have been missing for years), but there's mild grain in far too many shots and some scratches throughout.

The picture is fairly sharp overall, but the contrast is only adequate to good.

The audio has faint background pops and noises, but it's otherwise satisfactory.

Hairspray (1988) ★★★½
Director: John Waters
Running Time: 92 minutes

After making experimental movies for several years, Baltimore-based filmmaker John Waters gained national exposure with his audacious *Pink Flamingos* (1972), in which Mink Stole and David Lochary abduct women, force them to have children, and peddle the babies to lesbian couples. In the film's legendary climax, three-hundred-pound transvestite Divine (the late Harris Glenn Milstead) eats feces, straight from the dog, in one take. After three other films—including *Polyester* (1981), about a degenerate family, which was shown with scratch-and-sniff cards—Waters went "mainstream" with *Hairspray*.

"The Corky Collins Show" is a popular afternoon dance show in Baltimore of 1962, and it has no bigger fan (literally) than overweight Tracy Turnblad (Ricki Lake). Through an unexpected series of events, Tracy becomes a star dancer on the show and competes against gorgeous (and ruthless) Amber Von Tussle (Colleen Fitzpatrick) for the coveted title of Miss Auto Show 1963 (*sic*). Meanwhile, racial tensions explode on several fronts, as Tracy's best friend, Penny Pingleton (Leslie Ann Powers), dates a black teen, Seaweed (Clayton Prince), and Corky (Shawn Thompson) joins forces with black deejay Motormouth Maybelle (Ruth Brown) in an effort to integrate his show. An antisegregation protest at the studio lands Tracy in reform school, making Amber a shoo-in for Miss Auto Show ... or so it seems. As in films of the sixties, things work out for our Tracy.

In the midst of all the chaos and teenage angst, there's plenty of music and dance as well as Waters's outré sense of humor: a bomb hidden inside one character's Marie Antoinette hairdo; Penny locked in her room behind a jail-house door; Jerry Stiller as Tracy's novelty-gift salesman father, Wilbur, complaining that he lost a Silly Putty sale to watch his daughter on TV; Divine as Tracy's mother, Edna, *and* as WZZT station president Arvin Hodgepile; and Waters himself as Dr. Fredrickson, a quack psychiatrist.

Many longtime fans of the director feel he sold out with this film, a criticism that was also leveled at his next feature, *Cry-Baby* (1990), starring Johnny Depp as a teen from the wrong side of the tracks who's in love with a society girl. It would be more accurate to say that Waters has evolved, using camp and satire instead of shock to make his points about race and class—and to a wider audience.

Sonny Bono and Debbie Harry costar as Amber's parents, Franklin and Velma; Pia Zadora and rock star Ric Ocasek have bit parts as beatniks.

The Disc
Video: ★★
Audio: ★★★★ (Surround)
Chapters: No
Format: CLV
Source: RCA Columbia Pictures Home Video

The disc has more colors than a big box of Crayolas, but they're muted by a hazy brownish cast and a slight dusting of grain. The film isn't letterboxed, though panning-and-scanning is minimal (for example, at 24:09 on side two).

The stereo sound is heaven for oldies fans, and the rear speakers should be cranked up to get the full impact of the tunes.

Cry-Baby is also available on laserdisc, with a clearer picture and even better audio. *Polyester* is available only as a Japanese import, scratch-and-sniff card not included.

The Hallelujah Trail (1965) ★★½
Director: John Sturges
Running Time: 166 minutes

Inspired by the success of *It's a Mad Mad Mad Mad World* (see page 149), Sturges—a man known for his action films, not his comedies—decided to direct a big, dumb, Western spoof. He succeeded in three-quarters of his goal: *The Hallelujah Trail* is a big, dumb Western. As a spoof, it leaves a lot to be desired. Fortunately, even when the comedy doesn't work—which is often—at least there's Sturges doing what he does best: filling the screen with spectacular vistas (shot in Gallup, New Mexico) and thunderous action.

It's the fall of 1867, and the signs point to a hard winter. Denver is low on liquor, and though six hundred barrels are on the way from Philadelphia (in the hands of strike-primed Irish teamsters), bogus seer Oracle Jones (Donald Pleasence) suggests that a party of miners set out to meet it. They're not alone: Also heading to intercept the wagons are fiery temperance worker Cora Templeton Massingale (Lee Remick) and her band of women, as well as a large party of Indians led by Chief Five Barrels (Robert J. Wilke) and Chief Walks-Stooped-Over (Martin Landau). Setting out from nearby Fort Russell, Col. Thaddeus Gearheart (Burt Lancaster), Capt. Paul Slater (Jim Hutton), and their men have the difficult task of keeping the various groups from killing one another or stealing the liquor.

The movie isn't *Blazing Saddles*: The humor isn't as relentless, crude, or successful. Good ideas tend to go on too long: The Battle of Whiskey Flats, fought in a blinding sandstorm, has a few great laughs (an Indian dismounting on the wrong side of a cliff, Pleasence huddled by a rock and watching the enemies try to find one another) but also too much footage of people stumbling around blindly. Likewise, Sturges didn't know when to pack up and go home during the ill-fated wagon trip through Quicksand Bottoms.

As you'd expect from the man who gave us *The Magnificent Seven* (see page 179), the production is impeccable and the action scenes dazzling. There isn't a single process shot in the film: Close-ups of the actors on galloping horses or runaway wagons are actually the actors on horses and wagons, not special-effects shots. The stunt work and wagon crashes in the climactic chase are amazing (though there's a very visible cable that pulls the wagon over at 3/30.34). Watch for the shot of a wagon diving off a cliff and crashing toward the camera. It's the film's most spectacular stunt and it cost stuntman Billy Williams his life when he failed to get off in time with two other stuntmen.

Lancaster is stern and blustery in what's basically the straight-man role, the voice of sanity amidst the insane and inept. Looming large amoung the latter are Sergeant Buell (John Anderson), who takes most of the movie's pratfalls; Frank Wallingham (a marvelously crusty Brian Keith), who owns the liquor and wants it to get where it's going; Pleasence, who seems to drop in from another planet now and then; and Landau, a frightened deer of an Indian who's smarter than everybody around him. The late Lee Remick is prim as Massingale—though it's difficult to imagine her as a temperance worker after her brilliant work as an alcoholic in *Days of Wine and Roses* (1962). Pamela Tiffin is just pretty as Louise, Gearhart's daughter/Cora's disciple/Slater's lover.

No one writes music for movie Westerns as well as Elmer Bernstein, and the powerful, catchy score is one of his best.

The Disc
Video: ★★★★½
Audio: ★★★★½ (Surround)
Chapters: No
Format: CLV
Source: MGM/UA Home Video

Filmed in Ultra Panavision and Technicolor, on 70mm stock, *The Hallelujah Trail* was breathtaking on the screen: Now it's breathtaking in this meticulously transferred letterbox edition. The colors are eye-popping, the exterior detail is incredible (some of the interiors are on the soft side), and the print is in near-mint condition.

The digital sound delivers the goods, whether it's a soft, intimate moment between Lancaster and Remick, a heavenly choir singing whenever Oracle has a "vision," or the brass and percussion of Bernstein's score. The stereo separation is excellent, but the Surround aspect isn't fully utilized: Front and rear speakers simply get a different balance of the same material.

After the film's initial, disappointing Cinerama road-show engagement, approximately fifteen minutes were cut and the intermission was dropped. These have been restored, along with the overture and exit music.

The trailer is included, though it misstates the date of the movie's action by a decade.

Hamlet (1948) ★★★★★
Director: Laurence Olivier
Running Time: 155 minutes

Hamlet is considered by many scholars to be Shakespeare's greatest play. Written in 1601, it was based on the historical account that first appeared in the twelfth century *Historia Danica* and also, apparently, on Elizabethan playwright Thomas Kyd's play about the prince. (No copies of Kyd's work are extant, but contemporary writings suggest that it contained all the major plot points that appeared in Shakespeare's play.)

Hamlet is set at the Danish castle in Elsinore, where Claudius has poisoned his brother, the king, taken his throne, and married his (willing) widow, Gertrude. The ghost of the dead king appears to his grieving son, Hamlet, and describes the murder: After fits of indecisiveness and self-pity, Hamlet exposes his uncle's murderous act by having actors stage a play recreating the fratricide. Later, the embittered, frightened Claudius conspires with Laertes, the son of Lord Chamberlain Polonius—whom Hamlet has inadvertently murdered—to slay Hamlet in a "friendly" duel. During their swordplay, Gertrude accidentally drinks a cup of poison intended for Hamlet; Laertes nicks Hamlet with a poisoned sword and then is himself wounded with it; and Hamlet, told by the dying Laertes that the king was behind the plot, slays the murderous Claudius.

Though a magnificent film, *Hamlet* has always been a controversial one. For one thing, to keep the film from running over four hours, Olivier didn't just snip a line here and there, he dropped entire sections of the text—such as two important soliloquies, "O, what a rogue and peasant slave am I" and "How all occasions do inform against me"—and dropped Rosencrantz and Guildenstern—who, at Claudius's behest, were supposed to spy on Hamlet and then lead him to his death—as well as Fortinbras, an aspirant to the throne who, implicitly, ends up with the crown when all the carnage is through.

Olivier also turned lengthy passages of dialogue into thought and changed two dozen words to make certain passages more accessible to a mass audience. Shakespeare scholars were not happy, but Olivier parried their complaints by noting that they must also, then, "forbid the performance of Verdi's operas of *Othello* and *Falstaff*."

Finally, Olivier, at forty-one, was nearly twice the age of the troubled Dane. He did not even want to play the part, claiming, "My style of acting is more suited to stronger character roles . . . rather than to the lyrical, poetical role of Hamlet." Having already achieved success with *Henry V* (1944), in which he starred and also directed, he simply wanted to direct *Hamlet*. However, after searching for "an actor of sufficient standing to carry the role on whom I could have impressed my interpretation . . . I thought it simpler to play Hamlet myself." He dyed his hair blond, he said, so that audiences would not say, " 'There is Laurence Olivier dressed like Hamlet,' but, 'That is Hamlet.' "

And that *is* Hamlet. Though the loss of crucial segments and characters is irksome, his performance is hypnotic. He speaks the lines in a way that is completely comprehensible to modern ears, and he carries himself with the kind of poise and grace that takes one's breath away. Though he was not an athletic actor, he directed and acted the climactic duel magnificently—something one might not realize upon first viewing because the drama itself is so captivating. (Olivier himself performed the jump from the top of the stairs onto Claudius: It was the last shot they did, in case Olivier was hurt. That's also Olivier's voice you hear as the ghost, slowed down to give it an otherworldly quality.)

Eileen Herlie, Basil Sydney, Felix Aylmer, and Norman Wooland are very good as Getrude, Claudius, Polonius, and Hamlet's friend Horatio, respectively. Terence Morgan is surprisingly passionless as Laertes, and Jean Simmons is pretty but bland as Hamlet's love, the doomed Ophelia. Film buffs will enjoy horror-film star Peter Cushing as a foppish Osric, and Niall MacGinnis (*Jason and the Argonauts* and *Curse of the Demon*) as the sea captain.

The sets are imposing, abstract, and haunting; the early part of the film, including the appearances of the ghost, rivals the eerie best of the Universal horror films. The cinematography is amazing: Without detracting from what Orson Welles achieved in *Citizen Kane* (see page 48), it's shocking that Olivier's swooping, prowling, innovative camerawork has not been revered in the same way. (It's not *quite* technical perfection, though: Watch how the pond reverses itself at 9:10 on side two—Olivier hadn't shot enough footage for the dialogue to be laid on over it—then goes into a poor dissolve at 9:23.)

The Disc

Video: ★½
Audio: ★★
Chapters: No
Format: CLV
Source: Paramount

This movie must have been something to see when the prints were new and unscathed. As it is, the source material for this laserdisc is severely scratched in many places, moderately scratched in others, and rarely completely clean. The whites (especially the faces) are irridescent (except, absurdly, the ghost). In many cases, they lack any detail at all. The blacks are fairly solid and there is a decent but far from satisfactory range of gray tones. The image varies between sharp and fuzzy, with the most satisfying stretch occurring in the first third of side two.

The audio has many crackles and some hiss, but all of the words are audible. William Walton's extraordinary score is frustratingly tinny.

Director Franco Zeffirelli's 1990 remake is also available on a letterboxed laserdisc, and it features excellent performances by Glenn Close as Gertrude and Alan Bates as Claudius. Alas, Mel Gibson is as awful a Hamlet as you are likely to see, full of sound and fury with nothing of pain or canniness behind those eyes. Give him an *A* for effort ... though the poison came 134 minutes too late. The video and audio on the remake are both ★★★★; if only the condition of the two films was reversed!

The best Hamlet of recent years has been Kevin Kline's, a 1991 PBS presentation in modern dress, which is not available on laserdisc.

Hardware (1990) ★★½
Director: Richard Stanley
Running Time: 93 minutes

It's the twenty-first century and the world is poisoned by pollution and radiation. In the cities, where only a remnant of order survives, sculptress Jill (Stacey Travis) lives in a high-security apartment, where she's visited, occasionally, by her Corpsman lover Moses (Dylan McDermott). Unknown to both, surveillance expert and pervert Linc (William Hootkins) spies on them from another apartment.

Returning after a long absence, Moses brings Jill a gift—a broken-down M.A.R.K.-13 robot (check your New Testament)—which, unknown to them both, is a self-repairing combat drone. Jill uses the head in a sculpture and, after Moses leaves, the heat-seeking robot comes to life, reassembles itself, and stalks her through the apartment, trying to kill her. Voyeur Linc comes to her aid and is brutally murdered by the thing, which continues to hunt Jill in the small, inescapable apartment. Pretty soon, it seems as if half the city is trying to rescue her. She *is* saved, though not before, *Alien*-like, the drone returns over and over and ...

Based on the story by Steve MacManus

and Kevil O'Neill published in the British comic book *2000 AD*, the low-budget film was shot in London and Morocco and makes good use of both locations. It contains narrative and visual elements reminiscent of *Mad Max* (1979), *Alien* (1979), and *The Terminator* (see page 272), though it has its own unique, dreary vision of the future and some interesting characters. The special effects are fine, and the movie does not want for disembowelings, eyeball gougings, and other staples of splatter SF. (No surprise there: Producer Rachel Talalay was the co-producer of *A Nightmare on Elm Street 4: The Dream Master* [1988] and wrote and directed *Freddy's Dead* [1991]).

Unfortunately, that unique vision is dulled by a script that leaves too many questions unanswered and allows some improbable twists (along with some clever ones) in the final confrontation. You'll enjoy the film, but you'll be annoyed at how far short of its potential it falls.

The Disc
Video: ★★
Audio: ★★★½ (Surround)
Chapters: Yes
Format: CLV
Source: HBO Video/Image Entertainment

The disc has an alternately reddish and grainy look, problems inherent in the source material and not the fault of the transfer. There's a serious noise problem in the reds and browns, though, which is particularly troublesome in the opening scenes set in the desert.

The lack of a letterbox doesn't create any problems.

The sound is extremely clear, though there aren't as many zingy directional effects as you'd expect in a film of this type.

The Hard Way (1991) ★★★½
Director: John Badham
Running Time: 111 minutes

It's a joy watching two good actors play off each other, and though James Woods and Michael J. Fox aren't exactly Peter O'Toole and Richard Burton in *Becket*, they overcome a pedestrian script and yet another psycho-on-the-loose story line to generate real entertainment.

In order to give his lawman roles more authority, Nick Lang (Fox), a Cagney-like action star, arranges to spend two weeks with a real cop, John Moss (Woods). Moss, who's on the trail of a serial killer known as the Party Crasher (Stephen Lang), can't stand having the pampered star around him—especially because his own girlfirend, Susan (Annabella Sciorra), gets along better with Nick Lang than with him. Though Moss does everything he can to shake the little twit during his investigation (including handcuffing him to the bed in his apartment), Nick Lang is there for the hair-raising showdown with Moss, Susan, and the Party Crasher atop an animated Nick Lang billboard in Times Square.

The movie was a box-office flop, which was surprising. There's something for everyone here: engaging performers, terrific action scenes, romance, and humor (the highlight: Nick Lang taking the part of Suan so Moss can rehearse what to say to win her back). Director Badham (see *Dracula* and *Bird on a Wire*) keeps things moving; as zippy, mindless movies go, you couldn't ask for a better one.

The Disc
Video: ★★★★½
Audio: ★★★★ (Surround)
Chapters: No
Format: CLV
Source: MCA/Universal Home Video

There are letterbox and pan-and-scan editions, but the action absolutely requires the wide-screen version. Both feature perfectly sharp images and solid colors. The occasional color noise and sprinkling of grain here and there are a minor distraction.

The audio is wonderfully clear and dimensional and there are some head-turning directional effects.

Harlem Nights (1989)
★★½
Director: Eddie Murphy
Running Time: 118 minutes

It's fashionable to knock *Harlem Nights*. Eddie Murphy was ripe for attack: He came to the film with more hits than Pete Rose, and was making his directorial debut. And Murphy made the attack easy: Despite the fact that the movie takes place in 1938, his characters speak in 1980s jargon—for example, "Let's get this shit out in the open" and "I'll let you have your space." There are also countless slips in continuity, such as Murphy putting his finger to his cheek in chapter six, 45.04, and it not being there in the next shot. Murphy obviously had very little respect, if not outright contempt, for the intelligence of the audience.

Despite all of that, the film has many assets. It's tough to get over the flaws and *enjoy* them, but they're there. For one thing, Murphy gives Richard Pryor his best role in years, and the ailing Pryor turns in his last really fine screen performance. Murphy is also surprisingly good, playing an interesting hothead of a character and does far, far less mugging than in most of his films. There's meticulous attention to the physical details of the period (including a spectacular face-lift for the New York Street at the Burbank Studios) and a fun, very clever *Sting*-like story.

Eddie Murphy plays Quick, the two-fisted sidekick of Sugar Ray (Pryor), owner of Club Sugar Ray in New York's Harlem. Powerful rival club owner Bugsy Calhoune (Michael Lerner) and his partner, crooked police sergeant Phil Cantone (Danny Aiello), want to take over the profitable after-hours spot, but Ray and Quick don't intend to knuckle under the pressure—which includes a come-on from Calhoune's sexy hit-woman mistress, Dominique La Rue (Jasmine Guy). With the help of coworkers Bennie Wilson (Redd Foxx), Vera (Della Reese), and others, Quick and Sugar Ray come up with a scheme to sink the downtown bullies.

Murphy the screenwriter is no Damon Runyon, and his characters lack the slangy individualism of such characters as the Lemon Drop Kid and Harry the Horse. But he has great performers in his corner, giving the characters much more weight than there was in the script. He also has—in a very small part—Arsenio Hall as a gangster gunning for Murphy. The Hall subplot comes out of left field and disappears almost as quickly, but while it's there it's the film's magnificent, dumb highlight.

The Disc
Video: ★★★★
Audio: ★★★★★ (Surround)
Chapters: Yes
Format: CLV
Source: Paramount

It's ironic that Murphy's two least-successful projects—*Another 48 HRS.* (1990) is the other—have been given the best transfers of all his films.

The colors of *Harlem Nights* are radiant, from the wardrobe to the bright lights of the street scenes. There are stretches of speckling here and there, and a number of the night scenes are so dark they look like moving mud. But video noise and grain are minimal, and the good outweighs the bad.

There's *nothing* wrong with the audio, from the perfectly clear dialogue and sound effects to the striking stereo separation. There are many entertaining Surround effects as well, including chatter at the club, the roar of cars, and the *pop* of guns.

Harlem Nights is available in both letterbox and pan-and-scan versions. Though Murphy tends to employ close-ups a lot—which look fine in the pan-and-scan edition—there are two shots where the reactions are as funny as what's being said—for example, Pryor listening to Murphy's colorful description in chapter two, 11.02. Cropped, these scenes simply don't deliver the goods.

Harper (1966) ★★★½
Director: Jack Smight
Running Time: 121 minutes

Author Ross Macdonald's private eye Lew Archer is an honest cop who quit the corrupt LAPD and went to work as a private eye, specializing in divorce. He made his debut in *The Moving Target*, published in 1949, and went on to star in seventeen other novels.

Afraid that filmgoers would think he was like a modern-day Robin Hood, the filmmakers renamed the character Harper—confident, one supposes, that no one would think he was a musician. (Paul Newman also had had some luck with *H* movies, such as *The Hustler* [1961] and *Hud* [1963], and perhaps wanted to stick with the letter. The film's success vindicated his superstition.) The filmmakers also jettisoned Archer's art and music–loving sensitivity and gave him a quick tongue and a fondness for accents (long before Chevy Chase's Fletch became the preeminent master of disguises). It's not Macdonald, but the characterzation works and, except for a totally misguided, unbelievable, stupid-as-they-come ending, the film does, too.

At the suggestion of attorney Albert Graves (Arthur Hill), Mrs. Sampson (Lauren Bacall) hires Lew Harper to find her millionaire husband, Ralph, who disappeared from the Van Nuys airport when pilot Allan Taggert (Robert Wagner) left him alone for a few minutes. During the course of his investigation, Harper talks to Ralph's daughter, Miranda (Pamela Tiffin), fallen movie star Fay Estabrook (Shelley Winters), her sadistic husband, Dwight Troy (Robert Webber), jazz-singing junkie Betty Fraley (Julie Harris), and many other quirky sorts. In time, he learns that Ralph has been kidnapped, but that's just the tip of the proverbial iceberg. Practically everyone is guilty of *something* in this film, though who and what and how they're all connected makes it a lot of fun.

The film is weak on action but strong on barbed dialogue, and wonderfully awash with the look and feel of Southern California in the sixties. It boasts terrific performances—many, such as Harris's and Webber's, against type. Newman is fine, playing a character that he has described as a cross between Humphrey Bogart and Robert Kennedy. Those blue eyes have never looked better, and the filmmakers have fun with the fact that most of the women he meets can't stand him. Talk about "against type...."

Janet Leigh provides some astringent moments as Harper's bitter, estranged wife, Susan, and Strother Martin has fun as the mountaintop religious fanatic Claude. Newman's scenes with him are funny and incisive.

Watch for the gaffe at 4/15:26 on side one: the "now you see it, now you don't" food in Newman's mouth.

Newman made the second Archer novel, *The Drowning Pool* (1950), in 1976, with his wife Joanne Woodward costarring.

The Disc
Video: ★★★★½
Audio: ★★★★★ (monaural)
Chapters: Yes
Format: CLV
Source: Warner Home Video

You won't believe the beauty of the picture and transfer, which is perfect, save for some minor imperfections and a bit of washout in portions of the source material. The blacks are deep, the whites are bright, and everything in between is positively stunning, particularly the flesh tones. There isn't a trace of video noise, and barely any grain. The letterboxing shows off the film's striking compositions.

The digital audio is stunning. No details are lost, and Bacall's catty drawl and Webber's hissing evil *really* come across. Jazz fans will particularly enjoy the music played at the club and on the sound track.

Havana (1990) ★½
Director: Sydney Pollack
Running Time: 145 minutes

The place: Cuba, just before Castro's overthrow of the corrupt regime of President Batista. Gambler Jack Weil (Robert Redford) has come to Havana to play poker, feeling that the political turmoil will make people take risks that ordinarily they wouldn't. There, he meets Roberta Duran (Lena Olin), the wife of Castro sympathizer Arturo Duran (Raul Julia), and they share a definite sexual attraction. When Arturo is believed to have been killed by Batista's men, Jack and "Bobby" fall into bed and even make plans to return to the United States together. Then all hell breaks loose, Arturo turns up alive, and the unprincipled Jack must find out whether he has the courage to do something for someone other than himself.

Sound familiar? It should. It's an update of *Casablanca* (coincidentally, the female leads were both born in Stockholm, Sweden). Only it's *Casablanca* copied with Silly Putty, stretched to an inordinate length, robbed of color, populated with stereotypes and caricatures instead of characters, and for the most part *dull*. Redford plays Jack's world-weariness as boredom, which isn't the same thing. Lena Olin has some fire, but she fails to spark off either the lethargic Redford or the hollow, self-righteous Julia. It's a remarkable, chauvinistic conceit, by the way, to have the attractive young Olin drawn to Redford's character. We're expected to buy into that just because he *is* Robert Redord—but frankly, he looks like hell, worn and ragged and lacking the old Redford charisma.

There are a few tense and exciting scenes, mostly involving the supporting players, such as Alan Arkin as Mafia flunky Joe Volpi, Mark Rydell as gangster Meyer Lansky, and Tomas Milian as secret-police chief Menocal. These characters, like the settings, ring true. Unfortunately, the leads do not, and the movie sinks with them.

Opulently staged and shot in the Dominican Republic, the film was supposed to win the Triple Crown for the director, coming after *Out of Africa* (1985) and *Tootsie* (1982). Though photos show that the man was on the set, directing the film, you've got to wonder whether executive-producing two other movies that year (*Presumed Innocent* and *White Palace*) had left him just a little overextended.

The Disc
Video: ★★★★
Audio: ★★★★ (Surround)
Chapters: No
Format: CLV
Source: MCA/Universal Home Video

Except for the fact that the exquisite art direction is hurt by cropping, the transfer is ideal. The colors are vivid and radiant, and the subtle halos and glow that suffuse many of the scenes are captured with delicate precision. The film is largely free of grain and noise.

The audio is extremely clear and atmospheric, and there are numerous Surround effects, many of them quite unique (given the casino and locales), and most of them very effective. God knows you'll be listening to them *very* carefully as you try to stay focused on the film.

Head (1968) ★★½
Director: Bob Rafelson
Running Time: 86 minutes

It's always been in vogue to slam the Monkees, the rock group assembled in 1966 to star in a Beatles-inspired TV series. True, the members were chosen from the hundreds of hopefuls who answered a newspaper ad, but Michael Nesmith, Peter Tork, Davy Jones, and Micky Dolenz weren't the novices their detractors made them out to be. Nesmith had been writing songs and cutting records since 1961 (and wrote the hit Linda Ronstadt song "Different Drum"); Tork was a guitarist who'd been playing the Greenwich Village coffeehouses for years; Jones had appeared on Broadway in *Oliver!* and had also made several records; and Dolenz was a child star who'd played with several bands.

Once they were thrown together, the foursome meshed quickly as a group and, with the help of songwriters such as Neil Diamond, Carole King, and Harry Nilsson, turned out some of the best pop tunes of the sixties.

Their eponymous TV series lasted two seasons, after which the Monkees made a feature film. Rather than duplicate the formula of the series, in which they played struggling musicians who were always getting into trouble, they made a plotless film whose stream-of-consciousness vignettes commented on everything from war to fame to their "plastic" image to movie clichés.

Highlights of the nostalgically psychedelic film—which was written by Jack Nicholson and Rafelson (who went on to direct *Five Easy Pieces* and *Mountains of the Moon* [see pages 100 and 190])—are Micky's jump from a suspension bridge and mermaid rescue (accompanied by the wonderful "Porpoise Song"), Davy Jones's black and white dance, the trip up a vacuum cleaner, and the rippin' concert scene. The film features guest appearances by Sonny Liston, Terry (Teri) Garr, Victor Mature, Annette Funicello, Divine, Frank Zappa, and Nicholson.

Head hasn't got the innocence or energy of the Beatles' *A Hard Days Night* (1964) or *Help!* (1965), which inspired the Monkees TV series. But the film is ambitious and eclectic, and you won't come away unentertained.

The Disc

Video: ★★½
Audio: ★★½ (monaural)
Chapters: No
Format: CLV
Source: RCA/Columbia Pictures Home Video

Though the disc is primitive by contemporary standards, it's better than other films of this vintage (1986). The picture's a little soft and there's a hint of grain in many scenes. But the colors are bold and the action is dead-center, so that cropping isn't a problem.

The audio is a solid but unspectacular presentation of the good tunes and unusual sound effects. Some digital cleaning and stereo rechanneling would have been nice, but it's not bad at all.

There are three collections of the Monkees TV series (two episodes on each), and these are recommended as entertainment—though the colors have gone a bit reddish over the years.

The two well-known Beatles films are available on excellent Criterion discs, both CLV and CAV editions.

Henry & June (1990) ★★★★
Director: Philip Kaufman
Running Time: 136 minutes

In 1931, unpublished author Henry Miller went to Paris for what turned out to be a nine-year stay. While he was there, he wrote, among other works, his sensational *Tropic of Cancer*—a metaphoric and sexually explicit autobiographical work about his degradation and triumphs in the French capital. During this time, he also met and had an affair with critic and writer Anaïs Nin, whose detailed diaries chronicled the affair and provide a fascinating insight into the minds and lust of Nin and her lover.

What is remarkable about the film is how it evokes the tone and voice of Nin's diaries. If you read them, the film will replay itself in your mind—and vice versa. Though *Henry & June* was originally given an X rating, it actually shows far less than Nin tells in her writings, and Kaufman was right to refuse to cut it. To its credit, Universal backed him and was prepared to release the film unrated; the MPAA responded by creating a new NC-17 rating.

Still, the film is not short on eroticism, both heterosexual and homosexual, as it examines the relationship between Nin (Maria de Medeiros) and Miller (Fred Ward) and, peripherally, her ambitious banker husband, Hugo (Richard E. Grant), and Miller's actress wife, June (Uma Thurman). Despite some hammy and overwrought moments, *Henry & June* effectively chronicles Nin's growing self-awareness—sexual, creative, and otherwise. Maria de Medeiros is brave, vulnerable, sensuous, and strong as Nin—and looks amazingly like her. Ward's Miller (with a shaved head and bad fake hair pasted on the sides) tends to expound a lot, not always making valid points or sense, but you'll be won over by his passion and by the actor's charisma. Thurman is sexy and raw, an interesting character who should have had more screen time (she does, after all, share the title of the film). The shallow Hugo gets too *much* screen time. And the psychoanalyst, Dr. Allendy, so important to the diaries, is eliminated entirely.

The French locations and art direction are magnificent, vividly evoking prewar Paris.

The Disc

Video: ★★★★
Audio: ★★★½
Chapters: No
Format: CLV (sides one and two), CAV (side three)
Source: MCA Universal Home Video

Considering the dark and often monochromatic tones of the original film, the transfer is most impressive. Though there's a dusting of grain in many scenes—particularly on side three—the picture is generally sharp, with solid colors and glossy blacks. Video noise is rarely a problem, and the letterboxing allows the viewer to savor the careful positioning of the characters and the inspired flow of the editing.

The audio is a little soft, but stereo separations are good. The rear channels are sparingly but effectively used for emphasis in key scenes and for the lush score.

Henry: Portrait of a Serial Killer (1990) ★★½

Director: John McNaughton
Running Time: 90 minutes

When Becky (Tracy Arnold) leaves her husband and goes to Chicago to stay with her drug-dealing brother, Otis (Tom Towles), she's instantly taken with his roommate, Henry (Michael Rooker), a quiet, brooding young man who protects her from her brother's abuse (the husband must *really* have been a winner if she gave him up for Otis). But Henry has a life of which she's totally unaware: When he's not working as an exterminator, he's busy exterminating people—young women, mostly.

One night, Otis is present when Henry kills a hooker, and joins him on subsequent escapades—the two of them videotaping their atrocities and watching them later in their living room. Ultimately, Henry and Otis have a deadly falling-out over Becky, with Otis the bloody loser. Henry and Becky leave together, dumping Otis's body as they go.

Director McNaughton, an advertising executive turned music-video director, raised the film's $125,000 budget from a Chicago home-video entrepreneur, and loosely based his film on the career of murderer Henry Lee Lucas. He got his cast from the Organic Theater Company, and they're fine: Rooker has gone on to costar in films such as *Sea of Love* (see page 242) and *JFK* [1991]. Unfortunately, *Henry: Portrait of a Serial Killer* never went into general release because it could not get an R rating—which is absurd. Two of the killings *are* gut-wrenching: the recreational murder of a young man who stops to help Henry and Otis with their "stalled" car and the savage slaughter of a family. However, nothing in the film is as sensationalistic or sick as *The Silence of the Lambs, Cape Fear, Blue Velvet,* or other "mainstream" films. Killers don't always live in carefully monitored cells or spend fourteen years plotting delicious revenge or cackle like the Joker. They frequent malls and eat at local diners. They're a part of society, though out of synch with it, and this film suggests reasons why. It's a twisted buddy picture, a sort of *Beckets of Blood* (note that *Becket* is showing on the TV when Otis kicks it in), and it should be seen.

Which isn't to say it's a *great* film: The plot is thin, and some scenes go on far too long (the home videotape of Becky and Henry horsing around, for example). But it's a hell of a first effort. Studios keep giving money to David Lynch, Spike Lee, and other directors who make controversial films. Someone ought to get McNaughton back into the arena.

The Disc
Video: ★★★
Audio: ★★★ (monaural)
Chapters: No
Format: CLV
Source: MPI Home Video

The original film had some grain in many of the interior and nighttime scenes, so the transfer is slightly gritty. However, the daylight scenes are fairly strong, the transfer is relatively sharp, and the colors are generally lifelike. Since the film was designed for eventual video release, the lack of a matte isn't detrimental.

The digital audio is crisp, and the musical cues before each murder reverberate ominously (and loudly: Keep that remote handy).

This is the original, unrated version of the film. *Accept no substitutes!*

Henry V (1989) ★★★★★
Director: Kenneth Branagh
Running Time: 138 minutes

The artistic and commercial success of *Dead Again* (1991) proved he was no fluke. But in 1989, as a stage actor with only two minor films to his credit (*High Season* and *A Month in the Country*, both 1987 and as an actor only), the twenty-eight-year-old Branagh deserves credit for daring to refilm a play that Laurence Olivier had done so memorably in 1945. (The audacious Branagh quipped, "It happens all the time in the theatre. This time we did it on film.") He deserves even more credit for having pulled it off.

Henry (Branagh) is a young English king who, new to the throne and eager to show his strength, presses an hereditary claim to the French crown. This claim is naturally rejected by the French king (Paul Scofield), so Henry resolves to go to France and take the throne. With the devoted Exeter (Brian Blessed) at his side and a motley band of commoners, Henry meets and bests a vastly superior enemy force at Agincourt, then woos and weds the French Princess Katherine (Branagh's real-life wife, Emma Thompson).

The Life of King Henry V was written in from 1598 to 1600, at the height of William Shakespeare's fame. Unlike his better-known works, it labors under a unique burden: Because drama is one of the later plays among the playwright's nine works about the English kings, it assumes some audience familiarity with the characters (including Henry), which had been introduced in *The First Part of King Henry IV* and *The Second Part of King Henry IV*. Thanks to Branagh, this is not the problem it might have been, as his script incorporates bits of those works in his *Henry V*. Branagh is helped by the fact that this Shakespeare used a chorus to preface every act (dynamically acted in the film by Derek Jacobi), giving the playwright (and Branagh) a chance to brief the audience.

Branagh changed the play in other ways that are less satisfying. Characters have been dropped, as is customary when the Bard is translated to the screen (for example, the French queen Isabel is gone) and speeches have been truncated (Henry's chat with the French herald Montjoy before Agincourt has been shortened by more than half). But the *heart* of the play is still here, unforgettably played by all. (Is there *anyone* who doesn't feel like rushing out and signing up after Branagh's St. Crispin's Day speech?)

Just one question: Why did no one get *these* people to make *Robin Hood: Prince of Thieves* instead of the ghastly Costner and company?

The Disc
Video: ★★★★
Audio: ★★★★ (Surround)
Chapters: Yes ... but they're mislabeled.
Format: CLV
Source: CBS Fox Video

So much of this film was shot in overcast or fiery settings that the colors in the original print tended to be somewhat dull or monochromatic. Given that liability, it's amazing the disc possesses the subtleties it does. The dark segments are comparatively rich in detail, with surprisingly little grain, and usual trouble spots such as the reds and browns—of which there are plenty in the film—are relatively quiet, noisewise.

Though the disc is letterboxed, the matte is so mild that there are still bits and pieces missing from the fringes of the image—nothing crucial, and it is, after all, better than *no* matte.

The sound and stereo separation are crisp and excellent, though you may have to scan back a few times to catch some of Shakespeare's knottier phrases. And you'd best turn the Surround down a bit: The music, especially during the speech before Agincourt, tends to be overpowering.

In addition to the trailer, there's a featurette on the making of the film. It's enlightening, but beware: Once the "making of" cameras show you the modern buildings visible behind the action, you won't look at the film quite the same way again!

Branagh also directed *Dead Again* (1992), a masterful chiller starring himself and Ms. Thompson. The film is available in both cropped and letterboxed editions, each of which boasts superb color (with some crisp black and white segments) and excellent Surround sound.

Hercules
(1957; U.S. release, 1959)
★★★
Director: Pietro Francisci
Running Time: 107 minutes

There were athletes turned movie stars before Steve Reeves: swimmers Johnny Weissmuller, Esther Williams, and Buster Crabbe, boxer Max Baer, and others. But Reeves was the first championship bodybuilder to become a leading man (his contemporary, Gordon Scott, made a lesser impression in some fine Tarzan films), and his impact on action films of the 1950s and 1960s was profound. Kids loved him, women adored him, and men admired him; Reeves was one of Winston Churchill's two favorite movie stars (the other being John Wayne).

The winner of Mr. America, Mr. World, and Mr. Universe titles, Reeves had been in competitive bodybuilding for a decade when he was approached to star in an Italian-made film about the Greek hero Hercules.

Hercules begins with the hero en route to Jolco to serve as master-at-arms at the request of King Pelias. After alienating the king, Hercules travels with Jason and the Argonauts to find the Golden Fleece, then returns to Jolco, where he helps to unseat Pelias and marries Princess Iole (Sylva Koscina). Along the way, he partakes in two of his famous labors, slaying the Nemean lion and battling the Cretan bull.

Reeves makes a majestic, aloof demigod, and the image of Reeves just before his final feat of strength—chains wrapped around two pillars, muscles flexed as he prepares to pull down the facade of the palace—became one of signature icons of the 1950s.

Ironically, though Reeves was the only one in the cast who spoke English, his voice was dubbed along with everyone else's: The Montana-born actor sounded too American to play a Greek hero.

In a wonderful sequel, *Hercules Unchained* (1959), the hero drinks from the Waters of Forgetfulness, is captured by the evil queen Omphale (Sylvia Lopez), and escapes just in time to save the city of Thebes from destruction.

Both films were box-office titans, and Reeves followed them with other brawny hits such as *Goliath and the Barbarians* (1960), *The Thief of Bagdad* (1961), *Morgan the Pirate* (1961), and *The White Warrior* (1961). Inspired by his success, bodybuilders such as Reg Park, Alan Steel, Dan Vadis, and Mark Forest appeared in a flood of Italian sword-and-sandal epics. Reeves's success also encouraged young Arnold Schwarzenegger, who recently said, "Steve was a great inspiration to me."

Reeves is presently retired from the screen and raises horses on his sprawling ranch.

The Disc

Video: ★★★
Audio: ★★½ (monaural)
Chapters: Yes
Format: CLV
Source: VidAmerica/Image Entertainment

With characters and action spread across the screen, it's great to have this film available in a letterboxed version. However, the only wide-screen, English-language print was *not* the print shown theatrically and on TV in the United States but, rather, an alternate English-dubbed print made for the European market. Thus, the Reeves voice here is different from the one with which his fans are familiar (it's not as sonorous or monotone), and some of the dialogue is different. It all takes some getting used to.

Using this print caused other problems, as well. The titles weren't in English, so those on the disc were cribbed from another copy of the film and are "squeezed" rather than wide-screen (too bad; they're lovely). The opening sound track is also terrible, the melodic theme gurgling as though it's being played underwater.

A more serious problem occurs toward the end of the film, during the fight for Jolco. Where the print was damaged, Image used "fill-in frames"—that is, rather than causing a jump in the action and in the sound track, they simply repeated previous frames, causing the action to freeze for a moment. It's distracting, but it was the only way to retain the material on the sound track where the picture was tattered.

Those caveats aside, the rest of the print is in generally fine condition. The flesh tones are natural and the night and storm scenes are vivid and largely free of grain. The colors range from vivid to a *touch* pale.

The audio is scratchy in spots and a bit tinny throughout: Image did the best they could with digital processing, but, again, the source material wasn't exactly pristine.

Hercules Unchained is also available on disc, though it's not letterboxed (finding, repairing, and transferring the first film went *way* over budget, precluding a similar effort on the sequel) and much of the movie's spectacle is lost, not to mention numerous characters—including Hercules himself in several shots! The quality of the transfers is on a par with the first film.

Morgan the Pirate is also available on laserdisc, and it suffers less from panning-and-scanning because Reeves is usually front and center. The loss of any business on the sides, while annoying, is not crucial to the plot—if the word can even be applied to this energetic but rambling movie that is based less on history than on the second half of *The Sea Hawk*. The print is in good condition, though the colors are on the soft side.

The Hindenburg (1975) ★★★½
Director: Robert Wise
Running Time: 126 minutes

Why did the German dirigible *Hindenburg* blow up as it attempted to land in Lakehurst, New Jersey, on May 6, 1937? The official explanation is that St. Elmo's fire ignited the hydrogen in its gas cells—though many airship buffs have never accepted that. The zeppelin was the pride of Hitler's Germany and a big, relatively accessible target for anti-Nazi activists. That was the theory put forth in Michael M. Mooney's book *The Hindenburg*, and Robert Wise used it as the basis for this much underrated film.

George C. Scott stars as Col. Franz Ritter, assigned to fly on the dirigible after the government learns that it may be sabotaged. Also on board are Ritter's old flame the Countess (Anne Bancroft), Gestapo agent Martin Vogel (Roy Thinnes), and the obligatory array of misfit passengers, each of whom seems to have a reason for wanting to blow up the ship.

What sets *The Hindenburg* apart from other disaster films of this era (see *Earthquake*) is Scott's fine performance as a man torn between responsibility for the lives on board and a loathing for the Reich, and also Wise's masterful evocation of the brief era of airship travel.

The director's one questionable call was incorporating the actual black and white newsreel film of the explosion into the movie. "That footage is so well known and so powerful," says Wise, "audiences wouldn't have been satisfied with a recreation." That's arguable, since the rest of the special effects are so convincing—including a recreation of the dirigible's famous passage over lower Manhattan. Unfortunately, Wise dilutes the impact of the newsreel footage by constantly freeze-framing and cutting away from it to show what's happening to his characters (in black and white, to match the newsreel film). The *Hindenburg*'s demise is more interesting than their's.

The Disc

Video: ★★★★
Audio: ★★★★½ (Surround)
Chapters: Yes
Format: CLV (sides one and two), CAV (side three)
Source: MCA Universal Home Video

The Hindenburg was shot without vivid, primary colors (the big ship is silvery gray, after all), and the subtle pastel look of the film has been handsomely transferred to the letterboxed disc. There are a few patches of grain and video noise, though these are minor intrusions.

The Dolby Surround Sound is *very* effective, though you'll want to turn down the rumbling rear speakers when characters converse in the zeppelin's noisy metal framework. Or maybe you won't: the sense of being on the *Hindenburg* is more exciting than what most of the people have to say. Viewers with subwoofers will be thrilled with the disc.

Because the explosion is in CAV, you can study the original footage in detail. Watching frame by frame what on-site photographer Murray Becker described as "spectacular madness" is a chilling experience.

The trailer shows in color several of the recreated scenes of disaster that ended up as black and white.

Home Alone (1990) ★★
Director: Chris Columbus
Running Time: 103 minutes

This is the third most popular movie in history, right behind *E.T.* and *Star Wars* (see pages 87 and 263). How that happened is a mystery. The movie is small and inconsistent: It tries to be both Frank Capra's *It's a Wonderful Life* (see page 151) and *National Lampoon's Christmas Vacation* (1989; written by *Home Alone*'s screenwriter, John Hughes) but succeeds only modestly on both counts.

In a stupidly unlikely scenario, eight-year-old Kevin (Macaulay Culkin) is left behind in the Chicago suburbs at Christmastime when his mother, Kate (Catherine O'Hara), his dad, Peter (John Heard), and the rest of the McCallister family fly off to Paris. Not only must Kevin fend for himself while his mother tries desperately to return to the States, he has to protect the house from a pair of burglars, Harry (Joe Pesci) and Marv (Daniel Stern), guys so inept that they practically do themselves in. That's the *Lampoon* stuff. Meanwhile, Kevin befriends neighbor Marley (Robert Blossom), who is said to be the infamous Snow Shovel Murderer. Turns out the old fellow is anything but murderous or curmudgeonly, and he ends up saving young Kevin's hide (the Capra touch).

Even if you buy the premise and accept the fact that Kevin can't get help and Kate can't get home and the police can't be convinced to do anything—unlikely as all that is—the movie has little to offer other than Culkin being cute or sad, then turning into Rambo Junior as he defends his home. These scenes have some wonderful slapstick, and Pesci and Stern are funny (they seem to have been modeled after Jasper and Horace in Disney's 1961 feature *One Hundred and One Dalmations*). John Candy as Gus Polinski, who helps Kate get home, is also funny.

But the number-three movie of all

time? A holiday classic? Only if you haven't seen very many good movies.

Director Columbus, a Spielberg protégé, wrote *Gremlins* (1984) and made his directorial debut with *Adventures in Babysitting* (1987). He also directed the 1991 John Candy flop *Only the Lonely*.

The Disc
Video: ★★★★
Audio: ★★★½ (Surround)
Chapters: Yes
Format: CLV
Source: Fox Home Video

Perfectly sharp and clear, the letterboxed film has strong, true-to-life colors and is marred only by traces of video noise.

The audio is equally as crisp, with incredible range and precision from top to bottom. Though the rear speakers don't produce any show-off effects, John Williams's gushy, familiar score will embrace you like an quilt.

Horror of Dracula (1958)
★★★★
Director: Terence Fisher
Running Time: 82 minutes

During its nearly thirty years of active production, Hammer Film Productions made nearly 150 films. The studio was founded in 1948 to make low-budget British films for British theaters. A 1956 science fiction film called *The Quatermass Experiment* became a hit in the United States as *The Creeping Unknown*, and Hammer realized that a good horror film, with name value, filmed in color, would probably find an even bigger international market. They were right. The handsomely mounted, bloody (for the time), deadly-serious *Curse of Frankenstein* (1957) was a huge success and established Peter Cushing (Baron Victor Frankenstein) and Christopher Lee (the Monster) as bankable genre stars.

Hammer followed it with *Horror of Dracula*, a very loose period (1885) retelling of the 1897 Bram Stoker novel. When English vampire hunter Jonathan Harker (John Van Eyssen) disappears while working as a librarian for Count Dracula (Christopher Lee) at his castle, his friend Dr. Van Helsing (Peter Cushing) investigates. Van Helsing finds that Dracula has turned Harker into a vampire and gone to England to dine on Harker's fiancée Lucy (Carol Marsh). After staking Harker, Van Helsing enlists the aid of Lucy's brother, Arthur Holmwood (Michael Gough), to hunt down and destroy the vampire.

Though produced on a limited budget, the film has glossy, solid production values, a crashing and ominous musical score, and two great stars. Cushing's Van Helsing is a man of intelligence, courage, and dignity, while Lee's Dracula is courtly one moment, feral the next, and introduced sex to the blood-drinking process.

Lee played the Count in six sequels. He skipped the superb *The Brides of Dracula* (1960), but made *Dracula—Prince of Darkness* (1966), *Dracula Has Risen from the Grave* (1968), *Taste the Blood of Dracula* (1970), *Scars of Dracula* (1970), *Dracula A.D. 1972* (1972), and *The Satanic Rites of Dracula* (1973). Cushing costarred in several of these (he was also busy in the Frankenstein series). As the titles attest, the films became increasingly sensationalistic, and a discouraged Lee has said he always tried to depict "the majesty and dignity of this immortal character as well as the savagery, ferocity, and, above all, great sadness." That he rarely succeeded, he has said was due to "poor scripts (and) people who never seemed to understand the full potential of the story."

In addition to the Frankenstein Monster and Dracula, Hammer spawned a third successful series with *The Mummy* (1959), in which the long-undead Kharis (Lee) is discovered in Egypt by John Banning (Cushing) and his party, and goes about murdering those who have defiled the tomb of Princess Ananka (Yvonne Furneaux).

The Disc
Video: ★★½
Audio: ★★½ (monaural)
Chapters: Yes
Format: CLV (side one), CAV (side two)
Source: Warner Home Video

Perhaps no laserdisc release has been awaited as eagerly as this one—which make its flaws, while not staggering, all the more disappointing. The colors are good but not great, the reds (of which there are, obviously, a lot) are extremely runny, and the image is a little soft in spots. Only the interiors of the castle have any real depth and beauty. Panning is minimal and well done; the titles are letterboxed.

The audio is alternately hollow and shrill (the latter, when the music starts pounding away), but background noise is minimal.

This is probably the best copy of the film Warner was able to find, which is distressing. What's even more distressing is that the bloody thing is cut—literally. Lucy's staking has been trimmed to eliminate the blood spewing from her chest. Could the people at Warner *really* have thought that anyone purchasing this disc would be offended?

The Mummy is in somewhat rougher shape: The night scenes are all *very* dark and lack the gloss the film had when it was originally released. The sound is acceptable. The print used for this transfer is the American release print, which doesn't show Kharis's severed tongue, visible in the British print.

MCA/Universal Home Video has released a superb transfer of Hammer's only werewolf film, *Curse of the Werewolf* (1961), starring Oliver Reed as the doomed lycanthrope. Though the film plods until its closing moments, Reed is terrific, the silvery werewolf makeup is masterful, and the transfer of the near-pristine print is bright, sharp, and very colorful.

MCA has also released a generally satisfactory *Evil of Frankenstein* (1964), the third and most lavish in Hammer's Frankenstein series. Cushing stars as the good doctor, Kiwi Kingston is a Karloff-like monster, and the movie is one of Hammer's best. Though the colors are somewhat washed out and the image is a bit soft, the print is in excellent condition and the sound is strong.

Image Entertainment has released a double bill of *Scars of Dracula* and *The Horror of Frankenstein* (1970). The quality of these discs is simply terrible, and the movies aren't much better.

How the West Was Won (1962)
★★★½
Directors: Henry Hathaway, John Ford, George Marshall
Running Time: 163 minutes

How the West Was Won was the last of the big traditional Westerns—nonrevisionist, unapologetic, bursting-with-pride entertainment. It follows the fortunes of two generations of the pioneering Prescott family, from their journey west on the Erie Canal to their role in the Civil War to the part they played fighting hostile Indians and notorious outlaws.

The likable, headstrong characters and parade of stars are enough to sustain interest through the episodic narrative, among them Debbie Reynolds, Jimmy Stewart, Gregory Peck, Henry Fonda, Andy Devine, Robert Preston (watch how his whip miraculously changes hands at 54: 28 on side one), George Peppard (who gives a very strong performance as a disillusioned soldier-turned-lawman), Richard Widmark, John Wayne (in a glorified cameo as William Tecumseh Sherman), and Eli Wallach (adding yet another notch to his bandit belt). Spencer Tracy narrates.

In addition to the sprawling story, *How the West Was Won* features several all-out action sequences: a raft trip down the rapids, a buffalo stampede, an Indian attack on a wagon train, the Battle of Shiloh, and the most spectacular train wreck this side of *The Greatest Show on Earth*. (Stuntman Bob Morgan—husband of actress Yvonne De Carlo—lost a leg, a portion of his spine, and suffered facial disfiguration while doubling for George Peppard on the shifting logs of the flatcar.)

Scenes featuring Hope Lange as Henry Fonda's daughter (and George Peppard's frontier love interest) were cut from the film before it was released, to speed up the second half. Gary Cooper had been cast but died before any footage had been shot; he was replaced by his close friend Jimmy Stewart. Alfred Newman's score is highlighted by one of the most memorable themes in film history.

How the West Was Won was shot in the old three-panel Cinerama format; see *The Wonderful World of the Brothers Grimm* for more information.

The Disc
Video: ★★★★½
Audio: ★★★★½ (Surround)
Chapters: No
Format: CLV
Source: MGM/UA Home Video

MGM/UA Home Video originally released this film in a panned-and-scanned version: The disc robbed the film of nearly two-thirds of its original image and was a loser.

Conversely, the more recent letterbox edition—which captures just over three-quarters of the film's original image size—is a must have disc. The sense of depth created by the Cinerama lenses is astonishing, particularly during the railroad-building scenes and the train wreck. The join lines where the three panels meet are visible in many scenes, often causing curvature of objects as they move from one panel to another. Ironically, this actually enhances the sense of depth by fisheyeing those objects and wrapping them around the viewer as they move.

Some of the night scenes lack detail, and the colors are a touch on the soft side. Moreover, they don't always match from panel to panel, a flaw inherent in the original Cinerama print. (Even today, subtle color differences are inevitable from print to print; we just don't notice them because the films aren't screened side by side.)

No apologies need to be made for the digital audio, however. *How the West Was Won* was presented theatrically with seven channel stereophonic sound, resulting in a disc full of marvelous directional effects and thunderous bass. The film's glorious overture, entr'acte, and exit music are included.

A surprisingly tame theatrical trailer is presented at the end.

The Hunger (1983) ★★★½
Director: Tony Scott
Running Time: 100 minutes

Director Tony Scott used to hold lots of promise. That was when he moved from TV commercials to feature films and made *The Hunger*. Since then, it's been *Top Gun* (see page 281), *Beverly Hills Cop II* (1987), *Revenge* (1990), and *Days of Thunder* (1990)—serious stinkers all.

Based on Whitley Strieber's novel, *The Hunger* is is about ancient vampire Miriam Blaylock (Catherine Deneuve), who takes lovers who, for one or two hundred years, become her mates and companions in bloodletting. Unfortunately, these companions don't possess her immortality, and the centuries have a habit of catching up quickly and unexpectedly. John Blaylock (David Bowie) is her present lover, and he begins to sense that his time has come. Learning about antiaging research being conducted by gerontologist Sarah Roberts (Susan Sarandon), he goes to see her. In a tragically amusing sequence, he literally becomes an old man while sitting in her waiting room.

Upon John's death, Miriam makes Sarah her next companion—though for the first time since her youth in Ancient Egypt, Miriam finds her companion to be much more than she bargained for. Sarah causes problems for the vampire—implicitly, the younger, sexier "rival" stirs long-suppressed insecurity—and as her control slips, so does her mind, as the rotted corpses return to life for one last embrace.

Has she subconsciously brought them back? Is their resurrection all in her mind? Is Sarah the one behind it? That's for the viewer to decide, and you'll have fun picking through the clues dropped by this sexy, stylish horror film.

If *The Hunger* has a problem, it's a lack of insight into Miriam's character and vampirism. Sure, she's supposed to be enigmatic—but someone who's around four-thousand-years-old should have *some* fascinating characteristics and insights. Her hedonism and artistic refinement don't tell us much: Miriam is nothing more than an *Elle* cover girl who happens to drink blood. The doomed John is more interesting as he wrestles with his sudden mortality, but he dies halfway through the film. And Sarah takes too long to accept what she's become to hold our interest.

But if he fails to sink his teeth into the characters, Scott does a good job mixing horror and sexual tension: The opening of the film is sleazy and hot (John and Miriam pick up a young couple at a club, go to their house, tease them sexually, then cut their throats), and the first liaison between Sarah and Miriam is delicately seductive (that's a body double for Deneuve, by the way).

Ann Magnuson (of TV's "Anything But Love") plays the disco pickup, Willem Dafoe is the punk at the phone booth, and silent film star Bessie Love is Lillybelle.

The Disc

Video: ★★★½
Audio: ★★★★ (monaural)
Chapters: Yes
Format: CLV
Source: MGM/UA Home Video

Scott creates an eerie, alluring world for his vampires, and the choice of harsh colors and the smoky, diaphanous images tell you more about these creatures than the script.

Regrettably, while the film is still beautiful to look at, and the letterboxing is perfect, the colors aren't *quite* as vivid as they were in the theaters. The blues in particular have been toned down. However, there's little video noise in the reds—important in a vampire film—and the image is clear and quite sharp. For a film with so many low-light scenes, there is surprisingly little grain.

The audio captures the wide range of sounds, very faithfully reproducing the percussive thuds and ethereal strains of the sound track. The vampires tend to speak very quietly, but you won't have any trouble hearing what they're saying.

The theatrical trailer is included.

The Hunt for Red October (1990) ★★★★

Director: John McTiernan
Running Time: 135 minutes

Tom Clancy's first novel, *The Hunt for Red October*, was published without fanfare in 1984 by the Naval Institute Press. It became a best-seller (thanks, in part, to a plug from President Reagan) and single-handedly established the techno-thriller genre—suspense fiction with a slavish attention to hardware.

The film follows the events in the novel and, stripped of Clancy's preoccupation with machinery, reveals itself to be very much in the tradition of the film from Alistair MacLean's novel *Ice Station Zebra* (see page 145), a tale of superpower confrontation, double-cross, and down-to-the-wire suspense.

In 1984, a new Typhoon-class Russian submarine, the *Red October*, sets out on sea trials, in which it will be hunted by other Russian submarines to test the effectiveness of its revolutionary new "silent drive." But the skipper of the *Red October*, Capt. First Rank Marko Ramius (Sean Connery), has other plans: When Admiral James Greer (James Earl Jones) and CIA operative Jack Ryan (Alec Baldwin) learn that the vessel is not on maneuvers but is actually fleeing the Russian ships, the debate is whether Ramius is defecting or whether he's a renegade who intends to launch his missiles at the United States.

The Soviets say the latter, and urge the United States to help them find and sink the silent sub. But Ryan knows Ramius and suspects he's defecting. Flying out to join the crew of the USS *Dallas*, commanded by Bart Mancuso (Scott Glenn), which is hot on Ramius's trail, Ryan tries to figure out how to prove his theory before the *Red October* is destroyed. Meanwhile, there's a saboteur on the *Red October* who is working to thwart Ramius from within....

Stylishly directed by McTiernan (see *Die Hard*), the movie is perfectly cast from bow to stern. Though he speaks with his Scottish accent instead of even attempting a Lithuanian one, Connery is completely convincing as the confident, somewhat-arrogant commander. Baldwin has leading-man good looks with an appealing touch of wimpiness, and Glenn is as sharp as ever.

Though the miniature submarines and torpedoes created by George Lucas's Industrial Light and Magic fail to convince, the movie manages to maneuver through complicated plot twists, communicate a good deal of exposition, introduce a lot of characters, and make you overlook some *big* plot holes (for instance, why does the saboteur wait until the very end to take a shot at Ramius?). Even the end of the Cold War doesn't lessen its appeal.

The Disc
Video: ★★★★
Audio: ★★★★★ (Surround)
Chapters: No
Format: CLV
Source: Paramount Home Video

There are both letterboxed and pan-and-scan editions: The latter is pretty disruptive, dramatically, as characters get lopped off and the underwater shots are truncated.

The picture quality on both discs is about the same. There's *very* slight grain on both, particularly at night, though there's just a bit less on the pan-and-scan version. Despite all the reds in the submarines, video noise isn't much of a problem.

The audio will have you smiling from start to finish, and you'll have to watch the film a second time just to savor the sounds, from ringing telephones you'll *swear* are in the room with you to the thunderous Surround Sounds of the submarines and helicopter.

Clancy's *Patriot Games* is an inferior film starring Harrison Ford as Ryan. The quality of the disc is fine, but for naught.

Ice Station Zebra (1968) ★★½
Director: John Sturges
Running Time: 150 minutes

There have been some terrific movies made from the novels of the late Alistair MacLean: *The Guns of Navarone* (1961—when is someone going to letterbox this film?) and *Where Eagles Dare* (1969) top the list. There have also been some truly terrible films made from MacLean novels: *Puppet on a Chain* (1970) and *Bear Island* (1980) can never be forgiven. Then there are MacLean properties that fall somewhere in between, such as *The Satan Bug* (1965, also from Sturges), *Breakheart Pass* (1976)—and *Ice Station Zebra*.

Comdr. James Ferraday (Rock Hudson, after Charlton Heston turned the part down) and the crew of the nuclear submarine USS *Tigerfish* are sent by Admiral Garvey (Lloyd Nolan) to rescue survivors of Ice Station Zebra, a polar base—and, more importantly, to recover film of American and Russian missile sites taken from space and deposited in the frigid north by a Soviet satellite. In addition to the captain, on board are British intelligence agent David Jones (Patrick McGoohan, making his Hollywood screen debut); Capt. Leslie Anders (Jim Brown); Russian expatriate Boris Vaslov (Ernest Borgnine); and Lt. Russell Walker (Tony Bill)—one of whom is working for the Soviets, who are also racing to recover the film.

MacLean knew how to plot a taut tale, and the late Sturges (*The Magnificent Seven* and *The Great Escape*; see pages 179 and 122) knew how to film one. Certainly Hudson, McGoohan, and Brown know how to act in them. Unfortunately, the film is *way* too long and is almost fatally undermined by bad special effects and North Pole sets that looked fake in their original super-wide-screen Cinerama presentation and look just as phony on the small screen. The "ice" settings were based on photos taken by the navy's USS *Skate*, but they look like plastic, and there may not be a scene in a big-budget movie as fake as the five miniature jets flying wingtip-to-wingtip as the rear-projected terrain flashes by.

The interiors of the *Tigerfish* are convincing enough, constructed from odds and ends found at marine salvage yards, and the entire submarine set was built on hydraulic rockers, enabling it to be tilted up to twenty-three degrees for the diving scenes and the flood caused by a sabotaged torpedo tube—the film's best action scene. Conversely, the submarine exterior is a *bad* miniature that looks good only after you've seen those fake jets.

Finally, there's Borgnine, who sabotages every scene he's in thanks to his ridiculous Russian accent. "I don't really use it consistently," he has admitted. "In a short sentence, I may use it just on one word—like *in-ter-estink*. The rest is intonation." Make that abomination, Ernest.

This one's only for viewers who are hungry for *something* big and busy after fully digesting *The Dirty Dozen* (see page 68), *Where Eagles Dare* (available on laserdisc), or *The Hunt for Red October* (see page 144).

The release of this film forced most Cinerama theaters to ditch *2001: A Space Odyssey*, which was still making money for them. The box-office failure of *Ice Station Zebra* left the exhibitors very unhappy, and they began showing other kinds of films on the big screen. The next three Cinerama flops killed the process once and for all: *Custer of the West* (1968), shot in Europe with Robert Shaw(!), which never even played many locations; *Krakatoa, East of Java* (1969), with its thin drama and thinner special effects; and *Song of Norway* (1970), the superficial biography of composer Edvard Grieg.

The Disc

Video: ★★★★
Audio: ★★½ (Surround)
Chapters: No
Format: CLV
Source: MGM/UA Home Video

Despite having been filmed in Metrocolor, *Ice Station Zebra* has strong colors and an image that is sharp, fresh-looking, and relatively free of video noise (even when the red emergency lights are on). The film is letterboxed, though a little of the Super Panavision image has been shaved off the sides due to a defect in the print.

The sound is good but is something of a disappointment. While much of it is clear, there are passages—especially a lengthy one nearly halfway through side one—that sound as though they were recorded through water. As for the supposed Surround effects, the front and rear speakers feed you basically the same audio.

Michel Legrand's epic score sounds very good, however, and the disc contains both his marvelous overture, entr'acte, and exit music.

I Love You to Death (1990)
★★★

Director: Lawrence Kasdan
Running Time: 97 minutes

Because we've become accustomed to exciting or provocative films from Kasdan—such as *Body Heat* (1981), *The Big Chill* (1983), and *Silverado* (1985)—*I Love You to Death* is something of disappointment. Based on a true story (improbable as *that* may seem), the film has two distinct parts: the first half, which is a long, only occasionally funny introduction to the two main characters, neither of whom seems particularly interesting; and then the darkly comic second half, which is frequently hilarious.

Joey (Kevin Kline) and his wife, Rosalie (Tracey Ullman), own a pizza parlor and a couple of rental apartments. When he isn't making pies, Joey is busy making women—though his trusting wife doesn't suspect a thing. When she finally discovers what's been going on behind her back, she and her mother, Nadja (Joan Plowright), decide that Joey must die. Unfortunately, they can't seem to accomplish that themselves, so young Devo (River Phoenix), who works at the pizzeria and has a crush on Rosalie, engages junkies Harlan and Marlon (William Hurt and Keanu Reeves) to do the deed. Rosalie and Nadja drug Joey's dinner, and while he's asleep the two space cadets come to murder him. They screw up and only manage to wound Joey, which leads to a bizarre reconciliation.

Viewers who expect Kline to be as off the wall as he was in *A Fish Called Wanda* (see page 99), or Ullman as wacky as in her TV series, will be disappointed. *They*'re not the lunatics this time around. Behind a goofy Italian accent, Kline is simply testosterone personified, which is why he's much funnier *after* he's been shot; robbed of his libido, he's a pathetically amiable shell. Ullman is a sunshiny, doting wife who struggles to become a single-minded killer; she's Donna Reed trying to be Lizzie Borden and, like Kline, doesn't really get to let go. Both leads are good but are limited by the roles.

The more interesting, more textured performances come from Plowright, Hurt, and Reeves. The latter two in particular look and act like figures from a funhouse mirror and are wickedly funny.

This is not a movie whose every nuance is apparent after one sitting. A few viewings, though, and you'll find a great deal of merit in the film.

Look for Phoebe Cates—Mrs. Kline—as one of Joey's lovers.

The Disc
Video: ★★★½
Audio: ★★★ (Surround)
Chapters: No
Format: CLV
Source: RCA/Columbia Home Video

The transfer is extremely sharp, with very little grain, although the many browns and reds are either dark or very noisy. The film has been letterboxed, which allows you to enjoy the many two-shots.

The audio is clear but the Surround Sound is simply *there*, offering no surprises and no special treats.

Impromptu (1991) ★★★★
Director: James Lapine
Running Time: 108 minutes

Fredric Chopin (1810–1849) was the greatest of the romantic composers. The Polish-born genius wrote primarily for the piano (the sole exceptions being his concertos), but he made it *perform* like an orchestra, with its textures, shadings, and power.

Set in 1837, *Impromptu* does not focus on Chopin the composer. It sees him primarily through the eyes of the brash, liberated Amandine-Aurore-Lucie Dupin, the Baroness Dudevant—a writer who wore men's clothes, smoked cigars, and published controversial novels under the name of Georges Sand (Judy Davis). After a series of unhappy relationships, Sand hears Chopin (Hugh Grant) playing from behind closed doors and falls in love even before she sees him. Sand makes sure she is invited to holiday at a country estate where Chopin will also be visiting—along with composer Franz Liszt (Julian Sands), his mistress (Bernadette Peters), painter Eugène Delacroix (Ralph Brown), Sand's ex-lover Alfred de Musset (Mandy Patinkin), and her unwanted but tenacious present lover, Felicien Mallefille (Georges Corraface). They've been invited to provide culture and wit, but their hostess, the Duchess d'Antan (Emma Thompson) gets fireworks—figuratively and literally—she didn't bargain for.

Sand gets what *she* wants, however. Six years her junior, Chopin is initially repulsed by her, then wary, then friendly, and then infatuated. They become lovers and the film ends with them happily so; they would remain together for a decade, until two years before Chopin's death (parting after disagreeing violently on matters concerning Sand's children).

Making his film debut, stage director Lapine (*Into the Woods*) works wonders with the medium: The scene in which Sand first hears Chopin play and literally melts at the door is beautifully sensual, and Delacroix's reaction to the dead horse speaks more than pages of dialogue could have achieved.

The dialogue is smart and prickly, the characterizations deep and accurate, and there's a great deal of humor, both bawdy and clever. The performances are note-perfect, with Sands looking eerily like Liszt. Anna Massey has a wonderful supporting role as Sand's mother, whose presence brings out the writer's compassionate side, and Thompson works wonders with the shallow Duchess.

The movie perfectly describes the nature of the artist/patron relationship and the mutual disdain the classes had for one another. If *Impromptu* has a flaw, it's the fact that Chopin's music gets short shrift. Through his work, the sickly composer expressed his many sorrows and few joys; more of it would have helped to explain both the character and Sand's legendary infatuation with him.

In that respect, *A Song to Remember* (1945) is a nice complement to *Impromptu*. The film stars Cornel Wilde and Merle Oberon as Chopin and Sand; though the story is heavily fictionalized and the drama is hokey, the Technicolor disc is handsome and the music—though occasionally abridged—is magnificent.

The Disc
Video: ★★½
Audio: ★★★½ (Surround)
Chapters: Yes
Format: CLV
Source: Hemdale Home Video

The biggest disappointment about the disc is that it's not letterboxed. A mild one would've been fine, allowing the large cast and the gorgeous sets to be seen as the director intended.

That aside, the disc—Hemdale's first—offers an image that isn't as sharp or clear as it should be. The colors are more muted than they were on the screen, and there's a fair amount of grain and a bit of noise in the browns and reds.

The audio is pleasing: clear, with nice separation and excellent tone in the period pianos.

Invasion of the Body Snatchers (1956) ★★★★½
Director: Don Siegel
Running Time: 80 minutes

Years before he directed *Dirty Harry*, Don Siegel made a classic film version of Jack Finney's novel *The Body Snatchers* (1955; expanded from his 1954 short story "Sleep No More"). The Body Snatchers are seedpods from another world that, after landing on earth, replace human beings with emotionless duplicates that grow inside the huge pods whenever people are sleeping. As psychiatrist Danny Kaufman (Larry Gates) explains the process in the film, "Suddenly, while you're asleep, they'll absorb your minds ... your memories ... and you're reborn into an untroubled world." (Also, a world without friendship or love.)

The film is told through the eyes of general practitioner Miles Bennell (Kevin McCarthy) of suburban Santa Mira, California. At first, there doesn't seem to be anything unusual among the trimmed lawns, bountiful shade trees, and sunny casualness of the town. Then small cracks appear in the facade: an "emergency" medical appointment canceled without explanation, the gothic look of an abandoned produce stand, and the upsetting cries of a boy who says his mother isn't his mother. Then Miles and lady friend Becky Driscoll (Dana Wynter), mystery writer Jack Belicec (King Donovan), and his wife, Teddy (Carolyn Jones), find Jack's pod double about to be born, and the threat becomes clear. The problem: convincing the outside world while somehow avoiding being taken over themselves. Only Miles manages to get out of town, and only a lucky accident that spills pods on the freeway convinces the authorities he's telling the truth.

Considering the era in which the film was made, many people naturally regard it as a treatise against the enslavement and dehumanization of communism. But that was not a conscious theme on the part of the director: In numerous interviews, Siegel said that he made the film because he personally knew too many people who lived lives with "no passion, no empathy."

The film was shot in nineteen days in and around Los Angeles and in Sierra Madre. The framing story, in which Bennell reaches the authorities and tells them the story, was shot after preview audiences found the film's original ending comical, as the wild-with-fear Bennell screams into the camera, "You're next!" Bennell's voice-over narration was also added to help the kiddies—at whom most SF films at the time were aimed—understand what was going on.

Director Sam Peckinpah appears as Charlie Buckholtz, the meter reader. Carolyn Jones went on to greater fame as Morticia on TV's "The Adams Family."

The 1978 remake from director Philip Kaufman (see *Henry & June*) is an honorable, ambitious failure, weakened by the already anonymous big-city setting and by a poor choice of actors. When pure, radiant Dana Wynter is "replaced" in the original, we're horrified; when Brooke Adams undergoes the transformation in the remake, tromping around in the nude and screaming grotesquely, that's not chilling—it's silly. Veronica Cartwright is so hyper, you *wish* she was taken over; and with laid-back Leonard Nimoy, it's difficult to tell whether he is or isn't. Star Donald Sutherland is good, especially in the interesting downbeat ending.

Both McCarthy and Don Siegel had cameos in the remake.

The Disc

Video: ★★★½ (Criterion); ★★★ (Republic)
Audio: ★★★ (Criterion); ★★★½ (Republic)
Chapters: Yes
Format: CAV or CLV (Criterion); CLV (Republic)
Source: Criterion or Republic Pictures Home Video

There are some scratches and splices visible on both version of the film, but the picture on both is sharper and more impressive than most surviving broadcast or theatrical prints. The contrast has a good deal of snap; if you've only seen the film on TV or tape, the letterboxing will be a revelation. It shows off the film's stunning design, the wide screen actually *increasing* the sense of encroaching claustrophobia.

The analog sound is acceptable; the CLV disc has digitized audio that is somewhat crisper than its counterpart. The digital audio track on the Republic version is slightly stronger.

There are extensive supplemental materials, including an alternate sound track lecture that is full of pretentious baloney. The CAV package also contains the theatrical trailer, an interview with Siegel, a demonstration of letterboxing versus panning-and-scanning, and a bibliography of articles about the movie.

The supplemental material on the Republic disc consist of a videotaped interview with Kevin McCarthy and the film's trailer.

It's a Mad Mad Mad Mad World (1963) ★★★★

Director: Stanley Kramer
Running Time: 183 minutes

Often, directors with "serious" credentials decide to make comedies and fail miserably. From the old pros such as John Huston, who made the James Bond send-up *Casino Royale* (1967), to younger directors such as Steven Spielberg, whose *1941* (1979) was a major misfire, they find out that comedy is best left to the comedians.

An outstanding exception to the rule is Stanley Kramer, whose credentials as a dramatic director remain among the most impressive in Hollywood: *On the Beach* (1959), *Inherit the Wind* (1960), and *Judgment at Nuremberg* (1961) are just a few of his films. When he decided to make a comedy—which was originally going to be called *Something a Little Less Serious*—he opted to go with tried-and-true Keystone Kops–style antics and, most importantly, to hire dozens of comedy pros and let them do what they do best.

The result is a movie that's not for all tastes; sophisticated it ain't. But if you enjoy slapstick comedy, they don't come any better.

On a deserted mountain road in Crockett County, motorists J. Russell Finch (Milton Berle), Melville Crump (Sid Caesar), Benjy Benjamin (Buddy Hackett), Ding Bell (Mickey Rooney), and Lennie Pike (Jonathan Winters) all come upon a thug (Jimmy Durante) who has cracked up his car and, before kicking the bucket (literally), tells them about $350,000 buried in Santa Rosita Beach State Park. Since the group can't decide how to divide the loot when it's found, they agree to search for it separately, with the finder taking all. Also searching for the men is the intrepid Capt. C. G. Culpeper (Spencer Tracy), who had been on the trail of the original thug.

That's just the first few minutes of the film: The rest is composed of everyone's frantic efforts to reach the money, including latecomers Otto Meyer (Phil Silvers) and J. Algernon Hawthorne (Terry-Thomas). Also adding to the confusion are Finch's mother-in-law, Mrs. Marcus (Ethel Merman), and her violently protective son, Sylvester (Dick Shawn).

Just about everything that's standing up gets knocked down, everything that moves crashes, and everyone in on the chase gets upended, thrown through the air, or dropped from a height. It's *Who Framed Roger Rabbit* with people instead of cartoons, and with an unbridled sense of *fun*. Once in a while, Kramer *does* lose control of things—the cast flying off the hook-and-ladder truck is just *too* dumb—but for the most part, he and his comics are very much in charge of the material.

Watch it once for the incredible chases and stunts (the airplane through the billboard is amazing), for Jonathan Winters's hilarious destruction of the gas station (painful belly laughs *will* result), Sid Caesar's and Edie Adams's desperate attempts to escape from the hardware-store basement, the wonderful control-tower sequence, and the endless cameos (Joe E. Brown, Jack Benny, Jerry Lewis, the Three Stooges, etc.). Not only will you laugh yourself silly, you'll be reminded just what a debt is owed to this film by movies such as *Silver Streak* (1976) and *Airplane!* (1980).

Then watch it again to study the cast of extraordinary comics at work. From Sid Caesar's roadside explanation of how to divide the money to Milton Berle trying to get a word in edgewise as his mother-in-law and wife (Dorothy Provine) badger him, to Terry-Thomas's classic "bosom" speech, the movie is a constant joy. Spencer Tracy is the dignified eye of the storm, while Ethel Merman's every outburst is a delight: If anyone can be described as the best in this ensemble film, she's it.

TV's greatest comedic genius, Ernie Kovacs, had been cast to play Crump, but died, tragically, and was replaced by Caesar. Kovacs' real-life wife, Edie Adams, stayed on as Mrs. Crump.

Legendary special-effects artist Willis O'Brien (*King Kong*) was also hired to work on the film, to animate the stop-motion miniatures used during the fire-truck sequence. He died shortly after filming began, and the work was completed by Jim Danforth (see *When Dinosaurs Ruled the Earth*).

Watch for the continuity blunder at 10.19, chapter thirty: Dick Shawn dangling from the fire escape, then standing on top of it in the next shot.

In 1975, Kramer tried—and failed—to raise money for what was to be another big, star-studded comedy, *The Sheiks of Araby*, in which an earthquake causes all the oil in the Middle East to shift to Israel. He says he'd still like to make the film. Frankly, we'd like to see it.

The Disc
Video: ★★★★
Audio: ★★★½ (Surround)
Chapters: Yes
Format: CLV
Source: MGM/UA Home Video

Considering the age of this film, it looks remarkably fresh. The colors are vivid, the print is almost flawless, and there's hardly any video noise. However, the picture isn't quite perfect.

After the film's original road-show presentation, a half hour of footage was cut; twenty minutes of that footage have been found and put back in the film. Motivations that seemed absurd to people who had never seen the original now make perfect sense (at least as much sense as anything is required to make in this movie)—for instance, why Tracy's character suddenly decides to go after the money himself. Other snippets are still missing (for example, a scene explaining how Jim Backus's character gets to the plane, and a funny shot of Durante looking back in desperation at the police—and the camera—in the film's opening minutes). All of the restored footage is somewhat washed-out, with minor blemishes and thin sound. However, let's not quibble: at least they're here!

The sound and stereo separation are exceptionally clear, and the Surround effects, though minimal, are dramatic at times, especially during the airplane sequences.

The overture (with its accompanying graphics), entr'acte, and exit music are included—though not the police bulletins that were broadcast in theaters during the intermission of the road-show run.

The film was the first to be shot in single-camera Cinerama—actually, Ultra Panavision—and Kramer filled the screen from end to end with spectacle and comedians. The very wide letterbox given the film is vitally important. In fact, watch the movie, then pay attention to the panned-and-scanned footage shown during the supplementary interviews. There's no comparison. (See *The Wonderful World of Brothers Grimm* for more on Cinerama.)

The extras exemplify what a labor of love the film (and the laserdisc!) were. They occupy just over one and a half sides of the five-sided set, and after the obligatory trailers come interviews with Kramer, the surviving stars, and key production personnel. It's a fascinating and informative: Even the expected mutual-admiration-society stuff clearly comes from the heart.

It's a Wonderful Life (1946)
★★★★★
Director: Frank Capra
Running Time: 160 minutes

This movie—which was Capra's favorite, his paeon to "the importance of the individual"—began as a Christmas card. In 1943, Philip Van Doren Stern wrote his tale "The Greatest Gift," printed it on 200 cards, and mailed them to friends and associates. One of them brought it to the attention of RKO executives, and the studio bought the little story for a movie to star Cary Grant. Three scripts later (one by Clifford Odets, another by Dalton Trumbo), they didn't have anything shootable and shelved the project. When Capra learned of it, he bought the rights to the story, had a new script written, and cast his friend James Stewart in the lead. The two had worked together on *You Can't Take It with You* (1938) and *Mr. Smith Goes to Washington* (1939), and Stewart was the director's only choice for the role.

Stewart is exemplary as George Bailey, who, upon the death of his father, takes over the family's small building-and-loan firm in rural Bedford Falls. Bailey believes in people and lends money freely—out of his own pocket when necessary. He is constantly crossing swords with wealthy Mr. Potter (Lionel Barrymore), who sees Bedford Falls as a cash cow and has no time for sentiment. Bailey marries Mary Hatch (Donna Reed), who shares his values; even their honeymoon money goes out the window when George uses it to fend off a run on the bank during the Depression.

Potter tries to close down George's business and hire George—all without success. Then George's uncle William (Thomas Mitchell) accidentally drops eight thousand dollars of the firm's money into Mr. Potter's newspaper, and the miser keeps it, leaving George to face bankruptcy and prison. Disconsolate, George stands on a bridge and contemplates killing himself. But George's ers), shows up and boosts George's spirits by showing him how horrible life in Bedford Falls would have been if he'd never been born. George is revitalized, the more so when the town chips in to pay off his debt.

Capra said that nothing garnered him more mail over the years than the fact that Potter went unpunished for holding on to the eight thousand dollars Uncle William dropped. And it *is* an unsatisfying aspect of the film. But the movie survives that and, in a way, is more topical and more moving than ever. If *Gone With the Wind* (see page 116) is the masterpiece of Hollywood storytelling, *It's a Wonderful Life* is the masterpiece of the American spirit. Good and bad, greedy and generous, everything we are is here.

Casting the other roles for the $2.8 million film wasn't as easy as the lead: Jean Arthur was slated to play Mary, but she'd signed to do a Broadway show. Ginger Rogers and Olivia de Havilland were also considered before Capra settled with MGM contract player Reed. Claude Rains, Vincent Price, and Raymond Massey were all also-rans for the Potter part, while Walter Brennan and W. C. Fields were finalists in the Uncle William contest.

The town of Bedford Falls was constructed on four acres of RKO's Encino ranch and features some of the most realistic fake snow ever used in a film: Painted corn flakes proved too noisy for the sound cameras, so shaved ice, gypsum, and plaster were mixed together. More than two thousand extras were employed in the film, many in the "pool" sequence, which was shot at Beverly Hills High. And yes, that's Carl "Alfalfa" Switzer turning the key to open up the dance floor.

The film was remade as the awful TV movie *It Happened One Christmas* (1977) starring Marlo Thomas in the Stewart role; it was sort of remade with more success as *Mr. Destiny* (1990), a delightful film starring Jim Belushi and Linda Hamilton.

The Disc

Video: ★★★★★
Audio: ★★★½ (monaural)
Chapters: Yes (only three: for trailer, feature, and featurette)
Format: CLV
Source: Republic Pictures Home Video

There are several laserdisc versions of the film: an earlier Republic pressing, a colorized edition, and a CAV release from Criterion. The Criterion edition has better extras—a Capra interview, and an audio commentary on the second channel—but this forty-fifth anniversary edition is the one to beat. It's doubtful the manufacturer could have done a better job.

Republic went back to the original negative and made a stunning transfer: There are some speckles on the negative, but these are easily overlooked. The picture is incredibly rich and sharp, with glossy blacks, vivid whites, and excellent contrast up and down the gray scale. The picture is so clear, you can see that Jimmy Stewart's mouth isn't moving when he talks at 27:16 in chapter two on side one.

Though the audio suffers from occasional dropouts, and the dynamic range is limited due to the recording techniques of the time, you won't be disappointed: The sound is better than you've ever heard it on home video.

The film's trailer opens the disc and an interesting if talky "making of" featurette closes it.

Mr. Destiny is available on a *very* grainy disc from Touchstone.

Jacob's Ladder (1990) ★★★★★
Director: Adrian Lyne
Running Time: 112 minutes

Is he live or is he memory? That's the question that plagues Jacob (Tim Robbins) throughout this sad, disturbing, provocative film. A Vietnam vet who suffered through some (initially) unnamed horror during the war, Jacob has a doctorate but is disinclined to use it. His young son has died, his marriage has fallen apart, and all he wants is to do his job at the post office and come home each day to his devoted girlfriend, Jezzie (Elizabeth Peña).

He can't seem to do that, however. He's haunted by nightmares, by daylight visitations from ghastly figures, by thoughts of death that won't let go. Believing that his visions and horrifying experiences are somehow rooted in the suppressed memory of what happened to him in Vietnam, he goes looking into that past and uncovers a horrifying (but rooted-in-fact) secret involving a drug program in which he was apparently involved. Without giving too much away, the question is, *Is* that program a part of what happened in the war, or is everything that happened after the war a hallucination? The answers will leave you stunned and shaken.

The script by Bruce Joel Rubin (who also wrote *Ghost*) kicked around the studios for years, earning a reputation as the best unproduced script in Hollywood. Part of the difficulty in bringing it to the screen was translating its imagery into something less abstract (Rubin had graphic visions of heaven and hell, reflecting the origins of Jacob's Ladder as a ladder that appeared to the biblical patriarch in a dream, rising to heaven). It took Lyne (pronounced Line), coming off the box-office success of *Fatal Attraction* (1987), to get the film made and keep audiences from being utterly lost as Jacob moves between what seems to be real and what clearly isn't.

He succeeded masterfully. The movie failed at the box office because it's not a slasher film (its horror transcends that genre) and demands our complete attention: Like *2001: A Space Odyssey* (see page 287), it asks you to remember things you've seen in order to make sense of what you're seeing now—especially at the film's sad, unforgettable conclusion.

Robbins is perfect as the tortured hero, and Peña is ideal as his concerned, independent girlfriend. Watch for Macaulay Culkin's brief but important appearance.

Following previews, director Lyne cut his film by nearly a half hour. The deleted footage includes a lengthy scene in which Jacob goes to a hotel room, takes a drug, and seemingly exorcises his demons as the room breaks apart and blood pours from the cracks. Believing himself to be cured, he heads to Grand Central Station, only to find out that there *is* no cure. (This leaves the film in the same place narratively, though minus a very powerful segment.) Also eliminated was a horrifying sequence that really explains the movie: Jezzie is revealed to be a force of evil, not a person, underscoring the fact that all of the present-day events are imagined and that the film is all about the denial of death. The laserdisc release would have been a perfect place to put this material back in, or at least tack it on as an extra.

The Disc
Video: ★★★
Audio: ★★★★ (Surround)
Chapters: Yes
Format: CLV
Source: Carolco Home Video/Image Entertainment

This would have been a much more enjoyable film on laserdisc if more care had been given to the transfer. The picture is not as sharp as it could have been; though the colors are solid and generally satisfying, there's frequent video noise. Speckling is a problem on a number of copies viewed.

Though the film has not been letterboxed, the image has been opened up top and bottom, so there's minimal cropping on the sides.

The audio goes a long way to making up for the disappointing video transfer. Though a few stretches of dialogue are a *bit* garbled, you'll forget them as the frequent sound effects punch you nearly as hard as they do Jacob (especially if you've got Surround).

Jason and the Argonauts (1963)
★★★½
Director: Don Chaffey
Running Time: 104 minutes

After working on *Twenty Million Miles to Earth* (see page 286), special-effects master Ray Harryhausen devised a method of creating his screen magic in color. Dubbing the process Dynamation, he created special effects for *The 7th Voyage of Sinbad* (1958), *The Three Worlds of Gulliver* (1959), and *Mysterious Island* (1961). After that, armed with his largest budget ($3 million), he worked on the film of the Greek myth of Jason's quest for the Golden Fleece.

The film follows Jason (Todd Armstrong) from his journey to Olympus and an audience with Zeus and Hera—played with wit and style by Niall MacGinnis (see *Curse of the Demon*) and Honor Blackman (see *Goldfinger*)—through his voyage to Colchis and battles with the bronze Titan Talos, the fierce Harpies, the Clashing Rocks, the seven-headed Hydra, and an army of sword-swinging skeletons.

Despite the advances in special effects since 1963, most of this film's wonders remains unsurpassed. Today, when batteries of technicians are required to create even the simplest effects, it's inspiring to think that one man, working alone, created every frame of this film's magic. You'll go back to the fight with Talos and the duel with the skeletons for repeated viewings—and never once will you fail to be wonder-struck.

Though Armstrong is a weak lead (his voice was redubbed to make it sound more heroic), he receives top-notch support from a host of British character actors, most notably Nigel Green as Hercules, Laurence Naismith as Argus, Gary Raymond as the traitorous Acastus, and John Cairney as Hylas.

Unfortunately, *Jason and the Argonauts* was released at the end of the Italian sword-and-sandal cycle that had begun with Steve Reeves's *Hercules* in 1959 (see page 138). The public failed to perceive a difference between this film and the cheap Italian films, and it died at the box office.

Harryhausen returned to Greek mythology with *Clash of the Titans* (1981). Except for the battle with Medusa, the film is a disappointment. Harry Hamlin is a weak Perseus, and a sickly Laurence Olivier was not up to the part of Zeus. The laserdisc is grainy and mediocre. A subsequent Harryhausen mythological project, *Force of Trojans*—a retelling of the *Aeneid*—was scripted but never filmed.

The Disc
Video: ★★★½
Audio: ★★★★ (monaural)
Chapters: No
Format: CLV
Source: Columbia Pictures Home Video

Though the quality of the print is excellent and the colors are rich, a slight matte would have helped open up the film's many spectacular vistas. CAV would also have been a dramatic plus, since so many of the scenes—Talos straddling the harbor, the god Mercury towering over his temple, the skeleton duel—cry out for a long, appreciative look.

The audio is more satisfying, particularly when Talos goes creaking across the screen. Bernard Herrmann's score also sounds great, especially the percussion and brass that dominate it.

A CAV edition, with audio commentary by Harryhausen, is due from Criterion. Included in that version will be the original opening title sequence (*Jason and the Golden Fleece*), notes and storyboards on deleted scenes, etc. For the true Harryhausen fan, even at $100, it's a must.

Jesus Christ Superstar (1973)
★★★
Director: Norman Jewison
Running Time: 108 minutes

When the original conceptual album of *Jesus Christ Superstar* was released in 1972, it was called everything from deeply religious to blasphemous. Composer Andrew Lloyd Webber, who wrote the rock opera with lyricist Tim Rice, says, "The idea (was) to have Christ seen through the eyes of Judas, with Christ as a man, not as a God." In spite of (or because of?) the controversy, the album was a huge hit, and stage versions played all over the world.

After directing *Fiddler on the Roof,*

Norman Jewison hadn't been looking to film another musical. But he says that when he was offered the film version of *Jesus Christ Superstar*, he couldn't resist "the most moving and important story of western civilization."

The story recounts the last seven days in the life of Jesus (Ted Neeley), and his relationship with apostle Judas Iscariot (Carl Anderson), Mary Magdalene (Yvonne Elliman, one of two holdovers from the original album), Pontius Pilate (Barry Dennen, the other holdover), King Herod (Joshua Mostel), and high priest Caiaphas (Bob Bingham).

Unfortunately, in bringing the story to the screen, Jewison made one bad creative call: To suggest the timelessness of the story and of Jesus's teachings, he mixed the old and the new—modern dress for the Roman soldiers, machine guns and tanks to symbolize Roman might, angels represented by airplanes, and a prologue and epilogue showing the actors arriving at and departing from the desert by bus to perform the drama. The mix is jarring, and, thanks to that as well as an uncharismatic lead and god-awful choreography, audiences stayed away.

However, there's still the great music and strong performances by Anderson and Dennen and the spectacular location photography in Israel—including the caves of Bet Guvrin, near where David fought Goliath. At roughly the same price as the CD, the movie is probably worth owning: You can always slip it in and ignore the picture.

The Disc
Video: ★★★★½
Audio: ★★★★½ (stereo)
Chapters: Yes
Format: CLV
Source: MCA/Universal Home Video

The new letterboxed transfer does justice to the original, very sharp Todd-AO 35 image. Though the colors are a *touch* on the pale side and there are hints of grain here and there—both the fault of the original print, not the transfer—the picture is a tremendous improvement over the grainy, pan-and-scan version.

The stereo separations are clear and stirring.

The Jolson Story (1946) ★★★
Director: Alfred E. Green
Running Time: 128 minutes

Born Asa Yoelson, Al Jolson broke into vaudeville as a child and never looked back. He was not only an incredible entertainer, he was a phenomenon: Broadway smash, top radio entertainer, first recording superstar, and motion-picture legend who appeared in *The Jazz Singer* (1927), the first talking film (really a singing film, silent except for the songs and Jolson's patter before them). And when he'd worn out his welcome as a star, his life story was made into a film and he became known to a new generation of admirers.

The movie follows Jolson from childhood (he's played by Scotty Beckett as a boy), where he yearned to sing on stage, despite the disapproval of his father, Cantor Yoelson (Ludwig Donath). Taken under the wing of entertainer Steve Martin (William Demarest), Al tours, joins the minstrel show of Lew Dockstader (John Alexander), makes it big on Broadway, becomes a film star, and marries singer/dancer Julie Benson (Evelyn Keyes). But their marriage is troubled: Jolson is miserable when he isn't singing and is jealous when Julie is. Eventually, the understanding woman leaves her husband to his one true love—the footlights.

The film is more fiction than fact. Jolson's mother Naomi (Tamara Shayne), did not avidly follow his career; she'd died when he was eight. His father, Moshe, was a rabbi, not a cantor. There was no mentor called Steve Martin; Jolson worked with a number of people on his way up. He had two wives before marrying "Julie"—actually Ruby Keeler, who wouldn't allow herself to be portrayed in the film (and whose parting from Al was considerably more acrimonious). Most significant of all, the real Jolson was not the generous, jovial fellow played by Larry Parks; rather, he was a driven, egotistical bastard and a satyr (he often demanded—and got—sex from the chorus girls before he went onstage each night).

But—he *was* a hell of a singer/dancer, and the idea for a Jolson film had first been proposed in 1943, after *Yankee Doodle Dandy* (see page 311) proved to be a big hit. It took two years to put the script and package together—and to convince Jolson that, at sixty years old, he simply couldn't play himself in the film. Instead, he settled for ten thousand dollars to record the songs that Parks lip-synched. However, Jolson nagged the producers to let him appear *somewhere* in the film, and that's the legend himself singing "Swanee" in the long shot on the theater runway. (It's also dancer Miriam Franklin Nelson doing the difficult "Liza" dance for Keyes.)

Despite its false portrait of Jolson, the film is wonderful entertainment, with all those great songs and an engaging performance by Parks. It was followed by a sequel, *Jolson Sings Again* (1949), which ends with Parks, playing Jolson, meeting Parks, and playing Parks as he begins filming *The Jolson Story*. (Jolson was banned from the set of this film after swearing viciously at Parks for the way he was playing him.)

Jolson died of a heart attack in 1950 at the age of sixty-four.

the dialogue sounds, at times, nearly as crude as it did in the *The Jazz Singer*. The musical numbers are slightly better, since Jolson recorded them under carefully controlled conditions in the studio.

The disc of *Jolson Sings Again* is marginally better but still extremely disappointing.

Jolson fans will also want to pick up MGM/UA's spectacular *The Al Jolson Collection*, a boxed set containing eight Jolson features: *The Jazz Singer* (1927), *The Singing Fool* (1928), *Say It With Songs* (1929), *Mammy* (1930), *Big Boy* (1930), *Wonder Bar* (1934), *Go Into Your Dance* (1935), and *The Singing Kid* (1936).

The Jazz Singer is, of course, the most important film in the collection, and MGM/UA has found as clear a print as one could hope for. Though the film that many consider to be the best of Jolson's later efforts has not been included—*Hallelujah I'm a Bum* (1933)—the set offers another gem, *Go Into Your Dance*, which costars Ruby Keeler and boasts the unforgettable "About a Quarter To Nine." The rest are all average, though Jolson fans will rejoice in every one of them.

Obviously, the older the films are, the more raw the picture and sound is, though the video and audio quality ranges from good to very good on all.

The Disc
Video: no stars
Audio: ★★ (monaural)
Chapters: No
Format: CLV
Source: RCA/Columbia Pictures Home Video

RCA/Columbia used the same master for this disc as they did for the videotape, which was poor to begin with. The disc amplifies the problems.

The image on the disc is washed-out and reddish, the focus is soft, there are no details, and the whole thing is just plain dreadful.

Though the film had been very effectively rechanneled for stereo in 1972, the disc is monaural. There's a fair amount of background noise on the sound track, and

Journey to the Center of the Earth (1959) ★★★
Director: Henry Levin
Running Time: 129 minutes

In 1880, Edinburgh geology professor Oliver S. Lindenbrook (James Mason) chips away crusted lava from a stone and finds a carved message about a natural entranceway in Iceland that is said to lead to the center of the earth. Together with his student Alec McKuen (Pat Boone), Carla Guttenborg (Arlene Dahl)—the widow of a onetime rival scientist—and the brawny Hans (Peter Ronson) and his pet duck, Gertrude, Lindenbrook sets out.

As they make their way to the center

of the earth, the group flees a rolling boulder, survives a flood, battles dinosaurs, negotiates a tunnel of winds, is caught in a volcanic eruption, and deals with the intrigue of the territorial Count Saknussemm (Thayer David), a descendent of Arne Saknussemm, who died on a similar expedition: It is his notes on the rock and markings carved inside the earth that Lindenbrook follows.

Except for adding Carla and some pruning—such as the loss of the towering Ape Gigans and the battle between a plesiosaur and ichthyosaur—the film is generally true to Jules Verne's 1864 novel. (Though you've got to wonder why they kept the name Saknussemm yet replaced Hardwigg with Lindenbrook and Henry with Alec.) Verne doubtless would have approved of how the filmmakers realized his inner world: dark and craggy caverns and precipitous ledges leading to gem-encrusted passageways, fields of tree-sized mushrooms, a nest of dimetrodons, the lost civilization of Atlantis, and the sunken sea lighted by an internal sun with the crust of the earth visible above. The sets and matte paintings are *still* impressive, and even the lizards dressed up with frills and fins and photographically enlarged are convincing.

The performances aren't as successful as the sets and effects. They are cartoon-broad, the duck earning more sympathy than any of the humans, and Mason shows none of the texture or fire he brought to his Captain Nemo in Disney's *Twenty Thousand Leagues Under the Sea* (1954), which this film clearly tried to emulate. Worse, a romance between Alec and Lindenbrook's daughter, Jenny (Diane Baker), and the song Boone sings to her seem longer than the four-thousand-mile journey into the earth—though Boone *was* a popular young singer, and the producers can be forgiven this sop to the young girls who were *not* the target audience for the film. But you won't miss much if you jump right to side two and the start of the journey.

Bernard Herrmann's score is both eerie and celestial in ways that only he was able to achieve.

The Disc

Video: ★★½
Audio: ★★★ (Surround)
Chapters: Yes
Format: CLV (sides one and two), CAV (side three)
Source: CBS Fox Video

The colors of this once-vivid film are disappointing. Though they're not *quite* as bad as you might expect from the Deluxe process, the flesh tones look flat enough to pass for colorized, and the streets of Edinburgh, the school, the lab, and Lindenbrook's home are washed out. *But*—the inside of the earth still has some of the punch, the reds still intense enough to kick up some noise in spots.

The print is in generally good condition. The letterboxed edition is a decided improvement over the original pan-and-scan version, which robbed the film of its considerable grandeur. In fact, wide as the letterbox is, it still loses a bit from the edges of the CinemaScope image.

The audio is rechanneled Surround: It goes to all four speakers, but apart from the music being louder in the rear there are no directional effects. However, Bernard Herrmann fans will experience heaven thanks to the opening chord of the score—which, if turned up high enough, would probably open a passage to the center of the earth.

The extras consist of posters, lobby cards, and a few scenes that were slightly different for the film's British release.

Khartoum (1966) ★★★½

Director: Basil Dearden
Running Time: 136 minutes

Gen. Charles Gordon (1833–1885) was one of those soldier/fanatics England seems to produce at regular intervals, men such as Lawrence of Arabia or Clive of India, and his diaries about the siege of Khartoum (edited by his brother after Gordon's death) are full of passion, insight, and the religious mysticism to which he was drawn. As star Charlton Heston has put it, the general "was a little mad [but] the single-handed capacity Gordon displayed again and again to control large groups of people, quite unarmed and alone, is almost magical; quite scary, in fact."

This surprisingly accurate film opens with the massacre of a ten-thousand-man British army by the fanatic Mohammed Ahmed ibn Abdullah (Laurence Olivier), also known as the Mahdi—the expected one. The Mahdi is waging holy war against the countries of the Middle East, and one of his initial goals is to pray at the mosque in Khartoum, the capital of the Sudan. To do so, he will have to subjugate the thirteen thousand Egyptians living there—which means killing a vast number of them, especially the soldiers. England's Prime Minister Gladstone (Ralph Richardson) refuses to send another army sailing up the Nile, but he *will* send one man: General Gordon (Heston), the strong-willed officer who ended the slave trade in the Sudan. (Though this is not mentioned in the film, Gordon was busy searching for Noah's Ark when he received his orders to go to Khartoum.)

Along as Gordon's second in command is Col. John Donald Hamill Stewart (Richard Johnson). Gordon arrives in Khartoum and boldly goes alone into the desert to visit the Mahdi at his camp (an event that never occurred). Though the men come away with a mutual respect, the Mahdi refuses to withdraw. While Gordon plans for the defense of the city, the Mahdi tightens his noose until evacuation is impossible. Though Gordon is informed that he is free to go, the Englishman refuses to leave. The Mahdi's forces, fifty thousand strong, level Khartoum—though within months the Mahdi is dead and his jihad has ended. (Though not explained in the film, this was due to disease in the rotting dead of Khartoum. Was this the inspiration for H. G. Wells' *War of the World* denouement?)

Rarely has so much historical exposition been presented as skillfully as it is in *Khartoum*. The script never stops to explain things: Information comes out in uncontrived dialogue. The costumes and sets are also accurate and quite stunning, as are the spectacular battle scenes staged by Yakima Canutt—though the miniature model used for the filling of the moat is pitiful, and there are a couple of tacky-looking process shots that cheapen the film. The actors were on location in Egypt: why was it necessary to go back to a studio and shoot these scenes?

Surprisingly, what keeps the film from being great are its two stars. Heston is effective at conveying the heroism and despair that Gordon exhibited in Khartoum—but the British accent, while *close* now and then, just doesn't cut it. Olivier has a different problem: He gets the Sudanese accent right, but his Mahdi always seems as if he wants to smile, hinting—accurately but far too overtly—that he may have been a charlatan driven by ego and not religious fanaticism. The film would have been stronger if Olivier had played Gordon and someone else (Omar Sharif?) had been the Mahdi.

Still, *Khartoum* is an entertaining, moving, often chilling film that—in light of recent international events—reminds us that as much as things change in the world, they're very much the same.

The Disc

Video: ★★★★½
Audio: ★★★½ (Surround)
Chapters: No
Format: CLV (sides one and two), CAV (side three)
Source: MGM/UA Home Video

Filmed in 70mm Ultra Panavision, and originally presented in Cinerama, *Khartoum* looks incredibly clear on this letterboxed laserdisc, just as sharp as can be, with colors that for the most part are glossy and beautiful. There are a few flaws in the print (such as an annoying strand of *something* that grows larger from 10:38 to 14:55 on side two), but they're relatively minor.

The audio is very clear and the Surround Sound is good, though the explosions get a little raspy if you turn the volume too high, and directional effects are minimal.

The disc includes Frank Cordell's exquisite original overture, entr'acte, and exit music.

King Kong (1933) ★★★★★
Director: Merian C. Cooper and Ernest B. Schoedsack
Running Time: 100 minutes (*The Son of Kong:* 70 minutes)

There have been many stories about apes and monsters menacing and/or loving women, tales such as *Beauty and the Beast* (see page 22) and Edgar Allan Poe's 1841 short story "Murders in the Rue Morgue," in which a large orangutan not only carries off a woman but climbs buildings. There have also been tales of lost worlds, including the 1925 film *The Lost World*, with special effects by Willis O'Brien, which was based on Arthur Conan Doyle's 1912 novel about an expedition to a time-forgotten island inhabited by prehistoric animals. In the film, the scientists even take specimens back to London—an apatosaur (brontosaur) and a pteranodon—that cause havoc in the modern metropolis.

So *King Kong* is not without precedent, yet the combination of its timeless story, unparalleled special effects, lavish sets, and lush and thunderous score have made it the preeminent story of its kind. The tale is familiar: A film crew composed of Carl Denham (Robert Armstrong), actress Ann Darrow (Fay Wray)—a poor, beautiful woman Denham found on the streets—Captain Englehorn (Frank Reicher), and first mate John Driscoll (Bruce Cabot) journey to ancient Skull Island, where the natives kidnap Ann and offer her as a bride to their fifty-foot-tall god, Kong. The crew chases the huge ape to its lair, Driscoll rescues Ann, and, when Kong follows them back to the native village, Denham fells him with gas bombs. Kong is taken to New York, exhibited in a theater (a baseball stadium in an early version of the story), escapes, snatches Ann from a hotel room, and vents his anger on the city before climbing the Empire State Building. Four navy pursuit planes are sent aloft, and they pepper him with bullets until he falls to his death.

(Look for Cooper and Schoedsack as the squadron flight commander and chief observer, respectively.)

The jacket gives a detailed and accurate history of the making of the $430,000 film (studio overhead and the cost of an aborted dinosaur project, *Creation*, were tacked on, bringing the total to $650,000) and the story behind its remarkable special effects, which were created by Willis O'Brien using stop-motion photography—the frame-by-frame articulation of metal-jointed eighteen-inch-tall puppets. (The characteristic bristling of Kong's rabbit-fur coat is due to the fact that the fur shifted when O'Brien handled the model between frames, making the necessary incremental movements.) Though a giant Kong hand, foot, and head as well as pteranodon talons were constructed for a few close-ups, more often than not scaled, miniature, stop-motion models of Wray, Cabot, and the other actors were used for scenes in which the people had to act with Kong or the dinosaurs of Skull Island. (Watch, in chapter twenty, at 7:00, how the stop-motion models pass behind foliage so that the real actors can replace them in the shot.)

The expansive jungles were sets, but many of the more impressive vistas were actually matte paintings. To create a layered effect, different elements of the jungles were painted on separate panes of glass and positioned vertically, roughly a foot apart, with the models positioned between them. (An excellent example of this is the view of Kong seen through the jungle at 16:29 of chapter twenty-four.) Rear-screen projection and miniature-screen projection were also used (that is, showing prefilmed dinosaur footage on a giant screen with the actors in front of it to make them look like they're a part of it, or projecting prefilmed footage of the actors on a small screen in a miniature set to make the monsters look large).

Interestingly, one of the film's most spectacular sequences was as an afterthought: the scene in which Kong attacks the elevated train. The finished film had ended up filling thirteen reels; and, being superstitious, Cooper ordered the scene shot to bring the film up to fourteen reels. Ironically, after the scene was shot and he viewed the fourteen-reel, nearly two-hour film, Cooper decided to *prune* it considerably. Small and spectacular sequences alike had to go: shots of dinosaurs, of Ann and Driscoll swimming down he river after escaping from Kong, of the bellowing ape climbing down Skull Mountain in pursuit, and many others.

Some scenes, wrongly assumed to have been cut at this point, had been eliminated *during* production. A styracosaur chased Denham's men onto the log where so many of them met their death, then tried to uproot it with its horn. Cooper canned this, feeling it was peripheral to the main story—though the dinosaur's unseen presence was the reason the men simply didn't back off the log when Kong arrived to shake them off. (The styracosaur model was later used in *The Son of Kong.*)

Likewise, giant spiders and insects waiting to eat the men at the bottom of the pit were dropped during production after some footage had been shot. Cooper felt the scene was so gruesome that audiences would forget about Ann and *her* problem and the story would have trouble picking up steam again. Instead, the men die with awful thuds when they hit the floor of the pit. A scene in which a triceratops and a giant snake terrorize Ann before the arrival of the tyrannosaur were also snipped. Later, in the New York segment, a shot of Kong falling from the Empire State Building, seen from the top of the building, was deleted because the superimposed ape did not look convincing.

However, all of the scenes clipped in 1938 by skittish censors are here, including Kong stripping Ann, crushing people in his teeth and underfoot, and dropping a woman to her death in the city when he realizes she's not Ann, seen more clearly than in the restored print first shown in 1971.

Brilliant though the film is, it *isn't* perfect—and a few slipups are pointed out here in the spirit of fun, not criticism. At 20:00 in chapter twenty-seven, the rock on the right of the screen was added later, over a black area that had been painted on glass. To the left of the rock, reflections of the lights are visible on the glass. Also, watch the bars at the bottom of the door in chapter thirty-one, 29:13: The sailors suddenly "pop in," as though O'Brien —after animating Kong for a while—realized that no one had turned on the projector showing the people. As Kong pushes open the door moments later at 30:08, he's visible *through* the leftmost panel of the door on the right, the result of faulty superimposition.

These are like flaws on the Pieta or David, however, not detracting one iota from the grandeur of the whole.

The Son of Kong is a different matter. It took over a year to film *King Kong;* the sequel was shot in just seven months at a cost of $250,000. Writer Ruth Rose (Mrs. Schoedsack), who cowrote the first film, once said, "If you can't make it bigger, you'd better make it funnier." *The Son of Kong* filled the bill.

Hounded by creditors because of the destruction caused by Kong, Denham sails back to Skull Island to find its legendary lost treasure. Englehorn is back, along with entertainer Hilda Peterson (Helen Mack) whom they meet on a layover, and greedy Nils Helstrom (John Marston). When the crew finds out where they're headed, the frightened sailors set the foursome, along with the cook, Charley (Victor Wong), adrift in a lifeboat. The quintet reaches Skull Island, where Denham and Hilda save white-furred little Kong from quicksand. He returns the favor by rescuing them from various prehistoric animals and helping them find the treasure. When the island is torn apart by an earthquake, the ape holds Denham aloft long enough for the others to row over and save him. As for little Kong, his foot stuck in a fissure, he goes down with the island.

Comical and downright stupid in spots, *The Son of Kong* is an unworthy sequel.

Both films, especially *King Kong*, benefit enormously from the scores by Max

Steiner. *King Kong* boasts the first full-blown score ever composed for a film, and it remains one of the greatest ever written (try to imagine *any* scene without it). Steiner went on to write the music for *Gone With the Wind*, *The Adventures of Don Juan* (see pages 116 and 2), and other classics.

A third film was planned by Cooper, detailing the trip from Skull Island to New York, with King Kong escaping en route. Schoedsack convinced him that the project was a bad idea, and Cooper shelved it. After World War II, they came up with a new project, *Mighty Joe Young* (1949), which gave the old themes and effects new twists. O'Brien created the effects for that film, assisted by a young Ray Harryhausen, who went on to create classics of his own such as *Twenty Million Miles to Earth* and *Jason and the Argonauts* (see pages 286 and 153).

When he was involved in the development of Cinerama, Cooper planned a remake of *King Kong* called *The Eighth Wonder*, but he left the company before the film could be put into production.

In the early 1960s, Willis O'Brien himself tried to launch a sequel called *King Kong vs. Frankenstein* (also known as *King Kong vs. Prometheus*), in which the ape battles fifty-foot-tall Frankenstein's Monster. He was unable to raise the money, though a producer who heard about the project approached the Japanese about teaming Kong with one of their monsters, and the result was *King Kong vs. Godzilla* (1963). In that film and its followup, *King Kong Escapes* (1968), Kong was played by an actor in a ratty-looking costume.

Dino de Laurentiis gave us a disastrous remake in 1976, featuring an actor in an ape suit, no dinosaurs, and the World Trade Center instead of the Empire State Building. The $25 million film was unbearable, though even *it* was better than the sequel, *King Kong Lives* (1986), in which the ape gets an artificial heart, marries a giant female ape, and has a son.

The Disc

Video: ★★★★★ (Turner); ★★★ (Criterion)
Audio: ★★★½ (Turner); ★★½ (Criterion)
Chapters: Yes
Format: CLV (*The Son of Kong* CAV, side two) (Turner); CAV or CLV (Criterion)
Source: Turner Home Entertainment RKO Classic Collection/Image Entertainment or Criterion

What's incredible about the new Turner transfer of *King Kong*—made from a recently discovered 35mm print—is that viewers who didn't see the film when it first opened can begin to appreciate why it made the impact it did.

The print isn't perfect. Though there are long stretches that are free of blemishes, there are numerous sections with scratches, breaks, and flaws of all sorts. It earns a high rating because this is likely to be the best print of the film we'll ever have, and the *contrast* in the print is exceptional, with a wide range of gray tones. There are still some shadowy patches here and there, and some of the effects will never be razor sharp due to the rear-screen process used to create them (the image, projected from behind, had to pass *through* a screen and be rephotographed with the actors in front, cutting down on brightness and clarity). But even the dark areas aren't nearly as bad as what we've been watching since new prints were struck for the second reissue (1942) from *existing prints* of the film, not the negative—reproducing the scratches, cuts, and all.

The digital audio is hiss-free, the dialogue sharper than ever. Due to recording techniques of the time (and subsequent digital rerecordings of the score on CD, which sound so *good*), Steiner's music sounds a little on the tinny side—a nitpick cited in the name of accuracy.

The Criterion edition of *King Kong* was made from a source cobbled together from various prints to get the best overall image available at the time. The result ranges from good to very good, but there isn't a shot in these editions that can touch the Turner disc.

There's another Image release of *King Kong*, though it's the weakest of the bunch.

The Turner package marks the debut of *The Son of Kong* on laserdisc, and the picture and sound are in the same fine shape as *King Kong*. What's more, all of the animation effects are on the CAV side two, allowing viewers to study them jitter-free.

Dino de Laurentiis's two films are available on laser, for those who have nothing better to do with their money. The Japanese films are available in superbly transferred, letterboxed imports.

The Lost World is available on an excellent laserdisc release from Lumivision, transferred from the only known 35mm print.

King of Kings (1961) ★★★★½
Director: Nicholas Ray
Running Time: 161 minutes

Someday, producer Samuel Bronston will get his due. A few of the films he made were huge moneymakers and a few were bombs—but none of them was truly terrible, a few were damn good, and he certainly merits better treatment than critics have accorded him.

A Sorbonne graduate, the Romanian-born Bronston gave up his position as a flutist with the Paris Symphony Orchestra to follow his first love—movies. He became a salesman for MGM in France, then went to work for Columbia before becoming a producer, making the films *Jack London* (1943) and *A Walk in the Sun* (1945), among others. Yearning for greater independence, he set up his own company in Spain using money provided by the du Pont family.

Cecil B. DeMille had always wanted to remake his own silent film about the life of Jesus, *The King of Kings* (1927), but died before he could do so. After the success of *Ben-Hur*, Bronston decided that *King of Kings* would be an ideal project and, in an inspired move, hired hip auteur Nicholas Ray—*Rebel Without a Cause* (1955)—to direct. Ray's hiring, plus the casting of young, blue-eyed Jeffrey Hunter, caused cynics to dub the film *I Was a Teenage Jesus*, which is neither accurate nor amusing. Hunter does quite well with what's essentially an unplayable part (he described his only "guidepost" as "absolute humility"). One of the world's finest actors, Max von Sydow, didn't do much better in *The Greatest Story Ever Told* four years later; Hunter's youthful power is in many ways preferable to von Sydow's quiet piety.

King of Kings tells the story of Jesus from birth to Resurrection, and features an intelligent and insightful script comprised of pieces from all the Gospels. There's intimacy amid great spectacle (having Jesus move among the people during the Sermon on the Mount makes for a powerful and personal scene), and there are excellent performances—particularly by Siobhan McKenna as Jesus's mother, Hurd Hatfield as Pontius Pilate, Frank Thring as Herod Antipas (he played Pilate in *Ben-Hur*), Ron Randell as the centurion Lucius, and Rip Torn as a troubled Judas. The film also has great visual flair: Regardless of one's religious convictions, *no one* who watches the shadow of Christ healing the sick will be unmoved (though, conversely, the cross formed by the shadow of the resurrected Jesus falling across the fishing net in Galilee is more hokey than reverent).

To be sure, the film is flawed. Barabbas (Harry Guardino) was opposed to Roman rule, but not in the brawling, streetwise manner portrayed here. Ambushing soldiers and starting rumbles are simply an excuse to work action into the film. Having Jesus visit John the Baptist (Robert Ryan) in prison, while tearjerking, is also improbably silly, as is the notion that Jesus had legal counsel (Lucius) arguing on his behalf before Pilate. His presence is not only inaccurate, it undermines the power of Jesus's purposeful silence and trivializes his suffering. And having Jesus on the cross, ticking off just about *every-thing* the Gospels say he uttered, makes it seem like he's dictating a concordance rather than giving up his life.

The film's overall impact is great, however, helped by a stirring and angelic Miklos Rozsa score and narration written by science fiction author Ray Bradbury (another quirky but successful choice) and read by Orson Welles.

The success of *King of Kings* and the even more popular *El Cid* (1961) encouraged Bronston to erect huge studios outside of Madrid, and the Spanish film industry owes much of its subsequent success to Bronston. Unfortunately, his next three pictures—*55 Days at Peking* (1963), *The Fall of the Roman Empire* (1964), and *Circus World* (1964)—though entertaining and, in the case of the second, extremely literate, were expensive failures. Hopelessly debt-ridden, Bronston canceled projected film versions of *Brave New World* and *Isabella of Spain* and folded up shop. Moving to Texas, he opened a distributorship and has made only a small thriller since, *The Mysterious House of Dr. C* (1979).

The Disc
Video: ★★★★
Audio: ★★★½ (Surround)
Chapters:
Format: CLV
Source: MGM/UA Home Video

Fans of biblical epics will rejoice in the letterboxing of *King of Kings*. Even though it cheats a little by dropping a portion of the sides, the presentation captures the film's grandeur, something the original panned-and-scanned version fails to do.

Thanks to the 70mm film on which it was originally shot, the movie is also supersharp. Why not five stars, then? Because the color is flawed in spots, having gone red and pale as a result of the Eastman stock that was used by Technicolor at the time. There's also noise in some of the reds—which, in a movie involving the Roman Empire, is a real problem.

The audio is generally very satisfying. It suffers from some dropouts and the dynamic range isn't quite what it was in the theaters, but there's clarity, excellent separation, and the wraparound celestial score. However, it's inexcusable that the laserdisc leaves off the overture, entr'acte, and exit music, since they could easily have been fit onto the three sides without spilling over to a fourth. They're present on the original panned-and-scanned version.

Despite what the jacket says, the trailer is nowhere to be found. But that's not the only misprint: The disc is listed as running 171 minutes, which would be correct *if* it included the cut music. Obviously, the decision to eliminate the overture et al. was made after the jacket had been printed.

El Cid, *55 Days at Peking*, and *The Fall of the Roman Empire* are available on stupendous looking letterboxed discs from Japan.

MGM has also released George Stevens' interminable, star-studded life of Christ, *The Greatest Story Ever Told* (1965). Though the 70mm picture looks beautiful and the stereo separations are excellent, this is one boring motion picture. (When the disc was first released, the cast list on the jacket included Keir Dullea as Bowman—which, of course, belonged on MGM's *2001: A Space Odyssey*. Not only is that wrong but the bozo copywriter gave him top billing over Max von Sydow as Jesus.)

A Kiss Before Dying (1991) ★
Director: James Dearden
Running Time: 93 minutes

A Kiss Before Dying (1953) is terrific little novel, the first by author Ira Levin (*Rosemary's Baby*, *The Stepford Wives*). It's the story of a young college man who plots to wed the young daughter of a copper tycoon. But she becomes pregnant and, knowing that her father will disinherit her, the boy murders her and moves on to her sister to try and get his hands on the family fortune.

The novel was first filmed in 1956, starring Robert Wagner and Joanne Woodward, directed by Gerd Oswald, and it's a lulu. Wagner's smooth, boyish charm makes him as unlikely a psychopath as you could want, and the script is taut and clever.

Given the strength of the source material and his own credentials, director James Dearden *should* have served up a powerful remake. The son of director Basil (see *Khartoum*), James had written *Fatal Attraction* (1987), which was based on his own forty-seven-minute featurette *Diversion* (1980).

So what went wrong? The script and casting did. Though he follows the original plot, more or less, Dearden eliminates one of the three daughters in the novel and gives us Sean Young as both Dorothy and Ellen Carlsson (not Kingship, as in the novel). Pregnant Dorothy gets pushed off a building by Jonathan Corliss (Matt Dillon), who romances Ellen in order to work his way into the good graces of Thor Carlsson (Max von Sydow). However, Ellen has never believed the official findings that her sister committed suicide, and eventually she learns that Jonathan was responsible, leading to a *Fatal Attraction*-like showdown.

There aren't just holes in Dearden's scripts, there are voids the size of Pittsburgh, such as the fact that none of the people in the lobby sees Corliss go up to the roof with Dorothy, or leave—walking right past her smashed body with barely a glance. Or that Thor, who has a private detective investigate every *boyfriend* Dorothy has, fails to look into Corliss's past when he *marries* Ellen. He takes Jonathan's word for the fact that he's an orphan (who killed the guy he's pretending to be).

The casting and performances are also weak. Young is so bland in both roles that you've got to wonder what was going through Dearden's mind as he watched the dailies. Dillon is trip wire-scary, but his performance pales beside memories of Wagner: You *expect* the gaunt, punky Dillon to play a nutcase. And von Sydow walks through another one for the paycheck: Is this the same man who was once considered one of the world's great actors? Diane Ladd tries but isn't able to do much with her brief role as Mrs. Corliss.

Given the shoddiness of the entire project, it's fitting that Universal misspells Carlsson on the back of the sleeve.

The Disc

Video: ★★★½
Audio: ★★★½ (Surround)
Chapters: No
Format: CLV
Source: MCA/Universal Home Video

The movie gets a very solid transfer, with a minimum of grain and very little video noise, despite the amount of browns and reds. The image is sharp throughout. Only the titles are letterboxed, but the film isn't compromised by the cropping.

The digital audio is very good, and there are some interesting Surround effects—though far fewer than you'd expect from a thriller.

The original film is not available on laserdisc.

The Krays (1990) ★★★★
Director: Peter Medak
Running Time: 119 minutes

The Hungarian-born Medak is one of the industry's most consistently interesting directors, as well as one of the most consistently overlooked. His *The Ruling Class* (see page 239) was a masterful satire of the English upper class, and *The Changeling* (1979; discontinued on laserdisc) is an exceptional ghost story.

The Krays is a riveting character study inspired by the escapades of Ronald (Gary Kemp) and Reginald Kray (Martin Kemp), gangsters who terrorized London during the 1960s. They were eccentric and brutal: Swords and daggers were their preferred weapons until the sheer numbers of people to be killed forced them to switch to machine guns.

Medak regards the brothers as victims of their era (the scene in the tubes during the Blitz is chilling), of their domineering mother, and of their sex: More than once, the women in the film remark that men remain children throughout their lives. The Krays' games just happen to be a little rougher, is all.

There are some annoying lapses in the plot (where *did* the brothers get the money to fix up the club, and just what kind of gangster activities were they involved in when they started?), and a bizarre *Snow White and the Seven Dwarfs* motif underscored by ever-present mirrors ("Mirror, mirror, on the wall ..."). But the actors get the film over these few stumbling blocks. Billie Whitelaw is superb as the boys' mother, Vi, and Gary and Martin Kemp deliver what *should* have been star-making performances as the twins. Former members of the natty rock group Spandau Ballet, the real-life brothers are in turn icy, loving, and cruel, and they play off each other like magnets, alternately attracting and repelling. Even when they're butchering people, it's difficult not to watch them—and, more absurdly, to *like* them! As Whitelaw has said, the film is "just the tip of the iceberg of the atrocities they committed. Peter has actually made a domestic film about a mother and her two sons."

Former members of the Krays' gang were on the set throughout the making of the film, advising cast and director for accuracy. As for the brothers themselves, Ronnie is presently in a hospital, under more or less constant sedation, and Reggie is in prison.

The Disc
Video: ★★★★
Audio: ★★★★½ (Surround)
Chapters: No
Format: CLV
Source: Columbia Pictures Home Video

Because the brothers are together in so many scenes—usually on opposite ends of the screen—the letterboxing is vital. However, the matte is *so* mild that people who dislike the format shouldn't be bothered by it.

Except for the scenes in the Krays' lush red club and the regular sprays of blood, the movie is in smokey grays, earth colors, or pastels. The disc captures all of their subtle variations and has no trouble with the bright reds. Grain is a problem in only one or two scenes, most notably when the American gangsters arrive at the boys' club.

American ears will have a tough time following some of the cockney dialogue, but that's not the disc's fault. The audio is sparkling, with some nice Surround effects, from the distant barking of dogs to the roar of car engines as the Krays tear off to their next murder.

Kronos (1957) ★★½
Director: Kurt Neumann
Running Time: 78 minutes

In Greek mythology, Kronos (aka Cronus) was one of the Titans, the father of Zeus, who ate his son in an effort to avoid being dethroned. But Zeus was rescued by his mother, Rhea, and Kronos had to step aside. Kronos was also a god of fertility, so it's appropriate that the robot in this film bears his name.

The mute, cubelike Kronos comes from a world that is dangerously low on energy and has sent the giant robot here to soak up as much as it can, be it electric or atomic. As Kronos stomps around the Mexican countryside, heading toward the United States and a nuclear stockpile, Phoenix's Labcentral scientists Les (Jeff Morrow), his fiancée, Vera (Barbara Lawrence), Arnie (George O'Hanlon), and the computer SUSIE struggle to find a way to stop it—urgency that increases when a hydrogen bomb not only fails to destroy the robot but actually increases its size. Ultimately, the trio find a way to turn Kronos's stored energy on itself, melting the automaton just outside of L.A.

Considering the film's low budget—which forced the elimination of many special-effects scenes that were in the script—the director and his team did a remarkable job. Neumann's films, such as *Rocketship XM* (1950) and *The Fly* (1958), all work hard to tell an interesting story, and *Kronos* is no exception. It's helped considerably by strong performances and special effects, which, though not always successful, are remarkably ambitious and inventive. They were accomplished using full-scale mock-ups, miniature models, and surprisingly effective cartoon animation (watch how the animators drew a cartoon section of a building, which crumbles at 31952 on side two). The design of the robot is also impressive: sleek, original, and ominous. The inspired camera angles help to emphasize its size and fearsome power.

Ironically, while the film is still a lot of fun to look at, it's dated by a script that failed, even at the time, to stay within the bounds of scientific credibility. As Les and Arnie study Kronos's flying saucer on a telescopic view screen—and it clearly is a flying saucer, smooth and white, with a rim around its bulging middle—these great brains, these Ph.D.'s, keep referring to it as *asteroid* M47. Later, when the huge pod bearing Kronos crashes into the sea off the Mexican coast, there's a nice-sized splash where there *should* have been a wave at least the size of Popocatepetl. And shouldn't a race capable of interstellar flight be able to split the atom or at least harness solar energy instead of sending a robot to our world to suck up power?

Well, this *was* the fifties, when all an exploitation film had to do was dazzle and entertain. Not only did *Kronos* fill the bill but, thirty-five-plus years later, it still glimmers with a sense of wonder.

Watch for Robert Shayne—Inspector Henderson of TV's "The Adventures of Superman"—as the general in charge of the H-bombing. Also, make sure you check out the nifty, clear one-frame shot of the destroyed Kronos at 45007, right before it explodes.

The Disc
Video: ½
Audio: ★★★½
Chapters: No
Format: CLV (side one), CAV (side two)
Source: Image Entertainment

If you watch this disc and fail to find it *quite* as captivating as described above, blame it on the dismal transfer. The source material is pretty awful. The first reel is badly marked and scratched, and there's a big, disruptive break when the saucer disgorges the pod containing Kronos. The picture ranges from moderately clear to incredibly fuzzy, and contrast levels are low.

More damning is the fact that over half the wide-screen image is lost to panning-and-scanning, which *really* compromises many scenes, as when the scientists land a helicopter on its head and the camera stays on the actors, losing much of Kronos. The vistas of destruction are also severely hurt by the cropping.

The only saving grace is the CAV side two, but even that's got a caveat, because three steady frames are always followed by two jittery ones.

Happily, the audio is very good. Sound plays an important part in scenes involving the robot, and the disc's audio is extremely solid, free of the crackle and hiss found in so many films from this era. You can turn up the volume without worrying about extraneous noise or distortion.

Kwaidan (1964) ★★★★½
Director: Masaki Kobayashi
Running Time: 164 minutes

Lafcadio Hearn (1850–1904) was a journalist and author who gained early fame for novels set in Louisiana and the Caribbean. Always looking for new experiences, he went to Japan in 1890 and was smitten with the nation and its culture; he became a Japanese citizen and published under the name of Koizumi Yakumo. His books include *Glimpses of Unfamiliar Japan* (1894) and *In Ghostly Japan* (1899).

In subsequent films, director Kobayashi—who was a POW during World War II—would depict the horrors of war in graphic, unrelenting terms. His second film, *Kwaidan* is a much broader canvas, comprised of four ghost stories that are about the soul, about love, about desperation, and about honor.

In "The Black Hair," a samurai leaves his wife to marry a wealthy woman; "The Woman of the Snow" is about a woodcutter who is saved from frozen death by an ethereal young woman with a chilling secret; "Hoichi, the Earless" opens with a savage, unforgettable sea battle between two clans, then tells the tale of a blind bard who is visited by the dead warriors he sings about; and "In a Cup of Tea" is the story of a warrior who sees the reflection of someone else in his tea.

All of the segments were shot entirely on soundstages, and they feature some of the most beautiful and surreal images ever put on film. "The Woman of the Snow" and "Hoichi, the Earless" are masterpieces of atmosphere and psychological terror; "The Black Hair" and "In a Cup of Tea" are less successful, a bit long for the thin stories they tell, but they're masterfully staged and photographed.

Kwaidan is deliberately paced and demands patience and attention. However, Kobayashi's amazing sets and backgrounds, his ability to tell his stories visually, with a minimum of dialogue, and his spare but dazzling use of sound will bring you back to the disc over and over.

The Disc
Video: ★★★★
Audio: ★★★½ (monaural)
Chapters: Yes
Format: CLV
Source: Criterion

The perfectly letterboxed film has been given a wonderful transfer, with solid colors, bright whites, and glossy blacks. The only flaws are occasional loss of detail in some of the night scenes, some bleeding of the flesh tones, and rare faint scratches in the film. The subtitles are presented in the black band below the image.

The sound is generally quite strong, with occasional pops and crackles that were present in the master element.

Lady Jane (1985) ★★★
Director: Trevor Nunn
Running Time: 140 minutes

When young king Edward VI of England was dying, his protector, the Earl of Northumberland, persuaded him to ignore the legitimate claims of both his half-sisters, Mary and Elizabeth, and to name as his successor Lady Jane Grey, the great-granddaughter of Henry VII. Since Jane was married to the earl's son Lord Guildford Dudley, Jane's ascension would suit the earl by shifting the succession from the Tudors to the Dudleys. However, Northumberland hadn't counted on Jane alienating powerful allies by looking after the welfare of the common people; her enemies rallied around Mary and, after nine days of rule, Jane and her husband were arrested and beheaded. The deposed queen was sixteen years old.

The film is an accurate portrait of the sixteenth-century court and its intrigue, and of the impoverished lives of people in the surrounding countryside. It hasn't got the power or performances of *Becket* (see page 23) or *A Man for All Seasons* (1966), but the story is a fascinating, well-told tearjerker.

Helena Bonham Carter has the right mix of innocence and backbone for the part, and there's excellent support from a stable of British pros: John Wood, Michael Hordern, Patrick Stewart, and others. However, what makes *Lady Jane* especially worthwhile is the performance of Cary Elwes, who went on to star in *The Princess Bride* and *Glory* (see pages 220 and 109). His Dudley goes from being a bleary-eyed hedonist to a devoted lover and coruler; it's a difficult transition, and Elwes makes it work. Another plus is the directorial debut of Trevor Nunn of the Royal Shakespeare Company, who also directed the Broadway plays *Cats* and *Les Miserables*, among others. He has a lush and intimate style well suited to this kind of period romance and, if we're lucky, he'll go back behind the camera someday.

The Disc
Video: ★½
Audio: ★★ (stereo)
Chapters: No
Format: CLV
Source: Paramount Home Video

Sadly, the disc undermines Nunn's attractive visuals. The image is only slightly better than you'd get on videotape, the colors somewhat pale, the focus a bit soft, and the picture too often grainy. The dramatic aspects of the film are not hurt by cropping, though the beautiful countryside and castles are.

The audio is clear and intimate, but the stereo separations are undistinguished.

Last Tango in Paris (1972)
★★★★
Director: Bernardo Bertolucci
Running Time: 129 minutes

Paul (Marlon Brando) is an American living in Paris. A former reporter, bongo player, actor, and revolutionary, he's tortured by the suicide of his wife, Rosa (Veronica Lazare) and sick of his own aimless lifestyle. Looking for an apartment on the rue Jules Verne (where fantasies live?) he meets Jeanne (Maria Schneider), who is half his age and happens to be looking at the same unit. The two are drawn together and make love; that Jeanne is engaged to young filmmaker Tom (Jean-Pierre Léaud) doesn't faze her. Paul's an energizing, irresistible life force, filled with hate and anger that he channels into sexual passion. They agree to meet in the apartment regularly, promising never to tell each other anything about their lives, not even their names.

After just three days, however, Jeanne realizes that while Tom is a self-absorbed buffoon, Paul is an incubus who will drag her down with him unless she can get away from him. Unfortunately, Paul has already lost one woman and has no intention of losing another.

Last Tango in Paris is misogynistic and fiercely erotic, and Paul's sexual inventiveness will shock some viewers. But the deeper question—how much of Paul is driven by selfishness and how much by a perverse need to give?—is fascinating. Though slowly paced and depressing, the X-rated film is never dull and Brando has rarely, if ever, been better. His pained, bitter soliloquy beside his dead wife is some of the most hypnotic screen acting you'll ever see, yet he's also surprisingly playful when he compares notes with his wife's ex-lover, Marcel (Massimo Girotti), or dances his last tango.

Fortunately, Bertolucci's style was perfectly suited to what was by then Brando's penchant for only approximating the text and improvising: While the movie took just three months to shoot, it took twice as long to edit, as the director restructured scenes to accommodate insights and exchanges his star had come up with.

Brando's Paris-born costar reacted wonderfully to the actor, while contributing her own pouty, petulant touches. Though Schneider has continued to make movies, most of them have been minor affairs, such as *Mama Dracula* (1980) and *Bunker Palace Hotel* (1989).

The Disc
Video: ★★★ (Criterion); ★★★½ (MGM/UA)
Audio: ★★★ (monaural) (Criterion); ★★½ (monaural) (MGM/UA)
Chapters: Yes
Format: CLV (Criterion); CLV (sides one and two) CAV (side three) (MGM/UA)
Source: Criterion Collection or MGM/UA

The Criterion edition of this moderately letterboxed disc will cause you some trepidation as it starts out, with scratches all over and a great deal of video noise. However, the scratches vanish quickly and while the red/orange noise is more or less constant throughout the film (and much of the lighting is in that end of the spectrum), the rest of the transfer is admirable. The colors are strong, exteriors are perfectly sharp, and whatever grain is there was present in the original film.

The audio is solid, free of extraneous noise, and is nicely detailed with the sounds of Paris.

The MGM/UA version has colors that are truer to life than the Criterion edition, but the letterbox isn't as full and cramps the image a bit.

The sound is a little muffled; given

Brando's tendency to mumble, this is a minor problem now and then.

The Last Temptation of Christ (1988) ★★★★½
Director: Martin Scorsese
Running Time: 163 minutes

The people who lined up to damn this film obviously didn't see it—or, if they saw it, didn't understand it. It's difficult to imagine a more triumphant and faith-affirming look at the final years of Jesus.

Paul Schrader—who wrote Scorsese's *Taxi Driver* (1976) and cowrote his *Raging Bull* (1980)—based his screenplay on a work by Greek novelist Nikos Kazantzakis (1885–1957), author of *Zorba the Greek* (see page 313). Kazantzakis believed strongly in freedom as the ultimate goal of life, though the search is often fruitless and tragic. That's very much the theme of *The Last Temptation of Christ*: not just freedom from Rome and hate but freedom from the temptations to which Jesus was very much a prisoner.

The film's challenging conceit is that Jesus (Willem Dafoe) the carpenter built crosses for the Romans. This avocation put him at odds with Judas (Harvey Keitel) and his fellow Zealots, and eventually set Jesus off on his own tortuous path of spiritual purging and discovery. Initially dispatched to kill him, Judas is at first intrigued and then impressed by Jesus' transformation, and becomes his most ardent supporter; ultimately, it's Jesus who *asks* the very reluctant Judas to betray him so that he can die on the cross, as he believes God has ordered. And it is there, hovering painfully between life and death, that Jesus withstands the last temptation as the Devil shows him how pleasant his life would have been had he lived it as a man, not as the Messiah. Yet, even now, Jesus does not leave the path he has chosen. Though he questioned himself and God each step of the way that brought him here, Jesus overcomes his final temptation and the last of his doubts.

Given the director's decision to use American actors in the parts, the cast is exactly right, while the unornamented costumes, simple sets, and dusty look of the film—which was shot in Morocco—evoke the era perfectly. From the U-shaped table used at the Last Supper, to the nailing of crucifixion victims through the wrists and ankles (so their weight wouldn't rip them from the cross), the film strives for absolute authenticity (though the vivid and bloody crucifixions are not for every taste.)

Mind you, the movie isn't perfect. The colloquial dialogue, conversational manner, and Brooklynese of several of the actors is distracting at first. There are also sections of the film that are too brief (the interrogation by Pilate, David Bowie) or too long (Jesus waiting for Mary to finish with her clients, or the last temptation, which makes its point several times over in a scene that's distractingly like the time-distorting "alien room" climax of *2001: A Space Odyssey*). The special-effects shots of Dafoe with the lion could also have stood some fine-tuning, and, thanks to *Monty Python's Life of Brian* (see page 188), the stoning of Mary may evoke some totally inappropriate memories. But these are all minor problems.

Blasphemous? Offensive? Ridiculous. *The Last Temptation of Christ* will uplift you as no biblical film before it—and, more importantly, it will make you think.

The Disc
Video: ★★★
Audio: ★★★★ (Surround)
Chapters: No
Format: CLV
Source: MCA/Universal Home Video

Though the scenes shot in bright daylight are generally very clear, a lot of the film takes place at night or in darkened rooms, which cause both grain and a loss of detail. And though no character is lost by the cropped image, a slight letterbox would have allowed several of the actors to keep the backs of their heads.

The audio is extremely satisfying, helping—through the wind, music, or silence—to underscore Jesus' isolation or, in the crowd scenes, closing us in along with him. The rest of the Surround effects—barking dogs and the like—are not flashy but effective.

Lawrence of Arabia (1962)
★★★★★
Director: David Lean
Running Time: 217 minutes

No movie could do justice to the enigma of Thomas Edward Lawrence, an English soldier/archaeologist/scholar who went to Arabia to fight for British interests during World War I and was caught up in the cause of Arab nationalism. How much of that was genuine and how much was posturing will never be known: His escapades, reported by journalist Lowell Thomas, who traveled with him, were painted in heroic strokes. To Thomas, the individual deeds were more important than the ideals that motivated them.

We will also never be able to do more than guess about Lawrence's private life—whether he was asexual or homosexual, a masochist or not—or whether his death was accidental, the work of Arabs who felt betrayed by him, or caused by British agents who were afraid his pro-Arab stance would conflict with their plans for the region.

Lean's film takes the view that Lawrence was a martyr for the Arab cause, and it is largely derived from Lawrence's epic account of the war in the desert, *The Seven Pillars of Wisdom* (1926), though he also flirts briefly and superficially with the questions of Lawrence's sexual preferences.

The film opens with the death of Lawrence (Peter O'Toole) in a motorcycle crash, followed by his funeral and a flashback to the events that bring Colonel Lawrence from an office job in Cairo to an observer's post in the camp of Prince Feisal (Alec Guinness). From there, Lawrence launches a brilliant raid on the Turkish stronghold of Akaba and becomes the preeminent leader of the disunited Arabs. He gets arms from the British, attacks Turkish forces, and enjoys great military successes, throughout which his four companions are his Arab conscience, Sherif Ali Ibn El Kharish (Omar Sharif), his British conscience, Colonel Brighton (Anthony Quayle), his moral conscience, reporter Jackson Bentley (Arthur Kennedy), and his personification of the stubborn Arab spirit he tries and ultimately fails to understand and dominate, the Howeitat sheik Auda abu Tayi (Anthony Quinn).

Lawrence's capture in Der'a and severe beating at the hands of a Turkish effendi (Jose Ferrer) squash his messianic ambitions, after which he becomes a confused pawn of the British, specifically Gen. Edmund Allenby (Jack Hawkins) and the devious politician Dryden (Claude Rains). Ultimately, the political tides wash Lawrence away, and when he abandons his comrades he becomes a shell with no future. The film suggests that he replaces real ambition with the false gratification of speed, which ultimately destroys that hollow shell.

After director Lean and producer Sam Spiegel made *The Bridge on the River Kwai* (1957), they began planning a film on the life of Gandhi. However, Lean wasn't satisfied that he could successfully tell Gandhi's story in even a four-hour film and so he abandoned the project. Coincidentally, the film rights to *The Seven Pillars of Wisdom* became available and Spiegel, who had read the book, snapped them up.

Initially, Albert Finney and then Marlon Brando were offered the part of Lawrence. Both wanted rewrites, and Lean refused. There was talk of Guinness doing the role—he'd played Lawrence in Terence Rattigan's play *Ross*—but the actor decided he wanted to be Feisal. So Lean went looking for an unknown and found Peter O'Toole, an actor of negligible film experience but a member of the Royal Shakespeare Company.

Desert scenes were shot primarily in Jordan (the "no prisoners" massacre was filmed in Morocco using the Camel Corps), interiors were shot in England, and exteriors of scenes set in Cairo, Damascus, and Jerusalem were shot in Spain. Due to modernization of the real location, the scenes set in Akaba had to be shot on a set in Spain, along with the attack on the Hejaz Railway.

Shooting lasted three hundred days and the film ended up costing $12 million—a reasonable sum, all things considered. It was a critical and commercial success, though the meddling Spiegel cut thirty-five minutes from the film to bring it closer to three hours than four. In 1989, with the cooproration of Lean, a fully restored 70mm print was released and enjoyed a successful theatrical run. (Missing sections of the sound track had to be redubbed, with actor Charles Gray speaking lines for the late Jack Hawkins.) Frankly, not all of those scenes are beneficial: For example, Lawrence's run-in with the billiards table at the beginning obnoxiously overstates his inability to fit in, a point that already made. Still, Lean's vision overall is preferable to that of the crass Spiegel.

The movie is awesomely beautiful, ambitious, and powerful; there is irony, tragedy, deft humor, and hypnotic performances by all. If this isn't quite the historical Lawrence (as Lowell Thomas often complained, though *he* should talk: He *created* the mythical Lawrence!), it's a fascinating study of an ordinary man trying hard to be much more—and very nearly succeeding.

The Disc

Video: ★★★½ (Criterion); ★★★★ (RCA/Columbia Pictures)
Audio: ★★★★½ (Surround) (both)
Chapters: Yes
Format: CAV or CLV (Criterion); CLV (RCA/Columbia)
Source: Criterion or RCA/Columbia Pictures Home Video

With the exception of the CAV capacity and extras, the RCA version is the disc of choice. (*Not* the old pan-and-scan version, which is still available. Not only is the scope of the film mangled, but the restored scenes are missing.) Both suffer from very slight color shifts in the added footage and occasional scratches on the source material, which are minor flaws. RCA offers an incredibly sharp picture with astounding colors. Criterion's disc is not quite as sharp and there's grain in a few of the darker scenes.

All versions are letterboxed—again, a must.

The audio is outstanding in both, with superb separation and Surround effects that give scenes such as the desert windstorm and train attack a breathtaking sense of depth.

The extras on the Criterion CAV disc consist of a disappointing still file; the CLV extras are different and better, including newsreel footage. The RCA/Columbia edition has no extras.

The Bridge on the River Kwai is a five-star film but is available only in a poor-quality pan-and-scan version.

The Leopard Man (1943) ★★½
Director: Jacques Tourneur
Running Time: 66 minutes

Producer Val Lewton was a one-of-a-kind filmmaker. A Russian émigré, he had published several novels, poems, and even pornography before going to work as an assistant to producer David O. Selznick in the early 1930s. In 1942, with the Universal horror-film machine slowing its output, RKO saw a niche and decided to fill it. The studio gave Lewton the task of producing horror films that would cost less and be more sensationalistic than Universal's Frankenstein/Dracula/Wolfman films. But the thirty-eight-year-old Lewton had other ideas, and he personally supervised movies that met those requirements and were also artistic triumphs.

His first film was *Cat People* (1942), directed by former film editor Tourneur. It was one of the duo's finest efforts, the eerie tale of a women who may or may not be turning into a killer cat. They followed it with the chilling *I Walked with a Zombie* (1943) and *The Leopard Man*, a faithful adaptation of the novel *Black Alibi* (1942) by Cornell Woolrich.

Entertainer Kiki Walker (Jean Brooks) and her companion/manager, Jerry Manning (Dennis O'Keefe), are stuck at a small nightclub in New Mexico, where dancer Clo-Clo (Margo) is the main attraction. To steal her thunder, Manning rents a panther from a local huckster, Charlie How-Come (Abner Biberman), and has Kiki walk it into the club during Clo-Clo's performance. Her entrance stops the show—for good when the panther escapes. Young women begin dying horribly, mauled to death at night, though Manning doesn't believe the panther is responsible. Though scoffed at by museum curator Dr. Galbraith (James Bell) and police chief Robles (Ben Bard), he goes searching for the real killer, aided by Raoul Belmonte (Richard Martin), the grieving lover of one of the victims.

The resolution is utterly predictable and the rationale for the killings is weak. Yet the movie is never dull; it's alive with atmosphere and suspense. Two scenes in particular will have even the hearts of the gore-hardened racing: Teresa Delgado (Magaret Landry) having to cross—not once but twice—the impenetrable dark beneath a railroad trestle where the killer may be hiding. When something *does* pursue the girl, there are her frantic pleas for her disbelieving mother to hurry up and let her into the house. Also very effective are the scenes in which victim Consuelo Contreras (Tula Parma) is locked in a cemetery and Clo-Clo searches the dark streets for money she's lost. Throughout, the use of sound is unnerving, from the drip of the water under the trestle to the skeletal *clack* of Clo-Clo's castanets.

By the way, a panther is a black leopard, so, technically, the title *is* correct!

Later Lewton classics include *The Curse of the Cat People* (1944, which marked the directorial debut of Robert Wise), *The Body Snatcher* (1945), *Isle of the Dead* (1945), and *Bedlam* (1946). Lewton died at the age of forty-six, after having abandoned horror movies to try his hand (unsuccessfully) in other genres. He was the inspiration for the Jonathan Shields character played by Kirk Douglas in *The Bad and the Beautiful* (1952).

The Leopard Man was edited by Mark Robson, who went on to become a successful director (*Champion*, 1949, and *Peyton Place*, 1957).

The Disc
Video: ★★★★½
Audio: ★★★★½ (monaural)
Chapters: Yes
Format: CLV
Source: Turner Home Entertainment/ Image Entertainment

Apart from a few scratches and marks, this is as perfect a print as you could ask for, with deep blacks, bright whites, and solid gray tones. You'll be able to pick out details and subtleties even in darkest night scenes.

The digital sound also couldn't be clearer, whether it's the deep voice of the cat, hollow footsteps on deserted streets, or the evil clicking of the castanets. The train will definitely get your attention.

Licence to Kill (1989) ★★
Director: John Glen
Running Time: 135 minutes

After the producers of TV's "Remington Steel" refused to release actor Pierce Brosnan from his contract, the producers of the James Bond series turned to Timothy Dalton to pick up the mantle, following the departure of Roger Moore. Dalton made a wonderful debut in *The Living Daylights* (1987), playing Bond as a wry sophisticate, and the film was a hit. But the script had been written with Brosnan in mind, and Dalton wasn't crazy about the glib tone.

For the next outing, the producers created a Bond "for the nineties"—a tough, vengeful man who was actually closer in spirit to the Ian Fleming original. Unfortunately, the new Bond was a critical and box-office bust.

Teamed with longtime CIA colleague and friend Felix Leiter (David Hedison), Bond captures drug lord Franz Sanchez (Robert Davi). Sanchez escapes with the help of crooked DEA agent Milton Krest (Anthony Zerbe) and, seeking revenge, kills Leiter's wife and feeds Leiter to a shark. Now it's 007's turn to strike back: Ignoring orders to the contrary, he goes after Sanchez, assisted by CIA agent Pam

Bouvier (Carey Lowell) and a moonlighting Q (Desmond Llewelyn). With their help, Bond infiltrates the drug organization, which is operating in South America, fronted by a church run by Professor Joe Butcher (Wayne Newton). Bond destroys the operation and kills Sanchez with—what else?—a lighter.

Apart from the kind of eye-popping action scenes you expect from a Bond film—Leiter's helicopter roping Sanchez's plane and reeling it in, Bond waterskiing behind a seaplane that's taking off, a two-fisted barroom brawl, and the climatic eighteen-wheeler chase—the movie is a washout, sadistic and inane. How many times does Bond insist that he works alone? And how many times does Bouvier save his hash? *Too* many. The scene of the shark feeding on Felix goes *way* beyond what was necessary to sell Bond's motivation, while gory little touches such as Krest's head exploding in a decompression chamber are gratuitous nods to the tastes of the *Friday the 13th* crowd.

Pay attention to the bullets hitting the tanker at the end: Tune sound familiar? Also, note how Pam Bouvier uses the Kennedy name as an alias.

The Disc
Video: ★★½
Audio: ★★½ (Surround)
Chapters: No
Format: CLV
Source: CBS/Fox Home Video

The biggest problem with this letterboxed disc is the red noise. It's like a plague, with grain running a close second. The image is fairly sharp after a rocky first side (there are three), but the colors never pack the wallop they did in theaters.

Though some of the humdinger action scenes feature nice Surround Sound effects, the whole is surprisingly tepid. Stereo separation is okay—but *Die Hard* it isn't.

The only extras are the trailers for Dalton's two Bond films. Curiously, the *Licence to Kill* trailer is panned-and-scanned, while the trailer for *The Living Daylights* is letterboxed. Go figure.

MGM/UA has recently released *The Living Daylights* in letterboxed form, with a sharp picture, solid colors, and knockout Surround sound. In every way, it's an improvement over the previous, somewhat muddy pan-and-scan edition.

Lionheart (1987) ★★★
Director: Franklin J. Schaffner
Running Time: 105 minutes

In 1985, Talia Shire was all abubble about her new production company, Taliafilm, which she said was going to produce "Quality films, the kind of films I want to see."

Her first effort was *From Another Star* (1987), which failed at the box office. Her brother, Francis Ford Coppola, served as executive producer for her second production, *Lionheart*, which was also a commercial disaster. While it is by no stretch of the definition a *great* film, *Lionheart* is a good one, especially if you like period dramas.

Eric Stoltz stars as Robert Nerra, a young knight who sets out to find King Richard and join his Crusade. Traveling with him are the young fortune-teller Blanche (Nicola Cowper) and the knife-thrower Michael (Dexter Fletcher), whom he meets on the road. En route, the trio encounters a large group of children hiding from the evil Black Prince (Gabriel Byrne), who sells young people to the Saracens as slaves. Robert agrees to protect the band from the Black Prince, their Children's Crusade joined by young Mathilda (Deborah Leigh Moore), who runs away from home when her family forbids her to become a warrior.

Director Franklin Schaffner, who gave us *Planet of the Apes* and *Patton* (see pages 213 and 205) hadn't worked since the back-to-back flops of *Sphinx* (1980) and *Yes, Giorgio* (1982). He seems a little unsure here (not to mention hampered by a low budget): The battle scenes and joust lack vitality (especially the climactic fight between Robert and the Black Prince), and he didn't shoot enough film to edit some scenes properly. For example, the ambush of the Black Prince's men would have had more oomph if there had been a few more camera angles to cut to, especially during the rock slide, and we barely get to see Richard's face when he speaks at the end of the film.

But *Lionheart* looks great, shot in some lovely locales in Hungary and Portugal, and it skillfully evokes the alternately bright and dark, muddy medieval world. While some of the children's accomplishments strain credibility, the characters are well drawn and interesting.

Stoltz is perfectly cast as the boy who becomes a man, and Byrne—who played the fierce Uther in *Excalibur* (see page 88)—gives a reserved performance that projects infinite cruelness. The rest of the cast is also very good, though the marvelous Nicholas Clay (Lancelot in *Excalibur*) has much too small a part as Richard loyalist Charles de Montfort.

The Disc
Video: ★★★★
Audio: ★★★★½ (Surround)
Chapters: Yes
Format: CLV
Source: Warner Home Video

Fairly spectacular primary colors—banners, costumes, and foliage—play against gorgeous pastels and earth tones in this handsome transfer. The disc is very nearly grain-free, and there is a minimal amount of video noise.

For the most part, Schaffner framed the movie with video in mind, and except for the fight between Robert and Mathilda, and between Robert and the Black Prince—both of which are terribly cramped—very little of the image is lost due to the lack of letterboxing.

The digital audio is also grand, booming out Jerry Goldsmith's memorable score and providing terrific rear-channel effects: storms howling, rivers flowing, wind blowing, horses galloping, and footsteps echoing down castle corridors.

Little Big Man (1970)
★★★★½
Director: Arthur Penn
Running Time: 149 minutes

Jack Crabb (Dustin Hoffman) is 121 years old, and he agrees to reminisce for a historian (William Hickey) who comes to visit. He tells about how his parents were killed by Pawnees when he was ten (young Crabb played by Alan Howardi), how he and his sister, Caroline (Carol Androsky), were taken in by the Cheyennes, and how Old Lodge Skins (Chief Dan George) made him his son. Though Jack likes living among the Indians, he returns to "civilization" after a run-in with soldiers and is taken in by Reverend Silas Pendrake (Thayer David) and his wife, Louise (Faye Dunaway). When Jack catches Louise having an affair, he's shocked and runs away: He falls in with con man Alardyce T. Meriweather (Martin Balsam), who has a habit of losing body parts in each new endeavor; meets his long-lost sister, who teaches him marksmanship; becomes a gunslinger, the Soda Pop Kid; and in quick succession becomes a drunk, meets Louise in a brothel, fails as a shopkeeper, marries Olga (Kelly Jean Peters), goes back to live with the Indians, weds Sunshine (Aimee Eccles), becomes a hermit, and serves as a scout for George Armstrong Custer (Richard Mulligan) at the Little Big Horn before returning to live with Old Lodge Skins.

Many of the segments are unforgettable, particularly the heart-wrenching massacre of the Indians and Jack's subsequent inability to bring himself to murder Custer. The film is an amazing tour de force for Hoffman, though Dick Smith's "old age" makeup, revolutionary at the time, is less convincing today. It's also an excellent showcase for Dunaway, Balsam, and Chief Dan George, who is dignity itself as the old Indian. His observations and self-effacing humor will put more than Jack's life in perspective for you. The only disappointment is Richard Mulligan, whose Custer is a cross between Alexander Haig and Bud Abbott.

The soldier was that arrogant but not that absurd.

Viewers who think that *Dances with Wolves* is the last word on white/Indian relations owe it to themselves to see *Little Big Man*. It must be pointed out, however, that as good as the film is, it isn't as effective as Thomas Berger's 1964 novel. The episodic nature of the tale works better on the printed page with Crabb's long, detailed narration to bridge it. There's also more of Crabb talking about life in the old West (which Berger researched extensively), and his wisdom, humor, and fascinating use of language are more enjoyable in their unexpurgated form. (When Crabb first contacts Ralph Fielding Snell, the writer who wants to tell his story, the crusty old-timer says he hates the old-age home: "If I had my single action Colt's I wd shoot my way out." You *know*, right then, you're in for quite a visit!)

The Disc

Video: ★★
Audio: ★★★½ (monaural)
Chapters: No
Format: CLV
Source: CBS Fox Video

The master for this disc was created in 1983, when the technology was in its infancy, and is not up to current standards. Though the picture is fairly crisp, it's also a bit grainy and pale throughout—the night scenes are *very* grainy. There were also a number of scratches on the source material.

The squeezed titles show you how much of the picture you're missing in this cropped presentation. The panning-and-scanning was done fluidly and with some sensitivity—but you're still missing a third of the picture. The locations—in Montana, California, and Alberta—evoke the old West like few films before, and this disc doesn't do them justice. Frankly, even one of Fox's overpriced wide-screen editions would be welcome.

The audio is sharp and very clear, with hardly any flaws or background noise.

The Little Mermaid (1989)
★★★★½
Directors: John Musker, Ron Clemente
Running Time: 83 minutes

After *The Jungle Book* (1967), which was the last animated feature film personally supervised by Walt Disney at his studio, the studio churned out such derivative or just plain uninspired films as *The Aristocats* (1970), *Robin Hood* (1973), *The Rescuers* (1977), *The Great Mouse Detective* (1986), and *Oliver & Co.* (1988). Who even remembers what most of those were about?

So expectations were low for the company's twenty-eighth animated feature, *The Little Mermaid*. But thanks to fresh blood in the executive chambers and at the animation boards, it's an *incredible* achievement, with fresh and enchanting characterizations, a witty and suspenseful script, knock-your-eyes-out animation, and a magical score by Alan Menken and the late Howard Ashman (cocreators of the musical *Little Shop of Horrors*).

Ariel (voice of Jodi Benson) is an impetuous young mermaid fascinated with the surface world. Her companion, the reggae-crab Sebastian (voice of Samuel E. Wright), doesn't share her fascination and is horrified when she falls in love with the human Prince Eric (voice of Christopher Daniel Barnes) and makes a deal with the witch Ursula (voice of Pat Carroll) to trade her voice for legs so she can be with him. What's more, as part of the deal, if Ariel doesn't get Eric to kiss her, she must become Ursula's slave for all eternity. This being a Disney film, all ends happily—though not before Ursula has tricked Ariel, defeated her father, King Triton (voice of Kenneth Mars), and become a monster of hideous dimensions.

The film retains many plot elements, if not the tone, of the original tale. The mermaid in the Hans Christian Andersen story has no name, and there's no Sebastian. But the little sea teen does fall in love with a human prince and makes the same dunderheaded deal with a sea witch. (The sorceress doesn't simply steal her voice, though; she cuts out the mermaid's tongue. Sure ... that'll show up in a Disney film.) The love-struck lass dies at the end, her heart broken when the prince marries another.

The Little Mermaid was a huge hit and set the look and style for Disney films for years to come, witness the even more successful copycat film *Beauty and the Beast* (1991). That said, filmgoers could have worse product from which to choose.

The Disc
Video: ★★★★½
Audio: ★★★★★ (Surround)
Chapters: Yes
Format: CLV or CAV
Source: Walt Disney Home Video

This is the ultimate animation disc, with a picture so clear and sound so enveloping that you'll never tire of turning it on and losing yourself in it. It's even more fun in the CAV edition, since you can single-frame your way through the breathtaking animation. Some of these single pictures, such as Ariel breaking the surface for the first time after swapping her tail for legs, are masterpieces.

The film has no grain and just a hint of video noise in the reds. The video would have received five stars was it not for the fact that it isn't letterboxed. Though the film was shot flat, many of the scenes are cramped. And while the larger image permits you to study things such as Ursula's grimace in greater detail, the complete image would have been preferable.

The stereo separations are colossal, and the Surround Sound is alive with all kinds of fish, bubbles, music, and you name it.

Note: Early pressings of the CAV version had the stereo channels reversed, though there aren't many of those left around.

Have a look at Disney's *Robin Hood* on laser, if you can borrow a copy. That, too, has a superlative transfer, but the gags aren't funny and the climactic escape from the castle couldn't be less exciting.

Lolita (1962) ★★★
Director: Stanley Kubrick
Running Time: 152 minutes

Taken as a movie alone, *Lolita* is interesting, kinky, slightly psychotic, well-acted entertainment. As an adaptation of Vladimir Nabokov's controversial 1955 novel, it's largely a failure that captures neither the book's droll voice nor the eroticism of Professor Humbert Humbert's deep passion for the twelve-year-old Dolores "Lolita" Haze.

Arriving at the home of writer Clare Quilty (Peter Sellers), Professor Humbert (James Mason) shoots him dead for unspecified crimes against Lolita. After this man of many faces dies behind another—a painting—Humbert tells us how he came to be here.

Offered a fall teaching position at a college in Ohio, he decides to spend the summer in New England, in the resort town of Ramsdale, New Hampshire. There, he becomes infatuated with Lolita (Sue Lyon) and not only rents a room from her mother, Charlotte Haze (Shelley Winters); he goes so far as to marry the widow—whom he despises—just to be around the girl. When Charlotte finds Humbert's brutally honest diary, she's horror-struck and runs into the street, where she's hit and killed by a car. (The film's most powerful scene.)

Humbert takes Lolita with him to Beardsley College in Ohio, where he becomes increasingly jealous yet is unaware that the eccentric Quilty has been her lover and is following them, appearing to Humbert in all manner of outlandish disguises while seeing Lolita on the sly. With Quilty's help, Lolita finally runs away, meeting and marrying a poor young man and becoming pregnant. When the girl contacts Humbert three years later, asking him for money, he visits and is horrified by what's she's become: a young, budding version of Charlotte. He leaves her with a small fortune, takes out his wrath on Quilty, and dies in prison.

In addition to coming up with a voice

far different from that of the novel, Kubrick fiddled dangerously with the story's structure. By having Humbert murder Quilty in the opening scene, and unfolding the tale in flashback, he robs the characters of their ability to shock and surprise us, a quality that helps give the novel its power. (Though Nabakov is credited with having written the screenplay, it was heavily rewritten by the director.)

Many of the scenes *are* involving, much of the dialogue is flinty, and there are marvelous performances from the blowsy Winters and from Mason, who is particularly good at conveying Humbert's erotic desires without making him seem like a dirty old man, using looks to suggest what is more clearly spelled out in the novel. Sellers is unnervingly effective whenever he's just plain, spoiled Quilty; when he's playing one of his characters—particularly Dr. Zempf—he's much too broad, using a caricatured style that would serve him better in Kubrick's next film, *Dr. Strangelove* (see page 72).

The biggest hole in the film, though, is newcomer Lyon, who is not only too old for the part (she was sixteen at the time) but plays the teenager's "vulgarity" as whininess and pique. She isn't fascinating, bitchy, or alluring: she's a very ordinary brat. Lyon made ten other films, including *The Night of the Iguana* (1964), *The Flim Flam Man*, and *Tony Rome* (both 1967). Ironically, Lyon wouldn't have had the part if Errol Flynn had had his way: The actor was Kubrick's first choice for Humbert, but Flynn insisted on his young girlfriend, Beverly Aadland, for Lolita, and Kubrick declined.

James Bond's Miss Moneypenny, Lois Maxwell, has a small role as Nurse Mary Lore. Also, watch for the shadow of a crewman on Mason's right arm at 29/36:52 and the amusing poke Kubrick has Quilty take at his previous film *Spartacus* (1960), which was an unhappy experience for the director.

The Disc

Video: ★★★½
Audio: ★★★½ (monaural)
Chapters: Yes
Format: CLV
Sources: MGM/UA Home Video

Given Kubrick's splendid use of the wide screen, it was essential for MGM/UA to matte the film—even though the letterboxing isn't quite as wide as it should be. The transfer itself is very good, with generally excellent contrast, bright whites, and shiny blacks. The picture is razor-sharp and largely free of scratches, though there's some image warping in places.

The sound track is crisp and clear, and the schmaltzy mock-Chopin score sounds fine.

The film's very corny, very early-sixties trailer is included.

The Longest Day (1962)
★★★
Directors: Ken Annakin (British scenes),
 Andrew Marton (American scenes),
 Bernhard Wicki (German scenes)
Running Time: 178 minutes

The miracle of D day—June 6, 1944—was not just the size of the operation (although that *was* incredible, involving four thousand ships carrying 176,000 troops, a six-hundred-ship escort, and nearly ten thousand bombers and fighter-bombers) but also the amazing deceptions used to persuade Hitler that the attack was coming elsewhere and at another time. These latter intrigues are only hinted at in this mammoth recreation of the invasion, which is unfortunate: If the film had encompassed the entire story instead of just the battles and the cavalcade of stars, it would have been something special.

Based on Cornelius Ryan's exhaustive account of D day, *The Longest Day* gives each star his close-up and bit before moving on to the next. Smothered in melodrama, these early scenes fail to create a sense of preinvasion tension but, rather, dish up soap opera and platitudes. There's John Wayne lecturing about patience, Richard Burton lamenting a lost flier (and doing it extremely well), Roddy McDowall waiting to sail and remembering how "Every June my old man used to take me camping..." and just about every name actor in Hollywood and elsewhere doing *something:* Robert Mitchum, Henry Fonda, Robert Ryan, Rod Steiger, Richard Beymer, Robert Wagner, Tom Tryon, Paul Anka, Sal Mineo, Mel Ferrer, Jeffrey Hunter, Peter Lawford, Sean Connery, Gert Frobe, George Segal, Stuart Whitman, Eddie Albert—the list is almost as long as the roster of men who fought the battles.

The Longest Day also does a pretty poor job of getting in exposition: The film literally stops and, for our benefit, the characters tell each other what they already know. The German side is infinitely more interesting than the Allied side, as the officers try to figure out what's brewing and how to present their suspicions to Hitler. In terms of drama and narrative, the whole thing would have been better with just one director, one point of view, and one or two stars.

When the filmmakers stow the clichés, the film can be fascinating and powerful. There are fascinating looks at the use of paratrooper dummies, the work of the Resistance fighters, the dangerous glider landings behind enemy lines, and the tragic paratroop drop on the town of Ste. Mère Église, where descending Allied soldiers are picked off by the Germans. The invasion itself is a combination of stock footage and spectacular recreations, though the surging battles bog down whenever the filmmakers take time to show us what's happening to each of those damned stars.

Apart from a truly spectacular train wreck, the special effects aren't, with some very unspecial superimposition of the stars in actual World War II footage and surprisingly shabby rear-projection shots.

The Disc

Video: ★★★
Audio: ★★★★½ (Surround)
Chapters: Yes
Format: CLV
Source: CBS/Fox Home Video

The stock footage is fairly grainy, as you might expect—but so is the rest of the transfer. Details that were present on the big screen are lost on TV.

Apart from this, the blacks, whites, and grays are generally strong and the print is in terrific shape. The letterboxing of the CinemaScope film cheats just a little, losing slivers of action on the sides but otherwise does a fine job capturing the spectacle of the invasion.

Though the Surround is basically the stereo sound channeled to the rear, the audio is gloriously clear, with some fine stereo separation. The many subtle sounds, such as a ticking clock, ringing phones, and knocking on doors, give the film a greater sense of depth than the big blanket explosions.

Love Among the Ruins (1975)
★★★½
Director: George Cukor
Running Time: 103 minutes

When he was studying in Canada in the 1890s, a young law student fell in love with a young actress. They spent three days together, and before she went back to England they pledged to marry upon his return the following year. Instead, loathing her poverty and unwilling to wait a year, the actress married a wealthy noble. Still carrying a torch, the young man never marries.

Forty years pass, and the former actress —Jessica Medlicott (Katharine Hepburn) —has been widowed for two years. The student, Sir Arthur Granville-Jones (Laurence Olivier) is now a highly regarded barrister. By chance, he and Jessica are brought back together again when a young gold digger, Alfred Pratt (Leigh Lawson) sues her for fifty thousand pounds, claiming she'd agreed to marry him, then broken it off after he gave up his career at sea. At first, Jessica doesn't remember the days she spent with Arthur, though he does—oh, how he does!—and his passion and her stubborness clash as he tries to win her case ... and her heart.

This was the only time Olivier and Hepburn acted together, directed by Hollywood veteran George Cukor (*Pat and Mike*, *My Fair Lady*, and many others), directing his first made-for-TV movie. The stars are wonderful, of course—in spite of a more hurried production schedule than they were used to—but considering the talents involved, the project isn't as memorable as you'd think or hope. A large part of the problem is the script, which was based on Angela Thirkell's novel and leaves out important elements of the story—most notably the closing arguments of the plaintiff's barrister, John F. Devine (Colin Blakely, who is splendid)—and allows Pratt to destroy his own case in a way that the original story (and *no* barrister) would not have allowed.

Watching the acting profession's two greatest practitioners is reward enough, however, and we could do with more television like this!

The Disc
Video: ★
Audio: ★★★½ (monaural)
Chapters: Yes
Format: CLV
Source: CBS Fox Video

There isn't one shot in the film that isn't fuzzy (and *not* just because it's soft focus on Ms. Hepburn), and, except for Jessica's red costume at the trial, the colors are washed-out. The film isn't grainy or dark, but the other flaws make the quality less than you'd expect from a videotape quality. The image warps badly at one point, though that's the only serious flaw in the source material.

John Barry's score is surprisingly subdued, and the dialogue is quite clear—so much so that it underscores how bad the picture is. Background hiss is negligible.

The Magnificent Seven (1960)
★★★★★
Director: John Sturges
Running Time: 129 minutes

Is it profound? No. Realistic? Not at all. Original? Again, no. Yet, there's never been a Western as monumentally entertaining as *The Magnificent Seven*. From the opening strains of Elmer Bernstein's heroic score to the outrageous hearse ride up Boot Hill to the gathering of the Seven and the climactic showdown, the action, humor, and sheer energy of the film are an irresistible delight.

The Magnificent Seven was based on Akira Kurosawa's epic *The Seven Samurai* (see page 245), the adventure transposed to a Mexican village where seven gunfighters square off against the evil Calvera (Eli Wallach) and his much larger band of marauders. Yul Brynner shines as Chris, the black-garbed leader of the Seven, with a youthful Steve McQueen as his cocky second in command, Vin. James Coburn is a standout as the knife-throwing, sharpshooting Britt, and there's excellent support from Charles Bronson as Bernardo O'Reilly, Robert Vaughn as Lee, Horst Buchholz as Chico, and Brad Dexter as Harry Luck.

Few directors mastered the action film genre as capably as John Sturges. A one-time RKO art department employee, Sturges moved up to the editing room and went on to apprentice with David O. Selznick and William Wyler before becoming a director in 1946. He hit his stride doing action-packed Westerns in 1953 with *Escape from Fort Bravo* and followed it with *Bad Day at Black Rock* (1955), the historically inaccurate but muscular *Gunfight at the O.K. Corral* (1957—available on a nicely transferred laserdisc), and *Last Train from Gun Hill* (1959). See the entries on his *The Great Escape*, *The Hallelujah Trail*, and *Ice Station Zebra*.

The $2.7 million film was a huge success and spawned three increasingly contrived sequels: *Return of the Seven* (1966), *Guns of the Magnificent Seven* (1969), and *The Magnificent Seven Ride!* (1972), none of which is available on laserdisc.

The Disc

Video: ★★★
Audio: ★★ (monaural)
Chapters: No
Format: CLV (sides one and two), CAV (side three)
Source: MGM/UA Home Video

Though the colors of the film are a bit reddish—not to recreate the dusty West, but due to the impermanent nature of Deluxe Color (a misnomer if ever there was one)—the film looks better than many its age. Apart from the color, the source material was in fine shape, the transfer crisp and clear.

The letterboxed disc presents Sturges's slam-bang action the way it was intended to be seen, and you'll find yourself drawn to this disc over and over (cursing MGM/UA all the while for failing to provide chapter stops).

The sound is scratchy and rough, which is a disappointment given the importance of the score and sound effects: You won't be able to blast this one out of the room.

The Manchurian Candidate (1962) ★★★★½

Director: John Frankenheimer
Running Time: 127 minutes

Captured by Communists in Korea, infantrymen Raymond Shaw (Laurence Harvey), Bennett Marco (Frank Sinatra), and their platoon are brainwashed by the Chinese and returned to the United States. However, Shaw has been given special instructions: He's to live a normal life until exposed to a specific stimulus that will turn him into an assassin. Easing back into society, Shaw frequently crosses swords with his mother (Angela Lansbury) over his hatred for his left-leaning stepfather, Senator John Iselin (James Gregory), who has his eye on the vice presidential nomination. He also falls in love with Jocie Jordon (Leslie Parrish), the daughter of his father's arch-rival, Senator Thomas Jordon (John McGiver).

Marco, meanwhile, has been suffering from nightmares about the brainwashing, and he falls in with a Pentagon group that is looking into what happened to the platoon while they were missing in action. He also meets and falls in love with Rosie (Janet Leigh), a woman who many have some secrets of her own (though the film doesn't delve into these, or her, nearly enough).

Eventually, Marco discovers the truth about Shaw's brainwashing, which involves the murder of the presidential nominee and placing the White House within reach of his stepfather—and the Communists.

Based on the novel by Richard Condon, *The Manchurian Candidate* has more suspense than a barrel of Clancys, and memorable characters fleshed out by an exceptional cast (Shaw's confrontation with his wife and father-in-law in the kitchen will haunt you for days). Sinatra considers this to be his finest film, and he gives a tour-de-force performance: tough, compassionate, and frightened. The film was also the high point for Harvey, whose icy demeanor and sudden outbursts add to the trip-wire tension, and for the late McGiver, a sadly underrated character actor (he also gave a short, riveting performance in *Midnight Cowboy*, 1969). Lansbury is also very good, even if she *was* only three years older than her "son."

After its initial release, the film was shelved for a quarter of a century. Contrary to popular rumor, that wasn't because it eerily foreshadowed the death of President Kennedy (with L. Harvey as the assassin!) but, rather, because of a contractual dispute between Sinatra and United Artists. Sinatra was the impetus behind settling the matter and giving the movie back to the public.

The Disc

Video: ★★
Audio: ★★½ (monaural)
Chapters: No
Format: CLV
Source: MGM/UA Home Video

Given the importance and reputation of this film, the transfer is disappointing.

The picture is a bit soft and grainy throughout and there are few details in the dark. Cropping doesn't damage the narrative, though it hurts the design of some scenes, especially the brainwashing scenes and kitchen assault. In theaters, the open area around the actors underscored the tragic inevitability of their "closeness" in the center of the screen. On TV, that intimacy is hurt.

The audio is clean but tinny.

The film is followed by a short interview session with the director, screenwriter George Axelrod, and Sinatra. The information imparted is minimal and the mutual-admiration society is nauseating.

Manhattan (1979) ★★★★½
Director: Woody Allen
Running Time: 96 minutes

This movie had the unenviable fate of being Woody Allen's first comedy after *Annie Hall* (see page 10). He made the dreary, Bergmanesque *Interiors* (1978) between them, and fans hoped that Allen had gotten all the ponderous serious stuff out of his system. He didn't, but at least *Manhattan* was a return to the kind of seriocomic tale Allen tells best. And while it lacks *Annie Hall*'s dazzling narrative style and insights, it's still a marvelous tour de force about life, sex, and relationships—the Allen oeuvre.

The film opens brilliantly as spectacular visions of Manhattan fill the screen to the accompaniment of Gershwin's "Rhapsody in Blue," followed by the overdubbed voice of aspiring novelist Isaac Davis (Allen) uttering the first lines of the novel he's writing ... and rewriting ... and rerewriting....

Davis can't get the novel right, and we see very quickly that he can't get his life right, either. He has been dumped by his wife Jill (Meryl Streep), who's taken up with another woman, and he's dating seventeen-year-old Tracy (Mariel Hemingway), who is more responsible and mature than he is; he drops Tracy when he falls in love with pseudointellectual Mary Wilke (Diane Keaton), the mistress of his married friend Yale (Michael Murphy). By the end of the film, Isaac has managed to alienate everyone except the viewer, who will identify with the poor schlemiel; then again, compared to the self-indulgent Yale and the fraudulently highbrow Mary, almost anyone would seem likable.

There are plenty of Allen one-liners throughout to brighten everyone's downward spiral, a gentle and deeply affecting performance from Hemingway, and Wallace Shawn in a delightful guest appearance as Mary's ex-husband, Jeremiah.

The Disc
Video: ★★★★½
Audio: ★★★★½ (monaural)
Chapters: Yes
Format: CLV
Source: MGM/UA Home Video

The original laser (and videotape) release of this film was a landmark: Allen insisted that they be letterboxed. He got his way—though the *gray* bands on top and bottom were curious.

Unfortunately, letterboxing was the only good thing to be said about the original *Manhattan* disc from MGM/UA. There was a great deal of grain and hardly any contrast: The whites ran together (the gorgeous shot of snowy Park Avenue near the beginning was heartbreaking) and shadows lacked detail (the first scene in Davis's apartment was sludge).

MGM/UA has finally remastered the disc, and if you have the old one it's time to trade up. The transfer is nearly perfect—just gorgeous. The blacks are glossy, the whites shine, and everything in between is rich with gray tones. The picture is also as sharp as can be, though a few scenes still suffer from grain, a problem inherent in the source material.

The sound is much better than the original, too. There is no hiss, and the dialogue's very clear. What's more, if you want, you can play the Gershwin music on the analog track sans Allen's narration and dialogue.

Maniac Cop 2 (1990) ★★★
Director: William Lustig
Running Time: 87 minutes

The original *Maniac Cop* (1988) was a clunky, campy slasher film about an honest policeman who's blackmailed, maimed, and becomes a criminal-abetting cop-killer. It was directed by William Lustig, who also gave us the grisly *Maniac* in 1980, among other genre films.

Maniac Cop was a surprise hit; and rather than simply reprise the first film, the director gave us something new and something rare for the genre: a movie with believable characters who say interesting things. (Don't worry: If you're not up on the Maniac Cop mythos, there's a recap.)

When colleagues of the Maniac Cop Matt Cordell (Robert Z'dar) begin to die, police psychologist Susan Riley (Claudia Christian) suspects that Cordell has returned from the dead. No one believes her until Cordell makes an attempt on her life—handcuffing her to the steering wheel of a car and sending it roaring away. She survives, and Detective Sean McKinney (Robert Davi) takes charge of the investigation. Meanwhile, Cordell falls in with serial killer Turkell (Leo Rossi), forming a deadly partnership that taxes the resources of the New York police and leads to an action-packed climax—a dizzying car chase followed by a fiery assault on a maximum-security prison.

The plot isn't much, but the stunts throughout the film and the fire effects at the climax—in which practically everyone onscreen is immolated—are among the most impressive you'll ever see. The dialogue crackles, the New York locations look terrific, and the performances are several notches above what you'd expect, especially the snide, intense Davi and the insane Rossi. Michael Lerner (*Miller's Crossing, Barton Fink*) does a typically fine job as the corrupt Deputy Commisioner Edward Doyle. Z'dar is hidden behind slashed-face makeup and doesn't get to do much emoting, but he *does* twirl a mean nightstick. Director Sam Raimi (*Darkman*) has a small part as a newscaster.

Treat yourself to this one: It'll surprise you.

The Disc
Video: ★★★★★
Audio: ★★★★★ (Surround)
Chapters: Yes
Format: CLV (side one), CAV (side two)
Source: Live Home Video/Image Entertainment

The film is going to knock your eyes out: The picture is bright and glossy, with a stiletto-sharp picture. Despite the many reds and bright blues, there's no noise and just a trace of grain in a few scenes.

The film is nicely letterboxed, and the CAV frames are perfectly steady.

You'll revel in the sounds, which are sharp and bell-clear. The Surround Sounds blaze from all sides and create a remarkable sense of depth in conversational as well as action scenes.

March of the Wooden Soldiers (1934) ★★★★½
Directors: Gus Meins and Charles Rogers
Running Time: 78 minutes

Composer Victor Herbert wrote his operetta *Babes in Toyland* in 1903 and it was a big success on stages worldwide. Producer Hal Roach and MGM held the film rights and, after the success of Stan Laurel and Oliver Hardy's version of Auber's comic opera *Fra Diavolo* (1933), it was decided to put them into *Babes in Toyland*. (The film got its current title when it was released, and it stuck when the film was sold to TV.)

Stannie Dee (Laurel) and Ollie Dum (Hardy) live with Widow Peep (Florence Roberts), who is unable to pay the mortgage on her shoe house. When Stan and Ollie try to steal the papers from wicked landlord Silas Barnaby (Henry Kleinbach), they're arrested. Barnaby agrees to drop the charges only if the widow's lovely daughter Bo-Peep (Charlotte Henry) agrees to marry him. She does so, breaking the heart of her fiancé, Tom-Tom (Felix Knight). To save her from Barnaby, Stan—heavily veiled—takes her place at the wedding. The enraged Barnaby frames Tom-Tom for the death of one of the Three Little Pigs, and the lad is banished from Toyland to neighboring Bogeyland. Once again, though, it's Stan and Ollie to the rescue: They find the pig tied up in Barnaby's house. Escaping to Bogeyland himself, Barnaby leads the fanged, hairy Bogeymen in an attack on Toyland. Only Stan's quick thinking saves them: He activates one hundred six-foot-tall wooden soldiers who march on the creatures and destroy them.

The original play is considerably different from the film: There are no Stannie Dee and Ollie Dum characters; the hero, Alan, arrives in Toyland after being shipwrecked; and Uncle Barnaby is in love with Contrary Mary, not Bo-Peep. Several songs were also dropped, such as "I Can't Do the Sum" and "Beatrice Barefacts," though the famous "March of the Toys" and "Toyland" were retained.

The movie is lavish entertainment, with Stan and Ollie in their prime and everyone else just right. Originally, Walt Disney's studio was involved with the project: The mouse that nettles the Cat and the Fiddle is Mickey Mouse (alternately played by a puppet and a monkey in a costume), while the theme song of the Three Little Pigs is "Who's Afraid of the Big Bad Wolf," which was from Disney's 1933 short subject. Disney was looking to get into feature films, and *Babes in Toyland* would have been an ideal coproduction. For reasons unknown (a desire to stick to animation?), he left the project and only the song and Mickey's likeness remained. (Disney never forgot the property and remade it as *Babes in Toyland* (1961), starring Ray Bolger, Annette Funicello, and Tommy Sands. Drew Barrymore also appeared in a TV movie in 1986, with new and terrible songs.)

The Disc

Video: ★★★★½
Audio: ★★★ (monaural)
Chapters: Yes
Format: CLV (side one), CAV (side two)
Source: Goodtimes Home Video/Image Entertainment

You hate colorization. On a purely emotional level, you feel that Ted Turner and his cohorts have no right to tamper with the work of filmmakers, be they Orson Welles or Joe Blow. On a practical level, virtually every colorized film you've seen looks lousy: The colors are too thin or too thick, the gray tones ooze right through them, making them look muddy, and the colors bleed. Even the best of the colorized films—*The Sea Hawk* and *Yankee Doodle Dandy*—leave much to be desired.

Until now.

Ethically, colorization is still wrong. Having said that, *March of the Wooden Soldiers* comes close to vintage three-strip Technicolor—*awfully* close. And it can be argued that if you're *going* to colorize a film, a movie set in Toyland is the one to do.

The colors are extraordinary: There's very little gray show-through, the skin tones have texture (instead of looking like pink masks), and every petal on the sunflowers, every button on the Wooden Soldiers' uniforms, every hair on Bo-Peep's head is vivid, natural, *and* holds the color perfectly when the camera or object moves. There's no bleed at all. The colors also bring out details in the background you may not have noticed before—for example, the candlestick streetlamps. Watching the film, you'll be reminded of Oz from *The Wizard of Oz*: The colors are *that* vibrant.

The print itself is in marvelous shape, spoiled by a few minor flaws here and there and a handful of out-of-focus shots (such as the Bogeymen's river crossing).

The sound track is good. There's hardly any background noise, and the reediness of the orchestrations is due to the film's age.

The Drew Barrymore version (with

Keanu Reeves and Pat Morita) is available on laserdisc from Orion Home Video/Image Entertainment. The quality of the disc, at least, is excellent.

The Marrying Man (1991)
★★★½
Director: Jerry Rees
Running Time: 116 minutes

In the 1950s, shoe mogul Harry Karl fell wildly in love with singer/actress Marie McDonald, despite the fact that she was the girlfriend of gangster Bugsy Siegel. Over the years, Karl and McDonald managed to marry and divorce each other four times; "the body," as Marie was known, went on to marry three other men (one time each) before taking her life at the age of forty-two.

Neil Simon based his screenplay for *The Marrying Man* on the Karl/McDonald relationship. It's 1948, and toothpaste heir Charles Raymond Pearl (Alec Baldwin) is just six days away from marrying sweet and lovely Adele Horner (Elisabeth Shue). When he and some pals stop in the Lariat Room in Las Vegas for a drink, Charley falls in lust with lounge singer Victoria Anderson (Kim Basinger); despite the fact that she's the girl of Bugsy Siegel (Armand Assante), and despite the fact that Adele's father, movie mogul Lew Horner (Robert Loggia), has threatened Charley with a fate worse than death if he *ever* hurts Adele, the cocky, smitten young man goes to Vicki's house. They end up in bed, Bugsy catches them together and—puckish gangster he!—forces them to marry, making sure the photo appears on the front page of the L.A. papers, where Lew will see it—and seek revenge.

Reports from the set of *The Marrying Man* suggest that Simon could have written an even better screenplay based on the antics of Baldwin and Basinger. They fell in lust early in the shoot and reportedly held up production day after day while they dallied in their dressing trailers. Whether they did or not, they sure strike sparks on the screen—Baldwin losing his easy charm and catching fire whenever he's around the hot, trampy Basinger.

The movie is much better than you may have been led to expect from its bad reviews and dismal box-office performance. It's *Pretty Woman* with bite. Though the second half of the film doesn't quite fulfill the comedy potential set up in the first half—practically losing Adele and resigning Lew to the background—there's a constant flow of terrific Simon one-liners and top-notch performances, especially by Assante and Loggia. (You've *got* to wonder how much of what these two throw at Charley and Vicki was acting and how much of it was aimed squarely at Baldwin and Basinger.)

The Disc
Video: ★★★½
Audio: ★★★½ (Surround)
Chapters: Yes
Format: CLV
Source: Hollywood Pictures Home Video

This was a *very* difficult picture to transfer, thick with very saturated primary colors, especially reds. The picture was darkened in an effort to tone the colors down a bit; while there's still some red noise, it isn't nearly as severe as it might have been. Though details are lost in the night scenes because of the darkening, the colors throughout are strong.

The picture is very sharp, with no grain to speak of, and cropping doesn't hurt it at all.

The audio is wonderfully clear, with some appealing (though relatively infrequent) Surround effects—wind and thunder, cars racing by, nightclub sounds, and music.

Meet Me in St. Louis (1944)
★★★★½
Director: Vincente Minnelli
Running Time: 119 minutes

St. Louis of 1903 is a comforting place, a place of close-knit families whose members turn to one another to survive personal disappointments. These begin almost from frame one. Mrs. Smith (Mary Astor) is busy making catsup when daughter Esther (Judy Garland) informs her that her older sister, Rose (Lucille Bremer), is expecting a call from her boyfriend in New York. The call comes when the family is having dinner, so everyone hears ... and knows that things don't go as Rose had hoped. But at least they're there for her. Meanwhile, Esther doesn't have much more success with *her* boyfriend, boy-next-door John Truett (Tom Drake). Even young sister, Tootie (Margaret O'Brien), can't seem to get what she wants, being told she's too young to go out and throw flour on people at Halloween (though she gets the last laugh by going to the house of the wicked Mr. Bankoff [Robert Sully] and flouring up his dog).

The film is comprised of "moments" like this that allow us to get to know the characters—and then hurt for them when lawyer Alonzo Smith (Leon Ames) comes home and tells his family that he's planning to move them to New York to further his career. They resist, not only because they love their town but because none of them wants to miss the upcoming St. Louis World's Fair! Tootie, in particular, is devastated, and on Christmas Eve, when she realizes she'll have to leave behind all of the snow people she's built, she rushes outside in her nightgown and destroys them all. Seeing this causes Alonzo to acknowledge that the good life is worth more than material gain, and he elects to stay in St. Louis. (Even without moving, Rose and her boyfriend are reconciled. Not terribly believable, but that's what the movies are *for.*)

Inspired by Sally Benson's *New Yorker* short stories *5135 Kensington Avenue*, the film features such standards as "The Trolley Song" ("Clang, clang, clang, went the trolley ...") and "Have Yourself a Merry Little Christmas," as well as Judy Garland's best performance outside of *The Wizard of Oz* (see page 305). Her artistry and sensitivity provide the film with its emotional core. As ever, her big voice along with her astonishing phrasing—as good as Sinatra's, and more openly dramatic—is utterly unique and satisfying. And though not a technically accomplished dancer, she's eager to please and sells herself completely. She later married director Minnelli and the union produced daughter Liza.

Margaret O'Brien is also delightful, providing—as always—an alternative for moviegoers who wanted more than the obsequious cuteness of Shirley Temple. Unfortunately, she didn't develop into a successful adolescent or adult performer, and her work was limited to scattered TV and minor film appearances.

Lucille Bremer was even less fortunate. *Meet Me in St. Louis* marked the former Rockette's film debut. Though she subsequently made *Yolanda and the Thief* (1945) and *Ziegfeld Follies* (1946), both with Fred Astaire, she never caught on as a star; her career was over in four years and she opened a girls' clothing store in California.

The Disc

Video: ★★½
Audio: ★★
Chapters: Yes
Format: CLV
Source: MGM/UA Home Video

The colors of this remastered edition are more intense than those of the earlier edition, but there's still a brownish tinge that compromises the impact of the Technicolor. The image is also extremely soft throughout due to the unsuccessful digital video transfer. Adherents of analog transfers have often argued that digital ones have less authentic resolution. Whether or not they're correct, that certainly seems to be the case here. From the reel change at 45:37 on side two until the end, the image is shockingly grainy and noisy.

The audio is merely acceptable. There's a thinness in the singing and orchestrations that is *not* due to the film's age but to a shoddy transfer.

This new edition offers a sound-track recording of Garland singing the unused song "Boys and Girls Like You and Me," with stills of Drake and Garland accompanying her singing (the original footage was lost). The disc also features a trailer for the 1950s rerelease.

Memphis Belle (1990) ★★★½
Director: Michael Caton-Jones
Running Time: 108 minutes

Pilot Robert K. Morgan named his B-17 after his girlfriend, Margaret Polk, and man and plane fought their way through twenty-four successful missions. The rules were that if you completed twenty-five raids, your tour of duty was finished. This is the story of the last mission of the Flying Fortress.

The original crew of the *Memphis Belle* wasn't particularly colorful, so the names and characters have been changed to work in every stereotype known to war movies: ladies' man Richard "Rascal" Moore (Sean Astin, son of Patty Duke and John Astin); Val Kozlowski (Billy Zane), who lied about his medical credentials but still has to come through in a pinch; the thinking man/college grad Danny Daly (Eric Stoltz); the rigid, humorless Capt. Dennis Dearborn (Matthew Modine); shy Phil Rosenthal (D. B. Sweeney); cathouse pianist Clay Busby (Harry Connick, Jr., who gets to sing "Danny Boy"); and the obligatory virgin, a reform-school dropout, and a religious nut—you get the picture.

But if the names have been changed to protect the boring, and events added for the sake of drama—such as the last-minute crank-down of the landing gear—the heart of the film is strong and true. The events of the May 17, 1943, flight are largely accurate—including John Lithgow as the PR officer who coordinates coverage of the last flight for *Life* magazine. You'll get a real feel for the ordeals these men experienced and understand just why the crews grew so tight.

The film was moderately successful at the box office but was ignored in Hollywood and at the Oscars (the special effects are breathtaking, as is George Fenton's score) due to the involvement of coproducer David Puttnam (*Chariots of Fire*), who made a lot of enemies during his stormy tenure as the head of Columbia Pictures. His problem: He has taste.

Coproducer Catherine Wyler is the daughter of director William Wyler, who directed, wrote, and cophotographed the classic documentary *The Memphis Belle* in 1944.

The Disc
Video: ★★★★
Audio: ★★★★★ (Surround)
Chapters: Yes
Format: CLV
Source: Warner Home Video

The image is clear and sharp; the disc has the original film's slightly brownish tint, intended to mute the colors a bit and suggest a vintage look. The extremely mild letterboxing frames the picture quite nicely.

The audio is crisp as can be and the Surround effects are magnificent. There are excellent directional effects involving the planes, and during the flak attacks the rear speakers will very definitely give you a sense of what the characters are enduring.

Metropolis (1926) ★★★★½
Director: Fritz Lang
Running Time: 87 minutes

After being wounded during World War I, the Austrian Lang spent a year convalescing, during which time he began writing screenplays. He sold several, and by 1919 he'd turned to directing. After filming *Die Nibelungen*—an ambitious two-part adaptation of Wagner's opera cycle *Der Ring des Nibelungen*, consisting of *Siegfried* and *Kriemhild's Revenge* (both 1924)—Lang came to visit the film centers in New York and Hollywood. While sitting in the harbor and looking at the awe-inspiring Manhattan skyline, he came up with the idea for *Metropolis*.

In *Metropolis*, the rich live a life of luxury in the towers of the glittering city, while the poor live in relative squalor as they keep the machinery of Metropolis running. One day, wealthy master industrialist, Jon Fredersen (Alfred Abel), is visited by Maria (Brigitte Helm), a self-styled social worker who urges him not to forget the children of the poor. Fredersen is unmoved, but his son Freder (Gustav Fröhlich) visits the bowels of the city to see conditions firsthand. He's shocked, and urges his father to do something. But Jon has other plans. He has commissioned the scientist Rotwang (Rudolf Klein-Rogge) to build a robot duplicate of Maria, with which he plans to breed unrest instead of unity. Rotwang kidnaps the real Maria and sends his robot out in her place. Unfortunately, the robot goes too far and does more than cause discord: She leads the workers in revolt. They destroy the machinery, sparking massive explosions and floods that threaten to bring down the city itself. Fortunately, the real Maria escapes, and her quick action prevents the children of the workers from perishing. Freder slays Rotwang, the robot Maria is immolated, and Fredersen—sobered by the near-destruction of his city—makes peace with the workers.

Metropolis took two years to make and, at the time, was the most expensive film ever made in Germany. Over the years, it has been cut and truncated, many of the scenes lost in the devastation of World War II. In 1983, fresh from the success of *Flashdance*, songwriter Giorgio Moroder decided to restore as much of *Metropolis* as possible, substituting still photographs for missing footage, presenting the film with tinted scenes and sound effects, and scoring it with synthesizer music and new songs sung by rock stars Pat Benatar, Bonnie Tyler, the late Freddie Mercury of Queen, Loverboy, Adam Ant, Billy Squier, and Jon Anderson.

The result is the definitive *Metropolis*, as overwhelming and powerful an experience as the day it was released. The sets and special effects are still breathtaking, and the music reflects both the mechanization and humanity of the film's themes. Portions of the film will seem corny to modern eyes, especially the scene at the Yoshiwara "house of sin," where the robot Maria gets her first public tryout and rouses the men to a sexual frenzy. Their wolflike leers are a bit much. Some of the robot Maria's evil expressions are also somewhat comical in their overstatement, as is Freder's hair pulling whenever he's in a quandary (which is surprisingly often for a movie hero).

These are minor quarrels, however. The film is stupendously entertaining and watching it you'll understand why it has had such a tremendous impact on the genre—and on Madonna videos!

The Disc
Video: ★★★★½
Audio: ★★★★½ (Surround)
Chapters: No
Format: CLV
Source: Vestron Video

The source material for *Metropolis* has its flaws, but considering what the film's been through it's in remarkably fine shape. The movie is presented at the correct speed (not sped up, as so many silent films are when projected at sound speed), and Moroder has wisely replaced the title cards, superimposing the dialogue on the film. This creates a noticeable change in the pacing, allowing the drama to flow unbroken.

There are many tinted scenes and even hand-colored elements in a few shots: The colors are vibrant and noise-free.

Except for an inexplicable softness in the beginning of side two, the audio is splendid. The music swells, ebbs, crashes, throbs, and perfectly underscores the action, and the modern sound effects—such as the swipe of the scythe at 8:53 on side two—are terrific.

Mr. & Mrs. Bridge (1990)
★★★½
Director: James Ivory
Running Time: 127 minutes

Author Evan S. Connell told his story of a wealthy Kansas City family in two volumes: *Mrs. Bridge* and *Mr. Bridge*, recounting the events in their lives from two different perspectives. The film combines the narratives and, beginning circa 1935, introduces us to stubborn, tight-lipped, morally conservative attorney Walter G. Bridge (Paul Newman), and soft-spoken housewife India Bridge (Joanne Woodward), who wants to experience more passion, freedom, and self-expression but is restrained by her husband.

The couple's relationship is the heart of the film, but they're surrounded by children and friends: Daughter Ruth (Kyra Sedgwick) is a rather Bohemian spirit who wants to go to New York and become an actress; daughter Carolyn (Margaret Welsh) is a college girl who wants to marry someone who is utterly unacceptable to Mr. Bridge; and son, Douglas (John Bell/Robert Sean Leonard), is a mirror image of his father, although he doesn't *want* to be, and goes off to fight in World War II. Prominent among their friends are banker Virgil Barron (Remak Ramsay) and his wife, Grace (Blythe Danner), an alcoholic who is India's best friend (and a personification of the confusion and unrest that Mrs. Bridge keeps inside).

The film has some significant flaws. *Mr. & Mrs. Bridge* is told in a series of vignettes, many of which leave plot points dangling for far too long or leave them unresolved altogether. The film also trots out so many characters that most are given short shrift.

It's also an uplifting experience, however. You've never seen Woodward or Newman (or Danner, especially) in roles like this, and though Walter's aloofness and stubbornness will frustrate you—as when he refuses to seek shelter during a tornado, endangering not only himself but his wife—it also makes his shows of affection more meaningful. India's triumphs are small but she savors them, and so will you.

There's an unshakable love that binds the couple and holds them together through their many trials; it's something many viewers will relate to, and the beauty of it will linger long after the film has ended.

The Disc
Video: ★★
Audio: ★★★ (Surround)
Chapters: No
Format: CLV
Source: HBO Video

The transfer is a disappointing one. The picture is slightly soft throughout, there's a fair amount of grain in many scenes, and the reds and flesh tones are pretty noisy. The film is slightly cropped, though the panning and cuts are generally unobtrusive.

The audio is *very* crisp, though rear-channel use is lackluster, the latter coming to life only during the tornado, party scene, and rainstorm.

Monty Python's Life of Brian (1979) ★★★½

Director: Terry Jones
Running Time: 94 minutes

The British TV series "Monty Python's Flying Circus" debuted on October 5, 1969, starring six veteran TV comedy actors/writers who had been working together in various combinations for years. The series—whose nonsense title was assembled from various sources—was a hit and spawned 2 motion pictures: *And Now for Something Completely Different* (1971), for which some of the best bits from the shows were not terribly successfully recreated, and *Monty Python and the Holy Grail* (1975), a brilliant, iconoclastic look at the Arthurian legend.

Monty Python's Life of Brian grew out of a joke that Eric Idle made toward the end of filming on their Arthurian film, that their next film should be called *Jesus Christ: Lust for Glory*. As they kicked the idea around, they decided to change the slant and make a movie about the thirteenth disciple, Brian, who was Jesus' business manager. But the story grew serious whenever Jesus was onscreen, so *The Gospel According to St. Brian* became *Brian of Nazareth*, the story of a contemporary of Jesus' who is mistaken for the Messiah.

The project was shopped around to various studios, but the subject matter scared them away; finally, former Beatles member George Harrison came up with the money for what became *Monty Python's Life of Brian*.

Shot in Monastir, Tunisia—where, ironically, the miniseries *Jesus of Nazareth* had been filmed—and in the desert at Matmata (which served as the planet Tatooine in *Star Wars*)—the movie follows Brian (the late Graham Chapman) from birth to reluctant Messiah-hood to his sing-along Crucifixion. Along the way, he falls in love, falls in with terrorists, and even falls off a tower into an alien spaceship. There's a stoning to which women aren't allowed, so they all don fake beards; two side-splitting scenes with Pontius Pilate (Michael Palin), whose speech impediment foreshadows Palin's character in *A Fish Called Wanda* (see page 99); a wonderful gladatorial bout, with the more powerful fighter eventually dropping dead from having to chase his timid opponent; and a lesson in Latin conjugation given by a Roman soldier (John Cleese) who catches Brian scrawling anti-Roman graffiti on a wall.

The finished film ran forty minutes longer than the distributor wanted, so a scene involving shepherds and their sheep, the abduction of Pilate's six-foot-nine-inch wife, and the Judean Peoples' Front's King Otto planning to "establish a Jewish state that will last a thousand years" were cut. (Otto does, however, show up briefly during the Crucifixion, to commit suicide with his men.) If you're a fan, you'll have wished this stuff had been put back in for laserdisc: The movie's a riot.

The film drew protests from Christian groups whose members hadn't actually seen it (most protested on opening day). As a result, the movie was banned in some regions of the South—publicity that only drove up its box-office take where it *did* play.

The Disc
Video: ★★★★
Audio: ★★★½ (stereo)
Chapters: No
Format: CLV
Source: Paramount Home Video

Except for a few dark scenes—such as the graffiti sequence, which is set at night—the disc has no grain of which to speak. The focus is quite sharp and the colors are extremely rich and true to life. (Note how even the red of Pilate's robe stands out against the red behind it at 2/18.20.).

The only major problem with the disc is the lack of letterboxing (only the titles are matted). Some important comedy is lost—such as the laughing centurion on the right at 2/22.36, and even Brian himself is missing at 2/26.00.

Though the stereo offers nothing in the way of dramatic effects, you couldn't ask for clearer sound.

Thirteen separate collections of the original "Monty Python's Flying Circus" have been released, and are highly recommended. Their first two films are not presently available on laserdisc; see *Monty Python's The Meaning of Life*.

Monty Python's The Meaning of Life (1983) ★★★½
Director: Terry Jones
Running Time: 107 minutes

While planning what turned out to be their last film together, the Monty Python troupe decided to abandon the narrative form of their previous two features (see *Monty Python's Life of Brian*) and make a movie based on Shakespeare's seven ages of man.

You won't recognize the Bard here; as usual, the Pythons went far afield of their original idea. They came up with sketches that display the extremes of the Python humor, though tastelessness very definitely has the edge over philosophy in the huge *Oliver!*—like production number "Every Sperm Is Sacred"; Eric Idle's short "The Penis Song"; the Victorian soldiers looking for Idle's gnawed-off leg; and the gross highlight of the film—perhaps the grossest in all of movie history—the fat Mr. Creosote (Terry Jones) visiting a restaurant and repeatedly vomiting into (or at least *near*) a bucket so he can continue to eat, driving the other patrons away as a French waiter (John Cleese) hovers officiously at his side. (The vomit was vegetable soup, which, says Cleese, after three days of shooting smelled very much like what it was supposed to be.)

The movie ends with a short masterpiece: Death arriving at a dinner party to claim its six members. His appearance not only fails to terrify them, they hardly break stride in their shallow philosophizing, assimilating the Grim Reaper into the conversation and frustrating the skeletal figure to no end. When he finally convinces them that they're dead, their ghosts leave—and, middle class to the last, climb into the ghosts of their cars to follow him.

Terry Gilliam directed the energetic pirate featurette that opens the film, "The Crimson Permanent Assurance," and the epic style foreshadows such later works as *Brazil* (1985) and *The Adventures of Baron Munchausen* (1989). Originally, this segment appeared in the middle of the film (where the pirates still reappear briefly), but after screening the rough-cut version of the picture they decided to move it up front.

The Disc
Video: ★★★
Audio: ★★★½ (Surround)
Chapters: Yes
Format: CLV
Source: MCA Home Video

Mild though it is, cropping this 1.66:1 film does it a disservice. Reaction shots are vitally important to Python films, and too many of them fall off the sides. This is inexcusable, since a very mild matte would have kept everything on the screen.

The quality of what's up there is good, though the picture is never free of *some* level of grain. The colors are very strong, though the picture could have been a bit sharper.

The audio is clear and features generally excellent stereo separation. The low-range sounds tend to be muddy at times, though the upper ranges are ringingly clear. Surround Sound effects are sparse, although you'll know it when they hit (such as the booming rear-speaker voices in elephant dance, or the wall falling on side two, at 4/19:22).

Mountains of the Moon (1990)
★★★★½
Director: Bob Rafelson
Running Time: 140 minutes

Bob Rafelson had previously created the rock group the Monkees and directed *Five Easy Pieces* (see page 100), *The Postman Always Rings Twice* (1981), and *Black Widow* (1987), among other contemporary films. To say that this powerful period piece was a surprise is an understatement.

Sir Richard Francis Burton (1821–1890) was one of the most remarkable men of his age. A diplomat/explorer/writer, he visited places in the Middle East and Africa that no European had ever seen before and recorded his observations in detail. He spoke twenty-nine languages and dialects and, among other things, was responsible for translating *The Arabian Nights* and the *Kama Sutra*.

Based on the the 1982 biographical novel *Burton and Speke*, *Mountains of the Moon* concentrates on Burton's (Patrick Bergin) daunting search for the source of the Nile. It also examines the two key relationships in Burton's life: one with fellow explorer Lt. John Hanning Speke (Iain Glen) and his romance with the worshipful Isabel Arundell (Fiona Shaw).

The movie and its stars couldn't be better. The locations are both desolate and awe-inspiring, and the dialogue is witty and illuminating. Bergin (the nasty husband in *Sleeping with the Enemy*—see page 253—and star of the made-for-TV movie *Robin Hood*—see mention in *Robin Hood: Prince of Thieves*—burns with curiosity, dignity, and inner strength; in contrast, Glen's Speke is a man of ambition and ephemeral courage. Shaw's Isabel, though devoted to Burton, is strongly independent and every inch his equal.

Like *Lawrence of Arabia*, *Mountains of the Moon* is an epic of power, insight, and majesty—once seen, never to be forgotten.

The Disc

Video: ★★★½
Audio: ★★★★½ (Surround)
Chapters: Yes
Format: CLV (sides one and two), CAV (side three)
Source: International Video Entertainment/Image Entertainment.

A pox on IVE and distributor Image for not letterboxing this disc. No significant plot or character information is lopped off, but a few key vistas—which are not only beautiful but are used to underscore the characters' isolation—have been robbed of their impact. Some scenes, such as the dinner party and the candlelit Burton/Isabel liaison, are also quite cramped.

That said, the image itself is extremely clear, brilliant in the daylight and relatively grain-free even in the many night and low-light scenes.

The digital audio is striking, with excellent stereo separation. During the jungle scenes—which are ripe with native and animal cries—the Surround Sound can be unsettling.

The disc includes the trailer and an informative "making of" featurette.

The Music Man (1962)
★★★★½
Director: Morton Da Costa
Running Time: 151 minutes

A flutist with John Philip Sousa's band, Meredith Willson based *The Music Man* on his youth in Iowa. He began working on the musical in 1951, originally calling it *The Silver Triangle* and using the rather unique gimmick of having hero Professor Harold Hill and heroine Marian Paroo sing songs based on the same theme to suggest that they had much in common that wasn't readily apparent (in the finished musical, "Goodnight My Someone" is essentially a slow version of "Seventy-Six Trombones").

Willson went through countless revisions of the material, writing more than thirty drafts of the libretto and a total of forty songs before settling on the final version. (One of the last things to go was a subplot about a janitor and his crippled son; the boy was replaced by Marian's lisping little brother, Winthrop.) But the long haul wasn't over: Before the show opened on Broadway in 1957, the producers and director Da Costa struggled to find a star. Danny Kaye—who would have been ideal—was making movies and turned them down, after which they got nos from Dan Dailey, Phil Harris, Ray Bolger, Jackie Gleason, Milton Berle, Jason Robards, Art Carney, Bert Parks, Lloyd Bridges, Van Heflin, James Whitmore, and Andy Griffith. Finally, they offered the part to Robert Preston, who had zero singing and dancing experience. But he moved like a marionette, every joint alive and kicking with such infectious energy that he won a Tony Award for his performance and was allowed to recreate the role in the film version.

It's 1912, and con man Hill arrives in River City, Iowa, to create a boy's band—even though he doesn't know the first thing about music. His scam is selling families the instruments and uniforms and then splitting with his profit. River City embraces the huckster, who learns the ins and outs of the town with the help of his onetime partner, Marcellus Washburn (Buddy Hackett), who happens to live there. However, the unexpected happens: After selling everyone their uniforms and instruments, Hill falls in love with Marian (Shirley Jones), the local librarian, whose withdrawn brother, Winthrop (Ronny Howard), comes out of his shell at Hill's coaxing. He tarries too long, and traveling anvil salesman Charles Cowell (Harry Hickox) shows up. Cowell resents the bad name Hill is giving the profession and so exposes him. Hill is handcuffed and brought up on charges, but before the townspeople can toss him in jail the kids show up in their uniforms, instruments in hand. By some miracle, the double-talk he gave them about being able to play music just by thinking it works allows them to perform as a band. Hill is saved and, presumably, settles down with Marian in River City.

Except for the abrupt ending and one number that doesn't quite come off ("My White Knight" was replaced for the film by "Being in Love"), this is a nearperfect, all-American musical—consistently entertaining, witty, brilliantly choreographed, and wonderfully evocative of small-town America (even though it was filmed entirely on Warner's Burbank lot: The town square is still there). And it isn't dated at all: The musical's Rockwellian vision of America may not be with us anymore, but the emotions and sentiments it exudes are timeless and guaranteed to bring equal measures of tears and goose bumps.

Preston is immortal in the part, giving one of the most buoyant, galvanizing musical performances ever. Astonishingly, the filmmakers were concerned about his lack of box-office appeal and originally offered the part to Cary Grant: To his credit, Grant told them, "Not only won't I play it, but unless Robert Preston plays it, I won't even go to see the picture." Shirley Jones is also glorious, as are the adorable young "Opie" Howard, Paul Ford as the dithering Mayor Shinn, Hermione Gingold as his prudish and domineering wife, Eulalie, and the Buffalo Bills, a barbershop quartet transported from the stage play.

Another standout is Timmy Everett, who plays the Russ Tamblynesque delinquent band member Tommy Djilas. Unfortunately, Everett died of a drug overdose shortly after the film was completed.

The Disc

Video: ★★★★½
Audio: ★★★★ (Surround)
Chapters: Yes
Format: CLV
Source: Warner Home Video

This is a sharp, beautiful transfer, with every detail beautifully rendered. Just two drawbacks. Although the colors are extremely vibrant, the many reds and blues aren't *quite* as blazing as they were on the big screen. Also, a few of the night scenes are slightly washed-out. But these are small complaints, given the overall beauty of the transfer.

The letterboxing, which is about 10 percent shy of what it should be, is still very, very satisfying, All of the terrific choreography is nicely framed, and the film's many two-shots—with characters on opposite ends of the screen—are intact.

The earlier pan-and-scan version, while giving you a closer look at the wonderful Preston, loses so much else that it fails to satisfy.

The audio is perfectly clean and devoid of extraneous sounds, and the separations are fine. However, there *is* a problem with the Surround Sound during the musical numbers: The instruments, especially in "Seventy-Six Trombones," overpower the singing rather considerably. You'll have to turn your rear speakers down for a proper balance.

Mutiny on the Bounty (1962)
★★★★
Director: Lewis Milestone
Running Time: 186 minutes

As set out in the Nordhoff/Hall trilogy about the event, and Captain Bligh's own log, on April 28, 1789, four months after sailing for Tahiti to procure breadfruit to feed the slaves in Jamaica, officer Fletcher Christian and the crew of HMS *Bounty* mutinied against their driven (but not sadistic) captain. Bligh and eighteen loyal crew members were set adrift in a boat: Incredibly, they crossed 3,618 miles to the Dutch East Indies, losing only one crew member, and were able to make passage back to England. Though ships were sent in pursuit, the mutineers had settled on the mischarted Pitcairn Island, where their descendants live to this day. Christian died shortly after landfall—he may have been murdered for suggesting the mutineers return to England to present their case—and the *Bounty* was sunk.

MGM made this film with their *Ben-Hur* profits (see page 27) and managed to lose a fortune. The problem was not with the quality of the film but with the public's expectations. Thanks to MGM's 1935 version (available on laserdisc), Charles Laughton's Bligh and his "Mister Chris*tian*" had become synonymous with screen villainy, and Clark Gable had played (the English!) Christian as staunch and righteous, classically heroic. Trevor Howard's quietly obsessed Bligh in the later film is closer to the historical captain (who, after the mutiny, was exonerated by the Admiralty and went on to lead a distinguished career), while Brando's dandified Fletcher Christian, though ultimately heroic, is also sly, sarcastic, wishy-washy, and effete. He's also infinitely more interesting than Gable's mate. Hugh Griffith, Richard Harris, and the crew of character actors are also excellent.

The *Bounty* and Tahiti are both beautiful to watch (the ship leaving the Portsmouth harbor is dazzling), and there's a storm at sea that'll leave you exhausted. The *Bounty* was recreated for the film, built 115 feet long as compared to the 85 of the original to allow for cameras and lights. Because of delays in building the ship and completing the script, the crew ran into the rainy season in Tahiti. Very little footage was shot, director Carol Reed resigned, the company returned to Hollywood, and Milestone came aboard for the return to Tahiti four months later—the budget having grown from $8.5 to $18.5 million. Milestone and Brando did not get along; when it came time to shoot Christian's death scene, Milestone stayed in his dressing room and Brando took the helm.

The film is spectacular, and the script is sprinkled with wit and insight. It's a better film than the original or the 1984 *The Bounty* with Mel Gibson as a manic Christian and Anthony Hopkins as a fatherly Bligh; give it a chance.

The Disc

Video: ★★★★½
Audio: ★★★★½ (Surround)
Chapters: No
Format: CLV
Source: MGM/UA Home Video

The film is available in both letterboxed and panned-and-scanned versions. The close-ups look fine in the panned-and-scanned edition, but *Mutiny on the Bounty* was shot in Ultra Panavision, a sprawling 70mm wide-screen process. The vistas *demand* letterboxing; panning-and-scanning also loses many of the reaction shots so crucial to the relationship of Christian and Bligh.

The colors are rich and saturated, but the more monochromatic scenes—such as the Tahitian twilight and the storm—are also full of subtle colors. Grain and noise are rare, and the focus is very sharp in the letterboxed version. The print used for both discs is in excellent condition.

The digital transfer does justice to all the splendid sounds and the score sounds incredible; an enlarged orchestra was used, which gives it incredible body.

The trailer is included but, inexplicably, a prologue has been omitted from the disc. In 1808, the British ship *Topaz* arrives on Pitcairn Island, where botanist William Brown (Richard Haydn) is the sole survivor among the mutineers. He tells the story of the film (which accounts for the otherwise-inexplicable narration that crops up now and then). MGM has no explanation for why this material was not on the print used for the transfer.

The Naked Jungle (1954)
★★★
Director: Byron Haskin
Running Time: 95 minutes

This is one of those films that everyone who has seen it *remembers*: It's the one with the *ants*.

Long before he was starring as epic heroes, Charlton Heston was a terrific screen heel. After working in TV and on the Broadway stage, he headed west to begin his film career as a scam artist in *Dark City* (1950). Nor was he Mr. Warmth in his second film, playing the hardheaded circus manager in Cecil B. DeMille's *The Greatest Show on Earth* (1952). However, no Heston role approaches the stubborn arrogance of Christopher Leiningen in *The Naked Jungle*.

Based on the short story "Leiningen Versus the Ants" by Carl Stephenson, the film, set in 1901, is about a South American plantation owner (Heston) who orders a mail-order bride, Joanna (Eleanor Parker), from New Orleans. When she arrives, Leiningen discovers that she was married before: This offends his Victorian morality, and he prepares to ship her back home. However, Joanna elects to stay when the plantation is besieged by *marabunta*—lethal soldier ants. Ultimately impressed by her courage, Leiningen learns to love her before confronting the "forty square miles of agonizing death" bearing down on his land.

The film was produced by George Pal (see *War of the Worlds*). Though the script doesn't give the characters much substance, Pal demonstrated a DeMillian flair with the spectacular ant attack and ultimate destruction of the plantation. And yes, the ants were real: The actors wore plastic suits under their clothing. (The doomed floodgate keeper had his eyes, ears, and nose taped to keep the ants out.)

The Naked Jungle may not be a classic, but you'll be scratching for days afterward. (And read the story, if you can find it: It's a corker.)

The Disc
Video: ★★★½
Audio: ★★★★ (monaural)
Chapters:No
Format: CLV
Source: Paramount

Paramount has given us many disappointing discs; happily, this isn't one of them. The print is mint and the Technicolor is generally lush, especially in the jungle scenes. Even close-ups of the ants have an oily, multicolor beauty.

The noise-free sound is superb. The jungle is alive with screeches, hoots, and cries of all kinds, and a very satisfactory Surround-like effect can be achieved simply by pumping the sound through four speakers. In a key scene, when the jungle suddenly goes grave-quiet, you'll understand just *why* the characters are so frightened. The explosions and crashes in the climax are as memorable as the spectacular visuals.

Near Dark (1987) ★★★½
Director: Kathryn Bigelow
Running Time: 95 minutes

Bigelow—the former wife of director James Cameron (*Terminator 2*; see page 273)—had already had her directorial up and downs. The downs were the Jamie Lee Curtis cop film *Blue Steel* (1990) and the meandering Patrick Swayze bomb *Point Break* (1991). The up was *Near Dark*, a vampire thriller that adheres to the legend while adding a few twists of its own.

When southwestern farm boy Caleb (Adrian Pasdar) spots comely young Mae (Jenny Wright) at a local dive, he cozies up to her—unaware that she's part of a vampire clan that crisscrosses the country in stolen vans and Winnebagos, killing at random. Mae fancies Caleb and nips him so that he, too, becomes a vampire. Family leader Jesse (Lance Henriksen)—who has been a vampire since before the Civil War—doesn't trust newcomers but takes Caleb into the family on probation.

Meanwhile, when Caleb fails to return home, his father, Loy (Tim Thomerson), goes searching for him, which leads to a tense showdown and a satisfying, if tough-to-swallow resolution, as Caleb and Mae become normal people again: There are just some basics of the vampire legend that shouldn't be tampered with. (Human regeneration also gets stretched to the breaking point, as Loy's hand is very clearly and audibly crushed in the motel confrontation but is fine in the next scene.)

Pasdar is convincing in his "vampire as a blood junkie" role, and Henriksen is his usual, wild-eyed self. But Bigelow's stylish direction is the real star and her set pieces are marvelous, especially the vampire attack on the bar (*much* more satisfying than Cameron's retread of the scene in *Terminator 2*) and the daylight assault on the small room where the undead have taken refuge, the troopers' gunfire sending vampire-sizzling lances of sunlight through walls, doors, and windows.

The technical razzledazzle compensates for the thinness of the script: You'll have a good time with this one!

The Disc
Video: ★★½
Audio: ★★★½ (Surround)
Chapters: Yes
Format: CLV
Source: HBO Video/Image Entertainment

Though the picture is fairly sharp and the colors are satisfactory, grain is a real problem, ranging from mild to fairly thick. There's also a loss of detail in a number of the exterior night scenes—though, considering how dark the film is, the problem could have been a lot worse.

For the most part, the audio is wonderfully clear, and there are a few show-stopping Surround effects, especially during the two big fires and the attack on the vampire's motel room.

Nicholas and Alexandra (1971)
★★★★
Director: Franklin J. Schaffner
Running Time: 172 minutes

Robert Massie's 1967 book *Nicholas and Alexandra* is an exhaustive account of the last years of the Romanov dynasty and the rise of Russian communism. The book reads like a thriller, full of drama and strange, extraordinary characters. At the center of the storm was the well-meaning but weak Czar Nicholas II; his strong, proud wife, Alexandra; their hemophiliac son, Alexis; and the mad monk Rasputin, who saw Alexandra through trying times with her son, while his profligate lifestyle brought shame on the dynasty and helped to bring it down.

Coming off the success of *Patton* (see page 205), director Schaffner created this much underappreciated film, the last of the big road-show, reserved-seat films: Perhaps the backlash against epics in this era of *Midnight Cowboy* was responsible. *Nicholas and Alexandra* serves up a great deal of history without ever seeming expository, and it never loses sight of the human drama: The couple and their love, their devotion to family, the strain of Alexis's illnesses, and the people who were working for and against them—including Lenin and the moderate Kerensky (who ruled briefly between the fall of the Czar and Lenin).

The casting is perfect. The resemblance of London stage star Michael Jayston to Nicholas is uncanny, and he does a fine job capturing the power and insecurity of the Czar. His breakdown when he's alone with Alexandra after abdicating (side two/chapter eight) is heartbreaking. South African–born Suzman is also ideal, though she's much prettier than Alexandra. Rasputin was as out-of-control as Tom Baker plays him—and he really *did* survive all those attempts to kill him. (Baker went on to star as British TV's Dr. Who.) Laurence Olivier, John Wood, Jack Hawkins, and Harry Andrews are all effective in supporting roles: Michael Bryant (see *The Ruling Class*) and John McEnery (best known as Mercutio in *Ro-*

meo and Juliet [1968] are excellent as Lenin and Kerensky, and Roderic Noble is proud and sad as the doomed czarevich Alexis. Julian Glover, Curt Jurgens, Alexander Knox, and Roy Dotrice have small roles.

As in every Sam Spiegel production (see *Lawrence of Arabia*), no expense was spared in the making of the film. Portions were shot in Madrid, where the architecture resembled that of St. Petersburg, while familiar structures were reconstructed outside and in. Interestingly, the palace sets look unusually authentic because the floors were built using real marble, which was cheaper to get in Spain than a marblized substitute.

See also the entries on *Anastasia* and *Doctor Zhivago*.

The Disc
Video: ★★★
Audio: ★★★ (monaural)
Chapters: Yes
Format: CLV
Source: Pioneer Special Edition

The previous panned-and-scanned edition from RCA/Columbia was terrible—fuzzy, with flat colors. This one's much better. The wide-screen production has been presented in its *very* wide original aspect ratio. The magnificent sets, battles, crowd scenes, and shots of the entire royal family are intact.

The bad news is that the film is not as striking as it should be. The image is slightly soft—losing some details in the intricate costumes and sets—and there's a small amount of grain and a fair amount of video noise in many scenes.

The colors are good but not as splendid as they were when the film was originally released. It's difficult to tell whether this is the fault of the transfer or of the source material (likely), though the end result is the same.

The audio, though very clear, has a faint background hiss that will force you to keep the volume down.

The disc's one extra is a nice one: the lovely Richard Rodney Bennett score isolated on the right digital and analog audio tracks.

None but the Brave (1965)
★★½
Director: Frank Sinatra
Running Time: 106 minutes

Capt. Dennis Bourke (Clint Walker) and his crew crash-land on a South Pacific island inhabited by Japanese soldiers. The two units vacillate between bloodshed (an attempt by the Americans to steal a boat the Japanese are building) and cooperation (Chief Pharmacist Mate Maloney, Sinatra, visiting the Japanese base to treat a wounded enemy soldier before the film reaches its tragic, inevitable climax).

This is a frustrating movie. It's good, with some powerful moments and an antiwar message that was a few years ahead of its time. But director Sinatra wasn't up to the task of making this a *great* picture. Technically, there are cuts that just don't flow and scenes that could have used a few more or a few less close-ups. He also had trouble moderating his actors. Walker is *so* stolid that his scenes with antagonistic Second Lieutenant Blair (rabidly overacted by Tommy Sands) are embarrassing. Sinatra is good as the drunken, world-weary soldier, but he has a relatively small role; only Brad Dexter shines as the brawling Sergeant Bleeker. Sinatra wisely opted to have the Japanese speak Japanese with subtitles, and the voice-over narration by Lieutenant Kuroki (Tatsuya Mihashi) provides astute commentary.

The movie boasts some excellent special effects by Godzilla's creator, Eiji Tsuburaya, most notably the plane's spectacular crash landing and a devastating monsoon.

The Disc
Video: ★★★★½
Audio: ★★★½ (monaural)
Chapters: Yes
Format: CLV
Source: Warner Home Video

The sun-drenched colors of the island are breathtaking to watch on the letterboxed disc, and even the night scenes are clear and crisp. Only a hint of video noise keeps the film from a five-star rating. The master element is in nearly perfect shape.

The digital sound is surprisingly muddy in spots, compounding the preexisting problem of Walker's marbles-in-the-mouth delivery. However, the gunfire, explosions, and storm pack a wallop.

A minor point: Why are there *two* Brad Dexters coming out of the plane on the jacket?

North by Northwest (1959)
★★★★★
Director: Alfred Hitchcock
Running Time: 136 minutes

After filming the dark psychological thriller *Vertigo* (1958), Hitchcock planned to make the seagoing mystery *The Wreck of the Mary Deare*. However, he scuttled that project and decided to go with a lighter chase film, *North by Northwest*. (Michael Anderson directed *The Wreck of the Mary Deare* that year and botched it all up.)

It's fitting that when advertising executive Roger O. Thornhill (Cary Grant) enters the Plaza Hotel for his rendezvous with destiny, the musicians in the Palm Court are playing "It's a Most Unusual Day." Flunkies working for enemy agent Philip Vandamm (James Mason) mistake Thornhill for American spy George Kaplan. Though Thornhill escapes their clutches, he is framed for a murder and tries to elude both the police and Vandamm while searching for the real George Kaplan.

On the Twentieth Century Limited from New York to Chicago, hot on Kaplan's trail, Thornhill meets Eve Kendall (Eva Marie Saint), with whom he falls in love—unaware that she's very much more than she appears to be. The search for Kaplan (and some important mircofilm) brings Thornhill, Eve, and Vandamm together at Mt. Rushmore, where—as hero and spies crawl up, down, and all over them, fighting for their lives—the Presidents inadvertently help to preserve the nation they forged.

In terms of its tortuous plot, lightning pace, dry humor, and action, *North by Northwest* was very much the model for the James Bond films that followed three years later. And except for some really pathetic special effects (the car chase with its poor rear projection, people badly composited into previously filmed location footage, and the climax with its shockingly awful matte paintings), this is nearly a perfect film. It seems that every time Cary Grant turns around, he's not only in danger but in another scene that has become a classic: the United Nations murder, the chilling crop-duster attack in the cornfield, the restaurant shooting, and the finale on Mt. Rushmore. Impeccably cast down to the smallest role and beautifully designed from the opening credits (which foreshadow the up-and-down Rushmore finale) to the final cut of Grant helping Saint up the cliff and into a sleeper berth, it's breathtaking to watch. It's equally satisfying to listen to, with endlessly clever dialogue and one of the all-time great scores, composed by frequent Hitchcock collaborator Bernard Herrmann.

Not only does the movie hold up extremely well on repeated viewings, you'll *need* to watch it more than once just to appreciate all the abrupt reversals! There's Thornhill, the advertising man who specializes in persuasive lies, unable to convince anyone that he isn't George Kaplan; Thornhill, the in-charge executive who emerges confidently from the elevator in the film's opening moments, then subsequently rushes from an elevator like a scared rabbit; Thornhill, sent on a deadly rendezvous with a plane by Eve (named after the biblical betrayer?), then hurrying to save her from dying in one.

Though the film's title is a play on the name of the airline Thornhill uses to get to South Dakota, it was actually derived from Hamlet's line, "I am but mad north-north-west." There is no such direction, meaning that Hamlet's not mad ... and neither is Thornhill, despite appearances. (Incredibly, except for the visit to Glen Cove in the beginning, all of the action in the film moves north or west—even the trips along city streets: north up Madison Avenue, west to the Plaza, and so on.)

Make sure you watch closely when Eve

shoots Thornhill (19/29143 in the Criterion CAV edition) in the cafeteria at Mt. Rushmore: The kid in the background plugs his fingers in his ears *before* the gun goes off. (His fingers are *out* of his ears when Hitchcock cuts to another angle.) Also, look for Edward Platt (the Chief of "Get Smart") as Thornhill's lawyer, Victor Larrabee. Not so coincidentally, there was an agent by that name in the TV series.

The Disc

Video: ★★★★ (both)
Audio: ★★★★ (monaural) (both)
Chapters: Yes
Format: CLV and CAV (Criterion); CLV (side one), CAV (side two), MGM/UA
Source: Criterion and MGM/UA Home Video

North by Northwest was filmed in VistaVision, and the clarity that the process gives each shot is dazzling; The print used in the Criterion edition is exceptionally clean. Though the brightly lighted film is slightly washed-out in spots, these shots are a very minor annoyance. The letterboxing shows off Hitchcock's wonderful composition, from simple shots—Grant and the bus passenger on opposite ends of the street near the cornfield—to the more complex *Vertigo*-like shot down the face of the UN, the plane attack, or the view along the struts supporting Vandamm's house.

The video on the MGM/UA edition has punchier colors, though the picture isn't *quite* as sharp. On the other hand, the print used for this transfer doesn't have the occasional nicks and tears present in Criterion's offering. (MGM/UA's letterboxed remastering is superior in every way—framing, color, sharpness, audio—to the company's earlier, fuzzier pan-and-scan version.)

The audio of both discs has a wide dynamic range (important, given the heights and depths of the Herrmann score), and there are no dropouts. While there's no hissing, many of the Criterion discs have pressing-related problems with crackling. No such problems have turned up on the MGM/UA offering. Further, the latter offers both digital monaural and simulated analog stereo. Purists may cringe, but the latter isn't bad! (The music was recorded in true stereo, but only the title music is presented that way.)

Fans of the film and/or of Hitchcock will deem the Criterion CAV edition worth the $125 price tag. Not only can you freeze the more impressive shots (as well as handwritten notes and newspaper front pages) but it offers behind-the-scenes photos, a Hitchcock interview, the trailer, a Bernard Herrmann biography, and a remarkable series of storyboards. Hitchcock planned every detail of his films on paper before the cameras rolled, and you'll be amazed at how closely the finished footage follows the comic book–style illustrations—even to Grant's uncertain turn before running from the biplane.

The one-third-as-expensive MGM/UA edition offers only the trailer.

The Nutty Professor (1963)
★★★½
Director: Jerry Lewis
Running Time: 107 minutes

How good is this movie? So good that you'll forget for 107 minutes how Jerry Lewis has made you cringe by pontificating on talk shows, by fancying himself a singer, and by making like Eisenstein and writing the book *The Total Film-maker* ("Film, baby, powerful tool for love or laughter ...").

Lewis (who cowrote the screenplay) drew on *Dr. Jekyll and Mr. Hyde* as inspiration for this tale of nerdy, buck-toothed chemistry Professor Julius F. Kelp, who, in an effort to impress student Stella Purdy (Stella Stevens), creates a potion designed to turn him into a manly man. Instead, it turns him into a manly heel, Buddy Love, who not only woos Stella but bullies everyone in sight. The cad gets his comeuppance when he reverts at a most inopportune time—but, like the frog who became a prince, Kelp ends up with the love he desperately sought.

Kelp is a unique and wonderful creation: intelligent and butterfingered, with the demeanor of a frightened rabbit. He is Lewis's comic masterpiece.

There are a lot of funny lines (extolling the virtures of chemistry, Kelp says, "Carbon dioxide has always been a gas") and wonderful lunacy, such as Kelp sinking into the chair (literally) during a dressing-down from Dr. Hamius R. Warfield (Del Moore), the pre–Buddy Kelp working out at a gym, Kelp's first hangover from Love's drinking, and the disastrous senior prom. What prevents *The Nutty Professor* from getting a higher rating is too much Buddy: He's *supposed* to be annoying, but we got the message after his first visit to the student club, where he pushed everyone around, and, secondly, Jerry allows Buddy (read: Jerry) three songs too many.

Look for future "Rowan & Martin's Laugh-In" star Henry Gibson as student Gibson, and Richard Kiel (Jaws in the James Bond films) as a member of the health club.

See *The Errand Boy* for more on Lewis's career.

The Disc

Video: ★★★
Audio: ★★★
Chapters: No
Format: CLV
Source: Paramount Home Video

Though the image is a little soft and there's a loss of detail in some of the darker scenes (Buddy playing for Stella in the club, for example), the colors in *The Nutty Professor* are extremely bright. The lab scenes, with beakers and test tubes full of red, yellow, and blue liquids and belching Technicolor smoke, are lots of fun.

The disc is not letterboxed, but the loss of information is minimal, limited to props and sets rather than to actors. Panning is used sparingly, as in the faculty meeting.

Though there are occasional audio pops, the sound track is otherwise clean and very sharp.

Ocean's Eleven (1960) ★★★
Director: Lewis Milestone
Running Time: 127

Frank Sinatra doesn't sing in the film (Dean Martin and Sammy Davis, Jr., do, though), there's seemingly endless exposition and some sickeningly chummy camaraderie, and most of these guys couldn't act their way out of high school detention. Yet...

There's something irresistible about this caper flick as Danny Ocean (Sinatra) sets about bringing together his old buddies from the Eighty-second Airborne to pull off a heist that will net them each a million dollars. Using their skills in demolition, electronics, and so on, Ocean plans to black out Las Vegas and hit five casinos simultaneously. The other operators in the plan are Sam Harmon (Martin), Josh Howard (Davis), rich boy Jimmy Foster (Peter Lawford), former con Tony Bergdorf (Richard Conte), "Mushy" O'Connors (Joey Bishop), Roger Corneal (Henry Silva), Peter Rheimer (Norman Fell), Louis Jackson (Clem Harvey), Vincent Massler (Buddy Lester), "Curly" Steffans (Richard Benedict), and Spyros Acebos (Akim Tamiroff, who overacts pitifully, and most of whose lines were postdubbed by himself for clarity).

The unexpected death of Tony and the muscling in of Foster's mobster stepfather, Duke Santos (an excellent Cesar Romero), lead to some tense moments, quick improvisation, and the film's classic surprise ending. (Avoid the chapter listing if you don't know what happens and don't want to know!)

Thanks to the easy charm of the stars, even scenes that serve no structural purpose (such as Angie Dickinson as Ocean's estranged wife, Beatrice) are watchable, and the "job" itself is lots of fun—despite the holes (such as, where did Howard get the keys?). Because of the Lawford/Dickinson/Sinatra locus, the film benefits from implicit ties to the blooming Camelot era, giving it an emotional edge for those who are wistful about the time.

There are delightful cameos by Red Skelton, George Raft, and Shirley

MacLaine, though the exploding power tower is such an *awful* miniature, you half-expect to see Reptilicus slither by.

The Disc
Video: ★½
Audio: ★★★ (monaural)
Chapters: Yes
Format: CLV
Source: Warner Home Video

Though the film takes place in Beverly Hills and Las Vegas, two of the most colorful towns in the United States, the colors are flat in this transfer. You'd almost welcome a bit of noise if the rest of the tones had been pushed a little! For the most part, the image is fairly sharp; that's not entirely due to the transfer, however, but to the diminished picture size due to letterboxing.

The wide-screen presentation is welcome, of course. Though the sets are surprisingly sparse (no jazzy late-1950s decor for these hipsters?), the letterbox keeps you from missing any of the Rat Packers.

The audio is clear and free of hiss or extraneous noise, though there are occasional (insignificant dropouts.

The Pack's *Robin and the Seven Hoods* (1964) has also been released in a letterboxed laserdisc, and while this film about 1928 Chicago gangland hasn't the dumb charm of *Ocean's Eleven*, it's a lot of fun and the transfer is sharper and more colorful.

On Dangerous Ground (1951)
★★½
Director: Nicholas Ray
Running Time: 82 minutes

Jim Wilson (Robert Ryan), a cop who lives in a world of brutality and degradation, has no one in his life but lawbreakers and fellow police officers—no family, friends, wife, or lover. He lives only to track down violent criminals. In his small room, he places photos of suspects beside the dinner plate, or shuffles through them obsessively, or examines them continually in the backseat of a prowl car.

Wilson doesn't realize it, but he's losing his perspective and control of his life. After beating a suspect and carelessly endangering a witness, Wilson is temporarily reassigned to an out-of-town case. There, he meets a blind woman, Mary Mauldin (Ida Lupino), whose vulnerability opens him up. Meanwhile, in the person of Walter Brent (Ward Bond), Wilson sees a reflection of what he's become. Brent's daughter has been killed by a homicidal maniac, and his monomania, anger, and emotional ugliness hit the policeman hard. He begins to change, and even Brent is reformed by the accidental death of the murderer, whom they discover is an insane adolescent.

On Dangerous Ground has some riveting moments and, while its execution doesn't quite live up to its premise, it's a fascinating work in the evolution of its director, perhaps the leading figure of the auteur cultists. It was Ray's seventh film; his magnum opus, *Rebel Without a Cause*, was still four years in the future. An architectural student who'd studied under Frank Lloyd Wright, Ray segued into the arts, directing radio plays for John Houseman at the Office of War Information and acting in stage plays directed by Elia Kazan. After working on movies in various capacities, he made his film directorial debut with *They Live by Night* (1949), about young thieves.

The nearly fatal flaw of this film is an unfortunate, early shift from the tough-minded to the sentimental: It's painful to see Ryan's moral blindness contrasted with Lupino's physical blindness. Guess which one of them sees more clearly.

Despite the clunky symbolism, *On Dangerous Ground* is a thing of beauty, from its neon and shadows to the vast light of snow-filled landscapes. All of Ray's early work is characterized by camerawork as agitated as his rebellious antiheroes, and in his use of the landscape and sets to reflect what his characters are undergoing. In this film, Ray is particularly successful at conveying passage through time and space thanks to a hypnotic series of dissolves, the movie's main stylistic feature.

The actors are all seasoned pros who

deliver what's asked of them, and Alfred Hitchcock's favorite composer, Bernard Herrmann, contributed a typically moody score.

The Disc
Video: ★★
Audio: ★★ (monaural)
Chapters: Yes
Format: CLV (side one), CAV (side two)
Source: Turner Home Entertainment/ Image Entertainment

It's a pity better care wasn't taken with the transfer of this little-seen work by an important director. It's barely better than average, with no special attention paid to the gray tones that are so important to the film's atmosphere. Often, the picture is much too soft and there are some major scratches: At times, it seems as though parts of the source material have actually flaked off.

The CAV side features two or three steady frames, followed by two or three unsteady ones.

The audio is acceptable; the dialogue is soft and there's background hiss, but at least Herrmann's score has the power it should.

On Her Majesty's Secret Service (1969) ★★★★½
Director: Peter Hunt
Running Time: 135 minutes

Extremely faithful to the eleventh James Bond novel (published in 1963), *On Her Majesty's Secret Service* is a special Bond film. Not only does this sixth 007 movie feature the much-maligned Australian model George Lazenby as Bond, it boasts stronger characterizations than any film in the series and has a decidedly downbeat ending.

The film, like the novel, interweaves two stories: Bond attempting to outwit his archenemy, Ernst Stavro Blofeld (Telly Savalas), who plans to unleash a sterility-causing virus on the world, and 007 courting beautiful young Tracy (Diana Rigg), the daughter of powerful mobster Marc Ange Draco (Gabriele Ferzetti). Bond succeeds in thwarting Blofeld and marrying Tracy, though the film ends tragically as the villain murders her shortly after the ceremony. (Bond is seen visiting her grave in the opening moments of *For Your Eyes Only*, 1981)

Sean Connery retired from the series after *You Only Live Twice* (1967)—though he was coaxed to return for one more film, *Diamonds Are Forever* (1971), after *On Her Majesty's Secret Service*. Lazenby was cast just weeks before filming began, after the producers considered countless newcomers and seasoned actors such as Richard Burton, Lee Marvin, and even Adam West. (First choice Roger Moore was shooting "The Saint" for TV and was unavailable.) When it came down to Lazenby and John Richardson (who had played the caveman Tumak in *One Million Years B.C.* [1966]), Lazenby won because of his graceful agility during the action tests.

Long before anyone had seen a foot of film, the poor fellow was pilloried by the press, which wondered how *anyone* could succeed the charismatic Connery. Unaccustomed to the scrutiny and discouraged, Lazenby announced his retirement from the role even before the film was finished. (He did, however, make a cameo appearance as Bond in the 1983 TV movie *The Return of the Man from U.N.C.L.E.*)

Lazenby doesn't deliver his lines with quite the slyness of Connery, and he lacks the same magnetic screen presence. In fact, he looks distractingly like a young Dan Rather reading the news. But he handles the action scenes exceedingly well, and he has enthusiasm and energy—qualities seriously lacking from Connery's previous performance in *You Only Live Twice*. Given the choice between an eager Lazenby and a bored Connery, Lazenby wins.

Actually, the film's biggest problem isn't Lazenby but Telly Savalas. He's a second-rate Blofeld, cross instead of malevolent, smarmy instead of smooth. (Charles Gray, in *Diamonds Are Forever*, is far better.) Diana Rigg is splendid as Tracy and is far more human than her Emma Peel character on TV's "The Avengers," handling the love scenes with aplomb and the action scenes with her patented (and beloved) awfulness.

Despite the undercranked camera that speeds up some of the action scenes and tends to make them look comical instead of thrilling, the movie's chases and fights are corkers. The opening tussle on the beach is beautifully staged and edited, there's a terrific ski chase (with Bond on just one ski), a car chase through a stock car race that becomes a demolition derby, the commando attack on Blofeld's mountain fortress, and a bobsled chase, which, despite some obvious rear projection, is one of the action highlights of the series. (The faked close-ups aside, that's *someone's* head being dragged against the wall of ice in the long shots!)

For all its flaws, the film is not the aberration those critics in the don't-know would have us believe. On the contrary, it's one of the best films in the series.

The Disc
Video: ★★★★
Audio: ★★★½ (monaural)
Chapters: No
Format: CLV
Source: MGM/UA Home Video

This disc was produced from a European print of the film and contains a few minutes of footage not seen in the original panned-and-scanned editions made from an American TV print. (The audio track of existing American wide-screen versions was deemed too weak for a high-quality laserdisc.)

The opening scenes are a bit dark (not just because they take place at night) and some of the interiors are a little reddish, but the transfer and print have no other flaws of which to speak. The colors are very strong and the image is quite sharp.

The letterboxing works wonders for the carefully composed action scenes and mountain vistas (shot in the Swiss Alps; a revolving restaurant doubled as Blofeld's headquarters).

The digital audio is a bit reedy on side one but gets better as the film progresses.

On the Town (1949) ★★★½
Directors: Gene Kelly and Stanley Donen
Running Time: 98 minutes

Among Gene Kelly's films, the public adores *Singin' in the Rain* (see page 252), while the extravagant *An American in Paris* (1951) seems to be the darling of the critics, the story of poor American artist Jerry Mulligan (Kelly) who falls in love with Lise Bouvier (Leslie Caron), the fiancée of a friend, and spurns the advances of his patron, Milo Roberts (Nina Foch).

The long shadows of those two films have kept Kelly's earlier *On the Town* from enjoying the attention it deserves. Kelly himself has said, "I agree it may not be as good as *Singin' in the Rain* or as much as an achievement as *An American in Paris* . . . but in 1949 the idea of believable sailors dancing and singing in the streets of New York—using the city as a set—was new, and it paved the way for musicals like *West Side Story*." Actually, the connection between *On the Town* and *West Side Story* (see page 297) is more direct than that: Leonard Bernstein wrote the music for both, *On the Town* enjoying a healthy Broadway run in 1944 after starting out a year and a half before as *Fancy Free*, a ballet written by Bernstein and choreographed by Jerome Robbins. Entertainers/writers Betty Comden and Adolph Green were impressed with it and came up with the book and lyrics.

The film opens at the New York Naval Yard just before 6:00 A.M. on a summer day: sailors Gabey (Kelly), Chip (Frank Sinatra), and Ozzie (Jules Munshin, who had costarred with Kelly and Sinatra earlier that year in *Take Me Out to the Ball Game*) go on a whirlwind tour of Manhattan while singing the incomparable "New York, New York." Gabey spots and falls in love with Ivy Smith (Vera-Ellen), June's subway poster girl "Miss Turnstiles," after which he and his friends go to the natural history museum, accompanied by cabdriver Brunhilde Esterhazy (Betty Garrett), who's smitten with Chip. At the museum, they meet anthropology student Claire Huddesen (Ann Miller), who is fascinated by Ozzie, whom she regards as a living specimen of prehistoric man.

Unable to forget Ivy, Gabey goes off on his own and finds her taking ballet lessons at Symphonic Hall. They make a date, the sailors and their ladies rendezvousing that night at the Empire State Building. After they hit a few nightclubs, Ivy suddenly departs; meanwhile, pursued by the police for having wrecked a dinosaur skeleton at the museum, the quintet hides out in Coney Island. There, Gabey finds Ivy dancing in a seedy cabaret: She'd been too ashamed to tell him that she was not the high-society girl he imagined but has to work here to pay for her lessons. Gabey couldn't care less, and there's a sweet parting before the lads head back to their ship.

The film hasn't the wit of *Singin' in the Rain* or the polish of *An American in Paris*, but it's got a cast of fun, daffy characters and it moves from one dazzling dance number to the next. Miller is a knockout in the "Prehistoric Man" number, and Kelly gets to show off in the lengthy "A Day in New York" ballet, which summarizes, in dance, their day.

Kelly had a fair amount of power at MGM in those days, and it was at his insistence that the crew was allowed one week of location shooting in New York. That helped boost the cost of the film to a then-hefty $1.5 million—though these scenes give the film weight and credibility that could never have been achieved on the back lot.

The Disc

Video: ★★★½
Audio: ★★★½ (monaural)
Chapters: Yes
Format: CLV
Source: MGM/UA Home Video

The new, remastered disc is an improvement over the original, released over eight years ago—but it's not *quite* the vibrant disc it should be. The colors are strong and the image is precise and clear, but it lacks the breathtaking, full-bodied look of *The Band Wagon* (see page 17) and *Singin' in the Rain*.

The digital audio is relatively noise-free, although it's a little on the soft side.

The disc has a terrific extra: The lengthy featurette "Mighty Manhattan: New York's Wonder City," a spectacular, nostalgic tour of the city in 1949. It's presented in the beginning and will put you in the right mood for the film.

Our Man Flint (1966) ★★★
Director: Daniel Mann
Running Time: 108 minutes

After the first James Bond film, *Dr. No*, single-handedly established the superspy genre in 1962, filmmakers raided literature for every secret agent they could find, giving us Michael Caine as Harry Palmer in *The Ipcress File* (1965), Dean Martin as Matt Helm in *The Silencers* (1966), and more.

Derek Flint was created for the screen to spoof all the other secret agents. Not only is he a master spy, he's a gourmand, teaches ballet in Moscow, has mastered martial arts, fencing, and Zen, and—unlike so many other spies—he's "Our Man," an American. He also eschews traditional weapons, preferring a cigarette lighter that has eighty-two functions—"eighty-three if you want to light a cigar."

When we first meet Flint (James Coburn), he's an exagent for Z.O.W.I.E. (Zonal Organization World Intelligence Espionage). Though Flint's former boss, Lloyd Cramden (Lee J. Cobb), can't stand the agent's independence, he calls him back when a situation arises that requires his talents. A trio of scientists—Dr. Krupov (Rhys Williams), the Caucasian Dr. Whu (Peter Brocco), and the Oriental Dr. Schneider (Benson Fong)—known collectively as Galaxy (and described by agent 0008 as "bigger than Spectre")—have invented a weather-control device and threaten to cause a second Flood unless the nations of the world disband their armies.

Flint reluctantly takes the case, and the trail of clues eventually leads him to Galaxy Island—the most exotic land this side of George Pal's Atlantis—where he must stop the scientists, their murderous aides, Malcolm Rodney (Edward Mulhare) and Gila (Gila Golan), and their anti-American killer eagles.

Coburn is ideal as the alternately deadpan and explosive Flint. Though his martial-arts displays seem tame by modern standards, Coburn—who was taught by Bruce Lee—knew what he was doing. Cobb is perfect as the blustery spy chief, though the steel-fisted Mulhare is dull compared to Bond's flamboyant nemeses, and Israeli actress Gila Golan—whose only other noteworthy film was special effects artist Ray Harryhausen's *Valley of Gwangi* (1969)—is pretty but no actress.

The sets are impressive, the script is witty, but the action—except for a fight in a men's room—is lame by contemporary standards.

A sequel, *In Like Flint* (1967), was as misguided as the original was clever. Flint and Cramden reunite to battle women who are attempting to take over the world, but Coburn seems bored and the satire has given way to corn (for example, using a bowling ball to "strike" an enemy down).

The Disc
Video: ★★
Audio: ★½ (monaural)
Chapters: Yes
Format: CLV
Source: CBS/Fox Home Video

Except for a few scratches, the print is in very good shape. However, the Deluxe Color has faded as if they've been out in the sun for nearly three decades. Those multicolored sets on Galaxy Island *should* have registered like stained-glass windows; instead, they look drained.

The letterboxing is generous, though the edges of the CinemaScope print are missing.

The digital sound is on the thin side, which is a shame: The explosions on side two should really sing!

A slightly squeezed trailer for *In Like Flint* is included. Including it was a very bad idea: It does *not* make you want to see the film.

Pacific Heights (1990) ★★
Director: John Schlesinger
Running Time: 103 minutes

Daniel Pyne says he based the screenplay for this film on his own frustrating efforts to get rid of a tenant in a building he owned in San Francisco. When Pyne discovered that the law was on the side of the nonpaying tenant, he began talking to other landlords and discovered that everyone had a tale like his.

Pyne's script is based on a worst-case senario in which young Patty Palmer (Melanie Griffith) and Drake Goodman (Matthew Modine) buy a small building in San Francisco and take in two tenants in order to meet the monthly payments. They get one nice couple, Mira and Toshio Watanabe (Nobu McCarthy and Mako), and one psychopathic nightmare, Carter Hayes (Michael Keaton), who not only knows the law intimately but has an ulterior motive (stop if you don't want to know): Provoking Goodman to violence and winning the building in a settlement.

Director Schlesinger is no stranger to social misfits and thrillers, having directed *Midnight Cowboy* (1969), *Sunday, Bloody Sunday* (1971), and *Marathon Man* (1976), among others. He certainly keeps the tension turned up, though he's got two major obstacles: The worst-case scenario stretches credibility more than a wee bit, and Hayes is a more interesting and intelligent character than the dull and dull-witted Goodman. (How many times can Hayes dupe this guy? Plenty.) The movie sags in the middle and doesn't pick up until Palmer musters some pluck, figures out how to get back at Hayes, and does so.

Michael Keaton was wise to follow the megahit *Batman* (see page 19) with *Pacific Heights*, and his intensity blows the two-dimensional Griffith and Modine off the screen. Tippi Hedren (Griffith's real-life mother) has a nice small role as Hayes's unwitting victim Florence Peters.

The Disc
Video: ★½
Audio: ★★★½ (Surround)
Chapters: Yes
Format: CLV
Source: CBS Fox Video

Schlesinger shot the film with generally drab colors, and the transfer is even duller still. The image is somewhat soft, there's a fine coat of grain in almost every shot, and when it's dark it's *very* dark—no detail at all.

Though the film isn't letterboxed, the transfer dips into the safety zone so that everything that was on the theater screen is on your screen.

The audio is sharp and satisfying, with excellent stereo separation and enough rear-channel effects—sirens, traffic, music, and so on—to hold your attention even when Hayes's bag of tricks wears thin.

Patton (1970) ★★★★½
Director: Franklin J. Schaffner
Running Time: 176 minutes

Gen. George S. Patton was a frank, critical man, driven by patriotism, personal boldness, and daring (a quality he also demanded from others). He had an insatiable lust to *understand*, and he was particularly fascinated by archaeology, ethnology, horses, and, of course, military history. In his diaries, *War as I Knew It* (1947), he wrote, "One's spirit enlarges with responsibility," and he believed that waging war was the greatest responsibility a person could undertake.

George C. Scott was offered the part of Patton after it had been turned down over a four-year period by Spencer Tracy, Lee Marvin, Burt Lancaster, Robert Mitchum, and even Rod Steiger—Lancaster and Steiger objecting to the film's militarism in a period of strong antiwar sentiment. John Wayne wanted the part, but that would have been overkill. Scott had had a series of flops—*The Bible* (see page 30), *Not With My Wife You Don't!* (1966), *The Flim Flam Man* (1967), and *Petulia* (1968)—and hadn't worked in theatrical films since then. Though he didn't feel that the script by Francis Ford Coppola and Edmund H. North was particularly insightful or coherent, he made the film, complaining all the way.

Despite Scott's reservations, and despite a lot of necessary condensing, the picture is free of war movie clichés and is a masterful evocation of Patton and his time, particularly his admiration of Field Marshal Erwin Rommel (Karl Michael Vogler), his admiration/resentment of General Omar N. Bradley (Karl Malden), and his resentment/hate of Field Marshal Bernard Law Montgomery (Michael Bates), on whose ego the real-life Patton blamed thousands of needless Allied deaths. The film follows Patton's career from his arrival in Tunisia in March 1943, to take charge of U.S. troops, through the Battle of the Bulge and the end of the war—including Patton slapping a young soldier who was in the hospital for a case of nerves, which Patton simply couldn't abide. (Played by Tim Considine, the nameless soldier was a synthesis of men involved in two separate slapping incidents). The negative publicity caused by the slap nearly destroyed the general's career; Patton didn't do himself much good even after reaching Berlin, creating quite a stir when he tried to convince General Eisenhower to rearm the Germans and turn them against the Soviets, feeling it was better to fight them now rather than later. (The remaining months in the general's life are covered in the overlong but above-average 1986 TV movie *The Last Days of Patton*, also starring Scott. It isn't available on laserdisc.)

Scott's performance is electrifying and incredibly accurate and tends to overshadow the superlative work of Malden and the rest of the cast. The second-unit and special-effects crews also deserve credit for the memorable battle scenes.

The film was a huge success: Ironically,

Patton's heroics made him a symbol for the hawks during the early 1970s, while his rebelliousness earned him a large following among the anti-Establishment doves.

Scott declined to accept the Oscar he was awarded for the film, declaring the awards a sham and a "meat parade." Instead, he watched a hockey game and went to bed.

The Disc
Video: ★★★
Audio: ★★★★ (stereo)
Chapters: Yes
Format: CLV
Source: CBS Fox Video

Filmed in the wide-screen D-150 process, the screen is packed with people, tanks, planes, and sets (built in Spain) that would be seriously compromised without letterboxing. As it is, the edges of the letterboxed picture are missing, though nothing crucial is lost.

The pan-and-scan edition gives you Scott's performance but little else.

The colors are very good and the picture is sharp, though not *quite* as sharp as other films of this type (for example, *The Battle of the Bulge* and *The Dirty Dozen;* see pages 20 and 68). There's little video noise, even in the reds of that huge American flag at the beginning of the film, though there are some minor blemishes and image warping here and there.

The film boasts smashing directional effects, and, considering its age, the digital audio is quite clear.

The disc includes four Movietone newsreels about Patton, his death, and his legacy.

Penn & Teller Get Killed (1989)
★★
Director: Arthur Penn
Running Time: 90 minutes

Penn Jillette and Teller (that's his full name; it says so on his driver's license) are the bad boys of magic, comedian/magicians who reveal how classic tricks are achieved, who debunk fakes, and who will find a high-tech or bloody twist to old standards wherever possible. In their stage act, they don't just pull your card off the top of the deck: Penn drives a dagger through Teller's hand and impales the card on his bloody palm. And no ventriloquist's dummy for these guys: Onstage, they're accompanied by the electrode-wired head of Mofo the amazing talking ape.

Because the duo is so inventive, fans expected a lot from their feature film debut. And it starts out with great promise: a terrific trick on a TV talk show, followed by Penn suggesting to the host that life sure would be exciting if someone was trying to kill him. That's followed by a hilarious scene at an airport, with Teller ingeniously causing the metal detector to go off every time the increasingly irate Penn tries to goes through. After that, things go downhill. Someone *is* trying to kill Penn, and he goes into hiding, leaving it up to Teller to find out who it is.

The plot is devoid of clever twists and witty repartee until the very funny climax. But by that time, Penn & Teller fans will be so steeped in disappointment that *nothing* will cheer them, while nonfans won't even make it that far.

Caitlin Clarke does a very good job as the duo's manager, Carlotta, and there are some fine Atlantic City locales. David Patrick Kelly (the psycho killer from *Dreamscape*) is extremely effective as the nut who's stalking Penn (or is he?). Arthur Penn, who gave us *The Miracle Worker* (1962) and *Bonnie and Clyde* (1967), brings absolutely nothing to the party.

The Disc
Video: ★★★
Audio: ★★½ (Surround)
Chapters: Yes
Format: CLV
Source: Warner Home Video

Though several scenes are a bit grainy, the picture is generally sharp and bright, the colors solid, and there's very little video noise. Nothing crucial is missing from the cropped picture. Obviously, the director knew this one was going to be seen mostly on tape.

The audio is snappy and there are some nice directional effects, but, for the most part, the Surround speakers get to sit this one out.

The Perfect Weapon (1991)
★★★
Director: Mark DiSalle
Running Time: 85 minutes

When his mentor Kim (Mako) is slain, kenpo karate master Jeff (black belt Jeff Speakman)—a drifter—goes in search of his killer, aided and occasionally blocked by his kid brother, Adam (John Dye), a "stay within the law" cop. Their search brings them into the camps of rival gangsters, one of whom seeks to become the only game in town by tricking Jeff into attacking mobsters who had nothing to do with Kim's death. When Jeff finds out he's been duped, it's showdown time!

It's tough to figure out just *why* this film bombed at the box office. The plot isn't bad: There are a lot of twists and turns, and God knows there's enough martial-arts combat. The fact that Speakman isn't as bone-breakingly bloody or mean as Steven Seagal or Jean-Claude Van Damme may have had something to do with it. However, he's an appealing star (even women who don't like the genre seem to like Speakman) and the many fight scenes are lulus.

DiSalle obviously learned a lot from the mistakes he made directing Van Damme in the formless *Kickboxer* (1989). Hopefully, he—and Speakman—will be back.

The Disc
Video: ★★½
Audio: ★★★½ (Surround)
Chapters: No
Format: CLV (side one), CAV (side two)
Source: Paramount Home Video

Despite some video noise and a loss of detail in a number of the darker scenes, the transfer is good, with a generally sharp picture. The film was shot TV-safe, so cropping isn't a problem.

The stereo separation is excellent, and the rear channels shine during the car chase and other action scenes.

Peter Pan (1953) ★★★★★
Directors: Hamilton Luske, Clyde Geronimi, Wilfred Jackson
Running Time: 76 minutes

Back in 1939, Walt Disney realized that James M. Barrie's *Peter Pan* would make an ideal animated film, and he bought the rights to it. However, between various other projects and World War II, it wasn't until 1949 that he was able to put the $4 million feature into production.

One night, Peter Pan (voice of Bobby Driscoll) and the fairy Tinker Bell show up in the London nursery of the Darling children to reclaim Peter's shadow, which had been captured on a previous visit by Wendy (voice of Kathryn Beaumont, who was also the voice of Alice in Disney's *Alice In Wonderland*, 1951). His arrival wakes the children, who include Wendy's younger siblings, Michael (voice of Paul Collins) and John (voice of Tommy Luske). Sprinkling fairy dust on the trio so they can fly, Peter takes them to Never-Never-Land where they battle and defeat Pan's nemesis, Captain Hook (voice of Hans Conried), and his fumbling mate Mr. Smee (voice of Bill Thompson).

Peter Pan is one of Disney's most underappreciated films. For years, it was overshadowed by the annual TV presentation of Mary Martin's *Peter Pan* (aired annually from 1955–1972). Disney's film sticks less to the Barrie play than the TV version (for example, the audience is not required to clap to save Tink's life when she's injured), and, for the first time in film or theater, Peter was "played" by a boy. It's also the first time Tinker Bell was shown as something other than a beam of light, the Disney artists modeling her after Marilyn Monroe (they deserved to have some fun during the long animation process).

Peter Pan hasn't the same kind of virtuoso animation found in the early Disney films: Characters are rendered with uniform rather than molded colors, and there are very few multiplane shots—animation filmed through several levels of foreground art to give the scene a three-dimensional effect. The major one here is a doozy, though: Peter and the kids flying through the clouds over London, with the Thames sparkling below them. Viewers with a fear of heights are advised *not* to watch this scene.

What makes the film work are the characterizations and the comedy. The emphasis on slapstick is wildly successful: Pan's rescue of the Indian princess Tiger Lily from Hook is one of the funniest sequences ever created by the Disney animators, with the final duel a close runner-up. Poor Hook ranks with Donald Duck as the top Disney character, who, every time he thinks he's in control, ends up with a pie in the face. He's an utter delight.

This is a timeless film for children and adults alike: Along with *The Three Caballeros* (see page 278), it deserves far more attention than it's usually accorded by Disney buffs.

The Disc

Video: ★★★
Audio: ★★★ (Surround)
Chapters: No (CLV), Yes (CAV)
Format: CAV and CLV editions
Source: Walt Disney Home Video

The colors of the film are brilliant, though it doesn't have lines that are *quite* as sharply defined as later films, such as *The Little Mermaid* (see page 175). This, plus a bit of video noise, causes the colors to look just a bit runny in places. The frames on the CAV edition are jitter-free.

The audio is clear and free of background noise, and the rechanneled Surround is for sound effects and music only, not dialogue. That's okay: When they tamper that way with the audio of old movies (as they did for *Bambi* [1942] adding directional dog barking), the results are jarringly out of place.

The Mary Martin version is also available on laserdisc, though the quality is severely compromised by the pale condition of the source material.

Phantom of the Opera (1943)
★★½
Director: Arthur Lubin
Running Time: 93 minutes

What's amazing about this movie is what the filmmakers elected to do with the material: Turn it from a gothic romance to a Nelson Eddy musical, softening the horror element so it's flavorless pap. (Eddy and costar Susanna Foster even get top billing over Claude Raines, who plays the Phantom!) This isn't to say the movie is without merit; it's simply not the masterpiece it could have been.

Gaston Leroux's novel *The Phantom of the Opera* (1908; curiously referred to as a "composition" in the movie's credits) is about Erik, who, hideously ugly at birth, runs away from home and eventually ends up in Paris, where he helps design the Paris opera house, which includes a secret residence for himself. Falling in love with singer Christine Daae, he gives her lessons, kills to further her career, then decides he wants to marry her—which doesn't sit well with her lover, Raoul de Chagny. Eventually, the spurned Phantom releases Christine from any obligations and dies of a broken heart.

The first version of the film, made in 1925, starred Lon Chaney, Sr., in his most famous role. The movie is a faithful, if abbreviated, version of the novel, with the exception that the Phantom is chased by an angry mob, beaten, and thrown in the Seine. (Preview audiences had reacted negatively to the broken heart ending with which the film had originally ended.)

The second version, with sound and color, uses the same opera set built for the Chaney film (indeed, the set still stands on a soundstage at Universal; other sets are built inside of it), but very little remains of the Leroux tale.

Erique Claudin, a violinist with the Paris Opéra, is dismissed when an ailment in his fingers makes it impossible for him to play. Sadly, Erique has no money saved up: For three years, he has secretly been paying for singing lessons for aspiring diva Christine DuBois (Foster). Hoping to raise money by selling a concerto, Erique takes his manuscript to Louis Pleyel (Miles Mander). Pleyel (who was, in fact, a noted music publisher in nineteenth-century Paris) regards Erique's music as second-rate and tells him to leave. Hearing Franz Liszt playing the music in another room, Erique wrongly assumes Pleyel has stolen it. As the violinist strangles him to death, the publisher's alarmed girlfriend, Georgette (Renee Carson), throws etching acid in his face. The disfigured Erique runs from the building and crawls into a sewer, where he turns to murder to further Christine's career. Eventually, the Phantom abducts her, and her two suitors, singer Anatole Garron (Eddy) and Inspector Raoul de Chagny (Edgar Barrier) pursue him. They corner the Phantom in the catacombs beneath the opera house, where Chagny foolishly fires his gun and causes a cave-in. The Phantom is buried, and the two men escape with Christine.

This was the first film Eddy made without his longtime singing partner, Jeanette MacDonald, their sweet operettas having fallen out of favor during the war. He seems uncomfortable here; and he gets no help from Susanna Foster, who's appealling but is no Jeanette MacDonald.

Because this film was designed first and foremost as a Nelson Eddy vehicle, there was no room for a third leading man–type. Thus, the producers cast distinguished character actor Rains as the forty-eight-year-old Erique. He's good—when was he not?—but there's very little drama in a Phantom who's no longer a dynamic madman but a kindhearted, silver-haired violinist who is so decent that he does all his killing (except for Pleyel) offcamera. His disfigurement and first appearance as the Phantom occur in brightly lighted rooms, and he's almost never seen in shadow; when he's finally unmasked, his "horrifying" face looks like a cheekful of pizza—not a shinning moment for Jack Pierce, creator of the legendary Universal makeups such as the Wolf Man, the Mummy, the Frankenstein Monster, and so on (though he was obviously under orders not to scare off Eddy's fans by making Erique *too* grotesque).

So *Phantom of the Opera* (no *The*) is not a horror film and it's barely tolerable as a romance. Yet, the film is entrancing to look at thanks to the lavish sets, colorful costumes, and brilliant Technicolor photography. It's also fun to listen to, full of charming pseudo-operas: Eddy and Foster sing Tchaikovsky's Symphony No. 4, Chopin's famous Nocturne in B-flat Major, and other compositions that have been transposed to the operatic form.

Fritz Leiber—father of fantasy writer Fritz Leiber, Jr.—does a nice job as Franz Liszt, while Hume Cronyn is sturdy in a small role as Chagny's aide, Gerard.

A third theatrical *Phantom of the Opera* features Herbert Lom as Professor Petrie of the London Opera. Though this Hammer film is truer to the Rains film than to the novel, it is very much a horror film. The big, moronic twist in *this* version is that the Phantom sacrifices his life to save his lover from a falling chandelier. A fourth version stars Robert Englund (of Freddy Krueger fame) as the phantom and has neither atmosphere, romance, nor class, emphasizing the slasher aspects of the tale.

The Disc

Video: ★★★½
Audio: ★★★½ (monaural)
Chapters: Yes (Keyed to the musical sequences)
Format: CLV
Source: MCA Home Video

Since the physical trappings and music are about all the film has to offer, it's a good thing the disc looks and sounds as good as it does. Though the Technicolor print doesn't have *quite* the punch of *The Adventures of Don Juan* or *The Band Wagon* (see pages 2 and 17), and there's a bit of noise in the red dresses, it's still a visual feast, with a tremendous sense of depth in the opera and especially in the catacombs.

The digital audio is superb, remarkably full-bodied, given the age of the film.

The trailer is included; and though the colors are muddy, you'll be treated to a different take of the gunshot scene that brings down the roof.

The Chaney version is available in two laser editions, the best of which is from Lumivision and was transferred from the George Eastman House's beautiful 35mm acetate print, which was struck from the original nitrate negative before it fell to pieces. The presentation also features an early and impressive two-color Technicolor sequence—the masquerade ball—spliced in from UCLA's Film and Television Archives, and an organ score recorded in 1989.

The Englund film is available and is to be avoided.

The Philadelphia Story (1940)
★★★★
Director: George Cukor
Running Time: 112 minutes

Apart from a good "boo" and a spectacular train wreck, one of the cinema's greatest pleasures is a strong cast doing brilliant ensemble work. That's what you get in *The Philadelphia Story*, along with a plot that could have been torn from today's tabloid headlines.

Young blue blood Tracy Lord (Katharine Hepburn) is about to marry for the second time, and her ex-husband, C. K. Dexter Haven (Cary Grant), is piqued. To get back at the publicity-shy woman, he arranges for reporter Macaulay "Mike" Connor (Jimmy Stewart) and photographer Liz Imbrie (Ruth Hussey) to arrive at the Lord estate on the eve of the wedding and provide complete coverage for *Spy* magazine.

In the hours before the wedding, events and realizations (albeit, mightily telescoped) cause people to change dramatically: Mike finds himself repulsed by his job and yearning to write short stories, C. K. concludes that alcohol is not the answer to life's problems, and Tracy finds herself torn between three men—Mike, her ex-husband, and her fiancé, George Kittredge (John Howard), a self-made man who is nonetheless not in her social class.

Hepburn had done the wise, catty *The Philadelphia Story* on the stage in 1939 (with Van Heflin as Mike and Joseph Cotten as C. K.) and bought the screen rights from playwright Philip Barry. Despite several offers, she refused to sell them unless she got to star, along with Stewart and Grant (her previous two films had been with Grant, *Bringing Up Baby* and *Holiday*, both 1938); Hollywood wanted the project and finally buckled. Grant donated his $137,500 salary to the British Relief War Fund.

The film was remade in 1956 as *High Society*, with Grace Kelly (in her last screen performance), Bing Crosby, and Frank Sinatra. Despite some great Cole Porter songs, it doesn't have the wit or style of the original.

The Disc
Video: ★
Audio: ★ (monaural)
Chapter: No
Format: CLV
Source: MGM/UA Home Video

Discs such as this one are *not* what laser video is all about, and it's shocking how little respect studios have for their old films.

The Philadelphia Story—both the original transfer and a barely better remaster—is presented with all the care and affection of a B movie: Scratches and dirt abound, particularly around the reel changes and especially on side one and the first third of side two. The levels of contrast are satisfactory, but that isn't soft focus for Ms. Hepburn: The entire film is slightly fuzzy (made, it seems, from a 16mm print).

The audio is alive with pops and crackles; at the very least, the sound should have been cleaned up so the viewer could enjoy Hepburn and Grant in their prime delivering great lines.

High Society is also available on laserdisc. The newly remastered, mildly letterboxed film boasts generally solid color and excellent stereo sound.

The Pink Panther (1964)
★★★★
Director: Blake Edwards
Running Time: 116 minutes

Originally, the eight-film Pink Panther series wasn't intended to be a series: Inspector Clouseau (Peter Sellers) wasn't even the main character in the first film. Nor was Sellers the director's first choice to play him—Peter Ustinov had been cast, but he left after Edwards refused to cast Ava Gardner as Princess Dala. Edwards had in mind someone younger and a bona fide European. The movie was just a few weeks from going before the cameras, and Sellers came aboard with little preparation.

The characterization came to the actor while he was flying to Rome, where the movie was being shot. There was a picture of a mustachioed, virile Englishman on a box of matches, and Sellers decided he would use the mustache as a veneer of viriltiy for the character. Though the script described the inspector as a "complete idiot," Sellers felt Clouseau should have "great dignity, because he thinks of himself as one of the world's best detectives. Even when he comes a cropper, he must pick himself up with that notion intact."

Edwards liked Sellers's ideas, though he insisted that the character remain extraordinarily clumsy: The director felt that that would make the character's unflappable dignity all the more amusing. Sellers hadn't done much slapstick in his previous two dozen films, but he agreed to give it a try. The rest is comedy history.

Dashing cat burglar Sir Charles Layton, the Phantom (David Niven), is determined to steal "the most fabulous diamond in all the world," the Pink Panther (named for a panther-shaped discoloration) from its owner, Princess Dala (Claudia Cardinale). He follows her to the Cortina D'Ampezzo ski resort, intending to get to know her and learn where the gem is kept. Realizing that the jewel will be a tempting target for his old nemesis, Inspector Jacques Clouseau also heads from Paris to Italy in an effort to catch him. Complicating matters are the fact that the inspector's wife, Simone (Capucine), is in league with Layton *and* is his lover, and that Layton's nephew George (Robert Wagner), newly arrived from Hollywood, also lusts after Simone.

From the charming opening credits, which feature an animated Pink Panther (the future cartoon star's first appearance), to the climactic masquerade ball that ends with an hilarious car chase in which everyone's in costume, the movie is a constant delight. Though Layton's seduction of Princess Dala goes on *far* too long, and George is an annoying, extraneous character, Sellers, Niven, and Capucine are splendid.

The Pink Panther—like most films in the series—tends to get better with repeated viewings. Anticipating the falls or social gaffes or Clouseau's unrelenting ineptitude (as an inspector, lover, and violinist) allows you to savor them as he heads toward disaster like a "meurth" to flame.

In addition to *A Shot in the Dark* (see page 250), Sellers starred in *The Return of the Pink Panther* (1975), *The Pink Panther Strikes Again* (1976), and *Revenge of the Pink Panther* (1978); after *A Shot in the Dark*, the films became increasingly worse. *The Romance of the Pink Panther* was in the planning stages when Sellers died in 1980.

The non-Sellers films are *Inspector Clouseau* (1968), starring Alan Arkin, *Trail of the Pink Panther* (1982), which criminally uses outtakes and previously unseen footage of Sellers, and *Curse of the Pink Panther* (1983), starring Ted Wass.

The Disc
Video: ★★
Audio: ★★ (monaural)
Chapters: No
Format: CLV
Source: MGM/UA Home Video

The film has been remastered and generously letterboxed, the latter working wonders for the comedy (try to imagine, panned-and-scanned, the scene with the two apes cracking the safe). Too bad the transfer isn't as satisfying. The image is a little soft and the colors slightly washed-out. Grain and video noise are minimal. ("But of course, my dahling. The reds are so pale!")

The audio has an insistent hiss that will encourage you to keep the volume down. The film's trailer is included.

The Return of the Pink Panther and *Revenge of the Pink Panther* are available on laserdisc, the latter letterboxed—an okay transfer of an excruciatingly bad film.

The Pirates of Penzance (1982)
★★★★★
Director: Wilford Leach
Running Time: 112 minutes

English composer Arthur Sullivan and librettist William Gilbert wrote more than two hundred songs in their fourteen operettas. Two of their works—*H.M.S. Pinafore* (1878) and *The Mikado* (1885)—have been worldwide favorites since their premieres. Conversely, *The Pirates of Penzance*, which premiered in New York in 1879 and was successfully revived on its centennial (with largely the same cast that appears in the film), was never one of their more popular works.

Part of the problem was that it followed the successful *H.M.S. Pinafore*. In fact, the creators were forced to make concessions to audience expectations. Originally, the new operetta was to be called *The Robbers of Redruth*, and there wasn't a privateer in sight. However, feeling that audiences would want another seagoing locale, Gilbert reworked the libretto. Unfortunately, using the familiar setting only invited comparisons.

Another problem was that, despite Sullivan's accurate assessment that this play was "of a higher class altogether," the score is more like grand opera and lacks the light, catchy tunes of the previous operetta (with the exception of the stirring "With Cat-Like Tread," better known to audiences as the 1917 reworking "Hail, Hail, the Gang's All Here").

Finally, as opposed to the proper Victorians of *H.M.S. Pinafore*, the characters in *The Pirates of Penzance* are all slightly mad—not what audiences of the day were interested in. Yet, it is the characters' timeless ineptitude that helps to make the operetta so appealing to modern audiences. *The Pirates of Penzance* could easily have been filmed using Bugs Bunny and the Warner Brothers cartoon stable and *still* been true to Gilbert and Sullivan.

Apprenticed to pirates, young, handsome Frederic (Rex Smith) is twenty-one years old and finally free of his indentures. He departs the ship of the brash but dim-witted Pirate King (Kevin Kline), accompanied by his erstwhile nursery maid, Ruth (Angela Lansbury). Going ashore at Cornwall, Frederic falls in love with the beautiful Mabel (Linda Ronstadt), one of the daughters of the stuffy Major General Stanley (George Rose). Being an honest lad, Frederic deems it his duty to destroy the pirates—until the Pirate King realizes that Frederic was born in a leap year, meaning he must remain a pirate until 1940. Frederic rejoins the group and it's up to the chickenhearted constabulary to pursue and engage the pirates, though the battle ends happily when Ruth reveals that the pirates aren't pirates at all, but noblemen. The buccaneers agree to go straight, marry Stanley's daughters, and all ends happily.

The film was shot more or less like a stage play, complete with theatre-style sets and broad performances. But it works—gloriously. The clever lines, inventive rhymes, and delightful plot twists are all here, and Kline couldn't be more blithering, appealing, or athletic. Smith is appropriately dense and heroic, and Tony Azito stops the show as the rubber-limbed Sergeant of Police. Ronstadt looks and sounds fine in her role as the precious, porcelain Mabel, and Angela Lansbury has yet to give a less-than-magical musical performance. Only purists will mind the few minor changes, which include extending "With Cat-Like Tread" to allow Kline a welcome extra few measures of dance at the end, and borrowing the song "My Eyes Are Fully Open" from Gilbert and Sullivan's *Ruddigore*.

A nonmusical version of the play, *The Pirate Movie*, was released the same year, starring Kristy McNichol and Christopher Atkins. Pray that this awful film is never released on laserdisc.

The Disc
Video: ★★
Audio: ★★★ (stereo)
Chapters: Yes
Format: CLV
Source: MCA/Universal Home Video

The movie is moderately grainy during the night scenes, which occupy the bulk of side two. This was a problem in the original film (which was shot entirely on soundstages), so don't blame the transfer. On the other hand ...

There's a sequence (chapter six, 16:08–12) when Kline and Lansbury are on opposite ends of the screen, Smith is in the middle, and each is singing alternately. In order to get them all in, the telecine operator pans the print *so* fast that you glimpse everything while seeing nothing. In scenes before and after this, the operator simply loses Kline and Lansbury off the sides. During "With Cat-Like Tread," Kline is actually out of the picture entirely on the right while leaping a hedge!

Shouldn't it have been obvious to MCA that letterboxing was called for? The core audience for the disc (and tape) are fans of the show, and those viewers would surely want to see everyone who is singing and dancing.

If that wasn't bad enough, while the sound is perfectly clear and the stereo separation is excellent, the channels are reversed. This is so annoying that it's a good idea to switch your cables before watching the film.

The original stage version starring Kline, Ronstadt, and Lansbury, taped in 1983, is also available, with the stereo channels piped from the proper sides. The camera angles and sets aren't quite as interesting, but at least the play was staged for a TV camera, so there's no panning-and-scanning.

Another filmed stage version, starring Peter Allen, sticks more closely to the original Gilbert and Sullivan arrangements and choreography. Be advised, though, that acrobatically and vocally, Allen is no Kevin Kline.

Planet of the Apes (1968)
★★★★½
Director: Franklin J. Schaffner
Running Time: 112 minutes.

In 1963, the publicist-turned-producer Arthur P. Jacobs was ready to make his first motion picture and was looking for a property like *King Kong*. In Paris, a literary agent showed him a brand-new book by Pierre Boulle, author of *The Bridge on the River Kwai*: It was called *Planet of the Apes*, a cautionary tale of astronaut Ulysse Merou who lands on the planet Soror, where apes are the rulers and humans the inarticulate savages. The astronaut eventually returns to earth, only to discover that it, too, is now run by apes.

Jacobs optioned the novel, had sketches made of the ape characters, hired science fiction author Rod Serling to write a script—but he wasn't able to interest a studio in backing the film. He ended up making *What a Way to Go!* (1964) and *Doctor Doolittle* (1967) before Twentieth Century–Fox agreed to do a screen test, showing how the astronaut would interact with someone wearing ape makeup—not a mask but "appliances," a lower muzzle, upper muzzle, nose, and cheeks that would move with the actor's face. Charlton Heston and Edward G. Robinson believed in the project and agreed to appear in the test as the astronaut and as Dr. Zaius, the Minister of Science and Chief Defender of the Faith. When no one in a selected audience laughed at the footage, Fox gave the project the green lighted. There was, however, one stippulation. Serling's screenplay described a modern ape city in which everything was like our world but built to simian proportions. The sets would have been very expensive, so, in a new draft, writer Michael Wilson came up with the primitive city seen in the finished film. Unfortunately, before the project got under way, Robinson told Jacobs that he'd felt claustrophic in the ape makeup and declined to do the film; likewise Julie Harris, who was originally cast as Zira.

Astronaut George Taylor (Heston) and three companions crash land on the ape world, which is ruled by fear and religion, with science tolerated as long as it serves official doctrines. One of the astronauts died en route, another is lobotomized, a third is taxidermied and placed in a museum. Only Taylor survives, and chimpanzee scientist Zira (Kim Hunter) and her fiancé, Cornelius (Roddy McDowall), are astounded by his simian-level intelligence. Their superior, the orangutan Dr. Zaius (Maurice Evans), fears Taylor and orders him castrated so there won't be any more like him. Taylor escapes with the help of Zira and Cornelius and they venture into the Forbidden Zone, followed by Zaius and gorilla soldiers. There, they find proof that intelligent humans inhabited the world before intelligent apes. Zaius orders the evidence destroyed: He wants no trace of that brutal breed of human to survive. Alone, Taylor and a woman savage, Nova (Linda Harrison), venture deeper into the Forbidden Zone, where they discover why Zaius fears knowledge and humans alike: The ruins of the Statue of Liberty tell them that this is earth, staggering back to civilization after a nuclear holocaust.

Heston has never been better than as the cynical Taylor, and Hunter, Evans, and McDowall are excellent. The expressions they generate from beneath John Chambers's detailed rubbery appliances are truly amazing.

Jacobs was vindicated by the success of *Planet of the Apes*, and it spawned four sequels, the first two of which are available on letterboxed laserdiscs. In *Beneath the Planet of the Apes* (1970), James Franciscus plays Brent, the head of a rescue mission, who finds Taylor, along with a society of telepathic mutant humans, living underground and worshiping an atom bomb. The planet is destroyed in a nuclear holocaust triggered by Taylor, but not before Zira and Cornelius use one of the spaceships to flee to modern-day Los Angeles in *Escape from the Planet of the Apes* (1971). Apes employed as slave labor revolt in *Conquest of the Planet of the Apes* (1972), then fight for world supremacy in *Battle for the Planet of the Apes* (1973). Movies cobbled together from episodes of the hour-long TV series (which ignores the continuity of the films) are not available on disc.

The Disc

Video: ★★★
Audio: ★★★ (Surround)
Chapters: Yes
Format: CLV
Source: Twentieth Century–Fox

The colors on the wide-screen edition are fairly washed-out, but the image is very sharp and the letterboxing captures the film's imposing landscapes and sprawling ape village, though the picture has been opened up slightly to lessen the severity of the matte.

Though the film was recorded in stereo, Fox was unable to locate the original tracks. Thus, they've rechanneled the audio for stereo Surround, doing a good but not perfect job. Though the digital audio is clear and the stereo effects impressive—particularly during the crash of the ship—you'll notice that in spots they've got it backwards: Dialogue rather than "effects" and ambient sounds have been sent to the rear speakers. They also haven't been properly balanced: Small sounds are often *way* louder than they should be, competing with dialogue and music for our attention.

The extras on the disc are pitiful, consisting of reproductions of posters from two of the sequels—and not very good posters at that.

For the record, the photo below the text inside the jacket is from *Beneath the Planet of the Apes*.

Plan 9 from Outer Space
(1959) ★★★
Director: Edward D. Wood, Jr.
Running Time: 78 minutes

This is not a good movie by any means. In fact, it is a shockingly amateurish film that has appeared on countless "Worst Movies of All Time" lists. Yet, as has been pointed out wherever the film is discussed, its badness is so extreme, it becomes a merit in itself, a fascinating ugliness, if you will, and the movie can be entertaining as long as you understand what you're seeing and know what to look for.

In the twilight of his career, actor Bela Lugosi made two films for the ambitious and sincere but hopelessly inept Edward D. Wood, Jr.: *Glen or Glenda?* (1953), the director's semiautobiographical film about transvestism, and *Bride of the Monster* (1955), a supercheap but moderately entertaining mad-scientist opus. In 1956, in very poor health and needing money, Lugosi began a third film for Wood, *The Vampire's Tomb*. Lugosi died shortly after filming got under way.

The few minutes of Lugosi footage sat in Wood's home until he wrote a new screenplay entitled *Grave Robbers from Outer Space*, which was ultimately released as *Plan 9 from Outer Space*. The film incorporated the Lugosi footage, with a double (chiropractor Tom Mason, who looked nothing like him) helping to link it to the rest of the film.

Lugosi appears as a nameless old man who, while silently mourning his late (also nameless) wife (Vampira), is run down by a truck (offcamera). Concurrently, pilot Jeff Trent (Gregory Walcott) sees a flying saucer. Back at the cemetery, the dead wife rises from her grave, frightening a pair of grave diggers to death; Inspector Clay (Swedish wrestler-turned-actor Tor Johnson) investigates and he, too, is murdered by the woman. Her dead husband also walks the earth again, his face hidden behind a Dracula cape. And what's the reason for all of this zombie activity? A group of extraterrestrials—Eros (Dudley Manlove) and Tanna (Joanna Lee), who answer to the Ruler (John "Bunny" Breckinridge) back home—have been resurrecting the corpses by means of "long-distance electrodes shot into the pineal-pituitary glands of the recent dead" in order to convince earthlings that the aliens exist (the saucers weren't enough?). This dramatic Plan 9 (no mention of plans 1 through 8) is intended to persuade us to discontinue research into Solaronite bombs, which detonate particles of sunlight and have the power to destroy the universe—or something to that effect.

The script is not terribly clear or consistent. However, it *is* enjoyable, with its alternately arch and elevated speech—that is, the revved-up narrator with the Frostee-whip coiffure (Criswell, a Burbank mystic) intoning, "Death, the proud brother, comes without warning," or "The ever-beautiful flowers she had planted with her own hands became nothing more than the last roses on her cheeks."

Fortunately, the movie's merits are not restricted to the loony screenplay. Breckinridge and Manlove seem to think they're in a Shakespearean drama, albeit different ones: Breckinridge's style is rhapsodic, as though he was playing Prospero in *The Tempest*, while Manlove's is elegiac, like *Hamlet*. In a movie filled with classic moments, a highlight is Manlove, with his deep baritone voice, ramrod posture, and a filigree flourish of the fingers, offering up a graphic description of the ultimate fate of humankind.

But it's not the only great moment. The highlight *has* to be poor Colonel Edwards (Tom Keene), who's put in charge of fighting the flying saucers and is warned by General Roberts (Lyle Talbot) that he could be court-martialed if he expresses a belief in them.

Then there are the film's special effects: The modified (but not very) hubcaps that serve as flying saucers follow some peculiar aerodynamics, blowing when caught in an updraft (1/25:10–25:22), or the patio furniture jerked aside by wires representing a saucer's powerful exhaust.

The movie is chock-a-block with things to be savored—not the least of which is Vampira (Maila Nurmi), the short-skirted Scandinavian-born L. A. TV hostess who turned a million little boys into horror fans just by crossing her legs.

Wood made a few other low-budget films, turned to writing pornography in the 1970s, and died a homeless alcoholic in 1978. This is the only one of his films available on laserdisc. (Doesn't anyone realize how well a Wood boxed set would do, especially if it contained the recently discovered *Take It Out in Trade*?)

Note: The film was completed and shown to selected audiences in 1958, though it was not officially released until 1959.

The Disc
Video: ★★½
Audio: ★½ (monaural)
Chapters: No
Format: CLV (side one), CAV (side two)
Source: Wade Williams Productions

For a picture that's been kicking around for nearly a third of a century, and given very little respect during that time, the transfer is surprisingly decent. The print is in pretty good shape, with good contrast: You'll have no trouble seeing where the mats of fake grass are overlaid in the graveyard.

The audio is much shakier, and the mock-Stravinsky score with loping basses and blaring punctuations of brass sounds truly rinky-dink.

Incidentally, the jacket makes use of the original lurid poster art, which is actually a great improvement over most of the new work being done by marketing departments (see *First Men in the Moon*).

The Poseidon Adventure
(1972) ★★★½
Director: Ronald Neame
Running Time: 117 minutes

The late Irwin Allen made some pretty good science fiction films during his long career, such as *The Lost World* (1960) and *Voyage to the Bottom of the Sea* (1961). He also produced the TV series "Lost in Space" and "The Time Tunnel," among others. Then, in 1972, after a decade away from films, inspired by the success of *Airport* (1970), he shifted to the disaster genre and scored big with the $5 million *The Poseidon Adventure*. He followed it with the even bigger *The Towering Inferno* (1974). Unfortunately, Allen went to the well once too often and, in quick succession, made the megaflops *The Swarm* (1978), *Beyond the Poseidon Adventure* (1979), and the volcano epic *When Time Ran Out* (1980). Unable to launch his pet film *Circus*! and never able to come up with a big screen treatment of "Lost in Space" that satisfied him, he remained more or less in retirement until his death in 1991.

The Poseidon Adventure is based on the 1969 novel by Paul Gallico, about a group of passengers's efforts to survive after a seismic wave hits the liner three-quarters broadside and overturns it. The film retains most of the book's characters: the rebellious Reverend Frank Scott (Gene Hackman); Mike Rogo (Ernest Borgnine), a hard cop with a heart of gold; his wife, Linda (Stella Stevens), a former hooker with a sharp tongue and foul mouth (an actress in the novel); lonely bachelor James Martin (Red Buttons); young singer Nona "Nonnie" Parry (Carol Lynley); steward Acres (Roddy McDowall); Israel-bound Belle and Manny Rosen (Shelley Winters and Jack Albertson); and eighteen-year-old Susan Shelby (Pamela Sue Martin) and her plucky ten-year-old brother, Robin (Eric Shea).

The characters leave the overturned dining salon; as they try to make their way past the new waterline, where they *hope* they'll find an exit, they survive floods, explosions, and the deaths of several members of the party. What becomes obvious fairly quickly is that this is really a biblical parable disguised as a group jeopardy film, with an angel (Scott), a tempting devil (Rogo), sinners, and martyrs. Given the limited amount of time each character has onscreen, they're pleasantly affecting, memorable, and/or funny.

Director Neame deserves a lot of credit for the film's success, and Allen deserves a lot of credit for having hired him. Allen had experience with spectacle, and Neame —director of *Tunes of Glory* (1960) and *The Prime of Miss Jean Brodie* (1969)— fleshed out the characters in ways that subsequent disaster films failed to do. Don't misunderstand: The dialogue isn't Albee. But it isn't *Airport 1975* (1974) or *Earthquake* (see page 78), either. (Neame seems to have reached his peak on this film: His next disaster film, *Meteor* [1979] was one of the worst movies ever made.)

Everyone in the cast does a fine job, but Hackman is especially strong as the opinionated, iron-willed clergyman, and Winters is both touching and funny as Belle. Unfortunately, many viewers are going to have a tough time with Leslie Nielsen as the doomed Captain Harrison: He delivers his lines with the same seriousness that make him so funny in later movies such as *Airplane!* (1980) and *The Naked Gun* (1988).

Visually, the art directors did a magnificent job. They're always throwing something new at the audience, and the novelty of the upside-down sets doesn't wear off.

The film's exteriors were shot on the *Queen Mary*, while the dining-salon set was built on lifts to tilt it thirty degrees for the spectacular scene in which the ship rolls over. The shots of the full ship —even in the opening scenes—were done using generally convincing miniatures.

The Disc
Video: ★★★★
Audio: ★★★ (Surround)
Chapters: Yes
Format: CLV
Source: CBS/Fox Home Video

The letterboxed transfer is a very satisfying one, capturing the film's scope and getting everyone onscreen in the group shots. The wide-screen image is particularly effective in "selling" the rocking of the ship, which lasts for virtually the entire film.

The disc has grain and noise problems, but they're not severe, especially when you consider how dark most of the film is and how many fires and warning lights there are.

The jacket says stereo Surround, but the film sure sounds monaural. The audio is resonant and crisp, and John Williams's score and the sound effects get pumped out the rear speakers more loudly than from the front. But true stereo it definitely isn't.

The major problem with this disc, as with most Fox discs, is that it's *way* overpriced, at $49.95 for a single platter.

Predator (1987) ★★½
Director: John McTiernan
Running Time: 107 minutes

Arnold Schwarzenegger took the role of Dutch in *Predator* because he wanted to "expand his abilities." Though Arnold's not a guy you want to disagree with, isn't this film just another Schwarzenegger shoot-'em-up? "No," says Arnold. "I had to do more acting. I had to show fear."

Score one for Arnold: He *does* show fear when he goes one-on-one against the hunter from space at the end of the film. But until that point, the film is another Schwarzenegger shoot-'em-up. Not a bad one . . . but *High Noon* it isn't.

Dutch and his mercenary allies—Dillon (Carl Weathers), Blain (Jesse Ventura), and a handful of others—have been hired to head deep into a jungle in South America (actually Mexico) to rescue officials being held by terrorists. After assaulting the enemy stronghold, Dutch and Company realize that they're not the only aggressors in town: They're being stalked by a space creature (Kevin Peter Hall) who's come to earth on a safari, hunting humans. Suffice to say that not many of Dutch's party make it back alive.

John McTiernan had made only one film, *Nomads* (1986), before landing the assignment to direct *Predator*. His rapid cutting and gangbusters pace are saving graces, obscuring the fact that the leads are stiffly played by a trio of ex-athletes and that the story is just an uncredited update of Richard Connell's 1925 short story "The Most Dangerous Game," in which a big-game hunter visiting the Amazon jungle is stalked by evil General Zaroff (though *Predator* lacks the clever dialogue of the Connell tale and its various film incarnations).

The film's inventive special effects are another plus. The creature hides behind a force field that causes it to appear as a transparent, watery blur for the first three-quarters of the film. The light-displacement effect is startling. When forced from behind its shield, the creature turns out to be a dreadlocked insectlike humanoid, which—happily—isn't another rip-off of the H. R. Giger creature from *Alien* (see *Aliens*). The various dismemberments (especially Weathers's), flayings, and explosions are also extremely convincing; the film is *not* recommended for viewers who only know Schwarzenegger from *Twins* (1988) or *Kindergarten Cop* (1990).

The Disc
Video: ★★★
Audio: ★★★½ (Surround)
Chapters: Yes
Format: CLV
Source: CBS/Fox Home Video

The remastered disc is an improvement over the original release, not just because the action-packed film is letterboxed. The image is also sharper and the colors stronger, though there's a good deal of grain—some of which is present in the original film, some of it the result of the transfer. Many of the darker sequences lack detail.

The audio is as crisp and bombastic—sometimes the rear channels get a little *too* loud—though the Surround jungle and combat noises are a lot of fun.

Predator 2 (1990) ★★★
Director: Stephen Hopkins
Running Time: 108 minutes

This is a more ambitious and spectacular film than the original, better written and better acted. Unfortunately, there isn't a movie in memory whose climax falls apart as thoroughly as this one's does.

The year is 1997, and the place is not the South American jungle but Los Angeles (a fact established in a very clever opening shot). The Predator only attacks armed foes and has come here because the city's full of 'em. Los Angeles has been turned into a war zone by the police and drug gangs; even subway commuters pack heat.

Lt. Michael Harrigan (Danny Glover) is one of the city's bravest and most decorated police officers. When drug dealers and even the lieutenant's own people start dying in horrible ways, Special Federal Agent Peter Keyes (Gary Busey) shows up and Harrigan is rudely shoved aside. The reason? Keyes and his people have been hot on the Predator's trail for some time and have come up with an ingenious plan to trap and freeze the creature so they can study it. Not surprisingly, they haven't thought of *everything*, and, after the killer from space turns the tables on them, it's up to Harrigan to stop the monster.

Until Keyes and his men become victims, nearly three-quarters of the way through, the film is a crackling good thriller. That Harrigan is able to step in where a small army of trained Predator hunters has failed, take the punishment he does, and triumph is ridiculous. On top of that, the filmmakers come up with a kicker that provides a momentary jolt: After following the creature to its spaceship (unimaginatively designed, as it turns out), Harrigan finds himself surrounded by a slew of Predators. Unfortunately, the filmmakers choose *the* most boring and unlikely way to go with the confrontation, and the movie just peters out.

Glover and Busey are very good actors, and they bring along a lot of that wasn't in the script. Ruben Blades had a nice characterization too-short role as Harrigan's doomed pal, Danny. The special effects, too, are electrifying: There are a lot of tricks that weren't in the first film, such as the creature's walk through the puddle in the alley, scenes that have a sense of wonder evocative of the best of 1950s-style science fiction.

Kevin Peter Hall reprised his role as the Predator; the young actor died not long after finishing the film.

Check out the Alien-head trophy at 23/42.18.

Schwarzenegger was originally going to reprise as Dutch but couldn't come to terms with the producers. He would have been worth the roughly $15 million he'd have cost: The picture bombed without him.

The Disc
Video: ★★★½
Audio: ★★★★★ (Surround)
Chapters: Yes
Format: CLV
Source: Fox Video

It's too bad that there's a hint of grain in almost all the dark shots and a trace of red noise in spots; otherwise, the picture is as perfect as you could hope. It's stunningly clear, the letterbox is just right, and the colors are beautiful, especially point-of-view shots of the monster's "infrared vision."

Not only is the audio rich and solid but the Surround Sound is exceptional. There are so many audio "boos"—many from the rear—that the movie becomes even more unnerving. More mundane Surround effects also abound, from a gushing sprinkler system to the alien's scream. You're gonna love the audio so much, you *may* even forgive the film its moronic finale.

Pretty Woman (1990) ★★★½
Director: Garry Marshall
Running Time: 119 minutes

In this smart, entertaining update of George Bernard Shaw's *Pygmalion*, superrich takeover master Edward Lewis (Richard Gere) finds himself lost in Hollywood. He asks for directions from hooker Vivian Ward (Julia Roberts), who escorts him back to his Beverly Hills hotel. Lewis is taken with Vivian and, since his girlfriend, Jessica, has dumped him, he asks the hooker whether he can hire her to be his escort for the week. She agrees to be his "beck-and-call girl" and, of course, they fall in love. As much as Vivian changes externally, learning etiquette and wearing fine clothes, her "heart of gold" inside stays the same; Lewis, on the other hand, learns compassion, which poignantly affects his acrimonious relationship with elderly James Morse (Ralph Bellamy), who is resisting Lewis's takeover of his company. When the week is over, Vivian and Lewis part—for about ten seconds.

Predictable and sentimental as the movie is, the script is a constant delight, though it wasn't originally planned as the breezy romance it is. Originally called *Three Thousand* (the amount of money Lewis pays Vivian), it was a dark tale about prostitution until the film went from the underfinanced Vestron to Touchstone Pictures (Disney). Marshall signed on, the script was rewritten, and the film was a huge success.

Gere is perfect as the smooth, dynamic Lewis, and Roberts is sexy and sincere, if a bit too pixie-innocent, as Vivian. (She wasn't the filmmakers' first choice: Jennifer Jason Leigh was, but the actress preferred the original, darker script, feeling that prostitution was a poor subject for a "feel good" film.) The film also gets a lot of help from its supporting cast: Bellamy, Hector Elizondo as the hotel manager who goes from being indignant to paternal, Jason Alexander as Lewis's unscrupulous attorney Philip Stuckey, and Laura San Giacomo as Vivian's roommate, druggie streetwalker Kit De Luca.

The Disc
Video: ★
Audio: ★★ (Surround)
Chapters: Yes
Format: CLV
Source: Touchstone Home Video

The quality of this disc is very disappointing. Brightly lighted scenes range from clear to very clear, though the picture is rarely as sharp as it should be, and dark scenes tend to be muddy or downright opaque. There's also grain in some scenes

(5/51:07–51:16 looks as if it were shot through coffee grounds!). The film isn't hurt by cropping.

The stereo separations are good, though you'd expect more ambient sound in a film with so many party, restaurant, and street scenes.

The Princess Bride (1987)
★★★★½
Director: Rob Reiner
Running Time: 98 minutes

William Goldman's novel *The Princess Bride* (1973) is a quirky romance full of delightful nonsense. ("There have been five great kisses since 1642 B.C., when Saul and Delilah Korn's inadvertent discovery swept across Western civilization.") Leaving out the boring parts, which Goldman summarizes in authorial asides (he has said these are as dull as the chapters on whaling in *Moby-Dick*), it tells the tale of young Buttercup, whose lover, Westley, leaves Florin for America to seek his fortune. Times passes, and the wicked Prince Humperdinck notices Buttercup and wants her to become his bride. However, she's kidnapped by a "criminal organization" consisting of the Spaniard Inigo Montoya, who's a master swordsman; the powerful Fezzik, a Turk; and the Sicilian genius Vizzini. They're actually working for Humperdinck, who wants the abduction and murder of Buttercup to be blamed on neighboring Guilder so that he can go to war with them. Fortunately, Buttercup is rescued by a mysterious man in black, aka Westley, who never reached America but became the Dread Pirate Roberts. With the help Inigo and Fezzik, Roberts brings down Humperdinck and his evil aide, Count Rugen.

There may not be a film that's more faithful to a book than *The Princess Bride*. The incidents, dialogue, and characters follow Goldman's terrific novel almost precisely. Reiner has said that this was his most arduous film—not just physically but creatively as well. Goldman's script walks a *very* fine line between realism and parody, but Reiner and his incredible cast pull it off magnificently. The film is equally suitable for children and adults and boasts one of the screen's greatest swordfights, when Westley and Inigo first meet as rivals (though there's a surprising continuity flub at &/24:16 on the CLV version, with Inigo's arm extended in one shot then bent in the next).

Cary Elwes had previously starred in a handful of films, including *The Bride* (1985) and *Lady Jane* (see page 167), and he makes an astonishingly good Westley—lithe, glib, and sophisticated. He has also appeared in *Glory* (see page 109) and *Days of Thunder* (1990). Mandy Patinkin is an equally remarkable Inigo. Thanks to films such as *Yentl* (1983), *Alien Nation* (1988), *Dick Tracy* (see page 67), and *Impromptu* (see page 147), he has emerged as one of our best character actors. Also delightful are Chris Sarandon as Humperdinck, Christopher Guest as the unctuous Rugen, Wallace Shawn as Vizzini, and wrestler Andre the Giant as Fezzik. Robin Wright isn't asked to do much beside pine and look worried as Buttercup. Peter Cook, Billy Crystal, and Carol Kane put in small but memorable appearances, and Peter Falk delivers just what you'd expect as the grandfather reading the story to his grandson (Fred Savage).

The Disc
Video: ★★★★ (Criterion);
★★ (Nelson)
Audio: ★★★½ (Surround) (Criterion);
★★½ (Nelson)
Chapters: Yes
Format: CLV and CAV
Source: Criterion or Nelson
   Entertainment

Except for the freeze-frame ability, there's no reason to select the more expensive CAV edition—and, frankly, there isn't all that much you'll want to stop and study in this film. This is a movie that *moves..*

Both Criterion versions are letterboxed. There's a *very* slight softness to the images in each and a hint of noise in the reds and browns. However, the rest of the colors sing, from the primaries to the many gorgeous pastels, and the flesh tones are lifelike. Day and night scenes are both equally vivid.

The perfectly clear audio delivers excellent, if tame, ambient sounds, fine directional effects, and Mark Knopfler's terrific score.

Another version of the film is available from Nelson Entertainment, which went into the safety zone in order to fill up the entire screen. While nothing is lost, the picture isn't as clear, nor is the sound as good, and it isn't recommended. Even antiletterboxers will find the matte so mild in Criterion's editions that they shouldn't go for this much inferior version.

The Producers ★★★★½ (1968)
Director: Mel Brooks
Running Time: 89 minutes

Before going into movies, Mel Brooks was a TV writer ("Your Show of Shows," "Get Smart") and stand-up comic (with Carl Reiner, he did the brilliant "2,000 Year Old Man" routine, among others).

Brooks wrote the Oscar-winning screenplay for *The Producers*, and it remains one of the most tastelessly inspired in movie history. Max Bialystock (Zero Mostel) is a down-and-out Broadway producer, and Leo Bloom (Gene Wilder) is his skittish but brilliant accountant. Together, the two come up with what they think is a foolproof money-making scheme: To sell 25,000 percent equity in a play, make sure it's a flop, then keep the money. They buy the rights to the most outrageously bad play they can find, one that portrays Adolf Hitler as a misunderstood hero; hire a hammy nutcase to portray the Führer (Dick Shawn); and turn it into a musical called *Springtime for Hitler*, complete with a Busby Berkeley swastika. Incredibly, the play is a smash and *now* the duo has *tsuris*.

Mostel is brilliantly manic in the part; the late, great comedian did not leave behind nearly enough work. (He was blacklisted after being called to testify before the House Committee on Un-American Activities in 1951). Wilder is at his whining and neurotic best, and Shawn's beatnik Hitler is a classic.

The Disc
Video: ★★★½ (Criterion); ★★★ (Nelson)
Audio: ★★★ (both monaural)
Chapters: Yes (both)
Format: CLV (both)
Source: Criterion or Nelson Entertainment/Pioneer

Max's flamboyance is reflected in his colorful surroundings, and these are well-served by the letterboxed Criterion disc. The technology also shows how *good* Mostel was: It captures every nuance in his expression, from the lying smiles to the twinkle in his eye, details that just don't come across on tape. Even the Nelson disc brings it all home.

Pioneer's less expensive version isn't letterboxed, but that *may* be a plus in this instance: No vital information is sacrificed, and Mostel's delightful mugging looms that much larger!

The sound is generally solid on both discs and really shines during the performance of the musical itself. The Criterion disc includes the theatrical trailer.

The Professionals (1966) ★★★
Director: Richard Brooks
Running Time: 117 minutes

It's 1917, and pretty young Maria (Claudia Cardinale) has been kidnapped by Mexican revolutionary Raza (Jack Palance), a brutal lieutenant of Pancho Villa's, who has demanded a huge ransom from her husband, American magnate Grant (Ralph Bellamy). Rather than pay the $100,000, Grant hires mercenary Fardan (Lee Marvin)—a former ally of Raza's—to go to Mexico and rescue Maria. Fardan hires three men to go with him: horse breeder Ehrengard (Robert Ryan), bow-and-arrow marksman Jake (Woody Strode), and explosives expert Dolworth (Burt Lancaster). Upon Maria's safe return, each man will be paid ten thousand dollars.

From that point forward, the film is wall-to-wall action, as the men create and avoid ambushes, witness Raza's savage attack on a government supply train, infiltrate Raza's stronghold, snatch Maria, and face the rebel's hot-in-pursuit army. Of these, the most memorable sequences are the spectacular attack against Raza's village—with the mercenaries using TNT lashed to arrows—and Dolworth buying time for the group by single-handedly holding off Raza's soldiers (in ways that only Burt Lancaster can!).

Though there's a neat surprise ending, the plot has several gaping holes—such as how did the Professionals and Maria get out of the train, *with* their horses, while it was surrounded by Raza's forces?—and neither Ryan nor Strode is given much to do. Lancaster and Marvin get all the character development, and Lancaster gets all the great lines.

Based on the obscure Frank O'Rourke novel *A Mule for the Marquesa*, the film was shot in Valley of Fire State Park in Nevada and makes excellent use of the locations. Be forewarned, though, that a big disappointment awaits you on side two, chapter four: In two separate shots, as Cardinale offers herself to Lancaster, a shadow added in postproduction covers her bare breasts. (Presumably, the obstruction was not present in foreign prints of the film.) Once again, Hollywood showed the skewed sense of morality that governed its thinking for too many years: It was okay to stab, hang, or blow people all to hell, but bared breasts were a no-no.

The Disc
Video: ★★
Audio: ★★★ (stereo)
Chapters: Yes
Format: CLV
Source: Pioneer Special Edition

This new transfer was made from a very clean print of the film, and the letterboxing allows all four characters to appear on the screen at the same time—unlike the original RCA/Columbia Home Video panned-and-scanned version.

Unfortunately, the image is terribly soft in places, the colors range from solid (about half the time) to washed-out to red, and almost all of the night scenes are grainy.

Considering that the film was made over a quarter of a century ago, the sound is surprisingly good, full-bodied, with impressive range and some fine directional effects. And those castanets that are part of the musical score sound as if they're in the room with you. There's no hiss or other defects.

Psycho (1960) ★★★★★
Director: Alfred Hitchcock
Running Time: 108 minutes

You know the story: Marion Crane (Janet Leigh) is given forty thousand dollars in cash to take to the bank. Thinking about how the money will help her debt-ridden lover, Sam Loomis (John Gavin), and enable them to marry, she takes the cash and drives from Phoenix, intending to start a new life in California. Unfortunately, she decides to spend the night at a desolate motel run by Norman Bates (Anthony Perkins). As Marion showers, what *seems* to be an old woman knifes her to death. Moments later, Norman rushes in and finds the body; horrified, he places it in Marion's car, which he drives into a swamp. Sam, Marion's sister, Lila Crane (Vera Miles), and insurance investigator Milton Arbogast (Martin Balsam) come looking for Marion and the money, respectively: The "old woman" kills Milton, and Lila learns that it's actually Norman dressed as his dead mother. Though he keeps her rotting body in the fruit cellar, she "lives on" through him. Fortunately, Sam is able to disarm Norman before he can kill Lila, and the schizophrenic young man is incarcerated.

People are fascinated by extremes of human behavior, and *Psycho* is the ultimate in murderous voyeurism. Hitchcock's use of the camera to give us the killer's subjective point of view not only satisfied this voyeurism, it led to far more sensational movies such as the slasher-type films *Friday the 13th* and *Halloween*.

Ironically, the brutal bathroom murder for which *Psycho* is (justifiably) famous doesn't occur until well into the film. Hitchcock takes his time, unnerving us with the eerie architecture—the ramshackle motel and the Gothic house beside it—and bringing out the tics and quirks of Bates, who is easily provoked, unpredictable, and frightening even before he raises a butcher knife. On a more subtle note, Hitchcock is constantly using mirror images, suggesting that there are two people in all of us, not just in Norman Bates. And viewers who bother to think about it should be unnerved to realize that Marion's last name is Crane (from Phoenix, another bird) and Norman's hobby is taxidermy. (Marion is very nearly an anagram for Norman, the symbolism of which is also intriguing.)

Anthony Perkins had portrayed several outcast or troubled young men previously, and he is ideal as Norman. Given the mad nature of the character, his performance is surprisingly well modulated—sort of a reverse Hamlet. Janet Leigh had been working in films for thirteen years and reached the peak of her fame with *Psycho;* fittingly, her daughter, Jamie Lee Curtis, began her career in the *Halloween* films. John Gavin was being groomed as a new Rock Hudson but failed to click with audiences. He ended up as Ronald Reagan's ambassador to Mexico. Balsam is so terrifically arrogant that, frankly, we can't *wait* until he gets it. About the only misstep is Simon Oakland as the psychiatrist, who gives us a long-winded explanation of Norman's psychotic state at the end of the film. Anything the viewer hadn't already figured out could have been explained in a less clunky way.

The film was based on the real-life escapades of Wisconsin killer Ed Gein, a murderer who was fond of dressing in the skins of his victims, and on horror author Robert Bloch's 1957 short story "The Real Bad Friend," which is about George and Roderick—two faces of the same schizophrenic man—who plot against their wife, Ella, so they can be the sole possessors of an inheritance. Scripted by Joseph Stefano (creator of TV's "The Outer Limits"), *Psycho* cost $800,000 and made a bundle. It also spawned a series of sequels: *Psycho II* (1983), in which the "rehabilitated" Norman is released and returns home; *Psycho III* (1986), directed by Perkins and offering nothing more than Norman as a slasher; and *Psycho IV: The Beginning* (1990), a look at Norman's troubled youth, written by Stefano.

Incidentally, since you can't single-frame through the shower scene, it took seventy-eight different camera setups and a week of shooting to get the one-minute scene. Leigh wore a bodysuit and was doubled in the more revealing scenes by Marli Refro. Hitchcock himself held the knife.

The Disc

Video: ★★★★
Audio: ★★★ (monaural)
Chapters: Yes
Format: CLV
Source: MCA Home Video

This recently remastered (1988) edition supplants an earlier one, which was merely adequate. The picture is much sharper than one might expect from a film this old, made from a generally unmarked print with a very good range of gray tones.

The nondigital audio is reasonably solid, though Bernard Herrmann's marvelously screechy score sounds a bit more shrill than it's supposed to.

The disc offers an enjoyable selection of short trailers at the end of the film.

Psycho III is available on laserdisc, *Psycho II* as a Japanese import.

PT 109 (1963) ★★★

Director: Leslie H. Martinson
Running Time: 140 minutes

At 2:33 A.M. on August 2, 1943, the PT (patrol torpedo) boat 109, commanded by

Lt. (jg) John F. Kennedy was hit and sliced in two by the Japanese destroyer *Amagiri*. Clinging to one half of the wreckage, Kennedy, Ens. Leonard J. Thom, and Ens. George H. R. Ross heard the cries of five crewmen stranded in the burning waters. Kennedy jumped in and swam toward a group of three men, while the other two officers made for the remaining pair. It took Kennedy over an hour to swim the one hundred yards back to the wreckage to rescue one of his severely burned men; though exhausted, he returned for the others and then made the difficult decision to abandon the sinking husk and swim toward a barely visible island four miles away—towing McMahon, who was deadweight, the entire time.

The events leading up to and following this dramatic event—the arrival of JFK (Cliff Robertson) in the Solomon Islands, whipping the PT 109 into shape, a daring nighttime rescue of stranded soldiers, the fateful patrol, and the crew's amazing rescue—are all accurately recounted in this film, which is based on the book by Robert J. Donovan.

When the film was first proposed to the President, he agreed to allow himself to be portrayed under four conditions: The facts were not to be distorted at all; any monies that were due him were to be sent to the survivors of the ship, or to their families; he could choose the actor who was to play him; and that the actor portraying him *not* do a Boston accent. Robertson recalls, "He felt that with all the nightclub comedians doing JFK impressions, it would be distracting to hear one coming from the screen. He wanted the accent to be nonregional."

Dozens of actors were given screen tests and the footage was sent to the White House. The President watched the footage and narrowed the selections to Warren Beatty, Peter Fonda, and Robertson. All three actors were dressed in uniform, given scenes to read, and retested; from this footage, Kennedy selected Robertson.

The scenes set in the Solomon Islands were shot off Key West and on Key Largo and were directed by veteran Lewis Milestone (*All Quiet on the Western Front* [1930] and *Pork Chop Hill* [1959]). After six weeks, frustrated by Milestone's slow, meticulous approach to filmmaking, the producers replaced him. TV director Martinson handled the remaining scenes and all of the action footage, though most of what Milestone shot remained in the film. It's also the weakest stuff: The treatment of JFK in these early scenes teeters on hagiography. The character doesn't really get to do anything other than smile until he takes over the boat, which is where Martinson came aboard.

Robertson is earnest and credible as the youthful JFK, though he lacks the gaunt, boyish looks of the young lieutenant. Ty Hardin shines as the quiet, supportive Thom, and Robert Culp is his entertaining, wisecracking self as Ross. Robert Blake and Norman Fell also costar.

The two big action scenes, the sinking of the boat and a Japanese air attack against Todd City (not Tood, as listed in the chapter stops) are superb. The former was shot with full-scale mock-ups and, though covered from just one camera angle, is quite effective. Cameras inside the Japanese zeros as they bear down on the island would have added some variety and interest to the latter scenes, and it's surprising the producers didn't bother. They had the planes, after all.

A small but annoying gripe: Continuity is terrible in this film. When Robertson is first introduced, he puts a book down, but he is reading it in the next shot. Watch the elbows at 3/16.36, check out the position of the head at 8/42.22, and so on.

According to Robertson, the President liked the film very much and invited the actor to the White House to tell him so—about as fine an endorsement as any movie could ask for.

The Disc
Video: ★★★★½
Audio: ★★★½ (monaural)
Chapters: Yes
Format: CLV
Source: Warner Home Video

For a film that's thirty years old, *PT 109* looks incredibly young. The colors are solid and subtle and the picture clarity on the letterboxed disc is remarkable: The sunsets alone are almost worth the price of the disc. The reflections of the flames on the water after the collision give those scenes a three-dimensional look.

Except for splice marks, which are surprisingly plentiful (and prevent the film from earning five stars), the print is in excellent shape. (These wouldn't have been visible if the manufacturer hadn't opened up the film into the safety zone to lessen the letterbox.)

The audio is hiss-free and sounds fresh. The only drawback is the volume of the terrible William Lava/David Buttolph score, which often drowns out even the explosions. The theme is unmemorable (a no-no for war movies) and the music comes in at all the wrong times (Nixon supporters, probably).

The Punisher (1989) ★★½
Director: Mark Goldblatt
Running Time: 88 minutes

In the popular Marvel Comics magazine, Frank Castle is a much decorated Vietnam vet whose wife and children witness a mob rubout. The gangsters kill them, as well, and Frank leaves the marines to become the costumed Punisher, waging a holy war against crime. The hero made his debut in *The Amazing Spider-Man* #129 (1974).

Former Marvel Comics editor Stan Lee is credited as Executive Consultant (what does an "executive" consultant do: preside over a battery of assistant consultants devoted to Punisher canon?). However, the movie strays so far from the look and narrative of the comic book, it's doubtful anyone *listened* to him.

The origin of the movie Punisher is the same, and the film has retained all of the violence for which the comic book is renowned. But this Castle (Dolph Lundgren) is now an ex-Seattle cop who does his punishing dressed in leather threads instead of the neat skull-face tights he wears in the comic. From his sewer headquarters, the Punisher has killed 125 mobsters in five years; meanwhile, his ex-partner, Jake Berkowitz (Louis Gossett, Jr... yes, it's Berkowitz), is trying to find Castle and convince him to knock off his vigilantism. (Jake is not a character from the comic book.)

A Japanese Yakuza gang led by the ruthless Lady Tanaka (Kim Miyori) is moving in on the drug trade dominated by mob boss Gianni Franco (Jeroen Krabbe). The Punisher is content to let them slaughter each other... until Tanaka abducts the innocent children of Franco's mobsters, intent on selling them into slavery. While Berkowitz stalks Frank to keep him from adding to the body count, the Punisher and Franco team up to rescue the children.

The movie never had a theatrical release, which is curious. The script has a *lot* of great lines and the acting is better than you'd expect. Though Lundgren delivers his lines like Rambo underwater, he's an imposing figure who handles the fight scenes well—and there are plenty of them, good ones, with the Punisher taking as much punishment as he gives out. (Though once again you're left to wonder why thugs with machine guns *never* shoot at tires.) The Punisher's first attack on the mob and the scene in which he's captured and tortured are particularly effective. And though the movie is violent, it's not as bloody as you might expect.

Gossett, as usual, shines in a supporting role, and Krabbe is also very good (quite a departure from his role in *Robin Hood;* see *Robin Hood: Prince of Thieves*).

Sydney, Australia, looks nothing like Seattle, but the locations are fresh and well used.

The Marvel Comics hero Captain America was the subject of another unreleased film, this one made in 1990 and directed by Albert Pyun. The script is better than both Tim Burton Batman films combined, as the evil Red Skull and Captain America clash during World War II, then again in modern times, when the villain abducts and plans to brainwash the President of the United States (Ronny Cox). The movie features excellent performances by Matt Salinger as Captain America and especially by Scott Paulin as the Red Skull, and there are some very effective action scenes. Unfortunately, the low budget forced a number of sequences to be scrapped, leaving big, distracting holes in the continuity. Still, it's well worth a look.

The quality of the video is excellent during the daylight scenes, murky and grainy at night; the Surround Sound is actually just stereo, and not terribly impressive at that.

The Disc
Video: ★★★
Audio: ★★★★ (Surround)
Chapters: Yes
Format: CLV
Source: Live Home Video/Image Entertainment

The disc has some problems with grain and some of the colors are a bit pale, but the transfer is generally very good. The film isn't letterboxed, but nothing has been lost and there's plenty of breathing room in the chase and fight scenes.

The digital audio is extremely clear (though you'll *still* have to strain to hear what the mumbling Punisher is saying), and there are some spectacular Surround effects involving the explosions, cars, crowds, and gunfire. Unfortunately, the music tends to overpower the dialogue in some scenes. (It may not be deathless prose, but you *should* be able to hear it!)

The back of the jacket shows photographs from the hooker scene referred to in the movie but cut.

Quigley Down Under (1990)
★★★★½
Director: Simon Wincer
Running Time: 121 minutes

Fresh from the success of the TV miniseries *Lonesome Dove*, Emmy-winning Australian director Wincer helmed this sprawling adventure film that died at the box office. Too bad. *Quigley Down Under* is not only a terrific action film, good for repeated viewings, it delivers a powerful, accurate, and moving view of relations between white settlers and Australian aborigines.

Tom Selleck is perfect as Matthew Quigley, a rugged American sharpshooter who travels to Australia circa 1860 to work for rancher Elliott Marshton (a snarling, unbridled Alan Rickman). When he learns that he was hired to kill aborigines, Quigley quits and, aided by fellow American outcast Crazy Cora (Laura San Giacomo), protects them from Marshton and his army of murderous ranch hands.

The film doesn't shy from scenes of savage, heartbreaking slaughter, but, unlike the overrated *Dances with Wolves* (see page 60), it doesn't paint all whites as evil. It also makes excellent use of Australian locations, which are as fresh as they are breathtaking.

It's a pity Selleck can't seem to connect with most of his theatrical films. They do extremely well on TV, which is why he continues to get parts, but, as with so many former TV stars, audiences just don't want to pay to see him.

The Disc
Video: ★★★★★
Audio: ★★★★★ (Surround)
Chapters: No
Format: CLV (sides one and two), CAV (side three)
Source: MGM/UA Home Video

The beautiful film is well served by the letterboxed disc, which boasts a perfectly sharp transfer, blindingly rich colors, and no grain or video noise. It's simply exquisite.

The digital audio and directional effects are also marvelous, with resounding Surround Sound: Be ready to catch hanging pictures when Quigley fires his custom-built cannon-loud rifle. The powerful score by Basil Poledouris (*Conan the Barbarian*) also sound great.

Raiders of the Lost Ark (1981)
★★½
Director: Steven Spielberg
Running Time: 115 minutes

Steven Spielberg was at a professional nadir after the flop of his huge-budget, vastly underpraised comedy *1941* (1979). (He has since hit another low with the back-to-back stinkers *Always* [1989] and *Hook* [1991], the latter being the most insultingly bad movie of the year, decade, and possibly all time.)

But while brainstorming with producer George Lucas, he plotted his return to the box office stratosphere by concocting *Raiders of the Lost Ark*, an homage to the pulp adventure novels of the 1930s and 1940s—in particular, Doc Savage—and the great movie serials of the 1940s—most notably, several Zorro chapter plays.

Originally, Tom Selleck was asked to play archeologist-adventurer Indiana Jones, but he couldn't make time in his schedule, thanks to his just-signed *Magnum, P.I.* contract. Harrison Ford got the part, and in this film, set in 1939, he searches for the Ark of the Covenant, competing against Nazis who want to tap the relic's supernatural powers for their own evil purposes.

The action is nonstop, but this seriously overpraised film is so derivative of specific serial stunts (and the rolling boulder from *Journey to the Center of the Earth* [1959]), has so many plot holes (Jones travels *how* far hanging onto the submarine periscope?), and offers so little in the way of character development outside of Jones that it's more like an amusement park than a film—eclectic, in-your-face entertainment.

The movie was followed by two unbearable sequels: *Indiana Jones and the Temple of Doom* (1984) and *Indiana Jones and the Last Crusade* (1989), with Sean Connery as Jones's cantankerous dad and a truly tasteless run-in with Hitler. (Book burnings are funny?) The former has some of the most improbable action ever (with dolls and dinky toys doubling for actors and mine carts), and the latter has some of the dumbest *and* worst executed action (a plane follows the Joneses into a cave, loses its wings, and scoots by them on the ground, the pilot giving them a wide-eyed stare).

Do yourself a favor and watch a bona-fide cliffhanger instead, such as *Zorro Rides Again* (1937) and *King of the Rocket Men* (1949), both from Republic Pictures Home Video. The former will be particularly revealing to Spielberg fans: that's where the horse-to-truck transfer came from, done spectacularly well. Also, John Carroll makes a better hero than Harrison Ford on his *best* day.

The Disc
Video: ★★ (nonletterboxed);
★★★★½ (letterboxed)
Audio: ★★★★½ (Surround)
Chapters: Yes
Format: CLV or CAV (nonletterboxed), CLV (letterboxed)
Source: Paramount Home Video

Panned-and-scanned, the movie's a disaster. The only qualities *Raiders of the Lost Ark* have are its sound and its visuals and the latter, when cut in half, are blah.

The long-awaited letterboxed edition was finally released in August of 1992, and it looks great: solid colors, a sharp image, mild grain in a few dark scenes and, most important, proper framing for the action.

The audio on all versions is killer, from the catchy John Williams score to the crashing Surround effects. There's a hint of tinniness in the upper ranges of the brass, so keep the treble down a bit.

The second and third films are also available in pan-and-scan and letterbox editions, in case you've got money to burn or a friend at Paramount Home Video.

Spielberg's breakthrough hit, *Jaws* (1975), has also finally been released in an excellent, gorgeously colorful letterboxed edition from MCA/Universal. The film is a marvel of editing (thanks to the late Verna Fields who, rumor has it, saved Spielberg's hash when the mechanical shark was giving them trouble and the footage wasn't looking too good), and is well worth owning.

The Rainmaker (1956)
★★★½
Director: Joseph Anthony
Running Time: 121 minutes

Not long after the turn of the century, a man with a name as big as the heavens, Starbuck (Burt Lancaster), rides his wagon onto the Curry ranch in the drought-stricken Southwest. For one hundred dollars in advance, he promises to bring rain within twenty-four hours. Siblings Lizzie (Katharine Hepburn) and practical Noah (Lloyd Bridges) oppose striking a deal with the con man; their happy-go-lucky kid brother, Jim (Earl Holliman), wants desperately to believe in Starbuck and is for it, and their father, H. C. (Cameron Prud'homme), sides with him. Why not? he figures.

While Starbuck goes through the machinations of rainmaking, he accomplishes the more important task of helping Jim to get out from under the shadow of his domineering brother and of convincing spinster Lizzie that she's a beautiful woman, helping her to win the attention of a local lawman, File (Wendell Corey).

The Rainmaker was written and directed by the same team that staged it on Broadway in 1954, writer N. Richard Nash and director Anthony (Prud'homme was also imported from the stage version.) Not surprisingly, the result is a very theatrical movie, with very little camera movement and few close-ups. But first-time movie director Anthony lets his world-class ensemble act, and they could have sold the story on a bare stage in modern dress. Hepburn is alternately proud, sweet, and desperate, and no one could play a charlatan like Lancaster. The fact that Starbuck *causes* so many of Lizzie's quick changes makes Hepburn's scenes with Lancaster especially lively. Prud'homme also shines. Elvis Presley was originally considered for the part of Jim.

The play later became a hit Broadway musical, *110 in the Shade*, which was also directed by Anthony.

The Disc
Video: ★★★
Audio: ★★★ (monaural)
Chapters: No
Format: CLV
Source: Paramount Home Video

The VistaVision film is sharp and the colors are fairly vivid, though the night scenes are darker than they should be. Cropping causes a bit of information to be sacrificed on both sides, though this only hurts a few scenes—for instance, when Starbuck enters the house to hear the others talking about him, his reaction (his entire body, in fact) is lost off the right side. The opening titles are windowboxed to the correct ratio, giving you an idea of just what's missing.

The audio is quite clear and relatively free of extraneous noises or defects.

Re-Animator (1985) ★★★★
Director: Stuart Gordon
Running Time: 86 minutes

H. P. Lovecraft wrote his short story "Herbert West—Re-Animator" in 1922. In his florid, very literary style, he told of how young college student West and his (unnamed) friend sought to resurrect the dead "by calculated chemical action after the failure of natural processes." The tale follows their work over many years, ending with West's murder at the hands of the zombies he's created.

The filmmakers retained the thrust of the tale, along with the name of the character and the school—Miskatonic—though they added sex and gore to the update. Daniel Cain (Bruce Abbott) is a brilliant medical student at Miskatonic, and his future is bright: Not only is he a favorite of Dean Allan Halsey (Robert Sampson), he's the lover of the dean's stunning daughter, Megan (Barbara Crampton). Enter West (Jeffrey Combs), who rents a room from Cain and involves him in his experiments. Unfortunately, the smug West incurs the wrath of powerful Dr. Carl Hill (David Gale), who plagiarized material from West's mentor, Dr. Hans Gruber (Al Berry), and who also lusts after Megan. West's research gets him bounced from the school and costs Cain his scholarship, though that doesn't stop the lads from fiddling around with the dead. When Dean Halsey stumbles upon them reanimating a corpse in the morgue, the out-of-control zombie kills him; though the men reanimate the dean, his mind is gone and he has to be committed.

Things go from horrible to worse when West decapitates Hill, then reanimates his body and severed head separately. Mistake: Hill is able to control his torso and, together, body and head plot to destroy West... and claim Megan for their own.

The movie is roguish, violent, funny, suspenseful, and irreverent (cat haters will have a *great* time with West's first subject); despite some problems with pacing and hammy theatrics from Gale, it's the best of the splatter films.

The film was followed by a sequel, *Bride of Re-Animator* (1990), which continue West's adventures—with all the gore but none of the wit or finesse of the original.

The Disc

Video: ★★½
Audio: ★★★★ (monaural)
Chapters: Yes
Format: CLV
Source: Vestron Video/Image Entertainment

The original film was fairly grainy, and the laserdisc is grainier still. Though the image is fairly sharp, details are lost in the darker scenes and there's considerable red noise in spots. Cropping doesn't hurt the film at all.

What *does* hurt are the misbegotten edits: though this is billed as the unrated version, it isn't the *original* unrated version, which ran two minutes longer. Missing are shots of Hill removing and handling a brain in the classroom, of the zombie biting off Dean Halsey's fingers, of West's bone saw killing of the zombie, of the climax of the notorious "head" scene, and more. What's the point of issuing a cut film for the collector's market especially a film whose appeal rests, to some degree, on its explicit but playful gore?

The sound is very good: resonant, clear, and nicely balanced. You won't have to keep adjusting the volume when it goes (frequently) from quiet to "boo."

The video and audio on the laserdisc edition of *Bride of Re-Animator* are somewhat better—though it's a borrow or rent film, not one you'd want to pay for.

Director Gordon's *From Beyond* (1986) is also available in an okay transfer. The film is another Lovecraft adaptation starring Combs and Crampton, an energetic but empty film in which a scientist's search for a sixth sense stimulates his pineal gland and turns him into a monster.

Rear Window (1954) ★★★★

Director: Alfred Hitchcock
Running Time: 113 minutes

Photographer L. B. Jeffries (James Stewart) had his leg and hip broken by a wheel that flew off a race car he was shooting. Confined to his New York apartment, he sits by the window and watches people in other apartments—one of whom, Lars Thorwald (Raymond Burr), apparently murders his wife (Irene Winston). Jeffries is unable to convince his old military chum, Detective Thomas J. Doyle (Wendell Corey), that something's amiss, but his nurse, Stella (Thelma Ritter), and his elegant girlfriend, Lisa Freemont (Grace Kelly), believe him and launch an investigation of their own. Unfortunately, Thorwald realizes what they're up to and turns the tables on the trio.

Rear Window is brilliantly made, as well as tremendously thrilling and filled with all kinds of interesting psychological subtexts—such as Stewart as Hitchcock's alter ego (voyeur, photographer, and lover of Kelly) and the possible futures Hitchcock presents for his hero and heroine via the neighbors. Depending upon what the couple decides to do—marry or separate, Jeffries continuing his globe-hopping or settling down and shooting portraits—they can become like the frustrated composer (played by Ross Bagdasarian, who went on to create Alvin and the Chimpunks), the hack sculptress, the childless and love-starved couple, the passionate newlyweds, the lonely beauty, the even lonelier spinster, or even the hate-filled Thorwalds (chillingly, they have a leg up in that respect: Jeffries travels to take pictures; Lars is a traveling salesman, his wife, a stay-at-home).

Repeated viewings kill the suspense, obviously, but the supporting characters remain fascinating, and nothing could dull the ethereal beauty of Ms. Kelly, to whom Hitchcock devotes a welcome amount of screen time. And even after a dozen times, you'll still feel a chill when Thorwald finally realizes his across-the-court neighbor has been spying and glares out the window at him—and us.

The film is also a stylistic marvel, and movie buffs will enjoy studying Hitchcock's technique. The camera hovers around the wheelchair-bound Jeffries, never leaving his side or the rear window: Hitchcock never even takes you into other rooms of the apartment.

Rear Window is based on Cornell Woolrich's short story "It Had to Be Murder" (1942), which was retitled "Rear Window" when anthologized two years later. The first-person tale has no love interest (just a housekeeper, Sam), but is otherwise quite similar to the finished film—cleverer, in fact, in many details. Woolrich also wrote the similar "The Boy Cried Murder" in 1947, about a boy who witnesses a murder from his fire-escape window. It was filmed as *The Window* (1949), as *The Boy Cried Murder* (1966)—though the setting was switched to a boat!—and *Cloak and Dagger* (1984).

The short story and film were also the basis of a lawsuit that went all the way to the Supreme Court: At issue was whether or not the makers of a film have the right to continue showing the film after their license to the source material had expired. The Court's answer was no. This means if you've got the disc, hold on to it.

The Disc
Video: ★★★
Audio: ★★★ (monaural)
Chapters: No
Format: CLV
Source: MCA Home Video

Although the picture has a very slight amber cast during the darker scenes, the daytime colors are fairly bright and strong, the image sharp. The print is in excellent condition except for a few flaws before and after several of the reel changes.

The audio has occasional crackles and a few minor dropouts in chapter three, but otherwise the dialogue and Franz Waxman's score came through just fine

What's most jarring about the disc, though, is a trivial thing: the inclusion of the Universal logo for its home video and theatrical rerelease. This was a Paramount movie; years before Spielberg incorporated the famous logo into the opening of his Indiana Jones movies. Hitchcock made it an intrinsic part of the *Rear Window* opening. It should have been retained.

Red River (1948) ★★★★½
Director: Howard Hawks
Running Time: 133 minutes

It has been called *Mutiny on the Bounty* out west, and so it is. But *what* a retelling!

Instead of a trip to Tahiti to acquire breadfruit, the hands of *Red River* start out leading ten thousand head of cattle one thousand miles, from Texas to Missouri. The drive is headed by rancher Thomas Dunson (John Wayne), who has been left penniless by the Civil War and for whom selling the cattle is the difference between survival and extinction. His "Fletcher Christian" is Matthew Garth (Montgomery Clift), an orphan whom Dunson has raised since childhood. Also on the drive are Dunson's longtime friend (and conscience) Groot (Walter Brennan) and gunslinger Cherry Valance (John Ireland).

Garth eventually sends the obsessive

Dunson packing, finishes the drive, and faces his mentor in the final reel.

Having begun his career in silent films, director Howard Hawks had already made several classics—*Sergeant York* (1941), *To Have and Have Not* (1944), *The Big Sleep* (1946)—when he decided to do a Western. At $3 million, *Red River* was one of the most expensive Westerns ever made. Hawks originally approached his *Sergeant York* star Gary Cooper to play Dunson, but Cooper disliked the character's cruel stubbornness; negotiations to hire Cary Grant for the part of gunslinger Cherry Valance also fell through. Among Hawks's first choices, only screen newcomer Montgomery Clift made it into the film. But Wayne was no slacker, and he gives a performance of amazing depth and orneriness.

Truth is, there isn't a weak performance in the movie. Brennan will annoy those who just don't like his style, but he's perfect. Noah Beery, Jr. and Chief Yowlatchie are delightful as hands Buster and Quo. Hawks' trademark overlapping dialogue is used to great effect, and the people hold their own against the majesty of the one thousand head of cattle the director used in the film.

Red River's only flaw is an abrupt, unsatisfying, unrealistic climax: Suffice it to say that Ireland should have shot Clift's love interest, Joanne Dru.

The Disc

Video: ★
Audio: ★★★ (monaural)
Chapters: No
Format: CLV
Source: MGM/UA Home Video

This is the restored director's cut, and it's good to have *Red River* complete. You'll want it for that reason alone. Unfortunately, much of the black and white film is downright fuzzy, and what *isn't* blurry tends to suffer from terrible contrast. The print is otherwise free of defects, which earns the movie its single star.

The digital sound is good, though; the dialogue is surprisingly clear and the stampede sounds as big as it looks.

Return of the Dragon (1973)
★★½
Director: Bruce Lee
Running Time: 91 minutes

Before landing the role of Kato in the TV series "The Green Hornet" (1966–1967), Bruce Lee—who was born in San Francisco to Chinese parents—had been a martial-arts instructor in Hollywood (one of his students was James Coburn, of *Our Man Flint*—see page 202). Moving into feature films, the martial-arts champion enjoyed a phenomenally successful but short career: He died in 1973 at the age of thirty-two, four years after his movie debut in *Marlowe*. He left behind just five movies, one of which was unfinished at the time of his death.

Critics tend to dismiss Lee as someone whose only talent was the ability to break arms and faces. That's snobbish nonsense, though any assessment of Lee is difficult for three reasons: For the most part, he starred in films that were shot cheaply and quickly; he was usually dubbed; and when he wasn't, he spoke with a speech impediment that has been so widely parodied on TV and in other films (such as *The Kentucky Fried Movie*, 1977) that it's difficult to judge him impartially.

The fact is, even at his worst, Lee had charisma and intensity that in time he might have learned to use to great effect. Indeed, he was so unhappy with the quality of most of his films that he decided to write and direct his own; *Return of the Dragon* was the uneven result.

The story is a slight but acceptable framework for the star and his many action sequences. Chen Ching Hua (Nora Miao) has inherited a Chinese restaurant in Rome (an improbable development, true—but it *does* allow Lee an indulgent climax). Local mobsters want Chen to sell the place to them, but she refuses and enlists the aid of Tang Lung (Lee), a friend of her uncle's. After beating up every thug who dares to show his sneering face, Tang tangles with black-belt-for-hire Colt (Chuck Norris) inside the Colosseum, after which he mops up what's left of the gang.

Lee, the tyro director, showed promise but made a lot of mistakes. His staging of the film is uninventive, and he uses the camera as though it were an extension of his flying fists, zooming in and out on faces (mostly his own) so frequently that you're startled when he actually holds a shot *still*. And not that this is his fault, but it's especially silly dubbing the Italian and Chinese dialogue into English ... and *still* having an interpreter explaining what's being said to each character!

Fortunately, the fights are staged with gusto, and Lee himself is a marvel to watch, whether he's high-kicking out a ceiling light or swinging his nunchucks.

Also available on laserdisc is *The Game of Death* (1979), a bigger-budget film that he was shooting when he died. The movie was finished years later with a double, Kim Tai Jong, and the American stars—Kareem Abdul-Jabbar, Dean Jagger, Gig Young, and Hugh O'Brian—also returned. Except for the dazzling climactic fight, which is all Lee, the movie has very little of the star.

The Disc

Video: ★★
Audio: ★★½ (monaural)
Chapters: Yes
Format: CLV
Source: CBS Fox Video

Except for a few scenes that are set in a dark apartment—when very little at all is visible—the colors are generally quite solid, with very little grain or video noise.

The condition of the print is another matter. There are marks and splices as well as fill-in frames; these wouldn't be so objectionable if they didn't show up during the action scenes. The second fight in the alley is especially choppy.

The letterboxing gives the fight scenes legroom and makes them much more enjoyable. It doesn't affect the drama one way or the other: This is not a film in which reaction shots matter.

The digital audio is of little consequence as far as the dialogue and corny music are concerned, but the *whoosh* of the nunchucks, the slap of the jackhammer blows, and Lee's famous cries sound just great to those of us who like that sort of thing!

The picture and sound quality on the letterboxed *Game of Death* are each a ★ higher, which should give consumers some impetus to buy that title.

Reversal of Fortune (1990)
★★★½
Director: Barbet Schroeder
Running Time: 109 minutes

When Claus von Bulow met future wife, Sunny, in 1964, she was rich, attracted to him, and unhappily married. They had an affair and were later wed, after which the relationship soured due to Sunny's reliance on pills and drink and Claus's numerous affairs. The relationship ended when Sunny slipped into an irreversible drug-induced coma, which brought charges of attempted murder from Sunny's children.

Enter attorney Alan Dershowitz, who agrees to take the case even though he doesn't believe that Claus is innocent. Based on Dershowitz's 1986 book of the same name, *Reversal of Fortune* recounts the attorney's meticulous, often inspired efforts to win the Supreme Court appeal, his talks with the courtly von Bulow, and flashbacks speculating on how events *may* have occurred. The way the information is gathered and the case constructed is fascinating, though the appeal and resolution are almost throwaways.

This intelligent, stylish film could really have been called *Reversal of Expectations:* By the time the nonsequential narrative has ended, the film has neatly shifted the viewer's opinion of the characters 180 degrees. Dershowitz (Ron Silver) comes across as moral and enthusiastic at first, then abrasive and self-aggrandizing; the comatose Sunny (Glenn Close), who should *really* have our sympathies, seems pathetic, then spoiled, then completely off-the-wall. Even most of Dershowitz's go-get-'em Harvard law students have that top-of-the-class cockiness that makes you want to smack them, and von Bulow's two lady friends are unbearable.

Then there's von Bulow (Jeremy Irons), who is secretive, arrogant, a philanderer, and possibly a murderer—yet he's also open and has a sense of humor (the only character who does). If you look beyond his mannered aloofness, he's by far the most appealing character in the film. When Irons is not on the screen, you'll find yourself paying a lot more attention to the picture quality and Surround effects. Interestingly, though Irons watched interviews with von Bulow, he did not want to meet him: "I knew that if I met Claus he wouldn't tell me anything I really needed to know. And I didn't want to feel the need to play an impersonation. I wanted to get a distilled essence of him." (Von Bulow himself had wanted Robert Duvall to play him, and Irons suggested that the producers hire Klaus Maria Brandauer. But, says Irons, "they wanted an Englishman.")

Watch the eyeglasses for a surprising slip up in continuity on side one at 9/33.22.

The Disc

Video: ★★★½
Audio: ★★★★½ (Surround)
Chapters: Yes
Format: CLV
Source: Warner Home Video

This film would have benefited from a mild letterbox, opening up the elegant sets a bit and getting rid of the minor but still-distracting pans, especially when Dershowitz and his team confer (at side two, 4/15.22, for instance).

That aside, the presentation is good. The colors are muted but not monochromatic, and the disc reflects them accurately. There are occasional problems with noisy reds, but otherwise the picture is sharp and relatively grain-free. There's a big vertical scratch down the middle of the picture throughout the opening aerial tour of Newport, Rhode Island—*really* annoying, that.

The audio is great and the Surround Sound is surprising in its depth and effectiveness. There are the sounds of the ocean at the von Bulow house, the noises at the hospital, and, most impressively, the Ping-Pong game at the Dershowitz law factory. The ball bounces around for a full minute and is a *lot* of fun.

Ride the High Country (1962)
★★★★
Director: Sam Peckinpah
Running Time: 96 minutes

People tend to have strong opinions about the late Peckinpah: His movies, famous for their stylized violence and driven heroes, are not for every taste. But his second movie, *Ride the High Country*, is a magnificent exception, the tale of an aging turn-of-the-century lawman, Steven Judd (Joel McCrea), who, searching for self-respect, accepts a fee of forty dollars to carry twenty thousand dollars' worth of gold from the Coarse Gold mining camp to a bank. He enlists the aid of old friend and present-day con artist Gil Westrum (Randolph Scott) and his young sidekick, Heck Longtree (Ron Starr), who ride with him for ten dollars each, though Westrum and Longtree plot to persuade Judd to run off with the gold—and, failing that, to steal it. Accompanying them is young Elsa Knudsen (Mariette Hartley, making her screen debut), whom the men reluctantly agree to escort to her fiancé, rough Billy Hammond (James Drury), who's working a claim with his equally brutish brothers. The tensions that build between Elsa and the Hammonds and Judd and his companions comprise the latter half of the film.

The film was originally going to be called *Guns in the Afternoon*, and the script was shown first to Scott; he agreed to do it only if McCrea would costar. A deal was struck, and it's a pleasure to see these great pros strutting their stuff. They have incredible chemistry and charisma and, seldom having had the chance to work in *A* features like this, clearly savored every minute of it.

Hartley and Starr are bland, and Peckinpah didn't seem to care much about them—obviously realizing that their relationship isn't nearly as interesting as that of the older men. But the supporting players are uniformly fine, especially R. G. Armstrong as Elsa's religious father, Joshua; Edgar Buchanan as the drunk Judge Tolliver; and—as Billy's brothers Sylvus, Elder, Jimmy, and Henry—L. Q. Jones, John Anderson, John Davis Chandler, and future Peckinpah repertory player Warren Oates.

Among Peckinpah's other movies on laserdisc are his classic *The Wild Bunch* (see page 300), *Straw Dogs* (1971), *The Gateway* (1972; available only as a Japanese import), and *Bring Me the Head of Alfredo Garcia* (1974, Japanese import only).

The Disc
Video: ★★½
Audio: ★★ (monaural)
Chapters: No
Format: CLV
Source: MGM/UA Home Video

The film was shot in CinemaScope and Metrocolor, which means two things: Despite the *generally* satisfying wide letterbox given the film, something's going to be lost at the edges (such as both heroes as they approach the final showdown from the left) and the image is going to be somewhat red. The trailer included on the disc gives a slightly truer reproduction of the film's original colors.

Filmed in the Inyo Mountains of California, near the Nevada border, the movie is rich with stunning scenery and a nicely detailed picture, but the colors *are* annoying.

Though all of the dialogue is extremely clear—a good deal of it was dubbed in post production—there is a hiss throughout, which is very distracting.

Robin and Marian (1976)
★★★★
Director: Richard Lester
Running Time: 108 minutes

Robin Hood (Sean Connery) and Little John (Nicol Williamson) have been fighting the Crusades for twenty years. Upon the death of King Richard (Richard Harris), they return to England and to their former hideout in Sherwood Forest. Only Will Scarlett (Denholm Elliott) and Friar Tuck (Ronnie Barker) remain of their merry band—though the wicked Sheriff of Nottingham (Robert Shaw) is still terrorizing the countryside. At the moment, he's aiding King John (Ian Holm) in his war against the church by driving disloyal members of the clergy out of England and arresting those who won't leave. Among those refusing to go are Maid Marian (Audrey Hepburn), who is the abbess at a local convent. When the Sheriff comes to arrest her, Robin rides to her rescue and the old rivalry resumes. The beleaguered people of Nottingham run to Robin's side, the Sheriff's army camps outside the forest, and Robin avoids massive bloodshed by challenging the Sheriff to a duel to the death.

Though director Lester doesn't strive to create the same kind of adventurous, ribald spirit he mustered for *The Three Musketeers* (1974) and *The Four Musketeers* (1975)—when *will* someone letterbox those five-star classics?—and the film has a few draggy moments, he creates sublime characterizations, including his trademark "mutterers," minor players who comically bitch or fret about this or that, such as the barber who's supposed to remove the arrow from King Richard's neck.

Connery is perfect as the brash but easily winded hero who comes to realize but not accept his limitations. The Sheriff is pretty much the way Robin left him, using guile rather than brawn, and Shaw effortlessly walks a fine line between admiration for his old foe and condescension. Hepburn's Marian—porcelain on the outside but tough inside—is also exactly right, and her resolution to the problem of Robin aging, and her realization she loves him more than she loves God, will take you through a box of tissues. A thick box.

The Disc

Video: ★½
Audio: ★★ (monaural)
Chapters: Yes
Format: CLV
Source: Pioneer Special Edition

Though *Robin and Marian* was shot 166:1, the lack of a letterbox is terribly distracting. There aren't jump cuts to characters, but the camera is *constantly* making little annoying "adjustments" to whoever is speaking: A static two-shot of Robin and Little John sitting in prison now has more pans than Wolfgang Puck. Worse, the camera doesn't *bother* to pan when Robin tosses away his ax in the fight with the Sheriff. Because the Sheriff is partly offscreen, we don't immediately realize the significance of the fact that the Sheriff is still holding his ax. The titles are letterboxed and, as the mildness of that matte indicates, there was no reason not to letterbox the entire film. What's the point of having a line of Special Edition discs for connoisseurs if the film is going to be reframed?

As for the transfer itself, there's nothing special, and parts are downright awful. The countryside (filmed in Spain) looks lush and green, with a lot of pleasing details; while bright exteriors are sharp, with just a trace of grain, the dark forests are slightly fuzzy and grainier, and interiors are softer and grainier still. Toward the end of the film, not only are the nighttime forest scenes *thick* with grain but some of the shots are noticeably out of focus.

The sound is good, though several copies examined have serious problems with the audio fluttering in the last few minutes of side one. You may also want to turn up the treble a bit, as some of the dialogue is a little muffled.

The beautiful John Barry score—long sought after by sound-track collectors—has been isolated on the right digital and analog audio tracks.

Robin Hood: Prince of Thieves (1991) ½

Director: Kevin Reynolds
Running Time: 144 minutes

Robin Hood is said to have been inspired by the real-life Robert Fitzooth, who had run into the forest to escape his debts and then became the advocate of all debtors. The earliest-known reference to Robin Hood appears in the fourteenth-century poem *Piers Plowman*, attributed to William Langland. In that poem, he became an outlaw after beating a forester in a display of archery; the forester was so sore that he attacked Robin, who stopped him with a goose shaft in the heart. Hiding in the woods, he was soon joined by other oppressed souls, who became known as his Merry Men. Perhaps the most famous telling of the legend was in *The Merry Adventures of Robin Hood* written by Howard Pyle in 1883.

There have been many film versions of the tale, both good and bad (see below), but none has been quite so wrongheaded and thuddingly bad as this one. The good points are fine sets and costumes and Morgan Freeman's excellent portrayal as the Moor Azeem; the bad points are everything else, as one of the greatest romances in history is turned into a brooding, politically correct, formless mess with everything from anachronistic dialogue to anachronistic props (*printed* broadsides three centuries before the birth of Gutenberg). Critics lined up to unload their quivers at this turkey; but whether it was a lack of competition, Costner's appeal after *Dances with Wolves*, or just a yearning for *any* kind of escapism, the thing was a hit.

The film starts in Jerusalem, where members of King Richard's Crusade have been captured by Saracens. Robin and the Moorish prisoner Azeem manage to escape; owing Robin his life, Azeem follows him to England. Back home for the first time in six years, Robin learns that his father has been killed by the evil Sheriff of Nottingham (Alan Rickman). Robin and Azeem hide from the Sheriff in the woods, where they meet up with Will

Scarlett (Christian Slater) and others who survive by robbing and poaching. Even though Will doesn't like Robin—turns out the two are long-lost brothers, and dad always liked Robin best—Robin becomes the band's leader. They're soon joined by his childhood friend and enemy of the Sheriff, the feisty Maid Marian (Mary Elizabeth Mastrantonio).

Aware of the threat the newly organized brigands pose, the Sheriff hires mercenaries to enter the woods and clean them out. Robin's forces are decimated and Marian is taken to the castle to become the Sheriff's unwilling bride. Azeem suddenly reveals that he knows how to make gunpowder, and the remnants of the Merry Men attack the castle. Robin kills the Sheriff as he's about to rape Marian—just in time to turn the realm over to the returning King Richard (Sean Connery).

Robin is some hero. He beats Little John in the famous fight with quarterstaves by hitting him in the back. He's able to kill the Sheriff only because Marian distracts the villain. He's a great archer, sure, but he isn't the show-off bowman we know and love (the archery contest used to smoke him out has been eliminated).

But then, what's the difference? Costner was the worst possible choice to play Robin. Much has been made of his lack of an English accent, yet one could live with that; Burt Lancaster didn't have an Italian accent in *The Flame and the Arrow* (see page 101). More important, what Costner lacks are enthusiasm, joie de vivre, cockiness, emotion, the carriage of a hero—the very qualities that *define* Robin Hood. (Why did he *do* a film for which he was so obviously unsuited? Quid pro quo: Director Reynolds is an old friend who helped Costner on *Dances with Wolves*.)

On the opposite end of the acting scale, there's the rabid Rickman, who, even without the idiotic dialogue (such as "Call off Christmas," "I'm going to cut your heart out with a spoon," and "Shut up, you twit"), chews the scenery like a beaver. Considering the gentlemanly evil he projected in *Die Hard* and even the manic megalomania he mustered for *Quigley Down Under* (see page 224), he was obviously *told* to play the Sheriff à la Gene Wilder. It's not surprising to learn he hated the film.

Freeman is the only one who manages to balance fun with sobriety, though the ready acceptance of a black Moor in white Christian England is dead wrong historically. Mastrantonio is also good, delivering her quips with aplomb; however, it's insultingly stupid to have such a liberated woman, who initially does not like Robin, become his best friend and lover after glimpsing his naked backside in a pond.

To say that there are better versions of the tale would be an understatement. The most famous film, *The Adventures of Robin Hood* (1938), stars Errol Flynn, Olivia de Havilland as Maid Marian, Basil Rathbone as Sir Guy of Gisbourne, and Claude Rains as Prince John—a vitally important character eliminated from the Costner film. Also on hand are Alan Hale as Little John and Eugene Pallette as Friar Tuck. The movie is full of swash and buckle, from Robin's breathtaking escape from the castle to the final duel with Sir Guy; the romance is pure Hollywood (Robin at Marian's balcony will soften even the most jaded viewer), and Flynn at his peak is a joy to behold in *anything*.

Robin Hood (1991), starring Patrick Bergin as dashing, intelligent Robin, Uma Thurman as a fiery Marian, Jurgen Prochnow as a deliciously evil Sir Miles Folcanet, and Jeroen Krabbe as Robin's friend-turned-foe Baron Daguerre, is *quite* a surprise. The film was shown on TV in the United States just prior to the release of the Costner movie, so as to avoid a doomed head-to-head confrontation theatrically. Despite a much smaller budget, it's a much better film, superbly acted and extremely evocative of the era, with more real history than any previous version. Except for a disappointing duel between Robin and Folcanet, it's a joy from start to finish.

Walt Disney's animated feature *Robin Hood* (1973) is also available on laserdisc, but apart from brilliant colors it's a dreary affair, easily the worst and worst-animated Disney feature.

The Disc

Video: ★★★
Audio: ★★★★ (Surround)
Chapters: Yes
Format: CLV
Source: Warner Home Video

The transfer is good but not quite as successful as you'd expect for a popular movie such as this. The focus is a bit soft throughout, and there's a hint of grain and red noise here and there. However, the colors are accurate and quite faithful to the original film, and the letterboxing frames the picture perfectly (even though the film works fine panned-and-scanned on videocassette).

The audio is top-notch, with excellent directional effects and a lot of ambient sounds for the rear channels to chew on. Michael Kamen's score is bit loud (or is Costner's muttering too soft?) and isn't as appropriate as James Horner's theme from *Willow* (1988), which was used in the trailer.

Included is the Bryan Adams video of his superhit song from the film, "Everything I Do (I Do for You.)"

The Adventures of Robin Hood is available on CLV or CAV discs from Criterion, and a CLV disc from MGM/UA Home Video. The Technicolor on all is breathtaking, and the CAV disc has some wonderful extras.

Fox Video's laserdisc of the Bergin film is exceptionally good, with a sharp, grain-free picture and terrific Surround Sound.

Romancing the Stone (1984)
★★★½
Director: Robert Zemeckis
Running Time: 106 minutes

It wasn't easy making *Romancing the Stone*. The film was shot in Jalapa, Mexico—a three-hour drive through the jungle, from the *already* out-of-the-way airport in Vera Cruz. Torrential rains and flash floods hampered the production, the heat was muggy and awful, and there were language difficulties with the natives and members of the crew. Michael Douglas and Kathleen Turner don't just *look* ragged, they *were* ragged.

Directed by Spielberg protégé Zemeckis—who went on to outstrip his mentor qualitywise with the *Back to the Future* series, *Who Framed Roger Rabbit* (see page 300), and *Death Becomes Her*—and penned by first-time screenwriter Diane Thomas (who died in a car crash shortly thereafter), the film is about New York-based romance writer Joan Wilder (Turner) who receives a note from her sister: Unless she brings a certain treasure map to Cartagena, Colombia, her sibling will die. Leaving at once, the repressed, timid Turner teams with down-and-out adventurer Jack Colton (Douglas), who wants the treasure for his own and works with her to outsmart the baddies.

The film offers action aplenty, engaging repartee, and surprisingly fresh characterizations, along with magnificent support from Danny DeVito as a bumbling thug: It's a scene-stealing role that sent the actor on his way to superstardom.

The three actors reteamed for the inferior *The Jewel of the Nile* (1985).

The Disc

Video: ★★★
Audio: ★★★ (Surround)
Chapters: Yes
Format: CLV
Source: CBS/Fox Home Video

The newly mastered, letterboxed disc is a welcome one: The original disc was grainy, pale, and badly panned-and-scanned.

Unfortunately, the new version isn't all that fans hoped for. The letterbox is just under 70 percent of what it should be. While *most* of the image is here, why did CBS/Fox bother reaching out to that segment of the market with a half-baked effort? Moreover, while the colors are generally solid, the image itself is a little on the soft side. There's also an occasional video noise and grain—the latter, often during *daylight* scenes!

The audio has some excellent rear-channel effects, though the dynamic range is not as strong as you'd expect from a film of such recent vintage.

A trailer for *The Jewel of the Nile* is included. All things considered, however, this single-disc item is still overpriced at sixty dollars.

The Jewel of the Nile is available on a panned-and-scanned disc more or less on a par with the original version of *Romancing the Stone*.

The Rookie (1990) ★★★½
Director: Clint Eastwood
Running Time: 121

The Rookie may have bombed at the box office, but it's a lot of fun. Eastwood stars as burglary and auto theft LAPD Detective Nick Pulovski, Charlie Sheen as his green partner, David Ackerman. Dirty Harry–like, they go outside the law in an effort to bring down big-time car thief Strom (Raul Julia) and his murderous lover, Liesl (Sonia Braga, both of whom costarred in *Kiss of the Spider Woman* in 1985). Just when it seems like the partners have them, David makes a mistake that not only lets the criminals get away but allows them to take Nick as a hostage, forcing the rookie to find his courage, go out on his own, and save his partner.

Eastwood, Julia, and Sheen are all fine (Julia is a great villain), and Tom Skerritt is good as David's super-rich father, Eugene, who disapproves of his son's career. Lara Flynn Boyle is underused as David's law-student lover, Sarah.

To be sure, the movie *does* have some serious flaws—such as a badly staged climax (other than the spectacular airplane collision) and a few inexplicable developments (how come Charlie Sheen gets beaten up on his first visit to the bar but is a martial-arts dervish on his second, able to take out everyone in sight?).

But the action is incredible, particularly the opening chase and the car that's driven off the top floor of an exploding factory. Sonia Braga's rape of Eastwood is memorable (if wildly unlikely), there's good chemistry between Eastwood and Sheen, and the story will hold your interest (as long as you don't stop to consider how many innocent bystanders get creamed as Eastwood pursues his prey).

The Disc
Video: ★★★★½
Audio: ★★★★½ (Surround)
Chapters: Yes
Format: CLV (sides one and two), CAV (side three)
Source: Warner Home Video

Except for some video noise, especially during the bar scenes—which are *saturated* with reds—this is a very good transfer. The scenes in daylight and darkness are vividly detailed, and the colors really pop. The letterboxing frames the action scenes beautifully, particularly the freeway chase at the beginning.

The audio is bursting with Surround effects, which are good—except for a tendency to be a *little* overpowering, especially when Strom's man comes for the ransom and the sound of the chopper all but drowns out everything that's being said.

Rosemary's Baby (1968) ★★★★
Director: Roman Polanski
Running Time: 137 minutes

Until William Peter Blatty's *The Exorcist* came along (see page 89), Ira Levin's 1967 novel *Rosemary's Baby* was the biggest horror story ever to hit the mainstream. Movie rights were bought by William Castle, a director who specialized in low-budget gimmick chillers, such as *The Tingler* (1959), with its shock-delivering seats, and *13 Ghosts* (1960), which required viewers to don special glasses to see the supernatural characters in the film. *Rosemary's Baby* was one of his first experiences producing the work of another director, and it brought him his long-sought respectability. Castle also wanted to make the movie because he was intrigued by the sexual angle. He later said, "*Rosemary's Baby* broke the barrier to openly deal with sex. The public was ready for it at that time, after having had years of Cinderella stories."

Castle's choice of Polanski to direct was perfect, the thirty-five year-old having directed the acclaimed *Repulsion* (1965)—which chronicles the declining mental state of a sexually repressed woman left alone in an apartment—as well as the underrated horror comedy *The Fearless Vampire Killers or: Pardon Me, But Your Teeth Are in My Neck* (1967).

Ambitious actor Guy Woodhouse (John Cassavetes; Robert Redford turned the part down) and his wife, Rosemary (Mia Farrow), move into a New York apartment, next door to the friendly Minnie and Roman Castevet (Ruth Gordon and Sidney Blackmer). There, Mr. Castevet—who is part of a satanic coven—approaches Guy with a bargain: He will achieve success as an actor if he lets the devil impregnate Rosemary. Guy agrees, and almost at once an actor who had won an important role over him goes blind. Guy gets the part and, in a nightmarish scene, the devil gets Rosemary. She, of course, is not consciously aware of what's happened, though disquieting visions, strange marks on her body, sickening elixirs, and Guy's inexplicable closeness with the pesky Castevets tips off her (and the viewer) that something wicked is afoot. Unfortunately, the more Rosemary looks into the situation, the uneasier she gets, especially when her dear friend Hutch (Maurice Evans) is murdered for what he finds out.

Rosemary's Baby begins in the light and among crowds and (seemingly) friendly, well-intentioned people. Everything about the setting is so normal that the slow, subtle intrusion of horror is all the more unnerving. Note the uneasy look on Guy's face after he's been left alone with Mr. Castevet for the first time, the proposition obviously having been made. That's the first small step down the ladder to hell, and it's more horrifying than even the very bloody death of the first surrogate mother, Terry Fionoffrio (Angela Dorian), a few scenes earlier. It's easy to relate to Guy and his Faustian temptation and to Rosemary and her mounting terror as the film progresses.

Cassavetes and Farrow are excellent, as are Gordon as the wiggy, intrusive Minnie and Blackmer as the dictatorial Roman. Maurice Evans is wonderful in his small role as Hutch, and Charles Grodin is seen briefly as Dr. Hill, the obstetrician Rosemary goes to before she's sent (unwittingly) to coven member Dr. Sapirstein (a superb Ralph Bellamy).

Because the movie doesn't use special effects or makeup, it doesn't date like *The Exorcist* or other films whose execution seems crude by modern standards. *Rosemary's Baby* is as chilling today as it was a quarter of a century ago.

The Disc
Video: ½
Audio: ½ (monaural)
Chapters: No
Format: CLV
Source: Paramount Home Video

This couldn't have been the easiest film to transfer, since the original film was so grainy and many scenes were dark. Unfortunately, the disc is even grainier and darker. There's also video noise throughout the browns and reds. The image is so fuzzy that if you hadn't put the disc in the machine, you'd swear this was videotape, recorded at long play to boot. The picture is cropped, eliminating characters from the sides and cramping many of the two-shots. It's watchable and it isn't *quite* as bad as *10* (see page 270), but that's the best you can say about it.

The sound is every bit as disappointing. There's hiss, the dialogue is frequently muddled, and portions of the movie sound hollow.

The Ruling Class (1972)
★★★★★
Director: Peter Medak
Running Time: 140 minutes

When the thirteenth earl of Gurney (Harry Andrews) accidentally hangs himself, the family is in a quandary: the earl's sole surviving heir, Jack (Peter O'Toole), believes he's Jesus Christ and is in a mental institution. But Jack *is* the only heir, and the family summons him back to the estate, where the deceitful and snooty Sir Charles (William Mervyn) plans to marry Jack off to the Earl's trusted and beautiful mistress, Grace Shelley (Carolyn Seymour). Once Jack has produced an heir, Charles plans to have the fourteenth earl declared insane and then run the estate himself for the babe.

The wedding takes place and a son is born, but Jack's psychiatrist, Dr. Paul Herder (Michael Bryant), acts before the Master in Lunacy can be summoned. He arranges a showdown between "Jesus" and another inmate, McKyle (Nigel Green), the "Electric Christ." Jack loses and is cured of the delusion that he's Christ. He now believes that he's Jack the Ripper, and secretly begins to act accordingly. Ironically, the British upper class believes him to have finally become one of them, and he's invited to take his seat in the House of Lords.

The summary doesn't do justice to the complex plot or the people in it. There are numerous subplots involving Communist servant Daniel Tucker (Arthur Lowe), Sir Charles's love-starved wife, Lady Claire (the late, magnificent Coral Browne), Bishop Lampton (Alastair Sim)—who has a *great* deal of trouble dealing with Jack as Jesus—Charles's dim son, Dinsdale (James Villiers), and the clash between the upper and lower classes in English society.

Moreover, to see *The Ruling Class* only once is a disservice to the ingenious dialogue, which ranges from the outrageous (Jack tells the bishop he promises to love his new wife "From the bottom of my soul to the tip of my penis") to the profound (asked to explain how he knows he's God, Jack replies, "When I pray to Him I find I'm talking to myself") to the silly (Jack remarks that he was first married, "In the year of me, 1961").

Peter Barnes based the screenplay on his 1968 play, which is somewhat more British and a bit longer, though there's also more of the author's wit to enjoy (even if it *does* lack the wonderful polygraph and Rorschach tests to which Jack is subjected).

And be prepared for Jack to break into song every now and then—happy and constructive ditties as Jesus, a destructive tune as Jack. It's a fitting idiosyncrasy for this pied piper, who, failing to lead people to happiness as the God of Love, leads them to death as a serial killer.

Peter O'Toole is amazing, but then *everyone* is superb. Like the script, the performances can be savored over and over.

The Disc

Video: No stars
Audio: No stars (monaural)
Chapters: Yes
Format: CLV
Source: Nelson Entertainment/Image Entertainment

To see a *bad* movie given such an abominable transfer would be disappointing; to see a great film look so bad is heartbreaking.

The picture is soft, the colors terribly faded, the image warps now and then, and there are negative dirt and splices. For the most part, the absence of a letterbox doesn't hurt the film.

The audio is so muffled, you'll find yourself turning the bass down and treble up to try to hear what's being said, and you'll definitely do a lot of scanning back to listen to sections over again.

This is a shameful presentation.

The Russia House (1990)
★★★½
Director: Fred Schepisi
Running Time: 126 minutes

This thinking person's thriller is not for all tastes. There's no action, the story is told out of sequence, and the plot is complex—despite being an abridgement (!) of the tortuous John le Carré novel. The script by playwright Tom Stoppard—who cowrote director Terry Gilliam's

Brazil (1985)—is literate and demands the viewer's attention. This has caused many people to describe the movie as boring; it is if you go to the movies only for escapism. *The Russia House* is not that. It's a thriller/love story unlike any other, a fascinating character study and an incisive look at government paranoia.

In the days just before the end of the Cold War, British publisher and lush Barley (Sean Connery) is sent a manuscript by a young Russian woman, Katya (Michelle Pfeiffer). British agents get their hands on the papers, which appear to be important revelations about the Soviet military written by Dante (Klaus Maria Brandauer), a scientist in a position to know. The question is, Is Dante telling the truth or is the manuscript intended to deceive the West? British and American intelligence—in the person of Russell (Roy Scheider)—want Barley to go back to Moscow, express interest in the manuscript, and get to know both Katya and Dante.

The twists and turns that follow are puzzling at first, then fascinating, then extraordinary.

Except for Scheider, who is embarrassingly ballistic, the movie is perfectly cast, with reserved, civil performances and mesmerizing Russian locations.

The Disc
Video: ★★★★
Audio: ★★★★ (Surround)
Chapters: No
Format: CLV
Source: MGM/UA Home Video

Considering how overcast the movie is, the transfer is exceptional. The colors are vivid, the image exquisitely sharp, and there's only a hint of noise throughout. The film is letterboxed, though the image isn't *quite* as wide as the original film.

The audio is sparkling; and though the Surround effects aren't especially resounding, they envelope you in a most satisfying and appropriate manner.

The film includes a "making of" short, as well as the theatrical trailer.

The Sea Hawk (1940)
★★★★★
Director: Michael Curtiz
Running Time: 128 minutes

In 1935, former New Guinea plantation overseer Errol Flynn made an explosive impact on the public in *Captain Blood*, a part the virtually inexperienced actor won when Robert Donat dropped out due to a contract dispute. The film was based on Rafael Sabatini's 1922 novel about a young English physician who is accused of treason, sold into slavery, and escapes to become a pirate. It was a huge success and established the twenty-six-year-old Flynn as one of the screen's greatest swashbucklers.

Sabatini wrote a number of novels that became successful motion pictures, most notably *The Black Swan* (1942), *Scaramouche* (1952), and *The Sea Hawk*. However, when Warner Brothers decided to put Flynn in another seagoing swashbuckler, they retained only Sabatini's title: Instead of the author's tale of Sir Oliver Tressilian, an English gentleman who becomes Sakr-el-Bahr, the Hawk of the Seas and the scourge of the Mediterranean, they opted to fictionalize the exploits of England's famed Sir Francis Drake. The decision was sensible enough: Europe was at war and the tale of England against an aggressive foe was right for the time.

Sent by Queen Elizabeth I (Flora Robson) to prey on the treasures being collected in Panama by her enemy King Philip II of Spain (Montagu Love), Captain Geoffrey Thorpe (Flynn) and his men are betrayed by spies. Sentenced to the galley of a Spanish galleon, the Englishmen eventually escape, secure proof that the Spanish are planning to attack England with a great armada, and return to England. Before he can reach Elizabeth, Thorpe must fight her trusted aide Lord Wolfingham (Henry Daniell), who has been working in concert with Spanish ambassador Don Jose Alvarez de Cordoba (Claude Rains) to overthrow the queen. Killing the traitor in a furious duel, Thorpe saves England—and wins the heart of Don Jose's niece, Donna Maria (Brenda Marshall).

The film cost a hefty $1.7 million (and would have cost considerably more if some sets and costumes hadn't been recycled from the previous year's *The Private Lives of Elizabeth and Essex,* also starring Flynn). It was shot on a huge new soundstage built to accommodate two full-scale ships and an "ocean" twelve feet deep. Curtiz, who had directed *Captain Blood* and Flynn's *The Adventures of Robin Hood,* used the sets masterfully, shooting the ships from every conceivable angle and packing them with dueling, swinging, clubbing, climbing extras. Excellent miniature models were used for the explosive sea battles.

Though Flynn brandishes a sword and swings from ship to ship with his typical panache, his Thorpe is dignified and mature, a subdued characterization much different from his cocky Captain Blood or Robin Hood, or the tired, aging swashbuckler he would play in *The Adventures of Don Juan* (see page 2). Considering the different colors Flynn gave to so many heroic performances, it's a pity he was never accorded greater respect as an actor.

Ms. Marshall is pretty but wasn't much of an actress (she retired from movies in 1950 after an undistinguished career), while familiar movie heavy Daniell obviously had fun giving one of his most unctuous screen performances. Rains is appropriately smug and sly, Robson is strong and imperious, and there's excellent support from regular Flynn costar Alan Hale as Thorpe's trusted lieutenant Carl Pitt, the thorny Una O'Connor as his reluctant love interest, Miss Latham, and Gilbert Roland in a brief but effective role as the Spanish Captain Lopez.

The Disc
Video: ★★★½
Audio: ★★★ (monaural)
Chapters: No
Format: CLV (sides one and two), CAV (side three)
Source: MGM/UA Home Video

Though there are scratches and other blemishes here and there, this is a generally satisfying transfer. The contrast is very good, and the original sepia-toned Panama sequences (more golden, actually, as befits the nature of the crew's mission!) are very impressive.

The digital sound has some weak and scratchy stretches, but this is the best you'll ever hear the film. Erich Wolfgang Korngold's score sounds gloriously full on this disc.

The print used for the transfer came from the archives of the British Film Institute and contains ten minutes of footage that had been cut from the film before its American release (the material was considered too British, even though the film was shot in Hollywood), as well as ten minutes more that had been trimmed for the 1947 reissue. The restored scenes strengthen the Flynn/Marshall romance, feature additional sequences involving character actor Donald Crisp, who plays the queen's loyal adviser Sir John Burleson, and offer a stirring call to arms delivered by the queen at the end of the film. The print even includes the original adults-only rating given the film by British censors.

Included is the theatrical rerelease trailer, *not* the original release trailer as described on the jacket.

This disc is considerably better than the previous CBS/Fox Video edition released in 1985, the picture of which was somewhat grayer (not to mention edited).

Sea of Love (1989) ★★★
Director: Harold Becker
Running Time: 113 minutes

Frank Keller (Al Pacino) is a bored twenty-year NYPD veteran who doesn't want to retire but can't find a reason to be happy with his life. When three men who had advertised in singles magazines are murdered, shot in the head in their beds, Keller and cop Sherman Touhey (John Goodman) place similar ads in the hope of smoking the killer out. Keller falls in love with one of his dates, divorcée Helen Cruger (Ellen Barkin), unwilling to believe the mounting evidence that she may be the murderer. (Try not to think of the parallels between Keller and Inspector Clouseau in *A Shot in the Dark*—see page 250—or you won't make it through the movie.) The film will have you doing the "is she or isn't she" dance right until the climax, which comes out of deep left field, reeking of red herrings, but makes sense and is consistent with the clues.

The simple story line is bolstered by snappy dialogue, excellent performances from the leads and the many supporting players, and terrific New York locations. There are also some surprisingly poignant moments, especially the interview scene in O'Neal's Balloon when Pacino meets several single women for drinks in quick succession. The embittered look from the older woman at the bar will dredge up memories of every friend who ever caught you lying.

Among director Becker's other films are *Taps* (1981), *Vision Quest* (1985), and *The Boost* (1988).

The Disc
Video: ★★★
Audio: ★★★ (Surround)
Chapters: No
Format: CLV
Source: MCA/Universal

The scenes set in bright daylight are perfect, but, unfortunately, there are only a handful of those. The many night scenes and interiors have all the mild grain that was present in the theatrical presentation; in spite of this, the image is commendably sharp. The colors are solid.

The film is available in both pan-and-scan and letterboxed editions. As virtually all of the action is staged in the center of the screen, the choice is more or less one of individual taste, though the letterboxed version is slightly darker in a few spots.

The audio is very good. There are no car chases or explosions, so the directional effects are limited primarily to dialogue. The rear speakers don't get much of a workout, used sparingly for crowd scenes, traffic, and music.

The Searchers (1956)
★★★★
Director: John Ford
Running Time: 144 minutes

It's arguable that John Wayne's performance in *Red River* is more textured than his Ethan Edwards in *The Searchers*. But Edwards is more memorable, and the film—though improbable, if you think about it—pulses with his anger and prejudice.

Returning to the Texas ranch of his brother, Aaron (Walter Coy), in 1868, Confederate veteran Ethan joins up with Reverend Sam Clayton (Ward Bond) and a small band of Texas Rangers who go searching for cattle rustlers. While they're out in the plains, the men come to a horrible realization: the cattle were taken by Comanches whose aim was to lure the men away so they could attack their homesteads. When Ethan returns, he finds his brother's family murdered, save for teenaged Lucy (Pippa Scott) and her young sister, Debbie (Lana Wood), who have been abducted.

The posse sets out to rescue the girls, but time cools the trail and hardship thins their ranks, leaving only Ethan and young Martin Pawley (Jeffrey Hunter)—a halfbreed whose life Ethan had saved—to continue the search. Ultimately, Ethan learns that Lucy is dead and finds the grown Debbie (Natalie Wood), who has embraced her adopted culture. After years of searching, Ethan must face the most wrenching dilemma of his life: whether to kill the last surviving member of his family or embrace her, despite the fact that she's been raised and corrupted by a race he detests.

Wayne struts some amazing stuff throughout the film: Watch, for example, as he realizes that by pursuing the rustlers, he's inadvertently left his brother's family to die. His expression—at 11/17:37—is a combination of helplessness and pain that will change the way you regard Wayne as an actor. Everyone else in the film is fine, but this is Wayne's picture. The actor was sufficiently satisfied with his work in it to name his son Ethan; Ford felt that *The Searchers* was his finest film and seriously considered retiring after making it, convinced he'd never direct a better one.

One question, though: What happened to the guitar between frames 4/11:55 and 11:66 on side two?

Interestingly, according to drummer Jerry Allison of the Crickets, he and singer Buddy Holly went to see the film and decided to write a song around the phrase Wayne repeated throughout the film: "That'll be the day."

The Disc
Video: ★★★★★
Audio: ★★★★ (monaural)
Chapters: Yes
Format: CLV
Source: Warner Home Video

The incredibly detailed VistaVision image gets a top-notch transfer with Technicolor reproduction that is candy for the eyes; it replaces a previous pan-and-scan version that was seriously faded and fuzzy.

There isn't a scene in the movie that doesn't *glow*, and the letterboxed image—though wider than the drama itself requires—captures the size and beauty of Monument Valley, Utah.

The digital audio is perfectly clear, the dynamic range limited only by the recording techniques of the time and not by the transfer. Max Steiner's score sounds magnificent.

The extras are corny fun, a series of "making of" documentaries that aired on ABC's "Warner Brothers Presents," an hour-long series of dramas based on Warner Brothers films. Each episode ended with a ten-to-fifteen-minute plug for an upcoming film, and the plug about *The Searchers* is included here. Gig Young is the host, interviewing Hunter and Wood and pretending to be in Monument Valley with the crew (actually a soundstage).

The film's trailer is also included.

Seven Brides for Seven Brothers (1954) ★½
Director: Stanley Donen
Running Time: 113 minutes

Inspired by Stephen Vincent Benét's "Sobbin' Women" (published in his first short-story collection *Thirteen O'Clock* in 1937), this musical is hopelessly sexist—so much so that many viewers may find it off-putting.

In 1850, big, brash Adam Pontipee (Howard Keel), a farmer in the Oregon Territory, comes to town and decides to leave with a bride, largely because he's tired of his cabin, which "is like a pigsty, and the food tastes worse." The baritone sings his way into the heart of restless waitress Milly (Jane Powell), who marries him and takes her job as big sister to Adam's six brothers very seriously. She not only cooks and cleans but teaches them manners and instructs them on how to win and woo brides of their own. The men acquire the outward polish but that's all. Heading to town, they *kidnap* the women of their choice, then cause an avalanche so the pass to their farm will be blocked until spring. Naturally, during their captivity, the abducted women fall in love with the well-meaning brothers and, come spring, there's a sextuple wedding.

Apart from being silly beyond description, the film has a surprisingly slow second half, the major dances and best songs having occurred before the abduction. One of these—the barn-raising sequence—is so extraordinary, it's almost worth the price of purchase; truthfully, even *Citizen Kane* would have trouble holding your attention after this showstopper, as the brothers try to outstrut rival suitors at a dance. Russ Tamblyn, as brother Gideon, and New York City Ballet dancer Jacques D'Amboise, as Ephraim, perform acrobatic steps that will have you going back to the scene over and over without ever getting bored. The Rube Goldberg–like fight that follows is nearly as much fun, but after that there are no flamboyant dance numbers and zilch to hold your attention.

Depending upon your point of view, the film's sets are a plus or minus: Most of the exteriors were shot on soundstages, which is great if you like idyllically fake Hollywood forests, mountains, and countryside. The singing is generally strong, but the acting is hammy beyond words—right for the film maybe but definitely not for the discriminating.

The Disc
Video: ★★
Audio: ★★½ (stereo)
Chapters: Yes
Format: CLV
Source: MGM/UA Home Video

The print used for the disc is virtually free of flaws, though the Anscocolor is uneven: The image is rather soft for the first four chapters or so, the colors not nearly as glossy as they should be. Things pick up significantly after that, though there are serious noise problems with the reds and browns of the brothers' shirts, especially during the barn-raising sequence.

Despite being generously letterboxed, the movie is still short of its original CinemaScope ratio and characters are sometimes lost—for example, Keel at his own wedding (side one, chapter three, 20:38) and characters on the left of the sled after the women have been kidnapped. Still, it's vastly better than the pan-and-scan edition, which loses much of the dancing. And losing that, the film hasn't got much else to offer.

The digital audio is solid and the stereo is satisfying without being especially spectacular.

The film opens with a ten-minute celebration of MGM film music featuring the MGM Symphony Orchestra. Theoretically, this should be a lot of fun. However, this isn't concert footage. The music and cinematography were done separately, so what exactly is the point? To show off CinemaScope's stereo speakers, which hardly makes for fascinating viewing or listening today.

This footage is scratched, the selections abbreviated, and the whole thing is about as interesting as the fake "jam" in *Fantasia* (see page 92).

The Seven Samurai (1954)
★★★★
Director: Akira Kurosawa
Running Time: 203 minutes

Unable to earn his living as an illustrator, the twenty-six year-old Kurosawa went to work for a film studio as an assistant director in 1936. After five years, he was writing scripts; in 1943, he made his feature debut with *Sanshiro Sugata* (*Judo Saga*). His first international success was *Rashomon* (1950), a film in which a rape and murder is told from several perspectives.

Kurosawa's greatest triumph is *The Seven Samurai*, a film that maintains human nature is flawed and will always remain so, though good can and is done in spite of human frailty.

In the sixteenth century, a community of small farms is continually being raided by a horde of bandits. Following the advice of the village elder, the farmers hire five samurai and two aspirants to defend them against further attacks. As the story unfolds, we learn that the villagers are not innocent themselves but have murdered wandering samurai in frustration for their own brutalization. Even their defenders are not treated with respect, as the villagers prevent their daughters from fraternizing with them.

Though suspicious of and confused by one another, the farmers and samurai unite in order to win their struggle against the outlaws. Events test and strengthen this union, culminating in a final battle, one of the greatest scenes in movie history: Tension is built over and over again as the warriors not only struggle with their human enemies but with rain, wind, and mud. The deterioration of skills in the face of these impediments makes the conflict more believable and suspenseful.

Although the film has a strong ethical base, it has an equally powerful visual style as well, from the opening ride of the plunderers—in silhouette, these brigands seem as much a faceless, unstoppable force of nature as the elements—to the final contrast of the desolate graves on the hill and the irrigated, fertile fields.

It's a long movie and not for all tastes. Unlike *The Magnificent Seven* (see page 179), which was inspired by Kurosawa's film, the director takes the time to look at subtle shadings in all his characters. He also indulges his visual sense as in a long take of a campfire, during which we watch, *very* slowly, as a rainstorm develops. It's also difficult to get close to the characters, given the language and cultural barrier, and most viewers will recognize only stars Toshiro Mifune and Takashi Shimura (the star of *Godzilla*).

Those who stick with the movie will not be disappointed, and repeated screenings enhance its impact.

The Disc

Video: ★★
Audio: ★½ (monaural)
Chapters: Yes
Format: CAV and CLV versions
Source: Criterion

This is a frustrating film to watch. Today, the Japanese take very good care of their movies, but in the 1950s this was not the case. The print is worn, lacking contrast and detail. It's okay but no more.

In compensation, this is the full-length version of the film (with subtitles), which is not commonly seen in the United States.

The audio is also on the unhealthy side, scratchy and raw in many places.

The CAV version has an informative audio-track lecture by Japanese film authority Michael Jeck. However, you might just want to pick up the CLV edition and discover the movie and its many layers and textures for yourself.

The Seventh Seal (1957)
★★★★★
Director: Ingmar Bergman
Running Time: 96 minutes

As a child, Bergman would sometimes accompany his father, a Lutheran minister, to the churches he visited in Sweden. Bergman has said that he was fascinated by the "mysterious world of low arches, thick walls, the smell of eternity" in some, and the medieval art in others—the images of Death, of knights, of "dark lands." And then there were all the people who came to the churches, looking for God.

Bergman broke into films as a scriptwriter in 1941, at the age of twenty-three, and began directing movies four years later. He gained international renown for *Smiles of a Summer Night* (1955), which he both wrote and directed; its success enabled him to make a movie based on a short play he'd written some five years before, inspired by his childhood and (he has said) by the 1920 film *The Phantom Chariot*, in which a man faces Death and argues for his own survival.

In the middle of the fourteenth century, knight Antonius Block (Max von Sydow) and his squire Jons (Gunnar Bjornstrand) return to plague-ravaged Sweden after ten years of fighting the Crusades. Tired and disillusioned, the knight encounters Death (Bengt Ekerot) but keeps him at bay by intermittently engaging him in a game of chess (Death playing the black pieces, of course) as they make their way to the knight's castle and his waiting wife, Karin (Inga Landgre). Along the way, Block and Jons also encounter a number of colorful characters, most of whom join them on their journey: actors Jof and Mia (Nils Poppe and Bibi Andersson); accused witch Tyan (Maud Hansson); seminarist-turned-thief Raval (Bertil Anderberg); and the blacksmith Plog (Ake Fridell) and his unfaithful wife, Lisa (Inga Gill).

Death and Block both know who is going to win, but the knight's goal is not victory: He hopes, ultimately, to gain evidence that God exists and to perform an act that will define his life. The latter, at least, he is able to accomplish, distracting Death by knocking over the chess pieces so Jof, Mia, and their baby son, Mikael, can escape. As for his attempts to make sense of the world and existence by proving that God exists (symbolized by the chess game, order amidst chaos), they're foredoomed: He has sought God for ten years and failed. When Death comes to take him, he *still* has nothing more than faith, and he rather hopelessly surrenders to prayer.

Filmed at Hovs Hallar and at the Svensk Filmindustri studios in Stockholm in just thirty-five days, *The Seventh Seal* has often been imitated (and parodied; see *Monty Python's The Meaning of Life*). The art direction, costumes, and lighting are visual poetry, and the script is filled with thought-provoking exchanges. The film made a star of von Sydow and a critical darling of Bergman; majestic, depressing, and uplifting, it remains as spiritual and moving an experience as one can have in film.

The movie's title is derived from the Book of Revelation (8:1), which says that knowledge will be revealed when the seventh seal of God's scroll is broken.

The Disc
Video: ★★★★½
Audio: ★★★ (monaural)
Chapters: Yes
Format: CLV or CAV
Source: Criterion

Both editions feature as fine a print as you could ask for. There is no grain, the blacks and whites are almost always glossy, and the gray scale is richly textured. The flaws are insignificant.

The only problem is the subtitles. Physically, they break up here and there or run over white areas and are difficult to read. More significantly, they do not represent everything that's being said—not by a long shot—and are often out of synch, appearing when the next person is already speaking.

The audio is inherently a bit tinny and there's faint background hiss as well as a few scattered crackles. None of this will detract from your enjoyment of the film.

The extras on the CAV edition include an enlightening right-track essay by respected film historian Peter Cowie, which runs concurrent with the film, and an illustrated filmography of the director, which includes clips from *Wild Strawberries* (1957) and *The Magician* (1958).

She-Devil (1989) ★
Director: Susan Seidelman
Running Time: 99 minutes

Someday, Hollywood and the critical establishment are going to wake up to the fact that Meryl Streep is a fraud. You want accents? She does 'em perfectly. You want tics and mannered little movements? They're yours. You want depth? Forget it. A fine stage actress, she's all style and rarely substance on the screen (*Manhattan*—see page 181—and *The French Lieutenant's Woman*, 1981, being those rare exceptions).

People who worked with Streep always said that she has a great comic sense that the public never gets to see, so expectations were high when she and director Seidelman (*Desperately Seeking Susan* [1985]) teamed for this screen adaptation of Fay Weldon's darkly comic novel *The Life and Loves of a She-Devil*. The film bombed, and a good part of that was due to Streep. The rest was due to her costar, Roseanne Barr.

Mary Fisher (Streep) is a wealthy romance novelist who casts her amorous eye on ambitious accountant Bob Patchett (Ed Begley, Jr.), husband of the ugly Ruth (Roseanne Barr). Bob becomes both business manager and lover to the gorgeous Mary; when he leaves Ruth for Mary, Ruth gives him the children, gets a job at the Golden Twilight Rest Home, becomes friends with nurse Hooper (Linda Hunt), and, with her help, proceeds to make a shambles of Mary and Bob's life.

Filmed on Long Island and in New York City (where Barr's escapades in and around the Mayflower Hotel with her future husband, Tom Arnold, gave the film plenty of press), *She-Devil* is handsomely mounted but empty. In the novel, Ruth had an affair with a priest and a judge to further her cause, and underwent plastic surgery to resemble Mary; her passion for revenge was absolute and exciting. Onscreen, it's mechanical and unconvincing. Streep is a flirty bird rather than Weldon's smart predator, and Barr's shrill monotone doesn't convince us that she's capable of Ruth's complex revenge. Hunt and Sylvia Miles—as Streep's mother—provide the film's best moments, but they don't have nearly enough screen time.

The film's failure seems to have consigned Barr to TV; at least it wasn't a total loss.

The Disc
Video: ★★★
Audio: ★★★ (Surround)
Chapters: Yes
Format: CLV
Source: Orion Home Video/Image Entertainment

She-Devil gets a good transfer, with a clean picture and accurate colors. There's very little grain or video noise, though the image could have been a bit sharper. Cropping doesn't hurt the film.

The audio is clear but unspectacular. There's good separation, though ambient sounds are on the skimpy side—like the script.

The Shining (1980) ★★½
Director: Stanley Kubrick
Running Time: 144 minutes

With strong characters and an engrossing story, *The Shining* (1977) is one of Stephen King's best novels; with awful acting and a drawn-out story, it is Stanley Kubrick's worst film. Not a disaster, mind you, but far less than it should have been.

The Overlook Hotel is located forty miles west of Sidewinder, the nearest town. Because it's so remote, the Colorado hotel shuts down during the winter and, this year, the Torrances—Jack (Jack Nicholson), wife Wendy (Shelley Duvall) and five-year-old son Danny (Danny Lloyd)—are going to be the winter caretakers. Jack plans to use the time and isolation to start a new career as a writer; they arrive as the last guests and employees are leaving, though Danny gets to spend some time alone with cook Dick Hallorann (Scatman Crothers). Hallorann has "the shining" and tells Danny he sees it in him—the ability to read minds and experience the paranormal.

As soon as everyone is gone, Jack begins to lose his mind: Ghosts of past guests appear to him, including that of the ax-murdering former caretaker, Charles Grady (Philip Stone, who played Alex's father in *A Clockwork Orange*), who urges Jack to off his family. Danny sees ghosts, too, and his fear reaches Dick—who leaves his home in Miami and heads back to Sidewinder. He arrives at the snowbound hotel as Jack, his mind completely gone, is busy hunting his family down with an ax. Jack kills Hallorann but Danny manages to get outside and runs into a snow-covered hedge maze, pursued by his father; Danny eventually gets out but Jack, exhausted, falls to the ground and freezes to death. Inside, his likeness appears in a photograph taken in 1921: He is now a part of the ghostly family, though, in his own spiritually depraved way, he always has been.

There are numerous serious problems with the film, the biggest of which is that Kubrick changed the novel for the worse. In the book, Jack's slide into insanity is gradual; in the movie, he starts off borderline nuts and goes downhill. There's no time to get to know Jack as a man before he becomes a demon, no chance to experience normalcy before we're hit with the paranormal.

In King's tale, Hallorann lives and the hotel is destroyed, which makes dramatic sense. Kubrick trivializes Hallorann and his mission: This guy who can read minds gets bad vibrations from a kid twelve hundred miles away but can't sense an ax murderer hiding around the corner? Come *on*. (There had to be a better plot device to get a snowmobile to Wendy and Danny.) And could Wendy be any dumber? It's tough to feel sorry for a character who is so blissfully stupid that she tries *twice* to squeeze through a window that is obviously too small for her; who blithely brings up the subject of the cannibalistic Donner party, then yells at Jack for telling Danny that they ate each other; and who wrestles with a pantry-door handle that is obviously locked very securely.

Second, even if he'd stayed away from the set, Kubrick couldn't have elicited worse performances from his actors. Not until Dennis Quaid's Jerry Lee Lewis in *Great Balls of Fire!* (1989) would there be a performance as overdone as Nicholson's. In Kubrick's defense, the actor himself has said Jack would "have been a lot worse if I'd had my way ... he was so nuts that even before he was doing anything, he liked scaring people." Still, it's just too much. Shelley Duvall goes from singsong happy to shrieking, with no stops in between, and Danny Lloyd is just plain *blah* without a hint of "shining" in his eyes. Crothers—who was miscast—once said that Kubrick "had Jack Nicholson walk across the street, no dialogue. Fifty takes. He always wants something new and he doesn't stop until he gets it." Unfortunately, in this film, Kubrick came up with interesting details without finding any real substance or humanity in his characters. For instance, he missed what is really the most interesting facet of the characters: Though Jack suffers the tortures of the damned trying to write a single word of usable prose, his son, through his imaginary friend Tony, is able to spin fantasies effortlessly. *That*, as a trigger for Jack's rage, would have been ideal motivation, making him a frightening father instead of just a frightening man. (Nicholson himself feels that the movie has "a Shakspearean quality" and is *really* about domestic violence ... that the supernatural aspects are simply a manifestation of Jack's decaying mind. Interesting, but it doesn't wash: Danny sees the things, too.)

Finally, the story proceeds at a crawl. The scenes between Grady and Torrance in the men's room and in the pantry move like the dead rotting, as does Hallorann's flight from Miami: Did we really need the slow pan back from his face just so he could ask how long until they arrive in Denver?

The sets and cinematography are stupendous, and Kubrick's gliding camerawork makes the hotel seem alive (which it certainly is in the novel). There are the famous, much-imitated shots of Danny riding his Hot Wheels through the empty hotel, the incredible flight through the maze (a topiary in the novel), and many subtle touches, such as the knives on the wall pointing down at Danny's head in several early scenes and the many shots of the hotel's chandeliers perched like hellish crowns on Jack's head—the creature of heat who dies, ironically, from hypothermia. (This hot/cold, living/dead, good/evil motif is also reflected in the characters' clothing. Wendy is wearing blue and red in the beginning, then Danny wears the colors, and finally Jack. The dead girls are entirely in blue.)

Many of the ghostly shocks are original and chilling, Kubrick brashly showing all of the apparitions in bright light rather than in shadow: the murdered girls suddenly appearing in the hallway, the rolling ball from nowhere, Nicholson embracing the rotting corpse, the flood of blood from the elevator.

You'll go back to the film now and then to savor its aural and visual pleasures, but dramatically, the movie's a horror.

The Disc

Video: ★★★★
Audio: ★★★★ (monaural)
Chapters: Yes
Format: CLV
Source: Warner Home Video

The film's colors have been accurately reproduced on the disc, though there's a hint of grain in some of the darker shots. Video noise is minimal and the picture is quite sharp; the backlighted scenes don't suffer from the fuzziness that hurts Kubrick's *A Clockwork Orange* (see page 50).

Despite the fact that *The Shining* isn't letterboxed, it was shot 1.66:1, so very little is sacrificed. Indeed, the picture has been opened up somewhat—enough to allow the shadow of the camera-helicopter to be seen in one of the opening shots.

The digital audio is very good, faithfully replicating the booming basses of the music, the hotel's "heartbeat," and having only the slightest trouble holding on to the high-pitched "screeches." There is no background noise or extraneous popping.

A Shot in the Dark (1964)
★★★★½
Director: Blake Edwards
Running Time: 103 minutes

Even before *The Pink Panther* was released, Edwards was so sure it would be a hit that he put this sequel into production with Inspector Clouseau (Peter Sellers) as the main character.

Based on the 1961 play written by Harry Kurnitz (which was based on the French farce by Marcel Achard), *A Shot in the Dark* drops Mme. Clouseau and any mention of the inspector's conviction at the end of the first film. This time out, the inspector must solve a murder at the mansion of wealthy Benjamin Ballon (George Sanders). Making the mistake of falling in love with the prime suspect, Maria Gambrelli (Elke Sommer), Clouseau struggles to prove her innocence in the face of all evidence; before he's through, several other people have died—one of them, Dudu (Ann Lynn), during a classic scene in a nudist colony. In the end, he assembles all of the suspects in a room and hopes that his plan for exposing the killer will work. When it does, no one is more surprised than Clouseau by what he learns.

And there are two hilarious subplots. The inspector's ineptness manages to drive Chief Inspector Charles Dreyfus (Herbert Lom) utterly bonkers, and his attempts to murder Clouseau became a cornerstone of the series. Ditfor Clouseau's housekeeper, Cato (Burt Kwouk), who keeps the inspector on his toes by attacking him when he least expects it.

Unlike *The Pink Panther* (see page 211), Clouseau is rarely offscreen in *A Shot in the Dark*. Despite having a much thinner plot and largely inconsequential supporting characters, it's a funnier film, the jokes and pratfalls constant and endlessly inventive. The "watch synchronizing" scene with costar Graham Stark as Clouseau's long-suffering aide, Hercule, is a case in point: Just when you think the men can't come up with another way to muck up the process, they do. Stark recalled, "(The) sequence wasn't even rehearsed: It was totally adlibbed."

A Shot in the Dark was cowritten by William Peter Blatty, the author of *The Exorcist*.

The Disc
Video: ★★★½
Audio: ★★ (monaural)
Chapters: No
Format: CLV
Source: MGM/UA Home Video

Like *The Pink Panther*, the newly mastered film has been letterboxed, giving the viewer a chance to enjoy the peripheral business Edwards cooked up for his other characters when Clouseau holds center stage. (This is especially noticeable during the interrogation scene at the end of the film: Watch the reactions of the other people gathered around, particularly Sanders, whenever Clouseau steps on a foot, falls through a door, or slips off a sofa). The loss of resolution in the faces is worth the gain in comedy.

The transfer, too, is very satisfying. The colors are fairly zesty; though they're not perfect, they aren't as pale as those in *The Pink Panther*. The whites are *extremely* bright, and the print is in good condition.

The audio will leave you cold, though; it's hissy, with occasional pops.

The trailer is included and stars a very funny animated bullet (with the voice of Mel Blanc).

The Silence of the Lambs (1991) ★★★½
Director: Jonathan Demme
Running Time: 118 minutes

Author Thomas Harris explored the life and times of psychiatrist and cannibal Dr. Hannibal Lecter in the novels *Red Dragon*—which became the stylish, underrated film *Manhunter* (1986)—and the 1989 best-seller *The Silence of the Lambs*.

In this sequel, which is extremely faithful to the novel, FBI agent Jack Crawford (Scott Glenn) finds himself with a serial killer on his hands. Buffalo Bill (Ted Levine) is a maniac who has been skinning his victims for reasons unknown. Lecter is behind bars, and Crawford would like to pick his brains about Bill, but Lecter plays head games with interrogators and invariably sends them off with nothing of value. Figuring that he has nothing to lose, Crawford sends attractive young agent-in-training Clarice Starling (Jodie Foster) to see whether she can get him to open up.

Lecter takes to the woman, and their unique relationship is the foundation of the film: Though she searches for Bill and Lecter tries—and eventually succeeds—in escaping from captivity, they are still bound together, mentally and spiritually.

The relationship is so extraordinary that it's almost bad form to complain about the lapses of believability—for instance, how does Lecter manage to use that makeshift key of his, all trussed up? And how does Bill, decked out in "night vision" goggles, standing right next to Clarice in the dark, manage *not* to kill the fumbling trainee several times over? Reading the novel will fill in these gaps for you—but they're not explained in the movie.

The performances of Hopkins and Foster are also great. As vile as Hopkins's deeds are, they're all the more horrible because of the intelligence that burns through his eyes and wicked smile: This is a brilliant, reasonable madman, like a fun-house Mr. Spock. Incredibly, white-trash refugee Clarice manages to get close to his towering genius, pulling herself up by her bootstraps, and Foster can't be praised enough for making the young woman believable.

Demme's previous films include *Something Wild* (1986) and the delightful *Married to the Mob* (1988). He came aboard this film after Gene Hackman dropped out as star and director. He shot the FBI scenes in Washington and Quantico, the rest of the film being shot in and around Pittsburgh. The sets for Lecter's cell and Buffalo Bill's basement were constructed in an abandoned turbine factory.

Look for film director Roger Corman as FBI director Hayden Burke. And take a close look at those moth pupae: They're Tootsie Rolls.

The Disc
Video: ★★½
Audio: ★★★ (Surround)
Chapters: Yes (but don't read the headings if you haven't seen the film)
Format: CLV
Source: Orion Home Video/Image Entertainment

The transfer is like the bugs found in the throats of Bill's victims: Depending on their stage, they're either loathsome slugs or beautiful things with glorious wings.

Parts of the film (mostly the latter half) look fine, relatively sharp with good color. Other parts look awful, with bleeding and/or inaccurate colors, a less than sharp image, and grain. How to explain it? Inattention. The film should have been "tuned" constantly to make sure dark scenes, scenes with saturated colors, scenes with stark lighting, were of a consistent quality.

The film is not letterboxed but plays well as is.

The audio is basically fine, with highs as clear as a wind chime and resonant lows. But directional and Surround effects that were present in theaters aren't on this disc.

Manhunter is available on laserdisc and is recommended, not so much for the transfer as for the film itself.

Singin' in the Rain (1952)
★★★★★
Directors: Gene Kelly and Stanley Donen
Running Time: 104 minutes

During the making of *An American in Paris* (1951), producer Arthur Freed and star Kelly were already looking for another project. The men were clearly on a creative roll, having made, in dizzying succession, *Ziegfeld Follies* (1946), *The Pirate* (1948), *Words and Music* (1948), *Take Me Out to the Ball Game* (1949), and *On The Town* (see page 202)—and MGM brass kept up the pressure for them to *keep* making hits.

No one remembers exactly *whose* idea it was to make a movie about the transition from silent to sound films, but Kelly has recalled that once the suggestion was made, everyone got excited and "all of us dashed around the studio asking the veterans what it was like in the old days and the script was built around the information we picked up."

For music, the filmmakers selected the best songs from the rich library of tunes written by lyricist Freed and his partner Nacio Herb Brown. (For example, the title song was composed in 1929 and used that year in the movie *The Hollywood Revue of 1929;* it was also sung by Judy Garland in the 1940 film *Little Nellie Kelly*). For Kelly's costars, they went with newcomer Debbie Reynolds, a Miss Burbank with limited film experience; Jean Hagen, who had appeared in movies such as *Adam's Rib* (1949) and *The Asphalt Jungle* (1950); and Donald O'Connor, a fifteen-year veteran of comedies and musicals (he also played Beau Geste as a child in the 1939 adventure classic).

The result was magic, the saga of Monumental Pictures film stars Don Lockwood (Kelly) and Lina Lamont (Jean Hagen), who are about to make their first talking picture, *The Dueling Cavalier*. As matinee idol Lockwood is fleeing some rabid fans, he meets and falls in love with aspiring actress Kathy Selden (Reynolds). The meeting proves fortuitous: Lina has a dreadful speaking voice and, at a preview, *The Dueling Cavalier* is laughed off the screen. Fortunately, Lockwood's friend Cosmo Brown (O'Connor) comes up with the idea of having Kathy dub Lina's voice. The salvaged picture is a smash, and romance blooms between Lockwood and Selden. (Ironically, it was actually Hagen, not Reynolds, who provided Lina's "dubbed" voice, while Reynolds's own voice—which still had traces of a Texas twang—was dubbed by another singer for the musical numbers.)

Singin' in the Rain has more classic moments than any movie should be *allowed* to have, but standouts are the Kelly/O'Connor duet "Fit as a Fiddle," O'Connor's incomparable "Make 'Em Laugh" with its still-dazzling run up two walls (he scoots up and does a flip not once but twice in one take!), and, of course, Kelly's "Singin' in the Rain," in which his rapture is contagious.

There are those who don't think much of Gene Kelly as a singer or as an actor, and there are those who don't care much for his muscular brand of dancing (compared, say, to the more graceful style of Fred Astaire or the dazzling footwork of the Nicholas Brothers). But there's no denying that Kelly was an exceptional athlete and a resourceful choreographer who always challenged himself and others and who had a knack for picking projects that lent themselves to his brand of dance.

In any case, *Singin' in the Rain* is irresistible fun, a perfect film for those who love movie musicals—and for those who hate them. It'll convert you!

The Disc
Video: ★★★★½ (Criterion);
★★★★★ (MGM/UA)
Audio: ★★★½ (monaural)
Chapters: Yes
Format: CLV or CAV
Source: Criterion or MGM/UA Home Video

It's a rare occurrence, but the picture on the studio release is actually better than the Criterion version of the film, which itself was pretty impressive. With the possible exception of *The Band Wagon* and *The Adventures of Don Juan* (see pages 17 and 2), the MGM/UA release may be the finest Technicolor film available on laserdisc. And while the Criterion disc has some worthwhile commentary on the audio track, MGM/UA's version offers, as an extra, Debbie Reynolds's "You Are My Lucky Star" number, which was cut from the film, along with the trailer and—best of all—the original version of "Singin' in the Rain" from *The Hollywood Revue of 1929*. You couldn't ask for much more—and the MGM/UA disc is less expensive to boot!

There is no discernable difference between the quality of the CLV and CAV versions from either company.

The digital sound is clean and generally rich, though both the Criterion and MGM/UA editions *are* hurt somewhat by the limitations of the original film. Kelly's voice, reedy to begin with, lacks body, and the brasses have a touch of tin in them.

Either version is preferable to the old MGM/UA edition of the film, which is good, though the colors pale by comparison.

Sleeping with the Enemy (1991) ★★
Director: Joseph Ruben
Running Time: 99 minutes

Sara Burney (Julia Roberts) has a wealthy investment counselor husband, Martin (Patrick Bergin), who's a loving, doting angel to her one second and a savage wife-abusing devil the next. She can't take it anymore and, after careful planning, fakes her death by drowning not far from their spectacular beach house. Returning home when he's not around, she gathers up some belongings, drops her wedding ring in the toilet, and resurfaces in small-town USA as Laura, where she strikes up a relationship with her neighbor, school drama teacher Ben Woodward (Kevin Anderson).

Holes in the "death of Sara" scenario begin to bother Martin (her wedding ring has been sitting in the bottom of the toilet for *how* long before he notices it?) and, concluding she's run off, he decides to track her down. He succeeds, and plays a few mind games with her before moving in for the final showdown.

Roberts was riding high on the surprise success of *Pretty Woman* (see page 219), and her popularity single-handedly dragged this mediocre thriller to box-office grosses out of proportion with its real merits. The painful, tense relationship between Martin and Sara keeps the early part of the movie afloat; after she gets away from him, things flounder. She and the two-dimensional dud Ben are boring together, she's unexciting when she's on her own, and the movie comes to life again only when the schizophrenic Martin returns—which, in a twisted sort of way, explains why she stayed with him in the first place.

The film was based on the 1987 Nancy Price novel, which delved more deeply into Sara's state of mind and fleshed out her small-town life.

Director Ruben has made better films: *Dreamscape* (1984), *The Stepfather* (1987), and *True Believer* (1989).

The Disc
Video: ★★★★
Audio: ★★★★½ (Surround)
Chapters: Yes
Format: CLV
Source: Fox Home Video

For the most part, the film has been given an excellent transfer, with zippy color and a sharp image. It's hurt by an excessive amount of video noise in several scenes and softness in a few others. The film is not hurt by cropping.

The sound is superb and the Surround separation is inspired, the pounding of the storm at sea and the busy carnival alternating with scenes of utter silence (reflecting, perhaps, the extremes of Martin himself?).

Some Like It Hot (1959)
★★★½
Director: Billy Wilder
Running Time: 121 Minutes

Some Like It Hot is a men-in-drag comedy set in Chicago during the Roaring Twenties. Two musicians, sax player Joe (Tony Curtis) and bass player Jerry (Jack Lemmon), accidentally witness the St. Valentine's Day Massacre and flee perpetrator Spats Columbo (George Raft) and his hoods by impersonating females and joining an all-female band bound for Miami.

Adopting a third, Cary Grant–like persona, Joe strikes up a romance with Sugar Kane (Marilyn Monroe) and, while on a drunken spree at a dance party, the swacked Jerry, still in drag, responds to the overtures of a millionaire named Osgood (Joe E. Brown). Spats is eventually blown away by a rival crime boss, and the boys end up with their lovers, Joe reverting to his true self, Jerry seemingly headed for the altar as Daphne!

Though *Some Like It Hot* is a fun, fondly remembered comedy, contemporary audiences encountering it tend to find it neither daring nor especially riotous. Transvestite comedy, though not unprecedented, was more shocking in the 1950s: At the time, it was very bold indeed. As for the humor, Monty Python and "Saturday Night Live" have pushed the boundaries of taste so far that the film *does* seem somewhat tame. But there are still the marvelous performances, from the broad comedy of Curtis and Lemmon to the delightful self-parody of Raft. And, of course, there's Marilyn.

Though Monroe desperately wanted to be taken seriously as a dramatic actress, no one did the kootchy-koo, thinking man's dream-girl act as well as she did. In this film, along with *Gentlemen Prefer Blondes* (1953) and *The Seven Year Itch* (1955), she was likable, earthy, and—though sexy as hell—devoid of sexual danger. A wife could trust Sugar Kane with her husband.

Curtis and Lemmon have always done their best work in light comedy, and the witty script by Wilder and I. A. L. Diamond gives them ample opportunity to strut their stuff.

Tame by modern standards, yes. But the film is energetic and entertaining, and an important part of Hollywood's transition from the innocence of the thirties and forties to the explosive liberation of the sixties.

The Disc
Video: ★★★½
Audio: ★★★ (monaural)
Chapters: Yes
Format: CAV or CLV (Criterion); CLV (MGM/UA)
Source: Criterion or MGM/UA Home Video

Whichever version you choose, *Some Like It Hot* is preserved in a form close to the way it looked when it first opened.

The Criterion version has a couple of splices, but there's a good deal of detail in the image, and the middle-range tones are very well reproduced. Both versions are amply letterboxed.

The MGM/UA edition is a bit clearer and sharper, though the image is a bit (?)

There are some pops and crackles on the sound track of all the different versions, but the digital sound is more or less what you'd expect from a film of this era.

The CAV edition has interesting supplementary material: color home movies of Marilyn Monroe and the cast shot at the Hotel Coronado; production and publicity stills; a Lemmon interview; the trailer; and interesting commentary by Howard Suber. The CLV disc contains the Suber lecture and the trailer.

Son of Dracula (1943) ★★★★
Director: Robert Siodmak
Running Time: 78 minutes

The Frankenstein/Dracula/Wolf Man/Mummy movies set in Europe were running out of steam, so Universal attempted to revitalize the franchise by setting both *The Mummy's Tomb* (1942) and *Son of*

Dracula in domestic locales. The efforts did not provide the necessary box-office transfusion and, thereafter, the studio usually wooed patrons by heaping their monsters together in efforts such as *House of Frankenstein* (1944), *House of Dracula* (1945), and even *Abbott and Costello Meet Frankenstein* (see page 1).

But *Son of Dracula* remains one of the standout efforts of the series. German director Siodmak employs the gloomy expressionism that would become his trademark in such crime films as *Phantom Lady* (1944) and *The Dark Mirror* (1946); the movie is so full of mysterious shadows it looks as if it was shot through latticework! (One thing it *doesn't* have, though, is a son of Dracula: The villain is Dracula himself. But since it wasn't Bela Lugosi in the role, Universal felt it had to make *some* kind of distinction.)

In Louisiana, a morbid young woman, Katherine Caldwell (Louise Allbritton), comes up with a Faustian scheme: She plans to become one of the living dead by wedding the visiting Hungarian vampire Count Alucard (Lon Chaney, Jr.). Upon becoming a vampire herself, she plans to destroy him and bite her real lover, Frank Stanley (Robert Paige), so they can live together in ghastly immortality. The ethical Stanley reacts violently when he finally figures out what's going on; finding the count's coffin, he burns it. The vampire turns to dust at sunrise; unfortunately, so does Katherine.

Son of Dracula is probably the best-looking of all the Universal horror films, and it contains many unforgettable images: the diaphanous mothlike figure of Katherine as she moves through the swamp toward the cabin of a witch, Queen Zimba (Adeline de Walt Reynolds); the Count taking shape from vapor, then gliding majestically across a dark pond; Katherine trying to shield herself behind Dracula when Stanley approaches with a gun, then falling dead when the bullets pass through the Count's phantom body; and the great gothic patterns and shafts of light in the tunnel that is Dracula's lair.

Chaney had already played the Wolf Man, the Frankenstein Monster, and the Mummy: By playing Dracula, he scored a coup no other actor has ever matched. Though a bit on the chunky side, he is foreboding with his thin mustache, icy stare, and slicked-back hair. Allbritton—a brunette here—was the blond "other woman" in several second features, and Evelyn Ankers, as her sister Claire, went on to become the queen of *B* horror movies in films such as *Weird Woman*, *The Invisible Man's Revenge* (both 1944), *The Frozen Ghost* (1945), and others. Samuel S. Hinds, who plays Judge Simmons (and was a lawyer before becoming an actor) is best known as the decent father in *It's a Wonderful Life* (1946) and Lew Ayres's father in several of the Dr. Kildare films.

This is a great horror film, too often ignored.

The Disc

Video: ★★★★
Audio: ★★ (monaural)
Chapters: No
Format: CLV (side one), CAV (side two)
Source: MCA Home Video

When the Universal horror films were sold as a package to television in the early 1950s, the contrast of most of the prints had to be reduced so that details in the darkest scenes would be visible on TV. The movies no longer displayed glossy blacks and consequently lost a lot of their impact.

For the laserdisc of *Son of Dracula*, MCA used a high-contrast print that restores much of its magical darkness. The source material was in very good shape and the movie looks far younger than its years. The only thing wrong with the disc is that some fine-grain speckling crops up on most copies past 42:00 on side one.

Unfortunately, stretches of the sound track are a little threadbare, causing it to *sound* like a half-century old movie. There are dropouts scattered throughout the first side and a few minor ones on the second side.

The disc contains a theatrical trailer as well as a very impressive file of eighty-seven stills, several of which are in color.

Sorcerer (1977) ★★★★½
Director: William Friedkin
Running Time: 121 minutes

There was a time when William Friedkin only made good—often great—movies. He gave us *The Boys in the Band* (1970), *The French Connection* (1971), *The Exorcist* (see page 89), and *Sorcerer*, one after another. He seemed able to do no wrong. But the seven movies he's made since then have been unqualified commercial and artistic disasters, from *Cruising* (1980) to his return to *Exorcist*-territory, *The Guardian* (see page 125).

What happened? Chaos in his personal life (two divorces, one of them drawn out and acrimonious)? Perhaps. But it's no coincidence that the string of uninspired films followed the critical and commercial flop of his most powerful and ambitious movie.

Sorcerer is based on the novel *The Wages of Fear* by Georges Arnaud, which was previously filmed in 1953 by French director H. G. Clouzot (to whom Friedkin dedicates his picture). In Friedkin's film, a "punk from Queens,'" Jackie Scanlon (Roy Scheider), is forced to flee New Jersey after robbing a church whose priest is the brother of a powerful mobster; a banking scandal causes Victor Manzon (Bruno Cremer) to leave Paris; and terrorist Kassem (Amidou) leaves Jerusalem after being connected with a bombing. All end up in South America, hiding out and working for enough money to get anywhere else. Meanwhile, anti-American factions blow up an oil well that can be shut down only by using dynamite. Unfortunately, the explosives are located 218 miles from the blast and are so old and unstable that the only way to transport them is to pack them in sand and move them over twisting, precipitous jungle roads by truck.

Scanlon, Manzon, Kassem, and Marquez (Karl John) volunteer to drive two truckloads to the site (in case one doesn't get through). When hit man Nilo (Francisco Rabal) kills Marquez, he's forced to take his place, riding with Scanlon. The nerve-racking trip through the jungle comprises half the movie, and Friedkin is constantly hitting his characters with some new and unexpected travail—the most extraordinary of which has the two trucks inching across a swaying rope bridge during a furious storm. Despite the nail-biting adventure, Friedkin never loses sight of his characters. Marred only by excessive length in the first half and a downbeat (if inevitable) resolution, *Sorcerer* is a stunning film.

So why did it fail? Largely because the marketing was all wrong. Incredible as it may seem, the studio hoped to capitalize on the huge success of *The Exorcist* by disguising what the film was about. They gave it a supernatural title and emphasized the demon-faced truck in the advertisements; even the trailer showed a monsterlike carving that had no relation to anything in the movie. The wrong kind of audience came to the film and, not surprisingly, word of mouth was awful.

Suffice it to say, *you* won't be disappointed. Friedkin said, "I worked longer and harder on it than on anything else," and it shows.

The Disc
Video ★★★★½
Audio: ★★★★ (Surround)
Chapters: Yes
Format: CLV (sides one and two), CAV (side three)
Source: MCA/Universal Home Video

Why did MCA/Universal do side three in CAV when side two has that remarkable bridge crossing? Who knows. Maybe they thought viewers would prefer to single-frame their way through one of the rebels getting shot in the head.

Friedkin himself supervised all of the creative aspects of the transfer, and the disc cost MCA/Universal Home Video a staggering $100,000 in transfer costs: Only *E.T.* cost more. Not only was the monaural film rechanneled for Surround Sound but the picture itself was greatly enhanced, every frame engineered for improved color.

The panning-and-scanning on *Sorcerer*

is very well done. Friedkin shot the film at 1.85:1 and was present during the transfer "to get all the important stuff in." In a way, the film is improved. In the film, each man is hemmed in by his surroundings—by the small, cheap rooms, the small, dirty town, the small, constricted cabs of the trucks, the big, verdant jungle. Now, the frame closes them in, as well. It works just fine.

Grain was (and is) a problem with the film, though in many cases that, too, actually enhances the grittiness of the scene. Given the conditions under which *Sorcerer* was shot, it's amazing there isn't more of it.

What's most impressive about the laserdisc, though, is the spectacular stereo Surround. Everything from the roar of the trucks to the driving rain to the pulsing score by the German electronic group Tangerine Dream will put a smile on your face!

The trailer is featured at the beginning of the film, and it does a good job whetting the appetite without giving anything away.

Criterion has released a splendid edition of *Wages of Fear*, subtitled, uncut, and transferred from excellent source material. The film is dazzling, though not quite as wonderfully "in-your-face" as Friedkin's version.

The Sound of Music (1965)
★★★★
Director: Robert Wise
Running Time: 177 minutes

The Sound of Music opened on Broadway in November of 1959. Like all the musicals of Richard Rodgers and Oscar Hammerstein II—*Oklahoma!*, *Carousel*, *South Pacific*, and *The King and I*, among others—this true story of the Trapp Family Singers was considered ideal material for the movies.

Originally, *The Sound of Music* was to be directed by William Wyler (*Funny Girl*) and star Doris Day, but negotiations with the actress broke down and delays forced Wyler to withdraw. With a long-planned starting date approaching, Twentieth Century–Fox quickly signed Robert Wise, who had codirected *West Side Story* (see page 297), and Wise went looking for a star. He'd heard good reports about a film that was just finishing up over at Disney, and he asked to see some footage: Julie Andrews's performance in *Mary Poppins* convinced Wise that she'd be perfect for *The Sound of Music*.

At first, Twentieth Century–Fox balked: Andrews had acted in *My Fair Lady* and *Camelot* on the Broadway stage but was unknown to movie audiences. (The directors of the film versions of those two musicals resisted casting her and went with those "famous" singers Audrey Hepburn and Vanessa Redgrave, respectively.) But Wise stood firm. He said she was a fresh face and, what's more, she sang like an angel. Fox relented; and when Andrews won the hearts of moviegoers worldwide, Fox executives fell over each other claiming prescience for having cast her.

Andrews plays the headstrong Maria, a failed nun in prewar Salzburg, Austria, who becomes the nanny for the seven children of widower Captain Georg Von Trapp (Christopher Plummer). At first, the martinet Georg resents the free-spirited Maria, who takes the children picnicking, tree climbing, and boating. But when he hears them sing, fond memories of a happier time return—so much so that he gives up his stuffy fiancée, Baroness Elsa Schraeder (Eleanor Parker), and marries Maria. But their happiness is short-lived: When the Nazis demand that the captain accept a naval commission, the anti-Nazi patriot leads his family on a daring journey from Salzburg to Switzerland and freedom.

Sweet and noble in spite of its sappiness, *The Sound of Music* serves up endearing characters, beautiful songs, and stunning location photography. It became the most successful movie in history until *The Godfather* seven years later. Ironically, though Andrews became typecast as a musical star, her subsequent efforts—*Thoroughly Modern Millie* (1967) and *Star!* (1968)—a gargantuan biography of Gertrude Lawrence, directed by

Wise—were box office duds. It wasn't until the quasi-musical *Victor/Victoria* (see page 292) that she was back on top.

The Disc
Video: ★
Audio: ★★★½ (stereo)
Chapters: Yes
Format: CLV
Source: CBS Fox Video

Fans of the film have a tough choice: bad or worse. In the pan-and-scan version, which has nice color and a sharp picture, watch the kids hop off the wall during "Do-Re-Mi." What kids, you ask? The ones you don't see because they're lopped off; likewise, the children dancing around the fountain later in that number. Because Wise packed kids into every corner of the big 70mm image, you rarely get to see all seven of them in any scene of the cropped version.

That's not all. In the early stages of the Andrews/Plummer relationship, Wise often places them on opposite sides of the screen to emphasize the distance between them: One of them is invariably lost. During the nighttime scene at the gazebo, when Andrews gets up off the bench, you can see her dress blowing in from the right, but that's it until Plummer walks over to her.

So, happily, along comes the letterbox edition, which gives us the full screen image—but at an awful price. Fox seems to have gone out of their way to do the absolute worst transfer possible. The print itself is free of flaws, but it's also free of color: The wretched Deluxe hues look so flat and downright faded that the print seems colorized. The awe-inspiring opening shots, so vibrant in the theaters, are pale green and blue; that dress the baroness is wearing on the balcony at night is *supposed* to be bright red, not maroon; skin tones have no subtleties and night scenes lose much of their delicate shading. For the sake of emotional impact, the letterbox disc is still preferable—but just barely.

The sound, at least, is extremely clear on both versions, and the stereo separation is *wunderbar*.

The Spy Who Loved Me (1977)
★★★★
Director: Lewis Gilbert
Running Time: 129 minutes

After Sean Connery returned for one last go at the role of James Bond in *Diamonds Are Forever* (1971), the search was on for a new 007.

Roger Moore had been a recurring choice of producer Cubby Broccoli each time Connery threatened to quit or actually did so, but Moore was always busy shooting a TV series—first "The Saint," then "The Persuaders." Now that Connery was really and truly gone for good and Moore was free he wasn't offered the role immediately. He had made a suspense film, *Crossplot* (1969), which had bombed for United Artists, the studio underwriting the Bond films. United Artists didn't really want him, and, after a meeting with Moore producer Cubby Broccoli felt that he was too fat. ("I was," Moore admits. "I'd fattened up in anticipation of making no money from *Crossplot*.")

Moore says that newcomers were tested "like mad," and there were discussions with both Burt Reynolds and John Gavin to take the part. Finally, however, Broccoli decided that Moore had credibility in the genre and at least was British: If he could lose twenty pounds fast, the part was his. Moore did, and though his first two Bond films—*Live and Let Die* (1973) and *The Man with the Golden Gun* (1974)—were only moderate box-office successes, Broccoli stuck with him. Good thing, too: Like Connery in *Goldfinger*, Moore's third was a smash.

To say that the film is nothing like the novel is an understatement. The tenth novel in the Ian Fleming series, *The Spy Who Loved Me* (1962) is unique, told in the first person from the *heroine*'s perspective: Vivienne Michel is unable to have a successful relationship with a man until she meets Bond (well past the novel's halfway point!), who not only teaches her how to love but saves her from hoodlums.

The filmmakers scrapped that story and came up with the saga of Karl

Stromberg (Curt Jurgens), who, from his submersible fortress *Atlantis*, steals submarines from the East and West in such a way that each blames the other. The reason? He wants to start a nuclear war and rebuild civilization under the sea. Bond and a Soviet Agent XXX, Major Anya Amasova (Barbara Bach) team up to stop him, defeating his army aboard the supertanker *Liparus*, in whose belly the captured submarines are being held.

This is a taut, clever, classy film, with one of the most breathtaking stunts in the series, Bond skiing off a cliff—the three-thousand-foot-tall Asgard peak on Canada's Baffin Island—and tumbling through the air until a Union Jack parachute opens. It also features the neatest car since *Goldfinger*, the gadget-laden Lotus Esprit, which is pursued by a helicopter and evades it by becoming a submarine, and the most formidable bodyguard since *Goldfinger's* Oddjob, the awesome, unstoppable, seven-foot-two-inch, metal-toothed Jaws (Richard Kiel). This towering character was so popular that he returned in the text Bond film, *Moonraker* (1979).

Moore finally finds a perfect balance of urbanity and drollness in this film, though he does manage to do some cruel butt kicking in the assault on the supertanker and in the showdown with Stromberg. Bach is both a better spy and a tougher cookie than Bond, and she's arguably the most beautiful Bond costar of them all. Jurgens is dull, but he has relatively little screen time. Movie scream queen Caroline Munro doesn't get to do much either as his hit woman, Naomi.

Photographed in Egypt, Sardinia, Canada, Malta, Scotland, Okinawa, Switzerland, and the Bahamas by Claude Renoir, grandson of the painter, *The Spy Who Loved Me* was the most expensive Bond film to date, costing $13.5 million—a figure that doubled for *Moonraker* and remained in the $25 million range for *For Your Eyes Only* (1981), *Octopussy* (1983), and Moore's last outing, *A View to a Kill* (1985).

The theme song, "Nobody Does It Better" was the most popular recording from a Bond film since *Goldfinger*.

The Disc
Video: ★★★★
Audio: ★★★½ (Surround)
Chapters: No
Format: CLV (sides one and two), CAV (side three)
Source: MGM/UA Home Video

The colors are extremely solid, the picture sharp-edged in the two-disc letterboxed set. However, many copies have a distracting amount of speckling on side three, which prevents the set from earning a five-star rating. At least the CAV side contains what most viewers will want to see: the tail end of the attack on the supertanker, Bond's one-man attack on *Atlantis*, explosions galore, and Barbara Bach in a low-cut dress. The letterboxed trailer is also on this side, allowing you to freeze on key scenes from earlier in the film.

The digital audio and stereo separation are very good, though the rear speakers could have been used to greater effect.

Except for *The Man with The Golden Gun*, the Moore Bond films are available in letterboxed versions from MGM/UA and in old, fuzzier, panned-and-scanned editions from CBS/Fox.

Stagecoach (1939) ★★★★½
Director: John Ford
Running Time: 97 minutes

John Ford was a successful director when he bought the rights to Ernest Haycox's short story "Stage to Lordsburg" in 1938. By then, however, the Western had become passé in Hollywood, and he couldn't convince any studio to underwrite his film. Independent producer Walter Wanger agreed to put up the money, with the stipulation that hot young star Gary Cooper star as the Ringo Kid. But Ford had other ideas: He wanted John Wayne for the part. Wanger balked. In 1930, the very expensive *The Big Trail* was supposed to have made Wayne a star. It bombed in a big way, and the actor was relegated to low-budget films such as *Girls Demand Excitement* (1931) and *Randy Rides Alone* (1934). Wayne had worked for Ford in the silent days as a propman and an extra, and the director refused to consider anyone else to play Ringo. Wanger capitulated: Even if Wayne were a stiff, this was an ensemble film and the first "adult" Western, qualities that he felt would overcome a weak lead.

In 1885, the stagecoach heading from Tonto in the Arizona Territory to Lordsburg, New Mexico, carries Dallas (Claire Trevor), a "dancer" who is driven out of town by the Ladies' Law and Order League; Doc Boone (Thomas Mitchell), a drunken physician; Hatfield (John Carradine), a gentleman gambler; Lucy Mallory (Louise Platt), a pregnant woman traveling to be with her soldier husband; Gateswood (Berton Churchill), a banker; and Mr. Peacock (Donald Meek), a timid salesman. Driving the rig is Bucky (Andy Devine), with Marshal Curley Wilcox (George Bancroft) riding shotgun. The Ringo Kid (Wayne) joins the party en route, heading to Lordsburg to settle an old score with three desperadoes. (The character was called Malpais Bill in the Haycox story.)

While the characters get to know and in some cases dislike one another, Indians stalk the stagecoach, finally attacking as it crosses a wide-open stretch of desert. There are fatalities on both sides, though Ringo and Dallas make it through. The gunslinger wins the shoot-out in Lordsburg, after which he and Dallas hurry across the border to start a new life.

Filmed in Ford's favorite cinematic stomping ground, Monument Valley, *Stagecoach* invented the characters and situations that have since become stereotypes and clichés. But the actors are so good and the film is so well directed that you'll have no trouble seeing the film through 1938 eyes and just enjoying the rousing good ride from start *nearly* to finish. The actors are great—mythically American, with Wayne giving an alternately tough and boyish performance that made him a superstar. (Take *that*, Mr. Wanger.) Whatever you may think of Wayne's later work (and his politics), the first shot of Ringo, twirling his shotgun to stop the stage, will make you a fan. The only disappointment is the final shoot-out: Ringo confronts his enemies and dives to the ground, firing away; cut to the shots, heard from a distance. Ford felt that the Indian attack had been so exciting, it would be wiser to concentrate on the suspense of the gunfight rather than the action. It's disappointing though faithful to the story, where the gunfight is also "offcamera."

If the resolution is a letdown however, the afterglow of the breakneck Indian attack will last for *days*. Legendary stunt actor and former rodeo rider Yakima Canutt doubled for Wayne and several of the Indians, executing stunts and horse falls that have rarely been matched. The most incredible of these has Yak, as Ringo, leaping from the stagecoach onto the running horses to retrieve the reins. (Once asked why the Indians didn't just shoot the horses to stop the stagecoach, Ford replied, "Because they would have also stopped the picture.")

The Disc

Video: ★★½
Audio: ★½ (monaural)
Chapters: Yes
Format: CLV
Source: Warner Home Video

It's likely (and sad) that we'll probably never see a better print of this classic film: Even the fiftieth-anniversary prints shown around the nation were made from a fairly wretched negative. (In the early 1970s, a search by the American Film Institute revealed that virtually every 35mm print of the film had suffered considerable damage; the best print was owned by Wayne, and it is from his copy—not from an original negative—that most subsequent prints were struck.)

The print isn't completely awful, but it's not very good. The picture is soft and the grays variable: Some scenes have a satisfying range of tones, while others look dark, foggy, or have whites that are much too irredescent. There are also numerous scratches and marks.

Everything is intelligible in the audio, though the sound is generally scratchy in spots, and downright raw in others.

Star Trek—The Motion Picture (1979) ★★★
Director: Robert Wise
Running Time: 132 minutes

Somewhere along the line, this film got the reputation for being a stiff—*Star Trek: The Motionless Picture*, some called it. Poppycock. Part of the bad publicity arose from the cost of the film, over $40 million. What *isn't* generally realized, however, is that a lot of that was due to the failure of the original special-effects team to generate anything usable. The meter started running overtime as *two* teams (headed by John Dykstra of *Star Wars* fame and Douglas Trumbull of *Close Encounters of the Third Kind*) rushed to finish the film in time for its long-scheduled release. Some material never *was* completed, forcing key scenes to be left out of the film. (These were later added for TV showings, videocassette, and the original, panned-and-scanned disc. They are not present on the letterboxed edition.)

Another complaint is that the film isn't "Star Trek"—meaning it isn't as overacted, overwrought, and self-righteous as the prime-time series that ran from 1966 to 1969. That's true. Robert Wise (see entries for *The Day the Earth Stood Still*, 1951, *West Side Story*, and *The Sound of Music*) was hired to give the project big-screen credibility and sophistication, to open it up in ways the show never had.

Conversely, many science fiction fans resented the fact that the somewhat existential story—reminiscent of Sanislaw Lem's classic novel *Solaris* (1961)—was mucked up by casting a bunch of hamfisted TV actors.

While flawed by overlength as well as performances that don't quite work (Spock is repulsively icy instead of amusingly logical, and, unlike most of his colleagues, Shatner hasn't toned his performance down for the big screen), *Star Trek—The Motion Picture* is nonetheless the best and most literate big-budget science fiction film since *2001: A Space Odyssey*.

Deep in space, a mysterious object at the heart of an immense cloud is destroying everything in its path, from Klingon ships to communications stations, and it's approaching our solar system. Adm. James Tiberius Kirk (William Shatner), former captain of the starship *Enterprise*, rejoins his former mates Spock (Leonard Nimoy), Dr. Leonard "Bones" McCoy (DeForest Kelly), Chief Engineer Montgomery Scott (James Doohan), Sulu (George Takei), Uhura (Nichelle Nichols), and Pavel Chekov (Walter Koenig) to determine its nature and mission before it unleashes its destructive powers against the earth. Also along for the ride are Captain Decker (Stephen Collins), a Kirk protégé who resents the admiral's return, and the bald-headed alien female Ilia (Persis Khambatta), a Deltan with an irresistible sexual aura.

The twenty-third century is created with wonderful realism, particularly where the workaday activities in space are concerned. And the depiction of the cosmic cloud remains an awe-inspiring sight: It's part crystal, part crustacean, part cirus—a weblike electronic array layered atop active meteorological events. It's truly spectacular.

Credit must also be given to Jerry Goldsmith's stirring score, which, though dropped for subsequent films, serves as the sound track for the syndicated TV series "Star Trek: The Next Generation."

Subsequent *Star Trek* films have been of variable quality. *Star Trek II: The Wrath of Khan* (1982), directed by Nicholas Meyer, is a sequel to the 1967 "Space Seed" episode of the series and is very much a big-screen TV show, cutesy and cheap-looking. In it, Kirk battles the genetically designed warrior Khan (Ricardo Montalban) for possession of the Genesis device, which is capable of creating a thriving ecology on barren worlds—or smothering the existing life. Kirk wins and Spock dies, though his body is deposited on the Genesis planet, where it is reborn in . . .

Star Trek III: The Search for Spock (1984), directed by Leonard Nimoy (his price for returning as Spock), also looks TV-cheap, but the story and characters manage to transcend the production values. Spock's father, Sarek (Mark Lenard), informs Kirk that Spock's spirit may still be alive and living in Dr. McCoy. Accompanied by Vulcan science officer Lieutenant Saavik (Robin Curtis), Kirk and his crew return to the Genesis planet, find Spock's regenerating body, and attempt to reunite spirit and substance. Meanwhile, the evil Klingon commander Kruge (Christopher Lloyd) is trying to learn the secret of the Genesis effect for his own greedy purposes. Director Nimoy found a depth in the relationship of the principals that went beyond the typical sarcasm and verbal abuse, making for a satisfying entry in the series.

Director Nimoy's *Star Trek IV: The Voyage Home* (1986) is every bit as good as the first film, as a gigantic probe (here we go again!) approaches earth, shutting down the power of everything in its path. Spock deciphers the probe's squealing sounds and realizes that it's the song of humpback whales, which are extinct. Unless it hears some cetacean reply, the probe is going to destroy our world. Kirk and company go back to San Francisco in our time to find whales and bring them to the twenty-third century. The dialogue has wit, the performances have pith, and the whole thing is an entertaining, poignant delight.

Then there's *Star Trek V: The Final Frontier* (1989), which Shatner was allowed to cowrite and direct. His intention was to make a straight-ahead action film, but all he created was lots of movement, noise, and embarrassing situations as the Enterprise and its crew are hijacked by Spock's half brother, Sybok (Laurence Luckinbill), for a journey through the Great Barrier and a meeting with God. Corny, badly written, and amateurishly directed, the film is a mortifying failure that'll make you squirm.

Thanks to the skills of director Nicholas Meyer, *Star Trek VI: The Undiscovered Country* (1991) managed to win back some of the franchise's lost dignity, as Kirk and company try to preserve Federation/Klingon peace talks by preventing the assassination of a Klingon official. The disc contains three minutes of footage not seen in theaters or on videocassette.

The Disc

Video:
Star Trek—The Motion Picture
letterboxed: ★★★½
panned-and-scanned: ★★★
Star Trek II: The Wrath of Khan
letterboxed: ★★½
panned-and-scanned: ★★½
Star Trek III: The Search for Spock
letterboxed: ★★★
panned-and-scanned: ★★★
Star Trek IV: The Voyage Home
letterboxed: ★★★
panned-and-scanned: ★★★
Star Trek V: The Final Frontier
letterboxed: ★★½
panned-and-scanned: ★★
Star Trek VI: The Undiscovery Country
letterboxed: ★★★★½
panned-and scanned: ★★★★½

Audio: (Surround)
Star Trek—The Motion Picture
letterboxed: ★★★★
panned-and-scanned: ★★★½
Star Trek II: The Wrath of Khan
letterboxed: ★★★½
panned-and-scanned: ★★½
Star Trek III: The Search for Spock
letterboxed: ★★★
panned-and-scanned: ★★★
Star Trek IV: The Voyage Home
letterboxed: ★★½
panned-and-scanned: ★★½
Star Trek V: The Final Frontier
letterboxed: ★★★★
panned-and-scanned: ★★½
Star Trek VI: The Undiscovered Country
letterboxed: ★★★★½
panned-and-scanned: ★★★★½
Chapters: No
Format: CLV (*Star Trek—The Motion Picture* and *Star Trek IV: The Voyage Home* have CAV side threes)
Source: Paramount Home Video

With the exception of the first film, which demands a wide-screen image to the size and majesty of the alien presence, all of the films work acceptably in both panned and letterboxed editions: They were, after all, staged and filmed more or less like TV shows. It depends upon the viewer's preference: Bigger close-ups of the stars or fuller views of space, the final frontier, and the generally fake-looking planet sets.

Also, with the exception of the letterboxed edition of the first film, all of the discs tend to be on the grainy side, with a *slightly* fuzzy look. Obviously, this is less true of the letterboxed versions, which fill a smaller area of the screen. The problems stem from the fact that the *Star Trek* films tend to be rather darkly lighted, and the special effects often generate graininess and softness due to the processes used and the limited budgets of the sequels.

The audio is a bit noisy and hissy on the panned-and-scanned versions of several films, hence their lower ratings. The second, third, and fourth letter-boxed editions also suffer from background noise. On the whole, though, the sound is generally clear and the Surround effects are usually excellent.

The boxed set is no longer available. While the colors are a *touch* stronger in these discs (which were pressed in Japan), it isn't worth the $250-plus that some dealers are asking.

Paramount has issued a director's edition of the fourth film, which is identical to the previous letterboxed version except that it contains fifteen minutes of Nimoy discussing the picture. Don't bother to upgrade if you have the original.

The nonletterboxed edition of *Star Trek VI* loses nothing on the sides and actually contains more image on the bottom of the frame.

Star Wars (1977) ★★★
Director: George Lucas
Running Time: 121 minutes

Back in 1975, fresh from the success of *American Graffiti* (1973), longtime science fiction buff George Lucas tried to obtain the movie rights to the comic-strip hero Flash Gordon. King Features Syndicate wanted a ton of money and control over licensing, so Lucas decided to create his own science fiction mythology. Ironically, after *Star Wars* became the most successful movie in history, King Features licensed Flash Gordon to Dino de Laurentiis: his 1980 film, which cost $25 million and is much better than its reputation, was a box office megadisaster.

To be sure, Lucas borrowed plenty from Flash Gordon as well as from author Edgar Rice Burroughs's Mars novels (Burroughs's Jeddak became Jedi, banths became banthas, and so on), Frank Herbert's *Dune* novels (the desert planet Tatooine and the skeleton of the "sand worm"), the movie *Metropolis* (the design of the robot C-3PO), John Schoenherr's drawings of the forest-dwelling Jaenshi (Chewbacca and the Ewoks), Marvel Comics' Doctor Doom (Darth Vader), and many more. Even the plot for *Star Wars* was lifted from both Kurosawa's *The Hidden Fortress* (1958) and the British film *The Dam Busters* (1954), and even the look of *Star Wars* owes a considerable debt to *2001: A Space Odyssey* (1968).

All of that said, what Lucas *did* do was to pull all of these elements together in a grandly entertaining fashion. That he did this all for just under $10 million is perhaps the most amazing feat of all.

A restless lad on the planet Tatooine, farmer Luke Skywalker (Mark Hamill) becomes embroiled in a rebellion against the tyrannical galactic Empire after purchasing robots that belonged to rebel leader Princess Leia (Carrie Fisher). Leia is now a prisoner of Empire henchman Darth Vader (voice of James Earl Jones, body of Dave Prowse) and, with the help of mercenary Han Solo (Harrison Ford) and aging Jedi Knight Obi-Wan Kenobi (Alec Guinness), Skywalker storms Vader's fortress, the planet-destroying Death Star, rescuing the princess and helping to prevent the annihilation of the rebels.

Currently, *Star Wars* remains the second-top-grossing film of all time, right behind *E.T.* (1982). In light of that, it seems churlish to chide the movie for not just its lack of originality but its faulty science (the sounds of explosions and engines in space, ships refusing to burn up when blazing through earthlike atmospheres, a "parsec" referred to as a unit of time rather than distance, etc.). It is a high-tech fairy tale for our times, bolstered by spectacular special effects, a classic John Williams score, and some terrific performances.

In the sequels *The Empire Strikes Back* ([1980] directed by Irvin Kershner) and *Return of the Jedi* (1983, directed by the late Richard Marquand after David Lynch turned down the job), Luke, Han, Leia, and the rebels continue the struggle against the Empire, ending in the rehabilitation and death of Vader and the fall of the wicked Emperor. Except for the fact that the characters and setting were no longer a novelty, the last film is the strongest, tying up all the loose ends and featuring a rousing attack on a new and more powerful Death Star.

The remastered, letterboxed *The Empire Strikes Back* and *Return of the Jedi* suffer from considerably more grain than the original film. Moreover, in the case of the latter film, the manufacturer has opened up the image to lessen the severity of the matte, thus revealing very visible edit and splice marks!

The TV movies *The Ewok Adventure* (1984) and *Ewoks: The Battle for Endor* (1985) are also available on laserdisc. Though both were costly and elaborate by TV standards, they pale beside the theatrical films and are aimed at a very juvenile audience. The special effects work, though the discs tend to be on the muddy side.

The Dino de Laurentiis *Flash Gordon* is available on laserdisc: The sound is excellent, but the picture is noisy, grainy, and poorly cropped.

The Disc
Video: ★★★½
Audio: ★★★★½ (Surround)
Chapters: Yes (but they're surprisingly minimal on sides one and three of the three-sided set)
Format: CLV
Source: CBS/Fox Video

The colors on the film's latest, letterbox presentation are very good, with video noise and grain kept to an acceptable minimum. Most of the film is fairly sharp, and the source material was in tip-top shape.

Happily, the letterboxing does a fine job of showcasing the movie's imposing sets and planetscapes and capturing all of Lucas's dizzying camerawork in the two big space battles. Kids who have seen the movie only panned-and-scanned and weren't impressed will have their minds changed when the ship passes overhead in the opening scene.

The audio is colossal. The stereo separation is delightful and the Surround effects are resounding. The trebles don't sing with *perfect* clarity, but that's a small complaint at best.

Stone Cold (1991) ★
Director: Craig R. Baxley
Running Time: 90 minutes

Brian Bosworth, the Oklahoma all-American and chronic member of the Seattle Seahawks injured roster, made his movie debut in this stupid action film.

After the obligatory "walking in on a holdup and kicking punk butt" opening (which is pretty unexciting, alas), suspended Alabama police officer Joe Huff (Bosworth) is asked by the FBI to infiltrate a biker organization that is planning to kill antibiker D.A. and gubernatorial candidate Brent "Whip" Whipperton (David Tress). Huff accepts the assignment and, posing as excon John Stone, he gets close to gang leader Chains (Lance Henriksen). However, Chains has a contact in law enforcement who runs a check on Stone and learns his true identity. Shortly before a combined bike/helicopter assault on the statehouse, Stone is sentenced to die by being tossed from a helicopter with a bomb lashed to him (overkill or what?). Needless to say, he doesn't die—but practically everyone else does before and after the bloody final assault, including Whipperton, Stone's love interest, and dozens of innocent bystanders. (Kind of undercuts Stone's credibility as an *effective* hero: Could that be why he was suspended in the first place?)

The beetle-browed Boz makes a good screen hero, terrific in the action scenes and managing to deliver his lines with tongue-in-cheek aplomb. Henriksen, as always, does a lot more than the part calls for. However, despite their charisma and some spectacular explosions and dazzling cinematography, *Stone Cold* isn't the kind of action that satisfies. In an effort to be different, the filmmakers have come up with stunts that are unbelievable and/or ridiculous beyond words, and have to resort to clever cutting to help objects defy the laws of physics. Only the most undiscriminating action fans will be satisfied.

Watch for the blunder at 19:52 on side one, when Stone hands his sunglasses to the same guy twice.

The Disc

Video: ★★★★½
Audio: ★★★★½ (Surround)
Chapters: No
Format: CLV
Source: RCA/Columbia Pictures Home Video

As is often the case, a fourth-rate movie gets a first-rate transfer. Though cropping hurts the film a bit, the image itself is pristine: glossy and sharp, with bright, accurate colors. There are some bright red lights in many scenes, but noise is not a problem and grain is rare.

The stereo effects—choppers and copters, mostly—are incredible and the Surround Sound is super. The only drawback is the music. The dialogue tends to be on the soft side, and you might be tempted to pump up the volume. *Don't* unless you've turned down the rear channels. The music comes up so suddenly and so loudly that you may blow a speaker or two, not to mention your eardrums.

A Streetcar Named Desire (1951) ★★★½

Director: Elia Kazan
Running Time: 122 minutes

Playwright Tennessee Williams won a Pulitzer Prize for *A Streetcar Named Desire* (1947), which was originally staged by Elia Kazan with Marlon Brando as Stanley Kowalski, Kim Hunter as Stella, Karl Malden as Mitch, and Jessica Tandy as Blanche DuBois. When the play was bought for the movies, Kazan—always looking for a fresh project—had no interest in directing it. But his friend Williams convinced him that he was the best man for the job, and Kazan relented. He hired most of the cast from the stage play, though Vivien Leigh was signed to play Blanche. Warner Brothers felt that the iffy commercial prospect needed a name star, and not only had Leigh played the part on the London stage, she *did* have a knack for playing Southern women.

Arriving in New Orleans after a ride on a streetcar named Desire, the phony, frail Blanche reaches the apartment of her happy, well-adjusted sister, Stella, and Stella's blue-collar husband, Stanley. Blanche and Stanley don't get along, and things are complicated when Stanley's card buddy Mitch falls for the new arrival. During a visit that stretches to five months, Stanley investigates Blanche's past and learns that she had lost the family estate, Belle Reve, to creditors and has been sleeping around (prostitution is hinted at).

Blanche had come to her sister's home seeking an illusion, something that will help the aging, love-starved woman pretend that time stopped long ago. Emotionally and geographically, she's at the end of the line (hence the streetcar allusion), and through brutish insensitivity Stanley does exactly the *opposite* of what she needs: He tells Mitch, who drops Blanche cold. Not long after that, Blanche is carted off to a mental institution.

Williams himself liked Kazan's film interpretation better than the stage version, feeling that the necessary "toning down" of the characters made them more sympathetic, more real. The film—like most of Kazan's movies—actually *is* very stagy, and it drags when the director lets his camera just sit and watch scenes that pulsed onstage but seem very static on the screen.

The story is still riveting and disturbing, however, driven by the tension between Blanche and Stanley, parts that are expertly handled by Leigh and Brando. Leigh exposes the real person behind the outlandish facade and manages the difficult task of giving emotional credibility to the character, despite Blanche's melodramatic personal style.

As for Brando, his performance is a triumph of technique, and his explosiveness, gift for reflection, and jitterbug humor have killed the part for every other actor for all time.

The Disc
Video: ★★
Audio: ★½ (monaural)
Chapters: no
Format: CLV
Source: Warner Home Video

Produced just before the big leap in master/transfer quality in 1991, the image on the disc is merely passable. The picture is too soft most of the time, especially lacking detail in the skin, clothing, and woodwork. The blacks aren't glossy, the white areas are neither pure nor shiny, and the print lacks any kind of tonal range. There are quite a few scratches and one ugly splice, though that's not unusual for a movie from the mid-century.

The audio is only fair, a bit hollow, with more or less constant noise from the aging sound track and from damage to the master print.

Sunset Boulevard (1950)
★★★★
Director: Billy Wilder
Running Time: 110 minutes

Right away, you know you're in for an unusual ride: The film is narrated by a corpse, as Joe Gillis (William Holden) explains—using language of the hard-boiled school—just how he ended up riddled with bullets, facedown in a swimming pool.

Gillis was an unsuccessful screenwriter who pulled into the driveway of an old mansion to elude two men who were trying to repossess his car. Getting out, he quickly realized he'd stepped through a time warp and entered Beverly Hills of thirty years before: The house was owned by silent-movie star Norma Desmond (Gloria Swanson), who, by living in seclusion with her butler/confidant, Max (Eric von Stroheim), fervently kept pretalkies-era Hollywood alive in the confines of her home.

Though Gillis was disturbed by her obsessiveness, Desmond convinced him to stay. She wanted him to help her revise *Salome*, a script she'd written for her return to the screen. A mixture of pity and impoverishment made the idea acceptable at first, but Gillis miscalculated when he thought he could walk away from Desmond unscathed. Ultimately, his condescending pity and willingness to desert Desmond provoked her murderous rage, which left him floating dead in the pool.

This is a funny, biting film that takes its time and belabors its point, but the characters make it all worthwhile. *Sunset Boulevard* is not about filmmaking per se, or about Hollywood society. It's about two people united by desperation—she to be what she once was, he to be what he never will be. For Gloria Swanson, the part was somewhat autobiographical. She'd been a silent-film star with Paramount and Cecil B. DeMille for seven years, and had also been directed by Erich von Stroheim in *Queen Kelly* (1929). But she never clicked in talkies and her career foundered. As for Holden, at the time he had more than a touch of Gillis in him. He'd been laboring in films for a dozen years before *Sunset Boulevard*, and even this film failed to put him over the top. It wasn't until he reteamed with Wilder three years later in *Stalag 17* that his career went into overdrive. The two stars mesh brilliantly.

Jack Webb (of "Dragnet" fame) has a small part in the film, as do DeMille and Buster Keaton.

The Disc

Video: ★★½
Audio: ★½
Chapters: No
Format: CLV
Source: Paramount Home Video

The picture on this disc is fairly sharp, revealing considerable amounts of detail in the clothes, settings, and so on. Unfortunately, the daylight scenes are awash in Los Angeles's Mediterranean glare, so the gray scales are rather washed-out. Most of the darker shots are okay, though a few are somewhat contrasty.

The audio track is extremely noisy, even taking into account the film's age. There are far, far too many pops and crackles throughout.

Superman (1978) ★★★★½
Director: Richard Donner
Running Time: 143 minutes

In 1933, Cleveland teenagers Jerry Siegel and Joe Shuster created a comic-strip character called Superman. After five years of being rejected by one newspaper syndicate after another, they finally found a publisher who agreed to run what was supposed to be a daily strip in the new comic-book format. Superman made his debut in *Action Comics* #1 and was a sellout, ensuring the survival of the fledgling comic-book industry and spawning a cavalcade of costumed heroes.

Superman was a success on radio, in a pair of movie serials, in theatrical and Saturday-morning cartoons, as the star of a long-running TV series, and, of course, as the hero in four huge-budget motion pictures. *Superman* and *Superman II* (1980) were smash hits and great entertainment; *Superman III* (1983) and *Superman IV: The Quest for Peace* (1987) were witless, misguided flops. All are available on laserdisc, if you've got money to burn.

Superman opens on the planet Krypton, where Jor-El (Marlon Brando) is prosecuting a trio of villains: Zod (Terence Stamp), Ursa (Sarah Douglas), and Non (Jack O'Halloran). All are found guilty and sentenced to a limbolike prison known as the Phantom Zone. Jor-El is less pursuasive convincing Krypton's elders that the planet is about to explode. Placing his infant son, Kal-El, in a tiny starship, the scientist sends him to earth before Krypton is reduced to planetesimals. Possessing superpowers on our world, the boy is found and raised by childless farmers Jonathan and Martha Kent (Glenn Ford and Phyllis Thaxter); upon reaching adulthood, Clark Kent (Christopher Reeve) moves to Metropolis, takes a job as a reporter for the *Daily Planet*, and, as Superman, uses his powers to benefit humankind.

In the first film, evil Lex Luthor (Gene Hackman) buys a vast amount of desert land that will become valuable beachfront property when he reprograms a pair of nuclear missiles to strike the San Andreas fault and drop California into the ocean. Superman pushes one missile into space but is unable to stop the second. However, he *is* able to seal the fault and turn back time to bring fellow reporter Lois Lane (Margot Kidder) back to life before carting Luthor off to jail.

In the sequel, an explosion opens the Phantom Zone and frees the Kryptonian villains, who conquer the earth while Superman is busy making love to Lois in his Arctic Fortress of Solitude. After battling the villains to a standstill in the streets of Metropolis, Superman figures out a way to deprive them of their superpowers.

The films were originally going to be shot back-to-back to save money. However, the producers felt that Donner had spent too *much* time and money ($55 million) on the first movie, so they shut down production on the second and, when the first film became a hit, resumed shooting with British director Richard Lester (*A Hard Days Night* [1964] *The Three Musketeers* [1974]). To cut the budget further, scenes featuring the "spirit" of Jor-El were refilmed using his wife, Lara, since actress Susannah York cost less than Brando.

Finally, to bring in a European location and hopefully bolster foreign box office, the opening was rewritten so that it's a terrorist attack on Paris, and not one of Luthor's two missiles, that causes a rift in the Phantom Zone. (Roughly a third of Donner's footage remains; you can pick it out by watching Margot Kidder, who had dental work done during the hiatus and looks different before and after. Just how vital Donner was to the success of the films is clear by how awful the all-Lester *Superman III* is.)

The success of the films is due to three factors. First, there was the casting of Reeve, Hackman, Kidder, Stamp, and some great character actors—particularly Ned Beatty as Luthor's bumbling henchman, Otis, and Jackie Cooper as Perry White. Each brings a different style to the film, but somehow it all meshes.

Then there are the special effects, which, while erratic, manage to sell the superhero and his feats of strength. It helped that Reeve is a pilot: Whether he was on wires or working with the front-projection system, he positioned himself in ways that took into account how the currents, thermal and otherwise, would affect Superman.

Finally, the first two films had magnificent scripts by Mario Puzo, David Newman, Robert Benton (*Superman* only) and Leslie Newman. Puzo's first drafts had all the clever touches that foreshadowed the eighties: the real estate boom, the "sensitive" man (and Superman), the ultraliberated woman, and the gotta-have-it-all Kryptonian trio. The Newmans took the essentially humorless Puzo screenplays and dressed them up with wit and appropriate moments of camp. (David had cowritten the wonderful Broadway musical *It's a Bird, It's a Plane, It's Superman* [1966] as well as cowritten *Bonnie and Clyde* [1967] *What's Up Doc* [1972] and other films.)

Capping it off is John Williams's alternately heraldic and sweet score, arguably his best.

The Disc
Video: ★★½
Audio: ★★ (Surround)
Chapters: Yes
Format: CLV
Source: Warner Home Video

In its original panned-and-scanned version, *Superman* had all the power of a comic book, its majestic images broken up into cluttered little panels. With the new wide-screen release, Donner's epic vision is restored: the bodies of Kryptonians hurled, balletlike, through the air as their planet crumbles; the carefully composed shots of the crowd looking up at the helicopter dangling from the *Daily Planet* building (actually the *Daily News* building); the Golden Gate Bridge popping its cables and swaying as cars crash into one another and a school bus dangles over the edge. This is how the movie was meant to be seen.

But—and this is a big *but*—the colors of the new edition are pale and unsatisfactory, there's a fair amount of grain and video noise in the reds (and what color is Superman's cape?), and an unacceptable amount of speckling, so be prepared for an exchange or two—or three or four.

The audio is shockingly crackly and frail, except for a few scenes: The *whoosh* of the Superman symbol in the opening credits will knock you back in your seat, and the helicopter crash and earthquake will keep you there.

The other three films are available on laserdisc, and *Superman II* was recently remastered, though in a pan-and-scan edition. The spectacular scenes of destruction and multicharacter shots are seriously hurt, despite the wonderful clarity of the picture and sound.

Tales from the Darkside: The Movie (1990) ★
Director: John Harrison
Running Time: 93 minutes

Inspired by "Tales from the Darkside," the anthology TV series, the film is a trio of tales with a wraparound story. The tradition for films of this type goes back to *Dead of Night* (1945), *Kwaidan* (see page 166), and *Tales from the Crypt* (1972), all of which are better than this one.

Things start out promisingly as Betty (Deborah Harry) gets ready in her nice suburban home to gut and cook a young boy, Timmy (Matthew Lawrence), for a dinner party she's having. Timmy forestalls his fate by reading her stories from a book he finds in his cell in the kitchen: "Lot 249," about college kid Andy (Christian Slater) facing a vengeful mummy on campus; "Cat from Hell," with Halston (David Johansen) pitted against a murderous feline in a gloomy mansion; and "Lover's Vow," in which an urban demon exacts a strange and deadly promise from artist James Preston (James Remar).

Betty's fate is predictable but, thanks to a deft performance by Harry, the wraparound story is fun. "Lot 249" is the best of the tales—a decent story with a neat mummy—while "Cat from Hell" has a few chilling moments and no story. "Lover's Vow" is a real loser, an inferior, unscary, uncredited rip-off of "The Woman of the Snow" segment of *Kwaidan*. The fake, Muppet-like demon doesn't help the story either, though Rae Dawn Chong is sexy as Preston's lover.

This one's only for undiscriminating horror buffs or Harry fans.

The Disc

Video: ★★
Audio: ★★ (Surround)
Chapters: No
Format: CLV
Source: Paramount Home Video

While the daylight scenes are acceptably bright and sharp, interiors and night scenes—meaning a lot of the movie—are slightly muddy and short on detail. The film was shot with video in mind, and the cropping doesn't hurt.

The audio is quite vivid, though Surround effects are not as plentiful as in most horror films of recent vintage. If you're thinking of picking it up for the shock sounds, don't.

Five discs have been released featuring a total of twenty-one episodes from the TV series. Though the picture quality and sound leave a lot to be desired, they are better, dramatically, than the film, with segments written by Harlan Ellison and Stephen King, and performances by Danny Aiello and Carol Kane, among others. These are available from IVE and Image Entertainment.

The Tall Guy (1989) ★★★★
Director: Mel Smith
Running Time: 92 minutes

Like *This Is Spinal Tap* and *A Fish Called Wanda* (see pages 277 and 99), *The Tall Guy* is one of those movies that has a fiercely loyal audience, and justifiably so. It's very funny. Make that *cripplingly* funny: There are times when you'll have to back-scan to hear lines you missed because you were laughing.

Dexter King (Jeff Goldblum) is an American actor in London. For years, he has played second fiddle to exceedingly abusive Ron Anderson (Rowan Atkinson) in the comedian's stage play, and he's at the end of his rope. At the same time, Dexter is tense because he's fallen in love with nurse Kate Lemon (Emma Thompson) and can't work up the courage to ask her out. He even lies about a pending trip to Morocco so he can spend a few minutes with her, getting immunization injections. Counseling from his nymphomaniac landlord, Carmen (Geraldine James), doesn't help, but a chance meeting with Kate in a restaurant does: Dexter drops his date, asks Kate out, and the two hit it off. Concurrently, Dexter becomes the star of a new show, a musical version of *The Elephant Man* titled *Elephant*—surely the most misguided tuner since *Springtime for Hitler* in *The Producers* (see page 221).

Things are looking up for the Tall Guy until he has a meaningless fling with a pushy costar, Cheryl (Kim Thomson), and his world begins to unravel. The movie's own weird credibility also comes apart at this point—as Dexter quickly and improbably wins Kate back—though there's a lot of very black humor as he does so, racing after her while still in full Elephant Man regalia.

There's one great line after another from start to finish, and the conventions and clichés of acting are perfectly riposted by Dexter's auditions and the rehearsals for *Elephant*. Nor has there been a funnier scene in years than Kate and Dexter's first night together. Dexter's career may not be going anywhere, but their sexual passion literally brings down the house.

Goldblum is manic and wonderful, Thompson is like a lusty Mary Poppins, and Geraldine James is terrific with her steady stream of lovers. The supporting cast is also top-notch, especially Anna Massey as Dexter's agent, Mary, and Emil Wolk as his friend Cyprus Charlie. Many viewers will recognize Atkinson, a BBC comic perhaps best known for his Blackadder portrayal and as the star of the TV series "The Curse of Mr. Bean."

The Disc
Video: ★½
Audio: ★★ (Surround)
Chapters: No
Format: CLV
Source: RCA/Columbia Pictures Home Video

You *know* the movie's good when you can recommend adding it to the laser library despite the grainiest transfer in recent memory. Colors are okay beneath the grit, though they still aren't anything to brag about. The picture is moderately sharp, and cropping doesn't hurt the film.

The dialogue is perfectly intelligible and the directional effects are good, if not especially dazzling. The score tends to get a bit too loud in the rear, though the musical excerpts from *Elephant* have a lot of body and the songs are quite catchy.

The man who gave us the Pink Panther films, as well as the splendid *Operation Petticoat* (1959), *Breakfast at Tiffany's* (1961), *Days of Wine and Roses* (1962), and *Victor/Victoria* (see page 292) also directed *A Fine Mess* (1986), and, in succession, the disappointing *Sunset* (1988), *Skin Deep* (1989), and *Switch* (1991).

Edwards's critical and commercial high point was *10*, the saga of George (Dudley Moore), a composer who seems to have everything: a thriving career, an adoring lady friend named Sam (Julie Andrews, the real-life Mrs. Edwards), and material wealth. But while he's out one morning, he spots stunning Jenny (Bo Derek) on her way to marry David (Sam J. Jones, who later played Flash Gordon). George is hopelessly infatuated with the woman and, unable to get her out of his mind, he goes to Mexico, only to find himself at the same resort as the honeymooning couple. After saving her husband from drowning, George ends up in Jenny's arms. However, after making out to Ravel's *Bolero*, he's unable to go further: Though *10* has been propelled along by lust, it ends up being a tale of fidelity and love.

Moore had enjoyed considerable success on the stage with partner Peter Cook (see *Bedazzled*), and had made a splash as a pervert in the Goldie Hawn hit *Foul Play* (1978). He joined the film at the last minute, when George Segal and Edwards had artistic differences, and *10*—followed by *Arthur* (1981)—made him a star. Sadly, he hasn't had a hit since *Crazy People* (see page 57). Bo Derek fared even worse, following *10* with the likes of *Tarzan, the Ape Man* (1981), *Bolero* (1984), and *Ghosts Can't Do It* (1990), which have pretty much ended her career. (Time for a TV series, Bo.)

But, like Bogart and Bergman, they—and we—will always have the delightful *10*.

---

10 (1979) ★★★★
Director: Blake Edwards
Running Time: 123 minutes

There may not be a more erratic filmmaker on the planet than Blake Edwards.

The Disc
Video: no stars
Audio: ½ (monaural)
Chapters: Yes
Format: CLV
Source: Warner Home Video

Sad to say, the remastered edition of this film is every bit as bad as the original version, which makes one wonder why Warner bothered. To sucker dollars out of unsuspecting laserphiles?

The picture couldn't be fuzzier or grainier, the panning-and-scanning looks as though it were done by a chimp, and the audio is hissy and muddled. The movie may be a *10*, but this disc is a 0.

The Ten Commandments (1956) ★★★½
Director: Cecil B. DeMille
Running Time: 245 minutes

Director Cecil B. DeMille had always wanted to remake two of his greatest silent screen successes: *The Ten Commandments* (1923) and *The King of Kings* (1927). He was able to do the former, but died while the latter was being reworked as *The Queen of Queens*, the story of Mary.

The Ten Commandments follows the life of Moses (Charlton Heston) from birth to death. Placed in a basket and set upon the Nile by his mother Yochabel (Martha Scott), Moses is discovered by the Pharaoh's daughter Bithiah (Nina Foch) and, a gift of the Nile God, is raised in the court of Egypt. There, he becomes the rival of Rameses (Yul Brynner) to succeed the Pharaoh Sethi (Cedric Hardwicke) and win the hand of the lovely Nefretiri (Anne Baxter). With the help of the Hebrew chief overseer, Dathan (Edward G. Robinson), Rameses learns the truth of Moses's birth and the Hebrew is banished. Rameses becomes Pharaoh and Moses, falling in with shepherds, is commanded by God to return to Egypt and free the slaves. Ten plagues later he succeeds, parting the Red Sea to escape the charioteers of the fickle Rameses and leading the Hebrews to Mt. Sinai, where he first heard the voice of God. There Moses receives the Ten Commandments, causes a small earthquake to swallow up the Children of Israel who have lost faith in God and forged a golden idol, and leads the survivors to the Promised Land.

This isn't a great film, but it's a lot of fun. The sets are spectacular, the story and characters move entertainingly (if improbably) from reverence to soap opera, and Elmer Bernstein's Wagner-like score is glorious. Heston is the definitive screen Moses, earnest and charismatic, Brynner is delightful as the wickedly proud Rameses, and Baxter is kittenish and sly—despite having some of the film's clunkiest dialogue ("Moses, you stubborn, splendid, adorable fool!"). Vincent Price is also a standout as Baka, the cruel master builder.

Despite what DeMille says in the film, the only scenes shot on location in the Middle East were Moses wandering in the desert, his descent from Mt. Sinai after seeing the Burning Bush, the Exodus, and a few shots of Rameses's pursuit of the freed slaves. Everything else was filmed in Hollywood, and the difference is obvious. Watch, for example, when Rameses escorts Moses to the desert: The shots of Brynner and Heston together were filmed at the Paramount studio, while the shots of Heston alone were filmed in Egypt. The lighting, focus, and color values are jarringly different.

There's also a lot of very sloppy special effects work in the film. The parting of the Red Sea was unconvincing in 1956; it looks worse today. Pouring 300,000 gallons of water into a tank and printing it in reverse was a good idea, but it's poorly superimposed over the Red Sea (actually a large tank of water at Paramount), and Moses and the Hebrews are badly composited with that footage. Indeed, *all* of the composite photography is shoddy, even simple shots such as Moses drawing aside the drape to reveal the statue of Sethi as it's pulled into the city of Goshen.

But the film is so sincere, and has such incredible forward momentum, that you forgive it its flaws and just hang on for the ride.

Eighty year-old actor H. B. Warner, who played Jesus in *The King of Kings*, has a small part as Amminadab, whose fig tree Bithiah promises to plant in the "new land." Charlton Heston's son Fraser plays the newborn Moses.

The Disc
Video: ★★★
Audio: ★★★★ (stereo)
Chapters: Yes
Format: CLV/CAV
Source: Paramount Home Video

The recently released boxed set is a vast improvement over Paramount's original fuzzy, bland, non-letterboxed release. That's the good news.

The bad news is, the transfer isn't as good as it should have been. The colors are a bit thin in too many spots: compare them to the same scenes in the trailers, where they're much more vivid.

The mildly letterboxed image is generally very sharp—a hallmark of the VistaVision process—and the print is in good shape. Video noise is minimal, though there's occasional jiggle on the CAV sides, which comprise roughly the last hour of the film.

The audio is full-bodied and, happily, the digital remastering has smoothed out many rough spots—for example, Joshua (John Derek) saying to Moses just before the Exodus, "We march, praising His mighty name," which was dubbed in post production and always sounded clearer and more resonant than the lines that came before it. Now, they're perfectly integrated.

The new edition features DeMille's pedagogic introduction, a "making of" featurette, and trailers from this film as well as from DeMille's *Samson and Delilah* (1949), *The Greatest Show on Earth* (1952), and *The Buccaneer* (1958).

Paramount has also remastered those films, with generally excellent results. The previous edition of *Samson and Delilah* was slightly fuzzy and a bit washed-out; the new version is absolutely stunning, mastered from a gorgeous Three-Strip Technicolor print and boasting excellent sound. The movie was shot almost entirely on soundstages, so it doesn't have quite the sweep of *The Ten Commandments*; it's also over an hour shorter. But the destruction of the Temple of Dagon is a knock-out, and the actors are all fun to watch, even as they ham it up.

The Greatest Show on Earth is a big, boring circus film, also mastered from a superb Three-Strip Technicolor print. Though the image isn't quite as sharp as *Samson and Delilah*, the colors are breathtaking.

DeMille produced but didn't direct *The Buccaneer*, a remake of his own 1938 epic, leaving the task to son-in-law Anthony Quinn. The production values are all classic DeMille, and Quinn gets solid performances from stars Yul Brynner as the pirate Jean Lafitte and Charlton Heston as Andrew Jackson, who become reluctant allies during the War of 1812. This is the first time *The Buccaneer* has been released on laserdisc and, like the other DeMille offerings, the transfer is stunning.

The Terminator (1984) ★★★
Director: James Cameron
Running Time: 109 minutes

It's the year A.D. 2029 and machines have nearly taken over the earth. But human resistance is strong, with John Connor its most potent leader. What to do about Connor? The machines think they have the answer. They send a powerful Terminator (Arnold Schwarzenegger) back to a time before John was born, giving the cyborg instructions to kill John's mother, Sarah Connor (Linda Hamilton). Aware of the danger, John sends his trusted lieutenant Kyle Reese (Michael Biehn) back in time to prevent the Terminator from succeeding.

The concept of warring soldiers from the future isn't unique to *The Terminator*; it was the basis of the "Soldier" episode of TV's "Outer Limits," among other stories. ("Soldier" author Harlan Ellison was subsequently credited in the closing titles of video copies of *The Terminator*). However, no one ever told the tale with as much gusto as Cameron, who came to this feature after having directed only the lame *Piranha II: The Spawning* (1981) and having cowritten *Rambo: First Blood Part II* (1985), of which he says, "The action is mine, the politics is Stallone's"

Technically, the violent, $6.5 million film isn't *nearly* as slick as its sixteen-times-more-expensive sequel, but it has more forward momentum and Arnold is more believable as an evil Terminator than as the benevolent one in the sequel. He obviously realized that himself, having turned down the Reese role in order to play the cyborg. (Schwarzenegger's choice cost Lance Henriksen the part of the Terminator. Cameron had always planned on giving Henriksen the role; but when Arnold asked for it, the powers that be went along. Since Henriksen couldn't play the heroic Reese, he ended up as a police officer. However, he was rewarded with a juicy role in Cameron's *Aliens* [page 7].)

Schwarzenegger is fabulous as the bad guy, Biehn is a wiry, soft-spoken hero—a contrast to the macho Stallone/Norris breed of superhero that dominated the decade—and Hamilton is excellent as the tough but not yet supermuscled heroine. Also interesting is the hardware that pervades the film, from answering machines to disco strobes to video cameras—an insidious look at that which was to prove our undoing. However, Cameron isn't entirely pessimistic: In the end, it's a machine controlled by a human that ultimately destroys the Terminator.

The Disc
Video: ★★★
Audio: ★½ (monaural)
Chapters: Yes
Format: CLV
Source: Hemdale/Image Entertainment

It's frustrating not to be able to rate this film higher, because the remastered, letterboxed edition is an improvement over the original pan-and-scan versions (one from HBO Video, a second from Image).

Unfortunately, the color is still rather washed-out and the image is slightly fuzzy in places, with a good deal of grain throughout. It's the best version we're likely to get, and a welcome one, but good intentions still don't make it a great disc.

The audio is disappointingly limp and also a bit raw and ragged in the upper ranges. The Image release had simulated stereo: This version will be particularly disappointing if you've gotten accustomed to that more effective audio.

Terminator 2: Judgment Day (1991) ★★★½
Director: James Cameron
Running Time: 137 minutes

The plot? If you were being generous, you'd call it threadbare. An advanced liquid-metal Terminator, the T-1000 (Robert Patrick), is sent from the future to kill ten-year-old John Connor (Edward Furlong), who will grow up to lead the human resistance against the rule of the machines. A less sophisticated T-800 (Arnold Schwarzenegger) is sent back to protect John; together with John's mother, Sarah (Linda Hamilton), the Model T Terminator and John spend the bulk of the film running from the T-1000, wrecking cars, trucks, buildings, and people in the process.

Schwarzenegger had always wanted to make a sequel to the film that put him over the top (see *The Terminator*), but the project was tied up in legal knots. When they were finally cleared up and everyone was finally available, Cameron had just over two months to come up with a script before shooting began. Incredibly—considering the complexity of the special-effects stunts, not the quality of the script—the film went from rough draft to finished movie in just over a year.

The $90 million spent on *Terminator 2* is all there on the screen, a lot of it spent on three Bond-quality action scenes: a truck and motorcycle chase through a flood-control channel; a battle with police at the Cyberdyne lab, for which a four-story building was actually blown up; and a truck and car chase across a bridge and into a steel mill.

Like the stunts, the special effects are endlessly fascinating. The computer animation of the T-1000 is miraculous, but three other scenes deserve mention. One is the metal "splash holes" constantly being blown in the T-1000. These were silverized foam on radio-controlled springs that popped open through the actor's pre-cut shirt. Another involves the truck going off the overpass into the canal. Upon seeing the footage, Cameron decided it would work better if the truck was headed in the opposite direction. The image was flopped, which is easy enough; however, the computer crew had to remove the Plummer Street sign and reverse it and also digitally fudge the fact that the driver was now on the passenger's side. (They missed one thing, however: The name on the truck, above the grille, is still backward.) Then there's the nightmarish nuclear-holocaust sequence, created using incredibly detailed miniatures and matte paintings; the vaporization of Sarah's flesh was filmed by packing pieces of black and gray napkin onto a skeleton ordered from a medical catalog, covering it all with tissue-paper "skin" coated with tempera paint, and blowing it all away with air mortars.

Like the script, the performances are not particularly inspired. Schwarzenegger, Patrick, and Hamilton are all charismatic; Furlong may be the most annoying child who has ever appeared on the screen (independent is one thing; did he have to be *so* snotty?); and Joe Morton, a fine actor who plays Miles Dyson, a scientist who helps the boy and his Terminator, is only around long enough to get shot at, shot at some more, and finally killed.

It's a shame Cameron didn't give us a more provocative, literate film—something more along the lines of his *The Abyss* (1989)—but, as science fiction spectacles go, they don't come any juicier than this.

The Disc

Video: ★★★★½
Audio: ★★★★★ (Surround)
Chapters: Yes
Format: CLV and CAV editions; pan-and-scan is CLV only
Source: Carolco Home Video/Live Home Video

The picture is immaculate, sharp as can be, though there are problems with both the letterboxed and pan-and-scan versions. The color levels are really spectacular on the latter; the letterboxed edition seems a touch pale by comparison. The pan-and-scan edition also has incredible—make that miraculous—resolution. Unfortunately, the action just doesn't work as well without the letterbox—a serious drawback.

Both versions have negligible levels of grain; the CAV frames are perfect.

Which ever *T2* you get, you're guaranteed mind-blowing sound: Be careful not to push the volume up too far, however, since moments of explosive sound tend to follow extremely quiet passages.

The thirty-one minute "making of" featurette comes with the CAV edition and is particularly informative regarding the computer graphics. It's also nice to see the filmmakers give credit to Schwarzenegger's stunt double.

When the disc was originally announced, extensive footage was supposed to be restored, such as surgery performed on the Terminator's head and a dream scene involving Sarah and Kyle Reese. Ultimately, Cameron decided that the former slowed the film down and that the point of the latter—Reese telling her "the future is not set"—was made elsewhere in the film.

Many other scenes were scripted but never filmed in order to save money, such as the Terminator driving a motorcycle into the elevator at the mall, causing it to explode in an effort to stall the T-1000.

That's Entertainment! (1974)
★★½
Director: Jack Haley, Jr.
Running Time: 134 minutes

Jack Haley, Jr. (the son of *The Wizard of Oz* star Jack Haley) had been an actor before becoming a documentary filmmaker bent on chronicling the history of Hollywood. He made the wonderful TV series *Hollywood and the Stars* (1963 to 1964). And when he went to MGM as director of Creative Affairs in 1973, he began working on his dream project, *That's Entertainment!*

No argument: This movie *is* entertainment. However, it's also *just* the movies of MGM. Now, the studio made the best movie musicals, but, to be fair, *West Side Story* (see page 297), *The Gay Divorcee* (1934), and even *The Jazz Singer* (1927) are *also* entertainment. So were the Marx Brothers and Abbott and Costello and the films of Walt Disney and James Cagney, and none of that's here. In fact, this film is MGM being *so* full of itself that many viewers will get tired of hearing hosts Frank Sinatra, Donald O'Connor, Gene Kelly, Fred Astaire, Liza Minnelli (who gets her name misspelled on the back of the boxed set), Mickey Rooney, Debbie Reynolds, Elizabeth Taylor, James Stewart, Bing Crosby, and Peter Lawford (!) saying over and over, "This was the greatest [such and such]" ever filmed, or "No one in the history of movies was as good as [so and so]."

Precious little real information is imparted: for example, the fact that during his floor-to-wall-to-ceiling dance from *Royal Wedding* (1951), Fred Astaire was moving more or less in place while the room and camera turned (and watch the shadow of something—crumpled paper?—falling up to the ceiling from 12643 to 12653, to the upper right of the painting).

Another bad call: Director Haley chose to truncate many of the numbers, most criminally O'Connor's "Make 'Em Laugh" from *Singin' in the Rain* and the barn-raising dance from *Seven Brides for Seven Brothers* (see pages 252 and 244), both of which have sizable chunks missing from their midsections. It would have been better by far to eliminate some of the clips (such as Lawford's nonentertainment screen appearances, Elizabeth Taylor lip-synching to a dubbed voice, or most of the back-patting narration) and let the sequences run complete.

The greatness of the stars shines through *despite* the edits, the moronic narration, and the parochialism of the selections, however. There are wonderful, often spectacular clips from the studio's earliest sound films, from the Kelly/Astaire musicals, the Esther Williams production numbers, the Mickey Rooney/Judy Garland danceathons, more recent films such as *Gigi* (1958), and much more. You'll return to the film over and over for a pick-me-up, for, all complaints aside, this *is* entertainment.

Ironically and sadly, the studio that these scenes and stars are touting—and whose fiftieth anniversary the documentary celebrates—is a shadow of its former self, having sold its back lot and (as of this writing) having no films in production.

The Disc
Video: ★★★★
Audio: ★★★★ (monaural and Surround)
Chapters: Yes
Format: CAV
Source: MGM/UA Home Video

Considering the vast number of clips and the different color intensity in most MGM/UA has done a fine job with the transfer. If you own the laserdisc of *The Band Wagon* or the MGM/UA edition of *Singin' in the Rain*, you'll notice that the colors on this disc are as rich as those glorious releases: That's because the manufacturer took the time to drop in scenes from those of its films that have been remastered since *That's Entertainment!* was released.

Even in older clips, however, video noise is admirably absent from most of the bright, troublesome reds, browns, and blues. There *are* exceptions, such as the climactic ballet from *An American in*

Paris, which has a lot of trouble with bleeding reds, but they're relatively rare. Grain is rarely a problem (though when it does pop up, it's a doozy, such as side five, chapter five, from 08757 to 09252).

MGM/UA has generously and correctly letterboxed the few scenes that require it, and the CAV frames are jitter-free.

Some of the film is monaural, and there's also a good deal of rechanneled stereo—for example, on *Singin' in the Rain* and *The Wizard of Oz*. It's actually well done, though one can argue that tampering with the sound is as sacrilegious as shortening the scenes. Despite the Surround Sound label on the box, there's no difference between the sound coming from the front and rear speakers.

The package also includes the overture and exit music, an interesting "making of" featurette, as well as trailers for this film and for *That's Entertainment, Part 2* (1976) and *That's Dancing!*(1985).

A CLV/CAV edition of *That's Entertainment!* released in 1988 is still available, but it was so poorly transferred, with drab colors and tinny sound, as to be virtually useless now.

That's Entertainment Part II (1976) and *That's Dancing!* (1985) have also been given deluxe releases from MGM/UA. Although there are some good clips on each, most are also-rans that simply pad out the sets. The quality of both is good-to-mediocre.

Them! (1954) ★★★½
Director: Gordon Douglas
Running Time: 93 minutes

In 1953, *The Beast from 20,000 Fathoms* brought the *King Kong* story into the atom age: What if a dinosaur is frozen in ice, still alive, and nuclear tests unleash it? *Godzilla* (1954) and countless other films ran with that theme, but *Them!* took it in another direction: What if nuclear tests cause *ordinary* animals to mutate and grow, turning them into deadly beasts? The answer is as follows.

New Mexico State Police Sgt. Ben Peterson (James Whitmore) finds a little girl (Sandy Descher) wandering in the New Mexico desert, her family missing and their camper wrecked. FBI agent Robert Graham (James Arness) is called in. When a strange footprint is found, Department of Agriculture entomologists Dr. Harold Medford (Edmund Gwenn) and his daughter, Dr. Patricia Medford (Joan Weldon), join the team. The group discovers nine-to-twelve-foot-long ants living in the desert and therefore deduce that bomb tests in Alamogordo in 1945 caused the mutations.

The desert nest is destroyed, but two queens escape: One nests on a ship and is destroyed by the navy; the other makes its home somewhere in seven hundred miles of storm drains under Los Angeles. Peterson and Graham lead the army into the pipes, not only looking for the ants but for two boys who took refuge there when their father was killed by the insects. Peterson finds the lads, sacrificing his life to save them; the army arrives moments later and uses flamethrowers on the ants. As they burn, however, Patricia can't help but wonder what other mutations the nuclear tests *since* 1945 might have caused.

Them! is a thrilling film, with top-notch performances from Whitemore and Gwenn, a literate script, and direction that maximizes tension. Never mind that the laws of physics were vaporized at ground zero, that the ants' legs would have been unable to support their weight (you can't simply increase the size of *everything* and have it still function the same way): The ants make terrific monsters and the special effects are marvelous.

The ants were created using full-scale mechanical models and occasional miniatures. (You can see the mechanical workings inside the back of the ant on the right at 1./35:54). Originally, *Them!* was going to be filmed in 3-D, but the process had rolled over and died shortly before the film went into production. However, many of the special-effects scenes had been designed for the process and still create a sense of depth, as the ants frequently charge the audience, knocking things into the camera. Warner also considered shooting the film in color. But that would have taken longer to light and shoot, and the studio felt it was more important to get the film out while *The Beast from 20,000 Fathoms* was still fresh in kids' minds. (In fact, the same artist was used to create the poster art, and he borrowed images from his previous work when he painted *Them!*)

The film was a great success, spawning a slew of inferior big bug films such as *Tarantula* (1955), *The Deadly Mantis* (1957), *Beginning of the End* (1957; giant grasshoppers), *The Black Scorpion* (1957), *Monster from Green Hell* (1957; giant wasps), *The Cosmic Monster* (1958; bunches of bugs), and *The Spider* (1958).

Fess Parker has a nice small part as Crotty, a pilot who's put in the loony bin because he saw the giant ants whiz by. Ironically, Walt Disney went to a screening of the film to check out Arness as a possible Davy Crockett. After seeing the film, he changed his mind and cast Parker in the role. Watch for Leonard Nimoy working the Teletype machine.

The Disc
Video: ★★
Audio: ★★★½ (monaural)
Chapters: Yes
Format: CLV
Source: Warner Home Video

Grrrr. This film was shot at a 1.66:1 aspect ratio, and it would have been nice if this remastered edition maintained that. Instead, we get the same picture we've seen before, with the edges missing and the picture looking cramped.

The image itself is surprisingly drab and grayish for the first eight chapters, after which it becomes relatively bright, with rich blacks and whites and a full range of grays. The print is generally free of scratches and negative dirt.

The audio is *very* satisfying, however: The ominous desert winds and the screech of the ants have never sounded better!

The splendid original theatrical trailer is included, with scenes not in the film and its incomparable acronymic description of the film as being filled with "Terror, Horror, Excitement, and Mystery!"

The *greatest* bonus, however, is the fact that the film's opening title is in color, something that hasn't been seen since the film's theatrical release. (So why couldn't they have mildly *matted* the thing and given it to us in a two-disc set, with the final showdown in CAV? Didn't Warner think that fans of the film would pay the extra few dollars for a definitive disc set?)

This Is Spinal Tap (1984)
★★★★½
Director: Rob Reiner
Running Time: 82 minutes

Back in 1964, David St. Hubbins (Michael McKean) and Nigel Tufnel (Christopher Guest) formed the four-man band Spinal Tap, which rode each new wave—folk, flower power, head banger—into the present. The band has had thirty-seven members over the years, most of them drummers who died from spontaneous combustion, choking on someone else's vomit, and so on. Only bassist Derek Smalls (Harry Shearer) has demonstrated staying power. Touring the United States to promote their new album, *Smell the Glove*, the group revered as "one of England's loudest" is followed and filmed by TV-commercial director Martin DiBergi (Rob Reiner) for a documentary.

DiBergi interviews the musicians and tracks them from gig to gig, starting with well-attended concerts and ending with the band second-billed to a puppet show. His cameras are there as high hopes turn to disaster, as flagging popularity, friction with Polymer Records, and resentment over David's girlfriend, Jeanine Pettibone (June Chadwick), tears them apart.

This "documentary," which expertly deflates rock and roll pomposity, was the first film directed by Reiner, who has become one of our most eclectic and reliable directors (see *The Princess Bride*).

He and his actors shot hours of vaguely scripted, frequently improvised footage, which was cut into this tight, hilarious film. McKean and Guest are amazing, from their accents to their pretentious palaver to glances that range from hate-filled to vacant. (Guest, a "Saturday Night Live" alumnus and one of Hollywood's great untapped talents, directed a superb send-up of his own, *The Big Picture* [1989] about a student filmmaker's brush with Hollywood.)

Look fast for guest appearances by Ed Begley, Jr., Bruno Kirby, Patrick Macnee, Howard Hesseman, Billy Crystal, Paul Benedict (of "The Jeffersons"), Dana Carvey (of "Saturday Night Live," as the mime waiter), Anjelica Huston (whose name is misspelled in the closing credits), Fred Willard, and Paul Shaffer (David Letterman's sidekick) in a hilariously fawning performance as Chicago PR man Artie Fufkin.

The Disc

Video: ★★★
Audio: ★★★½ (Surround)
Chapters: No
Format: CLV
Source: Embassy Home Entertainment

Considering that the film is supposed to have a raw, gritty look, the transfer isn't bad. There's slight grain throughout (as there was in the original film) but very little video noise—remarkable considering the amount of garish colors in the concert footage.

The film really could have used a mild letterbox, though. There's no panning-and-scanning, just a loss of whatever's on the edge of the screen (which includes Jeanine at 50:06 on side one and David at 3:10 on side two—both crucial to the scenes).

The digital audio has an intentionally hollow, filmed-on-location sound. It's very clear, though you'll probably want to keep your volume controls near: The Surround kicks in only during the concert footage, and the heavy-metal sounds get *very* loud.

The group actually recorded an album, which was released in March of 1992.

The Three Caballeros (1945)
★★★★★
Director: Norman Ferguson
Running Time: 71 minutes

Scoff if you want, but *this* is Walt Disney's most delightful and audacious animated feature. Less full of itself than *Fantasia* (see page 00), *The Three Caballeros* is a collection of lighthearted stories set in Latin America. Along with *Saludos Amigos* (1943)—a similar though less inspired film—it was made to underscore the U.S. Good Neighbor Policy during World War II.

The cartoon and live-action sections are framed by Donald Duck's Friday the thirteenth birthday celebration, which is attended by the suave parrot José Carioca and, later on, by the gunslinging rooster Panchito. With his friends as guides, the irascible duck visits Central and South America; standout segments include that "wolf in duck's clothing" riding a magic serape and dive-bombing live-action bathing beauties in Acapulco, and dancing with entertainer Carmen Molina and a chorus line of animated cacti. Even viewers who've been spoiled by the impeccable special effects in *Who Framed Roger Rabbit* (see page 300) will be impressed by the integration of cartoon and live-action characters.

The film leaps nimbly from slapstick to song and dance to scenes of breathtaking beauty to the surreal—as when Donald gets trapped in and distorted by the sound track and the "You Belong to My Heart" number in which stars, flowers, and the love-struck duck mutate and evolve in mind-blowing ways. And there may not be a more infectious musical number in the Disney catalog than the title song. You'll be humming it (maddeningly!) for days.

Children will enjoy the film's many comic moments, but adults will be mesmerized.

The Disc
Video: ★★★
Audio: ★★½ (monaural)
Chapters: No
Format: CLV and CAV versions
Source: Walt Disney Home Video

The Three Caballeros is a vivid film, though the colors don't quite sing: Kids will say it looks old compared to, say, *The Little Mermaid* (see page 175). The picture is sharp and in generally good shape, though there's some noise in the reds and blues.

The film was shot 1.33:1, so the lack of letterboxing is not a problem.

The sound is somewhat tinny, a result of the era in which the film was made. However, it won't detract from your enjoyment.

Thunderbolt and Lightfoot (1974) ★★
Director: Michael Cimino
Running Time: 114 minutes

This is a very different, very disappointing Clint Eastwood film. He stars as John "Thunderbolt," a Korean war vet and bank robber who's running from ex-partners Red Leary (George Kennedy—missing from the credits on the jacket!) and Goody (Geoffrey Lewis), who are under the misconception that he stole the loot from a previous job. Thunderbolt falls in with drifter Lightfoot (Jeff Bridges); and when Red and Goody catch up with them, Thunderbolt explains that the money is just where he left it: behind the blackboard in a one-room schoolhouse in a small town in Montana. Unfortunately when they get there, the school is gone, replaced by a modern building. The upbeat Lightfoot convinces the despondent group to rob the same vault again, and the second half of the film concerns the preparations for the heist, the job itself, and its aftermath.

The film marked the directorial debut of Cimino, who had cowritten the screenplays for *Silent Running* (1972) and *Magnum Force* (1973), and went on to make *The Deer Hunter* (1978) and *Heaven's Gate* (1980). The big problems with *Thunderbolt and Lightfoot* are massive, "can't overlook 'em" plot holes—that is, how do Eastwood's expartners keep finding him, where do they get the heavy artillery used in the heist, and how come no one's worried about leaving fingerprints anywhere? —sketchy characterizations—we know nothing about Lightfoot's background, and Thunderbolt's past comes out in one indigestible lump—and a very uneven blend of comedy and action. The buffoonish Kennedy and the somber Eastwood appear to be acting in two different films.

Cimino manages to generate some suspense during the robbery, and there are a few good action sequences. The opening, with Eastwood seeking anonymity as a priest, is fun. Other than that, there's nothing here. Bridges was widely praised for his performance, and he's good—but not *that* good. Catherine Bach, Gary Busey, and Vic Tayback have small roles.

The Disc
Video: ★★★
Audio: ★★★ (monaural)
Chapters: Yes
Format: CLV
Source: MGM/UA Home Video

This has *got* to be one of the most uneven transfers ever made. Parts of the film, such as the opening, are so sharp that you're willing to forgive the movie its many flaws. Then, beginning with the motel liaison in chapter nine, the picture goes seriously grainy every so often— usually, but not exclusively, during indoor scenes. The nongrainy scenes are glossy, with solid colors, deep blacks, and no video noise whatsoever.

Despite his failings as a director, Cimino has a good eye, and the letterboxing frames his interesting compositions nicely.

The digital audio has acceptable range and body and is free of extraneous noise. But it's nothing special.

A ratty-looking theatrical trailer is included.

To Have and Have Not (1944)
★★★
Director: Howard Hawks
Running Time: 101 minutes

Considering how important Ernest Hemingway's style is to his fiction, the author's work has fared pretty well on the screen. The 1946 version of *The Killers* starring Burt Lancaster in his screen debut is a brilliant adaptation of the Hemingway tale; *A Farewell to Arms* (1932; available on laserdisc) with Helen Hayes and Gary Cooper, *The Sun Also Rises* (1957) with Tyrone Power, Ava Gardner, and Errol Flynn, *The Old Man and the Sea* (1958) with Spencer Tracy are also very good (though the remakes of each are uniformly awful). Even the much-maligned *Islands in the Stream* (1977), starring George C. Scott, is good, where it sticks to the spirit of the author.

To Have and Have Not is probably the best-known of the Hemingway adaptations because of its casting of Humphrey Bogart and Lauren Bacall, making her screen debut (at the age of nineteen!). Shortly thereafter, she married her forty-four-year-old leading man. It is not, however, one of the more satisfactory adaptations.

After the fall of France, cabin-cruiser skipper Harry "Steve" Morgan (Bogart) refuses to help his friend Gerard (Marcel Dalio) smuggle in an important underground leader, Paul de Brusac (Walter Molnar) and his wife. Meeting American Marie, aka "Slim" (Bacall), who is subsequently stranded in Martinique, Morgan agrees to help Gerard in order to earn money for a plane ticket for Marie. Though the mission is successful, Morgan's lush of a sidekick, Eddie (Walter Brennan), is captured by Vichy police lieutenant Coyo (Sheldon Leonard) and Captain Renard (Dan Seymour). Rescuing his friend, Morgan flees with him and Marie.

To Have and Have Not has desperately little in common with Hemingway's tale, in which a Key West native rents his boat to fishing parties during the Depression and smuggles Chinese immigrants and illegal liquor on the side. He is shot and killed while helping bank robbers make their getaway. The film was made to capitalize on the success of *Casablanca* (see page 42) but, unlike Bogart's Rick, the implied explanation for Morgan's initial neutrality is selfishness and corruption, which make him a far less romantic character.

The plot and Bogart may be nothing special, but Bacall is. Discovered by Howard Hawks's wife, who saw her in a *Harper's Bazaar* layout, she dominates this film, and a Bacall fad swept the nation on its release. People repeated her risqué lines ("You know how to whistle, don't you, Steve? You just put your lips together and blow") and young women imitated her teasing poses. No wonder: She introduced a new kind of body language to the screen, lazy and leonine. She would stand, loose-wristed, elbows cocked at her sides like a female gunslinger. She didn't look ingenuously at anyone she liked; she stared up conspicuously from beneath her smooth brow or gave them a sly sidelong glance. In *To Have and Have Not*, her sway-hipped dance at the end of the film is one of the most unforgettable exits in movie history.

In many ways, what went on behind the screen was more interesting than what happens in the film. Bogart and Bacall fell in love early in the eleven-week shoot, and there was real chemistry between them—so much so that halfway through the making of the film, a budding romance with Morgan and the character Helene de Brusac (Dolores Moran) was cut and one with Marie was added. However, though Hawks was happy with what was on the screen, he was not happy at how devoted his stars were to each other. He and Bogart engaged in a quiet power struggle over Bacall, with the director trying—and failing—to control her career *and* her life.

Hoagy Carmichael contributes some nice moments as the cocktail pianist Cricket, though Brennan—who was always on the borderline of annoying/amusing—is definitely the former. Horror-film buffs will recognize actor Sir

Lancelot (see *Zombies on Broadway*), who appears briefly as Horatio.

William Faulkner and Jules Furthman collaborated on the screenplay, and Faulkner's love affair with whiskey undoubtedly contributed to the disappointing, barroom-banter level of the film's humor.

The Disc
Video: ★★½
Audio: ★½ (monaural)
Chapters: No
Format: CLV
Source: MGM/UA Home Video

This isn't a bad-looking disc, but transfers have reached new heights since this one was done, and *To Have and Have Not* isn't up to current standards. The contrast is pretty good, but there's a softness of image and a lack of low-level detail that's just not acceptable. The source material was in average condition, with scattered scratches.

The sound track is fair, with too much noise in spots; the audio on the videocassette has stronger sound than this.

The disc includes the original theatrical trailer and a cartoon, *Bacall to Arms*, a satire on the Bogey/Bacall relationship.

Top Gun (1986) ★
Director: Tony Scott
Running Time: 109 minutes

Until the same director/star team of Scott and Tom Cruise gave us the totally stupid *Days of Thunder* (1990)—in which Cruise plays stockcar racer Cole Trickle (*Cole Trickle*, for God's sake!)—their *Top Gun* was one of the most unendurable "big" movies ever made. It's an Air Force recruitment film, a paean to high-tech hardware and Tom Cruise. It's slickly shot and edited by former TV-commercial director Scott, but that can't save a movie that has the emotional clout of a Nintendo game.

Maverick (Cruise) and his flyin' partner, Radar Intercept Officer Goose (Anthony Edwards, who acts everyone else off the screen), are transferred to the Top Gun Naval Academy, to which only the best pilots are sent. There, flier Ice (Val Kilmer) and Maverick vie for Top Gun honors, while Maverick also sets his sights on one of his instructors, young Charlotte "Charlie" Blackwood (Kelly McGillis).

Because Maverick's father is wrongly presumed to have been a coward, skipping out on his comrades in Vietnam, Maverick is determined to succeed, but determination alone doesn't prevent Goose from buying the farm in an accident for which Maverick feels partly responsible. He quits the Top Gun program until his superior, Viper (Tom Skerritt), tells him how, contrary to popular belief, Maverick Senior died saving three other planes in combat. Inspired, Maverick returns to his cockpit and, though Ice has won the Top Gun trophy, Maverick saves his life in a showdown with enemy MiGs, and everyone—including Ice—knows who's *really* the best.

You don't have to be a snob to hate this movie. It's just a really bad film built on clichés, predictable plot developments, and flat performances. The filmmakers *might* have had a good movie if they'd put as much effort into the script as they did into staging the spectacular aerial scenes—hence, the one-star rating—or trying to disguise the fact that McGillis is taller than Cruise. But they didn't, and while Cruise fans and hardware freaks ate "Top Gonads" up, and it's one of the two best-selling discs of all time, that doesn't make it any good. The film was inspired by an article in the May 1983 *California* magazine, which is far more interesting than the film.

Ironically, preview audiences thought the love scenes were blah, so McGillis and Cruise were brought back to film their elevator encounter. However, McGillis had already cut her hair for her next film—hence, the cap. And despite what many articles have claimed, the close ups of Cruise in the cockpit were not shot in the air but were filmed on a sound stage, using rear-projection.

The Disc

Video: ★★★★
Audio: ★★★★★ (Surround)
Chapters: No
Format: CLV
Source: Paramount Home Video

Except for the fact that the disc is not letterboxed (undermining its sole asset, the stunning aerial photography), the 1990 remaster is a beautiful transfer (the earlier version was slightly fuzzy and grainier). The picture is very sharp, with very little grain. Colors are quite solid.

The audio is awesome, with window-rattling Surround effects that *almost* justify obtaining the disc in a moment of weakness (it *is*, after all, under thirty bucks). Be warned, though: You'll hate yourself in the morning.

Days of Thunder is also an audio ripsnorter (and available letterboxed), which is fortunate: You'll need the sound to stay awake.

Touch of Evil (1958) ★★★★½
Director: Orson Welles
Running Time: 108 minutes

When Charlton Heston agreed to star in *Touch of Evil*, he assumed that his costar, Orson Welles, was also going to be directing. Why else *hire* him? When Heston learned that the studio was planning to assign a house director, with the financially strapped Welles simply acting, he said uh-uh, He wasn't going to act in it. The difficult, "artsy" Welles was as welcome at the studios as an audit, but Universal didn't want to lose Heston; they let Welles direct. And *that*, kiddies, is how masterpieces are born! (Four years later, while shooting *55 Days at Peking* in Spain, Heston pleaded with producer Samuel Bronston to give Welles $100,000 and let him improvise a spy thriller using the magnificent sets. Bronston foolishly declined.)

Welles never bothered to read the Whit Masterson novel *Badge of Evil* on which *Touch of Evil* was based. He hated the script and reasoned that the novel on which it was based couldn't possibly offer him anything. He wrote an entirely new script, retaining only the basic idea of a corrupt lawman moving the setting from sun-drenched San Diego to the dark, dreary border town of Los Robles, and changing the book's assistant district attorney, Mitch Holt, to a Pan American Narcotics Commission agent, Mexican Ramon Miguel Vargas. He also changed Mrs. Holt from Connie to Susan and made her and Vargas newlyweds. After seeing the film, you'll find it difficult to believe that another scenario ever existed. Welles came up with strong, seedy, memorable stuff.

A car blows up on the American side of the border from a bomb planted on the Mexican side. Vargas (Heston) and his new bride, Susan (Janet Leigh), are witnesses, and the honest, upright Vargas quickly runs afoul of the investigating officer, Hank Quinlan (Welles), a corrupt sheriff who relies on instinct, not fact, to solve crimes, then finds (or plants) the evidence to support his feelings. When he frames a young shoe clerk by placing dynamite in his bathroom, Vargas is furious and seeks to prove the youth's innocence. Resenting Vargas's interference, Quinlan joins with narcotics dealer "Uncle" Joe Grandi (Akim Tamiroff), an enemy of Vargas's, to frame Susan on drug charges. Ultimately, Susan is vindicated, though so is Quinlan, who, it turns out, was right about the clerk's guilt.

Touch of Evil was shot in Venice, California, with art and invention that is still startling. The first scene, which begins with a close-up of the bomb, rides over buildings, introduces the Vargases, follows them across the border, and ends with the explosion of the car, is one three-minute, nineteen-second take; the choreography of the actors, the gliding and racing moves of the camera, and the alternately garish and shadowy lighting form a breathtaking tour de force. In another scene, the camera unobtrusively moves into a building, into a small elevator, rides up several floors with the characters, and emerges to follow the continuing action of the scene. You can't help but be humbled by inspired filmmaking like that.

Principal photography stretched over several months from late 1957 to early 1958, after which Welles edited and then tinkered with the film for months more. Eventually, the studio's impatience to see the finished product made him physically ill, and he quit. After looking at the film, the studio left it more or less alone, though they had TV director Harry Keller come in and shoot a few extra scenes—what Heston has described as "structural cement to clarify what the studio felt to be unnecessarily ambigious sequences in Orson's version of the film." Heston added that despite the half day's worth of shooting, "The picture is very close to Orson's original intent."

Almost without exception, the casting was as inspired as the filmmaking. Though Heston tries hard, he's seriously miscast (and unaccented) as a Mexican, and Leigh isn't quite up to the demands of the sarcastic Susan. Welles, however—complete with his false nose—is unnervingly good. So is Marlene Dietrich as Tanya, a former lover of Quinlan's, now the owner of a brothel, and, in smaller roles, Dennis Weaver, Zsa Zsa Gabor, Joseph Cotten, Keenan Wynn, and Mercedes McCambridge.

The Disc
Video: ★★★★
Audio: ★★★ (monaural)
Chapters: Just one, for the trailer
Format: CLV
Source: MCA/Universal Home Video

The film noir look of *Touch of Evil* is beautifully served by the disc. Welles's stark lighting looks very sharp, and for the most part the gray tones are faithfully reproduced. The source material has some scratches, but the beauty of the film isn't seriously compromised by these flaws.

The audio is driven—and often drowned out—by Henry Mancini's overpowering jazz score. The dialogue is occasionally muffled, but that's more the fault of the original recording than that of the transfer. (The film was extensively re-dubbed in postproduction.)

The disc features the restored version of the film, with a few minutes of footage that had been clipped by Universal prior to the film's release.

The Toxic Avenger (1984) ★★
Director: Michael Herz and Samuel Weil
Running Time: 100 minutes

Some films, like *Plan 9 from Outer Space* (see page 215), are fun because they're unintentionally stupid. Other films, like this one, are intentionally stupid and not as much fun. Not that *The Toxic Avenger* isn't enjoyable: The filmmakers roll more gutter balls than strikes, but there's parody that works here and, considering the low, low budget, some effective action scenes.

Homicidal bullies Bozo (Gary Schneider) and Slug (Robert Prichard) and their lady friends Wanda (Jennifer Baptist) and Julie (Cindy Manion) trick Tromaville Health Club janitor Melvin (Mark Torgl) into donning tights and a tutu for what he's told will be a sexual rendezvous. Instead, he walks into a room where all of the club members are waiting; humiliated, Melvin hurls himself from a window and lands in a drumful of toxic waste. He metamorphoses into the tall, muscular, deformed, articulate Toxic Avenger (Mitchell Cohen; voice by Kenneth Kessler); still wearing the tutu and tights, he sets out to rid Tromaville of evildoers.

Breaking up a robbery at a fast-food restaurant (the movie's best action scene), he meets blind Sara (Andree Maranda), who moves in with him at his shack in the dump beside the Collins Chemical Plant. Furious with the do-gooder, corrupt Mayor Peter Belgoody (Pat Ryan, Jr.) has the governor send in the National Guard to destroy the monster. The troops mass at the dump, but citizens who have been helped by the monster stand between him and the tanks, refusing to let them fire. The Guardsmen back down; and when the enraged mayor fires away, the Toxic Avenger kills him.

The toxic-waste jokes are clever and the jibes at fitness are generally on target; Sara's antics (a blind mirror, hitting the monster in the groin with her cane) and Bozo running over kids for points are not just in bad taste, they're achingly unfunny. The makeup effects are excellent—except for the gang leader at the restaurant, who's wearing a fake, soon-to-be-ripped-off arm from the moment he enters the eatery.

The laserdisc features the unrated version of the film. There's nudity and sex as well as extreme violence, such as the creature ripping out the mayor's intestines, a whirring milk-shake blender getting shoved into a criminal's mouth, eyeballs being poked out, and other delights.

The film was the first major hit for the eleven-year-old Troma Team, and it secured the company's title as the cinema "shlock kings," a label they lived up to with subsequent efforts such as *Class of Nuke 'Em High* (1986), *Stuff Stephanie in the Incinerator* (1987) and *Rabid Grannies* (1988).

The Toxic Avenger was followed by *The Toxic Avenger, Part II* (1989), which has the hero battling Japanese businessmen who raze a home for the blind, and *The Toxic Avenger Part III—The Last Temptation of Toxie* (1989), in which he's wooed by the forces of evil.

The Disc
Video: ★★½
Audio: ★★½ (monaural)
Chapters: Yes
Format: CLV (side one), CAV (side two)
Source: Vestron Video

Despite the movie's low budget, the picture is surprisingly clear and the colors are good. There's some grain (this *is* a low-budget exploitation film) along with occasional splice marks and scratches. The CAV side two (though it says CLV on the label) enables you to study the goriest effects one frame at a time, such as a drug dealer's head as it's crushed by weights.

Though the disc has problems with the higher frequencies, the digital audio has a nice resonance, with both the Avenger's voice and the music of Rossini and Mussorgsky sounding fine.

The second film is available on laser disc, the quality identical to the first. The other Troma films mentioned above are available on laserdisc, *Class of Nuke 'Em High* as a Japanese import.

Toy Soldiers (1991) ★★★
Director: Daniel Petrie, Jr.
Running Time: 104 minutes

The Regis prep school for boys is also known as the Rejects school, since half of its students have been expelled from other prep schools. Despite the confrontational nature of the kids who go there, the school's run with compassion by Dean Parker (Louis Gossett, Jr.)

Colombian drug lord Enrique Cali (Jesse Doran) is being tried in the United States, and his son, Luis (Andrew Divoff), wants him released. To this end, Luis and his band of terrorists take over Regis, where the son of the presiding judge is a student. If Enrique isn't released, the students buy the farm. Luis is ruthless and has considered every angle—except for the resourcefulness of a handful of kids, led by Billy Tepper (Sean Astin) and Joseph Trotta (Wil Wheaton), who happens to be the son of a powerful mobster, thereby adding an interesting subplot (though the unbilled Jerry Orbach is awfully corny as the New Jeresy mob kingpin).

The cornerstone of the kids' plan is for Billy to make a daring escape, inform the authorities about how the terrorists have set up their defenses, then sneak back in before he's missed (a student will be executed for each student who fails to appear at roll call). In the end, it's up to the kids to save the day when the military screws up.

Based on the carefully plotted novel by William P. Kennedy, *Toy Soldiers* has some holes the size of Medellin (the asthma attack that draws Luis out of his office at a crucial moment, as if the SOB would be concerned about something like that; the "shower" explanation Billy gives for his wet hair, after he's been crawling through a mucky storm drain; etc.). But you'll overlook most of them because the tension is unrelenting, the plot twists are surprising and often ingenious, and the action is real. There are no superhuman tricks, no bad guys shooting at heroes and never hitting them.

The characterizations and script are more solid than most films of this type, and the actors are uniformly fine—especially Astin, Divoff, and the ever-reliable Gossett. And it's great to see the *Full Metal Jacket* drill sergeant Lee Ermey in a small part as General Kramer.

The Disc
Video: ★★★★★
Audio: ★★★★ (Surround)
Chapters: No
Format: CLV
Source: SVS/Triumph

What a picture! No grain or video noise to speak of, a sharp and glossy picture, perfect colors, and details in even the darkest scenes. The film is a pleasure to watch (and probably makes it seem better than it really is). Shot TV-safe, everything of importance is there on the screen in the nonletterboxed film.

Stereo separations are very good; and though Surround effects are limited to a few key scenes, they're knockouts. The radio-controlled plane is especially good, and there are some coughs and ringing phones that'll startle you. The rear speakers also have some fun with helicopters and gunshots.

Tremors (1989) ★★★½
Director: Ron Underwood
Running Time: 95 minutes

Back in the 1950s, the "giant monster on the loose" genre was a staple of Hollywood, from high-class movies such as *Them!* and *Twenty Million Miles to Earth* (see pages 276 and 286), to low-class but entertaining rubbish such as *The Giant Claw* (1957) and *Attack of the Fifty Foot Woman* (1958).

Tremors sets out to recapture the lurking fear and relentless forward momentum of the best of those movies, and it succeeds admirably. Handymen Valentine McKee (Kevin Bacon) and Earl Basset (Fred Ward) are fed up with life in Perfection, Nevada, and decide to leave. But as they drive away, they're cut off by something nasty under the desert sands and heading toward town: huge wormlike creatures that sense the vibrations and pop up to eat anything that moves. Returning to Perfection, the two men—along with visiting seismology student Rhonda LeBeck (Finn Carter) and a handful of locals—hole up at a general store and try to figure out how to get out of town.

The movie is tightly coiled, fast-paced, mindless fun, with top-notch special effects (did the Academy of Motion Picture Arts and Sciences sleep through this film?) and, literally, one cliffhanger after another. Bacon and Ward are perfect as the heroic leads, but the real eye-openers are Michael Gross (of TV's "Family Ties") and singer Reba McEntire, who shine as Burt and Heather Gummer, *Soldier of Fortune* lifestylists who tangle with one of the creatures when it tries to invade their underground bunker. Some smart producer ought to put these two in a buddy picture.

The Disc
Video: ★★★½
Audio: ★★★★ (Surround)
Chapters: No
Format: CLV
Source: MCA/Universal Home Video

This is a movie that sounds better on laserdisc than it did in the theaters. The audio envelopes the viewer like the maw of one of the worms: You're in the midst of it, and you'll have the time of your laser-watching life. And it's clear as could be: Just listen to those shell casings clatter around you as the Gummers fight off the intrusive monster.

The picture isn't *quite* up to the audio quality. The image is very sharp and brightly lighted, day and night, but is somewhat grainier than the original film. The film isn't hurt at all by the lack of letterboxing.

Truth or Dare (1991) ★★★
Director: Alek Keshishian
Running Time: 118 minutes

A great deal—arguably too much—has been written about Madonna Ciccone, the self-promotion genius who turned a sweet but limited voice, some dance experience at the University of Michigan, and "boy-toy" sex appeal into a career of surprising breadth and duration.

Truth or Dare was filmed during her international Blond Ambition tour, with director Keshishian (reportedly) having full access to the star, her entourage, and her friends and family. "Reportedly," because, while there's some interesting and even sensational stuff here, Madonna prohibits the camera from following her into a business meeting, and you've got to wonder what else she didn't allow the director to shoot. Sean Penn is only mentioned in passing, and the one guy she sets out to seduce is married and turns her down. Was she celibate during the entire tour? Was Sarah Bernhardt in her hotel room just for a visit? What aren't we being shown here? She bares her breasts (though not for the first time) and performs oral sex on a water bottle and allows a longtime friend to call her a little shit ... but is *that* the real Madonna or just shock-effect stuff that she thinks *we*'ll think is honesty.

It's tough to say, so all we can judge is the woman we *do* get to see, who comes across as demanding, hardworking, brave, impatient, brusque, and immature. And there are some memorable moments: Warren Beatty offering some incisive comments about his then-lover; Madonna making an appropriate "finger down the throat" gesture after Kevin Costner pronounces her show "neat"; a cleverly edited battle with Canadian censors; and reverse discrimination involving the straight and gay dancers on her tour.

The concert footage is invigorating, and the film will give you an entertaining taste of the perks and drawbacks of superstardom. But *Truth or Dare* never manages to convince us that it's as much the former as the latter.

The Disc
Video: ★★★½
Audio: ★★★★ (Surround)
Chapters: No
Format: CLV
Source: Live Home Video

The film is black and white, with color concert footage, and there are problems with both. The black and white scenes are intentionally gritty, which is fine, though not much of a treat for laserphiles. The color segments are crisp when they aren't plagued with video noise in the reds and blues, which is about half the time.

The letterboxing, while welcome, doesn't affect the film much except during the concert scenes.

The audio is super during the concert scenes and a little muffled behind the scenes. Not surprisingly, the Surround Sound is omnipresent during the performance footage, but it's used sparingly and to great effect during the documentary segments. However, watch the sound levels: You'll find yourself turning up the volume to hear quiet conversations, only to be hammered with a speaker-blowing burst of sound (at 4:34 on side one, for example).

At the very least, the film should have had chapter breaks for the songs.

Twenty Million Miles to Earth (1957) ★★★
Director: Nathan Juran
Running Time: 83 minutes

The cycle of 1950s "giant monster on the loose" films began with *The Beast from*

20,000 Fathoms (1953), the saga of a dinosaur released from eons of hibernation by nuclear bomb tests. The special effects were created by Ray Harryhausen, who brought the monster to life using stop-motion animation, the same process employed in *King Kong* (see page 159), in which jointed miniature models are posed and filmed incrementally, as though they were flat animated drawings. Harryhausen followed *The Beast from 20,000 Fathoms* with special effects for *It Came from Beneath the Sea* (1955) and *Earth vs. the Flying Saucers* (1956), all of which are available on laserdisc (*The Beast from 20,000 Fathoms* on a crystal-clear remastered disc).

Harryhausen's finest work of this era is his animation of the monster in *Twenty Million Miles to Earth*. Upon returning from Venus, a manned rocket crash-lands off the coast of Italy. A small reptilian creature brought from Venus washes ashore, is found by a young boy, sold to a zoologist, and begins to grow due to earth's alien atmosphere. Escaping into the countryside, the monster is hunted and captured by American Colonel Calder (William Hopper), a survivor of the spaceflight. Brought to a zoo for study, the extraterrestrial—by now as big as a house—breaks free and does more damage to Rome than did the Persians before it makes its final stand atop the Colosseum.

Joan Taylor provides bare-bones love interest as Marisa Leonardo, Calder's physician. Like the rest of the plot, however, love takes a backseat to the stunning special effects. Harryhausen gives his creature more personality than the human actors, and the compositing of the monster in the real-life settings is nearly flawless. The hide-and-seek sequence in the barn is especially well done, though pay close attention to the scene in which the monster leaps from the barn loft. The floor on which it lands is a miniature, superimposed over the real floor. However, watch when the monster moves to the right and Hopper to the left. Since Hopper can't step onto the miniature floor, Harryhausen distracts the viewer by having the monster rub its face. Keep watching the left, though, and you'll see the miniature section disappear so Hopper can walk there.

See also the entries on Harryhausen's special effects for *Jason and the Argonauts*, *First Men in the Moon*, and *The Golden Voyage of Sinbad*.

The Disc
Video: ★★★★★
Audio: ★★★★ (monaural)
Chapters: Yes
Format: CLV (side one), CAV (side two)
Source: Pioneer Special Edition

A pristine print was used for the disc: There are no imperfections to speak of, and the images are sharp in the daylight and full of subtle shading at night. Even silhouettes against dark gray backgrounds stand out, and the Doré-like lighting as Calder stalks the monster in the barn will take your breath away. The CAV function on side two will let you study jitter-free stills of the monster standing behind buildings, raging through ruins, ducking flamethrowers, or fighting an elephant.

The sound, too, is exceptional, from the screaming rocket as it rips through the skies to the monster's roar to the artillery blasts and, alternately, to the hiss-free silence.

2001: A Space Odyssey (1968)
★★★★★
Director: Stanley Kubrick
Running Time: 149 minutes

In 1950, prophetic science fiction author Arthur C. Clarke wrote a short story called "The Sentinel," in which scientists find a pyramidal object on the moon. Its job is to signal the alien race that had left it there, once humans had reached a significant stage of their development (that is—once they were no longer "still struggling up from savagery" but were advanced enough to get to the moon and find the thing). Only then would humans be worth contacting.

Kubrick was fascinated with the idea and, together with Clarke, used it as a springboard for what was then called *Journey Beyond the Stars*. The film was originally budgeted at $6 million; the final cost was $10.5 million, as Kubrick labored over the special effects and devised new ways to shoot them, most notably using computer-controlled cameras that paved the way for films such as *Star Wars* and *Close Encounters of the Third Kind* (see pages 263 and 52).

The film begins with savage subhumans fighting to survive and learning about weapons after coming into contact with a black monolith. The picture jump-cuts (breathtakingly) from a tossed bone to a spaceship to the discovery of the "beacon" (another black slab) on the moon, which sends a signal toward Jupiter. The beam is followed by astronauts on board the gigantic ship *Discovery*. En route, the space travelers fight the malevolent computer HAL (voice of Douglas Rain). HAL kills the astronauts in suspended animation and sends Frank Poole (Gary Lockwood) spinning off into the void; only astronaut Dave Bowman (Keir Dullea) survives, after he manages to lobotomize the computer. (The apes made weapons that killed; the things we make are *still* killing us!)

Upon reaching Jupiter, Bowman is sucked into a time/space vortex that brings him into contact with the alien beings who planted the monolith. Bowman ages while under their care and is reborn as what the shooting script describes as a "star-child," a human/alien hybrid sent back to earth to watch over it. (The star-child was originally a naked young boy filmed against velvet; Kubrick didn't like how that looked, and so he eventually went with a bug-eyed embryo made of fiberglass. As initially conceived, the star-child was also going to detonate all the nuclear weapons in earth orbit, but Kubrick disgarded that as being too similar to the end of *Dr. Strangelove*—see page 72).

2001: A Space Odyssey became a huge hit in its road-show Cinerama engagements, largely due to the "psychedelic" trip through the star gate at the end of the film. Today, it's still a hell of a ride, but the film is appreciated more for its innovative visual and narrative style, which many people initially found puzzling and off-putting.

Kubrick has said, "I don't like to talk about *2001* much because it's essentially a nonverbal experience. How could we possibly appreciate the Mona Lisa if Leonardo had written at the bottom of the canvas: 'The lady is smiling because she is hiding a secret from her lover.'?"

Nonetheless, *we'll* talk about it, and here are some facts about the film that are worth mentioning.

- Before the premiere, Kubrick eliminated a prologue in which eminent scientists discuss the idea of extraterrestrial life.
- Kubrick also scrapped a score composed by Alex North in favor of using classical music.
- After the film opened, Kubrick cut eighteen minutes, consisting of short scenes, including a close-up of astronaut Poole being crushed to death by the claws of the HAL-controlled pod.
- The aliens were originally going to be portrayed by actors dressed in all-white costumes, photographically distorted. Kubrick decided not to show them at all.
- The director insists it's entirely coincidental that the name of his deadly computer is one letter removed from IBM.
- The dead zebra at the beginning of the film is a painted (dead) horse.
- At one point, Kubrick intended to project pictures onto the monolith found by the apes, as it *showed* them new ways of doing things.
- Watch as the flight attendant plucks the floating pen from the air: She has to give it a slight tug because it was pasted to a rotating sheet of glass.
- The director's daughter Vivian plays "Squirt," the daughter of Dr. Heywood Floyd (William Sylvester).

- When the flight attendant walks up the wall, she was actually walking in place; the camera and the entire set were turning.
- Watch for the blunder: When space station-bound Dr. Floyd sips his food through a straw and releases it, the food slides back into the container. In zero gravity, it should have hung there.
- The "surface" of the alien world at the end was filmed in both Monument Valley and the Hebrides in Scotland.

The film's sequel, *2010* (1984), directed by Peter Hyams and based on Clarke's novel, is a technically impressive, occasionally fascinating movie about a return to Jupiter, the abandoned spaceship *Discovery*, and a flood of alien artifacts that cause thermonuclear reactions on the planet and turn it into a star. The film was a box-office failure. Presumably, we won't be seeing a film based on Clarke's *2061*.

The Disc

Video: ★★★½ (Criterion); ★★★★½ (MGM/UA)
Audio: ★★★★½ (Surround) (Criterion); ★★★½ (MGM/UA)
Chapters: Yes (Criterion CAV); No (Criterion CLV, MGM/UA)
Format: CAV or CLV editions from Criterion
Source: Criterion or MGM/UA Home Video

Criterion's discs may have been supervised by Kubrick himself, but they leave a great deal to be desired. The transfer was made from a 35mm intermediate negative, not from the original 70mm negative; the resultant image is not always as sharp as it should be. The colors are fairly strong, but the reds and oranges tend to bleed, particularly in the "Dawn of Man" episode. There are also occasional problems with grain.

The MGM/UA disc was made directly from a 70mm print, and it shows. You can practically count the monkey hairs, and the colors are spectacular (though there's some video noise in the reds on board the *Discovery*). Grain is not a problem with this disc. For the price (thirty dollars), you can't beat it, even if you already own one of the Criterion editions.

The original six-track audio has been successfully reduced to four channels for both discs. Despite occasional background noise, the clarity of the Criterion editions is generally excellent, serving up everything from delicate *pings* to sonorous rumblings. The rear speakers are especially active when the apes clash. The music (including the overture) sounds great.

The MGM/UA audio is a trifle less sharp in the upper ranges and a bit muddier in the lower, but the improved picture quality still makes this the disc of choice.

The extras on Criterion's CAV edition are marvelous. They include interviews from the original prologue, an explanation of some of the special effects, documentary footage of the *Voyager* Jupiter flybys, and—most exciting of all—actual space footage from NASA's files juxtaposed with scenes from the film, showing just how prescient Kubrick and Clarke were! (Though there won't be any Pan Am space clippers, alas.)

The CLV edition contains just the film, which is letterboxed. (It also has had a spotty history—literally. Manufactured at 3M, a large percentage of the discs have suffered from rot, while many others have faulty chapter stops).

The only MGM/UA extra is the trailer. MGM/UA's new letterboxed edition is not to be confused with the pitiful panned-and-scanned edition the company originally released. *2001: A Space Odyssey* is a movie of awesome visual style and storytelling: It cannot be appreciated cropped—at all.

2010 is available, letterboxed, on laserdisc from MGM/UA. Despite the handsome effects and good performances from Roy Scheider, Helen Mirren, John Lithgow, and HAL (Rain, again), it's a major disappointment. Keir Dullea's return is effective.

Ulzana's Raid (1972) ★★★★
Director: Robert Aldrich
Running Time: 103 minutes

Back in 1972, a visitor to Burt Lancaster's bungalow on the Universal lot would have heard the actor complaining that his latest film was getting zero support from the studio and wasn't even playing in many markets. He was right. Though Universal knew that *Ulzana's Raid* wasn't going to be a comic book–style romp like the director's *The Dirty Dozen* (see page 68), the studio was horrified by the grim, graphically violent film they got.

Lancaster gives a wonderfully restrained performance as McIntosh, an aging scout who leads young, green Lt. Garnett DeBuin (Bruce Davison) and his men in pursuit of the band led by renegade Apache Ulzana (Joaquin Martinez) circa 1880. The film cuts back and forth between the groups, vividly contrasting their cultures and motivations as it moves toward a showdown that is definitely *not* for fragile nerves.

There's evisceration, torture, rape, and a painfully vivid suicide, images that will haunt you long after the movie is over. But not one frame of it is gratuitous, nor does the violence overshadow the literate, character-driven script.

Look for longtime Lancaster friend and costar Nick Cravat as one of the soldiers.

The Disc
Video: ★★★
Audio: ★★½ (monaural)
Chapters: Just one, for the trailer
Format: CLV
Source: MCA Universal Home Video

The colors range from vivid to somewhat soft, and night scenes tend to be a little grainy, especially in the opening. There are no major flaws in the master element.

Ulzana's Raid isn't letterboxed, but no crucial information is lost and the pans are executed smoothly.

The digital sound is crisp, if unexciting.

The theatrical trailer is included at the end of the film: Note how the word rape is skillfully cut from Lancaster's speech.

Uncle Buck (1989) ★½
Director: John Hughes
Running Time: 100 minutes

When her father suffers a heart attack, Cindy Russell (Elaine Bromka) and her husband, Bob (Garrett M. Brown), have to hurry from Chicago's northern suburbs to Indianapolis. Unfortunately, only Bob's irresponsible brother, Buck (John Candy), is free to watch the kids, and he hurries over from his apartment in the city. Unemployed and a gambler, Buck can't get his act together to marry his girlfriend of eight years, Chanice Kobolowsky (Amy Madigan), who wants him to come work in her tire shop. But Buck *does* have a big heart and, when he isn't busy wrecking the house and his relationship with Chanice, he takes the job of looking after the kids very seriously. Young Maizy (Gaby Hoffman) and Miles (Macaulay Culkin) adore Buck, but teenager Tia (Jean Louisa Kelly) hates him because he doesn't like her boyfriend, Bug (Jay Underwood). Eventually, though, she learns that Buck was right about Bug and, to repent, she helps him win back Chanice. When Bob and Cindy return, everyone is pals and Buck and Chanice are off to a fresh start.

There are a couple of good moments in the film: Buck arriving at the wrong house in the middle of the night, a sight gag involving his clap-on light, and Miles's efforts to find another word for *balls*. But the picture suffers from contrived sentimentality, long stretches of predictable or unfunny gags, and abrasive characters. Cindy barely disguises her dislike of Buck; Tia is so mean, you wonder why Buck bothers to talk to her at all; and Bug has a major attitude problem. Even the minor characters are annoying, from sex-starved neighbor Marcie Dahlgren-Frost (Laurie Metcalf of TV's "Roseanne") to the snooty assistant principal to whom Buck gives some painfully self-righteous advice. Nor are Buck's treatment of Chanice or her shrill reactions much fun to watch.

Candy gives *Uncle Buck* his all, and the *only* reason to see this film is to savor how, with a look, a nervous laugh, a shift of his massive body, a gesture, and his delivery, he spins gold out of straw.

The Disc
Video: ★½
Audio: ★★★½ (Surround)
Chapters: No
Format: CLV
Source: MCA Home Video

Uncle Buck looked fine in the theaters, and MCA usually transfers movies well, so this somewhat grainy disc comes as a surprise. Only the brightest outdoor scenes are sharp and glossy. The rest of the image lacks sharpness and detail. From 26:12 to 27:13 on side one, Candy's image constantly shifts from dark to light. Otherwise, the colors are fine.

The film plays perfectly well unmatted.

The audio is quite sharp and the stereo separations are nice, especially those involving Buck's bomb of a car. There are a number of fun ambient sounds, but you won't be able to turn these too far up or the music *slamming* from the rear speakers will drown out the dialogue from the front.

The Untouchables (1987)
★★★★★
Director: Brian De Palma
Running Time: 119 minutes

Thanks to his best-selling autobiography and the popular TV series, Eliot Ness was an American hero long before Kevin Costner played him in *The Untouchables*. Taken as a whole, his career didn't amount to much: His reputation as an ace crime fighter came solely from his short but successful campaign against gangster Al Capone.

By 1929, at the height of Prohibition, the Chicago gangster was operating twenty *thousand* speakeasies. Two of his criminal undertakings came under federal jurisdiction: income tax evasion (Treasury Department) and bootlegging (Justice Department). Both departments were rotten with people on Capone's payroll, but Chicago-based Ness—a twenty-six-year-old Prohibition agent working for the Justice Department (not the Treasury, as in the film; he'd been with them from 1927 to 1928)—was both an outspoken critic of the mob and known to be clean. On September 28, 1929, U.S. District Attorney George Johnson told him to handpick a special team and go after Capone. He pored over personnel files, selected fifty candidates, and narrowed these down to nine men, five of whom he had worked with previously. (Sorry: Those great guys in the movie are all fictitious.)

The group began its operations in mid-October, each man earning an average of two thousand dollars a year. In the spring of 1930, a Capone flunky offered Ness two thousand dollars a *week* to back off; Ness literally threw the man out of his office. Learning what happened, a *Chicago Tribune* reporter dubbed Ness and his squad the "Untouchables," and the name stuck. Despite attempts on his life (he was nearly run down, gunned down, and happened to notice the hood of his car was slightly askew, which kept him from being blown up by dynamite hooked to the starter) and threats against his parents (not his wife, as in the film; he wasn't married until late in the crusade), Ness had all but destroyed Capone's brewing operations by the spring of 1931; meanwhile, Treasury agents (*not* the Untouchables, as in the movie) had built an income-tax case against Capone, who was brought to trial on October 6, 1931. The mobster was sentenced to a long prison term, and, after the Untouchables handed him over to U.S. marshals on May 3, 1932, they were disbanded. Amazingly, not *one* of the more than five thousand Prohibition offenses collected by the Untouchables was ever mentioned in court.

Capone stayed in jail for seven and a half years; debilitated by untreated syphilis, he died in his bed in 1947. Ness held a variety of relatively minor positions and ran unsuccessfully for office; he died of a heart attack in 1957, at the age of fifty-four.

The film follows Ness's career from the establishing of the Untouchables to the guilty verdict against Capone. Vast dramatic liberties were taken. For example, it was an informer who suffered the fate of screen Untouchable Oscar Wallace (Charles Martin Smith), and the "cooperation" of the bookkeeper came through wiretaps, not a showdown at the train station. However, the film accurately captures both the spirit of the men and their deeds, including the destruction of the breweries, the interception of alcohol being brought in from outside the city, and even Ness's confrontation with Capone—though not in retribution for the murder of an Untouchable but, rather, for the killing of an ex-con who worked with Ness.

Sean Connery (as cop-turned-Untouchable Jimmy Malone), Smith, and Andy Garcia—in a star-making performance as Untouchable George Stone—are all wonderful in their roles, and Robert De Niro (who put on thirty pounds for the role) is powerful as the gruff, explosive Capone. Billy Drago is perfectly evil as Capone henchman Frank Nitti—even if that isn't what he looked like or how he died. As for Kevin Costner, he's not Ness but Kevin Costner (*can* this guy act anything but?). He presents the lawman as a square (which he was) who is deeply troubled at having to go outside the law to nail Capone (which he wasn't). Still, Costner is an acceptable anchor for the other characters, and De Palma directs with his usual class, style, and punch.

The Disc
Video: ★★★
Audio: ★★★½ (Surround)
Chapters: Yes
Format: CLV (sides one and two), CAV (side three)
Source: Paramount Home Video

There are the pan-and-scan version and a newer letterboxed edition; only the latter accurately conveys the drama and look of the film, though it does cheat a little, opening up the frame on the top and bottom to lessen the matte, in the process revealing flaws in the print that weren't supposed to be seen.

While the colors are acceptable on both discs, they suffer from video noise—not high levels, but persistent ones. The picture is fairly sharp, though there's slight to moderate graininess in many scenes.

Worst of all, however, Paramount chose *not* to put the crackling good railroad-terminal sequence—with its runaway baby carriage inspired by Eisenstein's *Potemkin* (1925)—on the CAV side three. If viewers were going to still-frame any sequence, that's it. What makes this even more amazing is that there was *room* for it on side three!

The audio is very good, with a number of nifty Surround sequences, though you'll have to keep adjusting the volume: The sound effects are extremely loud and dialogue comparatively soft. The alternately staccato and soaring score by Ennio Morricone sounds terrific.

Victor/Victoria (1982)
★★★★½
Director: Blake Edwards
Running Time: 134 minutes

Though Edward's film is based on the 1933 German movie *Viktor und Viktoria*, the director also drew on his own *Pink Panther* films for inspiration. Victoria Grant (Julie Andrews) is a starving singer in the Paris of 1934. By chance, she links up with compassionate gay singer Toddy (Robert Preston), who convinces her that the way to become successful is to pretend to be a female impersonator. Together, they come up with a fictitious Polish count named Victor and finagle an audience with superagent Andre Cassell (John Rhys-Davies). Cassell gets Victor a booking and the singer becomes a huge draw. Victor is especially intriguing to a powerful American gangster named King (James Garner), who doesn't believe that Victor is really a man. While King sets out to prove his theory, a suspicious club owner, Labisse (Peter Arne), hires a bumbling detective, Bovin (Sherloque Tanney), so that he, too, can learn the truth about Victor.

Though the happy ending is contrived and unbelievable and the musical numbers are wildly uneven—"Le Jazz Hot" may well be Andrews's shining moment in the musical cinema, but "The Shady Dame from Seville" and "Crazy World" drag—the rest of the film is an absolute delight, due in large part to the three leads. Garner deftly handles his character's machismo and sexual insecurity, and Andrews—though never entirely convincing as a man—is a sassy, smart, and sexy Victoria. As for Preston, he creates a role so sweet and endearing that you'll find yourself wishing the late actor had been given more chances to display his remarkable talents in motion pictures.

Bovin's many accidents, along with his *très* corny French accent, are very Clouseau-like; *Pink Panther* memories will also be evoked by the presence of a nameless waiter played by Graham Stark, who was Clouseau's aide, Hercule. Stark's deadpan delivery is hilarious. Also very strong are Lesley Ann Warren as King's jealous dumb-blonde girlfriend, Norma Cassidy (a performance that outditzes even Jean Hagen's Lina Lamont from *Singin' in the Rain*), and Alex Karras as King's bodyguard, Squash Bernstein.

Watch for the stuntman at 43/13:38, who clearly is *not* James Garner.

The Disc
Video: ★★★★
Audio: ★★★ (Surround)
Chapters: Yes
Format: CLV
Source: MGM/UA Home Video

While the movie makes perfect narrative sense panned-and-scanned, much is lost: reaction shots in conversations, Karras's or Warren's reactions off to the side, the lovely Art Deco sets, and the numerous chorus lines. Both versions are available, but the letterboxed is understandably the one that's always out of stock!

The picture on both versions is very clear and solid, with colors that are just a *bit* on the soft side at times and a trace of grain in some of the darker scenes.

The audio is very clear and the musical numbers sound terrific. However, the quality of the stereo/Surround is disappointing. There are no real directional effects, and the rear speakers give you little more than the music and louder ambient sounds (such as rain) that are already coming from the front. One Surround effect in particular has to be the worst ever: When Norma is busy tossing things at King in their hotel room, she throws a vase away from us—yet it crashes loudly behind us.

Viva Las Vegas (1964) ★★
Director: George Sidney
Running Time: 89 minutes

Beginning his career by touring as the Hillbilly Cat, Elvis Presley signed with Sun Records in 1954, moved to RCA in 1955, and became a national hit the following year. By the time of his death in 1977 at the age of forty-two, he'd sold more than 600 million recordings—still more than anyone else.

Presley had always dreamed of being a movie star, and before he was drafted in 1958 he made *Love Me Tender* (1956), *Loving You,* and *Jailhouse Rock* (both 1957), and *King Creole* (1958). Upon his return two years later, he found himself facing increasingly stiffer competition on the record charts; however, he had no trouble resuming his film career, which enjoyed its former success.

Viva Las Vegas was his fifteenth film and, both musically and dramatically, he seems to be sleepwalking through it. (Indeed, he didn't seem to put much heart or swivel into anything he did following *Blue Hawaii* in 1961; after that, the unavoidable "boy makes good against all odds" theme started to bore him.)

Elvis plays race-car driver Lucky Jackson, who can't enter the Las Vegas Grand Prix until he earns enough money to buy an engine for his car. Though time is running out, he manages to spend time and money romancing Rusty Martin (Ann-Margret), a local student and swimming teacher who wants him to give up racing before she'll marry him. Naturally, he just can't do that.

Lucky suffers a series of financial setbacks—waiting tables doesn't earn him enough, and when he wins a talent contest the prizes are goods, not cash—so Rusty's wealthy father (William Demarest) buys the engine for Lucky. Our hero wins the race *and* Rusty, making sure his chief rival, the slick, wealthy Count Elmo Mancini (Cesare Danova), has a doubly bad day.

There's some exciting racing footage, though too much of the action is sped up and the actors are photographed in close-ups with awful process photography. Musically, the title song is great fun and performed with verve, and "The Lady Loves Me" is a strong tune, but the rest of the score is uninspired. Even Ann-Margret's energy, gyrations, snug costumes, and pouty expressions can't keep things hopping.

Look for the gaffe at 1/4:04: Shorty Farnsworth (Nicky Blair) is holding the paper in the shot; when it cuts away, the shop owner is holding it. There's another blunder at 13/40:44: In one shot, Elvis's guitar is erect and out in front, then behind him in the next.

The Disc
Video: ★★
Audio: ★★★ (monaural)
Chapters: Yes
Format: CLV
Source: MGM/UA Home Video

This new letterboxed transfer is disappointing, due in large part to the original Metrocolor processing, which has left the colors pretty washed-out. The reds and flesh tones that *are* there bleed all over, the image is only moderately sharp, and details are lost in night and dark scenes.

The letterboxing is very welcome, however, nicely showcasing the "Viva Las Vegas" number, the dance in the gym, the race, and the handsome interior of Mr. Martin's boat.

The digital audio is clear and the music sounds better than in any previous incarnation. That alone is reason enough for Elvis fans to buy the disc.

Jailhouse Rock has been released in a handsome letterboxed disc. It is arguably the best of the "early" Elvis films, and the black and white picture looks very good indeed.

The War of the Roses (1989)
★★½
Director: Danny DeVito
Running Time: 116 minutes

Based on the novel by Warren Adler, this mean-spirited movie covers two decades in the lives of Oliver and Barbara Rose (Michael Douglas and Kathleen Turner), from their courtship and marriage to the disintegration of their love into hate. That metamorphosis makes up the first half of the film, after which a darker, faster change occurs as the Roses slide from unloving to spiteful to vicious to homicidal.

DeVito costars as Gavin D'Amato, a divorce lawyer who tells the cautionary tale of the Roses to a client (did it happen at all? one wonders). However, DeVito (the director) is not warning his audience: He's having fun telling a dark, moody, occasionally expressionistic horror story, a Yuppified *Titus Andronicus*—right down to Oliver's beloved dog being cooked and served to him (the shot of the animal safe and sound was inserted *after* test audiences reacted negatively to it being fricasseed).

Whether it's worth owning depends upon how much you like the stars and how often you'll get a kick out of watching Turner sock her husband, throw a plate at him, or run over him and his car with a four-by-four. (Quite often, probably.)

The Disc
Video: ★★★★
Audio: ★★★★ (Surround)
Chapters:
Format: CLV (sides one and two), CAV (side three)
Source: Fox Home Video

The movie has been given a very handsome transfer: mildly letterboxed, with an extremely sharp image, a bright, detailed picture, and generally solid colors. Traces of color noise scattered throughout the film represent the only major flaw.

The audio is very clear, with frequent directional effects that are fun.

In addition to the film, there's DeVito's

hilarious commentary that runs on the analog audio channel; the film is followed by outtakes, deleted scenes (the movie ran nearly one-third *longer* in the first cut), the script, storyboards, stills, posters—the works. In many ways, these are more interesting than the film itself, and it's commendable that DeVito took the time and interest to put the package together exclusively for laserdisc. But the price (seventy bucks) still makes this one tough to recommend.

War of the Worlds (1953)
★★★
Director: Byron Haskin
Running Time: 85 minutes

The late fantasy filmmaker George Pal is inexplicably ignored by many film historians and movie buffs, rarely put in the pantheon with Walt Disney or his latter-day imitators George Lucas and Steven Spielberg. This is despite the fact that Pal was the preeminent visionary filmmaker of his day, creating hard-edged science fiction and delicate fantasies with equal skill at a time when the rest of the industry had written those genres off.

The Hungarian-born filmmaker had fled the Gestapo in 1933 and, after stays in Paris and Holland, came to Hollywood, where from 1941 to 1947 he made forty-one Puppetoons—charming short subjects shot like animated cartoons, using carved wooden figures for every separate movement a character makes. When these films became prohibitively expensive, Pal turned to features, producing one innovative box-office hit after another. Unfortunately, his later years were plagued by a series of ambitious misfires, among them *The Power* (1968) with George Hamilton and *Doc Savage: The Man of Bronze* (1975), a much underrated film starring Ron Ely.

With the possible exception of *The Time Machine* (1960), the most admired and successful of Pal's films is *War of the Worlds*. In H. G. Wells's 1898 novel, Martians invade Victorian England and are well on the way to world conquest when they're felled by earthly bacteria. Paramount had purchased the screen rights from Wells in 1925, intent on having Cecil B. DeMille make the film. When DeMille declined, the studio tried and failed to interest Russian director Sergei Eisenstein in the project. Orson Welles's headline-making radio dramatization briefly brought the project off the back burner in 1938, but it wasn't until Pal single-handedly created the modern science fiction film with *Destination Moon* (1950) and *When Worlds Collide* (1951) that *War of the Worlds* finally went before the cameras, with all the eye-popping spectacle $1.2 million could buy.

Like Welles, Pal moved the story to the present. He also did away with the tripodlike war machines described in the novel, opting instead to use a sleek design more in keeping with the look of then-topical flying saucers. Finally, Pal shifted the location of the tale from England to Southern California, where Dr. Clayton Forrester (Gene Barry) of Pacific Tech investigates reports of a meteor that has fallen outside the town of Linda Rosa. It turns out the object in the pit isn't a meteor but a cylinder from Mars. The military is called in and saucerlike Martian war machines rise to greet them, the aliens having no trouble decimating the troops under General Mann (Les Tremayne). Forrester and friend Sylvia Van Buren (Ann Robinson) escape the carnage in a small plane, crash-landing at an abandoned farmhouse that is attacked by Martians. They eventually make their way to Pacific Tech and, after an atom bomb fails to stop the Martians, Los Angeles is evacuated. The extraterrestrials begin to "stamp the city flat," as one character puts it, but, as in the novel, they're soon destroyed by terrestrial germs.

The story and characters are interesting enough, but the film's main attractions are the special effects and staggering scenes of destruction. The incredible Martian death ray was created by filming wire disintegrating under a welder's torch, which was then superimposed on the miniature models of the ships; the vaporizating of men and matériel was created using cartoon animation. Large miniature sets were built and burned for the destruction of Los Angeles, including an eight-foot-tall model of City Hall. The saucers themselves were miniature models roughly a yard wide, suspended from thin (occasionally visible) wires on the miniature sets, or composited with real scenery and performers. To underscore how complex the effects were, consider the fact that the live-action scenes took a month to film, while the special effects required a year.

Sadly, one of Pal's really inspired ideas was nixed by the studio brass. When the scientists and military put on protective glasses to watch the nuclear blast, Pal wanted audiences to do the same ... and watch the rest of the film in 3-D. The studio felt that the process, which was then very much in vogue, wasn't worth the expense.

The Disc

Video: no stars
Audio: ★★½ (monaural)
Chapters: No
Format: CLV
Source: Paramount Home Video

War of the Worlds is often one of the first discs science fiction fans acquire, and, aftering viewing it, the inevitable response is, "For *this* I stopped getting videotape?" Except for the green lights of the saucers, the Technicolor hues aren't *nearly* as vivid as they should be, and the dark scenes are nearly featureless, especially in the interior of the church at the end. The focus is never particularly sharp, nor is the print in very good shape. There are scratches and dirt all over the place, most prominently in exterior shots of the barn during the attack.

The sound track, too, is rife with hisses and scratches, though these are only noticeable during the dialogue. Happily, the defects are swamped by the explosions and screeching sounds of the war machines and death rays, which sound fantastic.

Conversely, *The Time Machine* has been given an excellent transfer by MGM—letterboxed, with strong colors and wonderful stereo sound.

Weekend at Bernie's (1989)
★★★½
Director: Ted Kotcheff
Running Time: 101 minutes

Hardworking Richard Parker (Jonathan Silverman) and his fun-loving friend Larry Wilson (Andrew McCarthy) work for a New York–based insurance company run by high-living Bernie Lomax (Terry Kiser). When Richard discovers that someone has defrauded the company of $2 million, he and Larry present their evidence to Bernie, who invites them to come to his beach house for the weekend to review their findings. Later, Bernie asks his gangster friend Vito (Louis Giambalvo) to murder the boys when they arrive at his house. But Vito, who is in with Bernie on the embezzling scheme, orders hit man Paulie (Don Calfa) to whack Bernie instead, not only because the guy is getting careless but because he's sleeping with the mobster's girlfriend.

When Richard and Larry reach the house, they find Bernie dead; for a variety of reasons (which include having access to all the island's babes), they pretend as if he's still alive. Naturally, when Vito learns that Paulie has failed, he sends him back to finish the job.

This film is at the top of many people's "guilty pleasures" lists and it *is* completely dumb, from the failed mugging at the beginning (Larry just pushes the guy's gun away and tells him it's too hot), to Richard's romantic lighthouse interlude with his girlfriend, Gwen Saunders (Catherine Mary Stewart), in which he's blinded by the light and falls down the steps, to the boys' attempt to escape from the island on Bernie's boat—the corpse falling overboard, being dragged behind (unknown to Larry and Richard), and colliding with the channel markers. (*Bong.* "Did you hear something?" *Bong.* "There it is again." *Bong.*)

In the proper frame of mind, you'll have a great time with this disc. If you're watching it with someone who hates it, you'll probably think it's even funnier.

The film was shot in New York City and in Wilmington, North Carolina. Look for the director in the small role of Jack Parker.

The Disc

Video: ★★★½
Audio: ★★★★ (Surround)
Chapters: Yes
Format: CLV
Source: International Video Entertainment / Image Entertainment

The colors on the disc are extremely washed-out during the New York sequences. They were on the pale side in the movies (suggesting the heat of the Manhattan summer?) but not *this* bad. The picture becomes tip-top when everyone gets to the beach. The image is sharp throughout, with only a trace of grain during the night scenes and a bit of red noise.

The film is not letterboxed, but it was shot TV-safe. The Surround sound is fun, with crashing waves, the roar of the speedboat, and party chatter. The only drawback is the score by Andy Summers (of the Police), which is a bit overpowering.

West Side Story (1961) ★★★★½

Directors: Robert Wise and Jerome Robbins
Running Time: 151 minutes

In 1948, choreographer Jerome Robbins had an idea to do an updated, musical version of *Romeo and Juliet*. His version, called *East Side Story*, was set in Manhattan's Lower East Side and told about a Jewish and Catholic family warring during the Easter / Passover holiday. Composer Leonard Bernstein and writer Arthur Laurents worked with him on the project, though creative conflicts and other work forced them to give it up.

Nearly six years later, Bernstein and Laurents read a series in the *Los Angeles Times* about urban struggles between White and Hispanic groups. They contacted Robbins and suggested telling *Romeo and Juliet* with *these* groups. He agreed. Young lyricist Stephen Sondheim was brought aboard and the project was under way.

The story they came up with involved two warring gangs, the white Jets and the hispanic Sharks, who fight for turf in New York's Upper West Side. Deciding that the town isn't big enough for both gangs, Jet leader Riff and Shark leader Bernardo decide to a rumble. However, ex-Jet Tony and Bernardo's sister, Maria, have met and fallen in love, and Tony promises Maria he'll stop the rumble. Unfortunately, when he gets there, Bernardo kills Riff and Tony avenges his best friend's death by murdering the Shark leader. Maria is forgiving, and they plan to rendezvous and run away from all the madness. Unfortunately, Bernardo's lieutenant, Chino, finds and shoots Tony, who dies in Maria's arms.

Robbins called their collaboration "the most exciting I have ever had in the theater," and the result of their efforts, *West Side Story*, opened on Broadway on September 26, 1957. It ran 734 performances and was bought for films. At first, Robert Wise seemed an odd choice to direct. He had no musical experience, but he *did* excel in two areas that were essential to the film: editing (he cut *Citizen Kane*) and directing gritty street films such as *The Set-Up* (1949) and *Somebody Up There Likes Me* (1958). He also had experience with strong women protagonists in films such as *Helen of Troy* (1955) and *I Want to Live* (1958). Robbins was hired to codirect, concentrating on the dance sequences. (After less than three months of shooting, Robbins wasn't directing anything anymore, since his slow, methodical pace was causing the $6 million picture to fall behind schedule.)

Wise and Robbins had both agreed early on that teen heartthrobs Elvis Presley, Frankie Avalon, Fabian, and Paul Anka were wrong for the film, and they cast actor/dancers. Oddly, their choices of Natalie Wood as Maria (for box office) and Richard Beymer as Tony (he was an up-and-coming star) are not entirely successful: Wood had the right kind of sweetness but was obviously neither naïve nor Hispanic, while Beymer was too scrubbed and gangly for Tony. Also, both had to be dubbed with full, gorgeous voices that clearly didn't belong to them—especially Wood's, which belonged to dubbing "queen" Marni Nixon. Jim Bryant sang for Beymer, and Betty Wand sang "A Boy Like That" for Rita Moreno.

Happily, they received incredible support from the rest of the cast, especially the electrifying George Chakiris as Bernardo, the athletic Russ Tamblyn as Riff, and the sizzling Rita Moreno as Anita. (Though, when she won the Best Supporting Actress Oscar, shouldn't Wand have been given the mouth?) And, of course, there's Bernstein's jazz-tinged score, every song of which has become a standard. The only one who wasn't particularly well served by the film was Sondheim, whose lyrics were watered down so as not to offend mass audiences. Two examples: in "Gee, Officer Krupke," the line "My mother is a bastard/my pa's an s.o.b." became "My daddy beats my mommy/my mommy clobbers me" (*that*'s a less objectionable sentiment?), while in "Tonight," Anita's line "He'll come in hot and tired, poor dear/Don't matter if he's tired, as long as he's hot" became "... as long as he's here."

But the story's emotional impact was not blunted, and it also has invigorating dances that improved on the stage versions thanks to Wise's amazing editing (you'll feel like applauding, even though you know you're in your house, watching TV), stunning visuals—from the magnificent God's-eye views that open the film to the final street-level study of Tony and Maria—and an inspired use of color to reflect moods and sexual fire that couldn't be talked about in films of that era. The use of actual locations was also a plus, especially in the opening number. The filmmakers had several blocks on New York's West Side at their disposal, locations that were soon to be demolished to make way for Lincoln Center.

While there's death and urban decay in *West Side Story*, and though the names of some of the characters, such as Ice and A-rab, have a surprisingly contemporary ring, the film is very much rooted in its time. It would be wrong to suggest that *West Side Story* is *quaint*, but at a time when automatics are sprayed at gangs from moving cars, when teens fight over drug money instead of turf, when police are attacked instead of mocked in song, the movie has a certain alluring innocence. The deaths, then, were a tragic exception rather than the rule.

The Disc

Video: ★★★★ (Criterion); ★★★★½ (MGM/UA)
Audio: ★★★★★ (both Surround)
Chapters: Yes
Format: CAV, CLV versions (Criterion); CLV (MGM/UA)
Source: Criterion or MGM/UA Home Video

The three different versions of the film all feature bright colors, a generally sharp and solid picture, and hardly any video noise despite some *very* bright reds in many scenes. The plusses of the MGM/UA version is a slightly sharper picture, fewer scratches in the master element—and a lower price tag.

The audio on both discs is perfect, with oomph in the music and clarity in the dialogue and softer songs. You can turn it up as loudly as you like without worrying about distortion.

The extras on the Criterion CAV edition are informative and a lot of fun. They include casting notes (wait till you see some of the soon-to-be-famous names who were turned down, and why), photographic studies of the locations, the art director's illustrations, storyboards, interviews, film of the premiere, and more.

When Dinosaurs Ruled the Earth (1969) ★½
Director: Val Guest
Running Time: 96 minutes

One Million Years B.C. (1966) was a huge hit for England's Hammer Films, due in large part to the barely clad Raquel Welch, but also due to the impressive dinosaurs created by special effects artist Ray Harryhausen. When Hammer wanted to make another tale of life among the cave folk, Harryhausen was unavailable, so they turned to young Jim Danforth, who had worked on special effects for pictures such as *Jack the Giant Killer* (1962) and *The 7 Faces of Dr. Lao* (1964). Danforth utilized the same basic stop-motion animation process as Harryhausen, filming three-dimensional fully-jointed models one frame at a time and compositing them with live actors. Danforth also used matte paintings extensively, creating spectacular landscapes through the use of detailed paintings that were optically combined with the live-action footage.

It's a shame Danforth didn't have more showcases like this one; since he made *When Dinosaurs Ruled the Earth*, his work has been limited mostly to TV commercials and assisting Harryhausen on *Clash of the Titans* (1981). Unfortunately, he took much longer than expected (sixteen months) to do the animation, which accomplished two things: It forced the producers to eliminate some planned dinosaur scenes, replaced by footage of photographically enlarged lizards snipped from *The Lost World* (1960); and it convinced them to make their next cave film, *Creatures the World Forgo* (1970), entirely without dinosaurs.

Though Danforth's creatures don't have quite the personality of Harryhausen's, the fluidity of his animation is incredible, and his superimposition of miniatures and live action is often flawless, most notably the chasmosaurus butting the caveman into a somersault and, later, falling off the cliff and into a gorgeous sunset; the mother dinosaur nipping off a piece of the giant eggshell in which the cavewoman Sanna is sleeping; and the attack of the winged rhamphorhyncus. Danforth went so far as to double expose each frame of the flying dinosaur, moving just the wings between frames, to make the scenes more realistic. (Previous winged monsters, such as the pteranodon in *King Kong* and the Harpies in *Jason and the Argonauts* [see pages 159 and 153], look somewhat artificial due to the fact that the wings were actually "standing still" when each frame was exposed. Real wings look blurred on the screen, like those of the rhamphorhyncus; the wings of the other flying monsters seem to strobe.)

There are a couple of serious slip-ups as well, such as the smoke and fire that vanish when they hit the matte painted area on side one 3/17:55 to 59 and the dinosaur's reflection visible on the glass-painted scenery behind it at 3/18:28 to 29. But these and other flaws are minor. Danforth's effects are just great.

Oh yes—the story. Though his name is listed in the credits as J.B., author J. G. Ballard (see *Empire of the Sun*) cooked up this tale of Sanna (Victoria Vetri, a *Playboy* Playmate of the Year and Welch wanna be) of the Shell Tribe, who has second thoughts about being sacrificed to the rising sun. She flees, tumbles into the ocean, and is rescued by Tara (Robin Hawdon), who takes her to live with his people, the Rock Tribe. Sanna's arrival coincides with strange fires in the sky; she's blamed for these and so flees, Tara setting out after her. The two are not only reunited, they're saved when the moon is born and destroys their enemies. It's *Dynasty*, cave people–style, and it's also pretty silly. The cave people all have neat rows of teeth, trim beards, and blow-dried hair, and they coexist with dinosaurs that died out tens of millions of years before. They also do stupid things such as hiding in human-eating plants to escape enemies or jumping off cliffs to avoid being thrown from them. It's amazing there was anyone left to evolve.

In addition to Danforth's effects, there are some nice exteriors filmed in the Canary Islands (though they match poorly with the studio interiors).

The Disc

Video: ★★★½
Audio: ★★½ (monaural)
Chapters: Yes
Format: CLV
Source: Warner Home Video

This is an excellent-looking disc, with glossy colors in all but a few scenes. Some color washout and grain appear in many of the special-effects scenes; this is not due to the transfer but, rather, to the techniques used to composite the images. The source print has very few flaws, and the picture is generally sharp. (Note how the footage from *The Lost World*—a CinemaScope picture—was not cropped or scanned but left "squeezed" to fit the flat screen image of *When Dinosaurs Ruled the Earth.*)

The audio does very well with the bass, but the sound is somewhat muffled overall—not that you'll be paying close attention to the cave talk, but still. There's no hiss or extraneous noise in the digital sound.

White Palace (1990) ★★½
Director: Luis Mandoki
Running Time: 103 minutes

Twenty-seven-year-old, upper-middle-class Jewish ad executive Max Baron (James Spader) has a run-in with forty-three-year-old Catholic White Palace hamburger cashier Nora Baker (Susan Sarandon) at her restaurant, then bumps into her later at a bar. They compare notes about the respective tragedies in their lives (he's lost his wife, she her son) and stumble into a passionate sexual affair that develops into love. Their different values cause them to fight, learn, and grow, and his family nearly pulls them apart—but you know how it ends up. The White Palace isn't just a hamburger joint: It's where Sleeping Beauty and the Prince ride off to as true love conquers all.

Despite the best efforts of the actors, the pairing is never convincing. They have a great time in bed; she's "real people"; and there are Oedipal underpinnings (Nora's as crabby and demanding as Max's mother; he's a baby-faced reminder of her lost teenaged son). But none of that seems glue enough for them to end up together at the end.

What's far more interesting and credible is the interplay among Max, then Max and Nora, and his friends and family. The characterizations and dialogue ring absolutely true without ever crossing into stereotype, and the "African photo safari" dialogue with Heidi Solomon (Kim Meyers) is a gem, Yuppie babble underscored by the paintings of a camera and film on the apartment walls. Max is right to flee it—though Nora's arms still don't seem like the ideal sanctuary.

Eileen Brennan and Kathy Bates turn in fine supporting performances as Nora's psychic sister, Judy, and Max's boss, Rosemary, respectively. Glenn Savan, who wrote the novel on which the film is based, appears as the irate customer in the White Palace.

The Disc
Video: ★★
Audio: ★★★½ (Surround)
Chapters: No
Format: CLV
Source: MCA Universal Home Video

The transfer isn't painful to watch, but there's certainly nothing impressive about it. There are varying degrees of grain throughout, which are partly the fault of the original film, partly problems with the transfer; the image is on the soft side, colors are a little pale—especially in the bright daylight—and there's video noise here and there.

The image isn't letterboxed, but the TV-safe film is none the worse for it.

The audio is very nice; and though the bulk of the Surround Sound is limited to music, there are some snappy rear-channel effects at the film's several party scenes and at Nora's home.

Who Framed Roger Rabbit (1988) ★★★★
Director: Robert Zemeckis
Running Time: 104 minutes

In Hollywood of the 1940s, animated characters—known as Toons—roam the streets and soundstages and, at night, go home to neighboring Toontown, which operates according to animated cartoon reality; even humans who go there are subject to its laws, which often defy physics.

Human detective Eddie Valiant (Bob Hoskins) is assigned to investigate the murder of Marvin Acme (Stubby Kaye), the Hollywood gag king and owner of Toontown. All signs point to a Toon murderer, and Toon star Roger Rabbit (voice of Charles Fleischer) is the logical suspect, since he believes (wrongly) his wife, Jessica (voice of Kathleen Turner; singing voice of Amy Irving), was having an affair with Marvin. Though the local prosecutor, Judge Doom (Christopher Lloyd), insists that Roger is guilty, Eddie believes otherwise, and he hides the rabbit while searching for the real killer—efforts that take him to Toontown for a hazardous visit. Eventually, Valiant learns that Doom was behind the murder, having killed Marvin so that Toontown wouldn't go to the Toons, as stipulated in Marvin's missing will, but could be leveled instead for freeways that would line Doom's pockets. And now, Doom is not only out to get Roger but Jessica and Valiant, as well.

Roger was created by author Gary Wolf and first appeared in the novel *Who Censored Roger Rabbit* (1981). The novel is considerably different from the film: In it, Roger really *is* responsible for a murder, in this case that of unscrupulous cartoon syndicate head Rocco DeGreasy. Roger is subsequently shot dead by an evil genie, who is hunted down by Valiant.

The story in the film is more dramatically sound, if predictable. But the story isn't the draw here—it's everything else, from the reemergence of long-unseen characters such as Betty Boop (in black and white), Tinker Bell, and even the *Mary Poppins* penguin waiters, to the first-time pairing of characters such as Donald and Daffy Duck, to its virtuoso technical achievements—not just the perfect blend of live action and animation but also the attention to details, such as the faint reflections of the Toontown characters in the turpentinelike dip after the warehouse wall has been shattered. Hardly a scene goes by where there isn't something to savor. Even when the story drags so that the filmmakers can indulge in some special-effects magic, you won't mind.

Almost lost in the cavalcade of cartoon superstars and the steady onslaught of pratfalls and gags are the terrific performances by Hoskins (an Englishman doing a perfect American accent) and Lloyd. They make you believe they're interacting with the Toons, even though they were performing in a vacuum (the cartoon actors, props, and settings weren't added until much later).

The $75 million film spawned a pair of short subjects: *Tummy Trouble* and *Rollercoaster Rabbit*, which played theatrically with *Honey, I Shrunk the Kids* (1989) and *Dick Tracy* (1990), respectively.

Footage cut from the film—a scene in which Valiant's head is turned into that of a pig when he visits Toontown—has been added to TV prints but not to the laserdisc.

The Disc

Video: ★★★★★
Audio: ★★★★★ (Surround)
Chapters: Yes (CAV)
Format: CAV or CLV
Source: Touchstone Home Video

The film is available panned-and-scanned or letterboxed, but there really isn't a choice: Only the latter allows you to savor the animated characters that often pack the screen from side to side. The letterboxing is only offered on the CAV edition, which permits you to watch the film a jitter-free frame at a time—a *real* treat. For example, take a look at the overhead shot in Maroon's office as Roger takes a drink and rockets to the ceiling. At regular speed, the scene makes perfect sense. But single-frame through it, and there's nary a drawing of Roger that *looks* like the rabbit. Each is a Picasso-esque abstract, beautiful in its own way. Single-frame through just about *any* of the action scenes, including the Donald/Daffy duet, and you'll find yourself smiling at their beauty or nuttiness (often both). Freeze-framing also allows you to study the window dressing, such as the newspaper headlines on Valiant's desk (bet you never knew Goofy was a spy).

CAV aside, both discs feature gorgeous

transfers, with solid colors, no grain, and sharp pictures. Scenes that appear brownish or hazy were shot that way.

The audio is perfect, with smashing Surround effects. If you thought the movie was fun in the theaters, wait till you get it home: Your ability to control the balance will *really* put you in the middle of the action.

Wild at Heart (1990) ★★★
Director: David Lynch
Running Time: 123 minutes

David Lynch is a soft-spoken, charming man who makes quirky, often revolting movies about love, dignity, and self-discovery. *Eraserhead* (1978), *The Elephant Man* (1980), and *Blue Velvet* (see page 33) are especially affecting because of Lynch's unflinching use of powerful imagery; *Dune* (1984) is little more than stylish freak shows (and, in fact, Lynch took his name off the final film). (All but *Eraserhead* are available on laserdisc, though the *Dune* disc is almost as bad as the film itself.) Lynch also created the TV series "Twin Peaks."

His fifth film, *Wild at Heart*—based on the Barry Gifford novel—is a sweet love story wrapped in fire and bloodred ribbon. It follows young, devoted lovers Sailor (Nicholas Cage) and Lula (Laura Dern) as they drive west from the Carolinas, pursued by Lula's demented mother, Marietta (Diane Ladd—Laura Dern's real-life mother), and her hit-man lover. Among the memorable characters the couple meets are the oily, savage Bobby Peru (Willem Dafoe) and the mysterious Perdita (Isabella Rossellini), an old acquaintance of Sailor's.

This film will either stir you to repeated viewings or put you off your feed with its graphic gore (and/or overdone, too-silly allusions to *The Wizard of Oz* and Elvis Presley). Cage is frightening in his intensity, and Dafoe is even scarier. Dern has a tough job balancing borderline nymphomania with little-girl vulnerability, but she does so admirably.

The Disc
Video: ★★★★½
Audio: ★★★★★ (Surround)
Chapters: Yes
Format: CLV (sides one and two), CAV (side three)
Source: Image

An advocate of black and white films, Lynch tends to create monochromatic scenes broken up with splashes of color—usually red. The disc captures his visuals to perfection; the grain present in a few of the night scenes was present in the original film.

The letterboxing demonstrates Lynch's skill at composing shots for the Panavision screen: Watch, for example, how the director works Dafoe into the mirror when his character visits Dern in her hotel room.

However, as interesting as the visuals are, the sound is even better. You'll find yourself scanning backward a great deal to reexperience it. There isn't a disc on the market in which the audio plays a more integral part. Lynch exaggerates sound to underscore the mood or serve as a transitional device, whether it's lighting a match, buffing shoes, or cutting from Lula jumping on her bed, the mattress springs squeaking, to music and feet pounding as she dances in a bar.

The Wild Bunch (1969) ★★★★½
Director: Sam Peckinpah
Running Time: 145 minutes

In this ground-breaking, mesmerizing motion picture, the late Peckinpah returned to the theme of *Ride the High Country* (see page 233): the old giving way to the new. But while he was content to stress the eternal beauty of the land and the bittersweet changing of the guard in the earlier film, this descendant of pioneers had obviously soured on humankind in the intervening seven years (during which he made only one film, the post–Civil War, cavalry versus Indians, Northern veterans versus Southern veterans epic *Major Dundee*, 1965).

In *The Wild Bunch*, Peckinpah's oldtimers are not men trying to go gentle into that good night; they're iron men who want to abandon their old, unmechanized ways with a bang. He presents the resultant violence in what was to become his trademark fashion: slow motion, with blood leaving the bodies not in sprays but in waves. As he once explained, "Killing a man isn't clean and quick and simple—it's bloody and awful."

However, if *The Wild Bunch* is bloody, it's far from awful. Pike Bishop (William Holden) and Deke Thornton (Robert Ryan) were partners in crime until the law caught up with them. Thornton was caught, but Bishop managed to flee and form a new gang, consisting of Dutch (Ernest Borgnine), Angel (Jaime Sanchez), Sykes (Edmond O'Brien), and hedonistic brothers Lyle (Warren Oates) and Tector Gorch (Ben Johnson). Railroad boss Harrigan (Albert Dekker, aka *Dr. Cyclops* in his last role) wants the bunch captured, and he offers Thornton his freedom if he'll bring them in dead. He accepts the job and assembles a band of bounty hunters.

When Thornton foils a carefully planned robbery, Bishop and his men manage to escape and plan one last big job: stealing guns from an army train and selling them to the Mexican despot Mapache (Emilio Fernandez). They succeed; and though Mapache pays them, he orders his men to hold Angel, whom he believes (rightly) to be assisting the rebels. The bunch leaves, and though they've fulfilled their dream—pulled off the job and earned enough gold to retire—they realize (like the magnificent Seven before them) that there can be no contentment without honor. Returning to the village to demand Angel's release, they end up murdering and being murdered in one of the most violent shoot-outs in screen history.

The insights into the men—fleshed out through flashbacks—are intelligent and credible. And for all its explicit bloodshed, the climax is one of the most mesmerizing and poetic sequences ever put on film: The acting, cinematography, staging, cutting, and special effects blur into a seamless whole, like the teeth of a spinning buzz saw—and with much the same impact.

The film boosted Peckinpah's stock in Hollywood, and though he made one other first-rate film—*Straw Dogs* (1971)—and another commercially successful one—*The Getaway* (1972)—subsequent efforts, such as *Bring Me the Head of Alfredo Garcia* (1974), *The Killer Elite* (1975), *Convoy* (1978), and *The Osterman Weekend* (1983), are not examples of the man at the peak of his powers.

The Disc

Video: ★★★
Audio: ★★★ (monaural)
Chapters: No
Format: CLV
Source: Warner Home Video

The print used for the transfer is the unedited version, which restores scenes that had been cut both before and after the film's initial release. The cuts not only involved some of the more violent moments, but some of the flashbacks that were thought to slow the narrative down. It's good to have the film more complete than it's been in years.

Unfortunately, the thing is panned-and-scanned. The action in the opening gunfight is so tight that it's confusing at times, and more often than not part of the bunch (and their reactions) are off the screen. The two shots at 19.20/21 used to be one shot, and there's a long stretch—40.49 to 41.11—where Holden is offcamera entirely, and we can't see what he thinks about O'Brien's important speech. The climactic battle is considerably better than the first (it isn't shot or cut the same way), though it still suffers from the artificial close-ups created by the cropping.

The colors are extremely rich and the image is sharp, with only mild grain; video noise is well under control. However, the print is damaged in spots, with long vertical lines often staying for ten or twenty seconds.

The audio crackles on occasion, but the dialogue and sound effects are otherwise fine.

Wings of Desire (1988) ★★½
Director: Wim Wenders
Running Time: 130 minutes

According to *Wings of Desire* (known in the director's native Germany as *Der Himmel Uber Berlin*), angels have roamed the earth since the beginning of time, observing events without being able to affect them. With the coming of humankind, they were able to interact to a small degree, offering a momentary sense of wellbeing to troubled souls.

Angels Damiel (Bruno Ganz) and Cassiel (Otto Sander) wander about modern-day West Berlin, before the fall of the Berlin Wall, lamenting about the barrier that separates them from humans. Damiel wishes he could trade in his wings to experience love or sadness, taste coffee, see colors, or feel something tangible. His yearning grows as he spends time watching sad French acrobat Marion (Solveig Dommartin) of the near-broke Circus Alekan and doubt-riddled actor Peter Falk (playing himself), who is making a movie set in Nazi Germany. After wanting it badly enough for so long, Damiel finally manages to slip through to "our" side and becomes a mortal, making the acquaintance of both Peter and Marion, with some surprising (and disappointing) results.

This is a heartfelt, very personal film, but if you're not in a reflective mood you may feel as trapped as Damiel. The mind-reading angel spends a lot of time roaming the streets and homes of the city, picking up snippets of thought. All of it is very real and frequently moving, but the point is belabored after the first dozen or so people have bitched about their lives. Damiel spends *far* too much time watching Marion do her act, following her to a nightclub where the performance seems to go on forever, and ditto with Falk; he doesn't shed his wings until the film is two-thirds over. Likewise, the world as seen by children (a recurring theme) is important, but it gets awfully tiresome the third and fourth time the same point is made. Too often, the movie seems like little more than the director's encyclopedic cataloging of what's right and wrong with humankind.

Ganz is utterly believable as the angel, with one of the most compassionate faces you'll ever see on the screen; he is equally successful as a mortal, enjoying everything from graffiti to the taste of his own blood. Falk is also excellent, and viewers who know him only from his shyster roles or TV appearances will be delightfully surprised by his gentle, sympathetic performance. (And, right: He's flying *coach* to Berlin at the beginning of the film. It's easier to believe in angels.)

Wenders, a postwar baby who was raised on American music and movies, originally wanted to be a priest. He became a film student instead, and made his first feature—*The Goalie's Anxiety at the Penalty Kick*—in 1971. He came to the United States to direct *Hammett* (1982) for Francis Coppola, though he didn't get along with the producer and left the film before it was completed. Except for *Wings of Desire, Paris, Texas* (1984), and *Until the End of the World* (1991), little of this work has yet received broad exposure on these shores.

The Disc
Video: ★★★½
Audio: ★★★ (Surround)
Chapters: Yes
Format: CLV
Source: Orion Home Video/
   CinemaDisc Collection

Until the final third, the film is primarily in black and white—the way the angels see the world. These scenes have an overcast look, no strong blacks and whites but a lot of gray tones in keeping with the hazy, angel's-eye view of things. Color is used sparingly until Damiel becomes mortal; the sudden switch makes those segments seem much richer than they ordinarily would have been.

There's very little grain in either the black and white or color sequences.

Only the titles of the film are letterboxed, but there's no significant loss of information.

The audio is a touch hollow and uses the surround speakers sparingly—for example, in the circus scenes and nightclub—though these are very effective. Directional effects are minimal. The film is in German, English, and French, with yellow subtitles. (Someone should have proofread the things more carefully: We have *steam's bed* instead of *stream's bed*, *jaloppy*, and *angles* instead of *angels*.)

The Wizard of Oz (1939)
★★★★★
Director: Victor Fleming
Running Time: 119 minutes

It's fun to speculate what might have been. What would *The Wizard of Oz* have been like if MGM had convinced Twentieth Century–Fox to lend them the number-one box-office attraction of 1938, nine-year-old Shirley Temple, to play Dorothy. Not only would the film have been different, but would sixteen-year-old Judy Garland have become a star?

What if studio head Louis B. Mayer had had his way and the "slow" song "Over the Rainbow" had been excised? Or if lanky Buddy Ebsen hadn't been allergic to the silver makeup and been able to play the Tin Man?

Most likely, *The Wizard of Oz* would still have been a great film, because its merits are endless: memorable performances from top to bottom, a wondrous story, a great score, incredible sets, and inventive special effects—not just for the time but for all time. (Watch as the Winged Monkeys fly down and scoop Dorothy into the air in the one take.) Even if the movie had *only* Margaret Hamilton's shrill, spidery Wicked Witch of the West, it would still be more fun than a barrel of winged monkeys.

The familiar story bears only a superficial resemblance to L. Frank Baum's 1900 novel *The Wonderful Wizard of Oz*. When a twister hits her Kansas farm, Dorothy Gale and her dog, Toto, are carried, house and all, to the land of Oz. Because the house comes to rest atop the Wicked Witch of the East and kills her, the hag's ruby slippers pass to Dorothy: The only way her sister, the green-skinned Wicked Witch of the West, can obtain them is by killing Dorothy. The young Kansan doesn't care about the shoes or the witches: All she wants is to get home. The Good Witch of the North, Glinda (Billie Burke), tells her to follow the Yellow Brick Road to Oz and present herself to the Wizard who lives in the distant Emerald City. He will help her. En route, Dorothy is joined by the Scarecrow (Ray Bolger), who would like to get a brain from the Wizard; the Tin Man (Jack Haley), who wants a heart; and the Cowardly Lion (Bert Lahr), who yearns for courage. When they face Oz (Frank Morgan), he agrees to help them—but only if they bring him the broomstick of the Wicked Witch of the West. They manage to accomplish this, only to learn that the Wizard is a fraud. Fortunately, Glinda informs Dorothy that she can return to Kansas simply by clicking the heels of her ruby slippers three times and saying, "There's no place like home."

The movie omits sizable chunks of Baum's novel—for example, the battle with the tigerbears known as Kalidahs, the rather lengthy encounter with the Queen of the Field Mice, and the run-in with the Quadlings, stout little men with extendable necks. The delections were due largely to budgetary constraints; as it is, the film cost a hefty $2.8 million. There are other minor alterations in the tale, such as making ruby slippers from Baum's silver shoes, substituting "There's no place like home" for the novel's "Take me home to Aunt Em," and adding characters in the Kansas sections (only Aunt Em and Uncle Henry appear in the novel). No matter. The film is true to the spirit of the book, and the fantasyland it creates is unequaled in movie history.

Though *The Wizard of Oz* was critically praised and drew large crowds, most of the admissions were children at children's prices and the movie didn't show a profit until MGM sold it to TV in 1956 for the first of its popular annual airings.

Garland's daughter Liza Minnelli provided Dorothy's voice in *Journey Back to Oz* (1964), an unimpressive feature-length cartoon that also featured the voice of

Margaret Hamilton. Diana Ross played Dorothy in the all-black version of the story, *The Wiz* (1978), which was based on the hit 1975 Broadway musical. *The Wiz* is available as a Japanese import.

Disney's *Return to Oz* (1985) was much more faithful in look and details to the Baum tales. The film was a box-office disaster but is *highly* recommended for its story, sets, and superb special effects. It's available only as a Japanese import

The Disc
Video: ★★★½
Audio: ★★★★ (monaural)
Chapters: Yes: more than twice the twenty-four chapters found in the original novel
Format: CLV and CAV editions
Source: MGM/UA Home Video

It's difficult to be critical about the fiftieth-anniversary disc of the film. The Kansas scenes are presented in their original sepia tones and, apart from some minor flaws in the source material, these sequences look very good.

The scenes in Oz were filmed in rich Technicolor: Notice how the filmmakers rendered the interior of the house and Judy Garland's costumes in monochrome so that *they're* still black and white in the shot when she opens the door on colorful Oz.

The colors throughout most of the film are very good, though often the saturated colors become *very* noisy—for example, Judy Garland's red lipstick, the slippers, the Yellow Brick Road, and the Horse of Another Color. Unfortunately, if you turn down the intensity of the picture, you'll miss all the other great stuff, such as the pastel backgrounds, which have extraordinary depth. Some of the dark scenes also tend to muddy up, especially the Winged Monkey attack and sequences set in the Witches' castle. Still, this is *The Wizard of Oz* looking more vibrant than you've ever seen it, even with the flaws.

The digital sound is excellent, and the second (right) channel offers just the score (including incidental music) and sound effects.

There are some delicious supplements: a reissue trailer, moderately interesting clips from the 1939 Oscars, a less interesting visit with some of the cast members at MGM during the making of the film, and then some real gems: Buddy Ebsen singing "If I Only Had a Heart," a cut dance number called "The Jitterbug," and Ray Bolger's excised dance number from "If I Only Had a Brain."

Wolfen (1981) ★★★
Director: Michael Wadleigh
Running Time: 114 minutes

A rich industrialist is savagely murdered in the run-down South Bronx, and New York police detective Dewey Wilson (Albert Finney) has to find out why. Coroner Whittington (Gregory Hines) thinks a wild animal was responsible. With the input of criminal psychologist/contrived love interest Rebecca Neff (Diane Venora), Wilson concludes that the killing is related to the spate of deaths of derelicts and junkies in the slums. Helped by construction workers who are descended from Manhattan's original Indian inhabitants, the detective traces the killings to wolves that were driven underground by the original white settlers and have remained there ever since, feeding mostly on people no one will miss.

Knowing what the problem is and how to deal with the highly intelligent wolves are entirely different things, and the showdown is a thriller—eerie, majestic, and unexpected.

Based on Whitley Strieber's 1978 novel, the movie has the same serious flaw as the book: It's slow in unfolding, though part of the film's problem is that it has got another one of those yakky "what a mess the white man's made of things" scripts. Also, though he *looks* right, Finney isn't entirely convincing as a slovenly New York detective.

But it's a fascinating film just the same, with remarkable wolf's-eye views of the streets, exceptional gore effects (including a gross answer to the question, "Does the head survive after decapitation?"), and a wonderful screen debut for Hines as the jive-steeped medical examiner. The director himself plays the terrorist stool pigeon.

Wadleigh's previous film was *Woodstock* (1970).

The Disc
Video: ★★★
Audio: ★★★ (Surround)
Chapters: Yes
Format: CLV
Source: Warner Home Video

The colors are on the pale side and there are some flaws in the source material. Otherwise, the disc is quite nice, with a sharp image and hardly any problems with grain or video noise.

The letterboxing is generous and recreates the incredible sense of motion the director gave to his wolf's-eye-view shots.

Though the audio is somewhat tinny, the separation is very good and there are some surprisingly strong Surround effects, particularly in the wolf scenes.

Women in Love (1969) ★★★★
Director: Ken Russell
Running Time: 132 minutes

D. H. Lawrence considered *Women in Love* (1920) his finest novel. A sequel to *The Rainbow*, it continues the tale of Ursula Brangwen, a teacher, and her sister, Gudrun, a sculptor. Ursula falls in love with and marries school inspector Rupert Birkin, who is in the process of rebelling against intellectual inhibitions and searching for passion; Gudrun falls in love with the possessive Gerald Crich, a ruthless industrialist. Rupert also falls in love with Gerald, though Gerald is too repressed to return that love completely.

Birkin is supposed to be Lawrence's alter ego, while the other characters are based on his wife and on friends with whom they shared a home in England. The novel is poetic, absorbing, and sensual—qualities Ken Russell was able to translate to film.

Former TV director Russell made two feature films before *Women in Love*: the comedy *French Dressing* (1964) and the thriller *Billion Dollar Brain* (1967). *Women in Love* was his first commercial and critical success and he continued to explore interpersonal and erotic relationships in films such as *The Devils* (1971), *Crimes of Passion* (1984), *Gothic* (1986), and *Whore* (1991), albeit with increasing ham-fistedness and self-indulgence.

Women in Love is his best, most subtle film to date. Faithful to the novel and extremely evocative of the era, it's filled with unforgettable images, from the pathetic shot of Gerald's drowned sister to the legendary nude wrestling scene between Gerald and Rupert. It also boasts powerful performances, especially by Glenda Jackson as Gudrun and Oliver Reed as Gerald. Alan Bates and Jennie Linden are memorable in their less interesting roles as Rupert and Ursula.

Ken Russell filmed *The Rainbow* in 1989, with Sammi Davis and Amanada Donohoe; Glenda Jackson appears as Gudrun's mother. The film—good but nothing more—is available on laserdisc, nicely transferred.

The Disc
Video: ★★
Audio: ★★½ (monaural)
Chapters: Yes
Format: CLV
Source: MGM/UA Home Video

Whether in bright daylight or dark rooms, the movie has a somewhat grainy, home-movie look that gives it its feeling of naturalism ... and voyeurism. That doesn't make for the ultimate laserdisc experience, but it won't detract from your enjoyment of the film.

The Deluxe colors are on the pale side, which—inadvertently—imparts an unglossy realism to the film.

Women in Love was not a wide-screen effort and is not compromised by very mild panning-and-scanning.

Russell wasn't much of an audio stylist until he began making musical movies—such as *The Boy Friend* (1971), *Tommy* (1975), and *Lisztomania* (1975). Here, the digital sound renders all of the dialogue comprehensible, which is all the movie needs.

Women on the Verge of a Nervous Breakdown (1988)
★★★½
Director: Pedro Almodóvar
Running Time: 88 minutes

Almodóvar is a former phone company employee who was drawn to the avant-garde underground in Madrid and began making movies. He made numerous short subjects and three feature films—the best of which, *Dark Habits* (1984), is about a singer stranded in a convent full of crazy nuns—before enjoying his first international hit, *What Have I Done to Deserve This?* (1985), starring Carmen Maura as a housewife overwhelmed by her responsibilities. It was followed by *Law of Desire* (1987), about a gay romantic triangle; *Women on the Verge of a Nervous Breakdown*; *Tie Me Up! Tie Me Down!* (1990), a love story about a mental patient who kidnaps a porn star; and *High Heels* (1992). Almodóvar's trademarks are (obviously) borderline-campy plots populated by bizarre characters; his movies are (also obviously) not for all tastes.

Women on the Verge of a Nervous Breakdown is his most accessible work, despite lapses into the absurd, such as a climactic car chase. Actress Pepa (Carmen Maura) is in love with smooth-as-silk actor Ivan (Fernando Guillen) and is devastated when he jilts her for a new flame. Meanwhile, Ivan's homicidal wife is annoyed with *both* women; Ivan's love-starved son and icy fiancée go apartment hunting and happen to come to Pepa's place; and one of Pepa's friends, Candela (Julieta Serrano), having unwittingly aided a dashing terrorist, is wanted by the police and seeks refuge with Pepa.

The movie gets more delightfully convoluted still. In spite of their eccentricities and self-absorption, Almodóvar's characters and their crises are endearing and often hilariously funny. Maura's performance is delightfully low-key, a perfect contrast to the mad people swirling around her.

This is a disc you'll go back to now and then for a pick-me-up: After sharing Pepa's absurd burdens for a while, you'll gladly welcome your own again!

The Disc
Video: ★★★
Audio: ★★½ (monaural)
Chapters: Yes
Format: CLV
Source: CinemaDisc Collection

Though the image is generally sharp, it's *slightly* reddish—a problem the original film didn't have. The picture is free of grain and video noise is rare.

The director tends to spread his characters out, so the letterboxed presentation was a must; it also allows the yellow subtitles to run below the image.

The digital sound is clear, if unexciting.

Tie Me Up! Tie Me Down! is also available in a letterboxed edition, a lovely transfer with excellent Surround Sound.

The Wonderful World of the Brothers Grimm (1962) ★★★
Directors: Henry Levin; George Pal (fairy tales)
Running Time: 129 minutes

The Wonderful World of the Brothers Grimm was shot in the three-panel Cinerama process, which used a trio of interlocked 35mm projectors and a huge curved screen to present an image that covered 146 horizontal and 55 vertical degrees—virtually the breadth of human vision. Beginning with *This is Cinerama* in 1952, the process was used solely for travelogues until MGM and Cinerama teamed in 1959 and agreed to produce a storytelling film. *The Wonderful World of the Brothers Grimm* was the result, followed by *How the West Was Won* (see page 142); subsequent Cinerama presentations, such as *2001: A Space Odyssey*, *It's a Mad Mad Mad Mad World*, *The Hallelujah Trail*, and *Ice Station Zebra* (see pages 287, 149, 127, and 145) were shot in the single-camera Super or Ultra Panavision processes.

Searching for a new and commercial project, producer George Pal (see *War of the Worlds* for biography) considered a sequel to his hit *The Time Machine* (1960) and also *Lost Eden*, an historical drama about Captain Cook. Instead, MGM dusted off a seven-year-old project Pal had wanted to do about the Brothers Grimm and gave it the green light. Pal went to location to Rothenburg ob der Tauber and Weikersheim and Neuschwanstein castles to shoot the eye-filling exteriors, while seventy-five interior sets were constructed in Hollywood. The film *looks* great. Dramatically, however— that's another story.

Jacob Grimm (Karl Boehm) is a studious young writer, happy to be working on the family history of the Duke (Oscar Homolka), which the nobleman wishes to present to the king of Prussia. However, Wilhelm Grimm (Laurence Harvey) is a dreamer, less interested in the Duke than in gathering and writing down fairy tales. On the other hand, Wilhelm is devoted to his wife, Dorthea (Claire Bloom), and his two children, while Jacob is a social misfit, unable to see (until nearly two hours of film time have passed) how much lovely young Greta Heinrich (Barbara Eden) loves him. Breaking up the corny drama are three splendid fairy tales: "The Dancing Princess," in which a woodsman (Russ Tamblyn) promises the king (Jim Backus) to find out how his daughter (Yvette Mimieux) manages to wear out a pair of shoes every night; "The Cobbler and the Elves," about good-luck dolls that come to life to help an overworked cobbler (Laurence Harvey); and "The Singing Bone," in which knight Ludwig (Terry-Thomas) and his squire, Hans (Buddy Hackett), go hunting for a dragon. There's also "The Dream," in which fairy-tale characters yet unborn—including Rumpelstiltskin (Arnold Stang), Tom Thumb (Russ Tamblyn, who also played the title character in Pal's 1958 film), Snow White, Cinderella, and Hansel and Gretel—come to visit the feverish Wilhelm and urge him to get well or they'll never be born.

The saga of the brothers is painfully uninvolving, directed with a lethargy rarely encountered in major Hollywood productions. Part of the problem is the script, which, though very faithful to Dr. Hermann Gerstner's *Die Bruder Grimm*, a collection of their letters (covering most of the first half of the nineteenth century), talks down to the viewers. For example, the real-life Jacob had proposed to a young woman and been rejected, a trauma so severe, he never married. That was considered too "rough" for a film like this; ditto Wilhelm's heart condition, which made it *necessary* that he write, since he couldn't support his family any other way. The film result was toothless soap.

The casting is also a problem. Boehm wasn't comfortable acting in English, and Harvey's ascetic style wasn't right for the dreamer Wilhelm (though he's wonderful as the cobbler). Pal originally (and wisely) had wanted to cast Alec Guinness and Peter Sellers as the brothers, but MGM nixed that; they had Harvey and Boehm under contract.

Skip right to the fairy tales, which are delightful.

Casting wasn't Pal's only disappointment. For reasons of budget and running time, the studio made him drop three fairy tales he'd wanted to include in the film. He'd also wanted to direct the entire picture, but the pressures of producing and directing the fairy tales made impossible. And finally, the film was a commercial dud. Pal's stock in Hollywood dropped, and his three subsequent films—*The 7 Faces of Dr. Lao* (1964), *The Power* (1968), and *Doc Savage: The Man of Bronze* (1975)— also failed, sunk less by their quality (which was variable) than by studio disinterest.

The Disc
Video: ★½
Audio: ★★★½ (Surround)
Chapters: Yes
Format: CLV
Source: MGM/UA Home Video

To begin with, while MGM/YUA retained the opening narration, they show a black screen instead of the footage of the world at war. There were some spectacular battle scenes of the Napoleonic invasion of Germany and landscapes in that section, and dropping them is inexcusable (one shot of gunfire survives in the trailer).

Secondly, unlike *How the West Was Won*, the three panels of the original Cinerama image don't match up especially well. Now, this is not the fault of the disc's maker: They did the transfer from a 35mm print on which the three panels had already been joined for its non-Cinerama general release in 1963. But you'd better be prepared for the separate images to jump *and* for the colors to shift radically from panel to panel.

Finally, the letterbox isn't wide enough to accommodate the 3:1 Cinerama image. Nearly one-half of each side panel is missing, leaving some characters off the screen and making some panning-and-scanning necessary (for example, when the brothers are first introduced)! MGM/UA didn't want to end up with a picture even thinner than their fully letterboxed *Ben-Hur*, but this compromise—though infinitely better than a cropped version—is still disappointing.

Then there's the quality of the transfer itself. The colors are faded and/or reddish, the focus is extremely soft in all but the fairy-tale sequences, and there's a good deal of grain throughout, often *very* thick.

At least the audio is extremely clear and the stereo separations are very appealing. The Surround Sound is *not* the film's original seven-channel separations, which were spectacular, but a rechanneling.

The film's insipid general-release trailer is included.

The Yakuza (1975) ★★★★
Director: Sydney Pollack
Running Time: 112 minutes

In the hierarchy of feudal Japan, the *yakuza* were the gangsters; along with the *sanzoku*, or bandits, they comprised the lowest social order. Like their ancient counterparts, the modern Yakuza are a ruthless, violent breed whom few are willing to cross.

Ex-cop Harry Kilmer (Robert Mitchum) goes to Japan to help a friend whose daughter is being held by the Yakuza. The friend, businessman George Tanner (Brian Keith), is a corrupt, undisciplined man whose carelessness and dishonesty endanger all with whom he comes in contact (especially his daughter, since he has no intention of paying the ransom). In order to help Tanner, Kilmer must call in a favor owed him by Tanaka Ken (Takakura Ken), whose sister, Tanaka Eiko (Kishi Keiko), he helped during the postwar occupation of Japan. Kilmer's request causes Ken to violate important traditions and sets off a volatile conflict that destroys all but a few of the participants (though we get some terrific action scenes along the way).

The Yakuza features Robert Mitchum's last great piece of acting, his sense of urgency and exasperation helping to create a portrait of a spiritually exhausted but honorable man. Cowriters Paul Schrader and Robert Towne—two of the best screenwriters of this generation—collaborated on a concise, emotionally charged script, while Pollack (*Tootsie*, 1982, *Out of Africa*, 1985, and *Havana*—see page 133) made what may well be his best and certainly his most overlooked film.

The Disc
Video: ★★½
Audio: ★★ (monaural)
Chapters: Yes
Format: CLV
Source: Warner Home Video

The new letterboxed version of the film is an improvement over the panned-and-scanned import, but it still isn't wholly successful. The colors aren't very punchy, though part of that is due to the sorry state of just about every film that was shot in color in the early to mid-1970s.

Still, there's extensive grain throughout and a loss of detail and resolution in the dark scenes, the result of poor digital mastering.

The audio is acceptable, though a little

on the hollow side and noticeably lacking in dynamic range.

Yankee Doodle Dandy (1942)
★★★★★
Director: Michael Curtiz
Running Time: 128 minutes

George M. Cohan lied. The all-American song and dance man/composer (1878–1942) was born on the *third* of July, but, since he did indeed embody the American spirit, you've got to forgive him the indulgence. You've also got to get this disc. No matter how many times you've seen this film, no matter how jaded you've become, it will boost your spirits and make you proud!

The film opens during World War II, and the story proper is framed by Cohan (James Cagney) visiting the White House and telling President Roosevelt (Capt. Jack Young) his life story (the first time a living president was portrayed in a movie). Cohan talks about his days on the road with the Four Cohans—father, Jerry (Walter Huston), mother, Nellie (Rosemary DeCamp), and sister, Josie (Jeanne Cagney)—about his struggle to make it to Broadway, and about his subsequent success as a writer, producer, and star of hit shows. He also discusses his life with devoted wife, Mary (Joan Leslie), his retirement, and his comeback—playing FDR in a musical.

Released the year after the United States entered World War II, *Yankee Doodle Dandy* not only entertained, it reminded Americans who they were and what they stood for. A half century later, no matter how cynical you've become about America's place in the world, the film's power is unabated. That's due in large part to heart-swelling Cohan standards such as "Over There" and "Grand Old Flag," and also to Cagney's timeless, energetic performance. Cohan personally selected Cagney to play him on the screen, and the former hoofer couldn't have been better *or* bettered. He spent four months rehearsing the dance numbers and mastering Cohan's stiff-legged step and mannerisms, though he infused the part with his own brand of dynamism (Cohan was a more thoughtful, softer-spoken man). Not surprisingly, this was Cagney's favorite role, and he said that one of the greatest moments of his career was receiving a telegram from Cohan that read, "Thanks for a job well done." Cohan died shortly after the film was completed.

Walter Huston is also memorable as the elder Cohan, his quiet dignity serving as a counterpoint to his irascible son, and Joan Leslie is enchanting as Mary.

Cagney played Cohan again, in a small unbilled role in *The Seven Little Foys* (1955) starring Bob Hope. He declined salary for the work, stating, "Any Cohan part is worth the effort."

Look for the shadow of a boom microphone on the left side of the screen, chapter thirty-eight, at 3:17.

The Disc
Video: ★★★
Audio: ★★★★ (monaural)
Chapters: Yes
Format: CLV
Source: MGM/UA Home Video

In its newly mastered version (the original disc was from Fox), the movie looks as good as the source material will allow. The contrast ranges from good to very good, and the print is largely free of defects.

It's the audio that's the attraction here, however. Although there are obvious limitations to the monaural sound track, and it flutters briefly now and then, the digital reprocessing has worked wonders. The big production numbers in particular sound more robust than ever.

After the film are a defense-bond cartoon that features Bugs Bunny doing Jolson singing "My Uncle Sammy," the original theatrical trailer, and a short subject, *You, John Jones*, starring Cagney as an air-raid warden who chats with God about the suffering of our Allies in Europe and Asia. For such an overt piece of propaganda, the eight-minute short is surprisingly moving.

Young Man with a Horn (1950)
★★★
Director: Michael Curtiz
Running Time: 112 minutes

Young Man with a Horn was a property that had been kicking around at Warner Brothers for five years. The Dorothy Baker novel was inspired by the life of renowned jazz trumpeter Bix Beiderbecke, who headed one of the best-known jazz ensembles of the Roaring Twenties, the Wolverines. Unfortunately, Beiderbecke was a heavy drinker and died in 1931, nearly destitute, at the age of twenty-eight.

Warner couldn't find an actor they felt would be able to carry the film. But after Kirk Douglas gave a riveting performance as a boxer in his eighth feature, *The Champion* (1949), Warner offered him the role. He eagerly accepted.

A ten-year-old orphan, Rick Martin (Orley Lindgren) wanders the streets and is drawn to the Cotton Club, where he is fascinated by the jazz band of Art Hazzard (Juano Hernandez). Hazzard teaches the boy to play trumpet and, by the age of twenty, Rick (Douglas) is a dazzling virtuoso. He joins a dance band, where he is befriended by pianist Smoke Willoughby (Hoagy Carmichael) and Jo Jordan (Doris Day). The mundane music bores Rick, who is fired along with Smoke when they jazz things up one night.

Rick continues to play dance music by day and jazz by night, earning fame and respect. Then he meets an enigmatic young high-society woman, Amy North (Lauren Bacall), with whom he becomes infatuated. They marry and he lets his music slide: When she grows bored with him, he leaves her and starts drinking. Things get worse during a recording session with Jo, when he can't even hit the right notes, and he smashes his trumpet in frustration. Rick takes to the streets and is near death when Smoke finds him in a home for alcoholics. Thanks to the love of Smoke and Jo, Rick makes a dramatic comeback.

In the novel, Rick dies, which would have been a more realistic ending for the film. Indeed, the tone of the film is so dark that his survival is jarring and unacceptable. (This film came from the the director who left Bogart standing Ilsa-less on the tarmac in *Casablanca* because it was the *right* way to end the film.) But in these postwar years, people wanted happy endings, so Curtiz gave them one.

That aside, the movie is engrossing and surprisingly affecting—surprising because so many subsequent films used the same comeback plot, reducing it to formula. Douglas is earnest and completely believable, Carmichael *is* the real thing, Doris Day is the sweet, caring angel she'd get to play so often, and Bacall is a snide, confused, self-absorbed lynx without a single redeeming characteristic. Quite intentionally, she's the exact opposite of Rick's beloved trumpet ("Whatever you tell it to do, it does").

There's some great music in the film, and if you're a jazz fan you'll wish there was more. The sound track features legendary Harry James playing for Douglas, and if nothing else the film is a record of that man's towering talent.

Musician and composer Carmichael had known Beiderbecke well, and he was an adviser to both Douglas and Curtiz. Douglas studied the trumpet for three months under the tutelage of studio trumpeter Larry Sullivan and became what he once described as "an adequate faker." He played in his dressing room whenever he wasn't needed, causing consternation among the music-loving members of the cast and crew.

The Disc
Video: ★★★½
Audio: ★★★½ (monaural)
Chapters: Yes
Format: CLV
Source: Warner Home Video

A very clean print makes for a generally satisfying transfer of this black and white film. The contrast ranges from good to excellent (look at the subtle shades at 30.05 in chapter five, side two), and the film noir–like lighting during the jazz club scenes and Rick's fall is captured very well.

The dialogue is a little soft and muddled in spots, but the digital audio is free of hiss. Both the trumpet and Ms. Day's voice sound celestially pure.

Zombies on Broadway (1945)
★★★
Director: Gordon Douglas
Running Time: 68 minutes

How can *anyone* resist a movie with this title (even if the zombies are on Sixth Avenue, not Broadway)?

Press agent Jerry Miles (Wally Brown) and his dull-witted partner, Mike (Alan Carney), are signed to promote the Zombie Hut, a new night spot being opened by reformed gangster Ace Miller (Sheldon Leonard). Jerry and Mike have rashly promised to provide a real zombie for the opening, and they travel to the island of San Sebastian to find one. After a run-in with some natives, whose zombie rite they interrupt, the lads stumble upon the castle of Dr. Paul Renault (Bela Lugosi), who has been trying for twenty-five years to duplicate the native potion that turns people into zombies. Naturally, he selects the two rubes as his next victims. They escape—despite being zombified—and, thanks to Renault's experimental serum, manage to come up with a surprise zombie for the club's opening.

At least one person associated with this film—Gordon Douglas—went on to greater things, directing the science fiction classic *Them!* (see page 276) and *In Like Flint* (see *Our Man Flint*), among others. Bela Lugosi was in his declining years (see *Plan 9 from Outer Space*), and this was the sixth of eight films former vaudeville comedians Wally Brown and Alan Carney would make in their failed effort to rival the success of Abbott and Costello.

The film was inspired by the success of the serious *I Walked with a Zombie* (1943), and even used the zombie star (Sir Lancelot) and calypso singer (Darby Jones) from the earlier film. If you can look beyond the comedy pair's fairly lame shtick—which will have you pining for Bud and Lou—the picture is quite enjoyable. Lugosi is particularly surprising, displaying a lot of animation and a nice comic touch (though the stunt double who fights with Brown and takes a few other falls looks *nothing* like the actor). Anne Jeffreys is lovely and tough as a knife-throwing dancer who agrees to help the boys if they'll get her off the island. There are also some wonderfully atmospheric shots (such as San Sebastian seen from the boat), though the jungle sets—the same ones used for RKO's Tarzan films—are pretty thin.

The Disc
Video: ★★★★½
Audio: ★★½ (monaural)
Chapters: Yes
Format: CLV (side one), CAV (side two)
Source: Turner Home Entertainment/ Image Entertainment

The source material used for the transfer—an original 35mm nitrate print—is a stunner: Except for a bit of negative dirt and a handful of marks, the print is pristine. The image is perfectly sharp, the blacks are deep, the whites shine, and the gray tones are wonderfully varied. The CAV side jitters every fourth frame.

The audio is a bit of a letdown: Though the dialogue is extremely clear, there's a persistent hiss throughout. There are no other extraneous noises.

Zorba the Greek (1964)
★★★★
Director: Michael Cacoyannis
Running Time: 141 minutes

Zorba the Greek was written in 1946 by Nikos Kazantzakis. It was the first of the author's novels to be published in the United States (1952), and it was quite successful. to Kazantzakis, Alexis Zorba represented a Dionysus, a creature of the flesh, which the author admired and yearned for; he himself was more like Basil, the novel's reflective, spiritual, Apollo-like narrator. This dual nature of people was at the heart of all of the author's works, which also included *The Last Temptation of Christ* (see page 169).

When English writer Basil (Alan Bates) inherits his father's crumbling lignite mine on Crete, he goes there, intent on making it operative once more. En route, he meets the outgoing Zorba (Anthony Quinn), who is looking for work and happens to be an experienced miner. Basil hires Zorba, who divides his time between trying to obtain timber to shore up the rotting supports in the mine and sleeping with the aging cabaret daner Mme. Hortense (Lila Kedrova), who falls deeply in love with Zorba—though, when he can afford her, he prefers a tart named Lola (Eleni Anousaki). Meanwhile, Basil and the proud young "widow" (Irene Papas) engage in a tentative courtship that ends with her murder at the hands of a grieving father, whose son committed suicide over his spurned advances. The mine also fails, but Basil has been touched by Zorba's life force. He will leave Crete a richer man, despite the money he has lost.

In spite of an accent that is more Italian than Greek, Quinn is mesmerizing as Zorba. His movements and expressions are full of nuance and poetry; you'll find yourself missing him when he's not onscreen. Bates, on the other hand, is reserved, naïve, and weak. After he does virtually nothing to prevent the widow's murder, you won't care whether or not his mine succeeds. Bates is terrific, but what a thankless role!

The Russian-born Kedrova is excellent, and her performance has been much-praised, but Papas's work is also exquisite: Watch all that she conveys, without a word of dialogue, when Bates comes to her home and she offers herself to him. It's brilliant screen acting.

Cacoyannis has done little of note since *Zorba the Greek*, having directed *The Day the Fish Came Out* (1967), *The Trojan Women* (1971), *Attila 74* (1975), *Iphigenia* (1977), and *Sweet Country* (1986)—a dismally bad film set in war-torn Chile.

The Disc

Video: ★★★½
Audio: ★★★½ (monaural)
Chapters: Yes
Format: CLV
Source: Fox Video

Like Zorba himself, the film doesn't look its age. The black and white print is almost entirely free of blemishes and is sharply focused throughout. Contrast is very good, with a wide range of gray tones. The only problems are with scenes set at night, where the grays go black and swallow up details.

The audio is clear and solid, with hardly a trace of background noise. And oh, how good that infectious Mikis Theodorakis score sounds!

Tacked onto the end of the film is Movietone footage of the film's premiere in Paris. We *know* Papas was only playing a part in the film, but it's still surprising to see her looking so glamorous with Quinn!

Zulu (1964) ★★★★

Director: Cy Endfield
Running Time: 138 minutes

Based on a true incident, the defense of the mission station in Natal, South Africa, from January 22 to 23, 1879, *Zulu* is a thinking person's adventure film. The heroes aren't two-fisted legends but real, desperate, honorable, and very scared British soldiers facing vastly superior numbers of natives.

For its first half, the film explores the people engaged in the conflict, most prominently Lt. John Chard (Stanley Baker), Lt. Conville Bromhead (Michael Caine)—over whom Chard just barely has seniority, causing considerable friction—and the alcoholic missionary Reverend Otto Witt (Jack Hawkins) and his daughter, Margareta (Ulla Jacobsson), both of whom have worked with the Zulus and don't want to see them slain.

The rest of the film is total war: Wave after wave of Zulu natives under Chief

Getywayo (Chief Buthelezi) attack the poorly protected outpost. The military tactics employed by both sides, especially by the natives, are fascinating, and the reactions of the soldiers are profound and frequently moving. The attack on the makeshift hospital is unforgettable.

The acting couldn't be better, with Caine a real surprise as the effete, inexperienced officer. Patrick Magee is also superb as the overworked, horror-struck Surgeon Reynolds, and Nigel Green gives a typically sturdy performance as Colour-Sergeant Bourne. Richard Burton's narration imparts an added aura of drama and class.

The film's only flaw is, ironically, the paucity of bloodletting. It hurts the picture's credibility to see bayonets and spears press against uniforms and skin without penetrating, or soldiers and bare-chested natives clutching at wounds when clearly they haven't been shot. Other films of this era—*Lawrence of Arabia* (see page 170) and *Spartacus* (1960), for example—were more graphic without being repulsive. This may seem petty, but in a movie whose entire second half is violent combat it's distracting.

Coproduced by star Baker and filmed on location in Natal, the film looks gorgeous—though someone should have taken care not to show Michael Caine's fillings so often (especially at 13/22:05).

John Barry's score is one of his best and for years was one of the most expensive and sought-after sound tracks. It is now available on compact disc.

In 1979, Endfield cowrote a prequel called *Zulu Dawn*, which was directed by Douglas Hickox. The film explains the political and military blunders that precipitated the strife in South Africa, though the film lacks the powerhouse performances and relentless battle scenes of the original.

The Disc

Video: ★★★★½
Audio: ★★★★ (monaural)
Chapters: Yes
Format: CLV
Source: Criterion

Except for a few marks on the master element and an occasional lack of sharpness—excusable in a film this old—*Zulu* is a stunner. The bulk of the movie is extremely sharp and free of grain and the colors are saturated. The soldiers may not bleed, but neither do their red uniforms; there's barely a hint of video noise. The sense of depth created by the clarity of the exterior scenes is miraculous, especially in the opening shot of the defeated troops at Isandhlwana.

The film is generously and accurately letterboxed.

The audio is clear and—once again considering the film's age—the dynamic range is surprising.

The film's one extra is remarkable: extensive excerpts from the memoirs of Getywayo. (Criterion's politically correct editorial embracing the film but repudiating apartheid is heartfelt but patronizing. *Zulu* doesn't advocate segregation, and anyone who doesn't realize that isn't worth the ink.)

Zulu Dawn is available on laserdisc, with acceptable colors and a fairly sharp image, poorly panned-and-scanned.

Glossary

Aliasing Also known as *Shimmering*, this is a wavelike pattern that appears due to an incomplete resolution of details. In other words, details are running together and causing waves or moiré patterns. This can often be found on linear designs (such as steps, close together in the distance) or checkerboard patterns. The only way to eliminate the problem is through more careful digital video mastering or the use of three-line comb filters, digital time-base correctors, and other devices in the players themselves.

Analog Recording A method of recording without numbers (see *Digital Recording*). Sound information preserved in analog or wave form are subject to the flaws inherent in the recording medium, such as "tape hiss."

Aspect Ratio The horizontal dimension of the picture relative to its vertical dimension. Filmmakers have used many different aspect ratios over the years, but these are the most common:

1.33:1 Until the 1950s and the dawn of the wide-screen era—Cinerama in 1952 and CinemaScope in 1953—virtually all films were shot in this aspect ratio. Seen on TV monitors—which are 1.34:1—1.33:1 films are not compromised.

1.66:1 Popular in the 1950s to the 1970s.

1.85:1 The most popular aspect ratio now being used. Movies shot 1.85:1 give a film some sweep in theaters, while requiring a minimum of cropping (28 percent) for home-video presentation. *Letterboxed* laserdisc releases in this format include *Dangerous Liaisons, The Producers,* and *Empire of the Sun* (see entries).

2.05:1 The widest image possible without distorting the image to fit on the film (2.35:1). Not commonly used.

2.35:1 This gets away from "flat" images and into the *anamorphic* or "squeezed" images. In order to show wider pictures without having to reequip theaters with new projection systems, Hollywood compressed images onto "normal-sized" film; these were unsqueezed in theaters by a special lens. Seen without *letterboxing*, these films—most of them made in Panavision—lose 43 percent of their original image. Examples include *Die Hard* (see entry) and *Ghostbusters*.

2.55:1 The aspect ratio used by CinemaScope and other superwide-screen processes.

2.66:1 The wide-screen aspect ratio of Camera 65, used for films such as *Ben-Hur*.

3:1 The aspect ratio of films presented in Cinerama, the widest of all screen processes (see *How the West Was Won* and *It's a Mad Mad Mad Mad World*).

Bleeding Colors that look fuzzy and don't "stay in the lines" of an object on the screen. This is usually the result of color saturation that is much too high (see *Video Noise*).

CAV Constant angular velocity: Laserdiscs in CAV turn a set number of revolutions each minute, generate one video frame per turn, and can store up to a half hour of material (54,000 frames) on each side. They turn at a constant rate of 1,800 rpm.

CLV Constant linear velocity: Laserdiscs in CLV turn a varying number of revolutions each minute. They can store up to an hour of material on each side but don't allow freeze-frame and other time-shifting devices unless the player is equipped with digital frame memory.

They begin turning at 1,800 rpm and end up at 600 rpm.

Cross Talk When a disc is warped, the laser beam will have difficulty reading it. As a result, information is picked up from adjacent areas. Cross-talk shows up as a herringbone pattern or "barber pole" pattern, rolling across the screen. Recent models tend to handle warped discs better than older players.

CX Encoding A system of reducing noise such as hiss or crackles on analog sound tracks.

Digital Recording A process in which information is translated to binary numbers, which are read and reconverted to original wave form. The technique allows unwanted sound or picture elements to be removed and creates playback free of distortion. (A few laserphiles feel that the audio sounds slightly artificial, since, unlike analog recordings, fragments of whatever is being recorded "fall through the numbers," as it were. All things considered, the crispness and clarity of the sound is worth this infinitesimal loss.) Ironically, the first digital audio laserdisc was *Wings*—a silent film. The organ score sounded great, though.

Digital Sound-Field Processing A means of digitally recreating different listening environments, such as concert hall, arena, nightclub, movie theater, etc.

Dropouts A flaw in the manufacturing process that shows up in two forms. First, there are speckles or dots that appear on your screen. These are either *inclusions*, caused by dust or dirt caught in the acrylic layer of the disc, or *confetti*, in which the aluminum layer or plastic disc is defective. There are also fairly common *rolling dropouts*, in which a horizontal bar rolls up the screen. These are caused by flaws in the aluminum layer of the disc or by sloppy stamping at the plant.

Dual Channel Discs on which there's a second audio track that is used for running audio commentary or dubbing; this allows the viewer to play just the musical sound track, etc. Discs with monaural sound tracks occasionally use the right or left speaker for this purpose.

Dummy Side A blank, white side of the disc where the plastic has not been written on or covered up (see *Pressing*). This saves manufacturing costs when only one side of a disc is being used. (Don't be alarmed if a label's there: Discs are read from the bottom. *Do* be alarmed if *both* sides are blank, as occasionally happens. That's a manufacturing flaw.)

Eastman Color A process used to make color prints from negatives. Due to the dyes and technology used in this process, films made before 1965 fade and/or went pink within eight to twelve years. Prints struck after 1965 take longer to go bad but still go the way of all flesh tones. Trade names for virtually identical processes include Deluxe Color, Metrocolor, Anscocolor, Fujicolor, Warnercolor, and Gevacolor. Though not part of the Eastman family, Pathé Color tends to get pastel-like over time. Cinecolor was a process of laying one color over black and white creating a "tinted" scene.

Internegatives "Duplicate" negatives made to protect the original negative. The quality of prints struck from an internegative is invariably less sharp than that of prints made from the original negative. How much less depends on the quality of the *interpositive*—the fine-grain print, struck from the original negative, from which the internegative was made.

Laser Rot Discs manufactured by Pioneer, especially during 1984 to 1985, suffered from oxidation, causing speckles that increased until there was significant loss of sound and picture (showing up in the form of red and blue "snow"), while discs from 3M during 1989 to 1990 literally decayed because of glue that ate through the aluminum layer of the disc. This problem was eliminated, for the most part, when Pioneer switched from aluminum that was 99.9 percent pure (instead of 99.1 percent), virtually removing the threat of oxidation, while over at 3M they simply switched to a different type of glue.

Letterboxing A transfer process that recreates, either generally or nearly completely, the theatrical *aspect ratio* of a film. Black bands known as "mattes" mask off unused portions of the monitor top and bottom. Fine details are sometimes lost, since the picture area is reduced. See *Pan-and-Scan* and *Windowboxing*.

Matte   The black bands used to block off the *safety zone* of a film for its presentation on laserdisc.

Matte Painting   A painting of landscapes, buildings, skies, planets, etc., done on glass and composited with real-life portions of sets. Matte paintings are an inexpensive way of creating spectacle or of bringing distant locations to the studio. Not to be confused with "mattes" (see *Letterboxing*).

Nitrate Stock   A clear film base that recorded images with exceptional contrast and detail. Unfortunately, it was highly flammable and was replaced by acetate (though many countries, such as the then-Soviet Union, continued to use it well into the 1970s).

Pan-and-Scan   In order to fill home-video monitors completely, motion pictures are panned-and-scanned on telecine machines, eliminating all but what the technician feels is the heart of the action. Images are cropped in three ways. For example, if two people are holding a conversation on opposite ends of the screen:

1. The technician pans across the image, from whoever is talking to whoever is listening. You will not get to see the two of them at once.
2. The technician simply jump-cuts from speaker to listener, avoiding the pan. This is preferable in wide-screen films, since pans that cover the intervening space look jerky and artificial (which they are).
3. The technician doesn't pan at all but, rather, simply stays in one spot—usually the center of the picture—losing whatever happens to be on the sides. (For example, when Charlton Heston and Sophia Loren are reunited at the beginning of the domestic videotape version of *El Cid*, their hands come together in the center of the screen, but her face is missing on the right, his on the left, for *the entire scene!*)

In order to fit the opening or closing credits of a film, the image will be shown "squeezed" to fit the roughly 1.33:1 dimensions of the monitor, leaving the letters—as well as whatever is behind them—looking long and skinny. (See *Aspect Ratio*, 2.35:1.)

Pressing   After a "stamper" has been created (see *Transfer*), commercial discs can be manufactured or "pressed." Liquid plastic is injected into the mold, duplicating the master, after which it's covered with an ultrathin coat of metal beneath clear plastic. Since each "stamper" represents only one side of the disc, two sides must be glued together to make a complete laserdisc. Unfortunately, an excellent transfer does not in any way guarantee an excellent pressing, and vice versa.

Process Photography   Shots in which actors are photographed before prefilmed footage or a still photograph that is projected onto a transluscent screen from behind. (If the projector was in front, the light would throw the actors' shadows onto the screen.) This is also known as *rear projection*. The term is sometimes used to include *front projection*, in which the camera shoots through a one-way mirror that is used to bounce the prefilmed footage onto the screen from in front, and composites created with a *traveling matte*, in which the footage of an actor, building, vehicle, etc., are combined with the background in the lab. *Traveling matte* composites are generally sharper, though foreground objects are frequently surrounded by a black or yellow "halo" and thin objects (such as individual hairs) tend to get lost due to the technique used to join the images.

Pro Logic   A patented Dolby system involving five speakers: normal *surround sound* with the addition of a fifth speaker, a "center dialogue channel" that allows voices and sounds to come from the area of the screen itself, not from the side speakers.

Safe Zone/Area   When directors shoot their films, they film more image on the top or bottom than they intend to be seen in theaters. It was originally designed to give the film editor area to splice scenes together so that splice marks wouldn't be seen. However, opening up a film (that is, showing the image in the safe zone) is now used so that movies won't have to be cropped or panned-and-scanned to fill a TV monitor. As a result, hot splice cement marks can still be seen on occasion. Many directors resent having this "working area" (along with exposed microphones, the tops of sets, etc.) showing up on TV. Thus, they create a *hard matte* right in the camera, which blocks these areas off on the negative. (It also helps projectionists present the film properly in local theaters.)

Subwoofer A speaker that reproduces only bass sounds amplifying them so they're felt rather than heard.

Surround Sound A process in which, ideally, the foreground speakers deliver the main stereo sounds of the film and the two rear speakers serve up ambient sound or the sound of objects "passing overhead" as they move from the rear or sides onto the screen. In films made before 1977, surround sound generally consists of rear speakers delivering the same sounds as the front speakers, with a slightly different balance (for example, louder music). *Dolby Sound* is a trade name for high-fidelity, quality sound recording, including surround-sound; *Ultra-Stereo* is another brand name, though the sound isn't as clear and intricate as that of Dolby.

Three-Strip Technicolor A process in which the greens, reds, and yellows were developed separately and combined to create a print whose colors are bright and sharp and will never fade. The expensive process was not widely used after 1954, though it was still available through the 1960s. The Technicolor brand name is still in use. In the 1920s, when color movies were still in their infancy, two-strip Technicolor was the state-of-the-art process, using magenta and cyan to create a *semblance* of full color. (See *Phantom of the Opera.*)

Time Compression A process developed by the late James Maclachlan in the early 1980s that subtly sped up the running of taped TV shows and recorded songs; though most viewers or listeners were unaware of the change, it allowed broadcasters to air more commercials. Another form of time compression involves removing portions of the image, causing barely perceptible "jumps" in it. In the case of laserdiscs, time compression has been used to fit presentations onto a single disc or side, where they would ordinarily require more. It is an abhorrent practice.

Transfer Getting a program from the master element to a point where discs can be mass-produced. The process begins with the film or tape being put onto a "master element" (or "master tape"). This process can be done digitally or through analog processes. At this point, defects such as dropouts are eliminated (hopefully), and features such as chapter stops are entered. Colors can be punched up or "sweetened" during this phase to restore faded films to former glory. (See *Hercules.*) From this, the manufacturer creates a "master disc" by feeding the information into a laser beam, which writes the particulars on a blank disc in the form of billions of pits, arranged in LP-like tracks. The process of duplicating the master is known as the transfer. Before discs can be mass-produced, the master disc—known as a glass "photo resist master"—is given a metal coating that is used to create a "stamper." (See *Pressing.*)

TV Safe The framing of a theatrical movie, with the action centered or characters bunched together in such a way that, when it's shown on TV, everything essential to the narrative will appear on the monitor.

Video Noise Quite often, "speckles" or fine-grain "snow" (also known as "artifacts") appear in certain high-or low-frequency colors—most often reds, oranges, browns, and blues; or else these colors will seem to "sizzle." These problems are the equivalent of video static and result from severe brightness ("luminance levels") or a poor-quality *transfer* in which the colors were either contaminated (usually by white or gray) or saturated too much or too little ("chroma level"). *Dropouts* are sometimes categorized as video noise.

Warping   Defects in which the discs aren't perfectly flat. There are two kinds of warps: *cone warps*, in which the center is depressed (or raised), and *potato-chip warps*, where the outer section is deformed. Warpage can be caused by heat, too-tight shrink wrapping, stacked discs, or manufacturing flaws in which the glue used to assemble the disc does not adhere uniformly.

Windowboxing   A process that fully replicates a film's *aspect ratio*, with black bands bordering the original theatrical image on all four sides. See *Letterboxing* and *Pan-and-Scan*.